TOWARD A THEOLOGY OF EROS

TRANSDISCIPLINARY THEOLOGICAL COLLOQUIA

Theology has hovered for two millennia between scriptural metaphor and philosophical thinking; it takes flesh in its symbolic, communal, and ethical practices. With the gift of this history and in the spirit of its unrealized potential, the Transdisciplinary Theological Colloquia intensify movement between and beyond the fields of religion. A multivocal discourse of theology takes place in the interstices, at once self-deconstructive in its pluralism and constructive in its affirmations.

Hosted annually by Drew University's Theological School, the colloquia provide a matrix for such conversations, while Fordham University Press serves as the midwife for their publication. Committed to the slow transformation of religio-cultural symbolism, the colloquia continue Drew's long history of engaging historical, biblical, and philosphical hermeneutics, practices of social justice, and experiments in theopoetics.

STEERING COMMITTEE:

Catherine Keller, *Director*

Virginia Burrus

Stephen Moore

TOWARD A THEOLOGY OF EROS

Transfiguring Passion at the Limits of Discipline

EDITED BY VIRGINIA BURRUS AND
CATHERINE KELLER

FORDHAM UNIVERSITY PRESS ❖ NEW YORK ❖ 2006

Copyright © 2006 Fordham University Press

Library of Congress Cataloging-in-Publication Data

Toward a theology of Eros : transfiguring
passion at the limits of discipline / edited by
Virginia Burrus and Catherine Keller.
p. cm.— (Transdisciplinary theological
colloquia)
Includes bibliographical references and index.
ISBN-13: 978-0-8232-2635-1 (cloth : alk. paper)
ISBN-10: 0-8232-2635-2 (cloth : alk. paper)
ISBN-13: 978-0-8232-2636-8 (pbk. : alk. paper)
ISBN-10: 0-8232-2636-0 (pbk. : alk. paper)
1. Sex—Religious aspects—Christianity.
2. Love—Religious aspects—Christianity.
3. Sex.   4. Love.   I. Burrus, Virginia.
II. Keller, Catherine, 1953–
BT708.T69   2006
128'.46—dc22   2006028869

Printed in the United States of America
08 07 06 5 4 3 2 1

CONTENTS

ACKNOWLEDGMENTS

It goes without saying that a volume of this sort is the result of the collaborative efforts of a multitude. We are first and foremost grateful to the sixteen other authors who contributed to the text, responding patiently, warmly, and often quite amusingly to our repeated editorial requests. Most of them participated in the 2004 Transdisciplinary Theological Colloquium hosted by Drew University's Theological School, which bore the title "Transfiguring Passions: Theologies and Theories of Eros." Others not among our authors also took part in that memorably rich and lively conversation, and many of their words and thoughts have left traces on the pages of this book—Cheryl Anderson, Chris Boesel, Danna Nolan Fewell, John Hoffmeyer, Otto Maduro, Dale Martin, Anna Mercedes, Stephen Moore, Peter Savastano, Terry Todd, and Richard Whaite. Chris Boesel and Terry Todd were also members of the planning committee while Mayra Rivera not only participated in the colloquium but also served as its formidably competent coordinator. She was supported by an able staff of Drew doctoral students, including especially Mario Costa and Luke Higgins. Master of Divinity student Erika Murphy both assisted with the colloquium and helped with the formatting and editing of the manuscript; beyond that, her gentle wit kept the editors sane. Maxine Beach, Dean of Drew's Theological School—well, what can we say? She not only trusted our slightly unorthodox passions but funded them, yet again. We are so very grateful.

Last but not least, we offer thanks to Fordham University Press and its gracious staff, to John Hoffmeyer and one other (anonymous) reader who offered extremely helpful comments on the manuscript, and especially to our editor Helen Tartar, whose intellectual and aesthetic judgment is impeccable and whose enthusiasm for this collaboration has been unflagging.

Sadly, one of the contributing authors did not live to see this volume's publication. We mourn the passing and honor the enormous scholarly achievements of Grace Jantzen.

V.B. and C.K.

TOWARD A THEOLOGY OF EROS

ᕽ Introduction: Theology and Eros after Nygren

VIRGINIA BURRUS

What does theology have to say about the place of eroticism in the salvific transformation of human subjects, even of the cosmos itself? How, in turn, does eros infuse theological practice and transfigure doctrinal tropes? Veering off the well-worn path of sexual moralizing, this volume explores what is still largely uncharted territory in the realm of theological erotics even as it also deliberately disrupts the disciplinary boundaries of theology. Indeed, it invites and performs a mutual seduction of disciplines—theology, philosophy, scripture, history—at multiple sites charged by desires at once bodily, spiritual, intellectual, and political. It seeks new openings for the emergence of desire, love, and pleasure, while also challenging common understandings of these terms. It engages risk at the point where the hope for salvation paradoxically endangers the safety of subjects—in particular, of *theological* subjects—by opening them to those transgressions of eros in which boundaries, once exceeded, become places of emerging possibility. In other words, it takes discipline (in multiple senses) to its limits in a stretch toward transcendence. But what kind of transcendence is imagined or hoped for? The essays gathered here offer a variety of answers to this question.

To reach toward a theology of eros is already to question the binary opposition of divine love and human desire momentously inscribed by Anders Nygren in his magisterial tome *Agape and Eros,* initially penned in the 1930s and reissued in revised form in 1953. For Nygren, the essentially Christian concept of love, or agape, originally had no more to do with the essentially Platonic or Greek concept of desire, or eros, than it did, in his view, with the essentially Jewish concept of law. "There cannot actually be any doubt," he writes, "that Eros and Agape belong originally to two entirely separate spiritual worlds, between which no direct communication is possible."[1] Observing that Platonic eros is always already a sublimation of what he names "vulgar Eros," he insists that there "is no way, not even that of sublimation, which leads over from Eros to Agape."[2] Neither is more sublime than the other, and neither can be derived from the other; rather the two are born rivals, reflecting fundamentally different orientations. Eros is human-centered, manifesting as an acquisitive desire or longing that charts an upward path toward God as its most worthy object and transformative telos. In contrast, agape is God-centered, emerging as a plenitudinous overflow or sacrificial gift that descends on humans and renders them both worthy of love and capable of loving others selflessly. If the concept of eros leaves little room for imagining God as an active lover, argues Nygren, the concept of agape precludes the notion that humans can love God in the same way that God loves humans. "In relation to God, man is never spontaneous; he is not an independent centre of activity. His giving of himself to God is never more than a response. At its best and highest, it is but a reflex of God's love, by which it is 'motivated.' . . . [I]t lacks all the essential marks of Agape." Then is it eros? No, it is faith, insists Nygren, "a love of which the keynote is receptivity."[3]

Curiously, most Christians have failed to observe the distinctions that are so clear to Nygren. As he puts it: "The idea of Agape can be compared to a small stream which, even in the history of Christianity, flows along an extremely narrow channel and sometimes seems to lose itself entirely in its surroundings; but Eros is a broad river that overflows its banks, carrying everything away with it, so that it is not easy even in thought to dam it up and make it flow in an orderly course."[4] In fact, much of Nygren's study, like the history it relates, is in danger of being overwhelmed by the floods of eros. Between the Pauline and Johannine literatures of the New Testament and the reformation of Martin Luther, ancient and medieval writers forge "syntheses" of agape and eros in which eros almost inevitably sweeps agape up into its all-too-powerful currents, argues Nygren. This is nowhere more evident than in those theologians whose works betray ascetic or mystical tendencies. The third-century Alexandrian Origen and the fourth-century Cappadocian Gregory of Nyssa are prime examples of such erotic excess in the history of Christian thought. However, it is Augustine's theology of *caritas*, together with Pseudo-Dionysius's Neoplatonic erotics, that Nygren credits with ultimate responsibility for medieval Christianity's thoroughgoing lapse into a synthetic, and thus counterfeit, theology of love. If, with Luther, "the specifically Christian idea of love breaks through again and shatters the artfully contrived synthesis,"[5] the work of reformation is never finished. Nygren continues Luther's legacy, as he understands it, resisting the confluence of agape and eros with his own prodigious scholarly labors.

Yet a reader of Nygren's historical study might well wonder whether agape, now as before, does not require an overflow of eros in order to reopen its congested channels or, to shift metaphors, to shatter its repressive defenses. Is the posited distinction between agape and eros, as well as between carnal and sublimated eros, not itself in need of interrogation? Nygren's critique of synthetic theologies of love rests, of course, not only on his conviction that synthesis, or syncretism, is a bad thing, but also on his assumption that agape and eros can be located as originally separate and pure cultural essences, identifiable by their fundamentally definitive motifs. That most theologians, by his own account, have not historically perceived them thus *might* in itself inspire continued reassessments of the relation between carnal and spiritual, passive and active, ascending and descending, creaturely and divine love. The essays in this volume join the voices of other contemporary scholars in pursuing a theology of eros after Nygren, even as they also share Nygren's articulated commitments to both a historical-contextual and a philosophically rigorous analysis of concepts of love and desire.

Plato's *Symposium* has historically constituted a fertile matrix for dialogue and debate about physical and sublimated eros, as well as about the relation of Platonic eroticism to Christian love. By distancing Christian thought from Platonic theories of sublimation, Nygren denies any possible link between human sexuality and Christian love. Indeed, his argument implies that embodied sexuality ("vulgar Eros") is the originary site of a subsequently sublimated desire ("heavenly Eros") arising from a lack that is filled, eradicated, or simply superseded by the prior, unearned, and indeed unexpected gift of divine Agape. The essays in part I reopen the debate by restaging Plato's symposium on love, performing contesting readings of an ancient text that itself already encompasses a multiplicity of voices.

Here Daniel Boyarin directly engages Nygren's work, exposing a slippage in his interpretation of the *Symposium*. Nygren, argues Boyarin, falsely conflates the concept of a "heavenly eros" continuous with physical sexuality, as described in Pausanius's speech, with the more strictly asceticized eroticism attributed to the prophetess Diotima and ultimately affirmed by Plato. This is a distinction overlooked by others as well, not least Michel Foucault. On Boyarin's reading, Platonic love as defined by Diotima draws close to Christian love as interpreted by the ascetics of later antiquity. Evading the particular binary of agape and eros (or, in Nygren's terms, synthesizing them), both Platonic and Christian asceticisms participate nonetheless in a problematically elitist politics of philosophical truth positioned in opposition to the democratic politics of rhetoric or debate, Boyarin argues. At this point, Mark Jordan takes up the challenge offered by Boyarin. Where Boyarin sees in Diotima's speech a displacement of the heavenly (but still also carnal) eroticism advocated by Pausanias, Jordan perceives in the highly ironized and powerfully seductive exchange between Alcibiades and Socrates with which the *Symposium* concludes an unsettling of the certainties of all of the prior speeches—not least Diotima's cited doctrine of radical sublimation. If the *Symposium* is both less ascetic and less didactic on Jordan's reading than on Boyarin's, it both is and is not thereby less continuous with the erotic theories and practices of the Christians of a later antiquity: Jordan closes with a consideration of Augustine's *Confessions*, referring forward to Karmen MacKendrick's reading of that text later in this volume. In the final essay of part I, Mario Costa returns us to Diotima's speech, discovering an eroticism that lends itself easily to an explicitly Christian development, though Costa's interests (in distinction from Boyarin's) lie with the relevance of Diotima's doctrine for current theological arguments regarding the inadequacy of purely lack-based theories of desire—arguments that are, of course, resonant (though not simply conflatable) with Nygren's opposition of agape to eros. In dialogue with philosophical theologian

Jean-Luc Marion, Costa discovers in Plato's text a concept of eros that is not simply identified with lack or death but encompasses also the agapic emphasis on resourcefulness or plenitude, in an inherently relational construal of divine-human desire in which eros itself arrives, and is returned, as a gift. Costa's essay should also be read in company with the philosophically or cosmologically framed essays of part 4.

The essays in part 2 extend the symposiastic conversation, continuing to complicate the distinctions between the sexual and the sublimated by layering other distinctions on them—heterosexual and homosexual, two-sexed and intersexed, normative and queer—through engagement with the erotic pieties of ancient and medieval as well as contemporary Christians. As resonances between premodern and postmodern texts and practices are explored, questions are implicitly raised about the transhistorical and transcultural analysis of eroticism or sexuality. If the queer of contemporary discourse depends upon resistance to the hegemony of the normal, how does it intersect with other cultures that appeal not to norms but to nature and furthermore acknowledge a natural fluidity of gendered and eroticized identities? Is queerness necessarily linked to resistance or transgression? Such questions are relevant not only to the essays in this section but also to many others in the volume that work in an explicitly transhistorical register.

Here Diana Swancutt "outs" the unsettlingly androgynous and queerly erotic body of Christ harbored within the Pauline corpus, thereby implicitly challenging Nygren's representation of the apostle Paul as the poster child of an agapically asexual theology while also explicitly challenging more contemporary invocations of Paul that support the oppressive politics of heterosexism. Considering a figure far less familiar to most readers than Paul, Derek Krueger uncovers in the writings of the Byzantine monk Symeon the New Theologian evidence of a startlingly rich homoerotic imaginary that foregrounds the male monastic body as the site of erotic transformation or deification; his essay glances back toward Jordon's as he detects possible echoes in Symeon's work of the teasingly cloaked erotic exchange between Alcibiades and Socrates with which Plato's *Symposium* concludes. Amy Hollywood, in turn, explores the fascinatingly fluid, culturally transgressive erotic subjectivities emerging in

the recorded visions of female medieval mystics Mechthild of Magdeburg, Hadewijch, and Marguerite Porete, who represent themselves, respectively, as a bride of Christ, a knight errant in love, and a female Soul
seeking erotic union with a feminized divinity.

Other essays in this section raise the question of whether the focus on
the sexed or the sexual is too exclusive for an eroticism construed as
broadly and productively transgressive of difference. Marcella Althaus-
Reid's provocative exploration of Latin American "feetishism"—centered
around theological readings of the work of Brazilian poet Glauco Ma-
tosso—considers how the erotic traverses and transfigures, queers and
subverts, differences framed in terms of colonialism and nationality, class
and race, as well as sexuality and gender. Perching at the edge of secular-
ized eschatological fantasies already morphing queerly into realities both
ominous and promising, Sheila Briggs explores new economies of pleasure that emerge in the ongoing transformations of "digital" bodies at
once glorious and grotesque.

In Christian as well as Jewish tradition, the erotic is frequently attended
by the suffering of pain or violent coercion, an interest that unites the
essays in part 3 while also linking them with the prior essays by Althaus-
Reid and Hollywood in particular. At this point, other fault lines in Nygren's typology become apparent. He wishes to keep separate the active
human subject of desire that characterizes his eros type and the receptive
or passive human subject of faith that characterizes his agape type. Yet it
would seem that to be a subject at all is both to act and to be subjected
to constraint, in discursive and political contexts where agency is never
absolute. To be an *erotic* subject is, perhaps, to begin to transfigure—even
to pervert—the submission that inheres in subjection. Where submission
is *actively* courted, chosen, or willed, the complication of agency is inten-
sified to the point of crisis, jamming and repeatedly reversing the distinctions between subject and object, domination and submission, power and
resistance. As Yvonne Sherwood demonstrates, the very structures of
narrativity or (divine) emplotment, whether biblical or postbiblical, convey this predicament of subjectivity while also opening up possibilities for
an erotic transformation of submission that limits omnipotence, whether
human or divine. Behind the crucifixion of Christ looms the binding of
Isaac, and in front of it proliferate innumerable inscriptions of mimetic

self-sacrifice or self-emptying, where pain and pleasure, loss and gain, mournfulness and joy converge and mingle.

Especially in the painful disciplines of asceticism and the prayerful fantasies of mysticism, there emerges a sublimely sadomasochistic eroticism played out on a charged field of divine-human seduction that promises to take subjects to their limits and beyond, opening them in and to the cut of love. My own essay places the late ancient ascetic theorist Evagrius of Pontus in dialogue with philosopher Jean-Luc Nancy in such a way as to uncover prayer as the site of the advent of a love that cuts across, breaks, or shatters the subject. In the masochistic erotics of ancient asceticism, there is disclosed the collapsing of the binary of activity and passivity that anchors Nygren's dualism of agape and eros. Folding back on Jordan's anticipatory reading of Augustine's confessional erotics, Karmen MacKendrick in turn exposes the power of the divine seduction that lies at the heart of Augustine's complex theories of love and subjectivity, desire and submission, thereby not only interrogating current critiques of seduction but also illumining the striking coherence of the North African Church Father's thought, where Nygren saw merely "synthesis" and inconsistency. Both Evagrius and Augustine represent late ancient legacies that leave a strong imprint on medieval Christianity, especially its more mystical versions—as Nygren notes, albeit with marked disapproval. We are thus brought back again to Hollywood's essay on the thought worlds of medieval Christian mystics, even as we are also directed forward toward Elliot Wolfson's treatment in part 5 of the erotic suffering that attends exegetical practice in the understanding of medieval kabbalists.

The intense yearning for erotic dissolution, which by definition puts "selves" at risk, is here engaged more appreciatively than it was by Nygren, to say the least. Yet it must be acknowledged that more sinister dangers likewise threaten. A productive perversity can itself be perverted, and neither the extremes of oppression (including domestic abuse and political tyranny) nor the subtle seductions of consumer cultures, for example, lie altogether outside the field of the erotic. The dilemma is real: the desire for justice may seem at points to require the forcible constraint of the erotic, yet to foreclose on the inherent transgressiveness of eros is also to risk repressing the very potential for transformability that enables the emergence of new possibilities for justice, love, and pleasure within human community.

Eroticism is not, however, confined to the human or even to the human-divine sphere of relationality. Eroticism is not perhaps confinable at all, as Nygren intuited; it appears also to lie close to the heart of creativity and thus of cosmology, an insight that Nygren, however, resists in his attempt to distance creativity from eros by aligning it strictly with the agapic. The essays in part 4 bring our attention to the powerful flow of eros in and through the very torrents of nature, as uncovered by Robert Corrington's reading of Ralph Waldo Emerson, whose thought, argues Corrington, effects a radical "liquification" of the conventional "architectural" distinctions drawn between ascending desire and descending love. Catherine Keller, in turn, surfaces the productively disruptive potentiality mobilized within historically layered and highly eroticized representations of the parabiblical figure of Mary Magdalene. Keller ultimately invokes process theology, poststructuralist philosophy, and contemporary physics to point toward a new theological cosmology in which the pleromatic is transfigured as the khoric site of divine becoming and erotic creativity. Mayra Rivera also highlights intersections of the erotic, the feminine, and the cosmological in her theological revisiting of the debate of Luce Irigaray with Emmanuel Levinas, as she reaches for a fresh conceptualization of the transcendence encountered in the (divine) Other in which eros is no longer opposed to an explicitly desexualized and implicitly anti feminine love. In the final essay of part 4, Grace Jantzen discovers in biblical narratives of new creation a source for envisioning divine and human creativity as an erotic overflow arising from a "passion for transformation," a position that explicitly resists current theoretical tendencies—e.g., that of René Girard—to understand violence as inherent to creativity as well as desire. Janzten's essay thereby also returns us to a critical consideration of the ambivalent relation of eros to pain, suffering, and loss highlighted in the essays of part 3.

While Plato's *Symposium,* with which we begin, has constituted a privileged site for the development of philosophical theories and practices of eros, the biblical Song of Songs, which is the focus of the final part 5, has allowed for a poetic unfolding of the erotic within exegetical traditions—a topic already broached in essays by Swancutt, Keller, and

Sherwood. As Tod Linafelt shows, the Song opens up a modality of eros, and thus perhaps also of theology, that exceeds even the complexities of narrative through an irruption of lyricism that evades linear temporality by performing a rhythmic sensuality that seduces our participation and thereby promises transformation at the most intimate level of embodied passions. Richard Kearney, in turn, both explores and supplements premodern interpretations of the Song, uncovering at the intersection of Jewish and Christian exegetical traditions an eschatologically charged eroticism that subverts the Nygrenesque binary of agape and eros, descending and ascending desire, while also inviting engagement with a wide range of contemporary philosophical, psychoanalytic, and literary expressions of sublime desire. Finally, Elliot Wolfson's Kristevan meditations on erotic suffering as a form of hermeneutical poetics in the kabbalistic tradition turns on readings of Song 8:6 ("place me as a seal on your heart"), thus providing a fitting seal to this section, even as it also curves back toward our beginning point in the *Symposium*.

All of the essays in this volume engage theology while refusing to be disciplined by it; their conversation, indeed, takes place for the most part at or beyond the limits of the theological discipline. Yet, for those who choose to submit more directly to this discipline, what might a distinctive *theology* of the erotic look like? What are its most promising resources, its most hopeful transfigurations of doctrine—not least the doctrine of God? These are the questions to which Catherine Keller returns us in her theological afterword. For now, let me suggest tentatively that if "God is eros," as Pseudo-Dionysius (following Plotinus) insists in his erotic transposition of 1 John 4:8 and 4:16, then perhaps *eros is God*. Or rather: eros is the power or process of divine self-othering through which creation is ever emerging—that which at once differentiates and joins, orders and disrupts. A God in and of between-spaces, then, and also a God always incarnating, always subjecting itself to becoming-flesh. Thus, a God who is a Christ—ever incarnating, but also ever withdrawing seductively, eluding even the grasp of words that must (according to the logic of a "negative" theology) be unsaid as soon as they are said. If theology gestures toward a God-who-is-eros, that gesture itself partakes of the erotic. Like prayer—or perhaps *as* prayer?—theology cannot *grasp* God but it *can* hope to seduce and be seduced by God.

PART I

❦ Restaging the Symposium on Love

❧ What Do We Talk About When We Talk About Platonic Love?

DANIEL BOYARIN

In his celebrated study of Christian love, Anders Nygren identifies the emergence of heresy with the perversion of agape: "Agape loses its original meaning and is transformed into Eros; not, however, be it observed, into the sublimated 'heavenly Eros' of which Plato and his followers speak, but into that despised variety, 'vulgar Eros.'"[1] The implications of this framing require unpacking. To do so, we must return to Plato's *Symposium,* where the term "heavenly Eros" occurs in the discourse of Pausanias, signifying a practice of desire that begins with physical love but ultimately transcends the physical. Yet Pausanias is not the only, or even the most privileged, speaker in the *Symposium.* The famous speech of Diotima, cited by Socrates, arguably lays greater claim to representing Plato's definitive views on love. Thus, in referring to "heavenly Eros" as that "of which Plato and his followers speak," Nygren erases any difference between the Pausanian ideology of eros and that of Diotima / Socrates—the latter of which I take to be Platonic love.[2] Indeed, Nygren makes this conflation quite explicit: "In the *Symposium* Plato feels no necessity to make Socrates or Diotima speak about it, but entrusts to Pausanias the task of explaining the difference between what he calls 'vulgar (*pandē-mos*) Eros' and 'heavenly (*ouranios*) Eros.'"[3] For Nygren there is, then, no difference at all between Pausanian heavenly love and Platonic love. For me this distinction makes all the difference. In Pausanian heavenly love, there is room (to be sure at the bottom) for sex, a point glossed over by Nygren, while Platonic love deems *all* physical sex vulgar. [4] As we shall see, what is at stake is not only a sexual but also an epistemological and, finally, a political difference: Pausanias speaks not only for sex but also for the city—that is, for democratic Athens—while Plato, via Diotima / Socrates, advocates a philosophical flight not only from carnal sex but also from the indeterminacies of truth and power inherent to the politics of democracy.

Nygren is, of course, not the only one to have collapsed this distinction. For Michel Foucault, for example, there is also little difference between Pausanian heavenly love and Platonic love, though his reasoning is almost the opposite: "One should keep in mind that [Platonic] 'asceticism' was not a means of disqualifying the love of boys; on the contrary, it was a means of stylizing it and hence, by giving it shape and form, of valorizing it."[5] Where Nygren obscured the difference between Pausanias and Plato by denying the physicality of Pausanias's ideal, Foucault obscures that difference by downplaying the radicality of Plato's asceticizing of eros.

Kenneth Dover, in contrast, does make clear distinctions between Plato's Pausanias (as the representative of the "best" of Athenian eros) and his Diotima (as the conveyer of Plato's own views), arguing that in Plato's writings "heterosexual eros is treated on the same basis as homosexual copulation, a pursuit of bodily pleasure which leads no further . . . and in *Symposium* it is sub-rational, an expression of the eros that works in animals."[6] Dover thus discriminates plainly between the sexual practices of Athenians in general even in their most high-minded, heavenly form—and Plato's disdain for all physical sex. Below I will affirm and develop Dover's views on this issue, departing from the legacies represented by both Nygren and Foucault. Plato, I will suggest, promotes an erotics that is almost in binary opposition to the erotics of Athens as best represented in Pausanias's speech, and this is consistent with, indeed part and parcel of, Plato's whole stance vis-à-vis the life of the polis itself.

In Platonic love, queerness itself is queered. Heavenly (Pausanian) pederastic homoeroticism may (not unlike gay marriage) inscribe a realm of male relationality that is deemed superior to but still comparable with marital heteroeroticism. In contrast, Platonic eros sets itself against both pederasty and marriage in resistance to the conventions of the ancient city (and perhaps to sociopolitical "convention" per se) while at the same time disrupting the boy-versus-woman binary via the insertion of fictive female figures (Diotima, Philosophia) into the male-male erotic economy. Here, I suggest, we may find a genealogy for Christian sex: what Plato frames as the resistance of philosophy to rhetoric, late ancient Christians represent as the resistance of the ascetic to the everyday; for both, a celibate sex life is positioned in opposition to the domesticized eros (gay and straight) of the city.

Peter Brown has written, "Like long-familiar music, the *ideés recues* of the ancient world filled the minds of educated Christians when they, in their turn, came to write on marriage and on sexual desire."[7] Surely, then, one of the most important tasks in constructing a genealogy of late ancient writings on sex and sexuality would be to achieve the most nuanced understanding possible of those *ideés recues* themselves, and, in particular, of their conflictual dynamics. Here I would like to present a reading of the *Symposium* that points up the radical difference between Platonic and Pausanian love, disrupting not only Nygren's view but also a more recent (Foucauldian) scholarly consensus inclined to place Plato's theory of eros on a continuum with (rather than in opposition to) classical Athenian pederastic practice.[8] Such a reading leads to a suggestion that some aspects of early Christian thought about eros were even closer to Plato than is generally recognized now. In arguing thus, I reinstate a certain very traditional reading of Platonic love as a forerunner of the wholly celibate erotics of ancient Christianity[9]—as a Christian eroticism before Christianity, so to speak.[10]

PLATO AS AN EARLY PLATONIST

In recent years it is certainly the speech of Aristophanes concerning the spherical people of three sexes that has excited the most interest in scholarship of the *Symposium* centered on the history of sexuality or queer studies. However, Socrates's recounting of Diotima's speech is at least equally important, especially if we are seeking better understanding of the continuities between ancient Greek and late ancient Judeo-Christian cultural formations.[11] One of the most important of questions, as David M. Halperin has realized, has to do with the question of Diotima's sex. In a compelling discussion, Halperin has argued that Diotima is a woman because she represents or substitutes for a "real" woman, Aspasia (the much cherished lover of Pericles), about whom there was a strong, persistent pre-Platonic tradition that she had been Socrates's instructor in matters erotic. While I endorse Halperin's account of Diotima as a "cover" for Aspasia and his perhaps startling conclusion that she is a prophetess because she is a woman (and not the other way around), I think that this conclusion could helpfully be restated more trenchantly. Halperin puts it this way: "[Aspasia] would be quite out of place in the *Symposium*, where Plato clearly wants to put some distance between his own outlook on *erōs* and the customary approach to that topic characteristic of the Athenian demimonde."[12] Although I agree with the first clause, I quite sharply disagree with the last: It is not the Athenian demimonde from which Plato wishes to distance himself (or not only that) but the Athenian *polis* and its everyday life of marrying, having sex (with boys *and* wives), procreating, and being involved in politics. It is trivial for Plato to distinguish himself from the eros of the demimonde or even from what Pausanias dubs "vulgar" eros, but Plato is going for more here. He is putting some distance, on my reading, between his own eros and all eros that includes physical sex, and especially Athenian heavenly eros. It is not so much Aspasia as *hetaira* or courtesan that would be so problematic for Plato as Aspasia as the "wife" and the mother of Pericles's child, Pericles Junior (ultimately granted Athenian citizenship).[13] To be sure, "Plato had a primary reason for preferring a woman, any woman, to be the mouthpiece of his erotic theory." So far, so good. However Halperin goes on to say: "But in order to replace Aspasia with another woman who was *not* a *hetaira*, Plato had to find an alternate source of erotic authority, another means of sustaining his candidate's claim to be able to pronounce on the subject of erotics. . . . In the *Symposium*, however, he looks to religious sources of authority, to which some Greek women were believed by the Greeks to have access."[14] Although going on to more complex explanations of Diotima, Halperin does not reject so much as supplement the Diotima as Aspasia in priestess-drag account, allowing, rather, that the Diotima replaces Aspasia substitution may be true enough, but maintaining at the same time that it does not at all explain why Plato remains invested in that tradition.[15] For my part, I want to dwell on this account a bit longer.

On my reading, the relationship to Aspasia is crucial for understanding the counter-political eros of the *Symposium*.[16] Not only is Diotima a prophetess from Prophetville (in Halperin's delightful translation of Mantinea) and thus a source of authority but also, as such, she is totally out of the corporal politico-erotic economy of the city. Her Peloponnesian origin is not beside the point. This notion of Diotima as doubly marked "outsider" (as an apparently celibate woman[17] and as a non-Athenian) is key to my reading of the *Symposium*.[18] If, following Halperin's attractive suggestion, Diotima is a replacement for Aspasia, more of an attempt to account for Aspasia's place in Platonic discourse seems necessary in order to understand Diotima. One important clue to this location is Plato's dialogue, the *Menexenus,* in which Aspasia is presented ironically as a sort of teacher of rhetoric and the producer of a funeral oration that is a parody of Pericles's as given by Thucydides.[19]

Thucydides's original and Plato's lampoon are both marked by their close approximations (one serious and one parodic) of Gorgias's high style, a point of some importance since, for Plato, the theory of erotics and the theory of rhetorics are closely aligned. Socrates, throughout the corpus, has only two female teachers, Aspasia and Diotima. In the *Menexenus,* in a context in which Socrates is openly mocking rhetoric and speechmaking, he cites Aspasia as his teacher in rhetorics. In the *Symposium,* when Socrates wishes to laud dialogue over rhetoric, it is *Diotima,* his teacher in erotics, who represents dialogue, for Plato the very antithesis of rhetoric. Rhetoric and dialogue are, for Plato, positioned in an absolute binary opposition, with the former marked negatively and the latter positively. "Bad erotics" are associated with "bad" speech practice, rhetoric, and "good" erotics with "good" speech forms, dialectic. When we remember, once again, that according to more ancient tradition it was Aspasia who was Socrates's instructor in erotics, I think we are not meant to miss this binary opposition, the seductive, flattering, lying funeral oration (*Menexenus* 234c–235a) taught and given by the beautiful, sexual, political *Athenian* Aspasia versus the true dialogue of the holy alien *Peloponnesian* prophetess, Diotima.

Both Aspasia and Diotima are presented as having taught Socrates some *technē* in the form of a discourse. Both discourses are indicated, within the dialogues themselves, as not truly simply the products of these women—Aspasia speaks for Pericles, and Socrates will deliver Diotima's speech—so we are surely meant to look for significance here. Aspasia, Socrates's traditional instructor in erotics, becomes his instructor in rhetoric, while a new woman is produced to teach him proper erotics. As Allen, with his characteristic perspicacity puts it: "We know where we are [in the *Menexenus*]. Socrates in the *Gorgias* distinguishes two kinds of rhetoric. There is philosophical rhetoric, aimed at truth and the good of the soul, whether it gives pleasure or pain to the hearer, and organized like the work of an artist to attain its aim. Then there is base rhetoric, aimed at gratification and pleasure, organized randomly according to knack and experience, a species of flattery; its effect on the hearer is like witchcraft or enchantment."[20] The analogy (or better, homology) in the realm of erotics is only too clear. Aspasia can teach only the false use of language, just as she would have been able to teach only the lower erotics that pursue pleasure, procreation, and political power, while Diotima can teach true erotics, because her sexuality is entirely out of all of these realms, and thus, to complete the ratio, she teaches true speaking (dialectic), as well.

This reading is strongly consonant with but expands the scope of Halperin's second major point as to the femaleness of Diotima, namely that since Plato has supplanted the Athenian "male" model of eros as acquisition of the beautiful with a "female" one of procreation of the beautiful, it is appropriate that the "mouthpiece" be a woman. Halperin writes: "What Plato did was to take an embedded habit of speech (and thought) that seems to have become detached from a specific referent in the female body and, first to *reembody* it as 'feminine' by associating it with the female person of Diotima through her extended use of gender-specific language, then to *disembody* it once again, to turn 'pregnancy' into a mere *image* of (male) spiritual labor, just as Socrates's male voice at once embodies and disembodies Diotima's female presence."[21] The precise choice of woman, or better put, the remarkably absent woman, the absent *real* woman, Aspasia, the woman who wasn't there, as it were, is an essential aspect of the overall rhetoric of the piece. Since Plato is adopting a procreative model of erotic desire, but contemptuous of the physical procreation of corporeal children, the teacher cannot be a *gyne* (woman, wife) but must be a *parthenos* (virgin). Diotima may be a female, but in

Greek, I think, she is not quite a woman. She is, however, on this reading a real, if fictional, female.

The substitution of the Mantinean mantic for the Athenian partner, lover, politician, mother (not *demimondaine*), was a very marked one indeed. If Aspasia is the female version of Pericles, Diotima makes the perfect female version of Socrates, the anti-Pericles. Diotima has to be a woman, on this account, in order to negate Aspasia and all that she means.

THE PHILOSOPHER AGAINST THE POLIS

A somewhat more detailed reading of the *Symposium* will, I hope, further sharpen these points and also raise others. As a motto for a jumping off point for the following discussion, an oft-cited text of Socrates's speaking is apt:

> That leaves only a very small fraction, Ademantus, of those who spend their time on philosophy as of right. Some character of noble birth and good upbringing, perhaps, whose career has been interrupted by exile, and who for want of corrupting influences has followed his nature and remained with philosophy. Or a great mind born in a small city, who thinks the political affairs of his city beneath him, and has no time for them. . . . Our friend Theages has a bridle which is quite good at keeping people in check. Theages has all the qualifications for dropping out of philosophy, but physical ill-health keeps him in check, and stops him going into politics. . . . Those who have become members of this small group have tasted how sweet and blessed a possession is philosophy. They can also, by contrast, see quite clearly the madness of the many. They can see that virtually nothing anyone in politics does is in any way healthy. (*Republic* 496a–c)[22]

The opposition between the life of a philosopher and the life of the *polis* could not possibly be clearer than it is in this passage. The philosopher is an alien by birth or even by virtue of his ill-formed body that keeps him out of the erotic and political commerce described, for example, by symposiast Pausanias, or is one who is blessed with a certain mantic ability as Socrates is. Diotima has all three of these characteristics: She is certainly a very marked sort of alien, "a great mind born in a small city," and is a Mantinean mantic to boot. Andrea Nightingale has already connected this passage in the *Republic* with the *Symposium* at exactly the point at which it is of interest to my argument here. She writes: "What is the nature of this new brand of alien [the philosopher]? . . . One of the most prominent aspects of Plato's definition of the philosopher is the opposition he forges between the philosophic 'outsider' and the various types of people who made it their business to traffic in wisdom." Nightingale then goes on to remark that "the clearest and most explicit enunciation of this phenomenon in the Platonic corpus" is perhaps "the *Symposium*'s handling of the exchange of 'virtue' for sexual favors."[23]

Instead of Pausanias's description of a good eros from which virtue flows in exchange for semen (or better put, perhaps, in which semen is the material within which virtue flows), Diotima inscribes an eros that is entirely spiritual in nature, outside the circulation (the traffic) of the sociality of the *polis*. She is explicitly speaking against, above all, Pausanias, that ultimate representative of the highest-mindedness of Athenian eros, the one who sharply distinguishes between vulgar love (pederasty) and Uranian love (pederasty cum pedagogy).[24] Socrates, it will be remembered, explicitly rejects Agathon's request that he recline next to him, "so that I can lay hold of you and thereby enjoy the benefit of that piece of wisdom which occurred to you," to which Socrates replies that "it is not in the nature of wisdom to flow from one person to another like liquid flowing from a fuller vessel to an emptier one" (175c–e), thereby capsizing the entire self-understanding of the Athenian pederastic/pedagogical system.[25] I would like to suggest that the *Symposium* is utterly of a piece with Plato's entire oeuvre in its articulation of a doubled social-space (the *polis* versus the Academy—a full two miles away from the *agora*[26]) coarticulated with a doubled ontological space (the physical versus the immaterial) and a doubled epistemological space (what appears and what is true, *doxa* and *episteme*). There is a doubled female figure that corresponds to this doubling, as well: Aspasia who belongs to the *agora* vs. Diotima who belongs to the Academy, if not further than that.[27] Finally, there is a doubled space of *logos* as well: rhetoric corresponding to the first of each of these binary pairs and dialectic corresponding to the second.[28] This consistent and persistent doubling has much more crucial consequences for the history of sexuality than any details of permitting or forbidding of this or that sexual practice.[29] *Encomia*, beautiful speeches in praise of eros, stand for Pausanian, demotic sex in Plato's economy, while austere dialectic, with its fearless search for so-called truth, stands for the true eros of love of the Forms.

SEXUAL INTERCOURSE

The *Symposium* stages these oppositions on various literary levels, with respect to both the form of the discourse and its content. The *Symposium* is not at all a dialogue, but, in fact, a staged series of *encomia,* of epideictic rhetorical pieces. In fact it is signaled as such right at the beginning in Phaedrus's first utterance: "How *could* people pay attention to such trifles and never, not even once, write a proper hymn to Love" (177c).[30] To which plaint Eryximachus immediately responds that this is exactly what they will spend the evening doing.

This contrast between epideictic encomia and dialogue comes first between the speeches of Aristophanes and Agathon, where Socrates is represented as attempting to lead the conversation into a "discussion" or dialogue and Phaedrus interrupts: "Agathon, my friend, if you answer Socrates, he'll no longer care whether we get anywhere with what we're doing here, so long as he has a partner for discussion [*dialegesthai*]. Especially if he's handsome. Now, like you, I enjoy listening to Socrates in discussion, but it is my duty to see to the praising of Love and to exact a speech from every one of this group. When each of you has made his offering to the god, then you can have your discussion" (194d).[31]

In fact, the symposium (if not the *Symposium*) is conceived as a rhetorical competition, echoing the theatrical competition for which the party and Agathon's victory therein is a celebration. Moreover, the text is already inscribing proper pederasty, à la Socrates, as the *dialogue* of the older philosopher and a beautiful boy.

Halperin has already well articulated how radically Plato's view of eros departs from the Athenian norm, represented at its best in Pausanias's speech: "Because *erōs,* on the Platonic view . . . aims at procreation, not at possession, and so cannot be sexually realized, Platonic *anterōs* [the aroused desire of the *eromenos,* the "beloved"] does not lead either to a reversal of sexual roles or to the promotion of sexual passivity on the part of the beloved."[32] For Halperin, the great departure of Plato is from the hierarchical model of sex to one of mutual desire and pleasuring. Halperin goes on to indicate that this reciprocity of active desire, "Plato's remodeling of the homoerotic ethos of classical Athens," "has direct consequences for his program of philosophical inquiry." It results in an ethos of true conversation in which "mutual desire makes possible the ungrudging exchange of questions and answers which constitutes the soul of philosophic practice."[33] Halperin concludes, "Since any beautiful soul can serve as a mirror for any other, reciprocal desire need not be confined to the context of physical relations between the sexes (which Plato, at least according to one reading of *Phaedrus* 250e, appears to have despised). The kind of mutuality in *eros* traditionally imputed to women in Greek culture could therefore find a new home in the erotic dynamics of Platonic love."[34] I need to unpack Halperin's argument a bit here, for it is a complex one. On the one hand, he claims that Platonic eros is fundamentally reversed in its values from Pausanian (demotic Athenian) values, that there is a Platonic transvaluation of values.[35] Where Pausanian, Greek love founded its theory of even the highest eros on desire to possess, for Plato desire to procreate is the aim of eros. Since procreation (according to Halperin's Plato) is impossible to realize sexually, it follows, therefore, that there is none of the dominance and subordination, the binary of the penetrator and the penetrated, in Platonic eros, as there is in even the most elevated forms of Athenian pederasty. Moreover, on the physical level of eros (which Plato "despises" in both its hetero and homo avatars), the ambiguity of the pederastic object (he will grow up to be "one of us") virtually precludes him being represented in everyday Athenian thought as a mutually desiring subject, precisely because his desire would be then the "unmanly" one to be possessed and penetrated. Consequently, for this piece of his metaphor for philosophy Plato had to turn to the acceptably mutual desire of the heterosexual couple (since women will never grow up to be men, they are not dishonored—any more than they are already—by their love of being penetrated or love and desire for the one who penetrates them). While I accept that the procreative motive as Plato's new model for eros is a crucially important motive and that this surely contributed to the femalehood of Diotima—

Who better than a woman to understand a desire for procreation? Who indeed?—I cannot swallow Halperin's idealizing reading of the eros/anteros of the philosophical dialogue, any more than its idealizing reading of heterosex (or homosex) as mutual and egalitarian.

Since, of course, procreation can be realized sexually, if one partner is male and one female, as Diotima herself makes quite beautifully clear (206c–e), there is more, then, going on in the move from the physically procreative eros of the heterosexual couple (Pericles and Aspasia) to the purely spiritual and intellectual one (Socrates and Diotima) than Halperin has articulated, namely a strong displacement of procreation itself. Where Halperin's argument seems to assume that the thrust of Plato's innovation is to find a way to assimilate male-male love to that of male and female, and therefore Diotima must be a woman, I would read it almost in opposite fashion as a way of making male-female love "as good as" male-male love, by removing the sexual element from the former as well as from the latter. Hence, in my view, the "vulgar" understanding of Platonic love as love without sex, whatever the sexes, has much to commend it. The relationship between Socrates and Diotima, models, as it were, the possibility of a purely spiritual eros between a man and a woman while theorizing that nonsexual eros as procreative in both its same-sex and other-sex (but always no-sex) versions. The mutuality of the heterosexual couple is a chimera, since the only reason, so it seems, that the female is permitted to desire the male penetrator is that she is always/already of dominated, penetratable status. This would suggest that using this eros/anteros as the model for "mutual desire [that] makes possible the ungrudging exchange of questions and answers which constitutes the soul of philosophic practice" could raise as many questions as it answers, and indeed, in my view, it does, as a further investigation of the *Symposium* will disclose. In short, I shall suggest that the eros of philosophical dialogue is, for Plato, as much penetrative and hierarchical as Pausanian pederasty or Pericles's liaison with Aspasia. The move that Plato makes is a decisive one away from the body, both the body of pleasure and the body of procreation, to a disembodied version of both. The question of an eros of speaking is, therefore, at the very heart of the *Symposium,* as much or even more (for being partly disguised) as in any of the dialogues, including the ones that most explicitly foreground it, such as the *Gorgias*.

The first speech by Phaedrus, at any rate, can be profitably read as a sort of parody of epideictic rhetoric. Indeed, in one reading, at least, all of the speeches are such parodies.[36] Explicit thematizing of rhetoric, however, appears when Agathon begins his own speech by insisting that before speaking he will have to theorize about speech—about what is proper and improper form in such a speech. Plato is explicitly setting Agathon up as a *rhetor,* that is, as a sophist and not philosopher, one who allegedly is concerned with form and not with content or truth. This theme is doubled in Socrates's second interchange with Agathon:

> When Agathon finished, Aristodemus said, everyone there burst into applause, so becoming to himself and to the god did they think the young man's speech.
>
> Then Socrates glanced at Eryximachus and said, "Now do you think I was foolish to feel the fear that I felt before? Didn't I speak like a prophet a while ago when I said that Agathon would give an amazing speech and I would be tongue-tied?"
>
> "You were prophetic about one thing, I think," said Eryximachus, "that Agathon would speak well. But you, tongue-tied? No, I don't believe that."
>
> "Bless you," said Socrates. "How am I not going to be tongue-tied, I or anyone else, after a speech delivered with such beauty and variety? The other parts may not have been so wonderful, but that at the end!"

Socrates is speaking here with his usual high irony, because it is precisely the last part of Agathon's speech that was composed and delivered in high Gorgianic style, and even in an over-the-top parodic version thereof. However, lest we miss this point, Plato has Socrates go on and underline it: "Who would not be struck dumb on hearing the beauty of the words and phrases? Anyway, I was worried that I'd not be able to say anything that came close to them in beauty, and so I would almost have run away and escaped, if there had been a place to go. And, you see, the speech reminded me of Gorgias, so that I actually experienced what

Homer describes: I was afraid that Agathon would end by sending the Gorgian head / Gorgonic head, awesome at speaking in a speech, against my speech, and this would turn me to stone by striking me dumb."

Socrates insists that it is the gorgiasness of the rhetoric that stuns into silence, while others in other dialogues (Meno), to be sure, would accuse Socrates of using dialectic to stun them. At this point, after some further gibes at Gorgias's alleged willingness to say anything on any topic without any regard for truth, Socrates insists that he will speak only if certain conditions be met: "But I didn't even know the method for giving praise; and it was in ignorance that I agreed to take part in this. . . . Goodbye to that! I'm not giving another eulogy [encomium] using that method, not at all—I wouldn't be able to do it!—but, if you wish, I'd like to tell the truth my way" (198a–199c).[37]

Socrates declares that "you will hear the truth about Love, and the words and phrasing will take care of themselves." This is (or at any rate becomes) a standard diatribe against rhetoric, claiming that it cares more for the form than for the substance, if it cares for the substance at all. It seems at first, notwithstanding this jibe, that he is offering just another version or type of an encomium, perhaps one that will be less beautiful but all the more truthful for that, but then, quite unexpectedly, when given permission, what Socrates turns to is not encomium at all, but rather a dialectical interrogation of an Agathon turned virtual Protagoras.

For Leo Strauss what this means (somewhat ridiculously) is that "when people are too tired to make long speeches, they are not too tired to make conversation, engage in dialogue."[38] Jowett provides a much more cogent and revealing reading when he refers to "the ruling passion of Socrates for dialectics." Socrates, "who will argue with Agathon instead of making a speech, and will only speak at all upon the condition that he is allowed to speak the truth."[39] In other words, we might say, dialogue equals philosophy, that is, the search for truth,[40] while encomia, rhetorical speeches, are incorrigibly marred owing to their search for their own beauty, or, even worse, for mere crowd-pleasing effect.

I wish again to emphasize the parallel between Aspasian rhetoric, sophism, traffic in wisdom and Pausanian pederasty on the one hand and between philosophy, alienated wisdom, and Diotima's desire on the other. Agathon (the beautiful), that stand-in for Gorgias and through him for Protagoras (and indeed Isocrates), has been made out to be a false-speaker, because he delivers *encomia* and does not participate in dialectic, as opposed to Socrates who will use speech only to discover "truth." And indeed at the end, when Agathon has—predictably, indeed per-force—capitulated, Socrates intones with great solemnity and self-regard, that it is not he who is impossible to refute, but the truth (201c).[41]

Socrates proceeds with his typical (and as usual fallacious) demolition of the argument of his sophistic antagonist by means of dialectical brow-beating. The fallacy in this *elenchus* has been well articulated by Steven Lowenstam: "Agathon had argued that Eros embodied happiness, beauty, youth, tenderness, poetry, and the four virtues. In his dialogue with Socrates, however, he is forced to agree to three major premises: (1) desire always has an object; (2) one lacks what one desires; and (3) desire can be anticipatory. Socrates introduces the third point to preclude Agathon from arguing that a healthy man may wish for health. Hence, when Socrates asserts that the healthy man desires health not for the present but for the future, he is merely demonstrating that this case confirms the second point: The healthy man desires what he currently lacks, health in the future. After Agathon agrees to these points, he capit-ulates to Socrates's conclusion that Eros can be neither good nor beauti-ful."[42] Allan Bloom describes Socrates's victory here as "single combat, and at this Socrates is the unsurpassed master." Then he remarks, "Any-body who puts himself in the position of wrestling with Socrates always loses and goes away either angry, claiming that Socrates has cheated, or entranced by his unrivaled skill and strength."[43]

The fact that all of the speakers in the text up until Agathon refer to *doxa* marks them off as of the rhetorical/sophistic party. It is this demoli-tion by Socrates of Agathon's rhetoric, of his speechifying, that will set up the explicitly protreptic discourse by Diotima/Socrates/Plato in favor of the dialogical/philosophical *bios*. C. J. Rowe has described this se-quence perfectly: "S[ocrates] launches into the positive part of [Dioti-ma's] account; but it is still in the form of responses to S., so that in effect, although the final part is a long piece of monologue in reply to the briefest of questions (208b7–9), there is strictly speaking nothing by way of a continuous speech to match the others, . . . In short, he 'speaks his piece' in a rather special way, which has more in common with his preferred methods of conversation (*dialegesthai*; see esp. 194d5–6n.) than with the set speeches of the other contributors, even if it reaches what is certainly, in retrospect (and must in any case be) a predetermined conclusion."[44] Indeed, by only a slightly perverse argument, one could opine that the major theme of the *Symposium,* as indeed of virtually the whole Platonic corpus, is its protreptic discourse on dialectic/dialogue with its absolute and coercive "Truth," over against the shady and shaky claims of rhetoric or debate, with its very precarious grasp on the same.[45]

Socrates's treatment of Agathon (meaning good, beautiful) is meant as an acting out of proper pederasty—Agathon being the beautiful boy with whom Socrates would love to have conversation, as opposed to the presumably incorrect (however "heavenly") pederastic relationship between Agathon and his actual lover, *Pausanias.* The same relations of power and hierarchy apply as in Athenian man-boy love: Agathon must assent to Socrates's reasoning, but the realm is not of the body but of the soul.[46] If Agathon the *eromenos* gratifies the need of Socrates the *erastēs* to penetrate his mind with logos (as he does with his body and Pausanias's phallus), then, presumably Agathon will receive some of the same things that the ordinary *eromenos* is supposed to receive from his gratifying the need of his *erastēs* to penetrate his body with phallus.[47]

This reading puts, I think, quite a different spin on this philosophical eros than Halperin's with its idealizing description of perfect mutuality in the relations of philosophical *erastēs* and *eromenos.*[48] On the one hand, we can find here in philosophical dialogue, Platonic style, a strong model of male-male desire, as spiritualized and as intense as the male-male desire of a Byzantine monastery.[49] That nevertheless should not blind us to differences in the ways in which that model is constructed. My reading also raises problems for one of Halperin's explanations for Diotima's genitalia, as it does for Foucault's similar insistence on the mutuality of the Platonic "dialectic of love."[50] However, it clearly assimilates Plato's pedagogical ideal to pederasty in the sharp asymmetry of the penetrator, penetrated, taking the pederastic model of Athens at its best, as represented by Pausanias's speech, and turning it on its head from its bottom, as it were.[51] It is that transfer from anus, vagina, and womb to pure mind that explains why Diotima is not Aspasia. She is the possessor of neither a vagina for pleasure nor a womb for physical procreation but both, in her, are purely spiritual entities, metaphors that help us grasp the proper eros. Ideal eros, for Plato, is entirely a mind-fuck.[52]

Socrates completes his ventriloquistic peroration by insisting: "Such, Phaedrus, is the tale which I heard from the stranger of Mantinea, and which you may call the encomium of love, or what you please." By enacting in the discourse the substitution of dialectic (philosophy) for encomia (rhetoric), Diotima has matched in the form of her expression the form of its content as well, the replacement of the physical eros and the rhetorical, political, ethical socialization that is attendant on it— Pausanias's "heavenly love"—with a heavenly love that does not belong to the world of getting and spending at all.

For Foucault, the move to philosophical love (Socratic/Platonic style) is the product of a structural problem with pederasty. As he puts it,

> The preoccupation of the Greeks, on the other hand, did not concern the desire that might incline an individual to this kind of relationship, nor did it concern the subject of this desire; their anxiety was focused on the object of pleasure, or more precisely, on that object insofar as he would have to become in turn the master in the pleasure that was enjoyed with others and in the power that was exercised over oneself. It was here, at this problematization (how to make the object of pleasure into a subject who was in control of his pleasures), that philosophical erotics, or in any case Socratic-Platonic reflection on love, was to take its point of departure.[53]

Foucault allows that "one does find in Plato the theme that love should be directed to the soul of boys rather than to their bodies. But he was not the first or the only one to say this." Even so, "(and both the *Symposium* and the *Phaedrus* are quite explicit on this point) [Plato] does not trace a clear, definitive, and uncrossable dividing line between the bad love of the body and the glorious love of the soul."[54]

Diotima's Platonic love, however, is entirely different from that of Pausanias, first in that it begins, as we have just seen, in a love of bodies that does not involve touching, contact, or mixing at all but only the begetting of beautiful ideas. We thus find two types of soul-love, even setting aside the vulgar love of men for women or men for men which is primarily physically oriented and goes nowhere even according to Pausanias. Pausanian heavenly love is *philotimia* (208c), while Platonic love is *philosophia* (205d). Platonic love does not, therefore, begin where Athenian (and Spartan) love ends but somewhere else, in a love of beautiful bodies that is never realized sexually at all, and it is only this kind of lover, the philosopher, who could ever hope to achieve knowledge of "just what it is to be beautiful" (211d):

> When someone rises by these stages, through loving boys correctly, and begins to see this beauty, he has almost grasped his goal. This is what it is to go aright, or be led by another, into the mystery of Love: one goes always upwards for the sake of this Beauty, starting out from beautiful things are using them like rising stairs: from one body to two and from two to all beautiful bodies, then from beautiful bodies to beautiful customs, and from customs to learning beautiful things, and from these lessons he arrives in the end at this lesson, which is learning of this very Beauty, so that in the end he comes to know just what it is to be beautiful. (211c–d)

Now it is clear enough from this passage that this correct loving of boys does not involve physical sex, else we would have to imagine a Plato who sees having sex with two beautiful bodies a higher practice than having sex with one and having sex with all beautiful bodies an even higher rung than that.[55] It's a nice fantasy, but not, I think, Plato's.[56] We see, accordingly, not one ladder but two, one beginning with physical love and ending with good government (the Lesser Mysteries) and one beginning with an eros only of eyes and ideas and ending with contemplation of Beauty itself (the Greater Mysteries).[57] Pausanian love, rhetoric, running institutions, these are all the province of banausic man; only philosophy belongs to daimonic man.[58] The most that Pausanian heavenly love can engender is "images of virtue," those images afforded by an education in wisdom (Sophia, not philosophia).

We find this point most vividly exemplified, perhaps, in the *Phaedrus* (251e), where there is as eloquent a description of passion for a beautiful boy as one could possibly imagine, but its consummation is purely through the eyes and the soul. No penises or other touching organs need apply. In the *Laws,* moreover, Plato explicitly marks this as the love of a "philosophical pair," this love without sex, while the less philosophical, the lovers of *timē* (honor) even at their most honorable, engage in sex sparingly (256a–d). Lest one imagine, moreover, that this is not being presented there as Socrates's "true" view, his behavior with Alcibiades as reported in the *Symposium* bears out this interpretation. Finally, in the passage on love in the *Laws,* we find the same dichotomy between the lover who loves with the body and the lover for whom the desire of the body is incidental (837b).[59] By staging the opposition between Aspasia and Diotima, Plato is enacting precisely the opposition between the lover of bodies/*timē* and the lover of souls/*epistēmē*: Aspasia versus Diotima equals Pericles versus Socrates, a binary opposition.[60]

This is a crucial point that is sometimes overlooked: The progress for the philosophers (or even for nascent philosophers) is not from bodies experienced corporally to souls experienced spiritually. Instead for those in the category of philosophers (from infancy, practically, or by accident of ill-birth; the alien, the ill), it is progress from bodies experienced spiritually to souls experienced spiritually, then to the Forms. Such philosophers do qualify themselves to be philosopher-kings or the leaders of philosophical academies, but not citizens of the democratic polis.[61] The political body and the physically reproductive, sexual body are on one side of a line; the philosophical body that begets only in souls on the other. Foucault insists that Plato only "broached questions that would later have a very great importance for the transformation of this ethics into a morality of renunciation and for the constitution of a hermeneutics of desire," while Plato himself is "deeply rooted in the habitual themes of the ethics of pleasure."[62] My reading tends to suggest, in contrast, that Plato is not only an unwitting catalyst for this transformation but its very agent provocateur, as it were, that in the *Symposium* (and in the *Phaedrus*) Plato sets up precisely that dividing line (the line of a binary opposition between body and soul) and thus already manifests some of the most significant components of a late-ancient erotics that we associated with Christianity.[63]

It seems to me, then, that Jowett was exactly right in his conclusion that Diotima has taught him that love is another aspect of philosophy. The same want in the human soul which is satisfied in the vulgar by the procreation of children, may become the highest aspiration of intellectual desire. As the Christian might speak of hungering and thirsting after righteousness; or of divine loves under the figure of human (compare Eph.: "This is a great mystery, but I speak concerning Christ and the church"); as the mediaeval saint might speak of the "fruitio Dei"; as Dante saw all things contained in his love of Beatrice, so Plato would have us absorb all other loves and desires in the love of knowledge. Here is the beginning of Neoplatonism, or rather, perhaps, a proof (of which there are many) that the so-called mysticism of the East was not strange to the Greek of the fifth century before Christ.[64]

My reading affirms the defensibility (if not more) of Jowett's conclusion that the *Symposium* already strongly avows what will be a Christian (or more broadly, late ancient) theory of sexuality. Both Dover and Foucault are right in asserting that Platonic love is not grounded in a law in the sense that it will be for Jews and Christians.[65] However, much more important in my view is the essential positing of a spiritual love that is not only not physical but in important ways directly opposed to the physical. The bottom line of the *Symposium* is that Greek eros has been entirely transformed from the attraction to beautiful bodies into the interaction of souls through dialogue. Once again, rhetoric has been marked by Plato as the space of the specious, while Socrates's dialogue, which, as we have seen, is equally much a power play, has replaced pederasty. Pederasty becomes pedagogy. The break with the patterns of socialization in the Athenian polis is total.[66] For Plato, it would seem, the body's beauty, as well as language's beauty, and the beauty of the community of ordinary human beings sharing views and reaching conclusions and decisions, as well as sharing bodily fluids and sometimes making babies,[67] all belong to the realm of the false-seeming, the realm of appearance, the dreaded *doxa,* and all of them together are to be replaced by the eros of love of the Forms, *epistēmē.* Whether or not this has anything to do with the mysticism of the East, it does have everything to do with the conceptions of the relations of the political body to the spiritual one in late ancient Judeo-Christianity. Christian celibate eros—the eros, for instance, of a Jerome and a Paula[68]—is neither the antithesis nor yet the product of heavenly Greek love, but finds its genealogy rather in the total break with sex and the city initiated by Platonic love.

❧ Flesh in Confession: Alcibiades Beside Augustine

MARK D. JORDAN

Benjamin Jowett, squirming still before his bowdlerized rendering of the *Symposium*, concedes the obvious as a condemnation: "It is impossible to deny that some of the best and greatest of the Greeks indulged in attachments, which Plato in the Laws, no less than the universal opinion of Christendom, has stigmatized as unnatural."[1] Even the Platonic Socrates must be reproved so far as he "does not appear to regard the greatest evil of Greek life as a matter of abhorrence, but as a subject for irony, and is far from resenting the imputation of such attachments."[2]

Daniel Boyarin's rereading of the *Symposium* brings us back to Jowett's claims—though not, of course, to Jowett's mendacious translations or prudish strategies.[3] Boyarin thinks that Jowett got something right: There is indeed resonance between Plato's views, as expressed through Socrates's recollection of Diotima, and the early stirrings of "the universal opinion of Christendom." Boyarin also shows how many things Jowett got wrong, including notably the critique of Socrates. Boyarin's (Platonic) Socrates does condemn male-male copulation. He would indeed have resented the imputation of such attachments as a misunderstanding of his teaching and his life.

To the spirited discussion that Boyarin's reading will provoke, I offer here two preliminary responses.[4] The first is a meditation on a part of the *Symposium*, the speech of Alcibiades, that many readers neglect or denigrate.[5] The second is the juxtaposition of Alcibiades's courtship of Socrates with Augustine's account of his "conversion" in *Confessions* 8, a piece of relatively early Christian writing full of consequences for Christian sex.

WHY IS ALCIBIADES A DRUNKEN MAN?

Any persistent reader of Plato has to make certain judgments on his rhetorical choices—that is, on his erotic character.[6] How comprehensive is his decision to write dialogues? How complete is their irony? How thorough the arrangement of dramatic details in them? How important is the absence of Plato from among the interlocutors and actors? Or do the dialogues finally betray an irrepressible dogmatism, a ferocious desire to state at last the truth about the highest things?

The questions about poetry or character press especially on any reading of the *Symposium*, where arts of writing and erotic character are both topics and occasions. The dialogue's speeches in praise of Eros celebrate a tragedian's victory in civic competitions. The dialogue itself begins by describing how its own words come to be: They pass down through a chain of men (Aristodemus, Apollodorus, Agathon, [Plato]) who love Socrates's words enough to chase after him. Apollodorus rehearses the story once again in response to a question that the dialogue does not record—a question posed by a comrade or fellow disciple or lover (*hetairos*, 173d).[7] The rehearsal is further framed as a response to a later Agathon's frustrated desire to hear the words about love spoken when Agathon the tragedian dined with Socrates and Alcibiades (172b). The dialogue descends through an erotic genealogy. Near its origin stands Aristodemus, who was an ardent suitor of Socrates in those days (*erastēs*, 173b). Apollodorus gives every sign in the present of aggressive infatuation, despite his nickname *"malakos"* (173d): soft, gentle, self-indulgent—or effeminate. The occasion for the original banquet is the same as the occasion for its being retold: a network of passions in which erotic terms and roles are densely present and curiously reversed. Effeminates assert themselves as suitors, and young beauties pursue the old.

Within that double frame, the evening's climactic episode is the encounter between Socrates and Alcibiades (and not Socrates inventing Diotima). Alcibiades's love-song to Socrates displays the kind of erotic relationship that enables the dialogue to persist—that preserves the night's speeches for infatuated retelling decades later. Alcibiades appears in the dialogue as Socrates's original suitor—as an earlier Aristodemus, the source of the genealogy—and so he embodies the conditions under which Socratic teaching can take place or be remembered. Alcibiades appears, too, as the god of the feast—assuming that Eros is only a halfling messenger (as Diotima argues, 202b–203e).

The banquet being retold enacts the city Dionysia. It falls on the day after Agathon and the chorus have sacrificed in thanksgiving for his victory in the festival competition (173a). Because there was so much drinking the night before, the banqueters banish the flute girl and adopt the sober rule that there will be speeches before wine (176e). Alcibiades disrupts it all. Already drunk, he is helped to Agathon's banquet table in the company of the flute girl. He is dressed as Dionysus and she is one of "his people" (213a), the Bacchic train—or rather the festal attendants who accompanied the preferred images (*agalmata*) of Dionysus, the *phalloi*, into the city to inaugurate the festival.[8] Alcibiades-Dionysus settles on a dining couch between Agathon and Socrates. (Remember the exact question to Apollodorus: The evening will be remembered as the banquet of these three.) Alcibiades takes mixed wreaths from his head to crown Agathon. He suddenly sees Socrates (his eyes had been screened by the dangling embellishments) and then crowns him with flowers taken from Agathon, saying "his words have been too much for all the world—and all of his life too, Agathon, not just the other day likes yours" (213e). Socrates is more justly honored as word-maker than the winners of the Dionysian contests. Alcibiades further disrupts the sober and politic agreement of the evening by chugging wine. Eryximachus insists that Alcibiades atone for his boorishness by making a speech even out of order, after drink. The speech that follows proceeds under the omen of things reversed—just like the erotic relationships that transmit the speech in memory.

SATYRS EVERYWHERE

At the Dionysia, tragedians typically presented a tetralogy, that is, three tragedies and a satyr play. Alcibiades starts right in with a satyr play. Socrates, says Alcibiades, is like the statuaries' figures of a flute-playing Silenus: They open up to expose figurines or images of the gods (*agalmata theōn*, 215b). Silenus is the father of satyrs and companion to Dionysus.

The satyr Marsyas is the second character in this Satyric or Silenic drama (as Socrates will call it, 222d). Socrates resembles Marsyas physically, but exceeds him in power to make trouble. Marsyas needed a musical instrument to enchant, but Socrates can do it by words alone. The effect is the same: Marsyan music and Socratic words discover divinely those who need the gods and their rites (215c–d). Alcibiades will testify that Socrates's Marsyan words produce in him physical effects stronger than the frenzy of the (Dionysian) Corybants (215d–e). They are incantations—or, rather, initiations. As Marsyas passed on bewitching music to Olympus (215c), so Socrates's words can still enthrall when played years later.

Socrates is a satyr-statuette with divine images inside. Or Socrates is an ugly satyr who plays and passes on incantatory speeches. By both likenesses he is related to Dionysus—and so to a divine *erōs* that is not Diotima's. From the outside, Socrates appears to pursue beautiful bodies and to calculate the usual features of attraction (216d–e). Readers of the dialogue see Socrates in hot pursuit, when he pleads with Agathon not to let Alcibiades come between them (222d). In fact, insists Alcibiades, Socrates mocks the prevailing erotic economy. He views "us as nothing" (216e)—"us," the drinkers around the table, famous competitors in the city's erotic competitions. Socrates spends all of his public life "ironizing and playing" (*eirōneuomenos de kai paizōn*, 216e)—or, dissembling and jesting; performing his word music; flirting as a divine tease.

The evidence for this accusation is testimony. Alcibiades glimpses the *agalmata*, the figurines or images inside this Silenus. They are "so divine and golden and all beautiful and astonishing" that he is held in thrall (216e–217a). Alcibiades understands this as a chance to become Socrates's lover in scrambled exchange for complete initiation. So he sets up situations in which Socrates can easily (and conventionally) play suitor to Alcibiades as "boy" (*haper an erastēs paidikois*, 217b).[9] When Socrates fails to take up the approved role, Alcibiades risks trading them. He invites Socrates to dinner, "just like a suitor" plotting against the boy of the moment (*hōsper erastēs paidikois epibouleuōn*, 217c). The series of dinners culminates, according to plot, in one that lasts so late Socrates is persuaded to sleep over. When the slaves are gone and the lamps put out, Alcibiades states his proposition freely (218c). He becomes the mirror image of the *erastēs*—a boy forced to play suitor. After a brief dialogue, to which I will come back, Alcibiades imagines that his directness has succeeded. He goes over to lie down next to Socrates, wrapping them both in a cloak against the cold. He puts his arms around "this truly daemonic and amazing man, and [spends] the whole night" (219c). During this time he testifies that nothing happened, nothing more than if he had been sleeping with a father or an older brother.

Having offered this humiliating testimony of apparent rebuff, Alcibiades goes on to narrate Socrates's heroism on the battlefield and to assert that there is no one like him. The speech of simile, testimony, narrative, and prosecution ends with a charge of erotic reversal—and a pointed warning to Agathon. Socrates pursues as if he were a suitor, an *erastēs*, but in fact he knows himself the *pais*, the desired boy (222d). Socrates reverses erotic economy or polity. If Alcibiades wants to constitute the banqueters judges of his charge against Socrates for arrogance (*huperēphania*, 219c), he knows that they are also plaintiffs. This is a class-action suit on behalf of every proper *erastēs* and *pais* against Socrates's treasonous reversal of roles. Alcibiades, who has himself been prosecuted for performing the mysteries before slaves at symposia, testifies in shame to Socrates's misleading initiations.[10] He is ashamed because he—buff beauty with a killer wardrobe—is chasing Socrates—old, snub-nosed, ill clothed, shoeless, and notoriously self-absorbed. Public decency—Athenian homo-normativity—requires that it be the other way around.

Within the dialogue, Alcibiades's speech is reabsorbed by the prevailing erotic polity. Those listening take his humiliating candor as comic proof that he is still in love with Socrates (222c). Socrates himself professes to read the whole speech as a jealous lover's ploy to separate him from Agathon. The ploy consists not only in warning that Socrates cannot be trusted, but also in exposing his erotic play as contemptuously empty. However much Socrates feigns panting, he is not going to be Agathon's lover. He is not going to play the part. If anything, Agathon will have to take an embarrassing initiative, only to be rebuffed. Socrates, who has already asked Agathon to protect him (213c–d), now proposes to praise Agathon—if only he'll sit next to him (222d, 223a). Socrates accuses Alcibiades of wanting a neatly transitive three-way: Socrates as *erastēs* only to Alcibiades, Alcibiades as only *erastēs* to Agathon. As if. Socrates plans to play *pais* to both.

The end and immediate aftermath of the speech seem to confirm Socratic chastity and to mark Alcibiades as an object lesson in misplaced desire. The Dionysian speech confirms negatively Diotima's teaching about the need to transcend the bodies. Alcibiades could not transcend—and look what happened. On this reading (which is, curiously, both Jowett's and Nietzsche's), Socrates stands firm against the surging forces of Dionysus—as he stood in immobile contemplation outside Agathon's door or in the camp at Potidaea, as he showed invincible composure even during the rout at Delium (220c, 221b). Socrates seeks out hardships. He is never drunk (220a). Diotima was right: it's all about getting beyond bodies.

Or is it? The existence of the dialogue and the testimony of Alcibiades-Dionysus are evidence to the contrary. The string of lovers that brings the dialogue into existence is a line of men who chase after Socrates. They remember not only his words, but also his actions, his daily doings (Apollodorus, "what he says and does every day," 172e–173a; Aristodemus, "and I followed him as usual" on daily rounds, 223d). These *erastai* also fall in love with his satyr body, because the divine, golden, all-beautiful, astonishing *agalmata* are inside it. Here we must remember that the *agalmata* of the city Dionysia are . . . giant phalluses. The god himself settled their ritual use by punishing the citizens of Eleutherai with a genital affliction for rejecting them. To say that Socrates has golden *agalmata* inside does not imply transcendence of erotic bodies (*pace* Diotima). When Alcibiades's testimony is read within the frame of the dialogue, it shows not so much his moral failure as Diotima's rather selective, if not quite fantastical, teaching.

Alcibiades says that those bitten by philosophical speeches, those seized by "the madness and Bacchic frenzy" of philosophy, become suitors (*erastai*). They are not at first suitors of Socrates who then become lovers of philosophy. They pursue Socrates *after* being enchanted by philosophy. They are perfectly well aware how little his body or social connections are worth at the city's going rate. Indeed, they are astonished to find themselves playing reversed roles. Philosophic enchantment eroticizes discounted bodies. In Socratic teaching, as Alcibiades describes it and the frame of the dialogue shows it, there are no unambiguous transits from the love of one body to all physical beauty, then to minds and customs or institutions and knowledge, so that one can swim at last in beauty itself (Diotima at 210a–211c). Alcibiades might be taken as simply a bad pupil—too pathetic in his lust for Socrates—were it not that the existence of the dialogue depends upon just his condition. Without Alcibiades, no (Platonic) Socrates.

There are of course other reasons for doubting whether Diotima's speech is the central teaching of the *Symposium*.[11] Socrates mocks Diotima and retells her as a sophist (206e, 208e). Her prophetic abilities and origin are rather comically overemphasized (201d). The claim that she taught Socrates about *erōs* contradicts Socrates's self-descriptions elsewhere (e.g., *Lysis* 204c). It also falls before the pointed Socratic critiques of pretensions to morally improving instruction. (Tell me, Diotima, whether *erōs* can be taught, a smarter Meno might begin.) The language Diotima uses to describe her ladder is like Socrates's language for telling myths in *Phaedo*, the *Republic*, and *Phaedrus*. His myths are pedagogically important—both consoling and hortatory. They are not plain doctrine. Neither is Diotima's ladder. Moreover, and against the logic of the dialogue's own transmission, Socrates is obviously altering his memory of what Diotima said. As Aristophanes tries to object, Diotima responds too exactly to what the comedian and others have just said (212c; compare Socrates's admission at 201e). When Socrates concludes, "That's what Diotima said to me," he is ironizing. He is also declaring that he is not an *erastēs* of Diotima. He is no Aristodemus—or Alcibiades—to her Socrates. We are repeatedly reminded that Socrates can interrupt at any point when Alcibiades stops telling the truth (214e, 217b). We have no such guarantee for the "memory" of Diotima's didactic pronouncements.

THE ANTICONNUBIAL COUCH

The central teaching of the dialogue is not in Socrates's fiction about an impossible (and perhaps insufferable) mock-myth. It is in the appearance, through Alcibiades, of divine (Dionysian) images. What then of Socrates's refusal on the couch? Is it an attempt to help Alcibiades step up the ladder? A denigration of the erotic as mistaken fulfillment? Shouldn't we instead ask: What do we know of Socrates's actions that night?

Before Alcibiades crosses to embrace Socrates, there is a short dialogue. Alcibiades begins by trying to award Socrates the role of *erastēs*.

Socrates is worthiest to be his *erastēs* because he is most able to improve Alcibiades. In return, he will be rewarded not only with a beautiful body, but also with the help of a network of allies (218c). These are the approved sentiments of the noble Athenian *pais*. To which Socrates replies, in effect: No, I'm the *pais*, because I have more real beauty. You, Alcibiades, really are the *erastēs*—and not just by a strategic exchange of roles. You are consumed by desire for my beauty. Socrates rejects not bodies and their pleasures, but the conventional erotic economy that ranks exterior beauty over the beauty of the golden *agalmata* inside. Socrates refuses the conventions of exchange—but not necessarily what lies underneath their commodification.

It is after this exchange that Alcibiades makes his move—the move of an *erastēs*. He agrees in effect to assume the role that Socrates has required. He certainly does not take Socrates's words as precluding sexual contact. On the contrary, Alcibiades hears the conversation as evidence that he has succeeded. He has pretended to hand the decision over to Socrates, but in fact he makes the first move. And perhaps the final one. Is it possible that Alcibiades lies about what happens next? Still in love with Socrates, is he willing to humiliate himself in order to magnify praise for his "conquering hero" (220c)? And is it possible that Socrates, who has already been editing or inventing memories for the sake of pedagogy, collaborates with Alcibiades in a deception despite all the fuss about stopping if there are lies? Perhaps the fuss is ironic—the secret signal of a collusion.

To ask this differently: How, exactly, do we imagine that *Socrates* would tell the story of that night on the couch? A sweaty Alcibiades squirming next to his icy indifference? Elsewhere, Socrates gives his reflection of his heroism at Potidaea. On the very day he got back from the campaign, he went to one of his usual haunts—a gym (*Charmides* 153a). There his friends eagerly sought news of the battle in which so many had fallen. Socrates does not repeat what news he gave. He professes to have been more interested in the boys. The most beautiful of them, Charmides, was lured over on a pretext to sit beside him. Socrates saw what the boy had inside his robe (*ta entos tou himatiou*) and "caught fire" (*ephlegomēn*), burning with animal hunger (*Charmides* 155d). Is Socrates being ironic in this first-person account? Yes, of course. But would he tell his reaction to Alcibiades any differently? So are we to imagine a long night of restrained, but fully mutual desire? Or would Socrates say that it was finally Alcibiades who flagged when he realized that it wasn't Socrates's body he wanted? When he recognized that a law like that against incest prohibited Socrates's body to him? Alcibiades does not testify that Socrates stopped him. He reports only that nothing happened beyond what you would expect when sleeping with a father or elder brother—where the emphasis on age restores approved hierarchies and the message underwrites sexual decorum. Whatever was said, done, or not done is covered by Alcibiades's cloak, by his suitor's care for the reputation of an improbable *pais*. By the refusal of that *pais* to assume the politically prescribed role of *erastēs* in order to respond with his version of the tale, because doing so would really mock mysteries before outsiders. Alcibiades and Socrates conspire to hold the cloak in place. Inside it are *agalmata* the reader cannot (yet?) see.

The reader sees this much: Socrates, master of flirtation, never stops Alcibiades's plot. He allows them to be alone while wrestling. He attends the dinners. He permits himself to be persuaded to spend the night. He does not tell Alcibiades to shut up and go to sleep. He does not push him from the couch. He does not get up to go home—though he was perfectly capable of walking across frost at Potidaea and crossing firmly through the rout at Delium. The conquering hero and gym rat will not play the role of suitor, but will take on the role of compliant beloved—at least until things are covered by a cloak. Socrates refuses to reduce erotic desire to the conventional calculus. Does that mean that he rejects copulation altogether—or rather that he wants it to exceed the calculus? He ironizes the games of desire. Does that imply continence—or (Dionysian) disruption? The banquet at Agathon's has been unusually sober. How much did Socrates and Alcibiades drink that other night before the lamps went out?

A reader may now be ready to notice the beginning of Alcibiades's speech (215a). When he says he will speak through images (*di'eikonōn*), he recalls how indispensable images are in Socratic similes for learning (*Phaedo* 99e, *Republic* 509e–510a).[12] Alcibiades remarks as well on the rhetorical agency of the dialogue. What is the *Symposium* but an *eikōn* in words of the body of Socrates crafted by Plato, that great sufferer of suitoring-love (*philerastia*, 213d)? Plato refigures the body of Socrates from passionately remembered and erotically rehearsed words. He fashions for him a durable satyr-skin of initiatory words. Plato recites the new Socrates to us, so that we can join them on a couch.

PLATONIC LOVE IN A MILANESE GARDEN

Where does this leave the resonance that Boyarin's acute ear detects between Platonic love and some early Christian texts? There is a prior question: Aren't the readings of some early Christian texts as problematic as readings of the *Symposium*? Christian texts have suffered even more the fate of Alcibiades's speech in the *Symposium*, and the "universal opinion of Christendom" to which Jowett clings is after all the enforced simplification of his Christendom rather than the rhetorical complexity of some early Christian writers. In an eloquent essay below, for example, Karmen MacKendrick will argue that Augustine sought out his final deity, the God of Christian scriptures, in order to satisfy his erotic desires.[13] I want to follow her reading by juxtaposing Augustine's narrative in *Confessions* 8 with Alcibiades's speech.

Certainly Augustine constructs the scene we call too simply his "conversion" as a competition (or *synkrisis*) of seductions. "Old friends," "trifles of trifles," "vanities of vanities," pluck at his flesh and whisper, "'Are you going to send us away?' . . . 'From this moment forward we will never, ever be with you again'" (8.11.26).[14] Their shameful insinuations are broken by a vision, the second in a triptych (compare 7.10–11, 9.10). Augustine sees "the chaste dignity of Continence, serene and joyful in no dissolute way, enticing [him] honorably to approach and not to hesitate" (8.11.27). Continence appears to Augustine as a better mother than Monica, but also as an ideal lover, neither his unnamable concubines nor his prepubescent fiancée (6.15). Continence reaches out to embrace him. Augustine discovers in her arms "boys and girls, many youths and every age, dignified widows and elderly virgins" (8.11.27). He recognizes a perversely ample physical beauty, across the suddenly arbitrary divisions of sex and age, of a single, gendered body and titles to its property. Some minutes later, famously, there sounds that voice from the house next door (8.12.29): "Take up and read." Augustine cannot tell whether it is a boy or a girl, perhaps because it is one of the confusing children of Continence. The bodiless androgyne's singsong reactivates his initial seduction by words. Words are an instrument of seduction, but they can also impersonate an erotic body, as they can open the imagination to an *erōs* beyond hasty friction.

The tangling in Augustine of desire and persuasion, of willing bodies and pimping speeches, may lead to Gallop or Lacan (as in MacKendrick), but certainly to the rhetorical books Augustine taught for a living. Indeed, what had turned Augustine from the clanging of the "cauldron of shameful loves" (3.1.1) was the required reading of Cicero's (lost) *Hortensius,* a rewriting of Aristotle's (barely reconstructed) *Protreptic.* Reading Cicero's book, the desire for wisdom flames up in him: "How I burned, my God, how I burned" (3.4.8)—not for Carthage, and not yet for a named God, but for the wisdom promised in exhortation. Augustine is persuaded to seek wisdom, draw near it, hold it, squeeze it (3.4.8). So his rhythmic effects imitate excited pulse. His clauses cascade as if panting. His text blushes with passion.

Cicero's *Hortensius* rewrote Aristotle, but thus also responded with Aristotle to the Platonic project of seduction through Socrates. Near the beginning of *Confessions* 8, Augustine mentions his study of the Platonists while recounting his spiritual pilgrimage for Simplicianus, a long-time Christian. Simplicianus rejoices that Augustine did not fall into the texts of other philosophers, full of fallacies and deceptions. In the Platonists, by contrast, "God and his word are everywhere insinuated" (8.2.3). Augustine has read his way further, from the Platonists into the incomparable chorus of Christian scripture. By the start of book 8, he is already firmly convinced, through study and visionary experience both, that every corruptible thing comes from an incorruptible source (8.1.1, compare 7.10.16). This philosophic quest began with Cicero's *Hortensius* (8.7.17), but it has led into Christian revelation: The incorruptible Light above all is the God who sent his Son as humbled Word, who inspired the writings of Paul (8.1.1, carrying forward 7.21.27).

Augustine seems the happy opposite to Alcibiades. He has moved up the ladder of love to a vision of the supreme Light. The Light has convicted him as it consoled him, and so he seeks to become worthy of it. To become worthy, he must be unchained from what binds him (*vincula mea*, 8.1.1). He is tightly bound "by (a) woman" (*tenaciter conligabar ex femina*, 8.1.2). In one sense, Augustine is held by a marriage arrangement. He has described already how his sainted mother, Monica, pushed for an arranged marriage to an acceptable girl (6.13.23). Though she was two years under the minimum age (possibly twelve or younger), Augustine found his intended attractive enough to be willing to wait, though not without taking another woman for the interim—Monica having dispatched to Africa his longtime companion (6.15.25).[15] In another and more important sense, Augustine is bound by the lust of marriage, because marriage meant to him chiefly an arrangement of regular sex (6.12.22). His marriage contract will only shackle him more securely to sexual satisfaction. Indeed, when Augustine runs through examples of artful dalliance in obtaining "wicked and reprehensible delight," he ends with the example of a cunning bride who delays her wedding so that her future husband will not despise what he gets too easily (8.3.7). The wicked pleasure here is had in married intercourse.

Before Augustine sees Continence gesturing toward him in the garden, his anxiety to escape the shackles of sex, of desire for copulation (*vinculum desiderii concubitus*), is inflamed by a story of instant renunciation (8.6.13). To be more precise, it is a remembered story about the instant effects of a written story. The written story tells the conversion of Antony the Great, legendary first among Christian renouncers who fled to the desert. The remembered story concerns two imperial officials who chance upon a codex containing a life of Antony (8.6.15). One man reads the hagiography; he is so "astonished and inflamed" that he rebukes his friend for their uncertain ambition to become friends of the Emperor when they could instantly become friends of God. The man reads on; his reactions are described with as many birth metaphors as Diotima could want. Putting down the codex, he announces that he will commit himself to monastic life at once. His friend—perhaps having listened while Antony's life was read aloud, if it was—commits himself as well; he would "stick with his comrade [*adhaerere se socium*]" in such a reward and such military service. Each man, it turns out, was already engaged, but their fiancées, hearing the news, conveniently agreed to dedicate their virginity to God. The shackle is woman (*femina*), and the support is one's comrade, partner (*socius*). Abandoning the flesh does not mean abandoning same-sex friendship. Indeed, when Augustine is finally freed by reading a random (that is, providential) passage in Paul, Alypius, who had been "fixed" beside him, discovers a few words further on enough justification for his own commitment to a celibate Christianity (8.11–12).

In this narration, Augustine's reading of Paul mirrors the courtier's reading of the story about Antony. But Augustine's reading is prepared by the vision of Continence, an eminently rhetorical and philosophical vision. It is characteristic of the *Confessions* that this climax turns on a rhetorician's device of personified exhortation and a philosopher's ideal of self-control. Not to say, the hot language of desire: "Act, Lord, do it, excite us and call us back, inflame and ravish us, be fragrant, grow sweet: that we may love, that we may run" (8.4.9). And the Lord does it: "You turned me to you, so that I would not seek a wife or any other hope in this world" (8.12.30). What we call Augustine's "conversion" is not a change of belief. It is an amorous refusal of the prevailing economy of male-female sex in favor of (male-male?) celibacy with God.

MacKendrick diagnoses this as the blushing testimony of an imperial rhetor who aches to be used by divine suasion—and still cannot surrender his power of speech. A night on the unwatched couch whispering not to Socrates, but to the Lord God of Hosts. What He will do, no one can ever tell. Augustine, one-time seller of power-words, strives now to be sold as a willing slave to a rhetor God. The pleasures of succumbing to a divine rhetorical power, of becoming its ardent fan, of feeling its breath across the always open orifice of the ear, of awaiting its ever-renewed entry by vibration—Augustine *sold* those pleasures as a rhetorician, but *enjoyed* them more intensely as a convert-writer. He is converted, turned to the Christian God, but also to tropes more inventive than Cicero's, to the ladder of reliable beauties, to the determined formulas of an overeager slave empowered to testify without interruption or response.

MacKendrick is right to underscore these barely hidden rhetorical passions for submission. With them, Augustine only imitates Paul, slave of Jesus Christ (Romans 1:1), whose words seal Augustine's turn when, remembering the story of Antony, he does pick up and read: "Put on the Lord Jesus Christ and have no care for flesh in its cravings" (Romans 13:13, as in 8.12.29). The words are worth meditating upon. What exactly do they promise Augustine? Have no care, because the Lord Jesus has dominion over your body once you dress up in him? Or take no care because your flesh, now the flesh of Jesus, will not have cravings? Because God will take care of you as if you were the flesh of Jesus, his Son?

The quotation is surprising, because the body of Jesus has been curiously absent from *Confessions* 8, despite Augustine's preoccupation with tales of Christian liberation from bodily bondage. From Jesus, "from the mouth of truth," Augustine has heard that those who can should become eunuchs (8.1.2). Augustine has recalled the "opprobrium of the Cross" before which the child of Christ must bow when accepting the "yoke of humility" (8.2.3). Augustine mentions "rites (*sacramenta*) of the humility of your word," but he does not explain their efficacy or narrate their origin (8.2.4). In book 8, Jesus Christ is most often the Word who sets moral examples or who brings light and grace. Of Christ's body as a divine incarnation, as a human body with God somehow inside (and not merely as golden *agalmata*), Augustine says nothing. "Putting on the Lord Jesus Christ" does not mean slipping into his skin. Nothing so crude as that. It means submitting to his humble example in order to be free from meat's craving.

"Put on the Lord Jesus Christ." The command can make it seem that Paul is a blunter or more simple-minded Alcibiades. Perhaps he is—and to his credit. Alcibiades acknowledged that he spoke in "images" about images of the (Dionysian?) divine in Socrates. He meant to barter himself for what Socrates could tell him of those images. Paul, the slave of Jesus Christ, submits himself to a more direct identification—or inhabitation. He no longer lives, but Christ lives in him. Or he lives inside Christ's skin, which he has put on. And it is very much the crucified skin brought back to life.

Augustine, caught between some Platonic books and anxious heteronormative passions, construes Paul's command as liberation from the regular sex required by marriage—not to speak, as he will not, of marriage's other inconveniences (8.1.2). Augustine means to put on the Lord Jesus without touching any skin. He wants the words and their power, but not the flesh that gives them power. The turning he narrates in *Confessions* 8 is triumph over flesh by a nominally incarnate God, whose handmaid Continence begins to resemble Diotima entirely too much.

Augustine disdains the impotent arrogance of the Platonic books (7.9), but apparently not their imperative to safeguard the divine from corruptible flesh.[16]

In this fastidiousness, Augustine aligns himself with an already waxing Christian asceticism, which seeks to imitate Jesus as God without meditating on his body. If Jesus must be a man (so as not to be a woman), do not think what piece of flesh makes him male. Take the power to enact moral proscriptions, but not the incarnation that underwrites them. A God incarnate in a fully sexed human body raises too many dangerous possibilities, which it has been the business of many Diotimas to denigrate and of every Christendom to stigmatize.

Stigmata are the punctures in Jesus' skin.

❧ For the Love of God: The Death of Desire and the Gift of Life

MARIO COSTA

The central question of this essay concerns the desire for God. In taking this as my theme, I want to expand the possibilities for thinking and experiencing desire in general and the desire of God in particular. That this should be a concern for me underscores what I think are some limitations of current theories of desire. Two are particularly noteworthy.

First, the tendency to theorize desire or erotic love overwhelmingly in terms of lack and death is conditioned by, because it coincides with, the death of God and the abandonment of metaphysics. If metaphysical or ontotheological construals of desire can be characterized by the desire for ultimate satisfaction and completion in a plentitude of presence, then in the wake of the deconstruction of the so-called metaphysics of presence, which resolves itself into what might be called a metaphysics of absence, incompletion and indefinitely deferred satisfaction determine the very exigencies of desire itself. On this view, the desire of God presupposes, indeed it would seem to require, God's absence or, what in contemporary thought amounts to the same thing, God's death.

Second, and as a consequence of the first, contemporary lack-based theories of desire or erotic love are articulated primarily in secular and even atheistic terms. Because the structure and economy of desire are theorized in abstraction from any particular object of desire—for it is precisely the lack of the object that animates desire—the object has no material effect on the constitution and activity of desire as such. To desire God, then, is no different from desiring any other "object." Rather, it is only after having worked out a coherent theory of desire that contemporary theorists then proceed to the question of the desire for God.

In this paper I want to formulate the problem of desire differently, and in doing so challenge those theories that privilege lack and death, as well as challenge the secular conditions that support them. To that end, I will first contrast the metaphysical conception of eros as articulated in Diotima's discourse in Plato's *Symposium* with a few epitomes of post-metaphysical lack-based theories, whereby I will sketch out some of the limitations of these theories. I will then suggest and develop a post-secular alternative by drawing from current philosophical theologies of the gift.

• • •

The *Symposium* is commonly read as inaugurating the tradition of conceptualizing eros in terms of sheer lack. Such a reading finds initial support in the exchange between Socrates and Agathon that immediately precedes the account of Diotima's discourse. Here Socrates claims "that what desires, desires what it lacks, or does not desire if it does not lack"; this, for Socrates "seems remarkably necessary" to the nature of desire itself.[1] Lack is the necessary condition of desire: One can only desire what one lacks, for to possess what one desires would bring about the end of desire.

There is no question that at this stage in the *Symposium* Socrates defines desire or erotic love in terms of sheer lack; neither the presence of the object of desire nor the satisfaction of desire is a necessary element of desire; the opposite is rather the case. Simply put, desire is lack. The only thing present to desire is its own lack. But if Socrates here advances a lack-based conception of desire, it is merely a provisional one. And it is one that he did not learn from she who taught him "in the things of love," Diotima (201d). Although lack is an important ingredient in Diotima's discourse on eros, and although there are points of continuity between Diotima's and Socrates's conceptions of eros, her view of erotic love is ultimately more nuanced and complicated than the view put forward here by Socrates. Indeed, at times it is in critical tension with Socrates's view.[2]

This difference between Socrates and Diotima reflects the difference between their respective methods of discourse. Whereas Socratic dialectic proceeds according to the oppositional dualisms of metaphysics (empty/full, wise/ignorant, beautiful/ugly, mortal/immortal, human/god), by which one term is privileged at the expense of the other, Diotima, as Luce Irigaray has pointed out, "[f]rom the outset . . . establishes an *intermediary* that will never be abandoned as a means or a path. . . . She presents, uncovers, and unveils the insistence of a third term that is already there and that permits progression: from poverty to wealth, from ignorance to wisdom, from mortality to immortality."³ Unlike Socratic dialectic, where the two terms are mutually exclusive, Diotiman dialectic discloses and occupies the space *between* the two terms. This is a dialectic of passage and progress between terms, which, for Diotima, according to Irigaray, "always comes to a greater perfection in love."⁴ If, as I have suggested, Diotima's conception of love, or more precisely, erotic love, differs from Socrates's,⁵ then the basis of this difference is found here: For Diotima, eros does not operate according to a logic of exclusion; rather, it institutes a logic of relation and becoming.

From Diotima we learn that Eros, as the child of Penia and Poros, has the characteristics of both want, or lack, and resourcefulness. That Eros is both wanting and resourceful indicates its basic indeterminate and intermediary character. Because Eros is neither empty nor full, neither of these terms can be privileged or absolutized. Consequently, Eros cannot, as Socrates proposes, be conceived solely in terms of lack, nor can Eros be equated with lack. But if Diotima nuances Socrates's lack-based view of Eros—they do agree that Eros lacks, and thus desires, good and beautiful things—she does not simply replace it with a conception of Eros defined in terms of fulfillment and completion. It might be that Eros, out of his resourcefulness, "ever plots for good and beautiful things," but such things never become permanently present to him as possessions, for "whatever is provided ever slips away so that Eros is never rich nor at a loss" (203d–e). Eros forever stands between lack and fulfillment, and makes possible the passage between them.

On the basis of his indeterminate and intermediary character, Diotima asserts, to Socrates's surprise, that Eros is neither mortal nor immortal, and thus neither a human nor a god. Instead, Eros is a "great divinity" or daimon, and as such is "intermediate between god and mortal" (202d). Like all great divinities, Eros mediates the difference and the distance between the gods and mortals. This mediation is, according to Diotima's description, essentially hermeneutic: "Interpreting and conveying things from men to gods and things from gods to men, prayers and sacrifices from the one, commands and rituals in exchange for sacrifices from the other, since, being in between both, it fills the region between both so that the All is bound together with itself" (202e). It is striking—at least to more prudish religious sensibilities—that the relationship between the gods and humans is an erotic one, and that it is not one-sided. If we understand it in terms of desire, then the one desiring the gods does not desire out of pure or absolute lack, that is, the gods' absence. Rather, there is only the finest of lines drawn between the worshiper's desire for the gods and the gods' desire for the worshiper. It is because eros interprets and then conveys things of the earth to the gods and interprets and then conveys things of heaven to the earth that human beings can and do communicate with the gods and that the gods can, and do, communicate with human beings. This communication, viewed from the perspective of eros, constitutes a discourse as erotic intercourse.

In mediating the distance between mortals and the gods, such that "the All is bound up together with itself," eros does not dissolve the difference between heaven and earth, between the gods and humans, such that all things earthly or physical are absorbed into heaven (or the metaphysical and transcendent). Diotima states emphatically that "God does not mingle with man, but all intercourse and conversation of gods with men . . . are through this realm"—that is, the region between gods and humans mediated by the divinities (203a). The binding together of the human and the divine into the All does not erase difference, rather, it establishes a relationship in difference and across distance. Eros, in fact, like all divinities, can only exist as indeterminate and intermediate with the assurance and preservation of the irreducible difference and distance between the physical and metaphysical, the human and the divine. In mediating the difference and distance between these two terms, eros does not reduce them to the singularity of being. Rather, eros operates in the in-between space of becoming. Because Diotima does not absolutize the figuration of eros as either lack or resourcefulness, eros is always becoming both empty and full. Consequently, eros is not thought and cannot be thought in grasping, possessive, and conquering terms.

This last point seems to go against the traditional reading of the *Symposium,* where desire is construed as essentially acquisitive, and it seems to be contradicted by the text itself. In order to better clarify this point, it is necessary to consider carefully several salient points in Diotima's exchange with Socrates.

Against Socrates's assumption that it is Eros himself who is loved, Diotima claims that eros is not the object of eros or erotic love, but the loving itself (204c). Because eros lacks beautiful and good things, eros is neither beautiful nor good in itself, and thus cannot be the object of one's desire. Rather, eros is always eros *of something.* It is important to note here that erotic love is not self-reflexive or narcissistic; desire does not desire itself or its own desiring. To the contrary, eros always has as its object something other than itself. As intermediary and relational, eros mediates, as the *loving,* the space between the erotic lover and the object of desire. At issue here is the following point: Eros is not a blind force that seeks to acquire or consume whatever it lacks. According to Diotima's definition, rather, eros is eros of beautiful and good things. A lover is erotic, therefore, not by seeking and wishing to possess whatever it lacks; instead, a lover becomes erotic by desiring or loving only beautiful and good things. Eros is essentially correlational, its nature defined in terms of its objects. And as correlational, erotic love produces intimacy, rather than antagonism, between desirer and desired.

But why does one desire beautiful and good things? Diotima leads Socrates to the following answer: "to possess them for himself genesthai *autō*]" so that "he will be happy" (204–5a). To render *genesthai autō* as "to possess them for himself,"[6] as most translators do, accommodates a reading of eros as fundamentally acquisitive and possessive, the aim or *telos* of which is happiness. In other words, one desires beautiful and good things in order to possess them (here eros is reduced to a means of acquisition) so that one might ultimately be happy (the end). But as Andrea Nye has pointed out, this translation of *genesthai autō* is misleading; according to Nye, a more literal and faithful translation of the Greek is "to come to be for someone" or "to happen for someone."[7] Following this translation, Socrates would then be understood to be saying that one desires beautiful and good things in order that they come into being or happen for oneself. On this reading, beautiful and good things are not acquisitions made by erotic lovers; this is not what eros desires. Beautiful and good things could instead be viewed as gifts that animate desire, such that desire does not seek to fill a void or lack but rather seeks attachments to, or relationships with, those things that are beautiful and good. Happiness, too, then, is not a possession to be grasped, it "happens for someone" as gift.

Erotic attachments to beautiful and good things do not fill a void or lack in desire or the erotic lover. To the contrary, these erotic attachments are productive, or better, procreative. For the work of Eros/eros is "begetting in beauty, in respect to both the body and the soul" (206b). Here Diotima complicates Socrates's sheerly lack-based conception of desire. Everyone, she claims, is "pregnant in respect to both the body and the soul . . . and when they reach a certain age, our nature desires to beget" (206c). Both body and soul are pregnant, and it is this fecundity that conditions eros prior to procreation. It is out of their fullness that body and soul desire the beautiful, and because it is in the presence of, and intercourse with, the beautiful that body and soul can each give birth to—or have come into being—beautiful things. This, according to Diotima, "is a divine thing, and pregnancy and procreation are an immortal element in the mortal living creature" (206c). But as we saw earlier, eros is intermediate between mortal and immortal, and it is eros that facilitates the progression or passage from the one to the other. The desire to beget, therefore, is the desire for immortality. And yet, if the desire to beget is conditioned by the fecundity or abundance of body and soul, it is also conditioned by lack.

To desire immortality is indeed to desire what one lacks. Oddly enough, however, while existence in and through time brings with it the gradual loss of life, coincident with this loss is an ever-increasing fullness in both body and soul. There is significant and productive interaction between lack and abundance, or more precisely, between death and life inherent in human existence. As Diotima describes it, one "is ever becoming new while otherwise perishing" (207d), which is to say that as elements of the body ("hair and flesh and bone and blood and the entire

body" [207e]) and soul ("its character and habits, opinions, desires, pleasures, pains, fears" [210b]) are perishing, other and new elements are
coming to be. The coming to be or begetting of what is other and new
is the product of erotic intercourse with the beautiful. With respect to
the body, erotic intercourse between beautiful bodies produces children,
and with respect to the soul, erotic intercourse between beautiful souls
ultimately produces virtue. In both cases, what issues forth from this
intercourse brings to fruition and perfects—to a lesser or greater degree—what is immortal and divine in human existence.

It remains now to be seen how erotic love perfects this immortal and
divine aspect of human life.

The desire or erotic love of beautiful things follows two trajectories, a
horizontal and a vertical one. On the horizontal plane, the erotic lover
is initially attracted to beautiful bodies, or rather, *a* beautiful body.
The love of one beautiful body then gives way to the recognition "that
the beauty on any body whatever is akin to that on any other body"
(210b).

Here the narrow scope of the lover's erotic attachments widens to
include all bodies. Although desire is attracted to and pursues the singular
form of beauty itself, all bodies participate in this form, for beauty itself
is manifest in and mediated through a plurality of physical, bodily forms.
Thus the lover "is constituted a lover of all beautiful bodies and relaxes
this vehemence for one, looking down on it, and believes it of small
importance" (210b). What is looked down on here and considered of
small importance is not the love of physical bodies as such, but the narrow attachment to one body.[8] Even when Diotima claims that one "must
come to believe that beauty in souls is more to be valued than that in the
body" (210b), the difference in value between the physical and spiritual is,
on this horizontal plane, relative. To claim that beauty in the soul is of
greater value than that in the body does not entail that the love of physical bodies is degraded or devalued. Rather, both body and soul, insofar
as they are beautiful, are valuable and necessary objects of erotic love.

What is important here is that in one's progression from mortality to
immortality, one proceeds from a love of what is mortal (the body) to
what is immortal (the soul). The divine begetting in the body achieves

immortality by preserving what is mortal, "by leaving behind, as it departs and becomes older, a different new thing of the same sort as it was" (208b). The result here is the begetting of children. This, however, is of secondary importance to Diotima, for what achieves one's immortality, rather than merely preserving one's mortality, is begetting in the presence of what is most beautiful, the soul. Such intercourse is between bodies, but unlike the intercourse that begets children, this intercourse does not result in sexual consummation. For those "who are still more fertile in their souls than in their bodies . . . what it pertains to soul to conceive and bear" (209a) is more beautiful and immortal. Rather than physical or sexual intercourse, this intercourse is essentially dialectical, and what it produces are beautiful ideas. For Diotima, such an erotic relationship constitutes "a more steadfast friendship" than sexual relations, "because they have in common children more beautiful and more immortal" (209c). Erotic love and relationships are not defined in terms of lack or possession. While one might lack immortality, this lack proves resourceful in the erotic lover's relationships with others. Out of this resourcefulness immortality is produced not as something to be possessed, but as something new that comes into being.[9]

Despite these horizontal attachments, however, Diotima's discourse on erotic love of beautiful things culminates in an ascent to the beautiful itself, a vertical ascent that leaves behind it a love for physical bodies and the erotic lover's horizontal attachments. This, according to Diotima, is the "right way to proceed in matters of love, or to be led by another— beginning from these beautiful things here, to ascend ever upward for the sake of *that,* the Beautiful, as though using the steps of a ladder, from one to two, and from two to all beautiful bodies, and from beautiful bodies to beautiful practices, and from practices to beautiful studies, and from studies one arrives in the end at *that* study which is nothing other than the study of *that,* the Beautiful itself, and one knows in the end, by itself, what it is to be beautiful" (211b–c).

As the scope of desire and the range of its objects expand outward, desire itself also ascends upward. And in this ascent the physical is transcended. The physical objects of desire are continually displaced—one beautiful body gives way to all beautiful bodies, which eventually give way to the beautiful itself—such that they never become the possessions of the erotic lover. The physical gives way to what is seen and ultimately known, which is the divine and immortal imaged in all bodies. In this sense, then, eros ascends beyond the physical to the metaphysical, beyond the "images of virtue [to] true virtue" (212a). At this stage, erotic love takes a noetic turn, and the lover's erotic attachments to the multiplicity of beautiful physical bodies becomes knowledge and contemplation of the one, the form of the beautiful. The significance of this point cannot be underestimated. Eros is here conceived as being rational. Reason is at the heart of desire and desire is at the heart of reason. Desire is not irrational, nor is it blind and indiscriminate. Rather, it comes to perfection in its rational ordering in the presence of the beautiful. It is only through such ordering that the soul itself becomes perfect. Here desire comes to its end.

But how is the end of desire to be understood? No doubt in teleological terms. The divine nature of eros entails that human eroticism is of the divine. Accordingly, human desires must be understood first and foremost, indeed essentially, in their relationship to the divine. As was demonstrated, Eros/eros is correlational, such that the character and nature of desire are determined by the object desired. If desire reaches its end in knowledge and contemplation of the beautiful or divine, this end indicates the perfection of the divine elements in desire, the becoming divine of the erotic lover. For Diotima this means the becoming virtuous and immortal of the erotic lover. Nowhere in her discourse does Diotima claim that either eros or the soul comes to rest in the contemplation of the beautiful. She concludes her discourse by stating that "in begetting true virtue and nurturing it, it is given to him to become dear to god, and if any other among men is immortal, he is too" (212a). Knowledge and contemplation of the beautiful leads to the perfection of desire not that one might cease to desire, but that one's erotic nature might continually beget and nurture one's virtue. It is according to one's continued virtue that it is given to one to become dear to god. If eros comes to an end, it does not end in overcoming its lack through the possession of its object; it cannot possess its object. Desire does not end in completion, fulfillment, or ultimate satisfaction. It ends in an increased intimacy between the human and the divine. Desire for things divine is reciprocated with a divine gift: love from the god.

• • •

A thorough reading of contemporary lack-based theories of desire and the conditions that support them would be in order here. I am only able, however, to offer a brief sketch of some epitomes of such theories and trace a certain trajectory in post-metaphysical conceptions of desire. In what follows, then, I will briefly consider Nietzsche, Freud, Lacan, and Derrida.

It is in Nietzsche that one finds the repositioning and privileging of lack and death in the economy of desire. Nietzsche's claim that God is dead announces the death or end of transcendence, religion, and metaphysics. While hailed as the "greatest recent event"[10] of "a higher history than all history up to now,"[11] it results in a sense of overwhelming loss—the loss of value, meaning, and truth. Consider the famous section in *The Gay Science*, where the madman's desire for God—he is "crying incessantly, 'I'm looking for God! I'm looking for God'"[12]—is frustrated and thwarted. God is nowhere to be found because God is dead. The significance of this event is not lost on the madman, nor are its consequences: the destabilization and utter disorientation of our lives, drives, and desires. "Are we not continually falling? And backwards, sidewards, forwards, in all directions? Is there still an up and a down? Aren't we straying as though through an infinite nothing? Isn't empty space breathing at us?"[13] What is lost and mourned here is an external, suprasensible world, one toward which our lives and drives are correlated. The erotic dimension of life becomes detached from an external and transcendent object or aim.

This loss and fundamental lack do not, however, signal a slackening of desire. To the contrary, the death of God unleashes an abundant and excessive force, what for Nietzsche is the underlying force of life itself: the will to power. Out of the ashes of death emerges an overflowing and ever-expanding energy, but an energy predicated on and conditioned by lack. The determinative role lack plays in the ever-expanding force of desire cannot be underestimated. With the loss of a transcendent, metaphysical object, in a world lacking inherent value and meaning, eros, which is a manifestation of the will to power, first suffers this loss, then redirects its energies and drives from what is other back toward itself.

Desire is not affected and attracted by an external realm (physical or metaphysical), rather, it affects solely itself and desires the expansion of its own power. Consequently, the character of desire is not defined in terms of its object, is neither correlational nor relational (as it was for Diotima); it is defined in terms of its own activities. And these activities are predominantly violent. For Nietzsche, desire becomes a violent, destructive, even a deadly force. Whatever constructive and creative possibilities might exist for desire, such possibilities necessarily entail a form of violence. From out of the abundance of the will to power is expressed "[t]he desire for *destruction*,"[14] and thus one "who is richest in fullness of life, the Dionysian god and man, can allow himself . . . the terrible deed and luxury of destruction, decomposition, negation."[15] The reference to Dionysus is significant. For if, as Nietzsche argued in *The Birth of Tragedy*, the Apollonian and Dionysian impulses reflect the two elements of creativity, and it is an erotic and sexually charged striving,[16] the absence of the Apollonian in Nietzsche's later work suggests that the wild, erotic, destructive, and frenzied force of the Dionysian has achieved a position of preeminence in his thinking.[17]

The transformation of eros/desire wrought by Nietzsche strips desire of its inherently divine and intermediary status. There are at least two troubling consequences of this move. The first is that desire does not facilitate interhuman relationships. Rather, the Nietzschean interpretation of desire has deleterious effects on the nature of the erotic attachments between human beings. As a manifestation of the will to power, which has as its aim the (too often violent) expansion of its own power, erotic love, and more broadly, human desire, are construed as unavoidably, if not essentially, antagonistic and agonistic. Moreover, desire does not mediate the human and the divine; rather, the loss of the divine renders any desire for God virtually, if not completely, impossible. In the wake of the final death and absence of God, the desire for God can only express itself in the creation of new gods, gods created in our own image. Herein, it seems, lies the ultimate satisfaction of human desire: to become gods ourselves.

The significance of Nietzsche in the development of a theory of desire as lack is rivaled only by that of Freud and Lacan. Psychoanalytic theories of desire tend to empty objects of desire of all concrete content; that is, to downplay if not ignore the material importance of such objects in favor of their importance as symbols, symptoms, and signifiers. For Freud, and more explicitly for Lacan, there are no objects of desire—the object is of little importance—because there is no necessary relationship between a particular object and the aim or satisfaction of a particular desire. In "Instincts [*Triebe*] and Their Vicissitudes,"[18] where Freud outlines a theory of the drives, he identifies satisfaction as the aim (*Ziel*) of every drive and the object (*Objekt*) as that "thing in regard to which or through which the [drive] is able to achieve its aim."[19] Moreover, the object "is what is most variable about [a drive] and is not originally connected with it, but becomes assigned to it only in consequence of being particularly fitted to make satisfaction possible."[20] An object's ability to satisfy a drive is not the result of a particular quality inherent in the object itself. There is no necessary correlation between a drive's aim and its object. The pressure (*Drang*) of a drive might be constant—and it is an irresistible pressure[21]—with respect to its general aim, but the object is not. In fact, a drive need not find satisfaction in an object at all, for, according to Freud, the object of a drive is essentially a psychic object or representation. In addition, insofar as a drive can find satisfaction through sublimation, the object no longer plays a significant role in the satisfaction of a drive. On his reading of this Freudian text, Lacan concludes that "[a]s far as the object in the drive is concerned, let it be clear that it is, strictly speaking, of no importance. It is a matter of total indifference."[22] In other words, no material object is properly adequate to satisfy the drive; all such objects, in effect, are lacking. Therefore, despite their aims and their (missing) objects, drives are never exhausted; they are never satisfied.

For Lacan, the missing object of desire is the *objet petit a*. It is the source of his conception of desire as lack. With the introduction of the *objet a* into psychoanalysis, Lacan claims to have "produced the only conceivable idea of the object, that of the object as cause of desire, of that which is lacking."[23] The contours of Lacan's theory of the drive or desire can be sketched as follows. The source of each drive is located in the erogenous zones, which have the form of a hole or a void. This void is constituted by the separation from its object, the *objet a*.[24] It is lack or separation that causes the drive, and what it desires is (re)unification with this object, which according to Lacan is impossible. Thus, for instance, the oral drive has as its source the mouth which desires (re)unification with the mother's (lost and lacking) breast. Frustrated in its aim, desire circles or circulates from lack to lack, cycling through objects which serve as (poor) substitutes for the *objet a* and fail to satisfy the desire. In this case, the mouth becomes voracious, seeking continually to gratify, but without essentially satisfying, its desires with replacement objects. The mouth and its desires become acquisitive, consumptive. This failure of desire to attain its object and satisfaction results in a turning of desire back upon itself. This constitutes the basic narcissistic structure of desire. As such, desire comes to desire its own desiring. At issue here are the following points: Desire or the drive is caused and conditioned by lack and frustration with respect to its aim, satisfaction; dissatisfaction only serves to further incite desire to grasp more aggressively after replacement objects; and if desire seeks satisfaction in the final discharge of its energies, its ultimate aim is death, which is to say that the desire for satisfaction becomes a desire for death.

This conception of desire is not altered when translated into a religious register. In Freud's psychological etiology of religions and the contents of their teachings, for instance, he reaches back to the early stages of ego development. Originally, "an infant at the breast does not as yet distinguish his ego from the external world as a source of sensation flowing in upon it";[25] rather there is a sense that "the ego includes everything."[26] It is only when the infant is separated from the mother's breast, when the breast is lacking, that the infant comes to distinguish between its ego and the external world. For Freud, this separation is traumatic. But this original "feeling of an indissoluble bond, of being one with the external world as a whole"[27] can, and for many ostensibly does, persist to a greater or lesser degree throughout the development of one's mental life. The trauma of separation is counteracted by a wish for a return to this original ego-feeling of oneness and limitlessness, also known as the "oceanic feeling." For Freud, the oceanic feeling is synonymous with religious experience and sensibilities. All religions, consequently, are manifestations of a wish fulfillment, a desire to return to ego-life prior to separation and loss. This desire, however, is just as frustrated, because just as impossible, as any other.

As with Nietzsche, it is virtually impossible and virtually meaningless to speak of a desire for God according to this model of desire. But whereas Nietzsche dramatically announces the death of God, Freud and Lacan merely presuppose it. As an object of desire, God is no different from any other object: God is at best a psychic representation, a phantasm, or as Freud puts it, an illusion. Thus, a desire for God does not impact in any transformative way the dynamics of desire (except perhaps to impinge upon desire); rather, the very notion of God emerges from the same conditions that structure desire.

In many ways, Derrida mediates or synthesizes the thought of Nietzsche, Freud, and Lacan. But unlike them, he addresses the desire for God, or as he prefers, the desire of God, directly. In speaking of the desire of God, Derrida extends and thus transforms or translates the metaphors of abyss and lack into the desert or—to use one of its metonyms—*Khora*. It is not surprising, therefore, that in engaging the desire of God, Derrida's primary concern is with apophasis, which is for him virtually coextensive with desire. His most explicit treatment of the desire of God is found in *Sauf le nom*,[28] where, as a "mark of respect"[29] for God and/or God's name, Derrida's aim is to render the name of God "safe." But if the title of this essay attests to a certain desire, then the equivocity of the expression *sauf le nom* likewise attests to an equivocity in desire itself. By "sauf le nom" is Derrida alluding to a desire to ensure that the name of God is and will be "safe," that is, safe from all final determinations, from every determinate faith? Or a desire to keep "safe" for God everything "save" the name (of God)? This essential and irreducible equivocity both provokes and interrupts the desire of God. This desire, too, is no less equivocal, for as Derrida points out, "the double genitive marks . . . the equivocity of the origin and of the end of such a desire: does it come from God in us, from God for us, from us for God?"[30] In an effort to locate our discussion, let us acknowledge that for Derrida the equivocity of the desire of God translates us into the "desert."

According to Derrida, what has come to be known as negative theology operates according to two kinds of apophasis. The first is one "that can in effect respond to, correspond to, correspond with the most insatiable *desire of God,* according to the history and the event of its manifestation or the secret of its nonmanifestation."[31] This is an apophasis that,

despite its language of negation and rigorous attempts to avoid all positive predication of God, nevertheless subjects itself to a particular, determinate revelation, namely, the Christian revelation. As such, this form
of apophasis, according to Derrida's critique, succumbs to hyperessential-
ism, the positing of a being beyond being. If apophasis marks an insatiable desire of God, its desire is correlated to, and resolves itself in, a final
object of desire that to a greater or lesser degree gives itself to be known
to the desirer. This form of desire, and apophasis, could be characterized
as ontotheological: the names of God ultimately give way to the name
God, which becomes identical with Godself; this marks the final completion and satisfaction of desire. "The other apophasis, the other voice,"
the one Derrida is inclined toward, "can remain readily foreign to all
desire, in any case to every anthropotheomorphic form of desire."[32] This
form of apophatic desire is not adequate to its "object," it does not come
to closure or final completion in the full presence of God. Unlike the first
form of apophasis, which Derrida suggests is anthropotheomorphic, the
second does not, because it cannot, ascribe to "God" any final determinate meaning; it does not ascend to, and come to completion in, a final
determinate representation of "God."

According to Derrida, if apophatic theology is truly to be a language
of negation, an empty language without positive terms, then when one
speaks in the language of apophasis one must always ask "[t]o whom is
this discourse addressed? Who is its addressee?"[33] One could just as easily
ask in this context, whom do I desire? Who is the desired? These questions are, for Derrida, undecidable, for apophasis, like desire, is without
a final object and, strictly speaking, a final destination.[34] There is no strict
correlation between a name and what is named, between one's desire
and what is desired. Any such correlation necessarily collapses in the
desert. At stake for Derrida is to "[s]ave the name that names nothing
that might hold, not even a divinity (Gottheit), nothing whose withdrawal
[dérobement] does not carry away every phrase that tries to measure itself
against him. 'God' 'is' the name of this bottomless collapse, of this endless desertification of language"[35] and, one might add, desire. "God" is
the name of a trace, is a trace left "*in* and *on* language,"[36] the trace of
what is without presence and beyond being, of what is wholly other.
Thus, desire, like language, does not come to fulfillment or completion

in the full presence of God. Desire cannot "measure itself against" God; it cannot correspond or be adequate to its divine "object." If desire is intentional, which is to say, if desire is desire of something, then desire founders by virtue of God's withdrawal. To desire God is to desire that which is wholly other.

If there is a faith of the desert, a deserted faith, then it is one irreducible to certainty, one that always challenges and destabilizes "the authority of that sententious voice that produces or reproduces mechanically its verdicts with the tone of the most dogmatic assertions."[37] But in the desert nothing is as it seems; indeterminacy and indecision abound. The desert offers no context, nothing by which to determine reference and meaning. Every other is wholly other—*tout autre est tout autre.* Thus, Derrida claims: "The other is God or no matter whom, more precisely, no matter what singularity, as soon as any other is totally other. For the most difficult, indeed the impossible, resides there: there where the other loses its name or can change it, to become no matter what other."[38] The wholly other defies, has already defied, will continue to defy our meanings, our expectations, our representations, and every horizon of possibility. More importantly, the wholly other marks the limit or interruption of desire. The desire of God, as desire for the wholly other, "[carries] with it its own proper suspension, the death or the phantom of desire." In going "toward the absolute other . . . the extreme tension of . . . desire . . . tries thereby to renounce its own proper momentum, its own movement of appropriation."[39] At issue here is a desire beyond desire, a desire purified of its desire to possess its intended object, to possess a final and pure vision of God, by the very impossibility of God. In short, God is heterogeneous to desire. God, then, as a name and an intended object of desire is subject to the most rigorous, that is, never ending, "nonsynonymous substitution," what Derrida refers to as "exemplarism:" "[e]ach thing, each being, you, me, the other, each X, each name, and each name of God can become the example of other substitutable X's."[40] By the logic of exemplarism, God is the name of everything and nothing, everything is God and nothing is God. When one speaks of/to God, one speaks of/to *I know not what,* the "no matter whom." With respect to desire, God is that which eludes the final grasp of desire.

This is the situation in the desert, where God has withdrawn and rendered Godself absent and thus indeterminate and indeterminable. It is this radical indeterminacy that saves, according to Derrida, both the name of God and Godself from the claims of any determinate religion. Moreover, it is this indeterminacy, the indeterminacy of the desert, that both incites and frustrates our desire for God, and this by the very God-lessness of the desert, where God cannot show up in any distinguishable phenomenal form or mode. But in desiring to preserve the alterity of God, might Derrida go too far? In a paper on Derrida's conception of the desire of God, Richard Kearney asks: "In the name of a God of desire beyond desire, do we not perhaps lose something of the God of love who takes on very definite names, shapes, and actions at very specific points in time, the God of *caritas* and *humilitas* who heals cripples and tells specific parables, who comes to bring life here and now and bring it more abundantly?"[41] What is lost, it seems, are any distinguishing characteristics unique to God, any conception of *difference* between God and any (wholly) other. At stake here is not an argument for a totalizing concept, representation, or definition of God. Rather, it is a question of truly saving, of truly preserving the integrity of both the name of God and Godself. Without any discernable and describable characteristics unique to God, characteristics that would distinguish between God as the wholly other and any other wholly other, the very notion of the wholly other does not itself admit of difference but becomes a kind of metaphysical category that collapses difference. If one cannot determine, to a lesser or greater degree, how things are in fact different, then the notion of difference (as well as of *différance* and the trace) becomes a virtually empty and useless one. In the desert, where God withdraws and is absent, where God is indiscernible and indistinguishable from anything or anyone else, might this signal a kind of death of God, at least the end of any possible theistic conception of God? And what is the relationship between God and death, between the desire of God and death?

According to the equivocal logic of the statement, *tout autre est tout autre*, it is the irreducible singularity of the other that renders the other wholly other. This can mean two things. On the one hand, "the possibility of reserving the quality of the wholly other, in other words the *infinite other*, for God alone, or in any case for a singular other;" on the other hand, to attribute or recognize "in this infinite alterity of the wholly other, every other, in other words each, each one, for example each man and woman."[42] The absolute irreducibility and singularity of the wholly other, whether God or a man or woman, renders the wholly other as the impossible; that is, it defies meaning, conceptualization, appropriation, and every representation and horizon of expectation. As such, the wholly other is no less impossible than, because it is structurally similar to, death. One's irreducible singularity is constituted by the fact of one's death, by the fact that only I can undergo my own death. As Derrida puts it in *Aporias,* death "names the very irreplaceability of absolute singularity (no one can die in my place or in the place of the other), . . . all the *examples* in the world can precisely illustrate this singularity. Everyone's death, the death of all those who can say 'my death,' is irreplaceable. So is 'my life.' Every other is completely other. [*Tout autre est tout autre.*]"[43] For Derrida, then, "my life" is nearly synonymous with "my death," because what distinguishes "my life" from any other's is the irreplaceability of "my death."

In *The Gift of Death,* Derrida correlates this conception of death with God, or more precisely, the gift of God's infinite love: "It is the gift of infinite love, the dissymmetry that exists between the divine regard that sees me, and myself, who doesn't see what is looking at me; it is the gift and endurance of death that exists in the irreplaceable, the disproportion between the infinite gift and my finitude, responsibility, sin, salvation, repentance, and sacrifice."[44] The gift of God's infinite love is, in the end, the gift of death. Thus, to encounter God is to encounter one's own death, the two, God and death, being virtually indistinguishable. Not only does this radically reduce the scope and possibilities of God's love (God's love gives only death), it likewise reduces the scope and possibility of one's love or desire for God. As Hent de Vries has pointed out, "There is a structural similarity between my being toward death and my being toward God."[45] Thus, the ambiguity surrounding the expression "the desire of God"—is it I who desire God or God who desires me?—appears to resolve itself unambiguously in irrecoverable loss, in death.

• • •

From a Christian perspective, the figuration of eros or desire primarily, and even solely, in terms of lack and death is inadequate. Given that humans are (among other things) erotic beings, such a construal of desire defines human being primarily, if not solely, in terms of lack and death. The fact of death is indisputable, as is the fact that one desires those things one does not have. What is disputable is whether it is necessary to identify desire with lack and death. Insofar as it is a central tenet of Christianity that the incarnate Word of God as the Christ brings, or better, gives (new) life to the creation, it is possible to discover in the gift of life, given through the life of the incarnate Word, a supplement to those theories of desire sketched above. As implied in this formulation, the gift of life, while overcoming death, does not ignore death. Rather, it is because of the experience of the full weight of death—an experience fully realized in the death borne by Jesus on the cross—that the gift of life is given and must be cherished. This is not to say that the gift of life is determined in its singularity by the gift of death (*pace* Derrida); rather, the resurrection attests to the power of life over death. If the gift of life is renewed by virtue of the death and consequent resurrection of the Christ, that gift takes the form of agapeic love. The gift of life, then, is no less than the gift of love. By introducing agape into my argument, my intention is not to rekindle the debate concerning eros and agape, the former typically characterized as profane and even pagan love, and the latter as the truly and uniquely Christian form of love.[46] By turning to theories of the gift and givenness, I want to rethink this all-too-facile opposition between eros and agape, to show that there is a necessary interaction between them. To this end, I will draw upon the work of Jean-Luc Marion.

From the perspective of Marion's phenomenology of givenness, it is possible to theorize desire with greater phenomenological clarity and rigor than is achieved by most lack-based conceptions of desire. For instance, according to Marion, "in whatever way and by whatever means something can relate to us, absolutely nothing is, happens, appears, or affects us that is not first, always, and obligatorily accomplished in a mode of *givenness*."[47] Thus, eros as an affect is given, is an accomplished mode of givenness, even if it is an affect in relation to nothingness, possibility, obscurity, or the void—all of which likewise are accomplished modes of givenness in spite of their lack of substantiality.[48] Those things which are, strictly speaking, no-thing (that is, which have no material or concrete presence), do not issue from or manifest a pure nothingness; rather, that they have the power to affect us at all attests to the fact that they are in fact paradoxically given as positive phenomena. Seen in this light, if desire is or emerges out of lack, at stake here is not an absolute negation or negativity, the destruction entailed in a desire that grasps and seeks to conquer out of its lack and to fill its lack, but a desire which operates (that is, desires) within the phenomenal field of positive givenness. Marion makes this point as follows:

> When a phenomenon becomes an object of desire, it is defined at once by the lack of intuition [that is, the sensible apprehension of things] in it and, inseparably, by its obsessional givenness. It is intuitively deficient, but this deficiency continually troubles him to whom it is addressed; the latter (and not just any other) desires this phenomenon (and not some other) because he apperceives it as lacking. The lacking remains simply absent for everybody, but for the one who desires it, its intuitive absence still gives it, indeed more intensely. What is lacking shines by its absence—the latter, without intuition, gives itself all the more.[49]

Lack is not a general condition; it is rather particular to the mode of givenness of a desired object. In other words, even when an object or phenomenon is characterized by lack, desire is nevertheless correlated to that particular object. This is because lack is not defined as absolute loss. Rather, lack is a positive phenomenon that *gives itself as lack* (in a particular mode of givenness, in this case intuitional deficiency) to the particular desirer. Desire, then, is here construed as being in relationship with the phenomenal (given) world and not as being obsessed with its own circular and narcissistic movements.

The plenitude of the given or created world is, according to Marion, a gift of love (agape) given, ultimately, by God. The objects of desire, whether given as intuitional lack or excess, are gifts "liberated only in [their] exertion starting from and in the name of that which, greater than [they], comes behind [them], that which gives and expresses itself as gift, charity itself,"—that is, God.[50] If, according to my reading of Derrida, the desert where one desires God is ultimately a Godless place, where desire is frustrated by the absence of God, then for Marion the desire for God (and all desire for that matter) occurs in the plenitude of the God-given creation. What distinguishes Marion's thought from Derrida's, and much of contemporary post-Nietzschean or postmodern thought, is that unlike Derrida who only recognizes two modes of phenomenality, a deficiency of intuition or an adequation between intuition and intention (presence), Marion identifies a third mode: intuitional excess or saturation. While all three modes of phenomenality are accomplished modes of givenness, the saturated phenomenon introduces a plenitude or excess of givenness (and meaning) into the phenomenal field. It is as the saturated phenomenon *par excellence,* that is, the self-revelation of God in Jesus Christ, a phenomenon that defies conceptualization, representation, and presence, that God becomes an "object" of desire.[51] This is not to say that God gives Godself as an object in the strict sense of a concrete or material object made present. Marion is clear, as well as adamant, that in no way is God reducible to an object in this sense. He continually affirms the (absolute) distance between God and the creation.

This distance, however, is not a site of deferral where the gift gets hung up and delayed, caught forever between heaven and earth, where our desires are once again deprived of an object or given phenomenon and continually frustrated. Moreover, this distance is not a barrier, so to speak, behind which God hides. For Marion, this distance is essential to relationship between God and the creation. As he puts it, "Distance, as distance, underlines separation only in order to save its intimacy,"[52] and again, "between God and man, incommensurability alone makes intimacy possible, because withdrawal alone defines the Father, just as paternal withdrawal alone saves for man the sumptuous liberty of a son."[53] Withdrawal and separation must not be understood here as lack and absence. Distance defines the difference between God and the creation, and only by such distance and difference can there be intimacy between them. Moreover, and more importantly, it is in the withdrawal of the divine that the Christ is given as the form of the God's love (agape). At the center of this intimacy between God and the creation, an intimacy constituted in both erotic and agapeic love, is the Christ—which is to say that the Christ, as saturated phenomenon *par excellence,* is given as both an erotic and an agapeic "object."

It is on the basis of this last point that I want to propose a Christian conception of love as an interaction between eros and agape.[54] The gift of the Christ, as the complete and perfect manifestation of God's love, manifests two closely related dimensions of that love. On the one hand, God's erotic love for the creation (an erotic attachment to the creation) is attested in God's desire to reconcile the world to Godself. This erotic love precipitates, one might say begets, the gift of the Christ who performs this reconciliation. Christ is, in effect, the manifestation of God's eros. Thus, God's erotic love of the creation does not only want, it also gives. On the other hand, in desiring reconciliation, God demonstrates love (agape) for the creation in the giving of Godself in and as the Christ. While different and distinguishable, divine eros and agape are so closely aligned in Christ as to be nearly inseparable—indeed, it is nearly impossible to speak of God's eros without referring to God's agape, and vice versa. In Christ, an intimacy between divine eros and agape as well as between God and the world is achieved. Furthermore, the Christ is at the heart of the creation's love for God. One's desire for God's love (agape) is fulfilled in God's giving of that love in the form and life of the Christ. To desire God's love is to desire God, and this desire has as its "object" the Christ. But once again, one's desire or erotic love for God does not only want. The desire for God's love as manifested in the Christ resolves itself in a giving of love (agape) in return: a love for the Christ.

This return, however, must not be construed as the cancellation of a debt. To the contrary, return must be understood as repetition. To love the Christ is not, strictly speaking, to love a person, but to love a mode or way of life: the life of love manifested and exemplified in the life of Jesus of Nazareth (as narrated in the Gospels). Here it is necessary to return to a point made by Diotima in the *Symposium*. One's erotic attachments might initially be narrow in scope—attachment to one body or person—but those attachments gradually expand in a widening circle of relations as one's erotic love is perfected. Erotic attachments to others do not aim to possess the other; as Diotima makes clear, erotic love does not result in consumption or acquisition, but in reproduction. Desire for beautiful things results in the begetting of beautiful things, for beauty, it seems, initiates an unceasing generation of beautiful things.[55] Similarly,

erotic love for the Christ might initially be manifested in a narrow attachment to the figure of Jesus, but such love does not reach completion or
satisfaction in the possession of an object. As a saturated phenomenon
the Christ is not something that can in any way be grasped. To desire the
Christ, to love the Christ, is to desire and love the life of the Christ, a life
of love. Consequently, if Christ's love is to be returned, it is to be returned in the living out of a life of love. The living out of such a life
unfolds in ever-widening circles of relations to others. And if Christ's love
is indeed divine love, if it mirrors God's love, then it is a love that both
wants (eros) and gives (agape). On the order of human love, what I want
to suggest is that the interaction between eros and agape brings about a
richer and fuller love life. Erotic love wants—it wants others, but it also
wants certain (good) things for others. Agapic love gives—it gives to the
other in accordance with one's erotic love for the other.

It is not the case that agape completes eros so as to bring about the
final satisfaction or end of desire; nor does agape overcome eros and
render it "useless and vain."[56] Similarly, eros is not merely a voracious
void wanting to be satisfied. An "object" of desire might be given, but it
does not become the possession of, it is not appropriated by, the desirer.
Desire is not hollow; rather, through its interactions with agape, it is
hallowed. Something of the divine is here restored to eros. But its divinity
is not contingent on knowledge or contemplation of the divine; desire
does not take a noetic turn as it did for Diotima. The gift of love (erotic
and agapeic) in, as, and for the Christ is a phenomenon so rich with
givenness (and meaning), that it overwhelms any intentional act and
thereby defies knowledge, conceptualization, and language itself. But it
is nevertheless given and received. Thus, as Marion claims, the only response to the love of God in the Christ is neither philosophy nor theology; it is not speech. Rather, the only response is (to) love, a love that,
as I have tried to argue, is both erotic and agapeic. This love is not
said, it is done. As Marion puts it, "Love is not spoken, in the end, it is
made."[57]

• • •

If contemporary theories of desire privilege lack over resourcefulness as
the defining characteristic of eros, this is the result of the presumption, a

particularly postmetaphysical presumption, that the world itself has lack as a defining characteristic. Put otherwise, it is presumed that at the heart of reality is a certain frugality; things withhold themselves, their meanings, their significance. Within this context, eros or desire is correlated to an impoverished world, which results in a conception of desire as initiated by, and operating in accordance with, a certain void. My reading of the *Symposium* does not propose a return to Platonic metaphysics. Rather, it is intended to retrieve, although in a different form, something of a pre-postmodern construal of desire. Two points are particularly important. The first is that human eros participates in the divine. Eros opens up a site of mediation, what I have called erotic intercourse, between the human and the divine. The result of this intercourse is the becoming divine of the erotic lover. Moreover, and this is the second point, erotic love between the human and the divine orients interhuman erotic relations. The reproductive or procreative nature of these relationships indicates that erotic love is generative and generous. Erotic love responds to and contributes to a generosity in the world. And this generosity is the result of a very real divinity that imbues the world and the human life in it. Divinity, I want to suggest, is the condition of erotic love.

The *Symposium* offers a suggestive alternative to sheerly lack-based conceptions of desire. Marion's conception of the gift reintroduces generosity back into philosophical discourse, but unlike Diotima's discourse, this generosity takes the form of agapeic donation. It is within the context of generosity or excess that eros operates. For Marion, this divine generosity is attested in the sheer givenness of all phenomena. Agapeic donation is at the heart of reality. But tied to giving (agape) is wanting (eros). From the perspective of the divine, it is God's desire that prompts the giving of gifts. God's desire is (pro)creative, but not in the imposition of God's will upon the creation (which seems to be Nietzsche's model of creation: the investing of one's will into things), but in luring the creation into relationship through the giving of gifts. I have argued that the interaction between wanting and giving is exemplary in God, but as such initiates a similar interaction within human relations. Desire without resources is indeed a desire that merely wants. But a desire situated in a world of plenitude is a desire that operates in a context of rich and very real resources. One's erotic attachments provide the conditions for human relationships. And these relationships are fecund. A counterpoint to wanting the other is to give oneself to the other, not in an act of self-sacrifice, but in an act of gratitude, for the other always comes as a gift from elsewhere. The other, however, is not something to be possessed, but someone, a particular someone, to be loved.

Just as, according to Diotima, beauty begets beauty, so love begets love. There is an important dialectic at work here. Agapeic gifts of love enrich the world with good and beautiful things to be desired. Erotic love for, and attachments to, these beautiful and good things result in the creation of new good and beautiful things. These new good and beautiful things further enrich the world with gifts that attract and incite the desire of others. The economy of erotic love is bound up with the economy of agapeic love. There is a sense in which lack-based theories of desire are right: It is when desire is reduced to a void that wants little more than its own satisfaction and fulfillment that desire fails to achieve its aim—or more precisely, that desire fails to be erotic love.

PART II

❧ Queer Desires

❧ Sexing the Pauline Body of Christ: Scriptural Sex in the Context of the American Christian Culture War

DIANA M. SWANCUTT

Sexual difference is one of the major philosophical issues, if not the issue, of our age . . . [It] is probably the issue in our time which could be our salvation if we thought it through.
—LUCE IRIGARAY

If there are no hard and fast sex types, there can be no apartheid of sex.
—MARTINE ROTHBLATT

In the midst of war in Iraq and a color-coded campaign against terror, American Christians are waging an intense cultural battle over the sexual dynamics of sexual difference. Responding to the legalization of same-sex marriage in Massachusetts (2004) and civil union in Vermont (2000) and Connecticut (2005), some of the nation's largest Protestant denominations (e.g., the Southern Baptist Convention), evangelical political organizations (e.g., the Arlington Group, Focus on the Family, and the American Family Association), and the U.S. Conference of Catholic Bishops have devoted unparalleled resources to fighting similar threats to American moral values in other states. In 2003 the Christian Right likewise pressed President Bush to back a constitutional amendment defining marriage as "between one man and one woman." In December of 2004, CBS even rejected an ad that welcomed gays in the United Church of Christ because it "touches on the exclusion of gay couples . . . by other individuals and organizations . . . and the Executive Branch has recently proposed a

Constitutional Amendment to define marriage as a union between a man and a woman." America is embroiled in a religious war over sexual union, and conservative Christians and the current administration insist that the sexual difference between man and woman defines the good.

In the battle to save heterosexual unions, "what the Bible says" is one of the biggest guns conservative Christians fire: Genesis 1 and 2 to prove that "the two sexes" were created complementary and naturally heterosexual, and Romans 1 to prove homosexual sex contrary to nature. But such ideas cited as biblical truths are not self-evident renderings of scriptural treatments of sexual union. (Biblical authors applauded everything from procreative sex to trysts-in-the-grass, multiple wives, concubinage, intimate male friendships, and rape-as-hospitality.) Nor are they derived from some universal truth of human sexuality, as their proponents assert. Rather, they reflect a colonization of scripture by readers who import a set of assumptions that define "sexuality" for the modern West—namely, that humans naturally come in two genetic sexes, each of which possesses a constitutional orientation toward either the same or the other (opposite or complementary) sex. American Christians have writ the modern ideological hegemony of the two-sex model into the corpus of scripture, controlling both its meaning and the terms by which morally legitimate sex is determined.

This essay undermines that colonization: first, by showing that the modern concept of "two natural sexes" upon which "sexuality" is based deploys a fictive ontology of gender complementarity to stabilize the heterosexist social order; and second, by arguing that the inscription of the two-sex model into scripture as a warrant for heterosexuality is destabilized at its scriptural foundation in the Pauline corpus. Neither Paul nor his early readers thought that humans naturally came in two biological sexes; like other ancients, they believed in a hierarchical continuum of relative masculinity. Males/men and females/women occupied the poles of that natural continuum, which admitted multiple genders and allowed for endless (and endlessly troubling) mutations of gender. Thus Paul's earliest readers would have understood Romans 1:26–27 as a censure not of homosexual sex but of sex that threatened unnaturally to transform men and women into androgynes. Yet the Pauline letters also undercut this censure of gender shifting by queering gender difference within the body of Christ. Paul's Christ is the eschatological recreation of the original androgyne, a distinct sex within whose body believers were materially, collectively remade. By "putting on" Christ's body in baptism, they became "no longer male and female" (Gal. 3:28). As Christ's lovers, they participated in an erotic union of spirit more holy than that of Genesis 2:24 (1 Cor. 6:17). Finally, in Christ's Body, the decisive moral good was believers' upbuilding (*oikodomē*) of the body through acts of neighbor-love. Intercourse was one such act not because its partners were ontologically male and female, but when it welcomed people into the body. In short, in contrast to modern claims that the distinction of male and female is the foundation for morally sanctioned sex, Paul depicted the Christian practice of communal sex, seminally incarnated in the androgynous body of Christ, as disruptive of stable gender identities.

AT THE ALTAR OF THE TWO-SEX BODY: THE AMERICAN CHRISTIAN CULT(URE) OF HETEROSEXUALITY

Not all Christians agree that the complementarity of the sexes makes marriage holy, much less that it grounds the good state.[1] But the public nature of the American Christian discourse of heterosexuality suggests that the terms of Christian debate between progressives and conservatives are set by the wider culture:[2] Both progressive and conservative Christians tend to presume and to project onto scripture the modern ideology of two biological sexes and sexualities, and on that basis to fight a battle for the good society that pitches the scientific treatment of sexuality (whether hetero- or homo-) as an innate aspect of human identity against the condemnation of homosexuality encouraged by the ideology of sex/gender complementarity. In this debate, the conservative claim that God created two ontologically complementary sexes for heterosexuality functions as the theological trump card over progressives' equally ontological argument that God created homosexuals as well as heterosexuals in the "image of God."

The Script(ur)ed "Nature" of the American Sexual Hegemony

Progressive arguments for the full humanity of gays do not typically address complementarity but instead emphasize that homosexuality, like human sexuality generally, is inborn and natural.[3] According to the Presbyterian document "Keeping Body and Soul Together," sexual orientation is "established early in life, at least by the age of 4 years and probably earlier, through some combination of genetic, hormonal, and environmental factors."[4] The "Report of the Commission on Homosexuality of the Episcopal Diocese of Michigan" (1973) likewise states: "Homosexuals have been found in all societies of which we have any knowledge." The argument proceeds: If sexual orientation is universal and constitutional, then homosexuals are created with "sacred worth" and "God-given dignity." Even Pope Benedict XVI (formerly Cardinal Joseph Ratzinger), who has spearheaded the charge to root out seminarians with homosexual "tendencies," wrote in 1986 that the inclination to homosexuality is not sin and homosexuals have "God-given dignity and worth" because they are "made in the image and likeness of God."[5]

This belief in an inborn sexual orientation, conjoined to Genesis 1:26–28 as a natural warrant for homosexuality, stands behind progressives' conviction that "it is arrogance on the part of the church to elevate some people's relationship with God while denigrating that of others on the basis of *innate sexuality*."[6] It also allows progressives to emphasize the created goodness of gays over the few, terse scriptural censures of male anal intercourse (Lev. 18:22, 20:13, 1 Cor. 6:9, Rom 1:27, 1 Tim. 1:8–11) while noting that "there is no evidence that Jesus said anything on this matter."[7] Perhaps typical of progressive attempts to deflect the force of such texts is biblical scholar Robin Scroggs's argument that Romans 1:26–27 is not an "abstract comment about the ordering of male and female in creation," but a stereotyped historical censure of Greek pederasty. "There was no other form of male homosexuality [sic] in the Greco-Roman world that would come to mind."[8]

Like progressives, conservatives assume that nature is the source of sexuality and the basis for sexual ethics and read that assumption into scripture. The main difference between progressives and conservatives is that conservatives treat heterosexuality as the only natural orientation,[9] arguing that homosexuality violates the "biblical, heterosexual structure of God's creation"—the divine creation of two, complementary sexes for sexual and social union, as described in Genesis 1:27, 2:18–24.[10] The basis of this assertion is the assumption that heterosexuality is bound to inborn gender differences between men and women. In the words of an Exodus International representative, "There is no solid scientific evidence that people are born homosexual. The overwhelming majority of gay people are completely normal genetically . . . fully male or female."[11] The implication is that genetic sex is heterosexual. As Philip Keane, author of *Sexual Morality: A Catholic Perspective,* said, the "idea of male-female complementarity is a critical feature of sexuality because it expresses the view that men and women are different, and that their differences are the source of unique social and interpersonal contributions to human fulfillment."[12] Protestant Pauline scholar Richard Hays argues similarly that the created order objectively and uniquely supports heterosexual complementarity: "Genesis 2:18–24 describes woman and man as created for one another and concludes with a summary moral: 'Therefore a man leaves his father and his mother and clings to his wife and they become one flesh.' Thus, the *complementarity* of male and female is given a theological grounding in God's creative activity."[13] This warrant from creation functions to sanction heterosexuality as the only *scriptural* orientation: "From Genesis 1 onward, scripture affirms repeatedly that God has made man and woman for one another and that our sexual desires rightly find fulfillment within heterosexual marriage."[14] In short, linking the cultural definition of sexuality as an innate, object-oriented drive for sex with the creation of two opposite sexes in Genesis enables conservatives to claim that God created man and woman for heterosexual complementarity.

Pursued most vigorously of late by Robert Gagnon, the necessary corollary of this point is that homosexuality is unnatural, and the argument of Romans 1:26–27, that people "exchanged natural relations for unnatural," serves as a convenient prooftext.[15] The conviction that homosexuality is "contrary to God's creative intent for humanity's sexuality"[16] holds even for those like Pope Benedict XVI (Ratzinger) and Richard Hays, who believe that homosexuals are fully "persons" created in the image of God (Ratzinger); that homosexual inclination is not sin (Ratzinger); and that the writers of scripture say nothing about homosexuality because they lacked a concept of sexual orientation (Hays).[17] Reading Romans 1 as an abstract reference to humanity, Hays contends that "the charge that these fallen humans have exchanged natural relations for unnatural means nothing more nor less than that human beings, created for *heterosexual companionship* as the Genesis story bears witness, have distorted even so basic a truth as their *sexual identity* by rejecting the male and female roles which are naturally theirs *in God's created order.*"[18] Ratzinger, who avoids the Levitical prohibitions of "lying with males" because they weaken his case (Lev. 18:22, 20:13),[19] likewise uses Romans 1, natural law theory, and allusions to Genesis 1:26–28 to assert that "instead of the original harmony between Creator and creatures, the acute distortion of idolatry has led to all kinds of moral excess. Paul is at a loss to find a clearer example of this disharmony than homosexual relations."[20] Consequently, homosexual inclination is a "more or less strong tendency ordered toward an intrinsic moral evil" and homosexual acts are "self-indulgent," and "thwart the call to a life of that form of self-giving [heterosexual procreativity] which the Gospel says is the essence of Christian living."[21]

Simply put, conservatives believe that humans naturally come in two opposite sexes, and they read that "truth" into Genesis 1 and Romans 1 as proof that homosexuality is unnatural and heterosexual complementarity, God's creative purpose for the sexes.[22] The heterosexual complementarity of the sexes' functions as conservatives' ace in the hole over progressives' equally ontological argument that God created "homosexual persons" in the "image of God." Convinced that complementarity is natural, conservatives then make it a bulwark of the public good—lest Christian standards for moral sex be diluted, Christians' societal control diminished, and the civil order destabilized.[23]

Skinning "Natural Sex" from the American Christian Corpus
Challenging the pervasive cultural practice of projecting the ideology of sexuality onto scripture involves acknowledging how very modern (and thus how very alien to the biblical texts) this ideology actually is. "Sexuality" was born only after Charles Gilbert Chaddock coined the term "homosexuality" in 1892; psychologists argued that humans possess an innate drive for sex; and twentieth-century scientists invented genetics.[24] Before that point in the West, sex acts were treated as an aspect of gender identity. In nineteenth-century America, for example, "sexual inversion" referred broadly to gender deviance, of which what we treat as homosexual acts (but nineteenth-century Americans did not) was an indistinct

part.[25] "Deviant object choice was viewed as merely one of a number of pathological symptoms [of cultural non-conformity] exhibited by those who reversed or 'inverted' their proper sex-roles by adopting a masculine or feminine style at variance with what was deemed natural or appropriate to their anatomical sex."[26] Only with Chaddock's invention of homosexuality did sexuality begin to take skin as a concept independent of gender identity. Sexual orientation is therefore a modern invention that signaled a sea change in the meaning of intercourse, its relation to gender, and its role in social self-definition.[27]

More importantly, the concept of sexuality presumes the scientific definition of biological sex as a dual (female-male), genetic (XX or XY) trait distinct from cultural gender construction (woman-man). Put another way, modern medicine *created* the precultural two-sex body upon which the ontological concept of (hetero)sexuality depends. As Thomas Laqueur details, before the rise of modern medicine, the dominant Western ideology of the human body was a gender spectrum that conflated sex and gender, treated the ideal body as masculine, and ranked actual bodies hierarchically as more or less perfect versions of the ideal masculine body.[28] "In a public world that was overwhelmingly male, the one-sex model displayed what was already massively evident in culture more generally: *Man* is the measure of all things, and woman does not exist as an ontologically distinct category. . . . The standard of the human body and its representations is the male body."[29] Hence, elite men, defined as hard, rational penetrators, populated the top of the gender spectrum. Women occupied its lowest rungs because they were soft, leaky, and wild—the least perfect male-bodies, their vaginas deemed undescended penises.[30] But the spectrum also included androgynes who possessed both phalluses and feminine qualities. In short, the dominant ideology of the body in the premodern West was a one-sex/body, multi-gender model that reflected ancient gender norms for the distribution of power. Only with the rise of Western medicine and genetics has sex been conceived as dual and ontologically stable—male and female.

However objective it may seem, even the scientific framework for defining the "two sexes" is a cultural construction. As Judith Butler has shown, the dominant American ideology of the body affirms the existence of two sexes, two genders, and two basic sexualities that are treated as naturally distinct. But biological sex is not ideologically independent of the other terms; our culture defines our genetics, object-oriented genital joinings, and other gender practices in binary fashion in order to identify us dualistically as either male/masculine or female/feminine (where "normal" males and females are heterosexual).[31] Violations of these norms are deemed unnatural. So doctors have tended to define genetic sex dualistically, as XX or XY, and to label violations of the genetic dualism (such as XXY and XO people), including "mismatches" between genetics, hormones, and appearance, as "diseased." But as Anne Fausto-Sterling describes, there is a spectrum of such deviations, naturally occurring bodies with non-dual genital combinations and diverse physical expressions.[32] Hidden among the males and females living in America are so-called "true hermaphrodites," who possess both ova and testes, "genetically male" (XY) people with Androgen Insensitivity Syndrome who look like and are usually raised as women, "genotypically female" (XX) children whose genitalia are virilized at puberty, and "genotypically male" (XY) children who are anatomically female or androgynous at birth but at puberty develop testes, a fused scrotum, and secondary male sex characteristics.[33]

Further, the definition and number of sexes and genders vary across cultures. Dominicans call children virilized at puberty *guevedoche* ("penis at 12"), a third gender.[34] In Siberia, Chukchi shamans are a distinct gender revered for transforming into various animal and human forms.[35] In India, hijras are a third gender of "not-men" that includes born-males impotent with women and hermaphrodites raised as women until they prove that they cannot menstruate. Normally castrated after joining the hijra community, they take up women's dress, names, and sexual behaviors.[36] Finally, eighteenth- and nineteenth-century Navajo had a three-sex, multigender system that included the *nádleehí*, a "two-spirit" (bi-gender) person who had one of three anatomical birth-sexes (male, female, or androgynous), but was identified by a combination of masculine and feminine gender-attributes. Because Native Americans typically thought birth sex matured over time[37] and defined gender primarily based on work preference,[38] "two-spirit" people included non-dually sexed persons; born-males who adopted women's work, manners, and speech patterns; born-females who took up men's work and mannerisms; or those born either male or female who combined elements of women and men's cultural roles.[39] Finally, the Navajo did not denounce the *nádleehí* as unnatural because gender or sex practices did not fit an individual's birth-sex;[40] rather, they thought that all humans were spiritually androgynous, so they treated the *nádleehí* as a special but natural gender.[41] This evidence suggests that what counts as a natural expression of sex and gender is a function of the gender norms of the cultural system in which a person identifies.

Paradoxically, the very attempt to inscribe a rigid two-sex dualism in the West proliferated awareness of exceptions marked as deviant. As Alice Domurat Dreger details, late nineteenth- and early twentieth-century medical advances led to an increase in the number of named hermaphrodites and then to their erasure.[42] Doctors had previously identified people possessing physical characteristics associated with males and females as hermaphroditic. But in this period, studies of human anatomy produced "a virtual explosion of human hermaphroditism," and researchers who worried about the normalcy of a third sex and who felt pressure from "feminists . . . and homosexuals who vigorously challenged sexual boundaries" began to insist on tighter "definitions of malehood and femalehood."[43] Researchers argued that most hermaphrodites were really male or female and rigidly dichotomized the definition of natural sex in order to keep "males" and "females" distinct and to control what counted as acceptable sexual activity. Binarizing male and female and linking that biological dualism to sex practice had two primary effects. Hermaphrodites, thus defined, were eliminated in the West, not just culturally and ideologically, but materially: They were surgically corrected so that they would reflect our "natural" two-sex/gender standard.[44] As a consequence of this practice, which continues today, certain classes of people (males and females) are privileged over others (intersexed, transgender) and the heterosexist hegemony based on the two-sex model is reinforced as natural.

The West's dualistic sex/gender hegemony is thus revealed as unnatural (i.e., a cultural construction) to the very extent that it gives rise to its own subversion by producing third-sex categories. Consider, for example, the case of Daniel Burghammer, a hermaphrodite living in Renaissance Italy:

[He] shocked his regiment when he gave birth to a healthy baby girl. After his alarmed wife called in his army captain, he confessed to being half male and half female . . . Uncertain of what to do, the captain called in Church authorities, who decided to . . . christen the baby, whom they named Elizabeth. After she was weaned—Burghammer nursed the child with his female breast—several towns competed for the right to adopt her. The Church declared the child's birth a miracle, but granted Burghammer's wife a divorce, suggesting that it found Burghammer's ability to give birth incompatible for the role of husband.[45]

Note the ideological union of biological sex and gender identity in this pre-modern account: Burghammer lacked a sex apart from a gender role as husband. Since "husbands" by definition could not give birth, Burghammer's gender role as a life-giving husband was a conundrum to the gender standards of both society and the church. It highlighted the limits of the laws and conceptions of sex/gender in Renaissance Italy. (This example also forces modern Christians to ask what *they* will do when the intersexed ask to get married or request a divorce.)

Similarly, the nineteenth-century hermaphrodite Herculine Barbin underscores the contingency of the modern binary sex/gender/sexuality system. As Mary McClintock Fulkerson describes, Barbin was legally defined as female and male at different points,[46] and wrote journal entries expressing desire for girls. But as Fulkerson underscores, Barbin's sexual feelings cannot be naturalized (or declared unnatural) by means of binary sex or an object-oriented sexuality. Herculine's non-dually sexed body confounds any attempt to explain a desire for girls by an appeal to "male" or "female" anatomy. This means that any attempt "to unify this person as a sexual [and sexed] subject is a display of the normalizing heterosexual regime of knowledge / power that we bring to the body. If we are to take Herculine seriously without explaining" Herculine away as unnatural, we must reject the idea that desire is the function of a naturally unified, sexed/gendered body.

If we take people who do not identify as male or female seriously, we must acknowledge that the Western, medical model of the two-sex body is but a cultural artifact of our binary construction of gender.[47] Western assumptions that there are but two biological sexes, and that biological sex is distinct from social norms for gender difference ("man and woman"), are cultural fictions maintained through ignorance of other cultures' gender norms, our culture's erasure of bodies that do not fit the two-sex norm, and our failure to recognize the power of the gender binary to regulate the definition of the two sexes and the kind of sex they can "naturally" have. (Hetero)sexuality is an ideological artifact of the hegemonic bi-gender body. Declaring marital unions between man and woman natural is, therefore, not a natural claim, but a cultural safeguard preserving the fragile societal fiction that "man and woman" is a self-evident category or precultural given. By extension, the Christian claim that Genesis 1 and Romans 1 prove man and woman ontologically complementary is a modern innovation based on the prior invention of the two-sex body model, and it illuminates far less about God's will for the sexes than it does about the control of American gender norms over Christian morality.[48] By implication, Christians cannot unwittingly declare "the two sexes, male and female" naturally complementary; write that ontology into Genesis 1; or claim that Romans 1 condemns homosexuality or supports heterosexual complementarity. Although he did reinterpret nature throughout his corpus, we now know that the apostle Paul could have known nothing of sexuality, heterosexual complementarity, or the two-sex model of human nature. Neither the biological model of two opposite sexes nor a scriptural theology of heterosexual complementarity provides a natural basis for defining godly sex.[49]

BUILDING CHRIST'S SEX: THE COMMUNAL BODY OF CHRIST AND UNNATURAL GODLY SEX IN THE PAULINE CORPUS

Reading Paul in his ancient context does not do so either, for Paul's treatment of sex was built on the pre-modern, one-sex model of human nature. According to his early interpreters, Paul deployed this model in Romans 1:26–27 to censure the unnaturally androgynizing sex of Gentiles who had degraded God's masculinity through idolatry. But he also deployed it, contrary to nature, to identify Christ as the recreated original androgyne, into whose body believers were materially knit in baptism with a power so transforming that it regendered them beyond "male and female" (Gal. 3:28) and with an intimacy so complete that it surpassed the intercourse of "male and female" (1 Cor. 6:16–19). The sex the apostle Paul declared good was not two, individual, complementary sexes established in creation but one communal sex, the androgynous Body of Christ, in whom and with whom believers were physically united in a process of re-creation. Paul's Body of Christ was a collectively unnatural sex that, like that of Herculine Barbin and Daniel Burghammer, parodied and subverted the natural gender hegemony of his day.

Unnatural Body-Morphing: God's Body Emasculated, Gentile Idolaters Androgynized (Rom 1:26–27)

Claiming to be wise men they became fools, and they changed the glory of the immortal God into an image of the likeness of mortal man. . . . So God handed them over to impurity for the degrading of their bodies . . . to dishonorable passions. For their women exchanged the natural use for that which is contrary to nature. Similarly, the men, forsaking the natural use of the woman, were consumed in their yearning for each other, men cultivating deformity in men and receiving in their own persons the due penalty for their error.
—ROMANS 1:22–27

Putting paint to this canvas begins with Romans 1:22–27, which depicts God as allowing Gentiles who had emasculated His *doxa* ("glory") through idolatry to indulge in sex acts that deformed them into androgynes. I sketched this argument in "The Disease of Effemination," demonstrating that what linked Romans 1:26 and 1:27 is not same-sex intercourse, but gender transgression that led to somatic change.[50] I want here to clarify the gender dynamic of this argument, showing that Paul's first extant readers interpreted Romans 1:22–27, through the lens of the one-body model, as a somatic tit-for-tat—the unnatural androgynization of Gentiles (particularly men) who had first emasculated God's body through idolatry. As Ambrosiaster said, "Because the Gentiles deified images . . . dishonoring the Creator God, they were . . . handed over . . . [to] damage each other's bodies with abuse. It must be said that they changed into another order."[51]

The ideological basis for this argument is the notion, shared by most ancients, that sex acts impacted one's standing in the one-body gender hierarchy of human nature. As classicists and biblical scholars have long noted, ancients (including Jews and Christians) treated intercourse not as a function of sexual orientation but as a gendered enactment of sociopolitical status understood in terms of the masculinity or femininity of the actor's actions, irrespective of the sex of their sex-objects.[52] Greek and Roman citizen-men were defined as active, masculine penetrators, and their sex objects (women, slaves, youths) as the passive/feminine/penetrated. The gendered performativity of ancient sex was a product of the Greek and Roman political ideologies of human nature, which as Laqueur showed, assumed that the ideal body was masculine and actual bodies (manly, womanly, and other) were more or less perfectly masculine. As he describes, the reason ancients treated bodies not as ontologically stable and distinct sexes but as manifestations of relative degrees of masculinity was that all bodies contained better (rational, masculine) and worse (passionate, feminine) aspects. It therefore required constant self-mastery (*enkrateia*) of the passions to maintain the perfect male body.[53] "Each man trembled forever on the brink of becoming 'womanish' . . . man had to strive to remain 'virile.' He had to learn to exclude from his character and from the poise and temper of his body all the telltale signs of 'softness' that might betray, in him, the half-formed state of woman."[54] Thus, physical masculinity was domination over feminine aspects within bodies and sexual and social dominion over more feminine bodies lower in the sociopolitical hierarchy.

One significant consequence of this gender ideology is that ancients believed that less-perfectly male androgynes existed. Well-known but ambiguous figures, androgynes appeared in a variety of sources from Greek myths and Roman literature to Hellenistic and imperial period statuary.[55] On the one hand, positive accounts of original androgyny survive in sources ranging from Plato's *Symposium* to Philo of Alexandria's *On the Creation of the World* and *Genesis Rabbah* (a subject to which I return). The deity Hermaphroditos also appeared in a range of religious settings as early as the fourth century B.C. in Attica, in Ovid's *Metamorphoses,* and in art. Indeed, Hellenistic and Roman era artists had a proclivity for sculpting *hermaphroditos anasyromenos*, figures depicted in the act of lifting their clothes to reveal their androgynous form.[56] However, the surprise crystallized in this act of revelation points to ancients' ambivalence about the gender status of androgynes. On the ancient gender hierarchy, androgynes were treated as double-natured barely-men possessing a penetrating (masculine) penis and a penetrable (feminine) vagina. Just one step above the lowly ranks of women, they embodied the point of gender flux between masculine bodies of sociopolitical power and feminine bodies of submission. In other words, gender confusion and the specter of physical change was writ onto their "dual nature" (*diplēs physeōs*) as penetrable-penetrators.

Because of their femininity, Greeks and Romans stereotyped them as the embodiment of unnatural gender instability and sexual effeminacy. Livy (39.22.3–5) called them "unnatural" "monsters" and, like other Romans of his era, assumed they resulted from ethnic miscegenation.[57] Ovid implied that Hermaphroditos's appearance signaled effeminacy among his worshippers, and he interpreted the legend of Tiresias, a seer who lived in a state of gender-flux, as an explanation of feminine passion (*voluptas*).[58] Eunuchs, who were assimilated to androgynes, were likewise called "dually natured" (*diphuēs . . . kai androthēlus*) and accused of lustiness and adultery.[59] The link of androgyny to passion and gender-bending sex is clear in Diodorus Siculus, who describes hermaphrodites forced by their dimorphism into "unnatural intercourse." *Library* 32.11 describes an Epidaurian named Callo who was "obliged to submit to unnatural embraces" (*tēn de para physin homilian hypomonein anagkazomenē*) because she was incapable "of intercourse as a woman" (i.e., being penetrated). Elsewhere Diodorus describes an oracle warning King Alexander to "beware of the place that bore the two-formed one," the hermaphroditic Herais, who developed a tumor at the base of her vagina that split, revealing "a phallus and testicles." People who discovered her hermaphroditism assumed that "she had had intercourse with her husband as a man, since natural intercourse did not fit their theory [of androgynous sex]" (*Lib.* 32.10.2). Androgynes' gender-bending (or gender-blending) made them the embodiment of "unnatural," sexualized gender trouble.

Second, because ancients believed somatic form was an achieved state, they typically thought that gender-transgressive acts could unnaturally transform men and women into androgynes.[60] For example, Romans

thought women who indulged in penetrative intercourse could masculin-
ize, shape-shifting into phallicized beings (*tribades*) whose androgynization destabilized the natural gender hierarchy and the masculinist society
it sustained.[61] This is why Martial, in *Epigrams* 1.90, charges Bassa with
being a false matron who, in the tradition of Tiresias, at first appeared
womanly, but then revealed androgyny by penetrating matrons with a
monstrous "penis" (*uenus*).[62] Similarly, men who habitually engaged in
over-passionate acts—whether in the form of gluttony, anger, strife, cowardice, or effeminate (passive) sex—ran the risk of morphing, contrary to
nature, into *cinaedi* ("androgynous girly-men"). This fear of passion-in-
duced physical transformation explains why Paul's Jewish contemporary
Philo of Alexandria expressed his disgust at pederasts who habituated
their passive sex partners to the "disease of effemination," "transforming
the [boys'] male nature to the female" by penetrating them, thereby
violating God's law, which ordains that the "androgyne who debases the
currency of nature perish unavenged" (*Special Laws* 3.37–41). In the words
of the orator Hypereides, "Nature would be shocked and astonished that
any man would not think it a most blessed gift for him to have been
born a man and [then] spoiled Nature's kindness to him, hastening to
transform himself into a woman [when "he misused his own body in a
feminine way"]."[63]

This logic of gender-transgressive androgynization—a logic that presumes the traversable, one-body model of human nature—explains the
function of unnatural sex in Romans 1:22–27. Paul deploys its correlation
between degrading acts and physical change twice to demonstrate: that
Gentile idolatry emasculated God's *doxa*, degrading His immortal majesty as Creator into the effeminized status of mortal things; and that God
responded by allowing idolaters, especially men, to androgynize their
bodies through gender-morphing sex. This narrative of reciprocal effemination begins in verses 23–24 with the definition of idolatry as the weak-
ening or emasculation of God's majesty. Although modern translations
render verse 23 as the exchange of God's glory for idols, Paul uses the
present active indicative form of *allasō* to argue that idolaters *changed* the
glory of the immortal God *into* (*en*) an image of mortal things, thereby
degrading it. Significantly, early church fathers read 1:23 in this way. As
Origen said in *On Prayer* 29.15, "These people *lowered* to a body without

soul or sense the identity of the One who gives creatures not only the power of sentience but also of sensing rationally." Likewise, Ambrosiaster: "So blinded were their hearts that they *altered* the majesty of the invisible God . . . not into men, but what is worse . . . into the image of man" (*Corpus scriptorum ecclesiasticorum latinorum* 81:45, 47).

The fathers' somatic reading of God's *doxa* may seem odd to us, but we cannot ignore it. In the first place, in verse 23 Paul avoids using *metallasō*, the verb for "exchange" that he deployed in verses 26–27 to pun *allasō*. Nor does he use the present middle indicative of *allasō*, which does mean "to exchange." Rather, he uses the present active of *allasō*, whose meaning is clear and uncontested, "to change." Second, in Paul's eschatological rereading of Genesis 1 in 1 Corinthians 15:38–41, he uses *doxa* to connote bodily appearance. Paul argues that God created living things with different kinds of bodies, and "the *doxa* of the one is distinct from the *doxa* of another. There is one glory of the sun, another of the moon, yet another of the stars, and even they differ from glory to glory." *Doxa* connotes the appearance of a body—even an "imperishable" body like that of God (Rom. 1:23, 1 Cor. 15:42)—and when it is paired with *allasō* in Rom. 1:23, it refers to the immortal appearance of God that people damaged through idolatry.

The charge that God's masculine *doxa* as Creator could be "changed" in this way aligns with philosophical debates about theology.[64] Writers from Aristocles to Diogenes Laertius and Origen believed that Stoics thought God was a body, the active material principle that created the world order and acted upon passive bodies within it.[65] Epicurus also treated the gods as "imperishable" beings who appeared as human "images" and "likenesses" nature imprinted on the mind.[66] Consequently, worshippers' minds had to be free of unworthy beliefs lest "the holy divinity of the gods" be "damaged" and "do you harm . . . you will be unable to visit the shrines of the gods with a calm heart and incapable of receiving . . . the images of their holy bodies which travel into men's minds to reveal the gods' appearance" (Lucretius 6.68–79). Stoics like Seneca decried this theology of "images," lest the gods be reduced to deaf and ineffectual divinities, matter that is "passive" and "acted upon."[67] But Paul uses the idea that divinity could be degraded by foolish worship to imply that Gentiles *claiming* to be wise (1:22) were actually idiots (like the Epicureans); believing that they should worship the immortal God of Israel as "an image of the likeness of mortal man," they damaged the appearance (*doxa*) of His divinity, degrading His masculinity as Creator to the status of created things.

Verse 24 describes God's response to this emasculation of his *doxa*. In an act of divine reciprocity, God hands idolaters over to *damage* their bodies (as NEB rightly translates *atimadzesthai*) in what verses 26–27 depict as unnatural gender-role inversion and the deformation of idolaters' bodies. Bernadette Brooten argues incisively that Paul uses two rhetorical devises in verses 26–27 to highlight gender transgression as the problem: He presents women before men, a clear inversion of the ancient gender hierarchy; and he portrays the women as actively "exchanging" (*metēllaxan*) the natural use of intercourse for the unnatural, whereas the men passively "gave up [*aphēntes*] the natural use of women." In Brooten's words, "The active verb (*metēllaxan*) with a feminine subject is striking. . . . Verbs for sexual intercourse are usually active when they refer to men and passive when they refer to women . . . in the context of the . . . cultural view of women as sexually passive, for women actively to 'exchange natural intercourse for unnatural' stands out."[68] Romans 1 depicts unnatural *gender trouble* among the Gentiles.

That trouble was not same-sex intercourse but gender-role inversion, women's practice of active sex and men's acquiescence to effeminating sex. In the first place, the women of 1:26 *cannot* be identified exclusively as women-loving women. The adverb *homoiōs*, linking 1:26 and 1:27, does not reveal their identity,[69] and ancients described a variety of female sexual activities as unnatural. Roman censures of *tribades* deployed the cultural disgust for androgyny to describe the physical androgynization wrought by their penetrative sex as unnatural.[70] Further, while Ambrosiaster identified the sex partners of 1:26 as other women, he was concerned not with wrong orientation but with the use of "a part of the body" for an "unintended" (non-procreative) purpose (Corpus scriptorum ecclesiasticorum latinorum 81:51). As James Miller argues, many ancients derided non-procreative sex (of various types) as unnatural.[71] Augustine suggests the reason: It was a gender-transgressive indulgence of passion (*Nuptial* 5:4, 20:35).[72] As Clement of Alexandria put it earlier: "It is surely impious for the natural [*kata physin*] designs to be irrationally perverted into customs that are not natural [*para physin*] . . . the point of this parable [concerning the passion and sexual activity of the female hare] is to advise abstinence from excessive desire, mutual intercourse [*epalleōn synousiōn*], sex with pregnant women, reversal of roles in intercourse [*allēlobasias*], corruption of boys, adultery, and lewdness (*Paedagogue* 2.10)." Clement assumes that women who indulged desire would act contrary to nature (*para physin*) in *various types* of intercourse ranging from adultery and sex while pregnant to "mutual intercourse" and a "reversal of sexual roles." Clement's emphasis on "mutual intercourse" and the "reversal of sex roles" reflects his concern with women who assumed the active, penetrative role in sex.[73] What was unnatural about women's unnatural sex was not its sexual object but its lust-induced *activity,* which inverted the "design of nature."

In the second place, the women's gender transgression in 1:26 is merely rhetorical foreplay; the thrust of Paul's censure is 1:27, where the parallel but more important charge of male effemination is signaled through the piling up of emasculating acts.[74] As Dale Martin has shown, the first two acts, Gentile men's "*giving up of the natural use* of the woman through *their burning with passion* for men,*" implies that overindulgence in passion led them to invert the naturally hierarchical sex act, the penetration of a *woman* by a man, by *penetrating men* as though they were women.[75] To echo Hypereides, they spoiled Nature's kindness, hastening to transform each other into women by misusing their bodies in a feminine way. The third and fourth acts confirm that the problem is gender-transgression: "*Working degradation* [*tēn aschēmosynēn katergazomenoi*] in men, men received *in themselves* the penalty fitting for their error." As *aschēmosynē* indicates, the language of physical effemination wrought by these acts underscores the unnatural effects of such gender transgression on their bodies.[76] Thus, *tēn aschēmosynēn katergazomenoi,* "working degradation," connotes the *physical* emasculation that results from indulgence of passion.[77]

The danger of androgynous shape-shifting inherent in the one-body model of nature explains why early interpreters highlighted the language of "change" (1:23) to read gender-morphing in 1:27. Not only did Ambrosiaster argue that men "changed into another order."[78] So did the *Physiologus*: "You must not therefore become like the hyena taking first the male and then the female nature; these . . . the holy Apostle reproached when he spoke of men with men doing what is degrading.'" *The Epistle of Barnabas*, on which it may depend, argued similarly: "You should not eat the hyena. . . . Why? Because this animal changes its gender annually and is one year a male and the next a female."[79] Likewise, Novatian denounced pederasts who "deformed themselves into women" (*accusat deformatos in feminam viros*).[80] Finally, while Clement challenged the idea of gender-morphing, he revealed its popularity: "Desire is not natural . . . [but] it cannot be believed that the hyena ever changes its nature or that the same animal has at the same time both types of genitalia, those of the male and the female, as some have thought, telling of marvelous hermaphrodites and creating a whole new type—a third gender, the androgyne, in between a male and female."[81] Clement knew that his contemporaries treated physical androgynization as a result of overly passionate sex. The Naassenes confirm the relevance of these assumptions to verse 27. According to Hippolytus, they read *aschēmosynē* as a reference to "formlessness," and they argued that the men's intercourse shifted their gender to an androgynous state.[82]

Thus, early readers understood the unnatural sex of Romans 1:26–27, through the lens of the traversable, one-body model, as a stereotyped embodiment of Gentile effeminacy. Fools, all, they degraded the masculinity of the God of Israel—His immortal *doxa* and His natural gender hierarchy. The result, according to Chrysostom, was the abandonment of its natural genders:

> Both he who was to be a leader of the woman and she who is to be a helpmate to the man now behave as enemies to one another. . . . what shall we say of this insanity? . . . Not only are you made [by it] into a woman, but you also cease to be a man. Yet neither are you changed [fully] into that nature nor do you retain the one you had. You become a betrayer of both. . . . Just to demonstrate my point, suppose someone came up to you and offered to change you from a man to a dog. Would you not try to get away from such a degenerate? Yet you have changed yourselves from men . . . into a much more loathsome animal. . . . A dog at least is useful, but a softie is good for nothing . . . for it is not the same thing to be changed into the nature of a woman as it is to become a woman

while yet remaining a man or, rather, to be neither one nor the other. (*Homily* 4.1.3)

Insane Gentile idolaters inverted the Creator's gender hierarchy through gender-transgressive sex, transforming women into masculine leaders and men into their helpmates, androgynous gender-monsters of less worth than a dog. Hardly an abstract description of human homosexuality, Romans 1:26–27 was a deployment of the *Greco-Roman* ideology of masculinity that used the charge of physical androgynization to contrast the impotency of the Gentile rabble with the naturally superior masculinity of Paul's Jewish God.

Imperial Queer: Jesus the Effeminate, Christ the Original Androgyne
The irony of Paul's embrace of the Greco-Roman ideology of nature to censure Gentile androgyny inheres in the fact that Paul's *corpus* itself redefines and subverts "nature" christologically through the androgynous Body of Christ. Further, that redefinition was queer: In an act of resistance to imperial self-definition and the emasculation of the Messianic movement, Paul transformed several Greco-Roman discourses of masculinity, through the effemination of the cross, to name the crucified Christ as the androgynous last Adam, the new creation into whose body believers were materially knit and within whose body they were being materially transformed.

This reading begins with Jesus and his disciples, who were girls by Roman gender standards. Colonizing the one-body model to name themselves the Man, imperial-era Romans made man a *Roman* citizen-male, an indomitable dominator who maintained his virility (and the empire) by never allowing himself (or it) to be penetrated or beaten.[83] Those who were penetrated or beaten were labeled half-men (*semiviri*), effeminates derided for desiring penetration. As a Galilean Jew the Romans crucified as a royal pretender, Jesus embodied everything the Roman man was not—dominated, penetrated, scourged, and humiliated.[84] To Roman eyes, therefore, the crucified Jesus was not king of the Jews, but a barely-man whom Rome nailed as a queen. As Halvor Moxnes shows, the Roman specter of effeminacy attached to the crucified Jesus extended to Jesus' circle of disciples, their master's humiliation degrading them into "eunuchs."[85] The earliest believers, Jews who were convinced Jesus was the Davidic Messiah come to exorcise their Roman overlords,[86] understandably redefined Jesus' emasculating death and recreated themselves via a powerful christological counterdiscourse. Usurping "Son of God," a title Greeks and Romans deemed a divine name for the Roman emperor, they redefined the crucified Jesus as what Stephen Moore has called "The Colossal Christ," the powerful Son of God sacrificed for their good.[87] In short, this small band of messianic Jews (including Jewish-Christian Greeks) embraced and transformed a powerful title for the Roman emperor to resurrect their leader's reputation and give themselves status and identity. They remade their eunuch into the Man.

But as Eric Thurman and Chris Frilingos show, this act of "colonial mimicry" was incomplete and gender-underdetermined.[88] Building on an alternative rhetoric of masculinity that virilized necessary suffering—a redefinition of *vir*-ility by Cynics, ex-slaves, and populist leaders whose power as *men* had been diminished by the rise of one-man Roman rule[89]—early Christian writers insisted that Jesus "approximated the masculine identity of Messiah and Son of God precisely and paradoxically by enduring the feminizing shame and humiliation of the cross."[90] As Homi Bhabha argues, usurping an imperial title to empower the leader of a subject group is an (imperfect) act of mimicry because colonial subjects, commanded to be both like and unlike their colonizers, have a "partial presence" that replicates "the colonizer's culture incompletely." That underdetermination "eludes the colonizer's control and may subtly work to undermine his authority."[91] In other words, when subject people mimic imperial signs, they may perform gestures of silent or whispered insubordination that subvert the power of the colonizer's culture over them. Believers' elision of the crucified Christ with the Son of God was such a sign, a parody of empire that reinscribed and subverted Roman imperial gender ideology in a masculofeminized, penetrated-leader discourse of masculinity.[92]

Like other early Christians, Paul learned this lesson of resistance well. He too usurped the Roman title Son of God to empower the crucified Christ, renaming Jesus Messiah the royal seed of David commissioned "Son of God in power" on account of his resurrection from the dead (Rom. 1:1–4). But Paul added to this another layer of gender mimicry, superimposing on the Son the Greco-Roman myth of the first androgyne, an elite discourse whose original masculinity functioned to counteract and christologically empower the effemination of the cross. In fact, Paul repeatedly identified Christ as the Last Adam (*eschatos Adam*), the new creation androgynous-man who, through his effeminating death and resurrection, became a life-giving spiritual body that transformed believers into sons like him.

As several scholars have shown, the basis of this claim is the popular ancient notion that the first human(s) was an androgyne.[93] For example, in Plato's *Symposium* 189d–190b Aristophanes depicts the first humans as two-faced, double-bodied androgynes so powerful that the gods divided them, as a punishment, into males and females who forever after sought sexual union (in various combinations) with their other halves. Jewish authors of texts like *Apocalypse of Adam* 1:4–5 and *Jubilees* 2:14 usurped this high-status Greek tradition, interpreting Genesis 1:26–27 ("male and female he created them") as a reference to Adam as the original androgyne. Philo of Alexandria dismisses the Platonic account, but he nevertheless builds on it, depicting the generic human as an androgynous embodiment of "male and female."[94] Similarly, Genesis Rabbah 8.1: "Said Rabbi Jeremiah ben Leazar: 'When the Holy One, blessed be he, came to create the first man, he made him androgynous, as it said, Male and female he created them and called their name man (Gen. 5:2).' Said R. Samuel bar Nahman: 'When the Holy One, blessed be he, created the first man, he created him with two faces, then divided him in two and made a back on one side and a back on the other.'"[95] Jewish authors even argued that Eve's creation was only possible because one of androgynous-Adam's two faces was female.[96]

As Dennis MacDonald and Dale Martin argue, the key to understanding original androgyny is masculinity; ideal human nature not only had to be gendered masculine, but its masculinity given an origin. So, the first androgyne represented neither the physical embodiment of two equally good genders (as moderns typically imagine), nor the effemination Roman ideologues (and Romans 1) typically attached to androgyny, but an idealized masculine, form that perfectly assimilated inferior, feminine elements.[97] As Plato opines, the generation of women was a devolution from the perfect original human, a deformity resulting from men's indulgence of passion, cowardice, and injustice in a former life (*Timaeus* 42c, 90e). Likewise, Philo claims (*De Opificio Mundi* 151–52):

> Since nothing in creation is constant and mortal things necessarily receive changes and alterations, it was unavoidable that the first man (*anthrōpon*) should also undergo some disaster. And woman (*gynē*) becomes for him the beginning of a blameworthy life. For as long as he was one (*heis*) . . . he went on growing like to the cosmos and like God . . . but when woman was created . . . love supervenes, brings together and fits into one the divided halves, as it were, of a single living creature and sets up in each of them a desire for fellowship . . . that likewise begat bodily pleasure, which is the beginning of iniquities and transgressions, on account of which they exchange immortality and happiness for mortality and wretchedness.

For Jews riffing on the Greek ideology of original androgyny, the extraction of the female form from Adam marked the onset of passion and degradation.[98] The corollary is that return to Adamic androgyny (or the return of Adamic androgyny) marked the renewal of perfect oneness beyond the creation of "female" and its effemination of humanity. This corollary explains why "every woman who makes herself male [in Christ] will enter the kingdom of heavens," "becoming a living spirit that resembles you males" (*Gospel of Thomas* 114). In Tertullian's words, "You too (women as you are) have the self-same angelic nature promised as your reward, the self-same sex as man."[99]

The Pauline corpus mimics this masculinist Greek notion of androgyny to claim that Christ *was* the new creation, the androgynous body of the new Adam. 1 Corinthians 15 and Romans 5:14 offer the foundational element of this portrait, Paul's christological-eschatological rereading of Genesis 1–2. According to 1 Corinthians 15:

> What is sown is perishable, what is raised imperishable. Sown in dishonor, it is raised in glory. Sown in weakness, it is raised in power. Sown a physical body, it is raised a spiritual body. If there is a physical body [*sōma psychikon*], there is also a spiritual body [*sōma pneumatikon*]. Thus is it written, "The first man Adam became a

living being" [Gen 2:7]; the last Adam became a life-giving spirit [*pneuma zōopoioun*]. The physical comes first, and then the spiritual. The first man was from the earth, a man of dust; the second man is from heaven. As was the man of dust, so are those who are of the dust; as is the man of heaven, so are those who are of heaven. Just as we have borne the image [*eikona*] of the man of dust, let us bear the image of the man of heaven [Gen. 1:26–27, 5:2–3].[100]

Romans 5:14–21 adds that Adam was the type (*typos*) of the one (*heis*) Christ, whose just act (*dikaiōma*) of self-sacrifice resulted in reign in life for believers. Taken together, these passages imply that the high-status "image" of Christ's androgynous spirit was transferred to believers.

According to Galatians 3:28, baptism was the ritual route of that transfer, somehow recreating believers into actual members of the material body of Christ. "In Christ Jesus you are all sons of God through faith. For as many of you as were baptized into Christ have put on [*enedusasthe*] Christ. There is neither Jew nor Greek, slave nor free, male and female. For you are all one [*heis*] in Christ Jesus" (Gal. 3:26–28). As Meeks argues, "Galatians 3:28 contains a reference to the male and female of Genesis 1:27 and suggests that somehow the act of Christian initiation reverses the fateful division of Genesis 2:21–22. Where the image of God is restored, there, it seems, man is no longer divided."[101] As the masculine Greek *heis* implies, "putting on" the one, perfect androgynous-man dissolved the disunity and degradation represented by the gender pair, male and female.[102] "Donning Christ as a garment" (Gal. 3:27, Rom. 13:14) in baptism was therefore a somatic act of cross-dressing that conferred on believers the ritual state of spiritual androgyny.

To depict the agent of this transformation, the *material* spirit of Christ, Paul superimposed on the discourse of Christ's androgyny another high-status Greco-Roman idea, that of the *pneuma* he says believers received. As Dale Martin argues in *The Corinthian Body,* Paul's description of Christ's body as *pneumatic* ("spiritual") was not a metaphor, but a somatic claim evoking philosophic discourses about "spirit" as the most elite material stuff in the universe.[103] On the Stoic model of nature, this *pneuma* or spirit was a rational material essence that permeated the universe and resided within the human heart or mind (*kardia, nous*), guiding it as *hēgemonikon* to act morally by extirpating femininity (passion). (As Galen, parroting Chrysippus, said, "the soul is noble or base depending on the state of its *hēgemonikon.*"[104]) Plato's *Timaeus* 90a also describes a divinely gifted guiding spirit in the human mind that "raises us up away from the earth and toward what is akin to us in heaven, as though we are plants grown not from the earth but from heaven." Seneca built on this famously dualistic Platonic idea of the indwelling *daimon,* repeatedly describing a holy, immortal spirit (*spiritus*) that lived within and guided the human body in right living (*Moral Epistles* 31.11, 41, 66.1, 120.14). He even claimed in *De Clementia* that Nero Caesar *was* the hegemonic spirit that guided the body of the Roman Empire. Both this Romanized, somatic definition of *pneuma* and the equation of it with a divine spirit indwelling in human minds are metonymous with Paul's presentation of Christ as the pneumatic body of the Last Adam. Paul said repeatedly that the spirit of Christ *dwelt* in believers' minds (Rom. 8:9–27; 1 Cor. 12:13; Gal. 4:6): "we have received . . . the spirit from God . . . we have the mind of Christ" (1 Cor. 2:12–16). At the same time, in contrast to both Plato and Seneca, Paul claimed that *on their own* humans lack this spirit (Rom. 7). *Christ alone* possessed it, and God alone gave it to believers in baptism (1 Cor. 2:10–16, Rom. 8:26–27). In short, Paul's use of spirit mimicked a broadly recognizable, Roman philosophic notion in order to make the counter-imperialistic claim that *Christ* was the ruling spirit of the cosmos whom only the members of his body possessed.[105]

The main effect of this claim was to make baptism a high-status sex-change ritual: By actively putting on the *toga virilis* of Christ, believers became "sons of God."[106] An "awe-inspiring" claim according to Chrysostom, "if Christ is the Son of God and you put him on, having the Son inside yourself . . . you have been made one [*heis*] in kind and form . . . the former Jew or slave is clothed in the form . . . of the Lord himself and in himself displays Christ."[107] Consequently, "difference of ethnicity or condition or gender is indeed taken away by unity of faith."[108] Simply put, believers' gender was masculinized in baptism through the indwelling of Christ's spirit: Women were materially transformed into sons-of-God-women-in-Christ's-male-body; men morphed into sons-of-God-men-in-Christ's-superior-male-body; and hermaphrodites and virgins shifted to herms-and-virgins-in-Christ's-superior-male-body. The middle term of believers physical flesh (*sarx*) became but a tiny morsel of meat sandwiched between the masculine elements of their new gender, "sons-of-God" in "Christ's-male-body." "Christ is all and in all" (Col. 3:10–11) so that "all diversity of ethnicity, condition, and body is taken away."[109]

In short, by subverting *three* Greco-Roman discourses of masculinity (sonship, original androgyny, spirit), Paul collectively made believers the Man. To his audience of upwardly mobile, but mostly lower-status slaves and freepersons, this must have been a thrill-ride of a claim, implying that how believers were created or viewed by outsiders, even the "rulers of this world" (1 Cor. 2:8), no longer mattered in the Body.[110] They had been transformed into sons by their baptism into Christ's androgynous, new "Sex."

Moral Cross-Dressing in Christ's Androgynous Body

Significantly, however, believers' "sex-change" was not a once-for-all surgical operation that gave the baptized Christ's superior fleshly phallus, but a materially spiritual impetus for moral action. As Paul's call in 1 Cor. 15:49 for believers to "bear the image" of the Last Adam implies, even though the life-giving Spirit of the Son dwelt in their minds, they had constantly to cross-dress in Christ. The reason was that they lived in a physical-eschatological already–not yet, the spiritual Body of Christ in the fleshly world, and retained their own skin (*sarx*) and the feminine weakness that inhabited that bit of meat (Rom. 6–7). Because it was an element of this world, fleshly weakness imperiled the health of the Body of Christ, rendering it vulnerable, through the actions of its members, to bodily invasion by the world's evils.[111] Until they received the "redemption of our Body," Paul therefore called the baptized to moral action that perfected their new, collective "sex" (Rom. 8:23; cf. Rom. 2:7; 8:1–39; 13:8–10; 1 Cor. 13).

As Brent Nongbri and others have argued, Paul's call to moral action resonates strongly with yet *another* discourse of masculinity, that of *prokoptontes* ("progressors in wisdom").[112] A dominant Roman (Stoic) model of the pursuit of virtue, *prokoptontes* referred to men who were not already perfect ("wise men") but who sought through daily self-mastery over passion to perfect themselves and attain virtue. (As Philo of Alexandria claimed, "philosophical progress [*prokopē*] is nothing else than relinquishing the female gender by changing into the male.'"[113]) For Paul, this masculinizing process required believers to "hold true to what they had already attained," and "press on" to make themselves fully who they already were—the Body of Christ (Phil. 3:12–16, 21; Col. 3:10). Doing so, which Paul calls "working out their own salvation," was possible because the spirit of "God was at work in them, to will and work for his good pleasure" (Phil. 2:12–13). In short, because believers possessed the masculine spirit of the last androgyne, which purified less masculine elements within their bodies,[114] they could rely on it to guide them in good deeds, extirpate weakness from their flesh, and eventually, perfect them (Rom. 8:1–39).

The key to understanding moral progress in the Body, however, is that it required believers' effemination—it was moral cross-dressing. In the first place, only Christ was the Man. Unlike philosophers, Paul thought that without Christ's indwelling spirit, humans lacked the guiding *hēgemonikon* that enabled right action. However weak or strong, whatever their individual fleshly genders, all believers were therefore femmes to Christ's butch spirit. Acting virtuously required acquiescence to H/is penetrating spirit acting as Phallus through their communion with H/im (*koinōnia*, 1 Cor. 10:16–21). In the second place, the moral life in Christ was communal. Whereas philosophers treated *prokopē* as a largely individualistic pursuit, Paul (and his disciples) defined self-mastery as the collective building (*oikodomē*) of the Body of Christ. *No one* belonged to themselves. "We who are many are one body," Paul said repeatedly (1 Cor. 10:17; Rom. 12:5). As "God's fellow workers" (1 Cor. 3:9), the collective temple cemented together by Christ's spirit (1 Cor. 3:9–17), believers were called to "please his neighbor for his upbuilding" (*oikodomē;* Rom. 15:2). Doing so was agapeic love, the work of faith that fulfilled the law of God (Rom 13:10). For Paul, "love" was therefore not a feeling—much less a warrant for heterosexual weddings (1 Cor. 13). It was an embodied drive for peace and upbuilding, which constituted the reign of God (Rom. 14:17–19, Eph. 4:16).

Most important, the moral life of the communal Body was a *mimesis* of Christ's effeminating sacrifice for others, which meant that love took the form of believers' collective self-sacrifice to build up the lowly (Rom. 12:1–2, 16; 15:1–3). Put another way, the effemination of Christ's crucifixion inhered in the moral masculinization of the Body.[115] As Christ's body, believers were not to act like "kings" (1 Cor. 4:6–12), but to be a "living sacrifice"—associating with the lowly, blessing persecutors, living peaceably with all, not being haughty, and never avenging themselves (Rom. 12:2–3, 14–21).[116] The key to this claim is, again, baptism. Paul asserted in 1 Corinthians 15:36 that "what you sow does not come to life unless it dies." In Romans 5–6, he argued that baptism coplanted believers with Christ in the likeness (tō homoiōmati) of his suffering death (Rom. 6:5), thereby creating both the possibility of new life *and* the demand to live it (Rom. 5:15–21, 6:4, 8:4, 9). For the life of faith, the main implication was that Christian *prokoptontes* were called to *imitate* (*mimēsis*) Christ's death in their life (Rom. 15:1–3, 1 Cor. 11:1). As Jo-Ann Brant shows, the *mimēsis* to which Paul referred was not a mere copying, but a practice of repetition that inculcated the pattern of the original, Christ, into the souls of acting subjects.[117] Hence, collectively enacting Christ's sacrifice for others, a practice requiring an ecclesiologically synergistic self-mastery, inculcated the Son into the baptized in such a way that they actually became H/is Body (Rom. 8:17, 12:1–5, 15:1). Thus, the effemination of Christ's death was soteriologically central to the masculinization of moral progress, making Christian living a collectively queer moral process of becoming—the material transformation of the body through self-lowering into the recreated "image" of Christ's eschatological body.

In Ephesians 4:12–24, an interpreter of Paul captures well both the gender dynamic and the eschatological imperative of Paul's queer moral program:

> Equip the saints . . . for the building up [*oikodomē*] of the body of Christ, until we all attain the oneness [*henotēta*] of the faith and knowledge of the Son of God, to perfect manhood [*eis andra teleion*], to the measure of the stature of the fullness of Christ. So that we may no longer be children . . . Rather, speaking the truth in love, we are to grow up in everyway into him [*eis auton*], who is the head, Christ, from whom the whole body, joined and knit together by every joint with which it is supplied, when each part is working properly, makes bodily growth and upbuilds itself in love . . . Put off your old man [*ton palaion anthrōpon*] . . . be renewed by the spirit of your mind [*tō pneumatic tou noos hymōn*] and don the new man

[*endusasthai ton kainon anthrōpon*], created after the likeness of God in true righteousness and holiness.

INTERCOURSE WITH CHRIST (*KOINŌNIA*), INTERCOURSE IN CHRIST (*OIKODOMĒ*)

Ultimately, it was *this* quest to perfect the Body, to "bear the image" of the Last Adam, that led Paul to remind believers of the importance of having sex with Christ's spirit—and of the power of having sex with each other. I am not kidding. As odd as it may sound, it is the somatic logic of Paul's communal love ethic that made the baptized lovers of Christ and sex acts a sanctifying ménage à trois. Paul expresses both this truth and its dangers in 1 Corinthians 6:16–20, where he uses believers *sexual* union with Christ as the "new creation" warrant against intercourse with prostitutes:

> a man having sex (*kollōmenos*) with a whore   becomes one flesh
> with her (Gen. 2:24)

but

> a man having sex (*kollōmenos*) with the Lord   becomes one
> spirit with h/im

Paul reworks Genesis 2 ecclesiologically, using an explicit analogy between sexual intercourse and believers' sex with Christ to remind them that they are "not their own." Rather, they are members of Christ's body intimately united with H/is most powerful material spirit (6:19). The author of Ephesians repeats this association (Eph. 5:29–32): "For no man ever hates his own flesh but nourishes it and cherishes it, as Christ does the church, for we are members of his body. 'For this reason, a man will leave his father and mother and be joined to his wife and the two shall become one flesh' [Gen. 2:24]. This mystery is profound and I am saying that it refers to Christ and the church." In 1 Corinthians 6, Paul emphasizes the singularity of this collective body (*sōma,* 6:13, 19, 20) and the inextricability of individual bodies with it (6:16, 18) to underscore that the believers' body was one with the Lord's.[118]

Consequently, all Christian intercourse involved the Lord, making it both sanctifying and dangerous. The logic of this claim is, again, physical. Ancient doctors thought *pneuma* collected most potently in the "seed" or *sperma*, which means that spirit could be ejaculated in intercourse.[119] Since ancients thought men and women (as different embodiments of one basic human body) could *both* ejaculate *sperma*,[120] and since Christ's spirit dwelt within believers' bodies, *when believers had sex (and ejaculated), they sent Christ's spirit out with their sperm.* This physiological logic of spiritual ejaculation is the material rationale behind Paul's warning against having sex with prostitutes. It actually, materially, made Christ one with a whore (6:15)—injecting H/is holy spirit-phallus into a dirty receptacle and expelling H/is masculinizing essence into a barren world, spending seed on infertile soil.[121]

Because it involved a somatic union with Christ's spirit, morally good sex, by contrast, was (re)*creative*—used for H/is glory (6:20). By this, Paul did *not* mean that people should join in "heterosexual marriage"—nor even abstain from sex, although this was his preference (1 Cor. 7:1–7). Rather, he called them to have sex in order to control passions that effeminated the Body (1 Cor. 7:5, 9); or to sanctify unbelievers within it (7:12–16). Dale Martin has explained the philosophical logic of the first case, self-mastery by eliminating passion.[122] Let me unpack the second. Within a discussion of divorce, Paul said in 7:12–16 that believers with unbelieving partners should remain with them *not because* "male and female he created them"—in contrast to Mark 10, Paul included no warrant for marriage from Genesis—but *if* they consent to dwell with them (*suneudokei oikein met' autēs*, verses 12–13). In that case, the believer made the unbeliever and their children holy (7:14). Paul said the believing partner could even save the unbeliever in this way (7:16). In other words, Paul enjoined *missionary* sex *in* the Body (*en kuriō*). As in 1 Corinthians 6, Paul's unstated body-logic is that intercourse in the Body is a *ménage à trois* involving Christ's spirit, and that spirit is materially sanctifying of the unbelieving partner and their children. So what is the difference between the sex of 1 Corinthians 6 and 1 Corinthians 7? Why does the believer not make the prostitute holy with Christ's spiritual seed? In 1

Corinthians 6, the believer's (and Christ's seed) is sent out of the communal Body into the impure world of the flesh. In the latter case, the unbeliever comes to live in the believer's house (*oikos*), which is the gathering place of the Body "in the Lord" (e.g., 1 Cor. 1:16, 7:22–23, 16:15). Thus, Christian lovers are purified by their location in Christ's body.[123] The argument of 1 Corinthians 7 assumes that sex is sanctifying not *because* it is created or heterosexual or complementary or "natural" but *when* it brings people into and unites them with the Body. Paul's limited warrant for intercourse—any intercourse besides believers' spiritual sex with Christ—was that it be literally (up)building of the Body.

In sum, Paul never used "creation" or "nature" or Genesis 1–3 as a warrant for *any* kind of marriage. His interpretations of Genesis were christocentric, ecclesiocentric, and eschatological, mimicking and subverting Greco-Roman discourses of manhood via the effemination of the cross to convince believers that their eschatological purpose was to live who they were, the New Man, the androgynous body of their Savior (Phil 3:20–21). This unnatural rule of the new creation was so important that it applied even to God. As Eugene Rogers underscores, in Rom. 11:24 the same God who allowed Gentile idolaters to shape-shift unnaturally acted unnaturally in Christ by growing "naturally" disparate peoples, Jews and Greeks, together into a "cultivated olive tree." As Paul said, if Christ, as the root of that tree, was holy, so were all of them (Rom 11:26, 15:12).[124] This unnatural logic of divine growth—peoples' material transformation in Christ—explains why there is neither Jew nor Greek in Christ's Body. It also explains why Paul called the Body to be a living sacrifice who "pleases his neighbor for his good" (Rom. 11:24, 26, 33; 12:1, 4; 15:2–3, 12): *It is the basis of the eschatological hope* (Rom. 11:12). Paul presented God's ultimate purpose in Christ as the communion of all peoples with him in praise (Rom. 15:6), and he insisted that Christ's physical act of self-sacrifice alone made that possible, materially queering the binaries of "natural" humanity to recreate the perfect possibility for the unnatural "mixing of kinds." That is why Paul's Body of Christ was queer, "neither Jew nor Greek, slave nor free, no longer male and female," but one in his masculine-androgynous spirit. This is also why loving Christ was a sexual affair, the work of the Body was neighbor-love, and intercourse that united, furthering the Body as a whole, was good. The work of the Body of Christ was the material union of all different types of people to God, and this unnatural process of becoming ultimately ushered in the eschaton: the return of the original masculine androgyne.

CHRISTIAN SEX IN AMERICA: ON BODY-BUILDING LOVE

The careful reader will see that this queer reading of Paul's Body cannot offer Christians a universal sexual ethic—nor should it. Paul's gender ideology and worldview were almost incomprehensibly different from our own, and even though Paul did not address homosexual sex, he enculturated nature as thoroughly as we do, reinscribing in his conception of the Body and unnatural sex (Rom. 1) a sense of human nature that reeked of misogyny. Paul's followers quickly capitalized on that hatred of the feminine, reinstituting—even in his own letters—the gender hierarchy between male and female that Paul's Body logic undermined (1 Cor. 14:34–36; Eph. 5:22–33; 1 Tim. 2:9–15). Appropriated analogically, Paul's nature (literally) screws women (1 Cor. 11), to the extent that they must be silent (1 Cor. 14) and saved through childbirth (1 Tim. 2). It also underwrites a denunciation of softness in men, a complex of gender deviations (effeminacy, hermaphroditism, sexual passivity, dandyism) that extends well beyond the sexual sphere—implicating, by analogy, even those men among us who dress too daintily or are overly lenient with subordinates.

Perhaps most importantly, while this rereading highlights the extent to which modern notions about sexuality, biological sex, and God's nature have determined the meaning of Romans 1,[125] it also suggests that using a simplistically analogical hermeneutics to appropriate it will simply shift our censorious (scriptural) gaze from gays to the transgendered and intersexed. This would be a terrible result, not simply because to those of us committed to social justice this kind of interpretation signals a new turn in scripture-based oppression, but because even on an analogical model, the hermeneutical challenge posed by Romans 1 is significantly more expansive than a limited critique of gender minorities allows. The ancient reading of Romans 1 as a censure of gender-transgression and body morphing challenges all of us, regardless of our professed sexual orientations, to determine what counts as a godly gender expression, and it threatens to coerce us all to adhere to a rigidly role-based gender dualism lest we devolve into girls.

But the Pauline corpus represents a genuinely ambivalent heritage, as its repetition and subversion of Greco-Roman standards of natural masculinity is also suggestive for rethinking Christian sexual ethics in resistance to the hegemony of the two-sex model. In the first place, Romans 1 unseats the universality of a two-sex model of the human body through its very censure of a third gender. It forces all of us—straight, gay, or bi, male, female, intersexed, or trans—to wrestle with the question, how many genders can be godly? Answers to this question are by no means obvious. Westerners approve the surgical alteration of almost all of the 1.5 percent of "hermaphrodites" born every year, which means that most of us know nothing of these persons, much less their joys and daily struggles. How much more the joys and struggles of those with conditions that cause their bodies to change form from female to more male at puberty? Christians need to think carefully about how they will describe the moral worth of these persons. Christians need to ask whether and on what basis they will have a place of standing in the church, be allowed to serve it, and to marry.

Further, the Pauline Body of Christ also highlights the ideological blindness required to maintain that the "Bible contains [no] internal tensions and counterposed witnesses" to counter its censure of male anal intercourse.[126] For the Pauline Body of Christ unlinks the authority of creation, read in terms of biological dualism (male and female) or ontologized sexual identity, from its conception of sexual morality. Anatomical sex is ritualized as a baptismal gift of new creation, human nature redefined sacramentally beyond dualism as a uniquely Christian, one-body, multi-gender practice of becoming. Christian sex is thereby transfigured into a transfiguring enactment of God. This would mean, as Paul claims, that sexual ethics in the Body must revolve around communal recreativity rather than individual procreativity. If we took it seriously, neither "male and female," nor "male" and "female," nor heterosexuality, nor homosexuality, nor either kind of marriage would be a Christian good—only the sexual and sexed / gendered performances that unnaturally unite divided peoples, in the Body of Christ, for lives of Christian service.

To some this may be an unsettlingly open-ended vision of Christian morality. Certainly, Robert Gagnon and the pope (not to mention liberal progressives) should be afraid that such queer enactments of scripture would destabilize Christian society. Once freed of its misogyny, the open-ended gender-performance of the Body of Christ challenges the church to resist parroting society's rigidly dualistic gender hierarchy and to enact its own subversive visions, in imitation of the Last Adam's self-sacrifice, of Whom it will become—"girls who want to be boys, boys who want to be girls, boys and girls who insist they are both, whites who want to be black, blacks who want to or refuse to be white, people who are white and black, gay and straight, masculine and feminine, or who are finding ways to be and name none of the above."[127]

As Dale Martin suggests, "Once we destabilize the duality, all sorts of new ways of being [Christian], not just two and not just combinations of two, may be invented. The gender made possible by the new creation in Christ opens as yet unknowable ways of gendering human experience, combinations of which we cannot foresee as long as we retain the dualistic male-female limitation."[128] It is precisely the open-endedness of this eschatological vision that fulfills Augustine's standard for a good reading of scripture: "Whoever thinks he understands the divine Scriptures or any part of them so that it does not build the double love of God and of our neighbor does not understand it at all" (Christian Doctrine 1.35.40).[129]

❧ Homoerotic Spectacle and the Monastic Body in Symeon the New Theologian

DEREK KRUEGER

Symeon the New Theologian (949–1022), arguably the most important Byzantine religious thinker between John of Damascus in the eighth century and Gregory Palamas in the fourteenth, often presents salvation as a heavenly marriage.[1] Scholars have long noted Symeon's frequent use of erotic and nuptial imagery to explore the relationship between the monk and God.[2] What scholars have generally failed to notice or account for is that much of this imagery is homoerotic. In contrast to more common tendencies to celebrate the consummation of male divinity with a monk's feminized soul, Symeon emphasizes the masculinity of the monk's body. I will argue that Symeon employs same-sex desires in order to emphasize the male monastic body as a locus of *theōsis,* the deification of humanity.

In his Tenth Ethical Discourse, Symeon invokes a homoerotic parable to assist in the formation of monastic spirituality. Despite excellent scholarly work on Symeon's theology and on the striking images that he employs to describe the encounter with the divine, this passage has tended to be overlooked or set aside. The text in question is a performance of male same-sex desire and fantasy that structures expectations of salvation. In presenting the male monastic body as the object of God's eros, the parable invokes themes also found among Symeon's *Hymns on Divine Love.* As a whole, the Tenth Ethical Discourse explicates the meaning of the "Day of the Lord," and highlights the place of the repentant sinner in God's work of redemption. In his story, which Symeon terms a *para-deigma*, an "illustration" or "example," an emperor takes a repentant rebel to his bed.[3] To illustrate the joy that God might feel at the return of a rebellious subject, the story contains echoes of the parable of the prodigal son, but the narrative soon moves to the bedroom, where it remains.

Scholars have been unable to determine whether Symeon composed the *Ethical Discourses* while he was the abbot of the Constantinopolitan monastery of Saint Mamas between 1003 and 1009, or later, during his exile across the Bosporus, where he led a small community at the Oratory of Saint Marina.[4] The original performative context for the Tenth Ethical Discourse also remains unclear: We do not know whether Symeon preached it aloud or intended it for a reading audience beyond his monastery.[5] If the latter, the literary document mimics the form of an oral discourse complete with frequent performance indicators like direct address in the vocative to "my brothers" and "beloved ones."[6] Nevertheless, the category of performance, broadly conceived, provides an interpretative framework in which to consider the deployment of homoerotic imagery in ascetic instruction and raises questions about the place of homoeroticism in middle Byzantine male monastic formation.

The parable tells of "the emperor of the Christians" and a rebel who had fought for many years against him. "He received messages on several occasions from the emperor of the Christians that he should come to him, and be with him, and be honored with great gifts and reign with him" (*Ethical Discourses* 10.239–241). After many years, the prodigal became disillusioned with his rebellion and decided to obey the emperor, who had been sending him messages, believing that the emperor would not count the tardiness of his response against him; he had heard of the emperor's compassion and goodness. The imperial context may invoke Byzantine political and military realities during the reign of Basil II, with rebels changing sides in wars against the emperor. But Symeon's interest lies in the delights of reconciliation.

When he approached the emperor and embraced his feet, he wept and asked forgiveness. Seized by unexpected joy, that good emperor immediately accepted him, wondering at his conversion and humility. The man, instead of making bold as he had thought he would and demanding honors for the love and trust he had proven to the emperor by abandoning the rebel [leader] and approaching the other's kingdom, instead lies mourning over his tardiness and the crimes for which he had previously been responsible. Raising him up, the emperor "fell upon his neck and kissed him (Lk. 15:20)" all over and on his eyes which had been weeping for many hours. Then, when he had ordered that a crown and robe and sandals be brought out that were like the ones he was wearing, he himself clothed his former enemy and rival, and in no way reproached him for anything. And not only this, but night and day he was rejoicing in him and being glad, and embracing [him] and kissing his mouth with his own mouth [*kataspazomenos stoma pros stoma auton*]. So much did he love him exceedingly that he was not separated from him even in sleep, laying down with him and embracing him on his bed and covering him all over with his cloak [*chlanidion*], and placing his own face upon all his members [*kai epititheis to heautou prosōpon epi pasi tois autou melesin*] (*Ethical Discourses* 10.235–273; *On the Mystical Life*, 150–151).

At least two modern commentators have found this passage troubling. The French editor and translator, Jean Darrouzès, notes that the story falls into a sensibility that is "a bit questionable" and opines that Symeon "gives the impression of having forgotten the 'perfected sensation' that he argues for."[7] And the English translator, Alexander Golitzin, writes, "Sometimes the saint's gift for image will exceed his discretion and good sense. This appears to be one such instance. We leave it in solely out of respect for the integrity of the text."[8] These same critics (and others) have registered enthusiasm for, but little surprise at, Symeon's more usual cross-sex nuptial imagery.[9] We must resist the threat of expurgation, of course, in order to understand how different Symeon's sensibilities were from some modern and frankly homophobic expectations. Indeed, this passage offers important evidence for the erotic imaginary available to a middle-Byzantine monastic theologian.

Like Jesus among the disciples, after Symeon has related his parable, he supplies an interpretation. Symeon's own exegesis of the passage reads his parable as a type for the repentant monk: "Such is also our situation with God, and I know that it is in just such a manner that the good-loving God welcomes and embraces those who repent, who, fleeing the illusory world and its ruler, strip themselves naked of the affairs of this life and approach Him as King and God" (*Ethical Discourses* 10.274–278; *On the Mystical Life*, 151). This interpretation makes the embrace of God available to each ascetic, an ascetic who is described in a manner typical of the New Theologian as "naked." In fact, Symeon often describes the monk as "naked before God," either stripped bare of worldly things through rigorous discipline or resurrected naked before God on the day of judgment (*Hymns* 21.361; 28.51). Here, however, the nakedness carries an explicitly erotic charge, as the naked and repentant rebel is destined for God's bed.

In Symeon's parabolic narrative, the expectation of the day of the Lord figures as the expectation of perpetual erotic delights. Indeed, for Symeon the exegetical point of his parable is clear: It should arouse desire and expectation in his monastic audience. His performative utterance flirts rhetorically with what within a monastic context is strictly forbidden. All sexual activity, including same-sex sexual activity, would violate the discipline of the monastic life, yet Symeon trains his audience's desire by redirecting it. Symeon's exegesis of his own parable becomes an invitation, as he continues: "Therefore, my beloved brothers, abandoning everything let us run naked and, approaching Christ the Master, let us fall down and weep before His goodness [cf. LXX Ps. 94:6], so that He, indeed, having seen our faith and humility, may similarly—or rather, even more so—welcome and honor us, and adorn us with His own robe and diadem, and make us worthy celebrants of the bridal chamber [*nymphō-nos*] of heaven" (*Ethical Discourses* 10.304–311; *On the Mystical Life*, 152). The monk's movement, naked, from falling before Christ, to being adorned with robe and diadem, to entering into the bridal chamber, inscribes the progression from repentance to eternal salvation.

While Symeon often invokes divine eros in his understanding of the process of deification, it is debatable whether this parable and its interpretation are "consistent with the New Theologian's use of nuptial imagery elsewhere," as Golitzin has claimed (*On the Mystical Life,* 1.151 note 2). It is certainly true that Symeon calls on wedding and erotic imagery in his works, including the First Ethical Discourse, where he reads salvation as a wedding between God and a rebel's daughter. "It is the daughter of one who rebelled against Him, one who committed murder and adultery" (*Ethical Discourses* 1.9.23–25; *On the Mystical Life,* 1.53).[10] However, the parable in the Tenth Ethical Discourse is not so simply classified as nuptial, at least not in any conventional sense. Significantly, in this parable, Christ's beloved remains male; he is neither transgendered into a bride nor identified with his grammatically feminine soul. Even though Symeon's own exegesis asks his audience to read the parable as a type of marriage, at the very least, the passage encourages the reader to expand the meaning of "nuptial" to include same-sex nuptiality.

How then to read this text as part of the history of eros in Byzantine monasticism? In *The Sex Lives of Saints: An Erotics of Ancient Hagiography,* Virginia Burrus has observed the persistent deployment of desire in texts designed to describe, promote, and champion the ascetic life. Far from eschewing all desire, the narrative literatures of earlier Byzantine asceticism redeployed the erotic toward consummation with God and toward new conceptions of the ascetic self that seduced audiences to self-control.[11] An understanding of Symeon's parable within his work as a monastic leader benefits from following the course of multiple and convergent desires: God's desire for the monk, the monk's desire for God, and Symeon's desires regarding the formation of his monastic subjects.

INTERTEXTUAL TYPES

Before we contemplate the mysteries of the emperor's bedroom, it helps to consider some of the literary and typological allusions at work in the text. This paradigm of the repentant sinner both recalls and quotes the parable of the prodigal son. According to the Gospel of Luke, when the lost son returned home, "His father saw him and had compassion, and ran and fell upon his neck and kissed him." The father then charged his servants, "Bring quickly the best robe, and put it on him; and put a ring on his hand and sandals on his feet." Symeon thus links his own parable to this biblical illustration of repentance, confession, and forgiveness in which the Father, here a type for God, "falls upon" the sinner

and kisses him before dressing him in a stole and sandals.[12] As a reenactment of the parable of the prodigal son, this stage of Symeon's story
illustrates divine joy as akin to the joy of a parent's longing for his son.
Symeon's interest in the prodigal son also surfaces in Hymn Fifteen, part
of a corpus of some fifty-eight hymns composed in exile, probably after
1011, and thus possibly contemporaneous with the *Ethical Discourses*.
There, Symeon identifies himself as the prodigal son, the unworthy recipient of divine love. "While I weep and complain you surround me
completely with your light, / amazement! and upset, I weep more copi-
ously, / admiring your mercy toward me, the prodigal [*asōton*, compare
Lk. 15:13; also: "one with no hope of salvation]" (*Hymns* 15.15–17). In the
Tenth Ethical Discourse, Symeon calls his monks to understand themselves similarly as God's prodigal.

But as Symeon himself says in his parable, it is "not only this." Within
a few sentences, this image of parental love morphs into a depiction of
same-sex erotic longing and activity. How does Symeon proceed from
the model of a father embracing and dressing a son to a model of intimate bedfellows?[13] Symeon's quotation of the prodigal son arises in the
context of an emperor investing a subordinate in lavish garments. The
quick movement from a scene of investiture in the garments of redemption to the dressing and adorning of a bride or bridegroom for a wedding
recalls Isaiah 61:10. In the Septuagint, the text reads, "I will greatly rejoice
in the Lord, my soul shall exult in my God; for he has clothed me with
the garment of salvation, he has covered me with the robe of rejoicing,
as for a bridegroom he has placed around me a garland, and as a bride
he has adorned me with a jewel." Salvation here figures as a nuptial
celebration, an image echoed in the New Testament sayings of Jesus that
compare the kingdom of heaven to a marriage feast for a king's son, and
the frequent designations of Christ as bridegroom.[14] In Symeon's parable,
however, the rebel who is both prodigal son and lover is not Christ, but
a figure for the monk. Curiously, the penchant in Hebrew poetry for
repetition with variation renders the beloved in the Isaiah passage first a
bridegroom and then a bride, or perhaps simultaneously both. The resulting fluidity with respect to gender provides some biblical perspective
on Symeon's license to turn the monk into the bridegroom, rather than
the bride, of Christ.

In the course of the parable, the emperor covers the repentant rebel with two different garments. Through these garments, Symeon proffers two different models of salvation. The first, the coronation robe [*stolē*] that the emperor uses to elevate and adopt the former rebel, corresponds to the robes of light and the "robe of glory" that Symeon discusses elsewhere. In the Fourth Ethical Discourse, Symeon writes, "While it is one thing to be satisfied with cheap clothing and not to desire splendid robes, it is something else again to be clothed with God's own light." The passage continues by introducing themes both of lust and of sonship: "For many have despised the first [the splendid robes] while at the same time being dragged down by their thousand other lusts, but it is only those who have been arrayed in the second [the robes of God's light] who have been made worthy of becoming sons of the light and of the day."[15] In the Tenth Ethical Discourse the relationship between salvation and the donning of clothing pushes beyond conventional interpretations of baptism as illumination. Immediately after the parable of the emperor and the rebel, Symeon argues that it is not enough simply to have "put on" Christ in baptism: his monks' self-examination will reveal whether "they have received the power from Him to become children of God."[16]

The second garment in Symeon's narrative is a *chlanidion*, an outer garment or cloak that was also used as bedclothes. The term in this diminutive form has no direct biblical precedent, although in Matthew 27:28 Christ is dressed in a scarlet *chlamys*. The emperor covers the rebel with his *chlanidion*, keeping them warm and cozy together on the same bed and covering their physical contact. As in many premodern cultures, it was likely common for Byzantine men to share a bed without engaging in sexual activity. In the parable, however, the bed that the rebel and the emperor share becomes a marriage bed.[17] The covering of one person by another with a cloak has sexual overtones in some biblical contexts. Ezekiel 16:4–9 begins with a description of an abandoned child: "On the day you were born they did not swaddle your breasts [*sic* in LXX], nor were you washed with water." Such a child, ripe for adoption, becomes God's bride instead: "When I passed by you and saw you, behold, it was your time, the time for love [LXX: the time for unloosening]; I spread my cape [*pterygas*] over you, and covered your indecency; yea, I plighted my troth to you and entered into a covenant with you, says the Lord, and you became mine" (Ezek. 16:8–9).

In the book of Ruth, a text which Symeon does not cite anywhere in his corpus, the heroine lies down at Boaz's "feet" and instructs him, "spread your skirt [*pterygion*] over your maidservant" (Ruth 3:8).[18] "She lay at his feet until the morning, leaving early so that others would not know she had spent the night with Boaz on the threshing floor." Here the spreading of a garment is the precursor to presumed sexual activity. Ruth's narrative may also give the rebel's act of falling at the emperor's feet in Symeon's parable a sexual valence in retrospect. Both Ruth and the rebel approach their social superior's "feet" and are later covered with a cloth to engage in erotic activity. While these biblical loci may seem remote from our passage, they provide a frame for understanding theological connections between covering with garments and sexuality.[19] The activities on the bed, which Symeon himself interprets as an allegory of the "bridal chamber of heaven," enact the union of God and his chosen. In the end, the robe of glory and the bedspread convey the same salvation.

The covering of two lovers with a cloak may also contain an allusion to Plato's *Symposium*. Niketas Stethatos, Symeon's disciple and hagiographer, relates that the New Theologian's schooling stopped short of the curriculum in classical literature shared by highly educated men, and scholars have generally argued that Symeon's theology lacks evidence of direct knowledge of classical philosophy.[20] But one wonders whether the incident with the emperor and the rebel under the *chlanidion* is not also an ironic twist on Socrates and Alcibiades. In the *Symposium*, Alcibiades complains that Socrates refuses to engage in sex with him, even when, on a cold night: "I had thrown my cloak [*himation*] around him . . . and lay down under his philosopher's cloak [*tribona*]." Then Alcibiades embraced Socrates for the entire night.[21] In Plato, the covering with a cloak raises the expectation of delight, but the delight appears to be deferred or denied (unless constant embrace is itself the goal).[22] In Symeon's parable the delight under the cloak is perpetual.

THE PARTS OF THE MONASTIC BODY

Literary allusions, both biblical and possibly Platonic, do not suffice to explain the cloaked encounter between the emperor and the repentant rebel, and its implications for structuring Symeon's readers' relations with Christ as Christ's beloved. In the parable in question, this encounter is particularly intimate. Indeed, the intimacy imagined far exceeds acceptable levels of contact between the men under Symeon's own authority. Earlier, in a sermon delivered while he was a young abbot at Saint Mamas, Symeon strictly regulated contacts between monks, insisting that monks never enter another monk's cell without permission granted by the abbot or another officer of the monastery: "When you go there, endeavor neither to speak nor to hear a word apart from the necessity for which you were sent. When you have performed your errand, return quickly" (*Catechetical Discourses* 26.3). Even outside the cells, a monk was not to speak to a brother who was by himself. Intimacy between monks threatened a monk's solitude and focus on penitence.[23] The rule seems to assume that Symeon's monks, in contrast to monks at other Byzantine monasteries, did not share cells. For example, according to their mid-eleventh-century *typikon*, the monks of the monastery of the Theotokos Evergetis were to live two to a cell, usually a novice or younger monk paired with an older monk.[24] Intimate friendships between monks, even between a master and his disciple, could be a source of scandal. In his *Life of Symeon the New Theologian*, Niketas is at pains to portray Symeon's own close relationship to his eccentric mentor Symeon the Stoudite as above reproach.[25]

The parable of the emperor and the rebel suggests that Symeon had decided to employ the potent homoerotic environment of the monastery, rather than deny it. The parable uses allegory to construct the male monastic's body in its entirety as the object of God's desire. But what does it mean for the emperor of the Christians to place his face "upon all the members" of the penitent rebel? One problem is the use of the term *melos*, a word that in common parlance means "limb" as opposed to the torso or core of the body. But, as we shall see, Symeon's usage of the term elsewhere extends the meaning of *ta melē* (plural of *melos*) to other appendages of the body, suggesting that the translation "member" is more accurate. Under pressure from New Testament usage, Symeon's catalogue of the parts of the body in Hymn Fifteen and in the Fourth Ethical Discourse includes the "shameful members [*ta aschēmona melē*]." In these texts, Symeon argues strenuously that even these parts of the body are redeemed in Christ.[26]

Symeon's Hymn Fifteen, a text controversial in its own era, focuses on the monk's body as a locus of deification through the incarnation, and articulates themes also found in the Tenth Ethical Discourse.[27] Symeon called his hymns "The Love Songs [Hoi Erōtes]," and they often celebrate the mutual desire between the monk and God. An extended section of Hymn Fifteen reflects on the incarnation in light of Paul's discussion of the parts of Christian body in 1 Corinthians 12:14–26. Paul wrote:

> For the body does not consist of the one member [melos] but of many. If the foot should say, "Because I am not a hand, I do not belong to the body," that would not make it any less a part of the body. . . . The eye cannot say to the hand, "I have no need of you," nor again the head to the feet. . . . On the contrary, the parts [melē] of the body which seem weaker are indispensable, and those [parts] of the body which we think less honorable we invest with greater honor, and our shameful [parts] are treated with greater modesty, which our more seemly [parts] do not require. But God has so composed the body giving greater honor to the inferior [part], that there may be no discord in the body, but that the members [ta melē] may have the same care for one another. If one member suffers, all members [panta ta melē] suffer together; if one member is honored, all members [panta ta melē] rejoice together.[28]

In Paul's discussion, "all the members" (compare Symeon, Ethical Discourses 10.273) includes the shameful parts that are customarily covered out of modesty, that is, the genitals. It has been conventional in English translation since the King James (Authorized) Version to use the broader and euphemistic term "members" for ta melē in this passage.

Symeon uses this inventory of the parts of the body of Christ as a template for meditation on the deification of the monk's body afforded by the incarnation of Christ.

> We become members [melē] of Christ—and Christ [becomes] our members,
> Christ [becomes] my hand, and Christ, my miserable foot;
> and I, unhappy one, am Christ's hand, Christ's foot!

I move my hand, and my hand is the whole Christ
since, do not forget it, God is indivisible in his divinity.[29]

For Symeon, the incarnate presence of God within his own body serves
as an invitation for others to permit their bodies to become Christ's body:

If therefore you wish, you will become a member of him,
and similarly all our members individually
will become members of Christ, and Christ our members,
and all which is dishonorable in us
He will make honorable (*Hymns* 15.149–152).

Symeon's hymns were edited by Symeon's disciple Niketas. In defense of
Hymn Fifteen, Niketas offers a biblical basis for the work in 1 Corinthians
6:15–17: "Do you not know that your bodies are members of Christ [*ta
melē tou Christou*]?"[30] But the discourse of shame and honor loosely quotes
1 Corinthians 12.23, where Paul addresses the honor to come to the
shameful member.

Symeon stresses the radical shock of a promise of deification that extends to all the members of the body, including those that are regarded
as dishonorable. "Now, you thus acknowledged even my finger as
Christ / and [my] penis [*balanon*]—did you not shudder or blush?"
(*Hymns* 15.160–161). Modern English and French translations of this hymn
enter into an expurgation of the text by translating *balanos* as "organ."[31]
But *balanos*, literally an "acorn," was already used by Aristotle and Galen
to refer to the head of the penis. Symeon's text is not oblique. For Symeon, the shuddering or blushing of his imagined interlocutor has doctrinal consequences, since denying the presence of the entirety of God in
the penis tends toward a denial of the incarnation and thus heresy. Symeon says, "But God was not ashamed to become like you / and you, you
are ashamed to be like him?" (*Hymns* 15.162–163). Symeon then supplies
his interlocutor's words, "No, I am not ashamed to be like him, / but
when you said that he was similar to a shameful member [compare 1 Cor.
12:23] / I feared that you were uttering a blasphemy" (*Hymns* 15.164–166).
Echoing Paul, Symeon argues that there is nothing shameful in this, since
the genitals "are the hidden members of Christ for they are covered, /

and for this reason they are more honorable than the rest, / as hidden members invisible to all of the One who is hidden" (*Hymns* 15.168–170). The head of the penis, hidden from view, is thus paradoxically among the most appropriate signs of the hidden God.[32]

In creating a dialogue within the hymn between himself and a horrified interlocutor, Symeon asserts control of possible reactions to his theological investigation. Later, the interlocutor demands, "Do you not blush at these shameful [thoughts] / and above all to disparage Christ to shameful members?" (*Hymns* 15.193–194). By performing both voices in the dialectic, Symeon guides his audience through the ramifications of faith in the incarnation.

Symeon's interest in the divine and divinized penis extends beyond mere anatomy: He allegorizes its physiology as well. It is God,

from whom the seed [*sperma*] is given in divine union,
divine [seed] formed, awesomely [*phriktōs*], in the divine form
from the divinity itself entirely, for it is entirely God,
the one who unites himself with us, O awesome [*phriktou*] mystery!
(*Hymns* 15.171–74)

Symeon describes the emission of divine seed as *phriktos*, "causing to shudder," rendering his imagery shocking and abominable at the same time that it is frightening and awe-inspiring. This shuddering mystery is at once penetrative, ejaculatory, and nuptial, uniting the monk to Christ through the transmission of seed. "It is truly a marriage that takes place, ineffable and divine: / he unites Himself with each one—yes I repeat it, / it is my delight—and each becomes one with the Master" (*Hymns* 15.175–78). In short, the two become one flesh. Symeon also connects these themes of divine intercourse with images of covering with garments. He disparages his interlocutor for covering the soul with the "immaculate *chiton*" of Christ (*Hymns* 15.181–2), and yet remaining "ashamed of all the rest of your members" (*Hymns* 15.184). Symeon insists that far from being shameful, these parts of the body are "holy members."[33]

Symeon's theological interest in the monk's penis features in the *Ethical Discourses* as well. In a related passage in the Fourth Ethical Discourse, Symeon allegorizes a catalogue of the parts of the body into a body of virtues. As Golitzin has written, Symeon "likens the different limbs and organs of the human body to the virtues of the perfected Christian."³⁴ Symeon says, "Legs and ankles and calves and knees and thighs are non-possession, nakedness, voluntary exile, willing submission for the sake of Christ, obedience, and eager service."³⁵ Symeon includes the monks' genitals in his discussion, again recalling the language of 1 Corinthians 12: "The members and parts [melē kai moria] which one is obliged to hide are unceasing prayer of the mind, the sweetness which derives from the shedding of tears, the joy of the heart and its inexpressible consolation."³⁶ Far from being irredeemable, this section of human anatomy represents some of a monk's highest virtues and rewards. After addressing the rest of the body (except for the head, which comes next in his discussion) he declares the body, "complete in all its members."³⁷ The perfection of the body lies in its identity with the indivisible Christ. In Hymn Fifteen, Symeon declares that each will be "completely like Christ in our whole body, / and our every member will be the whole Christ" (Hymns 15.156–57).

It is difficult to know how Symeon's concern with the body "complete in all its members" squares with the suggestion of some scholars that the New Theologian might himself have been a eunuch, having had his testicles removed in childhood for service in the imperial household.³⁸ The evidence for castration is far from certain. Niketas states that Symeon was a spatharokoubikoularios, "a sword carrier of the bedchamber" (Life 3.9–10). While some have argued that this office was reserved for eunuchs, evidence also suggests that some spatharokoubikoularioi were bearded. Later in the text, Niketas reports that after Symeon's death, a certain Philotheos had seen Symeon in a vision, a "white-haired, handsome, and venerable eunuch" (Life 147.6–7) presumably identifiable, in part, because he was beardless. This vision may or may not reflect Symeon's appearance in life, and certainly coheres with Niketas's project to defend Symeon against detractors who found imagery in Symeon's works, including some under discussion here, troubling. The vision seals Symeon's success in transcending sexual desire. It is important to remember that in most cases, castration did not prevent erection, and certainly did not prevent the capacity for sexual desire.³⁹ In any case, nothing in Symeon's own writings confirms this hypothesis. And his interest in the intact body of the monk may provide important counterevidence. More to the point, in Hymns Fifteen and Sixteen and the Fourth Ethical Discourse, Symeon's image of the glorious body of the monk is persistently sexed. Far from calling on monks to become "eunuchs for the sake of the Kingdom," Symeon challenges monks to regard their own body in a way that conforms to God's desire for them in all their members.

THE PRACTICES OF DESIRE

Next to the elaborate imagery of the male body in Hymn Fifteen, the parable of the Tenth Ethical Discourse may seem quite tame. Symeon's interpretation of the parable as the consummation of a marriage raises questions about the practices of desire, both the sexual behavior and the acts of fantasy that Byzantines might have engaged in. In Hymn Fifteen, Symeon illustrates the union of the human and the divine by stressing the presence of God in the monk's body, including his penis. In the Tenth Ethical Discourse, God lies not within the monk's body, but rather next to it, desiring it and embracing it. From the perspective of the monk, God is not self, but rather a loving other. Another scenario of erotic encounter between the human body and the divine occurs in Hymn Sixteen, where Symeon depicts God as both within him and lovingly intertwined with him:

> He himself is discovered within myself
> resplendent in the interior of my miserable heart,
> illuminating me on all sides with His immortal splendor,
> lighting up *all my members* with brightness,
> entirely intertwined with me, He embraces me totally.
> He gives himself to me, the unworthy one,
> And I am filled with His love and His beauty,
> and I am sated with divine delight and sweetness.
> I share in the light, I participate in the glory,
> and my face shines like my Beloved's,
> and *all my members* become bearers of light.
> (*Hymns* 16.23–23; emphasis added)

Here, sexual embrace of the entirety of the body serves as a potent allegory for divine revelation and deification. The interpenetration of the human and the divine is accomplished from both the inside and the outside, through God's inhabiting of the monastic body and God's erotic possession of it.[40] All the members of the body glow with divine light. And as Hymn Fifteen suggests, for Symeon this glorious body persists explicitly as male, even as its soul is figured as female. Indeed, in Hymn Fifteen, Symeon admits some fluidity in the gender of Christ's beloved monk, when, despite his male body and its deified penis, the subject's soul becomes Christ's bride:

> For he becomes a bridegroom [*nymphios*]—do you hear?—each day,
> and the souls of all with whom the Creator unites himself
> become brides [*nymphai*], and they, in turn, with Him, and it is a spiritual
> marriage, a divinely befitting intercourse [*theoprepōs symmignymenos*]
> with them! (*Hymns* 15.220–225)

Thus Symeon's construction of the gendered beloved admits complexity, playing with gender binaries by oscillating between them. If Symeon had wanted to feminize the entirety of the male monastic subject in order to figure God's desire as heteronormative he could have done this; but his commitment to the deification of the male monk's body in its entirety leads him to ascribe both cross-sex and same-sex desire to God.[41]

When, in the Tenth Ethical Discourse, the emperor of the Christians "places his own face upon all the members" of the penitent's body, Symeon illustrates God's desire for the monastic body. This act figuratively consummates the union of monk and God. For the figuration to work, the audience must be able to enter imaginatively into the scenario. Symeon's allegory depends on a shared understanding of male same-sex sexual activities and their pleasures, even while such pleasures were illicit in the monastery. But what does it mean when a lover "is placing his face" on all his beloved's members? Our knowledge of middle Byzantine sexual vocabulary is limited, in part by the nature of our sources and in part by the questions that we have posed to them. Even more serious are the gaps in our knowledge of middle Byzantine sexuality and sexual practices. The conventions of same-sex erotic practices are particularly obscure.[42] If an understanding of the history of sexuality in Byzantium is to advance, it will, in fact, have to take account of passages like this; but expecting this passage to be either typical or normative engages in a circular logic.

Taken literally, and at a minimum, the passage describes a sort of nuzzling, a loving pressing of the face upon another's body. Elsewhere in the discourse, God's face in itself becomes an object of desire: "I saw joy and happiness overflowing in me at the revelation and appearance of his face" (*Ethical Discourses* 10.287–289). But from the perspective of the twenty-first century, perpetual nuzzling, even upon all the parts of the body including the genitals, seems insufficient to illustrate the consummation of divine desire. Is "pressing the face" a euphemism? There is evidence in the passage to suggest that Symeon means something more, such that "placing one's face" "on the members" of another involves kissing the parts of the body, including the genitals.

The scene on the emperor's bed is preceded by two previous descriptions of physical intimacy. First, in the initial scene of the rebels' supplications, the emperor falls upon the rebel's neck and "kisse[s] him all over" including on his eyes. Then, the activities that follow are expressed not with aorist participles, but with present active and mediopassive participles: Symeon is describing repeated and habitual activity. The passage states that "night and day," the emperor was "embracing and kissing" him, "mouth to mouth [*stoma pros stoma auton*]." Thus, oral contact with the rebel's body is already and habitually under way before the emperor begins taking the former rebel to his bed. The constant, "night and day," mouth-to-mouth kissing figures as middle Byzantine foreplay, the lead-in to the bedtime activities that express the emperor's superordinate love. This does not, in fact, clarify whether the subsequent and repeated contact in the sleeping chamber, the "laying down and embracing," involves kissing. But since the bedroom routine described continues the act of embracing and includes face to body contact, the text seems to extend the kissing onto the bed, rather than suggesting that once in the bedroom, the kissing stops, and is replaced by nuzzling alone.

Now sometimes a kiss is just a kiss, and in the medieval Eastern Mediterranean, men's kissing and embracing might indicate intense emotion and friendship. In his *Life of Symeon*, Niketas describes his master as having transmitted mystical knowledge to him "mouth to mouth [*stoma pros stoma*]," a metaphor for discipleship.[43] However, the emperor and his rebel are engaging in activity that Symeon cues his audience to regard as sexual, activity appropriate to "the bridal chamber of heaven." While it remains unclear whether the face-to-body contact under the cloak involves oral-genital contact, let alone oral incorporation, I would argue that the lack of clarity is part of the point. What is the emperor doing under the cloak? And with which part of his face? And to what part of the rebel's body? Does the rebel achieve orgasm, or is he in a constant state of arousal? What should a Byzantine monk imagine two men would do on their wedding night? In Hymn Sixteen, the speaker is penetrated and inseminated by God. On the other hand, the loving face-pressing of the parable, by itself, might disrupt reasonable expectations of nuptial delights. What happens in the emperor's bedroom is cloaked in mystery. Symeon invites rather than denies further fantasy.

The parable does not limit the reader's interest to the rebel's experience alone. It also figures Christ's love for the sinner as homoerotic longing. "Seized by unexpected joy," Christ does not merely welcome his prodigal, but embraces him and kisses him, refusing to be separated from him, lying down with him on his bed under his own cloak. Christ's passion, if you will, is fulfilled in the bedroom, in his desiring embrace. Moreover, Christ's perpetual nuptial activity involves (at the very least) placing his face on his beloved's members. The King of Heaven expresses his desire for the entirety of the monastic body by showing honor to all of it, perhaps giving greatest honor to the most hidden parts. The valance of such an act in Byzantium is not entirely clear. In general, ancient constructions of sexuality still obtained. Sexual activity continued to be conceived as something that a social superior did to a social inferior, for the superior's gratification.[44] In this instance, in concerning himself with the repentant sinner's gratification, Christ takes on the form of a subject. As in Christ's descent from heaven in the incarnation, his adoration of the monk's body performs humility.[45]

PERFORMANCE ANXIETIES

How then should we understand Symeon's engagement with inflaming and potentially inflammatory speech? That Symeon might engage in a rhetorical performance of homoeroticism should not be entirely surprising, especially in light of his flamboyant confession in Hymn Twenty-Four that in addition to having been a murderer, he had been "an adulterer in [his] heart / and a sodomite [*sodomitēs*] in deed and desire" (74–75). In the same text, of course, he confesses to having been a lecher, magician, and baby-killer, among other things (*Hymns* 24.71–79). And while the historicity of these claims is problematic, the rhetoric of Symeon's public confession of such deeds and desires effects the construction of a performed persona, a textual Symeon.[46] His performance of sodomitical desire for God in Hymn Sixteen and his efforts to engage similar desires in the Tenth Ethical Discourse reflect Symeon's willingness to form the monastic subject by cultivating the power of fantasy.

However, Symeon places boundaries on his metaphors even as he presents them as normative. Later in the Tenth Ethical Discourse, Symeon admonishes his monks not to "serve the flesh by making provisions for its desires [*epithymia*]" (*Ethical Discourses* 10.582). In Hymn Forty-Six, he qualifies an erotic metaphor even as he offers it:

Dispassion [*apatheia*] in the form of lightning united itself with me
and ever more remains—understand this spiritually,
you who read, lest you be wretchedly defiled!—
and produces in me the ineffable sweetness of consummation
and an infinite longing for marriage, for union with God.
(*Hymns* 46.29–33; *On the Mystical Life*, 3.92)

Symeon can barely contain himself; While he is saving himself for God, Dispassion has already become his lover. In Hymn Fifteen, Symeon's mentor, Symeon the Stoudite, figures as the ideal monk precisely in his indifference to the naked body, both his own and those of others.[47]

So there was, even now in these latter days,
Symeon the saint, the pious one, the Stoudite.
He did not blush before the members [*melē*] of any person,
neither to see others naked, nor to be seen naked,
for he possessed Christ completely, and he was completely Christ,
and all his own members and everybody else's members,

all and each he saw always as Christ;
he remained motionless, unharmed, and impassive;
he was all Christ himself and as Christ he regarded
all the baptized, clothed with the whole of Christ. (*Hymns* 15.205–14)

One wonders where in the monastery it was possible to gaze upon another monk naked or to show oneself naked to others.[48] The Evergetis *typikon* (28) prohibited bathing for all but the sick. Faced with the naked members of others, Symeon the Stoudite saw only the body of Christ, a covering for all humanity. Pointedly, he remained "motionless" and "impassive," unerect. Ironically, the perpetually flaccid penis becomes the object and the goal of monastic desire. Symeon heightens the contrast for his easily shocked interlocutor, as he sneers, "While you, if you are naked and your flesh touches flesh, / there you are in rut like a donkey or a horse" (*Hymns* 15.215–16).[49] While homoerotic desire may serve as a model for divine love and love of the divine, nevertheless physical desire in itself threatens to deflect the monk from the passionless desire for God. Eros remains ambiguously both aroused and disciplined.

CONCLUSION

On some very basic level, of course, the reader or hearer of the Tenth Ethical Discourse is not supposed to take the parable of the emperor and the rebel literally—it is, after all, a parable. But as a parable, it is a soteriological fantasy dependent on a series of plausible referents: an emperor and a rebel; rites of investiture; biblical passages regarding clothing, salvation, and weddings; and the desire of men for physical intimacy with other men. Indeed one might argue that homoeroticism is the parable's most important referent, since Symeon calls on his audience to identify with such desire in order to understand salvation. The text both models homoerotic desire and arouses it in its audience; then the text redeploys this desire by integrating it into the desire for Christ. Understanding the consummation with the divine in the age to come turns on a vivid same-sex erotic scenario, one that stresses that salvation is corporeal and complete, that God's love encompasses the entirety of the human body in all its members. Symeon places this emphasis on the body even as he deploys textual performance to distance himself and his audience from actual physical contact. Indeed, the homoeroticism may hold even more theological power because it is discursive and textual, because it is already mimesis and fantasy. A virtual or discursively performative sexuality becomes only more powerful in its subsequent contemplation. Removed from the surface of the body it forms thoughts in the mind.

The place of eros in the ascetic life remains a subject of contemplation. In an essay on "The Body's Grace," Rowan Williams has observed:

> To be formed in our humanity by the loving delight of another is an experience whose contours we can identify most clearly and hopefully if we have also learned, or are learning, about the object of the causeless, loving delight of God, being the object of God's love for God through incorporation into the community of God's Spirit and the taking-on of the identity of God's child. . . . All those taking up the single vocation must know something about desiring and being desired if their single vocation is not to be sterile and evasive.[50]

Symeon's performance incites desire for the desired and desiring Christ, forming in his audience an overwhelming and embodied longing both for Christ and for themselves as Christ's beloved. He locates God's love in the gendered body of the male monk. The performative character of this desire within the text allows Symeon to leave a peculiar tension unresolved: Homoerotic desire has a place in the monastery. It is a powerful tool in the making of his monks.

✢ Sexual Desire, Divine Desire; Or, Queering the Beguines

AMY HOLLYWOOD

You can reduce religion to sex only if you don't especially believe in either one.—MICHAEL WARNER, "Tongues Untied"

In the face of what the social historian Judith Bennett refers to as "the virtual absence of actual women from the sources of medieval lesbianisms," a number of literary and cultural scholars have recently turned to texts by or about women to uncover homoerotic possibilities within the metaphoric structures of women's own writings or in the practices ascribed to women or female characters within male- and female-authored literary and religious documents.[1] Karma Lochrie, for example, looks to a number of medieval devotional texts and images in which Christ's bloody side wound becomes a locus of desire.[2] According to Lochrie, not only is Christ's body feminized through its association with women's (and particularly the Virgin Mary's) nurturing breasts, as Caroline Walker Bynum famously argues, but religious representations also "genitalize" Christ's wound, associating it both imagistically and linguistically with the vulva.[3] When women mystics write about eagerly kissing the sacred wound, then, their relationship with Christ is queered, for the body they desire and with which they identify is both male and female.[4] For Lochrie, "neither the acts / identity distinction nor the focus on same-sex desire is adequate or desirable as a framework for queering medieval mysticism."[5] Rather, Lochrie argues, the complex interplay of gender and sexuality in medieval texts and images effectively queers simple identifications of sex, gender, and/or sexuality.

Bennett describes the work of Lochrie and other cultural and literary critics with care and enthusiasm, yet worries that while "as literary criticism, these readings reach plausible conclusions . . . as guides to social history, they are considerably less convincing."[6] "It's great fun, for example, to read Lochrie's impressive exploration of the artistic, literary, and linguistic ties between Christ's wound and female genitalia, and to speculate, therefore, that the kissing of images of Christ's wound by medieval nuns somehow parallels lesbian oral sex. Yet Lochrie very wisely does not claim that any medieval nun who contemplated Christ's wound ever, in fact, was thinking about last night's tumble in bed with a sister nun."[7]

Bennett's worries about "actual people" and "plausible behaviors" lead her to argue that queer readings like Lochrie's are "intriguing-but-not-fully-historicized." Bennett's argument depends, however, on assuming that the history of lesbianisms is or should be centrally concerned with same-sex acts or identities derived from the pursuit of such acts, precisely the categories of analysis questioned by Lochrie (and, Lochrie would argue, by at least some medieval texts and images).

Bennett herself introduces the notion of "lesbian-like" in order to broaden lesbian history beyond its focus on "certifiable same-sex genital contact." Where she differs from Lochrie is in her focus on "broadly sociological" affinities between contemporary lesbians and women in the past—"affinities related to social conduct, marital status, living arrangements, and other behaviors that might be traced in the archives of past societies."[8] The pursuit of these affinities is certainly important historical work, both for women's history and for what Bennett calls the history of lesbianisms. Yet Bennett's argument is problematic if she means to suggest that these sociological categories give access to "real women" in a way that attention to the religious imagery and desires found in texts written or used by medieval women do not. Some medieval religious women did use intensely erotic language and imagery to talk about their relationship to the divine. No matter how implausible it might seem to us to understand Christ's side wound as a bloody slit that feminizes and eroticizes his corporeality, this is in fact what some medieval women (and men) did.[9]

Lochrie and Bennett are surely right to resist an easy movement from the relationship between the woman believer and Christ to sexual relationships between women (or between men and women).[10] Yet why shouldn't the complex interplay between sex, gender, and sexuality in representations of relationships to the divine have as much significance for contemporary lesbian and/or queer history as the marital status of late medieval women—especially when the fluidity and excess that characterize discussions of divine desire may work to undermine the seemingly unquestioned supremacy of heteronormativity within medieval Christian culture (a heteronormativity itself also often seen within devotional language and imagery)?[11] Sociological questions might seem more "real" to us in the early twenty-first century, but for many Christians in the later Middle Ages, one's relationship to Christ and the language and images through which one attempted to achieve and convey something of that relationship had equal, if not greater, reality. So while Bennett and Lochrie no doubt pursue different kinds of historical questions, I think it is important that we recognize both as historically valid and as of significance to contemporary questions about sexuality and gender.

At stake here is not just the question of what constitutes reality, but also how we are to understand the relationship between the often highly erotic and sexual imagery used by late medieval religious writers to describe the soul's relationship to Christ and human sexuality. Bynum's magisterial work on late-medieval religiosity has set the tone here, for she argues against what she sees as a modern tendency to equate the bodily too quickly with the sexual. In an attempt to refute the widespread reduction of late medieval religiosity, particularly that of women, to sex, Bynum is in danger of denying even the metaphorically sexualized nature of many women's and men's religious writings. Her explicit aim, both in *Holy Feast and Holy Fast* and the essays collected in *Fragmentation and Redemption*, is to expand the meanings that we ascribe to corporeality in late medieval texts and practices. Yet as Lochrie and Richard Rambuss convincingly show, Bynum "herself can be quick to delimit the erotic—and especially the homoerotic—potentialities of her own devotional polysemy of the medieval body."[12] When Catherine of Siena writes of "putting on the nuptial garment," Bynum explains, "the phrase means suffering" and so is "extremely unerotic." She goes on to argue that in

Catherine's "repeated descriptions of climbing Christ's body from foot to side to mouth, the body is either a female body that nurses or a piece of flesh that one puts on oneself or sinks into. . . . Catherine understood union with Christ not as an erotic fusing with a male figure but as a taking in and taking on—a becoming—of Christ's flesh itself."[13]

Bynum makes many contentious (and, not surprisingly, vehemently anti-Freudian) assumptions about sexuality and erotic desire—most crucially, that erotic desire can be clearly distinguished from suffering, the maternal, and identification—yet as Rambuss suggests, perhaps the most salient point of Bynum's interpretation is her refusal to see same-sex desire as potentially sexual. If Christ's body is feminized (and so becomes a point of identification for women), Bynum assumes it cannot also be the locus of female sexual desire (or even of a desire for the divine *analogous* to sexual desire). Her insistence on the feminization of Christ serves two functions, then, both providing a locus for female identification with the divine and protecting the divine-human relationship from even metaphorical sexualization.

What I want to show here is that some late medieval women did use explicitly erotic language to discuss their relationship with Christ and they did so, often, in ways that challenged the prescriptive heterosexuality of the culture in which they lived. The challenge occurs not only through the feminization of Christ's body discussed by Lochrie, but also through an intense, hyperbolic, and often ultimately self-subverting deployment of apparently heterosexual imagery. This excess often involves a displacement of Christ as the center of the religious life and emphasis on a feminized figure of divine love. Among the beguines, semi-religious women who flourished in thirteenth-century northern Europe and are best known for their so-called bridal mysticism (and hence, it would seem, for a resolutely heterosexual, non-queer sexual imaginary) we find accounts of insane love and endless desire in which gender becomes so radically fluid that it is not clear *what* kind of sexuality—within the heterosexual/homosexual dichotomy most readily available to modern readers—is being metaphorically deployed to evoke the relationship between humans and the divine.[14] Rather, as Rambuss argues with regard to early modern male-authored religious poetry, the absence in these texts "of a polarizing system of sexual types tends to open these works in the direction of a greater plasticity of erotic possibilities, possibilities not entirely containable by our own (often only suppositiously coherent) sexual dichotomies."[15] The very inability to contain medieval divine eroticism within modern categories points to its potential queerness.[16]

Religious desire and sexual desire are not the same, as Bennett usefully reminds us. Yet, in the evocative words of Michael Warner, "religion makes available a language of ecstasy, a horizon of significance within which transgressions against the normal order of the world and the boundaries of the self *can be seen as good things*."[17] Moreover, religious writers often use the language of eroticism to express that ecstasy, excess, and transgression. Perhaps this is because erotic language is able, in ways that devotional language both exploits and intensifies, to engender affective states that push the believer beyond the limitations of his or her own body and desires.[18] At the same time, the intensity of divine desire forces sexual language into new, unheard-of configurations. Hence the emergence in the later Middle Ages of what Lochrie aptly calls the "mystical queer." These religious representations do not reflect, nor even legitimate, particular configurations of human sexual relations—they often indeed seem to involve a movement beyond sexed and gendered bodies, even that of Christ, as the locus of pleasure and desire—but they do denaturalize and destabilize normative conceptions of human sexuality in potentially radical ways.

The centrality of the Song of Songs to medieval Christian devotional literature, images, and practices sets the stage for an intensely erotic and, at least on the surface, heterosexualized understanding of the relationship between the soul and God. Origen (ca. 185–254), the first Christian commentator on the Song of Songs whose work survives, reads the series of erotic poems as an allegory both for the relationship between Christ and the church and for that between Christ and the individual believer.[19] The latter reading provides a central source for twelfth-century mystical exegetes like Bernard of Clairvaux (1090–1153), William of St. Thierry (ca. 1080–1148), and Rupert of Deutz (1077–1120), who increasingly emphasize the intensely erotic nature of the relationship between the lover and the beloved, the bridegroom and the bride, or Christ and the soul.[20] When undertaken by male authors, these allegorical readings often involve a kind of linguistic transvestitism, whereby the male devotee becomes the female soul joined in loving union with the male figure of Christ.[21] When undertaken by women, on the other hand, apparently normalized sexual roles often prevail.

So, for example, in Mechthild of Magdeburg's (ca. 1260–1282/94) *Flowing Light of the Godhead*, an understanding of the soul as the bride of Christ is joined with traditions derived from courtly literature.[22] In Book I, Mechthild describes the soul as a lady, who dresses herself in the virtues so as to be prepared to welcome the prince. After much waiting, in which the soul watches other holy people dance, "the young man comes and says to her: 'Young lady, my chosen ones have shown off their dancing to you. Just as artfully should you now follow their lead.'" The soul replies:

> I cannot dance, Lord, unless you lead me.
> If you want me to leap with abandon,
> You must intone the song.
> Then I shall leap into love,
> From love into knowledge,
> From knowledge into enjoyment,
> And from enjoyment beyond all human sensations.
> There I want to remain, yet want also to circle higher still.

Their dance is recorded in song: The young man sings, "Through me into you/And through you from me" while the soul responds, like the alternately joyful and despondent bride of the Song of Songs, "Willingly with you/Woefully from you."[23]

Mechthild makes explicit her preference for erotic over maternal metaphors in her conception of the relationship between the soul and Christ. Weary of the dance, the soul says to the senses that they should leave her so that she might refresh herself. The senses, wanting to stay with the soul, offer a series of refreshments in which they too might take part: "the blood of martyrs," "the counsel of confessors," the bliss of the angels, and finally, the milk of the Virgin enjoyed by the Christ Child. To this, the soul replies, "That is child's love, that one suckle and rock a baby. I am a full-grown bride. I want to go to my Lover." Although there the senses will "go completely blind," the soul asserts that her true identity is found in the nature of God:

A fish in water does not drown.
A bird in the air does not plummet.
Gold in fire does not perish.
Rather, it gets its purity and its radiant color there.
God has created all creatures to live according to their nature.
How, then, am I to resist my nature?
I must go from all things to God,
Who is my Father by nature,
My Brother by his humanity,
My Bridegroom by love,
And I his bride from all eternity.[24]

Just as Mechthild will insist that she is God's child by both grace and by nature (see 6.31), so here she claims to be daughter, sister, and bride of Christ, multiplying metaphors (all derived from the Song of Songs) without undermining the eroticism of the dance of love in which the dialogue appears.

Moreover, identification does not preclude, but rather seems to follow from the intensity of desire. After asserting the commonality of her nature with that of the divine,

the bride of all delights goes to the Fairest of lovers in the secret chamber of the invisible Godhead. There she finds the bed and the abode of love prepared by God in a manner beyond what is human. Our Lord speaks:

"Stay, Lady Soul."
"What do you bid me, Lord?"
"Take off your clothes."
"Lord, what will happen to me then?"
"Lady Soul, you are so utterly ennatured in me
That not the slightest thing can be between you and me. . . ."
Then a blessed stillness

That both desire comes over them.
He surrenders himself to her,
And she surrenders herself to him.
What happens to her then—she knows—
And that is fine with me.
But this cannot last long.
When two lovers meet secretly,
They must often part from one another inseparably.[25]

As long as the soul remains within the body, the lovers can only meet fleetingly. The intensity of her desire and fusion with the divine both demands the use of erotic language and subverts it, for the body cannot sustain the experience of the divine embrace. (Although, as I will show below, Mechthild insists that the body will ultimately be reunited with the soul and share in its final glory.) The suffering to which God's presence and absence gives rise is then itself taken up as crucial to the path of desire for and identification with Christ.[26]

The interplay of suffering and desire is also crucial to the poetry and prose of Hadewijch (fl. 1250) in ways that ultimately disrupt the heteronormativity of the relationship between the soul and the divine prevalent in Mechthild's work.[27] In a poem on the seven names of love, Hadewijch makes the spectacular claim that love, Hadewijch's favored name for the divine, is hell:

Hell is the seventh name
Of this Love wherein I suffer.
For there is nothing Love does not engulf and damn,
And no one who falls into her
And whom she seizes comes out again,
Because no grace exists there.
As Hell turns everything to ruin,
In Love nothing else is acquired
But disquiet and torture without pity;
Forever to be in unrest,
Forever assault and new persecution;
To be wholly devoured and engulfed

In her unfathomable essence,
To founder unceasingly in heat and cold,
In the deep, insurmountable darkness of Love.[28]

For Hadewijch, the constant "comings and goings" of Love are a source of continual suffering, for the soul is caught between the ecstasy of the divine presence, Love's unrelenting demands for fidelity, and the constant threat of God's absence. Suffering does not preclude erotic desire, but is central to it. As Lochrie argues, "aggression, violence, masochism, and dark despair are as fundamental to the visions of some women mystics as the tropes of marriage and . . . languorous desire." For Lochrie, this kind of excessive, violent desire is "queer in its effects—exceeding and hyperbolizing its own conventionality and fracturing the discourses of mystical love and sex."[29]

Hadewijch, like Mechthild, argues that this suffering love itself becomes a part of the soul's identification with Christ. As she writes in a letter to fellow beguines, "we all indeed wish to be God with God, but God knows there are few of us who want to live as human beings with his Humanity, or want to carry his cross with him, or want to hang on the cross with him and pay humanity's debt to the full."[30] Yet this demand that the soul identify with Christ in his suffering humanity does not preclude a desire for the divine best expressed through the language of eroticism. Again like Mechthild, Hadewijch, particularly in her visions, makes use of imagery derived from the Song of Songs as the basis for her understanding of the union between the soul and Christ. One day while at Matins, she writes, "My heart and my veins and all my limbs trembled and quivered with eager desire and, as often occurred with me, such madness and fear beset my mind that it seemed to me I did not content my Beloved, and that my Beloved did not fulfill my desire, so that dying I must go mad, and going mad I must die."[31] This leads Hadewijch to desire that her humanity "should to the fullest extent be one in fruition" with that of Christ, so that she might then "grow up in order to be God with God."[32]

The vision that follows is the fulfillment of that desire. Looking at the altar, she first sees Christ in the form of a child of three years, holding the eucharistic bread in his right hand and the chalice in his left. The child then becomes a man and administers the sacrament to Hadewijch.

> After that he came himself to me, took me entirely in his arms, and pressed me to him; and all my members felt his in full felicity, in accordance with the desire of my heart and my humanity. So that I was outwardly satisfied and transported. Also then, for a short while, I had the strength to bear this; but soon, after a short time, I lost that manly beauty outwardly in the sight of his form. I saw him completely come to naught and so fade and all at once dissolve that I could no longer recognize or perceive him outside me, and I could no longer distinguish him within me. Then it was to me as if we were one without difference. . . . After that I remained in a passing away in my Beloved, so that I wholly melted away in him and nothing any longer remained to me of myself.[33]

Full union with Christ, expressed here through intensely erotic language, leads to a fusion and identification with profound theological implications. Although heterosexual in its imagistic operation, moreover, the melting away of the soul into the divine radically undermines any stable distinction between male and female and, more importantly for Hadewijch, between human and divine. The incarnation, in which God becomes human, is the basis for humanity's full identification with the divine.

Yet Hadewijch's work also undermines the association of masculinity with the divine and of femininity with the human, particularly in her stanzaic poems, in which the divine is represented as Love (*minne*, which is feminine), the unattainable female object of desire, and the soul as a knight errant in quest of his Lady.[34] Love cannot be clearly identified with Christ, the Holy Spirit, God the Father, or the Trinity; Hadewijch continually shifts and overlaps various divine referents. These poems again stress the cruelty of Love and the anguish to which her demand for desirous fidelity reduces the knight.

> Sometimes kind, sometimes hateful,
> Sometimes far, sometimes to hand.

To him who endures this with loyalty of love
That is jubilation;
How love kills
And embraces
In a single action.[35]

Those who are "Knight-errants in Love" live in an endless oscillation between darkness and light, the divine presence and her absence.[36] The knightly soul is suspended between activity, "laying siege" to Love in desire and fidelity ("the brave," one poem advises, "should strike before Love does")[37] and recognition that his "best success" lies in the suffering he undergoes when "shot by Love's arrow."[38] Even as Hadewijch stresses the gap between the (feminine) divine and the (masculine) soul, then, she both undermines rigid gender distinctions and lays the groundwork for the eventual union of the soul and the divine through the soul's "mad love" and suffering desire—a union that occurs through Christ but is often poetically imagined without reference to his human body.[39]

In the dialogues that make up Marguerite Porete's (d. 1310) *The Mirror of Simple Souls*, Porete similarly employs the feminine figure of Love as the most prominent representation of the divine. She goes even further than Hadewijch, moreover, in suggesting that while Christ and Christ's body play a crucial role in the path of the soul to union with love, ultimately the role of the body and of Christ will be surpassed. Instead, the female soul engages in a loving dialogue both with Lady Love and with the feminine Trinity, giving the text an intensely homoerotic valence absent in Mechthild's heterosexual account of the love between the soul and Christ and Hadewijch's transvestitism, in which the female soul becomes male in order to pursue Lady Love. Porete's Love and Soul provide a representation of those souls who have become so free of all created things, including will and desire, that they are indistinguishable from the divine.

I have argued elsewhere that Porete's pursuit of annihilation is a result of her desire to escape the intense suffering engendered by endless desire and "mad love." Absolute union with the divine occurs through the sacrifice of desire by desire. Yet the resulting loss of distinction between

the soul and the divine also radically subverts, even erases, gender distinctions, a move both dependent on and subversive of the text's homoeroticism. (Porete uses the femininity of the Soul and Love to elicit
pronominal ambiguities in which the gap between them is erased.)[40] Porete's work, with its distrust of spiritual delights, ecstasies, and visions,
stands in a critical relationship to that of her beguine predecessors. This
is evident in her relationship to the imagery of erotic love. For Porete,
like Hadewijch, Love is the primary name of the divine and she at times
makes use of language and imagery derived from the Song of Songs, yet
always in ways that undermine the initial gendered dichotomy between
lover and beloved. This subversion seems dependent, as it is in Hadewijch, on a displacement of Christ's body.

The process can be seen most starkly in a crucial scene toward the end
of the *Mirror* in which a now masculine God challenges the soul concerning the strength of her fidelity. Nicholas Watson argues that the series of
hypothetical scenes recounted by the soul "are eccentric versions of the
love-tests found in the tale of patient Griselda." Just as Griselda is honored for patiently submitting to the various tests of her fidelity posed by
her distrustful husband, so the soul imagines a series of tests posed by
God. She asks herself:

> as if He Himself were asking me, how I would fare if I knew that
> he could be better pleased that I should love another better than
> Him. At this my sense failed me, and I knew not how to answer,
> nor what to will, nor what to deny; but I responded that I would
> ponder it.
>
> And then He asked me how I would fare if it could be that He
> could love another better than me. And at this my sense failed me,
> and I know not what to answer, or will, or deny.
>
> Yet again, He asked me what I would do and how I would fare if
> it could be that He would will that someone other love me better
> than He. And again my sense failed, and I knew not what to re-
> spond, no more than before, but still I said that I would ponder it.[41]

Using the imaginative meditative practices recommended within contemporary devotional treatises as a means of participating in and identifying with Christ's passion, Porete here enacts a Trial of Love reminiscent
of those within secular courtly literature.

The trial leads to the death of the will and of desire (that same desire more often elicited and exploited through such meditative practices). In acquiescing to demands that go against her desire to love and be loved by God alone, the soul "martyrs" both her will and her love, thereby annihilating all creatureliness and, paradoxically, attaining a union without distinction with the divine. In Watson's evocative words, Porete "out-griselded Griselda," taking the test of submission to such extremes that subservience becomes the means by which the soul forces God to merge with her.[42] Porete takes the cultural stereotype of the patient bride, who will submit to anything in fidelity to her bridegroom, and converts it into an account of how the Soul's fall into nothingness is itself the apprehension of her full share in the divine being.[43] Like Mechthild, who insists that the soul is God's child by nature, thereby challenging late medieval versions of the doctrine of grace, Porete stresses throughout the *Mirror* the ways in which the soul, by emphasizing and embracing her sinfulness, abjection, and humility, can become one with God.[44] Most crucially, as Watson argues, Porete shows the soul achieving "mystical annihilation of her own volition, *by telling herself stories.*"[45] This particular story both depends on and subverts the hierarchically ordered gender expectations of late medieval culture.

Porete's use of erotic and gendered language is, like that of her fellow beguines Mechthild and, particularly, Hadewijch, remarkably complex.[46] As the example offered here suggests, however, unlike Mechthild and Hadewijch—or perhaps better, more starkly than they—Porete posits the goal of the soul as the eradication of any distinction between herself and the divine. Porete evokes this union without distinction through the unsaying or apophasis of gender and the displacement of Christ's body as the center of religious devotion. With the overcoming of gender comes also the annihilation of desire and radical detachment from the body.[47] (Perhaps the starkest evidence of this detachment from the body lies in the fact that Porete never mentions the doctrine of bodily resurrection.) With the annihilation of gender, will, and desire, also comes an end to the painful and ecstatic eroticism that runs throughout the texts of Mechthild and Hadewijch.

Porete's subversion of gender difference (grounded, needless to say, in her desire to overcome the gap between the soul and the divine) leaves no room for the vagaries of desire expressed in the closing dialogue of

Mechthild's *Flowing Light*. There we hear the words of a body and soul who refuse, finally, to renounce their ambivalent and multivalent desires:

> This is how the tormented body speaks to the lonely soul: "When shall you soar with the feathers of your yearning to the blissful heights to Jesus, your eternal Love? Thank him there for me, lady, that, feeble and unworthy though I am, he nevertheless wanted to be mine when he came into this land of exile and took our humanity on himself; and ask him to keep me innocent in his favor until I attain a holy end, when you, dearest Soul, turn away from me."
>
> The soul: "Ah, dearest prison in which I have been bound, I thank you especially for being obedient to me. Though I was often unhappy because of you, you nevertheless came to my aid. On the last day all your troubles will be taken from you."
>
> Then we shall no longer complain.
> Then everything that God has done with us
> Will suit us just fine,
> If you will only stand fast
> And keep hold of sweet hope.[48]

This promise depends on the body's self-denial, for "the less the body preserves itself, the fairer its works shine before God and before people of good will."[49] It is precisely the intense suffering of this desire and the self-denial to which it leads that give rise to Porete's attempt to save the soul and body through the martyrdom of the will.

Porete's utopian vision involves an effacement of differences—between God and soul, uncreated and created (including the body, will, and desire), and male and female—that, paradoxically, both queers heteronormative desire and sacrifices the bodies and desires from which, in their multiplicity, contemporary queer theory and practice emerge. There is clearly no straight road from medieval mystical writings to contemporary practices and politics. In the writings of the beguines, desire is both a resource, an opportunity, and a problem—a problem to which Mechthild, Hadewijch, and Marguerite respond in very different ways. The divergence between them shows that although we cannot simply identify these women's accounts of religious experience with human sexual practices, what they write about their relationship to the divine originates in and remains tied to their experiences of themselves as embodied and desirous human beings. And even the most apparently heteronormative texts queer sexuality in that the object of this desire is not another human being, but (a) divine (Godman). The ecstasies of religion and those of sexuality are metaphorically linked at least in part because of their shared bodiliness, intensity, and tendency toward excess, an excess that, in the case of Marguerite Porete, leads to the subversion of the very grounds from which it emerges.[50]

⌁ Feetishism: The Scent of a Latin American Body Theology

MARCELLA MARÍA ALTHAUS-REID

Nem tudo está perdido: resta o cheiro
Que invade-me as narinas quando passo
Na porta do vizinho sapateiro.

Not everything is lost: The smell still
remains invading my nostrils when I
walk by the door of my shoemaker
neighbor.

—GLAUCO MATTOSO, "Soneto
 Lírico 26"

If noble Christians have beautiful
feet, Nietzsche speculates, "perhaps
light feet are even an integral part of
the concept 'god.'"

—ALISTAIR KEE

THE ADVENTURES OF A BRAZILIAN FEETISHIST

In 1986, Glauco Mattoso, the blind Brazilian poet and self-confessed foot fetishist,[1] wrote a book that has become almost an object of underground cult. *The Loving Feetishist Handbook: Adventures and Readings from a Guy Crazy for Feet* was converted into a cartoon and renamed *The Adventures of Glaucomix, the Feetishist*. Both books were very successful and even attracted international academic attention.[2] Glaucomix (recalling Asterix) is portrayed as a young university student and foot fetishist. In previous books and poems, Mattoso had deliberately mixed contrasting issues of marginalization and power. In these works, issues such as power and disempowerment are represented by the idea of the university as the guardian of elite knowledge, or by the privilege of certain social classes in Brazil. This stands in contrast with what might be called "fetishist knowing," which is presented by Mattoso as commonplace (although transcendental) and anti-institutional.

The Glaucomix books produced a fashion in Brazil at the time of their publication. It is said that pamphlets about the famous *massagem linguopedal* advocated by the book (literally, "tongue-foot massage") were distributed by Mattoso himself in the streets of Brazil. Mattoso invited people to experience this fetishist massage as a form of understanding issues of humiliation and arrogance by the exchange of places between the oppressor and the oppressed, producing a new synthesis of humiliation and power together with pleasure in the context of classist, heterosexist, and racist Brazilian society. The *massagem linguopedal* was to be performed on the perspiring and dirty feet of groups such as the police, homophobics, and frustrated people in general. The proposal was highly successful. It is said that hundreds of people joined the initiative of the feetishist massage at the time, thus engaging in a religious experience of a transgressive, yet sacramental nature. It is true that there is a long history of disempowerment in Latin American theology.[3] Liberation theology is a theology of disempowerment that in any case advocates a different type of and relationship with power. However, what is unique in Mattoso is the presence of theology as pornology. That is, using an erotic language, Mattoso's work has the ability to represent the deconstruction and confrontation of power by a street liturgy of multiple humiliations.

What Mattoso did so successfully was to produce a democratic fetishist event, which participated in dialogic elements and dramatized issues of power, pleasure, and work. Fetishism is a form of art that gathers together the commonplace and the transcendent experience in a unique way. So Mattoso says:

> To shit all the spiritual things
> till to make them touchable
> To spiritualize shit, to make it invisible
> That is all
> the secret of art[4]

Theology is also an art and a sexual art in the sense that it is mainly preoccupied with the location, the quantity, and the qualitative degrees of intimacy between God and humanity. Theology also measures the exchanges of grace, redemption, and repentance and organizes the mechanics of exchange. What theology historically lacks is a practicing knowledge of pleasure and a strategy that utilizes queer irony as part of its exchange mechanisms of redemption. Rereading Hegel, Hamacher said that art ends in irony, but in this ending art is also to complete itself.[5] The queer irony of the *massagem linguopedal*, with its emphasis on feeling the dirty, perspiring feet of the workers, for some, and the experience, for others, of feet lovingly kissed after a day of exploitation, is a whole theological art in itself. It has New Testament undertones. Was Jesus' washing the feet of his friends a *massagem linguopedal*? Did it have the mixture of a pedagogy of power and pleasure that sent hundreds of Brazilians to experiment with it? What form of religious aesthetics lies in Mattoso's feetishism and his construction of the poor, marginalized, homosexual body in Brazil?

Whatever is there in the *massagem linguopedal*, it has that quality that Roland Barthes describes as "acting the thing" and not merely acting a name.[6] Barthes's *Mythologies* differentiates between speaking and speaking about a thing. He gives the following example. A woodcutter can name the tree he is cutting; in so doing, as Barthes says, the woodcutter "speaks the tree," as he is linked by labor to the tree. However, someone who is not the woodcutter cannot speak the tree; that person would only be able to speak about the tree. In the same way, a feetishist like Mattoso can speak the feet with authority, and in producing the *massagem linguopedal* event he enables people to act the thing itself (the synthesis of pleasure, power and disempowerment) and not just to name it or speak about it. However, it has become the role of the church to name power and disempowerment as an aesthetic experience and to do theology as a meta-language, speaking about but seldom speaking the thing.

SHITTING THE SPIRITUAL IN THEOLOGY

Queer theologies are theosocial reflections that somehow feel at home with kissing the dirty feet of a worker, because the starting point of queering theology is always the body.[7] They understand very well the meaning of Mattoso's words that the secret of art is shitting on the spiritual while spiritualizing the shit. Queer theologies have a way of knowing / loving God that gives form to a different location of a theology of the spiritually concrete and the materially spiritual. In this, a theology of the body has gone far beyond unveiling the ideological discourses of heterosexuality in Christianity. Queer theologies have pioneered the value of using different sexual epistemologies in theological praxis. For instance, bisexual epistemologies that do not partake of indecision but of choices of displacement or the acceptance of different placements or locations of love are good sites for gathering together transcendence and immanence—with less probability of reductionism than a classical heterosexual theology. Michael Taussig, in his article on state fetishism, detects in fetishism a capacity to find the ghosts of everyday life. That is to say, the experiential commonplace of our religious, economic and affective lives fluctuates between "spirit and thinghood,"[8] or as Mattoso puts it, between feet and pleasure.

This understanding allows us not only to do a theology of the body from the margins of systematic theological decency, but also to discuss the ideological naturalization given in Christianity to the body, as prior to the body encountering thinghood. For instance, prior to the encounter between the body and clothes or shoes that regulate behavior and sexuality, theology locates love bodily. That location of love and pleasure is somehow the location of a way of knowing and loving God. However, prior to the dressing process of a dogmatic body of theology, there is also a body of God, hidden and undecidable. That God is the space provided, or the reliquary; it is the rosary beads in biker boots or the feet of the Brazilian workers. It does not matter where it is, for it is always a displacement. God partakes of the fetish in having a presence dislocated from its origin. As Christopher Kocela says in his article "A Myth Beyond the Phallus," reflecting on Kathy Acker's work,[9] fetishism carries a desire for transformation or for ultimate Otherness.

The point is that ultimately feetishism shits the spiritual because it breaks the discourse that attributes a particular (and universal) spiritual givenness to the body. That is, feetishism takes away the conception that there is a natural spirituality before systematic theological dressing fixes in it some identity and sexuality or before the body is articulated, as Yegenoglu claims, becoming territorialized by dressing codes.[10] In reflecting on desiring feet or shoes, theology comes to understand how the body can be placed in other kinds of inscriptions. Shoes do not so much articulate in this case the identity of the body who wears them, but become rather a location of identity closed to processes of othering. Othering becomes then the act of performing that borderline between thing and ghost without disguising it with mere naming. Othering acts as a process of identification and seeking of the traces of the forbidden body in theology. Feetishism works here as a body inscription that identifies these valuative processes.

Albert Ploeger has an interesting discussion of aesthetics and religious experience that we could use to understand the "otherization" processes in fetishism in general.[11] We should consider here that North Atlantic theology frequently acts as a value system; it remunerates believers according to a system of gifts that relate to a political and sexual ideological kinship. The ideology that informs the discourse of value, such as the discourse on valuable experiences in the world of art, providing the criteria used to determine when art is art, is not neutral. Ploeger mentions George Dickie's artistic criteria that include "unity, elegance, intensity and complexity."[12] These criteria are not far from classical theological principles of evaluation. For instance, unity in North Atlantic theology is given the sense of sexual coherence that theologies need to achieve. Elegance is also part of a selective aesthetics; the "Other's" body is an inelegant body; it is also inelegant as a way of knowing (the dogmatic corpus; the body of knowledge).

Opening up the theological text has carried expectations of edges, critical borders, authority, authorship, and a theological genre to be recognized. The traditional theology of the body that comes from heterosexual thinking would need to be revised more in terms of Mattoso's *massagem linguopedal*. That is to say, in a body of fetishist knowing/loving, as if setting readable columns of opposition without borders, in mixed formats and styles and with different understandings of edges. That is what Derrida did in his book *Glas*, by the way of formulating a general theory of fetishism.[13] Could fetishism then give to theology the scent of a different system of gift's remuneration? Could salvation, for instance, become acted, instead of just named, by changing the ordering of justice to bring it closer to the fetish economy (a gift without debt)? Derrida discussed the economy of fetishism as "blinded to contraries"[14] as the location of oscillation and undecidability. If salvation joins the event of the other in theology to the tension inherent in the process of divine intervention in human history, a fetish economy could contribute to theology a spirituality of nonsuppressed sensualism, a different odor of sanctity that acknowledges other processes of religious and social formations of identities. Let us suppose then that Mattoso's feetishism is an inscription in a transcendental religious experience that transgresses the North Atlantic gift system of value exchanges and meaning in theology. After all, Mattoso is Brazilian, from the land of *batuque* and *jurema* leaves, which are ceremonially burned during worship by the Pai or Mai do Santo to call the spirits. During the *batuque* ceremonies people gather to smell the powerful incense of *jurema* from charcoal braziers, to attract *jurema* spirits,[15] and to speak with them. An interesting element of *batuque* is that, somehow, the *jurema* is the smell and the spirit at the same time. It is the smell of ethnicity and class and the smell of transcendence, much like the smell of feet in the *massagem linguopedal*. The question to ask theologically here is how God is displaced by the oscillation of the fetish act. How is God saved; or does God save himself; or how does God participate in a different mechanism of exchange that unfixes God? And once this new location of God is presented, monotheism, for instance, becomes a divine impossibility. The body of God's knowledge (dogma) becomes disseminated like the work of Mattoso during the years of the mimeographic generation in Brazil.

Let us consider pursuing the question of feetishist theology by discussing the idea of art, especially the unity and internal coherence that a work of art needs to achieve in order to produce what has been referred to as the world transforming significance of the artistic piece[16] or the spirituality of the experience of a work of art. Feetishism may be seen as a spiritual experience that is based on a disunity with the ideologically constructed body as a heteronomous, compact, constrained body. To start with, it dissolves the limits between the body and spirituality with thingness. This is the image of Mattoso lovingly holding a dirty pair of trainers. This is Derrida talking with such tenderness about his tallith in

Sao Paulo that he ended up confusing his own theory of fetishism by fixing a theological personhood to his prayer shawl.[17] In *Velos*,[18] Derrida considers the need to develop what he refers to as "a tallith's politics" in the context of the dualistic discourses originated by cultures pertaining to the tallith and the veil.[19] This he does as part of a political discussion concerned with a campaign against the prohibition for Muslim women to use the *chador* (veil) in France. For Derrida, the tallith or the veil are originals; they come first, as perhaps for Mattoso shoes come first. The veil is the origin of dualism (a secular/religious or lay/religious organized society) and not a representation of it. In this sense, the fetish is always original, to be found in the paradox of being located in and also preceding any discourse of beginnings. For Derrida, the tallith (or should we say, his tallith?) is never the result of a reification process, but its origin.

This is an important point, especially if we want to consider what we can call "fetishist knowledge" as an original, independent praxis, or, in the context of Mattoso's writing, if we want to reflect on the originality of shoes in theology. Cixous's own text *Sa(v)er* is helpful here. Fetishist knowledge for Cixous is a retrospective movement (or unveiling), which Derrida likes to relate to the sacred choreography of the location and tearing of the veil, the temple's sacred space of transcendence, the Holy of Holies. We could then consider that the fetishist knowledge is an original one, but only in a second movement that refers us to a primal reference, a veiled original fetish knowledge undisclosed, yet present. But the point is that for Cixous, that veil in the temple represents a doubt, perhaps even the distrust of metaphysical presences. Is it then that fetishist knowledge reveals God distrusting God? Is Jesus' resurrection an event of fetish sacred knowledge, also as a tear in the veil that discloses God as an original, yet does so in a second movement? The tallith's politics and the Christian one merge in a God whose love/knowledge is part of that movement of discovery and rejection in search of another original. For Jesus, this may be a veil that does not separate, but on the contrary, a veil that rejects the dualism implied in revelations.

Following from that and in this discussion,[20] Derrida claims that fetishism is not a substitutive for truth (or God) but a knowing, albeit an expiatory or sacrificial one; therefore, a fetish Messiah (a Messiah constructed from fetishist knowledge) may find the door open. Interestingly, for Cixous, the removal of the veil from our souls is connected to the elimination of a fetishist knowledge that is the opposite of a blind trust or confidence in an ideological sense (a *confianza*, that is, a knowledge professing faith). But fetishist knowledge is not a substitutive or intermediary; it is an original, and therefore Derrida presents us with a messianic theory of fetishism. That is, the fetish takes upon itself the burden of our quest for knowledge, which cannot be exhausted except in the fetish itself. Fetishist knowledge exhausts the process of unveiling truth and becomes in this way an expiatory lamb. So Derrida says, "It is the veil which is exhausted in me, *in my place*. It has stolen my name."[21] The fetishist knowledge asks us to pay a price for this redemption—our fixed sense of identity, or the boundaries of our theology or knowledge of God—that is, the borders of thingness and sacrality. And that is precisely what happened to Derrida, lost in his own metaphysical presences when he writes of how he loves and blesses his tallith, and speaks of it as if it were a person who believes: "[my tallith] does not believe in my inconstancy, it does not affect it."[22] Derrida has denounced the shadows of the gods in philosophy but forgotten the enduring power of his prayer cloth.

However, in the thingness of the smell of shoes there are other issues that perhaps Derrida may have considered when he claimed that there is a need for a generalized theory of fetishism, or what we can call a biography of veils.[23] Such are the smell of social classes; of a body without deodorants; of the color of one's skin; of sweaty shoes amid the atmosphere saturated by incense in the church. But Mattoso explores them in his biography of fetishism; moreover, he produces a general biography of shoes considering foundational events. Whereas for Derrida the foundational events for the biography of the tallith were the Exodus, Saint Paul, Freud,[24] for Mattoso the foundational events of fetishist knowledge are capitalist oppression, social exclusion, and global injustice. As a silk veil transgresses spaces and fetishist knowledge is always a revelation, the fetishist body exceeds everything and does not make its nest anywhere. And it exceeds an ideological understanding of transcendence, a discourse on transcendence and an approved religious/spiritual experience including the economic background that lies hidden, configuring, conforming the spiritual experience.

Or combining shit and spirit, as Mattoso might suggest, in excluding ways. For instance, Dickie's definitions of what constitutes a work of art are informed by class concepts and bourgeois appreciation of beauty, as in the requisite elegance. The questions in theology and fetishism are similar to those which come from the Brillo boxes of Warhol, García Uriburu's painting of the Venice canals, or Mattoso's Glaucomix cartoons. All these artists reflect in their works what Danto has called "the transfiguration of the commonplace."[25] In theology, and especially in the configuration of a queer body theology, fetishism is the praxis of trans-figuration of reality in the sense that if it reflects something; it is the reflection of a spiritual Otherness. This is something akin to Derrida's reflections on masks and mirrors as necessary to confront ourselves, as developed in his study of Caravaggio's *Head of Medusa*.[26] To see oneself one needs a reflection and a hiddenness, a way to apprehend the slippery, ghostly reunion of thingness, spirit and love. This is something that Mattoso has explored in comic strips such as *Roxana, a Senhorita de Santana* (Roxana, a young lady from Santana) where the characters are shown only by their feet or legs, but never by their faces. The feet are like reflections seen through the masks or obstacles of prescribed experiences of the body, or the encounter of the body with spiritual issues such as pleasures and neoliberal forms of oppression. The hypocrisy of the Santana society, represented here by the high morality of the Santana ladies, for instance, is an integral part of the irony of the cartoon.

Issues pertaining to spirituality and thinghood are present in the love of feet and shoes. Feet and shoes manifest a location of knowing/loving that relates to the process of Otherness, especially by intuiting the presence of an Other God. The point is that by queering body theology we may be led to discover the traces of a queer God, and through that the traces of Other covenants, lost pacts and revelations of God in an underground history of love. In that sense, Glauco Mattoso's words, "not everything is lost," remind us that in theology the inscriptions of God are related to the inscriptions of bodies and the inventions necessary to effect power in the body of the church, in God and in people. In looking at feetishism we may be looking to the extravagant inscriptions of God as manifested in the body marginal, outside the accepted practices in Christianity of corporeal inscriptions.

KISSING EVITA'S CAR: HOW LIBERATION THEOLOGY LOST THE BODY

In Buenos Aires, late one cold July evening, Evita Perón was going home from the Ministerio de Trabajo y Previsión (Ministry of Work) when she saw a group of workers queuing for a bus. Her chauffeur at that time was Francisco Ernesto Molina. He is still alive and recently gave an interview in which he recalled how Evita felt compassion for the people and ordered him to take the workers to their homes in the official car.[27]

> When we passed by [Plaza de Mayo] . . . Evita started to say, "Oh, all these poor people [waiting for the bus] in such cold weather! Once you have dropped me off come back for these people and take them to their homes. And I want other members of the government passing by [these queues] to do the same. . . ." Therefore, once I had left Evita, I went back to invite the people who were queuing for the bus to get into the official car. There was one woman who didn't want to get into the car. I explained to her that this was the car of *la señora* and that a few moments ago she herself had greeted [Evita] as we passed by [the bus stop]. I told people that I had orders to take them home because the evening was very cold. Finally the woman decided to get into the car and I took her to Villa Lugano. When the people got out at Lugano they began to kiss the car all over.

Kissing the car of Evita. That was a time when few people from Buenos Aires had cars and many had never been in one. Only the aristocracy and bishops were driven by chauffeurs. Evita's official car that night was an excessive sign of blurred frontiers between the government and a handful of workers and between social classes. Evita's chauffeur was also a worker, as was Evita by origin and by election. Is the story that Molina tells, of men and women kissing Evita's car after having been taken home on a cold, dark evening, one of a *massagem linguopedal?* Few if any references to some kind of stability can be found there; everybody is poor and everybody is privileged. It is a humbling scene for the chauffeur (who after all is a worker like the others) and a site of pleasure for everybody. Thingness and spirituality come together in a car being kissed by the poor. An event was fixed in the act of naming Evita's car social justice, solidarity or compassion, while the distinction between private and public was erased. The government car became almost sacramental in the unique way that fetishes are sacramental.

There has always been a fetishist spirituality in Latin America because the sense of displacement and destruction associated with the end of the grand narratives of Latin America[28] produced a ghostly conviviality of simultaneous religious and economic signs in the continent. Basically, in Latin America people die hard. There is a political tradition of rebellious bodies in the popular discourse of justice that reconfigures the transcendence of shit and spirituality and displaces death and life alongside issues of justice. In Argentina, for instance, our dead usually refuse to die. Instead of resting in peace they struggle to resurrect at any inconvenient time, either completely or partially. Therefore the walls of Buenos Aires have been painted through five decades with slogans such as *Evita vive* (Evita is alive) and *Rosas vuelve* (Rosas is coming back)[29] and popular songs claiming that Che Guevara did not die. The corpse of Evita disappeared for more than twenty years from Argentina and came back one day from a graveyard in Italy with shorter hair and without her rosary beads. General Perón's hands also went missing from his coffin one day. Latin American theology has carried the irruption of this disorder of bodies into theology: the bodies of the poor, the bodies of the disappeared, bodies in pain, in hunger, and persecution, tortured bodies. Social justice and a spirituality of the struggle have been constructed upon a ghostly race of rebellious corpses, or body parts (as in the case of General Perón's hands).

In liberation theology, the Other of the discourse of Levinas was given a face, a name, and a surname, together with a refusal to accept its own destiny, the destiny of the body of the poor, the destiny of the marginal to be a nobody, the destiny to disappear from politics and theology alike. However, that concrete body of the Other in liberation theology might have lacked the ghostliness of other kinds of aesthetics present in the life, suffering, and love of the people. The problem was not the romanticization of the body of the poor—that liberation theology always avoided—but its organization. Even liberationists try to discipline resurrections. The process of disciplining resurrections is one of determining what sort of bodies come back, what location of love is pertinent there and how the fixing process of the body-meaningful occurs. In contrast, fetishist knowing/loving tends to unfix references and events.[30] Kissing Evita's car undid old Argentinean borders for a time, until Evita died.

Understandably, liberation theology centered its arguments on issues of social organization (the discipline of bodies under state terrorism) and strategies of disorganization (the destruction of bodies in opposition during political persecution), for instance, the process of disorganizing the body of the people as a political body (or the body of opposition) by a repressive regime in power during the 1970s. In the repressive regime as in the liberationist discourse, the Christian body was constructed around the filiative, amorous processes of the individuals who formed the nation. The Argentinean writer Martin Kohan says that the repressive regime, in torturing children, women, and men, worked as "an engine. It depended on very small parts that sometimes were not taken into account but which represented the paternal and filial personal links" of an individual with the nation.[31]

The filial adherence to a body theology working under highly questionable social and political conventions results in crimes of faith. It was not through a disembodied, abstract theology that those crimes were committed, but within a theology of bodies that reclassified hunger, pain, and torture under the heading of the redeemable. There was a disorder of bodies that although dead refused to die, bodies that had gone where coming back was part of a theological strategy of conflating shit and spirituality. In the final analysis, liberation theology lost the battle of the body, which was the battle for disaffiliation. It sold short the shitting of the spiritual, or at least failed to realize what Fraser refers to as a sacramental aspect of shit.[32]

By shit I refer here to whatever problematized the construction of the Latin American Christian body in the decent order in liberation theology, which I have criticized elsewhere, for instance, in the *Others* of love. Yet that sacramental aspect that according to Fraser is manifested in the irreducibility of the experience of shit in its concrete strength may still help us to relocate the spiritual, the loving experience and the knowledge of God. That sacramental aspect of a fetish is an excess that clings like the smell of the shoes lovingly held by Mattoso, or the touch of rubber or the smell of leather. This is the element of queer loving that fetishism redeems not by illuminating it but by obscuring it. By blurring the clear line of the body definitions in Christianity and using a rhetoric of camp irony and shocking quasi-confessions, queer theology becomes a fetish act. We need to encourage a fetishization of theology, that is, to produce a strategy of sexual displacement that contests heterosexual sociotheology by its ability to oscillate and destabilize binary oppositions.

I am claiming that the alliance of theology and sexual and economic ideology is one made of small alliances resting on a filiative process built around the conception of a natural body, fixing that body's loyalties in issues of hunger and pleasure. The body of God, or more precisely the construction of the body of God, as for instance in creation theology, functions as a signature. It gives us a metaphysical author and therefore authorizes the orders of production and consumption, where human bodies fix identities and construct their loyalties.

The question of doing theology in Latin America started as a process of questioning the loyal body, but construed loyalty to an ideology as an intellectual stand instead of an affective one. Liberation theology in Latin America was controversial precisely because it needed to deny that process of filiation between the dominant state and its allied church. At times it felt as if it were engaged in a heretical struggle against God the Father—and it probably was. However, if Kohan is right and ideologies depend on ties of affection rather than on intellectual conviction, this points to a problem with liberation theology in Latin America. For instance, it could not disaffiliate from heterosexual ideology or ecclesial essentialism. Liberation theology needed to construct the Latin American body with a discourse more preoccupied with grammatical discussions than with the wrongness of the theological givenness of the body in Latin American Christianity. It shared with official theology some elements that were under discussion, namely the administrative ethos.

It is at this point that, in order to continue the theological praxis of liberation, we need to turn to another route, a perverted turn in the road. This is the point when queer thinking is required. Queer theology is a theology of love and of justice, but its strength lies in neither of these but only in betrayal. One of the main issues for queer theology is that of love betrayed, and Mattoso's feetishism is the most powerful example of this. The givenness of the theological location of love is betrayed; the sexuality of the body is betrayed. Queer theology remembers the body of its former lovers, their departures and their contradictions. Beyond that, in a more general sense, it is the theology that remembers the love that has been betrayed by dogmatic traditions and by the theological teaching of the church informed by ideologies of sexual exclusion.[33] That is the crux of the longing and nostalgia among queer theologians, the permanent attempt to claim back the love that was negated or silenced.

However, from another perspective, the whole art of queering theology can also be thought of as a continuous attempt to betray systematic straight thinking about God, to betray the presupposition of a sacred givenness in ecclesiology and the ideals of heterosexual ideology in society. Straight thinking produces straight theologies and straight theologies assume straight love rooted in the geometry of straight bodies, such as bodies of theological knowledge. Therefore, queer theology is confronted by the paradox of attempting to redeem a betrayal of love by theology through an inquiry that leads it into high treason. That is, it involves the betrayal of the ideological allegiances of heterosexual theology that requires a process of affective disaffiliation from godfathers and associates.

John Caputo in his book *On Belief* affirms that "God and love go together." However, as Nietzsche has said, it all depends on what sort of feet God has.[34] Caputo's affirmation may make us wonder why when philosophers turn to religion, sentimentality seems to displace their quest for deconstructing given truths. Or, to put it in a different way, we may wonder why philosophy reads theology straight. Queer theology, which is a theology of contextual displacements and twisting exercises, would start with fetishizing as a theological strategy. It would be concerned not with establishing the parity of love and God but with questioning the location of love and of God. That is, queer theology would start by betraying the given sentimental location of love/God, while looking for closeted or hidden divine addresses that have not been considered as yet. Indeed, God and love may be seen sometimes together, but the question is, where and when. The betrayal of sentimental addresses in theology is unavoidable because love can only be dislocated and translated (transferred) if the traditional theological places of love are betrayed, that is, if we become disloyal to the given ideological assumptions in theology that come from sexuality, racial and colonial understandings, and class biases.[35] At the end, betrayal is needed in the translation (transferring) of bodies in love in the theological systematic body.

BETRAYING BODIES: LOVE IN THE SOUTH

It is unfortunate that in the Latin American theological discourse the construction of bodies in love has remained located in unresolved colonizing discourses. That is to say, the sexual conceptual apparatus of a form of imperial Christianity exercises power by retelling a knowledge of love and bodies in an exemplary way for public consumption. Imperial theology makes love and God exemplary together, as part more of a colonial discourse of law than of a theological one. Therefore, if locating bodies in love in theology tends to follow colonial relationships, queering theology should always start by betraying love, displacing the construction of bodies in love, and creating opportunities to find God in unexpected places.

However, the fact remains that the construction of bodies, love, and God in theology follows commonly assumed patterns of economic production. The fact that Caputo bases his argument for the unity of God and love on the claim that if someone does not love, then that person is "not worth his salt"[36] discloses the commonplace economic covenantal pact existing in Eurocentric thought between the construction of bodies and God. For "being worth his salt" means simply earning a salary, in the context of what Caputo calls the need to find God, love, and truth, or in his own metaphor, "our true north."[37] The problem is that in a discourse from the bodies of the "true South," such salary is linked to exploitation and genuine disregard for anything that could helpfully be called love. It is not linked to loving fulfillment but to *vaciamientos de empresa*, asset stripping procedures that entail emptying a center of production of its machinery, thereby bringing about the closing down of the means of living for entire populations. The "true north" location of a love linked to salary and God demands the deconstructive process of unveiling the true south, as a different understanding of kenotic movements of production, bodies, and theology.

In queering theology, the desire to find the sexual ideology behind theological reflections may take us to the subversive construction of the site of love, the body in love, among contemporary queer writers such as Manuel Puig in Argentina, Luis Zapata in Mexico, or Hilda Hirst and Glauco Mattoso in Brazil. The interesting thing about Latin American queer writing is precisely the construction of bodies at the intersection of several discourses: political, heterosexual, cultural, and religious. The queer poetry of Mattoso might dislocate a religious discourse by the mere fact of dislocating the given position of bodies in love in Latin American theology, being also the meeting point between those bodies and God. As Foucault called our attention to the location of power (as the institutional power to punish anybody), theology also needs to consider the location of power-love (*el poder amar*). *Poder amar* (literally, to be able to love / love-power) is constituted in theology by disciplining the location of love. There are, for instance, the designated locations of marriage and the home and the specific constitution of the bodies allowed to love each other according to prescribed expectations of sexuality, gender, class, race. There are stories of love, records of loving lives, including divorces and separations.

A queer liberation theology (or "indecent theology") needs to look for other love locations in the construction of the body in order to proceed with the disaffiliation necessary to allow an "original" body to emerge in theology. The body south of Mattoso is the body displaced, relocated within a different border in its love for shoes. In the same way that Mattoso belonged as a young man to the mimeograph generation of poets who dispersed their poems in mimeographed copies when confronted with the impossibility of printing their work under the censorship of military regimes, so he disperses love in his poetry. The relocation of love sites in his poems corresponds to thoughts about the relocation of capitalism and society in Brazil. Raymond Williams defines a "subjunctive" text as one characterized by a subversive impulse that is not validated socially, politically or theologically—a concept that could provide us with a new theological referent.[38] In this case, the referent of the feetishist concerns the displacement of love to shoes, but instead of stilettos with silver charms bought in exclusive London shops, he reclaims the ordinary, vulgar, and dirty shoes of the poor.

Mattoso's poems are an important queer theological source for the construction of the body-south, a body in disorder and in dissent with traditional religious locations as constructed by the alliance of a ruling church and its political interests. They are a resource firstly because of his ability to break the myth of the wholeness of the body (what Caputo would call the "true north" of love) by subjecting the male Brazilian body to different theological crossings-over. And they are a resource secondly because Mattoso practices a style of writing that, as if it were a kind of *écriture féminine*,[39] cannot be easily subjugated by or subordinated to the metanarratives of theological discourses of the body in Latin American narratology or theological discourses. Mattoso uses a criterion of criticoconcretism[40] in the construction of his poems and therefore of the body. This criterion is in conflict with logocentrism, trying to rescue what he calls the "verbivocovisual" text, that is, the material concreteness of the word. Because queer theology does not only start at the level of people's critical reality, but also questions the discourse accompanying such experiences, criticoconcretism could provide us with important clues for the construction of a theology of the body in love and for discerning God's presence in the integration between verbal and nonverbal elements of poetry.

In this sense, Mattoso offers an example for constructing a hermeneutics from the body and from the changes of the body. When he was still able to see, he wanted to show the visual aspects of the word, the concreteness of the images present in poetry and specifically in his poetry. When he went completely blind, he continued to be preoccupied with making poems that could disclose the visual character of poetry. He used literary techniques such as alliteration, paronomasia, cacophony, and euphony to produce metaphors and translations with the power to reclaim the translucidity of the body in love, in a context of economic globalization, political corruption, and heterosexuality, as viewed from the Brazilian closet. It is precisely this almost exilic quality of the construction of a subversive excluded body in Mattoso's poems that conveys a sexual liminality that makes possible the understanding of bodies in love in between and of a God also partaking of this betweenness.

By the use of criticoconcretism, Mattoso dislocates love and dislocates sexual sites of pleasure and signification. He redefines friendship and solidarity and criticizes capitalism. Theology also has inherited the construction of the body by criticoconcretism. Take, for example, alliterative techniques, the repetition of speech in a sequence of closely related sounds. Repetition increases meaning, as for instance in the phrase "mission and transmission of the Gospel" or conceptual alliterations such as "mission and racism." In biblical times paronomasia was responsible for associating the name of the city of Babylon with chaos and crime (in Hebrew the word Babylon sounds similar to "mixed up"). There are also sexual paronomasias. Does the name of Jesus immediately associate with Mary? And because of the association of Mary and virginity is the theological perception of Jesus automatically drawn to the assumption of celibacy?

Alistair Kee writes of Nietzsche's musings about a God who understood how to dance. Thus Nietzsche puts the following words in Zarathustra's mouth: "I should believe only in a God who understood how to dance."[41] The God of life has light, dancing feet not as an ornament but as a constitutive element of God's divinity. As Kee comments, Nietzsche considered that Jesus was a free spirit, the first and only Christian, representing a strong and joyful spirituality of life.[42] Jesus' divine, perspiring feet also danced when kissed by those who loved him. This God who dances and God's followers (the "Christians with beautiful feet") are to be found in a body theology of fetishism. Fetishism is deeply relevant to the search for the body in theology, especially the queer body that includes the out-of-the-closet heterosexual body too. It is relevant also to the search for the body of the queer God, the one who became Evita's car when Evita's car embodied social justice; when Evita's car had feet lighter than any other God; when love became leather seats and rubber tires and people kissed them reverentially; when God's lighter feet were perspiring after a day in the factory in Sao Paulo and were lovingly kissed by the followers of Glaucomix, with the tenderness of Derrida touching his tallith.

Has theology lost the body in the dealings of heterosexual ideologies? Has neoliberalism pervaded our theologies of eros with its own aesthetics of exclusion and indifference toward the poor and marginalized? *Mais nao tudo está perdido* . . . but not everything is lost. A fetishist way of loving and knowing can still inform our discourse of theology, economics and sexuality by finding other bodies, other loves and an *Other* God. The scent of a Latin American theology will always be the scent of a materialist theology that knows how poverty smells and understands how erotic revelations (revelations of divine love) occurred when some policemen kissed the feet of factory workers in Sao Paulo. And this is because a Latin American feetishist theology arrives as an erotic unveiling of God's love amongst the dirty, sweating bodies of the marginalized and excluded. It is queer and it is political, as it is driven by that sense of urgency for social justice that still characterizes the liberationist Latin American theological movement in its search for alternative orders—loving orders and theological ones.

❧ Digital Bodies and the Transformation of the Flesh

SHEILA BRIGGS

BODIES IN THE DIGITAL IMAGINATION

Bodies have always been the subjects of representation, sometimes written about in texts but more often carved in stone or painted on walls. Such images constitute a central feature of the visual culture from which most people in most historical periods have derived their knowledge of how the body is ordered in their society. As postmodern theories constantly remind us, the order of the body is also the political, social, economic, religious, and sexual order of a society. The discursive body has so devoured the flesh that the sensuality of the body is endlessly evoked only to be embalmed in writing and theory. But in the statue or stained-glass window what directly confronts the viewer is not discourses or ideas but the physical representation of a physical body, where the flesh has already been transformed within the realm of the physical. Not all bodies are equal in the realm of physical representation—one body in particular has undergone continuous translations. The *corpus* (as the figure of Christ on a crucifix is called in the Roman Catholic Church) is a physical signpost to multiple dimensions of the flesh. It is a historical reminiscence of a man executed by the Romans, but in a Catholic church it hangs above the altar where in the Eucharist several corporeal realms and orders intersect. There is the social order of the church with its ecclesial hierarchy in which priestly male bodies alone are held to represent the body of Christ but there is also the Body beyond representation, the flesh that transforms its own symbols, a transcendent corporeality entered through the Eucharist. Even the transcendent Body submits to the regime of physical representation and hence reassumes the instability and impermanence of the flesh. It can only be preserved by being consumed. The physical taste of transcendence passes and the *corpus* above the altar reminds us that we are back to the ordinary physical forms of visual representation.

The physical medium of a visual representation constrains it in a way that is very different from the way in which words are confined within textual boundaries. The paper and ink are not integral to the discursive construction of a text and a text can be transferred from one physical medium to another without alteration. Moreover, a text can be divided, excerpted, rearranged, and integrated into other texts so that its meanings are changed but not obliterated. Even in paraphrase and translation its structure and argument can be preserved. In traditional visual media, such as painting, sculpture, or tapestry, representation cannot be easily, if at all, detached from its physical form and this restriction of the medium makes visual artifacts less accessible and more vulnerable to loss than texts. However, this constraint also gives visual media an affinity to the bodies they represent. After all, they too are vulnerable and limited to one location. They cannot be dismembered without destruction and cannot be combined with other bodies except in Frankenstein and other horror stories. They cannot exist in two or several copies and be translated into other physical forms except in parallel universes, ancient myths, and science fiction. Yet already the mention of exceptions reveals the true difference between the body and its physical representations. Visual media are most often not employed to portray the body "as it actually is." Even certain forms of artistic realism, including photography, seek what is beneath the flesh as seen by the conventional or casual view. They bring to the surface and transform into flesh, passions and motives, the fantastic corporalities that lie just below our everyday skin. So art is populated by physical doubles of the human body that have broken out of its ordinary perception.

When thinking about how contemporary digital media have transformed the visual representation of the body, it is important to recognize that they stand in a historical trajectory in which visual media have always given the fantastic and the fabulous physical form. There have always been visual narratives of bodies that exceed ordinary corporeality. What has changed in the last two centuries is not so much how the body is represented but the physical medium of visual artifacts. The photograph not only enables a more realistic picture of its subject but also changes its modes of circulation. There now can be several exact copies of the same visual artifact that can be distributed to any and many different locations. Eventually, the photograph can be produced privately and is not dependent on finding a publisher (as in the case of woodcuts and engravings in printed texts). The photograph is an essential step in the democratization of visual culture since its low cost does not require a person or institution of considerable means to commission it.

Film intensifies the possibilities for realism of the photograph and adds a crucial dimension to the representation of the body: movement. The vitality of the body can now be given a direct physical correlate in the cinematic image. Although films can be shown all over the world and thus share the portability of the photograph, their modes of circulation were for several decades restricted. Television brought cinematic images into homes but it was not until the appearance of the video cassette recorder in the 1970s that the democratization of the cinematic image could begin. One of the problems of films had been that, despite their capacity for wide distribution, their accessibility was not guaranteed and only lasted for a short period of time. Films which did not reflect mainstream views or tastes often found few cinemas to show them and were withheld even from the viewers who would have been eager to see them. Moreover, the enormous costs of film and television production concentrated decisions of what films and television programs were to be made in the hands of very few institutions and individuals. Filmmakers were more dependent on patronage than artists using traditional visual media had ever been. The VCR made films accessible, independently of cinema release, and therefore greatly widened the audience for non-mainstream films (world cinema, politically progressive projects, etc.). This then had an impact on television in the eighties and nineties as heads of programming realized the size of audiences for non-mainstream productions. In the United Kingdom, the BBC began to show on a regular basis world cinema, and Channel Four commissioned its own non-mainstream films, some of which became general cinema releases.

Soon after the VCR became commonplace in homes, so did the video camera. By the eighties this consumer technology was being used for more demanding projects than making home movies of the kids and one's summer holidays. Documentary makers, among them academics, found filmmaking more easily accessible. At the same time, digital technology began to transform how images were made and how they were distributed, and to overthrow the distinction between realistic and non-realistic representation to the extent that visually reality was collapsed into virtual reality. This brought about changes not only in the physical representation of the body but also in the relationship of the body to its physical representation. The digital revolution in visual culture occurred simultaneously on several fronts. One recurring feature, however, is that a digital technology is first implemented at a high-end, professional level at great expense but then over a course of (sometimes only a few) years drops so drastically in price that it becomes available to nonprofessional "consumer" users. The end result is not only that the consumption of digital images becomes daily fare—at least in the countries of the North—but that their creation is also a common daily task.

The digital is the least physical of all forms of visual media. One can show it on a monitor, even print a copy of it, but it is invisibly stored in a file of "1s" and "0s." Yet the digital image is finally able to rival the written word in its independence from its physical medium. There is no distinction between original and copy. A digital image (even a short film) can be carried on a tiny piece of plastic or simultaneously viewed on the World Wide Web by people scattered all over the globe. Although a digital image can be exactly copied, it can also be easily manipulated—cleaned up, superimposed upon another, hue and tone altered. Digital visual media can emulate the realism of photography and film and, at the same time, one of their chief uses is to break out of that realism. The human body figures largely in this ability of the digital to juxtapose intense realism and equally realistic fantasy, in such a way that the boundary between realistic and nonrealistic representation evaporates. We all are aware of the stunning special effects in recent movies where human bodies are placed in surreal landscapes and endowed with superhuman abilities, all the while looking like the human beings we encounter in everyday life.

There is a special connection between the human body and the digital medium that represents it. Digital technology has become a vehicle for the human imagination that has always sought a hidden potential under the skin. Human beings do not usually see their bodies as live meat. Interestingly, when human beings are referred to as meat it is almost invariably in the context of them being subjected to the sexual predation of others or to violence or to a combination of both. Human beings tend—even in body-negative religious and philosophical traditions—to see their bodies at least as the dwelling place of the self and as trans-formed by that self. Human flesh transubstantiates, the earthly becomes heavenly. In Christianity we see this in the doctrine of resurrection, not only of Christ but of all saved humanity. The risen Jesus has a glorified body, one that exceeds the normal capabilities of human flesh, it can seemingly appear from nowhere. Such a body is also promised to Jesus' followers and as a foreshadowing of the glorious body of the resurrection the bodies of saints have often been declared to have the escaped the natural decay of a dead human body. Instead of decomposing flesh the body is recomposed in a narrative of endless life that has overcome not only death but the finitude of the universe itself, a happiness without interruption or loss in a blessed state of eternal union with the divine. Such longings for a glorified body are not limited to Christianity and theistic religions. In Buddhism the enlightened body of the Buddha is resplendent and the path to enlightenment overcomes the illusions of the body, especially its physical desires. Yet this is not jettisoning the body but removing its constraints so that its ultimate glory can shine forth.

The malleability of the human body is, of course, not only a great source of hope but also a reservoir of fear. The self may be trapped in a flesh that can only experience death and decay. At best, we fear oblivion in the eventual betrayal of our frail flesh to disease, aging and death. At worst, we fear that the self might be perpetually trapped in hideous or tortured flesh. This is the other side of the Christian doctrine of resurrec-tion. In medieval churches one of the most depicted scenes was the Last Judgment. Often carved in the wood or stone of the rood screen, it was placed on the partition between the nave, where ordinary Christians worshiped, and the sanctuary in which priests officiated in the eucharistic transformation of bread into flesh. On the right side of the rood screen, bodies rose out of tombs and proceeded upward to Christ, seated in judgment. On the left side, too, bodies came out of graves but they descended down toward the devil and the gaping hole of hell. What brings the body to this terrible fate? The physical appetites, especially sexual desire, are the most common path to destruction. The body as an endless site of torment is also not restricted to Christian art. In many cultures the human body is threatened not only by the dissolution of death but can also be dissolved into the monstrous. Bosch paintings capture our horrified fascination with the idea that the human could be joined to the nonhuman and that the order of the body could be subverted and its members rearranged and distorted. The zombies and monsters of horror film and television play on the same dynamics of simultaneous attraction and repulsion. The special effects of digital technology allow not only the creation of more elaborate and convincing monsters, they enable the rapid and seamless transition of ordinary human into monstrous bodies and the reverse. Such transitions and their reversals can happen in rapid succession, so that the line between the monstrous and the human becomes blurred. The recent television series *Buffy the Vampire Slayer* and *Angel* used digital special effects to make vampires inhabitants of an ordinary adolescent and young adult world without stabilizing difference through confining it to one representation (as happens when aliens are created through the simple and constant wearing of prosthetic makeup in science fiction space shows). The digital transformation of human into vampire can be so easily and cheaply realized in a script that this no longer needs to remain an occasional eruption of the monstrous. Thus, a frequent disruption of identity can be performed, so that the vampire/human can no longer be pulled apart as binary opposites. This also contributes to a more complex description of the vampire/human's sexuality than the fanged violation or seduction of the classical vampire.

Digital technology enables us to explore heaven and hell, the glorified body and the monstrous self in ways that are not discontinuous with the human imagination of previous ages, but the expansion of our visual resources extends the realm of the imaginary. The boundary between ordinary human flesh and its glorified or monstrous forms is no longer clear. The permeability of this boundary has important repercussions for

ty, the questions whether there is sex in heaven and whether
the risen body of Christ has genitals are thorny ones. Orthodox theologians in ancient and medieval Christianity wanted to assert that Jesus had
an ordinary body and that his and indeed every human identity persisted
beyond the grave. But how integral was sexuality to human identity?
Jesus' genitals marked his masculinity but were without sexual function.
Visual culture partially subverted this view when it followed the logic of
realistic representation. Renaissance art emphasized the sensuality of the
human body and, consistent with its realist imperative, did not exempt
Jesus' body from the realm of the erotic.[1] Yet even here the frank sexualization of Jesus' body has its limits. In Valentin's painting of the *Noli Me
Tangere,* which hangs in Perugia, Mary Magdalene stretches her hands
out toward Jesus' genitals but does not touch. Does the Risen Lord have
any genitals beneath his robe?

Since digital technology can be used to confuse the boundary between
the ordinary and the glorified body, the risen Christ can now be a sexual
being. In contemporary television we can see Christ, separated not from
sexuality, but from masculinity. In the series *Xena Warrior Princess* the gal
pals Xena and Gabrielle assume the traditional imagery of Jesus' crucifixion and resurrection. Their sexuality, although not portrayed as explicitly
lesbian, is definitely queer in the sense of not conforming to heterosexual
norms. Moreover, their risen bodies remain in the realm of ordinary
human life, vulnerable to death and dismemberment. But whether death
or any dissolution of their bodies can remain permanent is unlikely. After
their assumption of Christ's crucifixion and resurrection their bodies become increasingly portrayed (thanks to digital special effects) as superhuman, or more precisely as human superbodies. Both permanently
eroticized and permanently subject to suffering, their ordinary human
bodies are the source of their own transcendence. Human flesh can exceed its own corporeality. The self that can communicate and unite with
the divine is no longer surplus to the body nor is it that which escapes
mortality. The excess of the human superbody bears the divine within
itself and does not need to escape mortality because it can endure
through it. At various points in the series, it is suggested that Xena is

crucified across time and in multiple realities. Finite and mortal, nonetheless her corporeality cannot be suppressed but constantly erupts, raising the question whether ordinary human sexual bodies can achieve a transcendence that surpasses any immortality of the soul.

Traditional Christian theology has not been so optimistic about the fate of our sexual bodies. There is according to Matthew 22:30 no marriage in the life of the resurrection, and Christian theology long understood this to mean that there was no sex either. Modern theologians are not bothered by sex in the afterlife largely because they are uncertain about the resurrection of the body itself. Even where this is still asserted, it is left undetermined. Somewhat inconsistently some earlier conceptions of hell depicted the bodies of the damned as sexual. The saved, it seems, were raised to an angelic and asexual existence while the damned got a version of their old bodies back, in which they had given in to their sexual desires. The difference between their old bodies and the new is that the latter were indestructible, which seems to be a makeshift construction so that the damned could endlessly suffer sexual torments. The saved, on the other hand, were portrayed as released from the tribulation of sexual desire. For them the erotic is transposed from the body to the soul. For the soul can enter into an eternal love affair with God and enjoy the beatific vision. The eroticism of heaven and its vision of the divine is also prefigured in mystical experience, which is often expressed through a thick sexual imagery, as we find in the works of Teresa of Avila and John of the Cross. But do we have to wait until heaven and give up our physical sexuality for our bodies to be gloriously transformed? Can digital technology at work with our imagination provide us with a vision of human corporeality in which our human bodies are transformed by their own excess?

BIOTECHNOLOGY AND THE PATH OF TRANSCENDENCE

One answer to that question would warn us to beware of the illusory world that digital technology creates and alert us to the danger of so many of us spending so much time in this world. Such an answer presupposes that the digital world is thoroughly illusory and that psychological and social damage is done through playing video games and becoming engrossed in the special effects of film and television. But there is another way of looking at the reasons so many people (at least in the West) choose to inhabit virtual reality. It is not necessarily the case that those of us who engage in such pursuits want to escape the "real" world. Instead we are confronting the fact of contemporary social reality in which technology has compressed time. The future is always overtaking the present. Technology does not simply provide us with some new tools; rather it disrupts and alters patterns of life, creating new forms of social organization and infrastructure. The course of an individual's life no longer has predictable patterns. In the late twentieth century the set rhythms (as they were conceived) of marriage and career broke down. Fragmented lives, multiple selves, the postmodern condition, we all know the diagnosis of the contemporary sociocultural realm. Digital technology, by allowing us easily to transpose ourselves into another world, mirrors our actual reality. The construction of social reality changes so much that it has become unstable and we end up living in a succession of social worlds, which are punctuated by ever decreasing intervals of time. But digital technology can be more than a psychological coping mechanism. It can provide our imagination new resources for envisioning and planning our rapidly advancing future.

By concentrating on digital technology as visual culture I have stressed its aesthetic dimension but, of course, computers play a critical role in scientific research. There are many scientific and technological applications of digital images. Indeed complex digital models can be created in which what is visually perceived correlates with multiple other indicators, allowing the computer to duplicate, among other things, organic processes. The ability to construct ever more complex digital models is continually changing scientific experimentation, since long, expensive, and difficult laboratory tests can be simulated rapidly, cheaply and easily on computers, allowing laboratory resources to be concentrated on the most promising avenues of research. Since computers have come to dominate scientific research at the same time as biotechnology has become a preeminent field of research programs, there has been a convergence of computer science and biology, giving birth, for instance, to the discipline of computational biology. Biomedical research is one area where we find extensive use of digital imaging as part of complex computer models. In most cases what is being simulated on the computer are small-scale processes, such as the functions of the cell, that seem remote from the usual aesthetic representation of the human body on a much larger scale. However, some biomedical digital imaging occurs on the macroscopic level and the software and programming techniques developed in this sphere have some influence on computer simulation of the human body in aesthetic contexts, for instance, in 3-D animation. But could the influence go in the other direction? Could how the human body is represented in the computer-generated images of film and television have an impact on how biomedical research reshapes the physical reality of the human body?

The convergence of digital and biotechnology opens up the possibility that the expanded visual resources available to our imagination could not only create new forms of the physical representation of the human body but could translate these images into actual new forms of human corporeality. Our imagined bodies in visual culture have been endowed with a great many characteristics that differ not only from those of our ordinary ones but also from one another. There are no univocal cultural scripts to direct biotechnology in its construction of the new human body. Such freedom is inevitably attended by ambivalence: Although human beings may long for a transformation of their flesh, they also fear it. For instance, the biomedical advances that cumulatively are extending life spans and eventually could grant human beings virtual immortality are already a source of cultural anxiety. There is the paradox that although many Westerners are comforted by rather vague notions of an afterlife, the thought that their current ordinary human life might never end is profoundly disturbing.

In fact, our response to biomedical research is very much shaped by the long historical traditions of the collective cultural memory. Embedded in this are deeply rooted religious expectations and fears which often remain unconscious in a secular society until biomedical research threatens to cross a boundary that previously we were unaware existed. The complaint that scientists may attempt to "play God" reminds us that finitude, mortality, and bodily restrictions are what has been understand to demarcate the human from the divine. In traditional Christian thought our ordinary bodies are created by God and any corporeality that exceeds our created bodies is exclusively in the gift of God. If science can provide us with a human superbody, what need do we have of the glorious body of the resurrection? On the other hand, we doubt the promise of science and fear that if scientists "play God" they will fail and we will be punished for our hubris of encroaching on the power of the divine. The monster is the product of such transgression and is seen even in the secular guise of Frankenstein lurking in the biomedical lab as penalty for ignoring the constraints of being merely human. These cloaked but powerful religious anxieties are mingled with concern about what would happen to sexuality in a biomedically enhanced superbody. We remember that the historically imagined body of the Christian West was either asexual, if glorified, or often oversexualized in its monstrous form. Whatever the psychic bond between *eros* and *thanatos* may be, sexuality has been envisaged as coterminous with our mortal body. Remove or weaken the limit of mortality, then we are conditioned to fear that sexuality will either unrestrainedly engulf us or, the opposite, will become attenuated and finally disappear over a limitless life-span. In the secular genre of science fiction one encounters advanced intelligent life that has evolved into pure energy. Such pure energy seems remarkably akin to older conceptions of angels, and one suspects that life forms of pure energy have no more use for sex than angels.

Feminists have been particularly alarmed at the potential of biomedical research to separate the human from our ordinary physical bodies. They have viewed this biomedical future as a continuation of the deeply rooted prejudices against the body in the Christian West. The disembodied self is the patriarchal dream of severing dependence on the feminine Other, human mothers and Mother Nature. Feminist theologians and ethicists have taken up the task of defending embodiment against the body- and sex-negative traditions of Christianity but also against science, which remains organized within still heavily patriarchal institutions. Even in Elaine Graham's recent work, which takes a generally positive view of the posthuman condition, we find a caution against the "technological sublime," and "its predilection for the qualities of detachment, omniscience, immutability and incorporeality promote disdain for embodied contingency and foster technologies that are obsessed with cheating death, vulnerability and finitude."[2]

However, one can take a different view even of such a radical proposal as that of Frank Tipler, who sees human beings abandoning their flesh for continued existence in supercomputers.[3] After all, he points out that this is the only way that human beings could survive in the extreme conditions of the later stages of the universe. Such a migration might not be so much giving up the body but exchanging it for a new corporeality. It is not immediately clear that the only form of human embodiment is carbon-based and that we should prefer this form over silicon or other material bases for our physical body. Indeed, the admittedly remote possibility of Tipler's model of human transcendence presupposes the radical embodiment of our selves in our brains. It is precisely because human subjectivity and identity exists through brain function that this physical medium could be modeled and copied to other physical media such as the silicon chips of a computer. Obviously, if human beings adopted other forms of corporeality this would affect their sexuality, but this would not necessarily bring about the end of the erotic. Even human intelligent machines might have sex.

A NEW ECONOMY OF PLEASURE

The real question raised by new, technologically mediated forms of corporeality is not whether they would negate human embodiment but how they would be distributed within a global capitalist economy. Already longevity in the West increases the unequal consumption of resources—we consume not only more but also longer. The different course of HIV/AIDS crises in Africa and the United States has demonstrated on a massively tragic scale that access to medical treatment is very unequal. We can only assume that life-extension, gene therapy and other biomedical advances will be limited to the wealthy or, at best, to those in the West who have good insurance or a generous system of social medicine. There is also an environmental impact when human populations increase partly as a result of not being culled by death. Digital technologies have largely taken over their regimes of representation from earlier forms of visual culture and digital sophistication does not necessarily banish racism, homophobia and misogyny. If we can choose to make our imagined bodies reality, our choices may be guided by stereotypes and hierarchies of race and class. If everyone has blond hair and blue eyes, then such appearance would lose its cachet but at a terrible cost for human diversity.

The satisfaction of our desires is always fundamentally a matter of political economy and, as Marcella Althaus-Reid has reminded us, a political economy is always a sexual economy as well.[4] Digital technology cannot be divided into an ideological superstructure of visual culture and a material base of biotechnological production. Digital technology will become an increasingly contested space which will not only be determined by a logic of technological development. Projects and conflicts within the digital imagination will also direct its technology. The desire for corporeal excess does not have to implicate us within the current global economy of capitalism just as it does not necessarily cause us to reject embodiment. This point will be resisted by many Christians, even and especially those on the left. The Christian critique of capitalism often has an undertone of asceticism and therefore can only see our material desires as holding us captive to an unjust system. Political strategies for justice based on the denial of desire are ineffective because they ignore the fact that pleasures—gross material pleasures, including sexual ones— are what enliven most people's lives. The problem of contemporary culture is that it is still not hedonistic enough. If one thought of a just society as one in which the coordination of pleasure so occurred that every person could satisfy not just their needs but their desires to the maximum compatible with the pleasure of others, then we would have a richer and more vital sense of human solidarity. A political economy in which the goal was to maximize pleasure would not only be concerned with the production of material goods but also of material satisfactions and as a sexual economy could also critically ask whether the whole range of our social/political/personal relationships promoted sexual pleasure.

A new economy of pleasure would also not be one of scarcity. The human superbody does not have to supplant either the embodied self of feminist theology and ethics or the traditional Christian glorified body of the resurrection, but it does drastically alter their context. The human superbody, which already exists in the digital imagination of popular culture, does not remove us from the ordinary physical realm, nor does its internal transcendence preclude a further transcendence. However, mortality and physical restriction are no longer the boundary between the human and the divine and sexuality is no longer the boundary marker. A human superbody is a new location for physical existence that may allow us to experience the universe in ways unknown before. It can therefore be a location in which we explore our sexuality in ways which we could not previously envisage and may therefore be productive of new sexual desires that are not dominated by the hierarchies of gender, race, and class. I am not arguing that such optimistic outcomes are inevitable, merely that they are possible.

PART III

❧ Sacred Suffering, Sublime Seduction

❧ Passion—Binding—Passion

YVONNE SHERWOOD

PASSION

The seductive enigma of the word *passion*—and the Christian passion to which it is tied—seems to me to lie in the way in which it allows the subject at its center to function as subject and object both at once. Derived from Latin *passio* and Greek *pathos*, it is bound, in its first appearances in anything we would recognize as English, to passivity, suffering, affliction, and "the fact or condition of being acted upon or affected by an external agency" (OED). As if to illustrate this sense of passion as the subjection of the subject, the word was frequently applied to illness, so that a sixteenth-century English speaker could speak of bellyache as a passion of the belly or apply ointments to relieve a passion of the joints. But even as passion indicates a state of being the object of a verb / an action / an affliction that comes in—violently and forcefully—to you (from outside you, or from within that inside-outsider that is your body), it also indicates something forceful that comes from within and exceeds and overruns you. In its attempt to categorize this sense of *active* passion, the OED grasps for prefixes like *out* and *over*. This passion is overpowering; it is an overmastering zeal or an outreaching of the mind. Active and passive senses of passion cross around a sense of excess that applies even when we perceive ourselves as, in some always qualified sense, passion's origin and subject. In the idea of the sub-subject *and* the super/supra-subject, passion emerges as that which is too much for us—both overwhelming and undermining.

According to Erich Auerbach, we owe all our etymological debts of Passion, in all their seductive, pliable ambiguity, to Christianity.[1] It is Christianity that, in its very particular passion, pushes "passion" beyond its contemporary Greek semantic field of pathos-passion (firmly opposed to active, creative concepts like *praxis, poiesis, ergon*), and etymologically propels it toward its opposite: the realm of *epithumia* ("desire"). Fleetingly, but provocatively, Auerbach suggests that the passionate [*leidenschaftliches*] suffering in the world that is the special (paradoxical) form of the Christian flight from it is the main force that drives us into the fraught force field of our "passion." He argues that even as Christianity absorbs the Stoic sense of passive passion as the enemy of active life, it also inaugurates a new sense of passion as the active aspiration/consummation of life. Describing Christianity, provocatively, as a condition of "movement within the polarity of opposites," Auerbach effectively maps passion as that which resists what Gilles Deleuze calls the distributive characteristic of (nonparadoxical) good sense, dividing things into a neat "on the one hand" or "on the other" (*d'un part et d'autre part*).[2] For Auerbach, passion's etymological backflip happens in that strangely active moment in which the figure of "God's love which moved him to take human suffering upon himself" becomes a "motus animi without measures and bonds."

If we turn to look once more at the Christian Passion, we can see how it functions as a performance of this etymological ambiguity writ large. The figure at its center functions as extreme subject and extreme object. He is the grammatical subject at the beginning and the grammatical object at the end of this sentence of death. In the gospel of John, Jesus proclaims that no one takes his life from him but that he lays it down of his own accord, and does so as an expression of his (that is God's) very active passion (John 10:17–18; 3:16). Glossing the message of this gospel in the language of the OED, we can say that God so loved the world that he pursued it with an "overmastering" zeal or an "outreaching" of the mind. In contrast, the Jesus of Mark, weeping in the garden, crying against the abandonment by the father (14:33–36; 15:34), embodies most starkly that sense of passion as being afflicted, being affected, and being the object of verbs / actions that come at you without your bidding, like a heavy cross on your back, ropes round your wrists, nails through your hands and tears in your eyes. Jesus becomes the focus of our riveted attention precisely because he is such an unfocussed subject/object of passion. He is a figure of that extreme objecthood that we call victim-hood, the subjected subject bowed beneath the weight of life as a burden. But at the same time (a time that, as Derrida says, disagrees with itself all the time[3]) he is the Logos writing his own story, inaugurating pas-sion's new, active, sovereign-desiring sense.

If Julia Kristeva is right (as I think she is) to say that the realm of the sacred is the realm of borderline and fragile states of subjectivity,[4] then the power of the Passion (like the power of the word *passion*) lies in its ability to gesture to the dynamic zone of interhuman living in which we feel ourselves—and never simply *alternately*—as both subjected subject and sovereign subject (like a god). And it is interesting to note, at least in passing, the internal divisions that haunt the English words *subject* and *object*. Through sedimented layers of meaning a subject has become a vassal or a person bound to a superior authority (such as a monarch, government or religious superior), and also, oppositely, a "thinking or cognizing agent," an organizing and perceiving center, to which every-thing else is external or object. But a subject is also a "person or thing towards whom or which action, thought, or feeling is directed"—hence also an object, at least in the sense of object as a "thing or person to which something is done." To complicate matters further, subjective and objective reverse the sense of freedom and self-government assigned to the dominant modern senses of subject and object. To be objective is to "present facts [objects] uncoloured by feelings, opinions, or personal bias," whereas to be subjective is to be too close to your own center, subject to passion, hence "idiosyncratic "(OED).[5] Though I will not go further than an "as if "and stray into a dubious proof by etymology, it is as if the overdetermination and overlayering of subject and object some-how performs the confusion that attends any attempt to parse, in clear-cut etymologies and grammars, the self in all its relations to itself and (multiple) others. How to distribute those selves between the actor and the acted upon?

Stretching his arms out to embrace what we attempt to demarcate as either subjecthood or objecthood, Jesus on the cross is the extreme figure of the overdetermined self. The Passion attracts us because it is an unstill truth that will not yield to the sorting effects of sequence or distributive logic (*first* crucifixion and *then* resurrection, or on the one hand Mark and on the other, John). Instead it insists that we take in these images of supra- and sub-sovereignty simultaneously, as if forced to look at, say, the incompatible panels of Grünewald's Isenheim Altarpiece all at once.[6] The figure of Jesus commands our attention as supra- and sub-subject, but mostly (perhaps counterintuitively) as sub-subject. While Bataille is too one-sided in seeing the Christian passion *only* as the "representation of loss and limitless degradation,"[7] our cultural artifacts witness that we have been less moved by the transcendent agent of newly active passion than by the bound wrists, the child-corpse in the arms of his mother, and the body subject to intensely hostile forces militating against us from outside (and inside).

Another way of saying this is to say that the allure of the Christian passion has to do with its role as the *paradigmatic story*—at least according to an important, though little-known, theory of story laid out in Michael Roemer's *Telling Stories*.[8] Arguing that stories are not for positivists[9] (thus explaining, perhaps, the relative unpopularity of his theory of story, as well as offering an alternative reason for the widespread cultural suspicion of story), Roemer argues that the task of story is to perform the depotentiation of humankind. Stories perform, in an exacerbated way, the sense of human subjection and unknowing in which "much of the time we don't even know what is going on, or growing, in our own bodies.[10] Their task is to foreground human exposure. And they do so through plots in which we see even those special individuals whom we call (or miscall) heroes function as subjected subjects. The very conditions of narrative—the fact that it is impossible to tell, or even imagine, a story that has only one protagonist with events entirely of his[11] own making—mean that story becomes, by definition, a performance of the limitation of the subject (even, in fact especially, when he is a hero). Entering a plot that has already begun without him and that moves forward through what Balzac called a "concatenation of causes,"[12] the hero encounters his limitation in relation to the intractability of a past that has started without him and a future that is shaped by more than his desire. In Roemer's formulation, story is not a space for freedom, diversion, leisure, but a merciless, constricted space that amplifies conditions of human subjugation. His anthem is that plots do not shelter us—and yet, that they also do. For it is also intrinsic to the conditions of story that this extreme performance of human limitation takes place in a safe place (a narrative panic room). After empathetically confronting your limits/ subjection/death in the surrogate realm of story, you put down the book or stop listening and (in a microresurrection?) continue to live.

In a fact that perhaps goes some way to explaining the turn to what we call narrative theology and the nagging sense of the insufficiency of the supersufficiency of systematic theologies, the conditions of the Christian passion seem to be, in some fundamental sense, the conditions of story. The Christian crucifixion can be understood as a hyperstory: a pushing of the limiting conditions of story to their furthest extremity (or rather, tightest confinement). For here we experience a contingency so acute that *even God is not sheltered*, is not safe. In a theological scandalon that can be understood as an exacerbated case of the scandal necessary to the very conditions of story, we get to see the most sovereign of subjects entering into a world that is not just of his making; subjected to a dense concatenation of causes that go variously by the name of Romans, Jews, Pharisees, Satan, God, and humanity; nailed through the hands (that part of us most closely associated with doing/acting); confined in a tomb/coffin; and acting (or, rather, being acted upon) as a *suffering servant*.[13] And undergirding it all, in a way that does not negate it all, is the most tightly woven safety net of story. For the extreme victim is also (equally extremely) the creator-author who, as far as it is possible in story, crashes through the limiting conditions of story and saves/writes himself.[14] More than this, he is also the hypersurrogate who dies for[15] us, so the microresurrection at the end of this particular story is the promise of real resurrection, and the thought of a place beyond story and the contingent afflictions of story. Though ultimately logically impossible and theologically undesirable, glimpsed here is story's *consummatum est*, its definitive end. In the extreme paradox of passion, the violation/depotentiation of the subject is ended and transcended and, at the same time, frozen and endlessly replayed.

BINDING

In an intriguing formulation, Roemer claims that "story and god have the same purpose: the depotentiation of humankind."[16] Quoting Marie-Louise von Franz, he argues that in story, as in dreams, "death [as limit of constraint] . . . and God's image are *de facto* indistinguishable."[17] The formulation suggests some link between what he calls story and what Kristeva calls the "sacred," as if the sacred were an exacerbation of the conditions of story to the point where the subject becomes excessively borderline and fragile. As story reminds us that human justice is imperfect and that our most carefully executed plans are often counterproductive, so, Roemer argues, it becomes a chastising force that expresses something of what believers and unbelievers alike call acts of God.[18]

This implied equation between the divine and the subjecting counterforce of story resonates with a particularly striking statement that Carl Jung made in an interview in, of all places, *Good Housekeeping*: "To this day, God is the name by which I designate all things which cross my willful path violently and recklessly, all things which upset my subjective views, plans and intentions and change the course of my life for better and worse."[19]

Fabulously, Jung's use of the name of God for the force that radically dismantles self and shelter is flanked by lots of little advertisements for perfecting yourself and your cozy domestic idyll. The interview is surrounded by advertisements for a purse of many facets in gilded, rose-patterned brocade; a ten-day "in the pink" diet plan; Playtex Living Gloves (for keeping your hands "smooth, soft and lovely"), and important advice for the middle American housewife on how to make better-tasting ham.

It hardly needs to be spelled out that deeply disturbing consequences follow from the thought-reflex that uses God as the ultimate name for the "fact or condition of being acted upon or affected by an external agency" ("Passion," OED) or as that which "crosses my willful path violently and recklessly" (Jung). It means that God must be, at some level, the name of the force that "crosses" Jesus and nails the stripped and flagellated body to the cross. As feminist and womanist theologians have pointed out, charges of abuse raise their ugly head in the slightest gap that opens up between the son and father. In fact, their critique may have been kept on the peripheries precisely because it makes explicit a discomfort that has always been felt at the very center of the tradition. It is arguably because of this discomfort that father and son are quickly welded together in a move that finds its consummation in fully-fledged Trinitarian theology but that is already being anticipated in the gospels— particularly John. The fused subjectivity-objectivity in this very particular performance of passion combines the figures of extreme subject and extreme object and nips accusations of perverse, abusive love between the father and his *agapētos* in the bud. Because of the compassionate (apologetic?) subjection of Godself, as victim, to those dispotentiating forces that strike us as his acts, and because of the conflation of the extremes of human experience (passion) in a single figure, the scene has great cathartic (redemptive?) potential. But it is also deeply dangerous—dangerous because it goes out on the most extreme limb of fragility: the subject lacerated unto torture, unto death.[20] It is dangerous too because, according to the inexorable laws of narrative, the conditions of perfect redemption/solution are impossible. For it is impossible for there to be a sole protagonist who is subject and object (god and victim) and plot and author all at once. The scene is constituted at the site of extreme risk and vulnerability: the conditions of narrative writ large. But its attraction lies precisely in the fact that it is such an unsafe salvific scene, in which the dream of the very best that could happen to a subject is bound up with the danger and spectacle of the very worst.[21]

The binding together of dark threat and cathartic promise becomes clearer if we turn back several hundred pages to look at one of the Passion's key precedents: the Akedah ("The Binding"). The sacrifice of Isaac is interesting because the roles of father (in fact two fathers), son and ram/lamb are far more *loosely* bound together than in the Passion. Clear daylight shines between them. Whereas in the Passion extreme subjecthood and extreme objecthood are (at least imperfectly) fused in one body, here they are distributed between bodies. God demands not the holocaust of his own body, nor even Abraham's, but of a body that is, as it were, two bodies down the line. The text stretches the space between the extreme subject and the extreme object, the sovereign and the victim. God speaks to Abraham alone (Gen. 22:1–2); the son's consent is neither sought nor given as it is in the Qur'an (Sura 37:99–113); Abraham actively (cryptically) conceals the truth from Isaac (Gen. 22:8); Isaac (incredibly) says nothing on the altar then slips out of the story altogether (Gen. 22:19). Grammatically *and* narratologically speaking, it is possible for Isaac to be either the subject or the object of the sacrifice of Isaac, or both at once. But narrative details and omissions make it impossible to ignore the sense of objecthood and so the problem of what elsewhere I have called "martyrdom-at-one-remove." The verb *akad*, used nowhere else in the Bible and never applied to any whole burnt offering apart from Isaac, inevitably provokes the question "Why must Isaac be tied up and what does it mean that he is bound?"[22] The conventional commentators' gloss—that the act of binding foregrounds Isaac's willing agency and so subjecthood in the controlling sense—rules out the more striking sense of Isaac as a trussed object of sacrifice.[23] The act of the binding foregrounds the space of agency/passivity that opens up between the different bodies by showing how Isaac must be bound, or tied in, to a plot not of his making—a plot for which the willful upset of his "subjective views, plans and intentions" would be way too mild a descriptive phrase.[24] In contrast to the embarrassed disclaimers in commentary, the Jewish tradition deliberately tangles itself in difficulty by abstracting The Binding / The Akedah as the story's title. Similarly, post-Renaissance Christian art (arguably a mode of commentary whose tongue is loosened by its silence) highlights and multiplies the bindings. Think of the famous depictions by Caravaggio or Rembrandt where Isaac's face is forced down on the altar and his hands are tied behind his back.[25] Precisely because the roles are so spread out, this scene allows us to see what is veiled in the Christian passion. For, unidirectional truisms notwithstanding, it is also (in fact, often) true that the Old Testament reveals what the New Testament veils.

The Akedah is a graphic performance of the consequences of equating that which constrains, determines, binds the subject with God's acts: acts that we instinctively interpret as the external manifestations of God's will, that is, God's desire. Curiously, Jacques Lacan and biblical commentators agree (albeit in slightly different language) that what motivates this story is not need *simplicitas*. God does not *need* Isaac's body or a ram's body to feed any natural appetite.[26] What is at stake is the excess beyond need: God's (inexplicable) will, or God's desire. Jacques Lacan and Gordon Wenham (who are not often paired together) agree that God is looking to Abraham for Abraham to pay him the compliment of an unconditional yes. (I am using Wenham not because he is extraordinary, but precisely because he offers a variant of the traditional theological gloss when he argues that the sacrifice of Isaac is a hyperintensification of the symbolism of the holocaust offering, through which the offerer demonstrates that he is "giving himself entirely to God.")[27] Pushing the logic a little further than Lacan, and certainly Wenham, take it, though only following where they lead, we can add that an unconditional yes can only stress its unconditionality through the most excessive of *demands*—the excess therefore being not an unfortunate accident, but precisely the point. Only a demand that comes from outside the commandments (bound up with ethics and God's solicitous care) can be the marker of the absolute, unconditional yes. Abraham can only become the iconic image of the one who (impossibly?) gives that unconditional yes by consenting to become an unnatural father and an outlaw (or out-Torah). We might note, at least in passing, that an Abraham (let alone an Isaac) who can give God this extreme unconditional yes is the most amazing character in the story—more godlike, in a sense, than god. Those of us who live in the realm of (mere) human beings, as divided and haunted as we are, know that the one who asks for an unconditional yes is always disappointed. Our acts of the most extreme unconditional giving may be designed to temporarily mask the painful fact that our yeses, no matter however loudly they are proclaimed, can only ever be maybes in disguise.[28]

For Lacan, who can be more of a textual literalist and fundamentalist than the biblical commentators, a desiring God who seeks from the outcome of the text/test a confirmation that he does not have at the beginning (cf. Gen. 22:12) is curiously subject to an anthropomorphized anxiety or lack. Another way of putting this is to say that this is a God-in-narrative, or a God who, though he officially has no body (and so no natural appetite), does, strangely, seem to have an eye. In contrast to biblical commentators who deflect attention toward what humans beings see and learn,[29] Lacan talks of a God who wants to see himself held, steadily, unflickeringly, perfectly, in the eye of Abraham, who, God demands,

must focus exclusively on him, without blinking, without even a side-
ways glance at his most beloved son. It is seems more than accidental
that the Akedah is constructed around puns on seeing (ra-ah) and fearing
(yara); that it functions as a crucial part of the optic metaphorical nerve
that runs throughout the book of Genesis; and that it climaxes in God
(or his messenger/angel) praising the not-withholding that allows God
to know/witness Abraham's full fearing.[30] Mount Moriah, the mount of
Seeing/Providing is the place where, just before God counter-provides
the ram, Abraham provides this unconditional yes, so that (the angel of)
God can look at Isaac on the altar and say "now I know that you fear
God" (Gen. 22:12). If the eye is the most voracious organ in any body (cf.
Ecclesiastes 1:8),[31] if it is that part of the body which desires the other
(beyond need) and that looks for the fullest confirmation of my I in the
eye of the other,[32] then it is not illogical to imagine the divine eye as a
gigantic voracious figure of the insatiability of seeing. What God wants
to see is nothing less than Isaac, the only, the beloved, bound on the
altar, with the wood beneath him and the knife above him. And we, it
seems, are also keen to see this. We freeze Isaac on the altar as we freeze
Jesus on the cross. Both are bound and helpless but Isaac, as if picking up
a cue from Mark that portrayals of the Passion do not / cannot develop,
sometimes has his mouth open in a howl or a scream.[33] More frequently
and more overtly a child than the child-corpse in the arms of Mary, Isaac
becomes a figure of what Lacan calls the corps morcelé—the haunting
memory of the nascent infant body. In its insubordination to our control
this helpless child-body anticipates the dying body and chastens (binds?
crisscrosses?) us with a sense of "lines of fragilization" that cut across the
subject, and recall the "vital dehiscence" at the "heart of man."[34]

The Akedah, say Brian Hook and R. R. Reno, is no place for active
agent heroes, for it imposes extreme narrative conditions in which God
can be the only hero.[35] This claim echoes a much earlier and much mis-
understood essay, written at around the same time as his work on the
etymology of passion, in which Auerbach argues that the text and all its
participants are, from the very first verse, already narratologically sacrificed bodies, pared down to an absolutely adjectiveless, all-but-lifeless
state.[36] Auerbach claims that the skeletal narrative and its servile,
"kneaded"[37] participants testify to an absolute and uncompromising truth

to which all rival flesh/life must be offered up. Superficially, this may remind us of the extreme testimonies of martyrs or those fasting saints that we tend to nowadays diagnose as holy anorexics. But the difference is that in Genesis 22 the subjection is purged of any trace of that exultant submission that led Nietzsche to suspect narcissistic motivation in fantasies of extreme self-violation.[38] Because the subjection of Abraham and Isaac is eerily emotionless (we might say passionless—or passionate only in the passive sense of passion), this extreme test creates a curious act of testimony that is very difficult to reduce to projections of pure human desiring, legitimated by a mere projection of God as underwriter of human desire.[39] Because the text goes to such lengths to establish Isaac as the object of Abraham's love (not to mention his very self projected into the future), it outlaws an interpretation that sees this as an extension of Abraham's natural desiring—even less of Isaac's. It thwarts a certain kind of modernist reduction/demystification by pinning us between two alternatives: to believe in God (as the name of that which crosses our paths willfully and painfully) or to believe in extreme self- and love-harming desires. By binding so severely, God creates narrative conditions in which it is all but impossible to eradicate the idea and force of God from the proceedings. The story testifies to the force of God's acts and God's desiring by imposing conditions that are in some fundamental sense binding, even for readers—which is perhaps why we find such strange agreement between biblical commentators like Gordon Wenham and Jacques Lacan.

PERVERSION (CRIMES OF PASSION)

It is hardly surprising that people prefer to treat the Akedah as if it were the theological equivalent of the hapax legomenon, *akad*, from which it takes its name. But far from being an aberration it is, like the Christian passion, a very familiar irregularity in the Judeo-Christian grammar—as intrinsic as the always irregular verb *to be* (or, in this case, to be or not to be). The Akedah is simply the most famous of a series of tableaux in which God seems to be the name for "all things which cross my willful path violently and recklessly." Think of God meeting Moses and trying to kill him, or the wrestling and wounding of Jacob at the Jabbok (Exod. 4:24–26; Gen. 32:22–32). Indeed, so often is life compressed, squeezed and (almost?) suspended in Tanakh that the story could be summarized as a kind of existential minimalism, or a hyperstory. (Though much has been written lately on so-called historical minimalism, perceived by many as the ultimate threat to the very being of Old Testament / Tanakh, less has been written on what could be called OT/Tanakh's own existential minimalism, in which threat to being is the dominant [dominated] trope[40]). The emergent subject-nation, or the eponymous heroes who embody it, is at most an ironically qualified "hero" who is fragile in the extreme. As if to foreground his inconceivable liminality, this "hero" is conceived through an extraordinarily difficult birth process, beset by barren mothers, detours through foreign wombs, murderous siblings, and knife-wielding fathers, and comes out looking like a bare incarnation of the inherent fragility of the promise.[41] Then this precarious subject's possession of the territory of the second promise—Canaan—is opposed by a disproportionate mass of counterforce including God, death, a host of foreigners, and even the land itself, which looks all set to swallow him up (Num. 13:32).[42] The flaccid narrative of the nonentry into Canaan could be cast as a sexual tragicomedy: the male nation's humiliating inability to possess an already possessed non-virgin land, occupied by the foreigners who make him feel so small (and smallness is a characteristic frequently applied to Israel; cf. Numbers 32; Amos 7:3, 5).[43] At the center of Torah is a mountain not so symbolically far from Moriah, and a bond-relation, the tenor of which student essays (like the one which rolled into my office, fortuitously, this afternoon), regularly and happily summarize with quotations such as: "[The Jews] were [God's] servants—they belonged to Him and were his property. Until God Himself released them from that agreement, they were His."[44] This radical disproportion of relation is only exacerbated in the Prophets, which make commentators' gentle assurances that they are *mostly* about *sheltering* (the orphan, the poor, the widow) look like *Good Housekeeping*'s advertisements for ham, washing up gloves, and diet plans, trying (desperately?) to deflect attention away from the Jungian drama in which God is frequently depicted as the smasher of houses and the builder of hedges of thorns and constraining walls (Amos 3:15; 6:1, 9–11; 5:11, 19; Hosea 2:6). As I have argued elsewhere,[45] the central character at the very dehiscent heart of the Prophets seems to be the abject national body, which, as a kind of liquid self on the verge of dissolution, reminds me of nothing so much as Marc Quinn's *Self* (1991)—a self-sculpture made of the artist's own frozen blood, which threatens to decoagulate at the flick of a switch (cf. Isa. 1:16; Ezek 21:7; cf. 2 Sam 14:14). On the grounds that, as Judith Butler says, the body exceeds and disempowers, overruns and disciplines the very idea of subject,[46] the body forms a natural ally with the dispossessing forces of God and story (as we are here defining them). Seizing on this instinctive symbolic alliance, aspects of the Old Testament work out a darker incarnational theology of God as wound/pus/rot in the body as well as overpowerer and restrainer/binder of the body (cf. Hos. 5:12; Jer. 20:17; Hos. 2:6). In OT/Tanakh God emerges as something like the dispossessing force that we try to (wildly) gesture to in the tangled etymology of *passion*—at once overpowering and undermining the subject from inside and outside the skin.

It may well be, then, that Isaac on the altar haunts the imagination not because he is an anomaly, but because he is a hypericon of the very qualified subject that is at the center of the hyperstory of Tanakh. If the conditions of story are such that F. Scott Fitzgerald says "Pull up your chair to the edge of a precipice and I'll tell you a story,"[47] then perhaps the characters of Tanakh are walked along the precipice of normal/natural life. For it is on the cliff-edge of the natural and at the extreme borders of human agency that we encounter the necessity of the supranatural in scenes mortal, dark and stark. How to imagine a God who, desireless, simply underwrites life as normal?[48] (If that were the case, there would be no story.) But how to stop the supernatural from manifesting its difference in the form of the sub- or unnatural? How to prevent it from generating perverse creative scenes in which, for example, the almost-cutting / burning of the son by the father creates a gigantic act of testimony and a sky full of sons as numerous as stars (Gen. 22:17)? If perversion is the good, proper, reasonable, normal, and natural turned the wrong way (*per-versus*; OED), then there is something perverse about the unnatural supernatural of Genesis 22. Not only is it the most contrary perversion of justice and reason conceivable, but its process of conception is also highly dubious. As a sacrificial scene, where a burst of future sons is generated through an almost-cut in Isaac's body, Genesis 22 can be seen as a perverse displacement of birth.

It needs to be said more regularly and more loudly that the Bible is often a long, ironic way from being the spokesman[49] for that which public rhetoric most conscripts it: heteronormativity, family values, and straight(forward) sexual reproduction as the Good Lord allegedly intended. This accidental closeness between *akerah* and *akedah*—"barrenness" and "binding"—reveals what is at stake in Genesis 22, as if by a slip of a letter or the tongue.[50] *Akedah* is needed because of *akerah*. The pun nicely makes the point, but is not necessary to it. The proof text is rather the barren body of Sarah, and all those other remarkably infertile mothers incredulously unable to contribute to Genesis and keep the story going. Sacrifice is "birth done better" when birth cannot happen; binding is necessary because the body of the mother does not work.[51] Perhaps distinctions between comfortably (naturally?) sexual Judaism and uncomfortably (unnaturally?) asexual Christianity are not as clear-cut as we assume, for, in the narrative sequence in which post-menopausal Sarah is *paqad*-ed ("visited") by God and conceives with or without the help of Abraham (Gen. 21:1),[52] followed by a scene in which the life of more sons is produced through the (almost) sacrifice of the son by the father, we are already well along the symbolic *via dolorosa* to the virgin birth and the crucifixion (productive death as the site of deflected [re]birth).[53] This is not just a queer birthing scene in which, as in a scene from Shakespearean drama, the woman's part is played by a man (reminding us, perhaps, of that curious male C-section in Eden, or the gush of eucharistic blood and baptismal water from the body of Jesus that replace the merely natural, fleshy, womb-birth [Gen. 2:21–23; John 19:34, cf. 3:4–7]).[54] It is also a demonstration of the general symbolic logic by which the supernatural manifests itself as surrogate for, and bizarre (miraculous) extension/supervention of, the natural, and thus an extreme performance of the general surrogacy process through which cultures, civilizations, artifacts and stories change the givens of their worlds. Our first thought is that they do this because those givens are too restrictive, but it might also be because they are not restrictive enough.

Looking at the biblical hyperstory, it is hard to avoid the brutal disproportion between the extremes of all-powerful subjecthood and all-powerless objecthood. This means that, were we mad enough to attempt to sexualize the story of the Hebrew Bible, then we would have to use—in some sense as defining norm—those alphabetical ciphers *s* and *m*. The use of the crucifixion and the aesthetics of Catholicism as inspiration for s/m practices may be old news (at least in some quarters),[55] but arguably the Torah and the Prophets could provide similar inspiration, if the image of Isaac on the altar and the metaphorical assault of being bound, overwhelmed, constrained by walls and thorns or having the possessive "The Lord's" tattooed on one's hand (e.g. Hosea 2; Isa. 44:5) had made it into such a central position in the iconicity and ritual of the West. Nor does this perversion pass without uncomfortable, if covert, recognition. When Abraham Heschel asks, "Is the covenant a tether, chain, or living intercourse?"[56] something seems intimated, as well as fended off, by the very existence of that rhetorical question, not to mention the particular vocabulary in which it finds expression. What strikes me as I write this is how little one has to nudge the text-affirming descriptions of commentaries before they cross that little line separating the well-worn truism from the outrage. (Does not the God who says "You are my property and I will never release you?" sound just a bit like Wanda; and does not the formulation "You are the pot and I am the potter" [Jer. 18:1–11; Jer. 19] convey dimensions that the Christian song with the lyrics "Break me, melt me, mould me, fill me" all too blatantly, if unselfconsciously, picks up?).[57]

Modernity runs up against its limits at the point where, attempting to translate the Bible into human-centered, so-called secular idioms, we read the story of Tanakh as story of reverse creation, in which man makes God in the image of his desiring. One of the payoffs of using sexual idioms to translate the story of the Hebrew Bible is that it throws the modern project back on itself by producing a story that, in its very unmodern queerness, keeps something of the persistent, awkward remainder of the religious that modern translations are trying to transfigure or translate. If we aren't *careful,* the very uncareful story of Tanakh and the Passion will force us toward a deeply uncomfortable, post-Freudian place—the kind of place charted by Georges Bataille, Gilles Deleuze, Leo Bersani, Karmen MacKendrick, Lynda Hart, and Anita Phillips—where *eros* and *thanatos* no longer agree to be compliantly contradictory, as they are in Freud.[58] Willingly or unwillingly, it will tug us to a place where masochism (with unexpected assertiveness) moves out of its role as outsider and pariah and foists itself on us as of the determining conditions of sexuality and, in some (related) sense, biblical theologies and biblical texts. How not to read the Akedah as a demand for the unconditional yes and the amazing (temporary?) giving of the kind of yes that is "not an assent to this or that, but an assent to everything,"[59] even, especially, when that everything is outside reason, law, safety? How not to note that extreme pitch of not-withholding (Gen. 22:12) that is emphatically not the same as giving—for giving keeps the giver central and powerful, not least because it implies property, ownership, and the means and resources to place another in debt. How not to notice the unlimited submission here of two bodies/ subjects, one of whom submits to the demand for everything/anything (without caveat or limit, and without any promise in advance of the safety net or word of ram or angel), and the other of which/whom is offered, in silence.[60] Even as his body is laid out as the testifying sign of unconditionality, it is possible both that Isaac has said his unconditional yes (in which case he becomes Abraham's double) or that that yes may have been said for him, without consulting him (in which case he becomes something else).

The fact that the Akedah is not overtly sexual is granted. This is a *translation*, but one that the scene, like the crucifixion, seems, in a sense, to be begging. For this is a story about the not-withholding not of, say, a piece of land, or a precious crop, but of that which matters most to us, and is closest to us: bodies. Bodies never fail to get our attention, and whenever bodies are given (up), or taken ("not withheld"), eroticism lurks. While there may be some dubious aspects to Elaine Scarry's biblical criticism and theology, she is onto something crucial in the pervasive theme of God the Alterer who makes his invisible presence felt through the radical giving, taking and altering of a particular group of bodies.[61] The work of God the Alterer finds its consummation in an altar scene combining violent death with massive (miraculous) rebirth. Scarry's strangely desexualized and degendered stories of the altered body suggest that the Old Testament might have things to contribute to a colloquium like this, besides its usual defense mechanisms, or favorite texts. It can do more than claim the alibi of only taking a pragmatic (desexualized) view of sexuality, along the lines of "he came, he saw, he entered, she conceived, and the family was sustained as a productive and generative unit," or, alternatively proffer choice texts such as Ruth's threshing floor or the Song of Songs—much loved precisely because they offer the most tantalizing possibilities of conforming to modern sex as mutuality and pleasure.

It is no surprise that those who looked for a sexualized biblical story that they could approve of assembled in the soon overcrowded Song of Songs. As it came out of theological allegorization, blushing, the Song first offered a plausible site for mutual sex between two subjects (in the best, autonomous sense of the word).[62] It then blossomed into a fertile garden for what, more than a little tongue-in-cheek, I am calling Jouissance Studies. Though there are multiple dimensions of the new branch of Jouissance (Song of Songs) Studies, the aspect that interests me here is the idea of deprivation/procrastination/pain—in moderation, and for good reason, that is, for a purpose. The Song became an accomplished practitioner of a principle established by an unlikely cohort including Bataille, Žižek, Barthes, Lacan, Gregory of Nyssa, and Wallace Stevens, that not to have is the beginning of desire.[63] Aspects of this sexual story had something in common with literary biblical studies, which tended to cast the Bible as an excellent literary performer. The theory of productive suspension of desire was in fact very close to conventional narrative theory going back to Aristotle, insofar as it cast suspension/complication/deferral as a *useful pain, needed by the plot*. While having something just a bit perverse about it, this theory still managed to fall into what MacKendrick describes as "the everyday (nonecstatic) economy of investment" whereby "expenditure is loss (and desire is lack, founded upon the need to fill what is empty, replace what is lost)."[64] The suspension of teleology is still a telos. Lack/withdrawal/pain is necessary, because once it is gone, the story or the desire will be over.

This approach did considerable work in turning the Bible into something capable of pleasuring the reading subject—rather like a sophisticated lover who knows that, in readerly and sexual terms, we all need our suspensions and complications. It took the Bible to bed in a space where we mercifully did not have to think about that dominant (and dominated) part of the love story of Israel that involves "writhing on a too short bed, with too short covers" (Isa. 28:19). But having started out as an antithetical space to the Prophets,[65] even the Song began to edge closer to the Prophets as biblical studies began, in its own way, to stumble over a sense of the masochistic as disturbingly intrinsic to sexuality and biblical texts. The uncomfortable turn came with more searching analysis of the watchmen scene in 5:6–7, which in turn led to rotation of the axiom just very slightly, so that not-having as the beginning of desire shifted into the far less countenanceable desire not to have, or to be hurt or deprived. For Linafelt, the watchmen are tropes intimating the element of "vulnerability, violation, assault" that characterizes all sexual relationships, drawing us towards a Bataille-like understanding of passion in which the "whole business of eroticism is to destroy the self-contained character of the participants" as they are in their "normal lives."[66] For Burrus and Moore the watchmen moment is the point where the Song equivocally qualifies its once unequivocal reception as a heterosexual consensual utopia and takes sex and theology into unsafe realms.[67]

Despite having led myself here, by various routes, I am still uncomfortable now that I have gotten here—though discomfort can produce interesting results. This piece of writing has talked itself into an interesting squeeze, somewhere between the cultural taboo about s/m, the last bastion of perversion, and the exacerbated taboo of imposing that on, of all things, the Bible. This discomfort must have to do with something more than divine violence, because we have been talking about that for years.[68] In fact, I wonder whether the scandal here is not so much *s* but *m*? Could it be that talking about God as violent superagent would be in some sense more congenial than exploring what is at stake in the converse position of the abject object? What is at stake in the scandal of this "m"? "M" is seen as particularly scandalous now precisely because it is perceived as willingly laying down the modern gift of autonomy, self-determination and pure subjecthood. It has the ability to make even those who "queery" biblical heteronormativity uncomfortable because, beyond resisting procreation in the name of pleasure, it is seen as mistaking pain as pleasure, and so giving up the sexual right to pleasure which is now a basic tenet of hard-won human rights. And the application of masochism to the Bible seems to only amplify masochism's perverse ability to be equally offensive to right and left. Analogies between masochism and the biblical subject foreground the bound or kneeling vassal-subject who somehow conveniently disappears in seamless elisions of biblical theocracy into democracy and human rights.[69] Despite all our smoothing efforts, cracks between modernity and biblical religions gape at the point where, say, biblical commentators accuse feminist protestors of being too much in love with autonomy to enter the biblical worldview that positions us at the feet of God, but then, at the same time, absolutely resist the submissive addressee position and instinctively ally themselves with the hypersubject: God.[70] This is more than an oversight. The advocated position—so easily sustainable as theological truism—becomes intolerable in practice, even in mere reading practice. Good, self-respecting scholar-subjects cannot identify with a position that is not a straight(forward) subject position at all, and is scandalously most like an m.

It is relatively easy—which is not to say unimportant—to engage with abusive or sacrificial texts in tones of unequivocal accusation. Feminists and traditional scholars find unexpected common ground in rejecting the position of Gomer in the book of Hosea, though they do it differently (one explicitly and one implicitly). The same could be said of Isaac.[71] It is relatively easy to say that fathers emphatically should not offer up the bodies of their sons to God, or that the book of Hosea falls not on radical feminist claims, but values as traditional and widespread as the modern heteronormative love story of caring intersubjectivity, or basic suffragette principles such as a husband should not imprison his wife to enforce conjugal rights. Conversely, it is possible to talk about the disempowered human addressees of the biblical text in exhortatory and celebratory terms as long as one sticks to the language of theology or ethics. Wenham can metaphorically and theologically underwrite Genesis 22's lesson that we must that "offer ourselves as a whole holocaust" without batting an eyelid. Similarly, recent (and important) work in biblical ethics can use Levinasian language about nonsovereign subjects "hollowed out" and ontologically preceded by the other. The master-servant narrative is somehow acceptable when it does not go any lower than the face, but becomes more scandalous as soon as we extend the metaphor beneath the neck. The sexual translation is important precisely because it gets under the skin, which is a very biblical thing to do. S/m is particularly useful because it gets at a biblical taboo through modernity's last bastion taboo. It gets at the kind of radical submission that one feels is impossible, outrageous, but that continues to be something that people stubbornly (theologically and sexually) want and accept.

TRANSFIGURING

Joining what is hardly a throng of voices,[72] I want to ask how we might begin to negotiate the fraught and painful gulf between feminist critiques and something other than straight critique—a question that becomes more pressing and also more fraught when it hovers around foundational biblical tropes and stories, rather than remaining as (yet another) perversion of the (peripheral, whimsical) Song of Songs. Might it be possible to explore the allure of restraint and qualified and bound power without the safety rail of the unequivocal pejorative and the self-arming caveat, There but for the grace of God/modernity goes my very solid and healthy I? On this issue I feel torn. Ten years in, I have become weary of simply crying out "abuse" through a loud megaphone, and I yet I feel that in a discipline where feminist critiques of abuse still remain off the general radar, and where these texts continue to have catastrophic effects on real human bodies, anything other than repetition might just have to have the respect and decency to wait. Clearly, any kind of attempt would have to go very carefully so that it did not emerge as a nonreflective *celebration* of the shattering effects of danger, or a translation into the hyperfreedom of the exotic zone of risk. If, from a different place, Frank Browning can advocate the pursuit of the sacred as a "journey separate from the path to equity, democracy and justice" and laud a "quality of knowing unavailable to the Rousseauistic mind of social contracts,"[73] the situation is more complicated for those who are employed to be responsible for public versions of a very potent version of the sacred and who spend considerable energy trying to thwart the fundamentalist dangers of cerebral submission and the unconditional yes. But yet it may be possible within what Anita Phillips maps out as a "strong self-confident, humorous, flexible feminism" that "can incorporate self-contradiction"[74] to explore subject positions that are reducible neither to pure autonomous subject or subject as vassal state. And it might be important to explore how, for better and for worse, the Bible is in some respects radically other to the modern project of the care and growth of the self. The promise/threat of the Bible as chastening, afflicting hyperstory might just lie in the way it lashes out against the belief, shared (in different ways) by believers and unbelievers, that the Judeo-Christian God is (but) the besotted lover of my I, the underwriter of my projects in this world and my eternal perpetuator in the next. It might pose some kind of alternative to the crusading gung-ho Christian and Jewish subjects all too visible on the contemporary stage. It might potentially upset the rather simplistic secular assumption that the biblical God is a straight(forward) narcissistic projection of my straight(forward) desiring. At best (and worst), these images intimate some kind of release from "my" salvation/redemption. It might provide an antidote to what often looks like contemporary religion's loss of the element of losing, taking away.

On this score, biblical studies and theology might have something to learn from what Anita Philips and Karmen MacKendrick tell us about what is meant by, and felt in, "masochism," beyond the cultural clichés in which masochism functions as an "emotional and sexual wastebasket"[75] and outside the pathology implied by a man's name reduced to lowercase. To (crudely, if not brutally) summarize, they sketch masochism as resistance to the sturdy subjective center; a mode of acting out, in an insistent and exaggerated way, the basic conditions of cultural subjectivity (in which we never feel like the pure agents we are meant to be); and an act that leans into the destructiveness of limits rather than shouldering the contemporary task of breaking, transgressing and extending them.[76] (One welcome service that such models might perform for us is to get us out of a certain wearisome postmodern trope of the erring, subverting, trespassing, actively deconstructing hypersubject, who vaults borders as heroically as King David and claims the shadow-spaces with the confidence of Victorian colonialists, claiming the dark spaces of the earth.)[77] In language that might recall biblical and theological tropes of the force of God and passion working through us, inside and outside the skin, Phillips and MacKendrick describe masochism as the performance of the vulnerability of the body in its susceptibility to bleeding/wounding/bruising—an act that proves particularly scandalous in times marked by the reinvestment of mass devotion in the body and the body's health.[78] They describe bondage as an extreme performance of living

through attachment (as if by way of a violent demonstration of the un-
bearability of Levinasian ethics), and talk of making overt the frailty and
receptivity of the (qualified) subject. For these are not lone pleasures but
acts, by definition, for more than one, which place an exaggerated emphasis on the other's strength. In their descriptions of that which thrives
on being unacceptable, outside or beneath the caring intersubjectivity of
good sex (and good theology), they may help to explain why the more
conflicted sites of crucifixion and Akedah may yet continue to exert a
deeper pull on the imagination than better theologies of, say, God as a
friend.[79]

By suggesting that what is going on in sadomasochistic performances
is not a simple (straight) performance and consolidation of (and submission to) extreme inequity and injustice, such descriptions may also help
us to understand what Judaism and Christianity really *do* with their, always in some sense "Old"[80] Testament. For no one, in truth, has ever
been crazy enough to insist on *sola scriptura*. Discomfort with figures of
extreme discomfort has meant that reception has always been marked by
the desire to transfigure, transform, rewrite, begin again.[81] What s/m
practitioners[82] do, as compared to what we think they do, is helpful for
thinking about what Jews actually do with Torah, in acts of reading and
observance a long way from the simple victimhood and vassal-subject-
hood that first-time readers of OT/Tanakh without any guidelines from
religious tradition often take to be the only position available to God's
love object.[83] In a way that ties into the preceding discussion of story and
hyperstory, MacKendrick and Phillips describe how s/m exacerbates and
amplifies the constrictive conditions of living, but relativizes this confinement by confining it in the zone of performance, story, game. And
because the positions of pure (lone) agent and pure (lone) object are as
impossible to perform in the act of sex as in the act of story, so *s* is never
purely *s* and *m* never purely *m*. In practice, s/m becomes an ambivalent
and complex site where roles are often switched; where, contra popular
perception, there is often less enthusiasm for being a top than a bottom;
and where the bottom is active in engaging his/her top and laying out
the contractual arrangements. S/m acts can be, simultaneously, an exaggeration of law and order and an extended joke on law and order, and

submission is always conditional submission, in the knowledge that s/he will always be untied at the end.

In all its complexity, this is in some sense analogous to the Jewish transformation/transfiguration of the extreme living conditions of the Hebrew Bible into something more livable—in moves that, in my opinion, are nothing short of brilliant. Without denying or erasing the sense of extreme encounter with one's limits, Judaism relocates this encounter in the realm of mutual contract, story and (though this can be overemphasized) joke and play. The meanings of the covenant at the heart of Torah are expanded to include a reciprocal, contractual, *mutually conditional* "I choose you and you choose me: You will be my God and I will be your people; you will be the master, and I will be the slave."[84] Beneath the whole hyperstory is stretched the safety net of resurrection (Sheol, the place of shadows, being too thin a safety net to catch us when we emerge from the extreme exposure of Torah's hyperstory). Thus we can enter into scenes of abjection and bondage knowing that we will be untied at the end. More profoundly, stretched out beneath everything that happens in Torah is the larger idea of Torah as the ultimate safe word, to which, crucially, God the qualified Master is also subject. The multiplicity of Torah means that God can be restrained/criticized in the excesses of his desire and that, in midrashic responses to the Akedah for example, Torah can be used to speak words that discipline and bind God and allow him too to feel the necessary limits of living in intersubjective space. Fascinatingly, Midrash interprets the moment where the hand of the angel restrains the hand of the father as an image of God himself bound in a necessary limitation of his desire.[85]

Midrash insists that God must submit to Torah: Torah both in the sense of text/story (and the conditions of text/story that make it impossible for anyone, even God, to be a pure agent) and Torah as the boundary of ethics/commandments which insist that even God must submit to the bar.[86] Torah does not replace the idea of God understood in the sense of the last (lone) word of authority. On the contrary, it is a safe word, paradoxically, because it is binding but also the enabling site for what could be called, in the true sense of the word, "masochistic" hermeneutics: the kind of question-asking that actively seeks out acute difficulty, restriction, the double bind of an impossible contradiction, encounters with the limits of one's thinking and the exposure of one's most precious concepts to death.[87] (Adapting Karmen MacKendrick's words from a different context, one could say that, in its chosen relation to difficult texts, Judaism chooses not anarchy/rebellion but the "fascinating spectacle of self-immolating form.")[88] As a realm for more-than-one's, Torah becomes a zone where words, verses, and people switch roles between slave and master and where even, in the most extended joke on law and order, God himself sometimes plays slave/student/bottom to Israel's / the Rabbis' / Torah's / the Law's top. In a movement that is becoming possible in the Hebrew Bible, but that becomes more marked and frequent in Midrash, God himself becomes a rather qualified hero—entrapped in the pathos of human existence, subject to "grief, frailty, presentiments of mortality"[89] and even failure as he is accused of not properly fulfilling the obligations of the contractual top. Thus, even as the traditional Jew binds the leather straps of tefillin around his body as a sign of submission to intractable commandments for which (so tradition has it) there is one for every limb/bone/muscle of the body, he becomes, at the same time, in the performative and reperformative zone of Torah, a highly active subject and a co-performer/participant with God.

This Jewish transformation of the Old finds its Christian analogue in the Passion, which also makes something more ambivalent, and livable, from OT/Tanakh's radical disproportion of power. Whereas Judaism works out its response by reworking the whole of Torah and, crucially, the complex conditions of binding-unbinding that define our (and God's) relations to Torah, the New Testament condenses its response in one (massively overdetermined) scene and one (massively overdetermined) body. As one s/m practitioner intimates when he describes Jesus as the one who "*set[s] himself up* to be on the receiving end of some very serious suffering,"[90] the power of the scene lies in the conflation of absolute, transcendent strength (godliness), and abject objecthood, rolled together in the one body, and the paradoxical sense of being the author and initiator of a story in which one's control is (exponentially) qualified and bound. Jesus becomes the focus of riveted cultural attention precisely because he is such an unfocused subject/object of a passion that is his, but also very much not (just or even) his. It is in this overwhelming and undermining of the limits of "him" that his passion resonates with the chaos of human passion in more than an accidental etymological sense. And, at the end of and through it all, his resurrection entails "an *exceptionally* forceful enhancement of the always unexpected resistant power of the body."[91]

❧ Praying Is Joying: Musings on Love in Evagrius Ponticus

VIRGINIA BURRUS

"Happy the spirit [*nous*] which attains to total insensibility at prayer," exults Evagrius of Pontus in his *Chapters on Prayer* (120).[1] The *Chapters*, like so many ancient texts, comes wrapped in the envelope of a personal letter (though we no longer know the name of Evagrius's addressee). A response to another letter, it begins suspensefully *in medias res*—in the midst of an epistolary exchange between friends and also in the midst of a charged moment for Evagrius himself. "It was so characteristic of you to get a letter to me just at a time when I was aflame with the hot urgings of my own impure passions and my spirit was afflicted with all kinds of vile thoughts," he exclaims with apparent abandon. A timely letter from a cherished friend has thus cut across the barriers of his self-enclosed misery, opening him to new possibilities, hailing another self. That friend, like Jacob, knows how to work hard in pursuit of "his heart's desire." His "command" has rekindled the flame of Evagrius's own desire. Left to himself, he had found nothing to say about prayer: "I have worked the night through and caught nothing."[2] But now, at his friend's renewed urging, he has cast his net again "and come up with a whole netful of fish." They are, he acknowledges, small in size but nonetheless great in number (153, to be precise),[3] and he sends them, "in the basket of charity [*agapē*]," to his friend. "So then, this is my way of carrying out your orders to me."

Evagrius's adoption of the role of a joyfully submissive lover is not an unusual rhetorical stance within late antique literature, and especially within the literary correspondences of ascetic men, who frequently represent themselves both as filled with erotic longing for their absent addressees and as able to write only under command. It is also not, however, incidental to the chapters that follow—a collection of aphoristic sayings on prayer. Indeed, the introductory letter goes on to perform a brief, but nearly ecstatic, numero-theological meditation that conveys Evagrius's newfound joy and fecundity of spirit, the marks of a truly prayerful monk. ("Prayer is a continual intercourse of the spirit with God [3], he notes later; it is also "the fruit of joy and thanksgiving" [15].) In addition, and still more significantly, the letter itself turns out to be a prayer, as well as a request for prayer.[4] Evagrius concludes his address to his friend: "Since you have the gift of preserving the fruit of kindness and charity for your true brothers, pray for a sick man that he may recover his health, pick up his mat and henceforth walk about freely by the grace of Christ. Amen." Freedom is, then, to be discovered in the exchange of "charitable" prayers, in the transfiguring acts of mutual interpellation invoked in a spirit of love. Of course, we hear only one half of this particular exchange. But is that not always the case with prayer?

This is why desire is not love. —JEAN-LUC NANCY, "Shattered Love"

Evagrius, as we have seen, assumes a distinction between "impure passions" and the state of spiritual love (*agapē,* but also *erōs*) that is both the precondition and the goal of prayer—that is, indeed, virtually identical with prayer. He is famous for his advocacy of passionlessness (*apatheia*) as the necessary first stage on the ascent toward prayerful contemplation.[5] "The state of the spirit can be aptly described as a habitual state of *apatheia*. It snatches to the heights of intelligible reality the spirit which loves wisdom and which is truly spiritualized by the most intense love [*erōs*]" (52). The notion of an *apathetic eros* is not of course unprecedented within ancient thought (whether non-Christian or Christian); nonetheless, the ambitious stretch of the paradoxical concept invites interpretative engagement, now as then.

For Evagrius, passion is, most generally, that which produces psychic disturbance and distraction, scattering creative energies and dissipating joy. In another work, he conveniently catalogues the "evil thoughts [*logismoi*]" that can, in the unguarded soul, stir up passions—gluttony, impurity, avarice, sadness, anger, *akēdia*, vainglory, and pride (*Praktikos* 6). Such "thoughts" cannot be banished. They can, however, be ignored, and it is the ability to ignore the "thoughts" that characterizes the soul that has attained *apatheia*. Anger—"the most fierce passion" (*Praktikos* 11)—receives perhaps the most airtime in the *Chapters on Prayer*. Yet it is "impurity"—the temptation of sexual unchastity—that here draws our attention. This is where Evagrius himself initially points us, in his opening invocation of his own "impure passions," performatively eclipsed by the renewal of his desire for prayer and his capacity for "charity." Furthermore, we shall see that "impurity"—though no more primal than gluttony or avarice, no more fierce than anger, no more debilitating than sadness or the despairing boredom of *akēdia,* no more insidious than vainglory or pride—nonetheless conveys a distinctive threat to prayer, from Evagrius's perspective. (This is a claim I am willing to make despite the well-taken warnings of Peter Brown that it is only with Augustine that sexuality per se is privileged within Christian discourse as a symptom of fallenness or imperfection in spiritual life.)[6]

Two passages in the *Chapters on Prayer* particularly interest me. The first emphasizes the tricksterish nature of "the demon of unchastity [*porneia*]," which can appear "even when you seem to be with God." Evagrius continues: "He is a cheat and most envious. He wishes to be swifter than the movement of your thought, more piercing than the watchfulness of your spirit. He would have you believe that your spirit is separated from God when in fact it attends him with reverence and fear" (90). What is intriguing about this passage is the suggestion that the demon of unchastity is not easily distinguishable from the love of God. Indeed, this sly rogue slips into the monk's prayer closet even when the monk is experiencing holy intercourse with God, far from the temptations of anger, sadness, boredom, or the like, one imagines. The demon outpaces thought itself and thus penetrates the ascetic's defenses—or perhaps it merely seems to do so (here as elsewhere, Evagrius's language is notably cryptic) and thus it is the *apparent* swiftness of the dart of desire that lures the monk falsely. Is divine penetration not, after all, what the watchful spirit awaits? The instability produced by the demonic mimicry of spiritual intercourse not only opens the praying monk to an unholy violation but also introduces confusion regarding the "real thing," so that divine presence itself is mistaken as distraction—a mere representation, an "impure thought." If the demon of impurity can cause the soul "to speak and hear words almost as if the reality were actually present to be seen" (*Praktikos* 8), perhaps it can also mime—and thus undermine via mimicry—the unmediated presence of God.

The chapter that follows this one—and that seemingly refers to the same demon—is less convoluted but no less instructive. Evagrius writes: "If you have a real interest in prayer then be prepared to withstand the assaults of the demon and endure with constancy the lashes he lays on. He shall attack you like a wild beast and buffet your entire body" (91). Here the aspect of erotic submission inherent to prayer is intensely foregrounded. One does not fight fire with fire when faced with demonic attacks. (And one who prays hard enough will inevitably be faced with such attacks.) One can only take it, and even take it to extremes, surrendering to an abysmal passivity. In the endurance of these strangely physical lashings and buffetings of the "entire body," the monk demonstrates his capacity for prayer; passivity, at its extremes, is also a queer kind of activity, enacting the power of resistance.[7] This is not, in other words, a mere ignoring of distraction or a vain attempt to repress; it is the embrace of a rigorous training regime. "Train yourself like a skilled athlete," reads Evagrius's next chapter (93). "The man who endures painful things will some day also find consoling ones," he continues (94). As the call to masochism overtakes the representation of *porneia*'s insidious ability to mimic divine love, that mimicry is itself mastered by the text. True submission finally renders the distinction between demonic assault and divine command virtually irrelevant, for to submit truly is to submit to God, no matter who is playing the top. To pray is to submit; to submit is to love. Praying is loving—an intense joying. "When you give yourself to prayer rise above every other joy—then you will find true prayer": thus, Evagrius's final chapter (153).

Is the sublime joying that is also a praying not then a passion, when all is said and done? If it is, it is a transfigured passion. To shift to more contemporary parlance: it is no longer "desire." "Love," unlike "desire," is neither a condition of lack nor an attempt to possess either an object or the subject. Rather, suggests Jean-Luc Nancy in his essay "Shattered Love," it is the cut across subjectivity that "breaks" the heart—that constitutes the "heart" as such in its very breaking—and thus exposes it to joy. Evagrius might almost have detected in Nancy's words the marks of a man of prayer: "Joy is the trembling of a deliverance beyond all freedom: it is to be cut across, undone, it is to be joyed as much as to joy. . . . For joy is not appeasement, but a serenity without rest. To joy is not to be satisfied—it is to be filled, overflowed."[8]

A proper name . . . does not behave like a sign —JEAN-LUC NANCY, "Of Divine Places"

Even those only passingly familiar with Evagrius will be aware not only of his promotion of *apatheia* but also of his sternly aniconic theology, which pervades his understanding of the practice of "true" prayer as contemplation.[9] "When you are praying do not fancy the Divinity like some image formed within yourself," he advises. "Avoid also allowing your spirit to be impressed with the seal of some particular shape, but rather, free from all matter, draw near the immaterial Being and you will attain to understanding" (66). Concepts, words, images—these are, from Evagrius's perspective, not merely limited (as interpreters of apophatic theology frequently frame the problem), but demonic distractions, impure penetrations: "Beware of the traps your adversaries lay for you. For suddenly it may happen when you are praying purely, free from all disturbance, that some unusual and strange form appears so as to lead you into the presumptuous thought that God is actually situated there as in a place" (67). "Prayer is a rejection of concepts [*noēmata*]," he notes succinctly (70). The problem of memory looms large for Evagrius, and indeed the seduction of thoughts (*logismoi, noēmata*) and images (*eidōla, eikona*) during prayer is largely a seduction of memory, which tugs the monk out of the present moment and thus out of the divine presence: "The memory has a powerful proclivity for causing detriment to the spirit at the time of prayer" (44). On a more positive note: "Happy is the spirit that attains to perfect formlessness at the time of prayer" (117); "happy is the spirit that becomes immaterial and propertyless at the time of prayer" (119). Prayer is thus approached through a kind of ascetic strip tease that leaves the spirit nakedly exposed to the pure presence of God.

"What greater thing is there," Evagrius queries rhetorically, "than to converse intimately with God and to be preoccupied with his company?" (34). But what kind of "conversation" is imagined between a naked spirit, stripped of all impeding veils of signifying practice, and an eternal God who by definition transcends language and all other images and is thus equally naked? The wordless conversation of lovers, perhaps—welling pools of silence watered by tears of supplication (78), lightly rippled by groans (42), vibrating with songs of praise (83, 85). Interestingly, however, Evagrius has surprisingly little to say about silence in his *Chapters on Prayer*. (Silence is, after all, difficult to capture in words.) On the other hand, he does offer advice about how to address Divinity properly: "If you wish to pray then it is God whom you need. He it is who gives prayer to the man who prays. On that account call upon him saying: 'Hallowed be thy Name, thy Kingdom come'"—a form of address for which Evagrius offers an explicitly trinitarian interpretation (58).

It is frequently unclear how we are to harmonize the uncompromising insistence on a particular trinitarian formula of divine naming (fetishized in creedal form and policed by the apparatus of "orthodoxy") with the strongly apophatic tendencies of the theoretically sophisticated Greek theologians of the late fourth century—most notably the Cappadocians, with whose intellectual circle Evagrius overlapped. Yet these tensely leveraged assertions arise out of the same matrix of theological thought and thus cannot be dissolved into sheer contradiction;[10] nor, I think, are they simply complementary (as if theology were here merely seeking a golden mean between apophatic and kataphatic strategies). In the case of Evagrius the tension is particularly acute, given his strong (even, ironically, "heretical") rejection of *all* images of God. Yet the *Chapters on Prayer* suggests an answer to the dilemma, namely, that trinitarian naming—the matter of divine address—involves a relational, rather than a metaphoric, linguistic practice. ("Oh my God!" is, after all, the ecstatic language of lovers as well as of those who pray—and, in the former if not also the latter case, few are tempted to interpret it as strictly referential.) What is at stake is precisely *not* producing a visual, verbal, or conceptual image or representation of God—how deadeningly unexciting.

What is at stake is something altogether different and far more thrilling, a "calling upon" God that is also an invoking of the very possibility of divine "presence." This calling inaugurates a theological language as pure as the prayer advocated by Evagrius.[11] Indeed, for Evagrius, prayer and theology are virtually identical (60).[12]

The name of God uttered in prayer is, in other words, a "proper" name. And, as Nancy points out, a proper name is not "part of language . . . in the way a common noun is." He muses, "Perhaps its nature is that of a *Wink,* of a gesture that invites or calls. On that score, the lack of proper names has nothing whatever to do with the metaphysical surfeit of the thing over the sign, of the real over language. The lack of a proper name is a lack of a *Wink,* and not of signifying capacity. . . . Thus all names could be given to the gods, so that if there is a lack of sacred names, it is not because certain names are lacking. There is a lack of naming, of appellatives, of address."[13] Nancy's essay "Of Divine Places"—consisting of fifty-one "chapters" as gnomic and ambiguously jointed as Evagrius's own *Chapters on Prayer*—pronounces the lack of "divine names" (reflected in the "madness" of philosophical discourse since Nietzsche) and thus the impossibility of prayer in our own historical moment. Nancy's message is not, however, despairing any more than it is triumphalist. (It is not, in other words, apocalyptic.) His essay unfolds to offer, in the place of divine names, the promise of "divine places." "This is why we shall not call this presence 'god,' we shall not even say it is divine: we shall not say it—we shall leave it to set out the places of its reserve and its generosity. . . . These places, spread out everywhere, yield up and orient new spaces: they are no longer temples, but rather the opening up and the spacing out of the temples themselves, a dislocation with no reserve henceforth, with no more sacred enclosures."[14] Here, as in the essay "Shattered Love," Nancy remaps (divine) transcendence as a cutting across, an opening up, or a breaking into all "sacred enclosures"—above all, the enclosure of the perversely sacralized (linguistic) "subject." "But this transcendence is not the one that passes into—and through—an exteriority or an alterity in order to reflect itself in it and to reconstitute in it the interior and the identical (God, the certainty of the *cogito,* the evidence of a property). It does not pass through the outside, because it comes from it."[15]

Perhaps Nancy has after all recovered a language of summoning, a language that invites "the opening up and the spacing out of the temples themselves"—effecting a "dis-location" that, in Evagrian terms, refuses "the presumptuous thought that God is actually situated there as in a place" (67) and, in so doing, discovers a "place of prayer" (71, 102, 152).[16] If Evagrius anticipates Nancy's suspicion of the madness (the demonic character) of linguistic idolatry, he also anticipates his hope in the invocation that opens divine places—that exposes us nakedly to the advent of love. (At this point, Nancy's two essays begin to speak to each other, as well as to Evagrius, as I imagine it.) "Love does not stop, as long as love lasts, coming from the outside."[17] Yet for Evagrius, the place of prayer is also "the perfect place of God" (57). For Nancy, the "divine places" are "without gods, with no god."[18] Has Nancy (unlike Evagrius) not mandated the end of theology, not least by refusing the temptation of a "negative theology"?[19] The answer to this question cannot be simple. Yet an "atheology" that pivots on the withdrawal or death of god and the loss of divine names is, arguably, still a form of theology, in so far as it remembers precisely what it has lost. In Nancy's "absenting divine we hear the whisper of the silent word. . . . A silent word is a word still, a specific absence," notes Karmen MacKendrick; it is also a "forgetful remembering," she suggests, that brings us to the borderline where time intersects with eternity, "the instant of rupture with duration."[20] That brings us, in other words, to the "place of prayer." And, as Evagrius puts it, "If you truly pray, you are a theologian" (60).

HISTORICAL-THEOLOGICAL POSTSCRIPT

Evagrius is an idiosyncratic thinker (though, historically speaking, by no means isolated or without influence). His texts are not particularly juicy, even by Patristic standards; on the contrary, they are notably arid.[21] Yet his very purity provides an opportunity to gaze with clear vision at the erotic ambition at the heart of Christian practices and theories of prayer—unobscured by the steam rising over the prayer closet of Augustine's contemporaneous *Confessions,* for example. (Indeed, Augustine's *Confessions* is arguably the more idiosyncratic text, in relation to ancient ascetic practice.)

Richard Rambuss has made the "prayer closet" a household name in a least a few queer scholarly families. His *Closet Devotions* exposes the flamboyant eroticism of early modern mappings, both literary and architectural, of an interiorized space of prayerful intimacy with God (a space that Evagrius, as well as Augustine, did much to clear).[22] Rambuss has laudably refused to dismiss such erotic devotions as either "merely metaphorical" or instances of "sublimation." (As Nancy phrases it: "Love is what it is, identical and plural, in all its registers or in all its explosions, and it does not sublimate itself, even when it is 'sublime.' It is always the beating of an exposed heart.")[23]

In the course of his readings, Rambuss both builds on and critiques the historical periodization inscribed by Foucault's *History of Sexuality,* as I have also done in a work dealing with late ancient Christian eroticism (though not, in that instance, with prayer per se).[24] Given Foucault's capacity for ambiguity, especially when dealing with Christian texts, it is almost always possible both to agree and to disagree with him—often in the same breath. In relation to sexuality, Foucault's Victorian modernity frequently seems to arrive much earlier than he imagines. But, by the same token, so does his implicitly postmodern escape from modern sexuality. He himself was, after all, captivated by Evagrius's western disciple John Cassian, whom he was seemingly inclined to situate at once at the beginning of modernity and at the beginning of modernity's demise. Highlighting Cassian's elaboration of (Evagrian) techniques of self-examination ("what he is concerned with is the nature, the quality, and the substance of his thoughts"), he calls our attention to "the apparition of a new kind of self" produced by a "hermeneutics of the self" that is in many respects continuous with the judicial, medical, and psychiatric discourses of the modern era. Yet Foucault also marks the distance separating ancient Christian "technologies of the self" from the deeply problematic modern attempt "to constitute the ground of the subjectivity as the root of a positive self." Christianity, he asserts, posits not a positive but a sacrificial self, resulting in a curious paradox: "We have to sacrifice the self in order to discover the truth about ourselves, and we have to discover the truth about ourselves in order to sacrifice ourselves." Foucault repeats the point, while also confessing his own ambivalent attraction: "And that is, I think, the deep contradiction, or if you want, the great richness, of Christian technologies of the self: no truth about the self without a sacrifice of the self."[25]

I am clearly strongly attracted to Foucault's subversively postmodern[26] reading of the sacrificial subjectivity at the center of ancient ascetic practice—at the center, indeed, of a practice of prayer that is also, I have suggested, an art of eroticism (even a distinctly sadomasochistic art). The embrace of a postmodern reading is, of course, already implicit in my interpolations of the voice of Jean-Luc Nancy into the discussion of Evagrius's text.[27] The contemporary—and stubbornly modern—appeal to Christian tradition as a source for the sexual morality enshrined by "family values" is an instance of astonishing (and willful) selective memory at best—though not simply preposterous (for indeed when Christianity finally found a place for carnal sex, most notably with Augustine, it was in the context of a strictly circumscribed marital ethic of procreation). As Mark Jordan has pointed out, the primary contribution of early and medieval Christianity to theories and practices of erotic pleasure has centered more on the masturbatory theater of private prayer and the sadomasochistic excesses of asceticism than on the marital bed. Indeed, one is hard put to find any Christian discourse of pleasure or joying that touches upon marriage. "Our union with God in prayer," Jordan suggests (explicitly drawing on ancient tradition), "is the fulfillment of our capacity for erotic pleasure." He continues: "Many Christian traditions have prescribed austerities of various kinds to those who want to pursue God in prayer. Some of the austerities have exactly resembled the rituals of sadomasochistic sex." In both cases, "pain or subjection is used as a way beyond ordinary consciousness—a way to reach the point where the apparent relations of dominance and subjection are dissolved in mutuality, intimacy."[28]

Does such a perverse proposal constitute good news? Perhaps it does. That Christian prayer is at heart *jouissance,* that *jouissance* is a kind of prayer—surely this possibility should enliven not only the monastic cell but also all other queer spaces and divine places traversed by love.

I would like to have brought this essay to an end with that last, hopeful sentence. But I am haunted by Nancy's critique—perhaps unfair in its context yet thereby rendered no less haunting—of those who turn "places of obscenity" into "altars": "To name God as Bataille did in the heat of love and in a brothel is still to yield to a modern temptation."[29] To make an altar of the bed, a temple of the brothel, or a cult of orgasm would indeed constitute an infelicitous relapse into "modernity." My intention is rather to affirm, with Nancy, that "there are no parts, moments, types, or stages of love. There is only an infinity of shatters." Moreover, love "is not in any one of its shatters. . . . It does not withhold its identity behind its shatters: it *is* itself the eruption of their multiplicity."[30] Love *is* the trembling touch of the flesh. Love *is* the joying of prayer.

❧ Carthage Didn't Burn Hot Enough: Saint Augustine's Divine Seduction

KARMEN MACKENDRICK

At the opening of Book 3 of Saint Augustine's *Confessions*, the author enters into young adulthood and into the city of Carthage, where all about him famously simmers a burning cauldron of unholy loves. Yet the ultimate object of his desire, in these years when he indulges in theater and prays for chastity to come at some more convenient time, is neither theatrical nor narrowly sexual—nor is it God, who might have been the reader's first suspicion. "I was in love with love," Augustine writes, though he adds that he is a bit confused about what "love" might mean.

He distinguishes love from lust, contrasting "love's serenity" to the search and struggle of "lust's darkness."[1] What we expect, if we don't know enough to know better, is that his religious conversion several books later will neatly free him from lust, leaving him in the pure and serene state of love, directed appropriately and rewardingly toward a God who keeps him always satisfied. But if this simple story were true, even Augustine's rhetorical brilliance would be hard-pressed to save him from the fate of being boring—and, whatever else we may think of him, boring he most decidedly is not. In fact, the relation he finds or creates with the Christian God, in constant tension between love and lust, seems rather closer to his characterizations of the latter, with their striving and frustration and bewilderment.

I want to suggest that Augustine stays in love with love—more exactly, that he seeks a constant and potent seduction of and by his God, and that the *Confessions* is mutually illuminating when read with contemporary theory on seduction. Only seduction will allow Augustine to retain his love of the created world as good while refusing to immerse and gratify himself in its beauty. Augustine's relation to God exemplifies at least three characteristics of seduction: the manipulation of the will beyond a simple opposition of consent and coercion; the persistence of the elusively promising within the representational and discursive; and, relatedly, the necessary incompletion of both meaning and desire. The fires of worldly lust are too easily quenched for one who wants to be seduced, and the complexities of seduction in relation to desire, complexities of coercion and pleasure alike, are fully present in Augustine's complicated quest.

To make this argument properly, perhaps I should begin with a definition of seduction, which turns out to be quite an elusive term. The Latin *seducere* indicates being led aside or away. Augustine himself uses the word fairly restrictively, to suggest being led *astray* and not merely turned aside—for example, "To tie me down the more tenaciously to Babylon's belly, the invisible enemy tramped on me (Ps. 55:3) and seduced me because I was in the mood to be seduced."[2]

His use is a neat fit as well with the first sense given by the OED, "To persuade (a vassal, servant, soldier, etc.) to desert his allegiance or service"—Augustine is turned from the position of a "slave to lust," as he says, to an urgent quest for enslavement by God. Once seduced by the world (turned away from his proper allegiance), he seeks a stronger seduction (a return of all his service to his master). The term indicates both turning around and drawing toward, and a duality of force and direction: being turned toward something by being drawn away from something else; toward the seductive object and away from some other demand upon one's time or attention or desire. It implies will and resistance, not simply between seducer and seduced but within each party involved, because no one who enjoys seduction wants to accomplish it too soon.

Ultimately this distance and distinction is itself to be overcome, at least on certain models of seduction: "The activity of seduction," writes Alicia Ostriker, "is quite a subtle matter. It differs on the one hand from the act of rape, where X subdues Y by force, and on the other from the proposal, where X promises Y an exchange of goods and services: come live with me and be my love and I'll give you this and that. In both rape and the proposal, X and Y remain distinct beings with separate sets of wishes. In the seduction this separation is less certain, less absolute. . . . Seduction depends on X convincing Y that she already secretly desires the same amorous play that X desires."[3] Seduction, rendering subject boundaries untidy, cannot be a one-sided play of power.

Pamela Haag has persuasively noted how deeply our models of consent, particularly sexual consent, are caught up in our notions of the individual and our various liberal understandings of individualism. "Some feminist critics . . . leave the reader with a choice of seeing herself as a 'free creature' or a 'victim' because standards of individual autonomy and consent in sexual relations are so caricatured that feminists who *would* like to speak about subtler forms of coercion, pressure, and so on seem to these critics to be making annoying, wimpy assaults on women's very identity as competent and autonomous individuals. The criticism, to some extent, is liberal feminism falling on its own sword."[4] But subtle seductions are more complex still than coercion. If we move beyond individualism and autonomy we are, as I've noted elsewhere,[5] in very delicate territory indeed—precisely the place of Augustine's religious sensibility.

Much of the controversial nature of seduction, for right-wing Christians and radical feminists alike, seems to stem from the question of agency in this turning and traveling. Clearly, if I simply decide—particularly if I decide on rational grounds—to turn my attention away from one matter and invest it in something else, it is difficult to argue that I have been seduced. But if on the contrary I am forced or even severely constrained, say by the threat of lasting bodily harm or long-term unemployment, to attend to what would otherwise not have drawn me, it scarcely seems that I have been seduced—though there are many who have found this distinction less evident than I do.

Seduction is often associated with complicity attained under false premises—that is, with being duped. But neither coercion nor duplicity quite describes seduction, which seems rather to entail a realization that the drawing of desire, though it cannot be accomplished by force, also cannot be brought about by reason alone; that the will is never singular in its direction. It is here we see the limitation of well-intentioned "positive consent" policies; seduction eludes not only simple concepts of agency but strictly discursive language as well—a subtle and interesting effect. It may well be, as stated in the Antioch code, that "the intent of the policy is yes," but as Haag notes, "the need to define women's agency—to have 'no' respected as a transparent and literal assertion of will—has strange effects on the status of 'yes,' or authentic consent. From a feminist perspective 'yes means yes' seems to occlude sources of coercion or pressure short of physical harm. . . . There are forms of coercion or even violence in addition to physical risk that literal, or fixed, parameters will not contain, or accommodate."[6] Seduction is so problematic an issue for agency because it does not fit the notions of agent and object that we still, even knowing better, tend to assume. There are not only forms of coercion that fixed parameters cannot accommodate; there are forms of consent and desire as well.

Augustine, of course, problematizes agency as thoroughly as anyone has ever done. While he heartily blames himself, taking on the burden of an agent, for his tendency to be drawn by worldly pleasures, Augustine is significantly less independent when it comes to God. Here, in fact, he seeks willfully to be enslaved, writing in Book 10, "My entire hope is exclusively in your very great mercy. Grant what you command, and command what you will. . . . O love, you ever burn and are never extinguished. O charity, my God, set me on fire. You command continence; grant what you command, and command what you will."[7] And again, later in Book 10: "Grant me now and in the future to follow gladly as you do with me what you will."[8]

This is not a simple matter of abdicating a responsibility that might become too much, but rather of continuing a seduction too enticing to make turning away again a tolerable option. One does not enslave inanimate or will-less objects, nor even animals; and in a *voluntary* enslavement complex intertwinings of will and intellect are required, and the possibilities of self-subversion that seem unique to human beings. To subvert selfhood may well be, in fact, Augustine's ultimate aim—if we may use "aim" of what would subvert the possibilities of agency and teleology alike.

Augustine must constantly strike a delicate balance in his desire. As I have noted, he cannot or will not condemn outright the beauties of the created, material world. When he does speak against his early pleasures, there is in this condemnation an interesting ambiguity. It is nothing so simple as an alignment of the somatic with evil. This in fact is something Augustine must carefully avoid, as it approaches too closely the Manichaeism he has only recently, if vigorously, rejected. I think too that it is not so simple as the worry that these are distractions that turn a limited supply of energy and desire away from God. His concern is not so much with the objects themselves as with the manner of enjoyment they invite.

Augustine worries about all of his sensual loves, struggling daily, he says, against the temptations of intemperance in food and drink,[9] of pleasure in music, in which he fears enjoying voice and melody more than the praises of God being sung;[10] even of light, and the sights illuminated by it.[11] He worries about being drawn into, and drawing to a stop in, the pleasures of the world, but he worries too in each case about too strict a resolve against pleasure, which in itself shows how good God's creation can be.

Augustine presents a fairly straightforwardly Platonic solution to his difficulty in appreciating beauty, and we could just make matters easy on ourselves and follow it. "I asked myself why I approved of the beauty of bodies . . . and what justification I had for giving an unqualified judgment on mutable things. . . . In the course of this inquiry why I made such value judgments as I was making, I found the unchangeable and authentic eternity of truth to transcend my mutable mind. And so step by step I ascended from bodies to the soul which perceives through the body, and from there to its inward force, to which bodily sense report external sensations. . . . From there I ascended to the power of reason. . . . So in the flash of a trembling glance it attained to that which is. At that moment I saw your 'invisible nature understood through the things which are made' (Rom. 1:20)."[12]

But this does not really seem to do justice to Augustine's own descriptions, or for that matter to the Plato of the *Symposium*, from which this image of ascent to abstraction is taken. The Neoplatonic tradition, which is at least as influential as Christianity upon Augustine's thought—which, indeed, is the only way in which he can view Christianity as having the philosophical sophistication he requires of a theological system—tends to turn away from bodies, but this turn is not self-evident in Plato (nor, I think, is it inevitable). Even in Diotima's description of divine ascent (a description conveyed in the *Symposium* by Socrates, layered about with so many warnings of its fictive character that we must take it very cautiously indeed), the love of the body of a single beautiful boy is a necessary, even foundational, step. Those who are not brought to their knees by such beauty can never be acolytes of the Beautiful itself; unable to perceive beauty even in its most evident forms, they are unseducible—stolidly, irredeemably secular. A straightforwardly Platonic reading, even of so abstract a notion as the ascent of the soul toward the Beautiful, must always be unfair to Plato's texts. Obviously, we cannot know whether Augustine regarded his ladderlike description as truly Platonic or not, but Augustinian complexity, subverting this description's seeming simplicity, is more true to Plato than the author may have realized.

Augustine is certainly sensitive to the beauty his senses give him. Indeed, the created world cries out to him, he says, though he's careful to avoid making that world itself into God: "And I said to all these things in my external environment: 'Tell me of my god who you are not, tell me something about him.' And with a great voice they cried out: 'He made us' (Ps. 99:3). My question was the attention I gave to them, and their response was their beauty."[13]

The nature of this question and answer intrigues me. "My question was the attention I gave them," Augustine says, and so it is clear that he has not sat down to have a theological discussion with the dandelions; he is merely noticing how very lovely they are. They respond precisely by being lovely; that is, the question is answered in advance, yet one senses that it has not been simply rhetorical. We know *what* the world tells him—that it was made by God; and we know that the world "says" via its beauty—its very power to draw us into itself. We know too that this saying is not verbal; he may be odd, but Augustine nowhere gives us evidence that he is prone to auditory hallucination.[14] Nor, despite the gesture toward a simplified Platonic ascent, does the beauty of the world offer us rational argument. Augustine may make rational arguments, but even there he admits that understanding when it arrives comes "in the flash of a trembling glance."[15]

Augustine's postconversion desire is always in a tense relation with corporeality. The somatic, and more generally the material, are not condemned as such, but neither are they valued simply for the satisfactions they might provide. Rather, their greatest value is in turning one toward something beyond them, or beyond their most obvious manifestations. The nature of this turning is important, because it is *not* a turning-away— "look at how lovely this is and then deny yourself the pleasure of it"— though I have to admit it is not impossible to imagine Augustine working that way. Nor is the turn referential, with worldly objects hinting that we ought to go check out this maker if the creation impresses us. The world speaks through neither direct declaration nor rational inference. Neither does it somehow represent a divine presence, either directly or symbolically. No one has stomped a cross like a crop circle into the fields, nor does the face of Christ appear to Augustine in a buttercup one day. And the beauty of the things of the world, exclaiming, "He made us," is not a representation of the maker, as if the image of God appeared there in a sort of organic shroud of Turin. Rather, the world can lead us into its own beauties and please us there, or it can turn us constantly toward the further seduction at which it always hints—a seduction already there, a different, more mysterious manner of enjoyment.

So Augustine attends to the world, and it answers with beauty, which of course is why he was attending in the first place, and this beauty tells him something that is not there, by some quite indirect means.

I will suggest again that the means is seduction, and that the turn toward God is an attempt to sustain the seductiveness of the world rather than allowing desire to be stopped and satisfied in worldly beauty. Here I want to draw, strangely perhaps, on theory about pornography. There's been much written, not all of it particularly good or useful, attempting to distinguish the pornographic from the stuff-that-looks-like-it-but-isn't. Most such efforts focus on content. "Pornography is about dominance. Erotica is about mutuality. Any man able to empathize with women can easily tell the difference by looking at a photograph or film and putting himself in the woman's skin."[16] The famous content-oriented definitions legally declaring pornography a civil rights violation offer nine different categories of unacceptable representation, with a note that women, men, children, and transsexuals may all be objects thus represented, though the language of the ordinances is geared toward women.[17]

But I suspect that the difference, insofar as there is one, lies neither in the subject nor in the act, but rather in the fact of representation itself.[18] This, as it happens, does not allow us to distinguish a pornographic representation from any other. Pornography is representational and discursive; it shows and tells. Jean Baudrillard writes that seduction, on the other hand, threatens discourse with its own, sudden reversibility, from meaningful language and explicit representation to that which shimmers somehow as always uncertain, which cannot be said or shown but renders saying and showing evocative rather than demonstrative,[19] which whispers, "Wait, there's more."

Pornography, some theorists have argued, is a means as well as a manifestation of power; as Adrienne Rich claims, "Where language and naming are power, silence is oppression, is violence."[20] The problem here is the association of silence with powerlessness. Baudrillard suggests that the seductive works against power, to undermine it; I would agree, though with the caution that what undermines is power too. I will not—and would not—try to name a difference between the pornographic and the erotic, but I would allow this difference, between representation and allusion, between the pornographic and the seductive, with a warning that the same stimulus may very easily be both, even to the same person. Representational pornography, when we view it as pornography, may move us to action or to contemplation or to laughter. The seductive moves us less directly; it draws us, but we do not quite know where.

Curiously, this is related to those opening questions of consent. Old laws governing seduction, at least in the United States, were in fact for many years laws about informed consent, variations on contract law.[21] The idea is that the seduced is being led somewhere, but is not so clear about where. Seduction as the term is negatively used suggests that the seducer lies about an implied destination—in these laws, usually marriage—but in its more positive sense it suggests simply an unknown. And because of this, the leading itself is indirect. Something in the words, the image, the sound, or the scent we find seductive arouses us and beckons to us, but without the specificity of the pornographic.

Now, one might want to argue that this just shows that Augustine has been regarding the world's beauty pornographically, and has been led by it straight to a specific and satisfying belief in God. There are, however, two objections to this possibility. The first is that the leading *is not* straight, or at least straightforward; how he gets from the beautiful to God is just not self-evident. More significantly, there is nothing definite about the God to which he is led. His own incomprehension is a constant theme in the *Confessions,* and while he is fairly sure about what God is *not*—such as physically bounded, or temporal—positive attribution is significantly more elusive. Augustine *worries* about relating to the beauty of the world pornographically—about being led there and not beyond. Yet he cannot reject or ignore the world's beauty, not only by temperament but also in fear of falling back into Manichaeism. In finding this delicate balance, he allows himself not to enjoy beauty and stop there, nor simply to use the beauty as a basis for argument, but to be seduced by the beautiful, drawn by it toward something that is not quite there, not quite yet. The world seduces him into wanting more.

Not yet and always more. Famously, many of Augustine's analogies for the love of God are quite somatic. Rejecting the idea that what he loves about God is something physical, he nonetheless declares, "a light, voice, odour, food, embrace of my inner man, where my soul is floodlit by light which space cannot contain, where there is sound that time cannot seize, where there is a perfume which no breeze disperses, where there is a taste for food no amount of eating can lessen, and where there is a bond of union that no satiety can part. That is what I love when I love my God."[22] The metaphors of the body in the love of God are metaphors not of gratification but of an infinite tease, of a hint toward satisfaction perpetually and necessarily incomplete. Later in the same Book he adds: "You called and cried out loud and shattered my deafness. You were radiant and resplendent, you put to flight my blindness. You were fragrant, and I drew in my breath and now pant after you. I tasted you, and I feel but hunger and thirst for you. You touched me, and I am set on fire to attain the peace which is yours."[23]

These are not images of satisfaction, but of a longing perpetually stimulated and enhanced. Augustine's desire before his seduction by God, his desire for sexual satisfaction, amusement, and the esteem of his peers, was potent and recurrent, but temporarily satiable. Worldly lust burns, and it can be reignited, but it does not burn constantly hotter.

To be sure, Augustine speaks of the possibility of God as a final rest, an end to restlessness: "our heart is restless until it rests in you,"[24] he declares in the very first section of the *Confessions*. But there is precious little rest in his love for God. The conversion process is inflammatory: "My God, how I burned, how I burned with longing to leave earthly things and fly back to you. I did not know what you were doing with me."[25] This is not, however, simply a purifying fire, burning away the last of his pagan tendencies; once he's encountered God it gets worse still. "Wherever I am carried, my love is carrying me. By your gift we are set on fire and carried upwards: we grow red hot and ascend. . . . Lit by your fire, your good fire, we grow red-hot and ascend."[26] Nor does God make things easy, being just as in love with love as the young Augustine: "Who will enable me to find rest in you? Who will grant me that you come to my heart and intoxicate it, so that I forget my evils and embrace my one and only good, yourself? . . . What am I to you that you command me to love you, and that, if I fail to love you, you are angry with me and threaten me with vast miseries?"[27] Yet not to love is still worse: "If I do not love you, is that but a little misery? . . . Do not hide your face from me. . . . Lest I die, let me die so that I may see it."[28] This love Augustine directs toward God is self-feeding, and he loves it. He is in love with love still, making the transition from a theatrical lover of the spectacle of suffering to a sufferer in love with his own agonies. His desire is incompletable, less a matter of Platonic lack than of a Neoplatonic overflow, less a Freudian diminution of excitation than a Lacanian dissatisfaction.

I will not claim much expertise on Lacan, but it does seem to me correct to suggest, as he does, that desire, unlike need, is inseparable from language. Thus it is also caught up in the interminable analyses that make up the search for meaning, meaning that is never in fact complete. If my desire is for desire, if I am in love with love, then I will look for it in the most seductively incompleteable places: in a will turned back upon itself, in material beauty that slips past itself and denies that it is everything—and in the effort to speak of God.

As Jane Gallop puts it, "This is Lacanian 'castration'—the sacrifice of 'complete satisfaction' [necessary to adulthood]. According to Lacan 'displacement' is metonymy (*Écrits*, 511), and 'desire *is* a metonymy (*Écrits*, 528). Thus this absence of 'complete satisfaction' coupled with 'displacements' characterizes what Lacan calls desire . . . (*Écrits*, 690)."[29] Desire in Augustine flows outward in order to draw in, overflowing without ever being filled full.

Like his love of God, his desire for knowledge burns hot in Augustine (he even declares at times that his mind is on fire); his passion for God is as much to know, to understand, as to encounter—indeed, it is not quite clear what the distinction would be, though I would not go so far as to say that there is none. I would say, however, that Augustine's is a religiosity unusually intense in both its intellectualism and its passion, and in the inseparability of those two. This, I think, has not only psychological interest but theological import as well.

To make sense of this, I want to look just a little longer at the relation of desire to knowledge—more specifically, to speakability. To quote Gallop again, "Since words elicit a desire for meaning, there is a drive to complete the sentence, fully reveal the signification. Yet any 'sentence' can always be added to; no sentence is ever completely saturated. The play of metonymy, the forward push to finish signification, to close meaning, creates the impression of veiled signification."[30]

Susan David Bernstein explicitly links this metonymic desire to seduction, noting of Lacan's own discussion: "By deferring meaning, Lacan's abstractions and puns facilitate the possibility of seduction in the form of a reading investment spurred by a desire to know."[31] Augustine too defers meaning, telling us in this remarkably inconclusive work less of a discovery than of a search. Indeed, the one certainty in the *Confessions* seems to be God, but in what manner this God is certain we are hardpressed to say. He *is*, but we can describe that existence only negatively (indeed, reading Augustine, I am increasingly uncertain as to whether even existence is properly predicated here, but that is a consideration for another place and time).

It may be evident where I am going with this. As Lacan writes, "To put it elliptically: that desire be articulated, precisely for that reason it is not articulable."[32] In fact, Augustine's desire is the insatiable demand for desire, in turn the impossible demand for articulation of the God who cannot be said. Meaning itself is full of desire, reaching toward an impossible completion.

The meaning of God is constantly elusive for Augustine, and thus seductive. The completion of what infinite perfection means is impossible. In language too, in language as it seeks understanding, divine seduction is dual. God draws Augustine's language, "I tell my story for love of your love," but his language is likewise an effort at seduction. Bernstein writes of "seduction via interpretation," "Thus, feminists have been led to ask to what extent the privilege to speak and to confer meaning, which might also be the power to seduce through language, is culturally encoded as a male prerogative. Indeed, one may well ask whether every account of seduction . . . is marked by gender patterns of dominance and submission."[33] I think this is not quite right, nearly inverted in fact, though it engages the right cluster of issues. Seduction is too deeply reversible to be a gender prerogative—and besides, it gets assigned to different genders on a fairly frequent basis. Seduction through language does not, cannot confer meaning; it is precisely what in language eludes the discursive and the representational. It is language's poetic element. Lacking the completion of meaning, Augustine has faith, not belief in dogma without understanding but a lived experience of the incomprehensible. Faith, as Baudrillard notes, "in the religious sphere is similar to seduction in the game of life. Belief is turned to *the existence of God* while faith is a *challenge to God's existence,* a challenge to God to exist . . . One *seduces* God with faith, and He cannot but respond, for seduction, like the challenge, is a reversible form."[34]

The theology appropriate to this faith is not necessarily the one Augustine will develop in his later works, where he speaks more as an ecclesiastical authority and not, or at any rate not so much, out of religious yearning. The theology appropriate to this incomplete and unsayable God can only be a saying of what cannot be said, a warning against the illusion of understanding. Full comprehension—of God or by God—is loss of distinction, fire to the point of melting-into. "You are my eternal Father, but I am scattered in times whose order I do not understand. The storms of incoherent events tear to pieces my thoughts, the inmost entrails of my soul, until that day when, purified and molten by the fire of your love, I flow together to merge into you."[35]

Perhaps this really is what Augustine wants; perhaps the only "completion" appropriate to seduction is, as Baudrillard claims, death—the loss, rather than the satisfaction, of the seeking self. Only God even holds—or, as I suspect, is—the promise of burning that hot, a promise that never precisely defines what it offers, made in the constant uprising of desire. The problem with Carthage is not, was never, that it burns. Nor is it that its burning is a distraction from higher pursuits. Carthage simply did not burn hot enough; all of the desires aroused there can be satisfied, and Augustine is not after satisfaction. He would burn with the seraphim, until his very self has been fully, unspeakably, burned out.

PART IV

❧ Cosmos, Eros, Creativity

◆ American Transcendentalism's Erotic Aquatecture

ROBERT S. CORRINGTON

There are two high-water marks in the self-unfolding of the depths of nature within Euro-American thought. The earlier occurred in the neo-Plotinian transfiguration of our experience of infinitizing nature in the metaphorical undulations concresced in the writings of Ralph Waldo Emerson. The latter emerged in the dazzling architectonic of the creator of pragmaticism and the greater triadic tradition of semiotics, Charles Sanders Peirce—overpowering the subsequent dyadic semiological trajectory inspired by Saussure. For Emerson, the astonishing and fecund power of nature naturing held forth the fitful and often explosive power of the great One, while for Peirce sheer firstness, the predyadic dimension of immediacy, traitless fecundity *an sich*, and nonsemiotic radiance, served as the brake on the manic centrifugal force of the phenomenological and ontological categories of secondness (dyadic causal impact) and thirdness (concrete reasonableness in an evolutionary context).

Peirce was profoundly transformed by the thought of Schelling, to whom he remained indebted, yet he sanitized the brooding and dangerous intuition Schelling had into the underconscious of nature—an underconscious from which even gods and goddesses emerge. While Peirce had a glimmering of the depth of nature, as the spawning ground of both signs and refracted light, he turned his back on this dimension over and over again in his flight toward evolutionary love and the conquest of sheer firstness by a blinding and self-enfolding categorial array awaiting him in the infinite long run of an evolutionary perspective that was only minimally Darwinian.

For Peirce, the universe is like a great breathing architecture gathering up its distressed foundlings and weaving them into an increasingly crystalline realm of thirdness. Rather than stressing the evolutionary principles of random variation, natural selection, adaptability, and a minimal form of self-organization under the rare conditions emergent from a surplus value of evolutionary competence, he imposed a Lamarckian mythos of evolutionary love in which all variation served the higher good of convergence. Peirce's fear of and complicit desire for the abyss of sheer firstness drove him into a titanic effort to pull thirdness out of a reluctant nature. This countermove to the Schelling-like domain of firstness was his biggest mistake—and one that Peircean scholastics reenact with him.

Like the Wittgenstein of the 1921 *Tractatus Logico-Philosophicus*, Peirce, a chemist by academic training, felt most at home in crystalline imagery. If the boisterous and fuzzy universe was not yet a pure self-reflecting crystal, it would be. And the method of science serves to bring the counterfactual *would be* into the infinite facets of the divine crystal. The primary metaphor in his philosophical anthropology, taken from Shakespeare, is that we are a "glassy essence"—our internal semiosis being a clear and distinct microcosmic mirror of the macrocosmic sign-series, always infinite, that molded it. The method of science provides the self-control necessary to align the optics of the self with the optics of God. Yet the God problematic remains curiously incomplete in Peirce's philosophical theology. It is truncated, contradictory, and self-masking. It reminds one of Michelangelo's unfinished slave sculptures in which the figures are almost pushing their way out of stone, but are somehow held back by a mocking opacity.

It may take another century for philosophy to fully grasp the legacy deposited in Peirce's writings, but the case for Emerson seems different— seems, but may not be. For surely Emerson's essays, journals, poems, and even translations have been the subject of much appreciative scrutiny. And they are certainly not as internally complex as are the writings of Peirce. But is this so, or only a delusion produced by an easy and lazy familiarity with a figure hoary with age and properly enshrined in the

North Atlantic pantheon of those who shaped the contours of our in-creasingly complex meaning horizons? The case to be made is a strenu-ous one, but not impossible; namely, that Emerson's writings are among the most difficult, profound, and evocative of the One in the English language. For a philosopher of some sophistication to be told that Emer-son's essays rank with the writings of Peirce in the above characteristics, would produce both a wry smile and a self-important incredulity. But the tale is yet to be adequately told and it may take another century before *this* story finds its proper measure within the continuing self-giving of the infinite light.

Stepping outside of the magic circle one last time—indeed, we have yet to properly enter into it—Peirce always writes within a Christian eschatological context. The universe, and the divine engine within it, is evolving from the less perfect to the more perfect, from the tantalizing but terrible fecundity of firstness to the clear, clean, crisp, and unambigu-ous realm of divine self-return in the glowing architecture of thirdness—god, as universe, sure and whole at the end of a journey that may not have been real in the first place. And even in his concept of evolutionary love, which has a highly muted erotics, the outcome is secure, the jour-ney marked with clear guideposts, and the relationality of the consum-mated realm prevailing without any dangerous movement that would tear into the serene divine mind.

A primal intuition tells us that a crystalline world is not an erotic world. It is not a world that surges, retreats, burrows into itself, explodes out of a tremulous underconscious, and lives as a boundary-in-the-mak-ing in an elliptical pluriform. Moving toward the charmed circle of Emer-son's writings, several striking features emerge as we turn away from Peirce's triumphalism toward the deceptively serene fields and streams of Concord. The pilgrim is struck by a great silence that envelops the problematics of history, god, progress, the scope of science and scientism, and the very concept of consummatory eschatology. Peirce's titanic unity has somehow splintered—tumbling away from the Christian metahistory that brooks no opposition. It is still here, but now scattered and under-ground, no longer forced along a great arc of history and compelled by a brutal hand to be an antientropic arrow pointing only to the divine mind. The convergent unified force of evolutionary love has devolved into the nonhistoric explosions of innumerable foldings and unfoldings within the orders of nature.

This great leap into the prehistorical was made in Emerson's youth by Schopenhauer, another slayer of the Christian eschaton. Radicalized in his vision by his encounter with the Upanishads, Schopenhauer created the first truly post-monotheistic philosophy of genius within the many Western traditions. Emerson did not need the Upanishads to find the measure of the midworld of Eastern Massachusetts, but it became his companion on subsequent journeys through much vaster landscapes. A curious internal mix started brewing while Emerson was intuiting his way toward the creation of Transcendentalism out of the ashes of a failed Unitarianism still wedded to a supernatural Christology and a progressive (ameliorative) eschatology.

Emerson had little genius for architectonic, for the gathering together of massive categorial structures into a grounded yet aspiring thought experiment. For the philosophical architect, grounds are available and even transformable into a structure that weds antecedent to consequent through the once-and-for-all bridge of sufficient reason. Bridges of this nature have a curious tendency to spawn historical consequents that flee from the self-giving ground and drive toward the gathering of a seductive and authoritative "not yet." After all, an edifice has to last, to hold to the last, and to find its measure in the solar power of a lucid and mirroring counter-light that shines in and as history. Architectonic in the Christian horizon is strangely moving toward the place within *chronos* where history finally comes to a stop—all light, all luminosity, and all burning fire. The earthly weight of architectonic marries itself to the fire of the eschaton and the very need for a vast categorial array dissolves in the plasma that is hotter than the heat of any sun, of any supernova, of anything whatsoever within the indefinitely ramified orders of the world.

Emerson would have none of this. His internal alchemy bodied forth something far more elusive and more tenuous (at least from the perspective of the not so discerning eye of the absolute idealist—hell-bent on establishing a vision of strict internal relations among the moments of a totalizing consciousness). Emerson took his world in small units, in small pulsations that emerged before and within him as he endlessly walked among the quotidian organic invitations of his midworld. Everywhere he looked he saw the dissolving waters that surround each order of nature. Metaphors, always his chief guide in probing into the infinitizing powers of nature naturing, were offered to him by each tree, each grove, each meaningful human act, and, most forcefully, by his vision of the sheer luminosity of the nighttime sky. His very notion of religion, of the cultic embodiment of the sacred, had its highest epiphany in a kind of people's astronomy. Were the stars to appear only one night in a thousand years, he opined, the memory of their photonic shower would be enough to fuel all of the religions of the world, making our contemporary historical religions but pale and all-too-human imitations.

Agape belongs to the architects, to those who always build for the solar array that pours its authoritative benediction on those laboring below. The philosophical architect wrenches metals and silicates out of the soil of sufficient reason and melds them into the structure that awaits solar transformation and blessing. Eros comes from a different dimensionality and is most clearly seen in its dissolving and binding power within horizontal midworlds that move not toward the agapastic sun but through the liquid steams and torrents of nature natured, always the dim refraction of nature naturing, from whence all liquefactions come. Emerson knew this, and knew it from the beginning as his Unitarian soul was carried over a cataract that only later received its proper name: nature naturing, or nature producing itself out of itself alone, never confined to what is created, to the innumerable orders of the world.

Five years after publishing his inaugural essay "Nature" (1836), an essay that brought human religious self-consciousness to its then highest level within the context of the emerging post-Protestant world, he delivered an important address in Waterville, Maine. This address, "The Method of Nature" (August 11, 1841), opened the sluice gates of his nascent erotic aquatecture. It is one of the most significant documents in the early prehistory of the world theology that is experiencing its birth pangs in the current era. For in it Emerson is carried into consciousness by forces that are but barely understood and are certainly not subject to the ameliorative self-control that drove Peirce's cosmology.

Nature is methodic, but in a way that shatters all that we mean by that concept. It is method *as* nature or nature *as* method, rather than being a detached nature that could *have* a method, as if in addition to some other possibilities. Peirce's nature has the method of instantiating thirdness—the power of which comes from the divine crystal consciousness. Emerson gives us something raw and untamed:

> The method of nature: who could ever analyze it? That rushing stream will not stop to be observed. We can never surprise nature in a corner; never find the end of a thread; never tell where to set the first stone. The bird hastens to lay her egg: the egg hastens to be a bird. The wholeness we admire in the order of the world is the result of infinite distribution. Its smoothness is the smoothness of the pitch of the cataract. Its permanence is a perpetual inchoation. Every natural fact is an emanation, and that from which it emanates is an emanation also, and from every emanation is a new emanation. If anything could stand still, it would be crushed and dissipated by the torrent it resisted, and if it were a mind, would be crazed; as insane persons are those who hold fast to one thought, and do not flow with the course of nature.[1]

Threads are forever, infinite sign series with neither beginning nor end. All is emanation but seemingly no emanator of all emanators, no ultimate ground, only groundings, better yet, only outpourings into vessels that can't long remain vessels. Even cornerstones have no place to land, no architecture to support, no fixed place on a soil that is forever dissolving under roaring cataracts that are inexhaustible—cataracts coming from we know not where, overpowering us and eternally fueled by rain, melting snow, or even, in the mysterious world of the underconscious of nature, by drought. Churning and erupting water is everywhere, but here there is no hint of the gentle Tao that also lives in the water world of indefinite elisions. The Tao is far too tame, a product of a mountain-high fantasyland that is safely above the turgid valleys below.

This indefinite and endless ramification of an aquatecture, that is unlike any other kind of architecture, is too frenzied, bereft of a whence and a whither, to provide, let alone sustain, the antecedent to consequent relation of sufficient reason. Emerson's vision sweeps away Leibniz, Royce, Whitehead, and all other architects who struggle to hold forth grounds when nature scoffs at their efforts. Whether the grounds be pluriform (monads, actual occasions, Cantorian self-referential infinite sets), or monadic, (absolute consciousness, substance), they stand but a moment before the all-dissolving aquatecture that is nature; that is, nature creating itself (endlessly) out of itself alone.

You search in vain for any hint of the arc of history, of the eventual "would be" that will conclude history and bring it into a final consummatory blaze of glory—and shame for those outside of the arch of the sacred. For where would history be if there is no initiating event, no mythos of founding heroes, no first cities, or no castrating tribal deities serving imperial and militaristic interests? What would be the goal of nature if all structures are little more than momentary and feeble constructs awaiting the inevitable dissolution from the universal solvent? As a chemist Peirce knew the name of this solvent, but he desperately wanted a world in which it would remain encased in a silicate, hidden under the chemist's work bench—always just out of reach.

Contrary to highly grooved and canned theories, Emerson's Transcendentalism is made of stern stuff, demanding the utmost in spiritual courage in the face of a nature that would as soon see our species snuffed out as give birth to yet another evolutionary random variation—a variation, alas, that will in all likelihood die almost as soon as it emerges. Decades before Darwin Emerson faced into the sheer raw power and absolute indifference of nature. Yet at the same time he saw that our attunement to the method of nature can save us from madness, fanaticism, and obsessional delusion. For we are mad to the extent that we attempt to impose our own feeble methods onto the "torrent" that ultimately comes from the underconscious of the world.

And where is erotics in this infinite liquefaction? Is not eros the bond that holds the modes of being together? Is it not, as Karl Jaspers argued, the bond of the modes of the encompassing—perhaps his term, seen through a glass darkly, for nature naturing? And what of the strange spatiality of eros as seen in traditional Christian dogmatics? For we are told that agape always comes down from above, a gift or blessing from the perfect to the imperfect—a gift always undeserved and somehow ontologically alien to finite creatures who face their nonbeing with anxiety. While eros, we are told, is a movement from the lower toward the higher, a movement not of gift giving but of longing. This longing is for an ecstatic infusion, a kind of positive psychoanalytic transference, in which the divine commingles with our nature. Down or up, that is the key discriminandum.

And what, for Emerson, are we to do with these spatial terms, terms obviously parasitic on a stable architectonic in which the directionality of the solar power is always above the horizon, on an ecliptic that never varies—constant and radiant, having no other stellar power in its domain? Clearly Transcendentalism has no place in its aquatecture for a vertical and aloof solar crystal that gives out all light. Agape, as traditionally understood, simply cannot prevail in a world of endless emanations where the very concept of *von oben* is rendered moot. As Emerson reiterates elsewhere, we are on a set of infinite stairs where neither their beginning nor their *telos* are in view, indeed, they never can be in view given the nature of nature. If agape has no between to traverse, standing as it does on a great height from which it pours its spermatic power down on the groundlings, where, on the other hand, is the little sprite eros to be found? Or is eros not such a Platonic messenger after all, not a denizen of the smaller between-world transiting between the mortals and the shining ones? Endless and recurrent personifications aside, what is eros that so much is made of it? Or are we on yet another fool's errand projecting our own traits, much magnified, onto the endlessly ramifying orders of infinitizing nature?

Before we can let eros enter into the erratic rhythms of the method of nature we need to open out the most important dimensionality of nature, a dimensionality that forms the ultimate clearing within Emerson's (and our) aquatecture. Three years after his Waterville address, Emerson published *Essays: Second Series* (1844), the text so beloved by Nietzsche. In the sixth essay, fittingly entitled "Nature," he unveils the Transcendentalist version of what Heidegger called the "ontological difference":

But taking timely warning, and leaving many things unsaid on this topic, let us not longer omit our homage to the Efficient Nature, *natura naturans*, the quick cause, before which all forms flee, flee as the driven snows, itself secret, its works driven before it in flocks and multitudes (as the ancient represented nature by Proteus, a shepherd), and in undescribable variety. It publishes itself in crea-tures, reaching from particles and specula [a small hard-pointed body], through transformation on transformation to the highest symmetries, arriving at consummate results without a shock or a leap.[2]

Implied here is also the obverse to *natura naturans*, that is, to this first dimension of nature in its unending self-othering fecundity. The second and unfolded manifest dimension of nature is *natura naturata*; namely, the innumerable orders of the world, orders that, in their endless ramifi-cations and ordinal locations, can never be counted, never contained, never unified into some alleged superorder or transordinal container. The domains of nature natured are never in something larger, nor are they enveloped by something manifest that would be of greater scope.

Heidegger's ontological difference between Being and things-in-being, for all of its multilayered complexity, lacks the more shocking and dra-matic sweep of Emerson's ontological, nay, natural difference between nature naturing and nature natured. In the spirit of Irigaray's water love, we can say that Heidegger's world, especially the ringing of the fourfold of earth, sky, gods, and mortals, lacks the universal solvent that could dissolve the manic mythos of the Teutonic tribe lost in reverie as it stands under the solar power that roots it in blood and soil.

And wherever Being goes its shadow self non-Being goes, a troubling disturbance that was quickly but artificially overcome by Hegel in the opening gambits of his great *Logic*. Non-being is a cunning obstacle to the sweep of Being, or perhaps a sweet underground lover that nestles into the heart of a blazing Being that yet strangely hides its brilliance from the object-intoxicated human process. Lover or cunning antagonist, non-Being is never far from the citadel of Being itself.

But what can be said of the depth-correlation between nature naturing and nature natured? Is it at all analogous to the love/hate relationship between Being and non-Being? Or is it something else entirely? And if it is something else, is it at all related to a nontribal eros that seems to demand its place in the pulsations of Emersonian aquatecture? We start with the relationship and move on to the relata. How does nature natur-ing, that ever elusive spawning ground, never itself a natural complex or order with traits, relate to that which is unfolded from within its seemingly closed-off infolding?

Being, non-Being, and things-in-being form a triad in which modes of self-othering and envelopment move back and forth in a circle that only seems open. Being and non-Being are different from each other, while neither is the same with those innumerable things-in-being that, for many, constitute the scope and boundary of that which has meaning. For Heidegger, leaps, abysses, and forms of nongrounding ground, hold open a deep between that, for us at least, lacks intimacy. The subtle and almost haunting transition to the experience of enownment (*Ereignis*) partly ameliorates the fierce power of the ontological difference, but still leaves us with a Nietzsche-like Homeric contest—an agonistic struggle in which the outcome is ensnared in the dark meshes of a self-giving and, above all, self-withholding history.

Eros is covered over in this historical Heideggerian world. But with Emerson we find something that allows eros into the free play of the natural difference. For while Being has its opposite, its oppositional non-partner (or hidden pseudo-partner) in non-Being, Emerson's nature has no opposite. There is nothing that is not natural, nothing that is somehow outside of nature. The fissure opened up *within* nature, namely that between nature naturing and nature natured is in no way disruptive of the absolute ubiquity of nature. It is a modal distinction within that which, *an sich*, is not modal. Nature is what it is, is only what it is, is never more than it is, and never less than it is—even as it self-fissures into the deeply bound modalities of *natura naturans* and *natura naturata*.

Strictly, you cannot separate out the two halves of the natural difference, any more than nature does. Nature naturing and nature natured are not held apart by the historicizing of history (a kind of *Heilsgeschichte* or *Seinsgeschichte*), but by a fissuring that is always and already bound together by the gathering potencies of eros. The depth-relationship, better put, the modalities of relevance, between nature naturing and nature natured is not held together by some kind of network of internal relations, nor by external causal relations, nor, finally, by the principle of sufficient reason which always brings in too much monolithic explanation too soon. Eros is the inner and entwined movement that holds the modalities of nature naturing and nature natured together, always and in all respects. Emerson's aquatecture is above all a depth-phenomenology of the erotic entwining of the twin primal dimensionalities of nature. Nature naturing is no more or less real than the innumerable orders of nature natured. The principle of ontological parity compels us to let go of any sense of the more or less real, any sense of a chain of Being in which some discriminanda participate in their own devolution as they somehow find themselves with less Being in the cosmic drama.

Eros lives in the fluidity of the natural difference. There is no spatial or temporal place from which eros is absent in the great self-fissuring. For Emerson, the depth-momentum of his aquatecture is prespatial, pre-temporal, and presemiotic. Eros lives in and through both dimensional-ities of the natural difference. Its most dynamic liquefaction is found within the eternally self-renewing nonhistorical giving of world. Aqua-tecture is what it is through its erotics, an erotics that sustains, but never conquers, the nonspatial torrent that lives in the great between, the mod-alizing of nature that comes to us in those rare and fitful moments of ecstatic release echoing forth out of ontological, not neurotic, melancholy.

The relationship between (if this word is not already too aggressive, too spatial) nature naturing and nature natured, is what it is in and through the erotics of an aquatecture that is neither hierarchal nor a form of greater consciousness. Eros prevails without intentionality, without a conscious sense of history, and indeed, is not conscious at all. The erotics that plays in and through the natural difference is effortless and unend-ing. Eros has no beginning and has no terminus. The predicates of time, space, causality, ordinal location, semiotic structure, and scope have no relevance in the aquatecture of the natural difference.

The greater torrent prevails in the entwining of the always already entwining natural difference. As torrent, it keeps open the aquascape that enables the natural difference to be at all. Eros, in this primal modality of all modalities, is the potency within the greater torrent, a torrent that comes from nowhere in particular and goes to no "wheres" at all. Eros is the potency that makes all subsequent actualizations possible, but eros is never a seedbed of eternal thoughts nor is it a blueprint of what nature builds. Eros is the *ur*-relationship that enables ordinal (worldly) relations to obtain at all.

The relata, the innumerable potencies entwined with the potency of eros (nature naturing), and the innumerable orders that have no outer boundary or inner core, are entwined erotically in their own way. But with the case of nature naturing, it is impossible to probe into its depth-dimension—this remains just on the other side of all phenomenological description or transcendental argument.

Within the primal relationship that is the natural difference, eros meets no resistance, no Peircean secondness, which would damn up its aquatic unfolding. But when the focus shifts to the partly knowable dimension of nature, the innumerable orders of the world (the second relation of the twin relata of nature naturing and nature natured), it becomes clear to our phenomenological reflection that eros is bound up with powers and structures of resistance that limit its scope (in this modality where scope is relevant) and seem to impose an ossification on its movement of encompassing. Metaphorically it is as if many orders of nature become armored against a moving aquatecture that is less "interested" in concresced vessels than with the potency of endless emanations. Here the lesser torrents that wash out the ossified internalities of the world's orders have limited scope, have more compressed channels within which to move.

Partly one could say that to prevail, to have traits that are in some sense unique (the principle of individuation) is to resist that which would dissolve or liquefy those traits. This being so, eros is confined, is blocked, is sometimes rendered powerless when it steps outside of the modalizing of the natural difference and enters into the provenance of the indefinitely ramified orders of the world. On this side of the natural difference, erotic encompassment is, perhaps by necessity, always within certain orders in certain respects, but subject to forms of entropy—not only of heat loss and disorder, but of the entropy of nonrelevance, of nonmeaning, or even antimeaning. The worldly aquatecture of eros is limited by structures of resistance, to forms of armoring that are antecedent and recurrent. In the world, eros is neither omnipotent nor omniscient.

Eros, the potency within the endless torrent of the aquatecture of nature, lives in, through and around the natural difference. In the ever-opening that is the natural difference eros is itself the measure, the giving of measure for the difference itself. Yet when it appears in the endless modalities, endless forms of semiosis, and endless traits of the world it is no longer effortless, no longer the ever-simple entwining that is at the same time strange liquidity. Eros, intraworldly eros, both gives and receives measure. It is indeed a nature sprite, moving horizontally among orders that resist its liquefaction. But it is a sprite of a higher order (if we may echo Schleiermacher). Ordinal to be sure, but somehow this eros is more than a wood sprite that plays the trickster for unwary mortals. Perhaps we could say that the eros of the natural difference *is* the between, while the eros of the world of indefinite and recalcitrant orders, is caught *in* the numerous betweens that punctuate its life.

The greater eros and the lesser eros are, of course, deeply bound together. But here we can say that the emanated, the lesser eros and its various ordinal locations, is intimately tied to the greater eros, the greater torrent. The greater eros is not a ground from which one could move. It is more like a momentum that makes emanations, unfoldings, possible. Yet as even Emerson knew, there is a prior of all priors, a light behind all lights, an erotics within all manifest erotics. Coiled within the unfoldings of our liquefied cosmos is the primal infolding that is deeper even than the natural difference itself. It is the *Quelle*, the source for all that is, of the four Greek elements and of all erotics that serve this infolded mystery.

❧ "She Talks Too Much": Magdalene Meditations

CATHERINE KELLER

As it has done all along, the sensuous icon of Mary Magdalene flashes through popular culture, but with a curious difference now: The saint has found her voice. The recovery of certain ancient texts over the past century has made her speech possible. Some of these, such as the *Pistis Sophia*, a lengthy third-century gnostic document, unfold such arcane mystical allegories that the speeches seem to lack all resonance with the familiar. But then an angry outburst disrupts the smooth psychopompic surface of the text. It brings us back to an all-too-familiar present—in some sense, to our own.

This is the scene: The recently resurrected Jesus is lecturing on the mysteries of Sophia, divine Wisdom, in her struggle with the primal chaos. Each time Jesus concludes a discourse, he invites his listeners' feedback. To each of his speeches his inner circle of disciples respond either with questions or with citations and interpretations of an appropriate biblical Psalm, thus producing a consistent intertextuality of two radically different styles of spiritual language, one Hellenized and esoteric, the other Jewish and biblical. And usually it is one Mariam, the Magdalene, who jumps in—a teacher's delight! After a couple of such contributions, Jesus names her "she whose heart is more directed to the Kingdom of Heaven than all her brothers."[1] Then, after another exchange, he exclaims: "Excellent, Mariam, you blessed one, you *pleroma*, you all blessed *pleroma*, who will be blessed among all generations."[2]

Heady praise! The *pleroma*, or "fullness," refers in the gnostic corpus to the indivisible radiance of the All, the effulgence of divine potencies and emanations. Whether by hyperbole, metonymy, or ontology, Mariam is said to *be* the fullness she articulates. And articulates a bit too fully, as it turns out.

Jesus discourses a bit further and again pauses for discussion. But before the teacher's pet can reply yet again, we read the following: "Peter leapt forward, [and] he said to Jesus: 'My Lord, we are not able to suffer this woman who takes the opportunity from us, and does not allow anyone of us to speak, but she speaks many times.'" Or, in a less literal translation: "She talks too much." Confronted with Mariam's pleromic verbosity, Peter can't get a word in edgewise. He explodes with resentment. With consummate pastoral skill, Jesus deflects Peter's view of the situation: "Let any in whom the power of their spirit has welled up so that they understand what I say, come forward and speak." Indeed he handles the outburst with the soothing evenhandedness we expect from a New Age seminar leader: "Nevertheless, Peter, I see your power within you understands the interpretation of this mystery."[3] Practically jumping up and down, Peter cries, "Lord, hear . . ." and quotes his Psalm. Jesus duly affirms Peter's input—though with noticeably less enthusiasm than he shows for Mariam's contributions.

The little scene with Peter encodes a churning set of inassimilable tensions within early Christianity, exposing bifurcations of hermeneutics and ecclesiology within an already highly differentiated tradition, of gender within a destabilized patriarchy, of sexuality along a spectrum of carnal and spiritual eros, and of the binding of these differences into the binary of orthodoxy and heresy. The power of a spiritual movement was already giving rise to the power drives of a new religion. In the conflictual transition, power—marked as both as the surging spirit, the "power within you," and as the communally conferred power to speak out—is getting negotiated in the Magdalene texts. In the following meditation I consider this and other early Christian texts, such as the Gospels of Mary and Philip, that are often dismissed as "gnostic"—not, as Karen King puts it so nicely, "to drown out the voices of canon and tradition, but in order that they might be heard with the greater clarity that comes from a broadened historical perspective."[4] My task is, however, more constructive than historical. In another time of conflictual transition—namely, our own—these narratives of tension and inspiration well up like the spirit, offering themselves to contemporary theological imaginations.

Indeed, we find ourselves in an extended magdalogical moment, a "resurrection of Mary Magdalene," as Jane Schaberg proclaims it.[5] Scholars have been plumbing the secrets of lost-and-found ancient texts. Some, such as Elaine Pagels, have divulged these mysteries to a wide audience hungry for a spiritual tradition with historical depth but without authoritarian clichés. Feminist New Testament scholars like Elizabeth Schussler Fiorenza, Schaberg, and King have exposed the sex-and-power scam that controlled the Magdalene image for most of Christian history and have lifted up an icon of women's ecclesial leadership. What King says of the *Gospel of Mary* holds true of a range of ancient Christian texts, canonical and gnostic: "It exposes the erroneous view that Mary of Magdala was a prostitute for what it is—a piece of theological fiction."[6]

At the same time, the Magdalene's cultural and spiritual effects have been escaping both academic and ecclesial supervision. My hippie adolescence was shot through with the melody from *Jesus Christ Superstar*: "I don't know how to love him." (Still don't.) In Nikos Kazantzakis's novel *The Last Temptation of Christ*, or the Scorsese movie version, the long-fantasized sexual sin of Mary similarly stimulates a fantasy of the incarnation turned carnal. In the Mel Gibson *Passion* footage of the Magdalene, on the other hand, her sex reverts to stereotype. At the same time, the neognostic fiction of Dan Brown's *Da Vinci Code* directly counters the reformed whore tradition with a dignified, matrimonial, sexual ritual. The stunning success of that novel reveals an immense collective yearning for a spirituality that depatriarchalizes Christianity by recombining it with a significantly feminized and sexually emancipated wisdom tradition. The appetite is also of course for a spirituality that might, for once, prove thrilling. Most academics respond with indignant condescension to its literalizable distortions. Not I: After reading Brown's *Da Vinci Code*, my nineteen-year-old niece shocked me. She actually wanted to talk to me for the first time about religion, even about Christian history. And why shouldn't the mysteries of Sophia make for exciting fiction? We may wish for a less erotically heteronormative and historically misleading tale.

But then one of "us" should write it. The dismissive approach to such phenomena of popular culture betrays our own failure as academics to reach a wide enough public—and to read its fickle, collective eros as inextricable from our own.

Excavating the ancient Magdalene, in other words, may help us decode a present desire. But there is little of interest about her in present theology. Feminist theology has had bigger fish to fry: like the sex of God, or the patrilineage of Father, Son, and church. In the meantime, New Testament scholars' historical quest for the women around Jesus has often remained tightly restrained by both the nature of the evidence and the discipline imposed by the methodology. But something else has been opened up by the refreshing strangeness of the gnostic texts. I find myself wanting to read the fullness, the *pleroma,* of the Magdalene, and not just in some historically, theologically, or politically purified version. I want to let her talk too much. But who *is* she? If she is not just a fragmented and distorted memory of a probably once living woman, what sort of representation is she?

Susan Haskins considers her as "myth and metaphor,"[7] and Schaberg calls her a "moving icon."[8] She appears in a disparate series of spontaneous, contradictory concrescences: both her canonical and her gnostic inscriptions, but also the endlessly narrated, painted, permutating penitent, and sometimes not so penitent, sinner, the later saint of sex workers, reformed or not, and now too the sensuous new age goddess with her own website. One is tempted to call her an archetype. Yet she encapsulates no timeless essence but rather encompasses too many times, evincing (not unlike such figures as Moses, Jesus, Peter, Mary the Mother)—a perilously continuous mutability. If not an archetype, then perhaps a prototype, as Schussler Fiorenza might suggest? Not quite. I do not want to shift interest backward onto a normative original. In order to account for the current Magdalene magnetism, we need a concept that captures how her strata of historical iconization expose, hide and cumulate. I propose the term *stratitype.* It suggests the layering effect of an iconic movement in time, as it recapitulates the past—and does so always differently, always presently. These strata can be read as the layered theological tensions of leadership, gender, sex, and power in the Christian tradition. Thus a hermeneutical destratification (by which Gilles Deleuze means not a reduction of layers but their differentiation) must precede the development of the stratitype as an icon within an emergent theology of Eros.

Leadership: What is the tension that irrupts between Mariam and Peter as two different leaders, symbolic at least but possibly also quite literal figures, of the early Christian movement? Was there an explosive divergence of direction between communities, a rift between Petrine and Pauline Christianity on the one hand, and Magdalene on the other? Schaberg proposes "the threatening thought" that "Mary Magdalene can be considered a—or the—founder of Christianity, if one wants to use such a term."[9] This tension was exacerbated by the opposition of the emerging church organization to the mystical movement now called gnostic and felt to be a dangerous rival. But the rift is already suggested by the divergent accounts of the resurrection in the synoptic gospels. Mary Magdalene is the first witness of the resurrection in John—hence her reputation as the *apostola apostolarum*. "It is striking that Mark, Luke, and John invite the reader to compare Mary Magdalene with Peter. In Mark she is on the same footing as Peter; in Luke Peter is clearly more important than Mary Magdalene, whereas in John, Peter pales by comparison."[10] Yet the Western church, and in particular the See of Peter, has brooked no competition with the Petrine rock. Such internal struggle over leadership belies the memory of a Christian golden age, of even a single generation united under the banners of Peter in Jerusalem and Paul on the road. No matter how radical the new beginning, difference is original.

Gender: Of course these are ancient texts, written in the Judeo-Greco-Roman matrix of unquestioned, if variegated, male supremacism. Peter's explosion about her talking is not just about talk. It is about a woman talking. Her rhetorical and spiritual acumen in the gnostic traditions much exceeds his. So does her courage (another classically male virtue) in John's gospel, as the one who does not flee, while cocky Peter betrays Jesus thrice before the cock crows. But it is in the gnostic texts that the gender theme becomes explicit; thus, later in the *Pistis Sophia*, Mary articulates a familiar double-bind: "My Lord, my mind is understanding at all times that I should come forward at any time and give the interpretation of the words which you spoke, but I am afraid of Peter, for he threatens me and he hates our kind."[11] The word for "kind" is *genos*, translated sometimes "race," but here agreed by scholars to mean "gender." In other words, the rock of Petrine misogyny is blocking her own ability to speak. Hatred inhibits hermeneutics.

The problematic of gender irrupts in the much more accessible little *Gospel of Mary* (Magdalene), written early in the second century and rediscovered a century ago. In the surviving fragment, the male disciples have failed to comprehend the post-resurrection teaching of Jesus. Peter has asked Mary if she is privy to some illumining revelation. "Sister, we know that the Savior loved you more than any other woman. Tell us the words of the savior that you know, but which we haven't heard."[12] She needs no further prompting, and generously shares her own experience of Jesus' after-death teaching. Andrew doesn't believe her, and asks the "brothers" their opinion. His is that "these opinions seem to be so different from his [the Savior's] thought"—dangerous difference again. Peter chimes in with an indignant: "Has the Savior spoken secretly to a woman and not openly so that we would all hear? Surely he did not wish to suggest that she is more worthy than we are?"[13] What a treacherous response—given that he had asked her precisely for some speech still unknown to the men. It seems to be the combination of the unfamiliarity of the mystical teaching with its female provenance that provokes such resistance. So Peter's protest anticipates (or perhaps coincides with) the hereticizing of gnosticism by church fathers of the late second century. Besides, how could any significant teaching have been shared in inappropriate—indeed for a Jewish male almost impossible—privacy with a woman not of his family? But, worse: might Mary be not only the most favored *woman*, but also the most favored *disciple*? She, the courageous and verbal one, finally bursts into tears—but also finds her tongue again. She asks if he is accusing her of making this up. Like the *Pistis Sophia*, the *Gospel of Mary* records the effects of misogynist pressure on the subject who is female and speaking.

A third male voice, that of Levi, unexpectedly intervenes: "Peter, you have always been a hothead, ready to give way to anger. And now you are treating the woman like an adversary." And like a good feminist male, confronting sexism man-to-man, Levi persists: "If the Savior considered her to be worthy, who are you to disregard her? For he knew her completely and loved her devotedly." Levi's stance, like that of Jesus in the *Pistis Sophia*, suggests that there was in fact some male support for the prominence of women in the movement. If no utopian moment of gender egalitarianism among the disciples, even around Jesus, is thus suggested, the *Gospel of Mary* "presents the most straightforward and convincing argument in any early Christian writing for the legitimacy of women's leadership," along with a "sharp critique of illegitimate power."[14]

In the first couple of centuries, however, it was not only certain proto-heretics, but also some forgers of the winning orthodoxy, who carried the memory of the Magdalene's leadership. It was Hippolytus, bishop of Rome (170–235), who granted her the title *Apostola Apostolorum*. Women can be apostles and disciples (though only as obedient "helpmeets," Eves to the Adams of the church). Tellingly, Hippolytus makes this move in the context of his *Commentary on the Song of Songs*, where he allegorically links her with the Shulamith and thus with the bride of Christ.[15] The hint of eros, sublimated but not suppressed, carries here no whiff of sin. She counts for him thus as an *appropriate* first witness to the resurrection. But this hint raises the question of what Levi meant by Jesus' *completely knowing love* of Mary.

Sex: The problem of gender wraps around that of sex, and sex curls around the margins of the early Magdalene texts. It is the *Gospel of Philip* that fuels the sexual curiosity of recent readers when it names Mary as Jesus' companion, *koinonos*, a term unique to the gnostic material and not attributed to any other disciple. Some scholars (e.g., Jorunn Buckley, following Menard) note that the Coptic term can mean "spouse" or "wife," but it is not used elsewhere in this gospel when the author signifies "wife." Marjanen suggests "spiritual consort." But, as Thimmes notes, "There is no scholarly consensus on this issue."[16] With this "issue" is secreted the sexual innuendo of readers still struggling to valorize sex in distinction from procreation and "family values." Great therefore is the interest in a subsequent scene in the gospel of Philip, which were it not for the Klimt cliché, we would call The Kiss. Once again, the Magdalene appears as the most loved disciple: "And the companion (koinonos) of the S[avior is] . . . Mary Magdalene. [But Christ loved] her more than [all] the disciples [and used to] kiss her [often] on her. . . ."[17] This is an intriguing lacuna in the manuscript. Scholars enjoy disputing just which body part was meant, although the mouth is the favored candidate. "The rest of [the disciples] . . . said to him, 'Why do you love her more than all of us?'" And the Savior returned their question with one of the great rhetorical questions of the ancient world: "Why *do* I not love you like her?" Far from reassuring the guys that he loves them all (at least) as much as *her,* his teasing mimicry leaves them and us to wonder at the meaning of the kiss! Despite the *Da Vinci Code* and other hopeful dramatizations of a sexual union, a *hieros gamos*, of Jesus and Mary Magdalene, scholars line up sternly on the side of a symbolic reading of the kiss. Kissing, as Robert Price notes, often stood for sexual intercourse, but the fact that in a gnostic text "it implied sexual intercourse is purely spiritual and metaphoric in nature."[18] At any rate, whatever this Jesus often kissed her upon and whether or not he loved her strictly for her *gnosis*, the passage certainly confirms the exalted status of Mary among the gnostic communities.

Something, however, is missing in this discussion of sex: the lack thereof. In the texts of the first centuries, nothing whatsoever was said of the penitent prostitute, great sinner or redeemed adulteress. It is becoming household knowledge that there is nothing in the Bible identifying the Magdalene with any sinful or sexual behavior. It is only said of her background that she had been possessed of seven demons. In other words, the encounter with Jesus was powerful therapy for a many-layered and troubled psyche. If the hints of *eros* in non-canonical ancient texts suggest surprising intimacies, they have quite literally nothing to do with the later legend of the reformed prostitute. That salacious portrait is a composite of Mary of Magdala, the anonymous woman sinner of Luke 7, and Mary of Bethany, who anointed Jesus in John 12.

This conflation of females under the name of the Magdalene, which never took place in Eastern Christianity, only became official in the Western church in the seventh century through the preaching of Gregory the Great in the prior century: "She whom Luke calls the sinful woman, whom John calls Mary, we believe to be that Mary from whom seven devils were ejected according to Mark."[19] The portrait of Mary Magdalene as the beautiful penitent had irresistible staying power. Indeed, by the seventeenth century, it became a fashion accessory—a whole string of English and French noblewomen, over a dozen of them mistresses of

Charles II or Louis XIV, had their portraits painted *à la Madeleine.* The theme allowed for poses at once provocative and pious. In other words, from the sixth century on, the sexual, indeed sexy, stereotype possessed the Magdalene stratitype.

Schaberg, who has guided the feminist deconstruction of the legend for over a decade, describes how this composite forms an ecclesiastical biography that "fulfills the desire—or the need—to downgrade the Magdalene as well as the desire to attach to female sexuality the notions of evil, repentance and mercy."[20] We might add that the very degradation of Mary allows her ascent; her humiliation heightens her sexual allure, indeed renders its endless depiction a work of piety. And of course in the light of the conflicts within an originally heterogeneous community and the elevation among one faction of a woman to model church leader, her subsequent negative sexualization cannot be a coincidence. Thus Rosemary Ruether argued in 1985, "The tradition of Mary Magdalene as a sinner was developed in orthodox Christianity primarily to displace the apostolic authority claimed for women through her name."[21] And as Elisabeth Schussler Fiorenza demonstrated in 1983, "the distortion of her image signals deep distortion in the self-understanding of Christian women. If as women we should not have to reject the Christian faith and tradition, we have to reclaim women's contribution and role in it. We must free the image of Mary Magdalene from all distortions and recover her role as apostle."[22] Even if we can never free this or any image from all distortions, as indeed such purification may not characterize how historical change does or should work, the reclamation of the Magdalene stratitype remains a sine qua non of a female- and sex-friendly Christianity.

Heresy: So far, however, feminist theology, as indeed most biblical scholarship by women, engages the content of these gnostic texts only as it sheds light on the social context of the struggle for power. The milieu formed by the tensions of gender, sexuality and rivalry for leadership is itself rich with interest. Pagels's *Gnostic Gospels* made a wide-reaching argument that the hereticization of the gnostics was not just a matter of theological difference, but of the orthodox rejection of the leadership roles women were playing in gnostic communities.[23] Indeed the inherent heterogeneity of early Christianity quickly organized itself into an opposition between heresy and orthodoxy, with the gnostic Christians as the primary heretics. So it is hard for feminist theology to ignore—even with the pressures of the politics of orthodoxy and academic marginalization—the links between female apostleship and the gnostic movements. Yet when one tries to enter into the gnostic side of the tradition more seriously, to consider not just its social and gender structures but also its theologies, perhaps even seeking spirited metaphors for feminist theology, one trips upon the obscurity of most of the texts, the Neoplatonic codes and deliberate psychopompic esotericism. Then we recall that in certain matters (like the goodness of the material creation, and the salvation of women as women) orthodoxy is sometimes preferable. So we may too readily settle for a feminist, revised version of apostolic succession. Nevertheless, it may not be possible (or necessarily desirable) to scrub Mary Magdalene down and present her as a right-on, progressive but properly de-eroticized Christian minister.

The sexual "charge" (as both intensity and accusation) of heresy, as having feminine and promiscuous associations, early electrified the boundaries of Christian orthodoxy. Yet boundaries by definition are shared on both sides: between the winners and losers, the insiders and the out. Thus the penitent prostitute became a needed skin of the Body of Christ, enabling a certain controlled penetrability, necessary for repentance and mission. Said to have been used first by others (Jews, pagans, outsiders), as penitent she symbolizes the conduit to the inside of the body. But to play this boundary function she must retain the taint and permeability of her illicit sex. She who had too much to say was framed as she who had too much sex: she who knew too much, that is, too many men. The heretic becomes the harlot. Here Virginia Burrus's analysis of the orthodox distribution of heresy and sexuality needs to be quoted at length:

> The fourth-century figure of the heretical woman, who is almost invariably identified as sexually promiscuous, expresses the threatening image of a community with uncontrolled boundaries. Just as she allows herself to be penetrated sexually by strange men, so too she listens indiscriminately and babbles forth new theological formulations carelessly and without restraint: all the gateways of her body are unguarded. . . . The figure of the orthodox virgin is the

counterpart to this figure of the heretical woman. . . . The virgin is typically described as maintaining the enclosure or privacy not only of her sexual parts, but also of her mouth (she is silent, diligently guarding the received tradition), of her physical location (she rarely leaves home or receives visitors), and of her social location (she does not presume to enter the public sphere of men or to challenge their hierarchical superiority)."[24]

In other words, both the speech of the heretic and the spatiality of the whore exceed the boundaries of orthodoxy—and so any heretic is marked with an illicit femininity. Any spirituality that slips beyond the prescribed limits, no matter how rigorously celibate and ascetic its practitioners, can be associated with off-limits sex. In this context, I am suggesting that Mary is a hybrid needed by orthodoxy not only as safety valve for an irrepressible eros but also as an icon of the penetrable penitent. Burrus does not discuss Mary Magdalene. Yet she has investigated a variety of holy harlots, such as Mary of Egypt, who may have helped to create the early template of the sexual-sinner-turned-saint by which the Magdalene would have been reshaped. It took a few centuries to make the holy woman into a harlot—indeed, into the figure of the harlot made holy woman. But if the Mary of orthodox legend reigns as the supreme case of the holy harlot, she straddles the very boundary between the orthodox virgin and the heretical whore.

That boundary is charged with eros. So the non-virgin woman, the woman with no hope of following the other Mary, the mother Mary, in her impossible virginity, has and so offers hope by way of her shamed and silent penance. Yet her eros, in its sublimation, remains all the more vivid, a warning and yet also a secret invitation, mysteriously attractive. The sinner still florid and flush with her sex, made licit by her penance, her devotion, and, above all, her silence? A bit of sexual advertisement for a theocracy always in danger, thanks to its triply masculine God, of spiritual sterility? Yet at the same time a zone of freedom from its fierce sexual denial? How else can we understand the fixation upon the image of the Magdalene, as, for instance, it grew its own aesthetic in early modernity? Her beautiful, often semi-naked, image was painted repeatedly, voraciously, without ecclesial protest. The legend gave her cover, draped her, veiled her in a submissive sanctity, a solicitude sweetly freed from solicitation. Mary of Magdala indeed would be ever seen and never heard. Her secret teaching—really, any teaching of women, any alternative, other, heterodox teaching—could be *sexually* shamed into silence.

If the erotic appeal of Mary Magdalene remains a fiction of orthodoxy, it has also allowed a certain exploration of eros itself—of an elemental potency neither separable from nor reducible to sex. That potency, in its plenitude and indeterminacy, its mysterious fluidity, invites conjunction and yet resists reduction to an object that can be possessed. In this ambiguity the eros opens into a cosmology, and beyond the boundaries of any particular *kosmos*, into a *pleroma*. Often the mystical side of Christianity, risking persecution, has straddled the boundary between outside and in, between proclamation and secrecy, between speech and silence, between male and female. At that boundary, it does not repress but rather channels the erotic charge. "Arise, my love, my fair one, and come away" (Song of Songs 2.10).

It was through association with the Shulammite, the female subject of the one erotically supercharged book of the Bible, the Song of Songs, that Mary Magdalene was in Hippolytus first made not sinner but rather apostle. Curious. Even Gregory the Great, the pope who formalized the composite legend and sealed Mary's fate as penitent whore, also follows elsewhere, in his mystical mood, that hermeneutical strategy, reading her love for Jesus as fully sacred, to be increased and emulated by men. He describes Mary's desperate search for Jesus in the tomb as inspired by her burning love. "Therefore, first she sought but found not at all. She persevered in her seeking and so it came to pass that she did find. This was done so that her expanding desires might grow and as they grew might take hold of what they sought. This is why it says of the Lover in the Song of Songs, 'On my little bed night after night I sought him whom my soul loves; I sought him and did not find him.'"[25] This passage conflates the Magdalene not with a prostitute, but with the single acceptably aggressive sexual female in the Bible. It does not seek to repress desire—but to expand the eros until it grows into a gratifying fullness. If these are teachings designed for the fulfillment of male celibates, it would seem nonetheless self-defeating to perpetrate a feminist reductionism on the tradition of spiritual eros here instantiated.

For feminism also cultivates a discourse of desire, of a desire whose fire does not consume self and other but rather energizes the more radical incarnations of love. Indeed we may find the male mystic's identification with a sexual woman pursuing her bridegroom, identifiable with Jesus or God, promisingly queer.[26] Of course much feminist and liberation theology has been predicated on a certain desexualization of the oppressed, a posture of purity, suggestive of moral superiority. My own initiation into the Magdalene question twenty years ago is illustrative. A well-known feminist New Testament scholar was leading a workshop for women on biblical hermeneutics. She had made the point—then truly startling—about how the penitent whore is a postscriptural invention. She divided us into groups to dramatize important scriptural scenes involving women. (I stifled the feeling of dressing up in a bathrobe for the Sunday School pageant.) The young woman playing Mary Magdalene at the tomb made the mistake of letting her rather long and lush hair down as part of the performance. And then, in front of everyone, she was asked in sternly repudiating tones: "What is it with the hair? Why do you repeat the patriarchal stereotype?" Thus, in the interest of liberating women from a tradition that shames us for our sexuality, a woman was shamed publicly for her sexuality. It took me a couple decades to bother with the Magdalene question again.

I did not, however, cease to pursue the possibility of a feminist inscription of gender within and not beyond the forcefield of an open-ended eros. Theologically this forcefield supports the discourse of an incarnate, indeed *incarnal*, love. Such eros is then neither purged of its sexuality nor reduced to a sexual role, performance, or identity. It is suggested by Marcella Althaus-Reid's queering of the Magdalene, a vivid scene in her challenge to the Christian "decency" retained even in feminist and liberation theology:

> What happens then is that if the shanty townspeople go in procession carrying a statue of the Virgin Mary and demanding jobs, they seem to become God's option for the poor. However, when the same shanty townspeople mount a carnival centered on a transvestite Christ accompanied by a Drag Queen Mary Magdalene kissing

his wounds, singing songs of political criticism, they are not any-more God's option for the poor. Carnivals in Latin America are the Christmas of the indecent, and yet they are invisible in theological discourse.[27]

As the poor must be tendered a halo of asexual innocence in liberation theology, so have women been cast in the role of innocent victim in much Christian feminism. The "indecent" alternative need not be read as a merely oppositional or defiant sexualism, no more than as a callow celebration of our goddess-identified sexual wholeness.

The Magdalene stratitype as an icon for a current theology concentrates in itself all the twisted, damaged, dignified, and unwhole layers of Christian eros: from a beneficiary of exorcism and her articulate vision, to her fictional harlotry, on through the gaze of male artists, to her patronage of both active sex workers and the Magdalene reform houses; right on into late twentieth century feminism, or to the neognostic new age priestess or goddess, sexy but dignified, of the sacred union with the male principle in Christ—and on to the festive Drag Queen. One cannot embrace these conflicting facets at once. Yet they are all there in the spectrum of her sex, filigreed into the present strata of this shifting icon. A stratitype cannot purge even its own stereotypes, as they are layered into its constitutive history. But it reveals them as such; it doesn't excise its own deformations but destratifies them, exposing them as potentials for transfiguration. I am trying to suggest, as a minor allegory for feminist theology: If we want to lift up the figure of a visionary and teacher of the early church, one who spoke eloquently, with vulnerability and courage, we do best to work with rather than against her erotic charge. We do not need to purify her—in either gnostic, orthodox, or feminist fashion—of the temptations of the flesh, but to amplify her desire lovingly, through our own. This amplification and this eros express, then, a present theology, a present unfolding of the Christian love-symbol.

"Christianity," writes Burrus, "did indeed change the state of things in the history of western sexuality, with its sternly ecstatic revising of lives translated into holiness at the shifting borderlines of sexual difference, in the movement of eros across the constructed limits of subjectivity. . . . Yet Christianity—to the extent that it continues to inspire new life, to inscribe new lives—is itself ever in a state of transforming love."[28] If love has often gotten stuck at the boundaries of a constructed interiority, waiting in impotence to be overpowered by some absolute Other, some exterior omnipotence, it has not yet lost its self-transforming capacity. Yet another plenitude, one that cannot be bottled up in the fixed contours of a divine or a human subject, has always pervaded Christian spirituality. In this opening of an eros that can no more be cut off from the gospel agape than from all queerness of sex, feminist historians of Christianity, practiced in the stratitypical complexity, have much to teach theology. Thus Amy Hollywood articulates the relation of mysticism to sexual difference within Christian history: "Poised between the desire to transcend the body's limitations and the recognition that transcendence occurs only through the body," women saints and mystics "hold out the possibility that endless, ceaseless, illimitable desire might be thought and lived outside of a phallic law of impotence. For this, neither politics nor religion will suffice."[29] Without this possibility, without its fulfilling but never finally fulfilled desire, we cannot decode the Magdalogical stratitype.

The incarnational eros powers a body-bound transcendence—what Mayra Rivera calls a "relational transcendence."[30] Its desire is always also desire for the divine—which, inasmuch as personalizing projections stick at all, certainly accepts female images of herself. Otherwise the *imago dei* must be restricted to males. But the transfiguration remains irreducible to any sexual ethic, even the ethics of a gender egalitarianism. Such desire encodes the open fullness of becoming. "Love of God has nothing moral in and of itself. . . . God forces us to do nothing except become. The only task, the only obligation laid upon us is: to become divine men and women . . . to refuse to allow parts of ourselves to shrivel and die that have the potential for growth and fulfillment."[31]

May we hear some resonance between this Irigarayan language of fulfillment and that of the Magdalene as the "all-blessed *pleroma*," she in whom no part was any longer impotent, shriveling or dying? She who lived an illimitable desire, and who also spoke it? And this—not any erotic practice—is what the gnostic gospels remember her for: "She spoke," according to the *Dialogue of the Savior*, "as a woman who knew the all." Not necessarily the know-it-all Peter sees, she remains one articulating her becoming as connectedness to everything else, to the all, to fullness itself.

Yet the thought of an illimitable becoming, of a self-exceeding finitude that takes part in an infinity beyond itself, does not necessarily harmonize with the gnostic "All." It is Emmanuel Levinas who has most definitively defined the infinite as both the effect and the aim of "Desire": "The infinite in the finite, the more in the less, which is accomplished by the idea of Infinity, is produced as Desire—not a Desire that the possession of the desirable slakes, but the Desire for the Infinite which the desirable arouses rather than satisfies."[32] This desire is never realized, satiated, done—for the Other whom it desires cannot be had, consumed, appropriated. Edith Wyschograd foregrounds the tension between this open infinity of desire and any imaginary of the whole, the *pleroma*. In her reading, the "pleromatic desire" of such philosophers as Gilles Deleuze, with his *"omnitudo,"* or One-All, would count as that of a totality that encloses the other within ontological sameness, and therefore within the self.[33] While this critique may not finally capture the radical nature of the gnostic pleroma or escape speed of the Deleuzian infinite, it does surely formulate the temptation of all ecstaticism, mysticism, gnosticism: to construct Fullness as an ultimate enclosure, a de-differentiating sphere of light. Alterity melts into the unifying medium of the All. This tendency toward a monism that dissolves particularity and its relationships—whether to the creaturely or the divine Other—is in part responsible for the orthodox Christian repudiation of gnosticism as well.

Moreover, the Jewish and Christian gnostics were branded heretics not only for their monism but also for their acute dualism, for the imagination of a *pleroma* outside of the cosmos, the site of a divinity too pure, too transcendent, too changeless to touch or be touched by a material world. It was orthodoxy in Christianity and Judaism that insisted on the goodness of the created order. Some forms of gnosticism indeed construe the *pleroma* as the highest reality because it is utterly separate from the world of affect and flesh; there, the preoccupation with Sophia is with a feminine element that has fallen into flesh, that symbolizes the feminine chaotic matter in its inferiority to the masculine light. Far from an incarnal eros, driving a transcendence within and among all bodies, let alone of a single incarnational body, a virulent spiritual antibody infects much

of what is called gnosticism (and of course much of what is called orthodoxy, as well, but the mirror-play of the church with its designated heres-
ies is a different topic).

At this point, however, we can hardly read gnosticism in its own
terms. It comes mediated by two millennia of loss and hearsay, defama-
tion and deformation—something like the Magdalene herself. And no
doubt it gets warped by its own need to hide, to protect its wisdom both
from those not ready for it and from those ready to persecute. So the
aura of esotericism, secret codes and global conspiracies still clings to its
recrudescent forms (making for a new genre of distinctly exoteric best-
seller). Indeed the elusiveness, the interiority, of mystical teachings can
all too readily be associated with a secretive sexuality, offering illicit
winks and clues. But however convenient it has remained to decry as
'gnostic' any kind of Western mysticism deemed excessive, alien, elitist,
pantheist, or just too fanciful, the fact is that women have more often
found voice within various forms of mysticism, orthodox or heterodox,
than in any other religious language—and in premodernity, than any
other public language at all. No doubt the veil of secrecy, the metaphoricity, elusiveness, and indirection of the discourse have given women
cover—which does not imply an intuitive or inward feminine essence.

However, between a reductive social explanation and a stereotype, the
feminist radiations of Mary Magdalene are making me curious about
the theological content—not just the social context—of the texts loosely
banded together as "gnosis." It is this lost-and-found library, after all, that
has delivered the strangely realistic sketch of a boldly articulate woman
driven to tears by misogyny in one text, and in the other putting into
language her own silencing by the misogyny of Peter, upon whom would
soon be erected a rock-hard male hierarchy, impatient with all mystical
exploration. For those of us outside of the specialized historical studies of
gnosticism and early Christianity, or of later mysticisms, it is a challenge
to bracket the millennia of repulsion and read the texts more experimen-
tally. This might mean—as a hermeneutical exercise in defamiliarization,
not as a formal comparison—reading it with some of the curiosity and
respect we practice if we read the *Tibetan Book of the Dead*, or the *Lotus
Sutra*. We do not so readily dismiss them as monist or dualist, even as
we are befuddled by their complex philosophical and mythical levels of

spirits, disciples, worlds, journeys. Indeed, given the trade routes opened by Alexander, historians do not exclude East Asian influence upon the second-century texts. In what follows, however, let me relinquish any claims to historical genealogy for the sake of a Magdalene experiment.

In the *Gospel of Mary*, the Savior is asked: "Will matter be utterly destroyed or not?" The question seems to presume an apocalyptic world-view among its hearers. Yet the answer comes in terms blending and decentering both Jewish apocalypticism and Platonism: "Every nature, every modeled form, every creature, exists in and with each other. They will dissolve again into their own proper root. For the nature of matter is dissolved into what belongs to its nature."[34]

The existence of creatures "in and with each other" invokes a radical ontology of relation. In Jean-Luc Nancy's formulation, "Being cannot be anything but being-with-one-another."[35] Karen King finds echoes in the passage of the apocalyptic tradition of 2 Peter ("since all things are to be thus dissolved") blended with a Platonic tradition of the origin of all things not in "nothing," but in a "matter" to which all things return.[36] One can imagine traces of, or perhaps only affinities with, the Buddhist *pratityasamutpadha*, "dependent co-arising" and "dissolving" of all phenomena within the shifting causalities of karmic interdependence. Indeed the dissolution of their forms might recall *sunyata*, the emptiness of form, to which all entities return, the serene participation in which is the ultimate dissolution of *nirvana*.

To Peter's question about the sin of the world, Jesus responds that "there is no such thing as sin. Rather you yourselves are what produces sin when you act in accordance with the nature of adultery, which is called sin." That startlingly unbiblical language might also sound something like Buddhist constructivism, whereby the karmic production of a clinging and insatiable ego, through the mechanisms of ignorance (*avidya*) and clinging, actively produces wrong action.[37] The ignorance that construes us as permanent and separate subjects cuts us off from our roots in a pleromic process. Gnosis, which, like enlightenment in Buddhism, means awakening from the ignorance, rather than an exterior grace, is what saves. Gnosis of course refers to no objectifiable knowledge, but is transforming insight, liberation from clinging delusions.

As another interpretive maneuver, might we dislodge the Magdalene *pleroma* from the Hellenistic metaphysics of a being or hyper-being that subsists changelessly *beyond* the cosmos? For the cosmos we now "know" bears little resemblance to the comparably tiny and tidy order of the ancients. The current expanding universe, or possible multiverse, comes closer to the darkly infinite, barely thinkable, mystery of the *pleroma* itself, the impersonal All, through which emanate various densities and grades of light energy. Instead we might, with the help of a process theology influenced from the start by the new physics, bring another sense of the "dissolving again" into play—as the "perpetual perishing" of Alfred North Whitehead. Every particle of matter becomes and perishes, as a momentary event of relationship amidst infinite waves of potentiality. A human is comprised of such momentary becomings, each of which takes shape and dissolves, bequeathing its particularity to the interrelations of which it is at bottom comprised: first of all in the "withness of the body." In its moment of becoming, it cannot be "simply located," but takes place as event of relation to all things that will maximize the good inasmuch as it increases in love toward all things. "In a certain sense," wrote Whitehead, receiving quantum theory early, "everything is everywhere at all times."[38]

Echoes of the Magdalene's "knowing of the All"? Yet in this new cosmology, knowledge remains perspectival and particular, enmeshed in the matrix of (all) interdependent materializations. They do not wash into a homogenous *pleroma*. Yet, nonetheless, one might trace in process thought a pleromatic sense of cosmos as composed of entities perpetually perishing into their "root" in the flux of becoming. Process theology effects a combination of a traditionally Christian creation-affirmation with the Timaean chaos or *khora* as the not-nothing from which all things arise, which Whitehead identified not with "God" but with the "creativity" in which God—the "eros of the universe"—is also becoming.[39] Process thought can help within the context of its own postmodern pluralism to effect a heterogeneous and fluent cosmos, a medium in which our distances and our intimacies may materialize as meaning. It is just one hermeneutic trying to minister to a desire, at once academic and popular, spiritual and secular, to live less wastefully, more lovingly, within the fullness of an All that is ever multiple, unfinished, *infini*, infinite.

Whatever cosmology she may support, Mary of Magdala, who "speaks as a woman who knows the All," gives guidance in a life that takes place amidst dissolution, amidst natural enough deaths and unjust, intolerable ones. The "resurrection of the Mary Magdalene" signifies at once the ascendance of speaking women in the face of long Christian injustice—and the remembrance of Mary's wordy *rabboni*, in the face of his insistent fullness of life. His resurrection is no longer predicated on a sadomasochistic torture willed by a father for a son, but on the pain-drenched transfiguration of our shared and violated mortality. Emblazoned in the withness and the witness of his body to John's Mary, the resurrection of one in whom the cosmic Logos, the translated Sophia, became incarnate, now inspires new desires. It would take flesh in our vital differences, in an eros carrying us across "the constructed limits of our subjectivities."

We might gather the whole Magdalene stratigraphy into a single elusive moment: this present tense shot through with our histories of exuberant desire and of desire nipped in the bud, of violation by the desires of others, of the adulteration and disfiguration of our own desire, and of its resistant, insistent freshness. In the tension of this moment can take place the transfiguration of desire at the roots of desire itself. This at any rate is a possible discourse of the All, a speech that always already goes too far, and never far enough.

Another second-century Nag Hammadi text insists itself. This stunning and ever more popular poem of a female Wisdom figure bears citation in this Magdalene context. For it does not fear but celebrates the gendered and sexed difference of a woman who speaks. Its title, "Thunder Perfect Mind," seems to hint at East Asian influence, but of this there is no evidence. Read stratitypically, it seems to anticipate Mary's reconstruction as holy harlot before, chronologically, it had happened—and in the same breath, to perform its deconstruction. Though it bears no identification of its female speaker, and certainly no allusion to any Mary, it reads as though the Magdalene herself is speaking as in the pleroma, or persona, of divine Sophia. This Wisdom discloses how she gets hated and silenced, humiliated and framed in terms of those familiar binary hierarchies of the patriarchy; and how through paradox she turns the binaries to her advantage. And that of All.

I was sent forth from the power,
And I have come to those who reflect upon me, . . .
You who are waiting for me, take me to yourselves.
And do not banish me from your sight.
And do not make your voice hate me, nor your hearing.
Do not be ignorant of me anywhere or any time. Be on your guard!
Do not be ignorant of me.
For I am the first and the last.
I am the honored one and the scorned one.
I am the whore and the holy one. . . .
I am she whose wedding is great
And I have not taken a husband . . .
I am the silence that is incomprehensible
And the idea whose remembrance is frequent.
I am the voice whose sound is manifold
And the word whose appearance is multiple. . . .
I am strength and I am fear . . . I am the one who has been hated
everywhere
And who has been loved everywhere . . .
I am the one whom you have hidden from
And you appear to me.
But whenever you hide yourselves,
I myself will appear . . .
I am a mute who does not speak,
And great is my multitude of words.[40]

I, for one, retreat into the thundering silence of her words. Before I say
too much, too soon.

Ethical Desires: Toward a Theology of Relational Transcendence

MAYRA RIVERA

"Eroticism is first and foremost a thirst for otherness. And the supernatural is the supreme otherness," writes Octavio Paz in *Double Flame*. The supreme otherness of God—theologians call it "divine transcendence." Eroticism thus suggests a link between human otherness and divine transcendence. In its most common versions, however, divine transcendence seems not to enhance the awareness of interhuman otherness, but rather to so relativize difference as to effectively absorb otherness into itself. Indeed, "transcendence" is assumed to be what God has and humans do not. Thus the otherness of God and the otherness of creatures, the love for God and interhuman relations are distanced from one another.

The work of Emmanuel Levinas reacts against this dichotomy. The "gleam of transcendence in the face of the Other," Levinas's crucial formulation, seeks to turn discourses of transcendence away from dreams of an otherworldly realm, toward the concrete reality of other persons. Bringing transcendence to bear on the ethical encounter between human beings, Levinas's work has influenced philosophies and theologies of liberation as well as poststructuralist thought. However, Levinas sets apart the sexual encounter and ultimately opposes ethics to eroticism. This is a common dichotomy that threatens Levinas's critical reformulation of transcendence. Luce Irigaray's reading of Levinas's *Totality and Infinity* not only exposes the problem but also opens his proposal toward the possibility of an "ethics of sexual difference." Her interrogation of the role that Levinas assigns to the feminine in the production of transcendence will help us uncover the implicit gendering of Levinas's transcendence as well as the spatio-temporality that it assumes. And yet her transcendence also closes itself around predetermined types of encounters.

After a brief synopsis of Irigaray's assessment of classic philosophical notions of transcendence, this essay will trace the move from Levinas's face-to-face to Irigaray's body-to-body encounter and its effect on the spatio-temporal imaginary of transcendence. We will explore the interpenetration of transcendence in the flesh and between persons as well as its broader cosmic dimensions, where transcendence appears as erotic cosmological incarnation. This breadth requires, paradoxically, greater singularity. The work of Chicana scholars Gloria Anzaldúa and Cherríe Moraga will allow us to move beyond Irigaray's images of the body, to see the body in the singularity of its multiple differences and limitations.

DISEMBODIED TRANSCENDENCES

Luce Irigaray argues that "the philosophers" rightly recognized their need for transcendence as a basis for the becoming of subjectivity, as an external limit to their subjectivity, but also as a telos for their intentionality.[1] These philosophers, Irigaray reminds us, "were men and they were debating between men. Their solution was, of course, a masculine one."[2] As we know, they conceived the journey toward transcendence as entailing the overcoming of their own bodies—indeed of materiality as such—which they viewed as constraints to freedom. They projected these constraints onto women, positing a God as the "opposite pole of their instincts and natural inclinations." God would be their external limit and the objective toward which their intentions could be guided.[3] They proposed: "The subject develops between . . . two extremes: nature and God, nature and spirit, mother-nature and father-Logos, irreducible birth and absolute creation."[4] An imaginary rift is thus opened between nature and God, which in turn divides spirit from nature and birth from creation.

God was their other, perhaps their only transcendent Other, for the masculinist culture ignored the transcendent character of the body, of bodies, of the cosmos. Thus, Irigaray calls us to turn back to the relation between the sexes for a sexual or carnal ethics—an ethics of the passions.[5] "Transcendence is no longer ecstasy, going out of the self toward the inaccessible, extra-sensible, extra-earthly entirely-other."[6] But Irigaray is not expounding pure immanence. Rather than choosing one side of the immanence/transcendence cosmological divide opened by the philosophers' transcendence, Irigaray interrogates its assumptions. She seeks a model for the relations between nature and God, nature and spirit, flesh and transcendence, that allows spirit to touch the most intimate spaces of life. A notion of transcendence in the flesh grounds Irigaray's vision of a relation between the sexes that is both "terrestrial and heavenly."[7]

LEVINAS'S EROS

Irigaray's most sustained discussion of transcendence unfolds in the context of her response to Levinas's *Totality and Infinity,* and so we shall turn to his depiction of interhuman transcendence in order to encounter Irigaray's difference.[8] In *Totality and Infinity,* Levinas takes us back to the singular encounter of the self with the other (whom I will never be) to reinscribe responsibility at the core of subjectivity. It is on the basis of such an understanding that he poses the question of transcendence—one that does not bypass the human Other, but is opened by "him." Levinas thinks of transcendence as the "welcoming of the other by the same, of the other by me."[9] Transcendence is found in the *face* of the Other. For Levinas transcendence "designates a relation with a reality infinitely distant from my own reality, yet without this distance destroying this relation and without this relation destroying this distance."[10] Transcendence is defined as separation. The relation established between the self and the Other is based neither on knowledge nor on a dynamics of revelation. It is a relationship of desire—of what he calls metaphysical desire. "Transcendence is *desire*."[11] Metaphysical desire is strictly opposed to the needs of the body, which, like hunger, are satisfied by the incorporation of the desired object into the self. Metaphysical desire "desires beyond everything that can simply complete it"; it does not aim at appropriation or consumption, nor even consummation.[12] This interpretation of the relation of transcendence in terms of desire represents a promising move towards a relational transcendence, where the irreducibility of difference is not in conflict with desire, and where desire does not seek the elimination of difference.

But before we get too excited by this metaphysical desire, we should note that Levinas carefully distinguishes it from eros—revealing his desire to be less *sexy* than *sexist*. Levinas does ponder the ethical import of the sexual relation between man and woman, at least for a moment, but ultimately eros fails his test of transcendence. Eros, he argues, like physical needs, seeks satisfaction, it returns to itself. For Levinas, ethics does not return; the desire of transcendence is always an outward movement, without cycles.[13] However, cycles, as Irigaray constantly reminds us, are intrinsic to the temporality of nature, to the life of the body. A purely linear transcendence is famously prone to leave the flesh behind. Admittedly, the abstract, progressive impulse is not the transcendence that Levinas seeks in the face-to-face encounter; nonetheless a common patriarchal anxiety about the workings of bodies seems to haunt his encounter with the erotic. He concludes: "The metaphysical event of transcendence—the welcome of the other, hospitality—Desire and language—is not accomplished as love."[14] The ethical relation is "primordially enacted in conversation," a discourse that, Levinas makes clear, is not love.[15] Love is thus relegated to the nether side of transcendence.

Indeed, Levinas's account of the sexual encounter is doomed from the start, for the feminine has already been given a role: The beloved is frailty, tenderness, vulnerability, irresponsible animality, infancy, equivocation.[16] Transcendence is not accomplished as love, except when love engenders the son. It is paternity that saves love, furnishing a transcendence that becomes incarnate among men—made possible by, but foreclosed to, women. The feminine here is only womb, an immanence from which transcendence has been plucked. In Levinas the promise of a philosophy of transcendence in the finite is thwarted by replicating the immanence/transcendence divide within the created realm—across sexual difference. The assumed chasm between God and creation of traditional conceptions of transcendence is displaced, but not its undergirding logic: the imagined chasm between a transcending man and an immanent woman. In consequence, a rift opens also between justice and passion, between responsibility and love.[17]

Commenting on the Song of Songs, Levinas writes, "Perhaps justice is founded on the *mastery* of passion."[18] Not only does Levinas reinstate the dichotomy between justice and passion—oddly, to be sure, while reading the Song of Songs. His description of the logic of this mastery also bears eerie resemblance to a well-known structure of subjection—domination over an Other on which the dominating one nonetheless depends. "The justice through which the world subsists is founded on the most *equivocal* order, but on the *domination* exerted at every moment over this order, or this disorder. This order, equivocal *par excellence,* is precisely the order of the erotic, the realm of the sexual."[19] Domination is thus invoked as the power that leads from equivocation—the order of the erotic, or the "epiphany of the feminine," as Levinas says in a different context—to justice.[20] Levinas continues, "Justice would be possible only if it triumphs over this equivocalness."[21] Mastery and domination over the erotic— what kind of justice could this found? Let me say in passing that it seems hardly irrelevant that one could use that same sentence to describe patriarchal or imperial logics. Patriarchy (or colonialism) is founded on women (or the colonized), more specifically on the domination exerted at every moment over them. Indeed, Levinas's advocacy of mastery over the erotic seems to be yet another instance of those discourses, to which Irigaray alludes, that imagine transcendence as an ascending journey from nature to God, from body to spirit, from an irreducible birth to an absolute creation—from eros to justice.

The dichotomy thus established between justice and the order of the erotic ultimately makes the status of the face uncertain. Is it still possible, as Levinas attempts, to prevent the call of the Other from becoming detached from his or her body? Would word and face-as-flesh not fall on different sides of the chasm thus opened? For Levinas, it is in the face of the Other that transcendence gleams. The face presents itself—it is seen and it is heard, it expresses itself visibly and/or audibly—but always across an infinite distance. It is precisely the need to protect the separateness of transcendence that leads Levinas to imagine the relation in terms of discourse.[22] Conversation "maintains the distance between me and the Other, the radical separation asserted in transcendence," Levinas explains. Light and sound travel through the divide between the self and the Other in ethical relation. In Levinas's depiction of the relation, light and sound reach out across the distance and touch the eyes and the ear drums of the subject—an approach of waves to skin, but never of skin to skin.

IN THE BEGINNING: TOUCH

The dichotomy between ethics and the erotic in Levinas's thought is certainly related to his problematic depictions of the feminine, but is not limited to that issue. The spatio-temporality of transcendence in Levinas's imaginary—its heights, exteriority, and straightforwardness—presupposes the exclusion of eroticism. It cannot quite accommodate encounters between bodies, where one is inside the other, where one embraces the other.

A model of transcendence in the flesh calls for other ways to conceive of the bonds between human beings. Like Levinas, Irigaray locates transcendence in the encounter with the Other. However, for her what protects the otherness of the Other is not separation, as it is for Levinas. *"Approaching* involves an irreducible *distancing;* which lies, insurmountable, in the drawing near to one another."* The distance that Irigaray imagines here, in contrast to Levinas's separation, defies common intuition; it is insurmountable in touch. It is a figuration of irreducible difference, an "elusive mystery of which the preservation is necessary," for transcendence, that is, "in order that desire *unfold* toward a blossoming."[23] This elusive mystery welcomes touch; it envelops bodies, within and without.

"Lovers' faces live not only in the face but in the whole body," Irigaray reminds Levinas.[24] The encounter between lovers does not fit the model of two planes facing each other   two facades, as it were—that the Levinasian account evokes, where the Other's transcendence is always exterior. The erotic encounter demands an imaginary that can accommodate bodily transcendence—as bodies in touch and within each other. Irigaray finds a metaphor for this spatiality in our own beginnings in the womb, in that intimacy of a shared membrane, contact between self and Other, before the word. That place, where we were welcomed before our offerings of any welcome, is the site of identification between mother and child as well as of differentiation between the two. In the beginning was touch, Irigaray reminds us.

The place of initial welcome, however, is no longer there; it does not call us back to it, to perform a regressive move like the ones that Levinas (like most masculinist thought) fears.[25] The imaginary return to the womb awakens us to the memories of its primordial caress inscribed in the flesh. And it is precisely in fidelity to that memory that subjectivity can become welcome and open to a "birth that has never taken place"— for both man and woman. "Sensual pleasure can reopen and reverse" the control-and consumption-oriented approaches to the world and to the Other. It moves toward an infinite empathy that abides "by the outlines of the other."[26] Neither grasping nor assimilating, the caress retraces the borders of the Other. Neither height nor one-dimensional separation describes the space between lovers. That space is traced by the contours of bodies.

Drawing near and unfolding—this movement follows a complex spatio-temporality where Eros "touches upon" transcendence. This space is multidimensional; the flow through it involves cycles and returns as much as forward movement—the morphology of the body challenges the privilege of the phallic imaginary. The caress of the Other summons me to recall the intimacy of a primordial communion that gives birth to difference. "Caressing me, he bids me neither to disappear nor to forget, but to rememorate the place where, for me, the most secret life holds itself in reserve. . . . Plunging me back into the maternal womb and beyond that conception, awakening me to another birth," again and again.[27] The erotic encounter thus opens the possibility of a new birth, where transcendence takes place.

Transcendence is not achieved through a linear straightforward development. Like cosmic life, transcendence takes place through cycles of repetition that bring forth new births, through remembrances that instantiate new possibilities. Transcendence repeats, and brings about the new. Transcendence does take flesh. Transcendence is neither deferral nor consummation, but a new outcome of the encounter mediated by eros: new conception, rebirth, regeneration. Indeed Irigaray challenges the way that Levinas's deferrals always maintain the separation "with the other in the experience of love."[28] For Levinas admits no time for returns and no space for communion. In his ethics, there is only desire, not love. The lovers never enter the place where "the perception of being two persons becomes indistinct," they never access the "energy produced together" to be born again. Levinas, Irigaray observes, turns toward "a future where no day is named for the encounter with the other in an embodied love."[29] As the actual encounter is deferred, love evades the responsibility of transcendence. Ethics is excluded from the realm of actual sexual relations. Perhaps, as Gayatri Spivak claims, "the hardest lesson is the impossible intimacy of the ethical."[30]

TRANSCENDENCE AS SEXUAL DIFFERENCE

Irigaray's account of the sexual encounter inscribes sexual difference as a difference between the feminine and the masculine. All other transformative encounters, distant or intimate, seem to be excluded. The place of new birth appears to be open only to sexual couples. Is the energy for transcendence absent from other encounters? "Who or what the other is, I never know," Irigaray admits. "But," she adds, "this unknowable other is that which differs sexually from me. This feeling of wonder, surprise, and astonishment in the face of the unknowable ought to be returned to its proper place: the realm of sexual difference."[31] Can there be, however, a "proper place" for wonder and astonishment? Can we set rules for surprise?

The status of the sexual pair in Irigaray's work is the subject of much scholarly debate, for Irigaray frequently appears to be subverting the sexual hierarchy while leaving its heterosexist assumptions in place. Levinas's depiction of the sexual encounter conforms to the patriarchal gendering: He imagines a male (active) lover in relation to a female (passive, settled) beloved. In contrast, Irigaray introduces other characters to the sexual encounter scene: the female lover and the male beloved. This seems to open the possibility for resisting heterosexist assumptions. Troublingly, however, Irigaray does claim that "pleasure between the same sex does not result in that immediate ecstasy between the other and myself."[32] Why would she want to impose such limits upon the possibilities of sexual experiences?

A Levinasian move might be at play here. Like Levinas, Irigaray wants to guard ethics from a logic of substitution. The Other and the self are not interchangeable. Levinas argues not only "that the same goes unto the other differently than the other unto the same," but that it is impossible "to place oneself outside of the correlation between the same and other."[33] I cannot take the place of the Other or include her within the reach of the self; the Other presents "himself." I approach the Other only as myself, with all the limits that implies. Levinas attempts to assure that directionality through the asymmetry of relation—the Other is the poor whom I cannot approach with empty hands. The relation is irreversible. The Other is the destitute one to whom I must respond. While it subverts the predominant social hierarchy by asserting the priority of the destitute person, it raises other ethical concerns: In his framework the Other is always in the position of victim.[34] This logic entails an unsurpassable hierarchical relation, even when its values are reversed. Indeed, Irigaray contends that in Levinas's work there is no "recognition of," or "interaction between, two different subjectivities."[35]

Like Levinas, Irigaray wants to guard against substitution. She does so by asserting not the asymmetry of the relation to the Other, but the irreversibility of sexual difference. She locates the relational boundary not between the propertied and the poor or between the citizen and the stranger, but between man and woman. She says, "I will never be in a man's place, never will a man be in mine. Whatever identifications are possible, one will never exactly occupy the place of the other—they are irreducible one to the other."[36] Although this move avoids the implicit hierarchy of Levinas's asymmetry, it still leads her to similar problems: The boundaries of otherness are structurally set. For "the confused and changing multiplicity of the other . . . begins to resolve itself into a system of intelligible relationships," to quote Irigaray's own comments regarding Plato's *Hysteria*.

WOMAN, MAN, AND THE THIRD

Irigaray's strategy tends to reify and indeed transcendentalize sexual difference, as Amy Hollywood has persuasively argued. Irigaray puts "sexual difference in the place once occupied by God." It is, she argues, "the universal and objective difference through which subjectivity can be discovered."[37] However, Irigaray's male-female dualism may be destabilized when the sexual pair is grounded in the other relations in which Irigaray herself seems to envision it. Focusing on Irigaray's allusions to "the third" may help us move toward a broader and more theologically promising notion of relational transcendence. The sexual pair is not one! The man-and-woman is always in relation to "the third"—a concrete reality beyond the sexual pair. This third is not, to be sure, an extra-mundane or extra-temporal reality that would submit both man and woman to its immaterial law. After all, we know that at the end of the day the dominant man slips into the position of such a god, proclaiming the supposed precepts of eternal and immaterial essences.

If the third that Irigaray alludes to liberates man and woman from the potential tyranny of the dyadic structure, it is not by escaping materiality, but by signaling the multiple relationalities inherent in men and women. The third relates both man and woman to their potential as well as to their own limits: "to the divine, to death, to the social, to the cosmic."[38] Or better: to the cosmic *as* material, social, and divine. To conceive these cosmic relations entails imagining space differently. An ethics of the passions requires a reconception of *place,* as Irigaray announces in the introduction to *An Ethics of Sexual Difference.*[39] Traditionally, woman has been the place for man. She has been his envelope. Without her own place, woman is only his thing. His world turns her into a seductive and threatening thing, into a container whose engulfment has been the source of innumerable male fantasies. If there is no third, Irigaray alerts us, she or he would become *all-powerful.*[40] And this provokes violent reactions: He attempts to contain her in his places that, unlike the womb, are neither alive nor open. Man has constructed a world where she has no place of her own, she has no third. At the same time, as a man's thing, without her own place in the world, woman has no access to transcendence. She becomes reduced to the immanent ground of his transcendence. If she is *his* place, how could she *offer* welcome to the Other? For her to receive the Other, for man and woman to welcome each other, each must have his and her own space.

A COSMIC PLACE

Each woman and each man must have her and his own place if they are to enter a common space for the erotic encounter—to enter and to emerge from it. If the relation between the sexes is to bring forth new births, if it will open the flesh to transcendence, it must, quite literally, take place. Incarnation, Christianity has taught us, needs its stable, its ass, its ox, and its star. Indeed, the *"work* of the flesh is never unconnected" from the world and the universe. The "work of the flesh" needs the energies of bodies and cosmos, but it also produces energies that contribute to its transformation, to the cosmos's continuous creation. Furthermore, as irreducibly relational, the work of the flesh is never without limits. Transcendence is always becoming within the limits and promises of embodied existence—never dislodged from it.

A common place in which the self and the Other would enter is not part of Levinas's depiction of the ethical encounter. Indeed, posing a space that could contain both self and the Other would for him amount to creating a totality. For Irigaray, however, the cosmos is never a closed totality, but a living ground.[41] The cosmos does not lead back to sameness. It is not "pure immanence," but quite to the contrary, the site of transcendence in flesh. Yet masculinist cultures have denied their "debt toward that which gives and renews life," just as they have foreclosed the body and the womb.[42] They have reduced the cosmos to a closed totality, as a once and for all product of creation.[43] "Believing that [the cosmos] is given once and for all, to be exploited endlessly, carelessly, irretrievably," human beings have ignored its transcendence. In this reduction of creation to the merely immanent we have also abandoned our own responsibility as mediators of creation, as agents of its transcendence. We have forgotten our own role in the becoming of the cosmos as well as God's concern for it.[44]

In addition to the place into which man and woman enter, and places for each one, there must be a space between them. "Desire can eat up place," Irigaray reminds us, in attempts either to regress to the womb or to consume the Other. The subsistence of the couple and the desire that unites them thus depends on the protection of the space between them. This idea of distance, introduced above, is neither static nor abyssal, but a dynamic interval subtended "toward and into infinity" by Godself. "The *irreducible.* Opening up the universe."[45] May we imagine God as the living and dynamic envelope that links us while protecting the space between us? An envelope that subtends the "space" of difference and opens creatures to a relational infinity that is transformed as a result of the relations across differences?

As mediators of the becoming of the cosmos, human beings meet the transcendence, not only of the sexual Other, but also of the whole creation. Indeed, the demise of the transcendence of the cosmos is most frequently inextricable from the implicit relegation of ethnic Others to sameness, to immanence. Irigaray does not explore these connections. The role of providing support for man's flight to the heights of ethics—of transcendence—is not exclusively assigned to women. This mechanism is the guiding principle of contemporary geopolitics and capitalist globalization. For instance, the Others of the south are increasingly confined to a closed space, to the role of supplying the material resources, indeed being the material resources, for satiating the desires and setting free the first world—not accidentally conceived as spatially higher. The south is conceived as being the place from which the north departs to pursue its own transcendence. In these encounters with the Others of the third world the cosmos continues to appear as given, once and forever, for incessant exploitation. We have yet to think of our encounters with those Others in light of transcendence of the flesh and of the cosmos. It seems crucial, indeed urgent, to find a model of encountering these Others of the third world—sexually different, but not only—where each is invited to enter a place and have a place, a cosmic dwelling. For the United States, desire has been consuming the cosmos, eating up place.

The relation between sexual difference and cosmological unity/multiplicity opens the space for a theological interpretation of the erotic relation. Rather than extracting the sexual pair from its relations to the cosmos, the social, and the divine, might "the third" link both partners to the multiple complexities of their existence? As a site of incarnation that participates and contributes to the continuous creation of the cosmos, the Irigarayan erotic encounter may be imagined as an instance in the infinite web of relations across difference that constitute a living creation.

THE SOCIAL BODY

In Irigaray's work, however, the implications of the social relations of each of the persons in the sexual relation remain undeveloped at best. Irigaray's analysis stays in the interstices of sexual difference. Indeed, at times she seems to define the space between the self and the Other as a simple frontier—in sharp contrast with her descriptions of that interval between the self and Other as a dynamic and living place subtended toward and into infinity.

Touch between sexually differentiated bodies provides us a key figure for the simultaneity of desire and transcendence, and a much-needed supplement to the Levinasian face-to-face. We have seen that the encounter between bodies opens up a more complex spatio-temporality and a richer model for imagining the transcendence in the flesh. And yet to predefine the basis on which the Other may induce "feelings of wonder, surprise, and astonishment," is a step toward occluding the excess, the infinity in the flesh of the Other.[46] Furthermore, an exclusive reliance on the sexual pair as the site of this bodily transcendence is at risk of exiling man-and-woman from their other relations, from the broader (social) world. If it loses touch with its social relations, this model may turn out to propose yet another *otherworldly* transcendence.

Otherness is multiple in its singularity. The Other is always already implicated in infinitely complex relations—sexual relations—which are always also political, ethnic, and economic relations. The transcendence of the Other might thus be imagined as that infinite relationality that appears to us at the present time, in this particular encounter. This relationality extends in time as much as in space. For the differences encountered at any given time—as differences that emerge from relations, from other encounters—also extend beyond this moment. They reach beyond the boundaries of sexual difference. The call of other Others is never merely exterior to the relation between the sexes. Other encounters fold into the sexual relation and sexual relations unfold into the maze of socio-political affairs.

Each singular encounter unfurls to an irreducible multiplicity. A singular encounter opens up to history, and a room to a whole country. I indicated above that for Irigaray the work of the flesh is never unrelated to the universe. I want to emphasize that the work of the flesh is never unrelated to other persons. Even inside the maternal womb, before conception and differentiation, the traces of the multiple relations that bring forth mother and child subsist. In *This Sex which Is Not One,* Irigaray turns to female morphology—"*neither one nor two*"; a nearness that does not long to become one—to provide an alternative vision for overcoming the phallic economy of the one: "The *one* form, of the individual, of the (male) sexual organ, of the proper name, of the proper meaning."[47] But she never pursues the potential of this multiplicity for a rearticulation of differences, along racial, ethnic, and cultural axes.[48]

The multiple relations (and their markers) that constitute the person have been of particular interest to feminists of color, whose experiences of racial/ethnic marginalization are as important as sexuality for their theorization of the body. For instance, the work of Chicana scholars Gloria Anzaldúa and Cherríe Moraga may be read as attempting to un- cover the transcending potential of the sexual relation and the power of touch to bring about new births.[49] However, their conceptualization of the sexual is always already also racial/ethnic.

Anzaldúa's use of the term *mestizaje* illustrates the intertwining of race/ethnicity and sexuality in a single body that is not one. Literally, mestizaje refers to the product of the sexual encounters between persons of different races, particularly between European and indigenous people. Nonetheless Chicana scholars have used it to refer to the myriad of rela- tions across difference that constitute the self—not only the racial mix- ture associated with Latina identity, but also other social relations that impinge upon and become inextricable from the self. Thus, in Anzaldúa's work, mestizaje refers not only to the relation between the Indian mother and the Spanish father, but also to the relation between the Mexi- can and the Anglo-American elements of her identity.[50] Multiplicity is, to be sure, riddled with ambiguities. In its attention to the complexity within the self, mestizaje resembles Irigaray's characterization of female sexuality. In their intimate relationship, the different elements of the mestiza are *"neither one nor two."*[51] And yet mestizaje extends the bound- aries of the body toward the social body. The body is inscribed by the multiple relations from which it emerges—at birth and beyond. "Pero es dificil differentiating between lo heredado, lo adquirido, lo impuesto"— Anzaldúa ponders, "just what did she inherit from her ancestors? . . . which is the baggage from the Indian mother, which is the baggage from the Spanish father . . . ?"[52] The socio-political becomes flesh, it is incarnate in and as sexed bodies. Irigaray is not oblivious to this fact, of course. But her privilege of the man/woman difference restricts the realm of the erotic. As we saw, Irigaray reminds Levinas that "Lovers' faces live not only in the face but in the whole body."[53] Anzaldúa and Moraga would add that the lovers' bodies live not only in their *individual* bodies but in the whole socio-political body.

Moraga's explicit thematization of the social production of desire and its inscriptions on bodies leads her to more complex and conflictive descriptions of the erotic than those Irigaray expounds. Moraga may, like Irigaray, imagine a sex that is not one. But writing from the conflicted space of racial and sexual wars, Moraga represents the social constitution of bodies through figures of multiple, but also of partial or wounded forms of embodiment. For instance, a woman's skin appears as the site of memories of the touch of the maternal dwelling, but also of painful and guilt-ridden separation—her light skin is a sign of her distancing from her brown mother and thus a reminder of her complicity with a racist society. Her skin is a "scar sealing up a woman," she writes. From another perspective, however, Moraga is brown. Her skin is darkened by her desire of women—Moraga's sex, she observes, is brown.[54] "By incorporating pain, difficulty, and failure in the re-imagining of a sexual and social world, [Moraga] represents a non-redemptive vision that obliges the reader or spectator to account for the conflictive social and cultural contexts providing the arena for sexual experience."[55] She imagines bodies as not yet whole, portrayed as dismembered bodies and amputated parts: as faces still searching for their bodies, for example. These bodies where conflicted relationships take place are still yearning to be reborn as one—or at least as a multiplicity capable of lovingly touching itself. For these bodies, to caress their own multiplicity is a promise not-yet-fulfilled.

Significantly, Irigaray's phrase, the "memory of the flesh," evokes a myriad of carnal reminders that Irigaray never considers: skin color, the texture of hair, the scars on the skin, one's body type—markers of racial difference. For the lover's flesh remembers. It bears the marks of histories of wonder and pain—even beyond the womb. Individual histories, in their relation to others' histories, mark the skin that is touching and being touched. They make possible (or foreclose) erotic desire. An account of transcendence in the flesh would need to acknowledge the transformative power of these wounded bodies, whose memories also open the self toward unforeseeable becomings, toward incarnate transcendence.[56]

Transcendence is a relation with a reality irreducibly different from my own reality. This difference is an elusive mystery in the whole body of the Other—singular in its irreducible multiplicity. The Other is not merely one who summons and judges, but rather one who incites feelings of wonder. Her/his otherness preserves the interval necessary for the unfolding of desire. Erotic pleasure and intimacy are thus returned to the realm of ethics, where transcendence does take place—in the singularity of each encounter, in a particular space. Flesh and cosmos open toward transcendence. Relational transcendence does not entail overcoming the flesh. It is a transfiguration that never bypasses the body in its complex historicity. To develop a notion of relational transcendence thus requires a reconceptualization of the interhuman encounter and of the body—one that foregrounds the links between the individual body and the sociopolitical body, between the single encounter and histories of communal encounters. Such a model may lead us toward a more inclusive theological articulation of the cosmic as material, social, and divine.

❧ New Creations: Eros, Beauty, and the Passion for Transformation

GRACE JANTZEN

The Genesis story in the Hebrew Bible, with its account of a beautiful garden forfeited by a descent into sin and violence, is often taken as the paradigmatic narrative of creation for Christianity. It is not the only biblical account of creation. The prophet Isaiah, for example, describes a vision of a new creation, made by God to transform the present world of trouble, destruction and pain. He declares the proclamation of God:

> For behold, I create new heavens and a new earth;
> And the former things shall not be remembered or come to mind.
> But be glad and rejoice forever in that which I create;
> For behold, I create Jerusalem a rejoicing, and her people a joy . . .

There follows a description of a utopian Jerusalem—so different from that conflict-ridden city in Isaiah's time or in ours—in which people live together in peace and harmony. All flourish together. Violence has no place: "They shall not hurt or destroy in all my holy mountain, says the Lord" (Isaiah 65:17–25).

Similar accounts of a new heaven and a new earth also occur elsewhere in the Bible, notably in the book of Revelation, where the writer describes "the holy city, new Jerusalem, coming down out of heaven from God, prepared as a bride adorned for her husband" (Revelation 21:2). All God's enemies have been defeated and shut out, and the people of God live with him in unimaginable beauty and splendor. The city has "the glory of God, its radiance like a most rare jewel, like a jasper, clear as crystal." Through the city flows a "river of the water of life," beside which grows "the tree of life with its twelve kinds of fruit . . . and the leaves of the tree were for the healing of the nations" (Revelation 22:1–2).

These visions of a heavenly Jerusalem of peace and beauty stand as parallels to the Genesis story of the first paradise. But whereas the Genesis story represents the beginning of all things, this new creation represents the end. It will not be a scene of sin, disaster and expulsion as was the Garden of Eden; nor will God exert his own violence upon it as he did in the flood that followed the sinfulness of early humanity. Rather, the new paradise will go on forever, with no more sin, pain, or violence, whether inflicted by God or by people. The newness of the new Jerusalem is a cancellation or forgetting of what has gone before: The anguish of the past no longer comes to mind, as "God himself . . . will wipe away every tear from their eyes . . . for the former things have passed away" (Revelation 21:4).

Nevertheless, it is obvious that the writers of each of these accounts have violence very much on their minds as they write. The ambiguity of the Genesis stories is paralleled by the ambiguities of these new accounts of creation, in which peace and beauty prevail only because others have been expelled. Isaiah represents the enemies of God's people as utterly crushed; the writer of the Apocalypse has opponents of true believers cast into hell with Satan. Just as in the case of the Genesis flood, violence and beauty appear in a tension that becomes unbearable once we put ourselves into the position of those who are outside rather than those whom God has favored.

Elsewhere I explore some of the specific forms taken by the tension between violence and beauty, necrophilia and natality, the preoccupation with thanatos and the passion for transformation.[1] Here, however, I shall restrict myself to an exploration of three theoretical accounts of violence that have been offered in relation to religion, with specific reference to the question of how that violence could be transformed. What is the relationship between creativity and violence? How does newness enter the world, the newness that is needed if there is to be transformation of the violence of the present world order? None of the thinkers whose ideas of violence I shall consider has much to say about beauty, creativity, or the erotic passion from which beauty and creativity flow. However, I shall argue that although beauty is ignored in their work, just as it has regularly been pushed to the margins in the Bible and in Christian theology, it still offers a place of resistance from which violence can be challenged. In the final section of this essay I shall begin an exploration of what that entails.

THE VIOLENCE OF CREATION?

Is creativity itself violent? Could there be creation without violence? At first sight it would seem that creativity is the very opposite of destruction, and therefore contrary to violence; yet, as I have already hinted, the ambiguities are already present in the biblical text. It might be thought, therefore, that when influential scholars have defined violence in ways that render creativity itself violent they are in fact faithful to the uncomfortable tensions of the Bible. However, I believe that things are not that simple. I propose to begin, therefore, by examining these definitions. I shall argue, in the first place, that they are incorrect or harmful as definitions; and shall show later how creativity is essential if we are to develop alternatives to violence; and that although no human activity is unambiguous, violence is not inherent in creativity itself. What I want to get at is how creativity has been displaced or stood in ambiguous tension with violence and the love of death. What are the forms which creativity has taken and perhaps can take again to bring newness into the world?

I begin with a definition of violence offered by Hent de Vries.[2] Before I address his account of violence directly, I want to pay tribute to the significance and timeliness of his work on religion and violence. Until relatively recently, religious scholars, like many others, tended to assume that the world was, for good or ill, becoming increasingly secular, at least in its public face, and that such religious belief and experience as there still is belongs in the private sphere. Religion, it was thought, is not (or should not be) involved in scientific experiments or in the stock exchange or in the master discourses and disciplines of modernity. But with the destruction of the Twin Towers in the name of Allah, and the military campaigns against Afghanistan and Iraq in the name of God Bless America, a new era has erupted in which it has became clear—as it should have been all along—that religion is a potent force in legitimizing violence. Many religious scholars were caught napping, with very little in the way of conceptual resources either to understand the eruption of violence in the name of religion or to see how religion could act as a counterforce. De Vries was one of the few scholars who had seriously focused on the relationship of violence and religion, and was therefore in a position to comment intelligently on what was going on.

Nevertheless, when it comes specifically to de Vries's definition of violence, I have a problem. De Vries says:

> Violence, in both the widest possible and the most elementary senses of the word, entails any cause, any justified or illegitimate force, that is exerted—physically or otherwise—by one thing (event or instance, group or person, and, perhaps, word and object) on another. Violence thus defined finds its prime model—its source, force, and counterforce—in key elements of the tradition called the religious. It can be seen as the very element of religion.[3]

I do not find this definition helpful. If, as he says, violence is involved in *every* exertion of force, even when it is justified and even when it is nonphysical; moreover, if this exertion is not restricted to the intentional exertion of force by persons but includes also events and even words, then nothing is left out. Everything is violent. Creation is violent; so is destruction. Religion is violent, but religion is also the "counterforce" to violence.

Now, it seems to me that it is vitally important to have tools for discrimination between violence and nonviolence, between those exertions of force, physical or not, which are destructive and those which are transformative. If we say that *every* exertion of force is violent, then the effect is to evacuate the term *violence* of all specific meaning, and with it all possibility of moral evaluation. The force of persuasion that a dog owner exerts in training, all her praise and puppy treats, could not be differentiated from the force she would exert if she were to beat up the puppy instead. The force of an argument and the force of a bomb would be the same, in quality if not in quantity.

I suggest that if violence is defined so broadly, then rather than being helpful, the definition becomes useless as a way of understanding the function of violence in the paths that religion is taking in the world today. De Vries draws on the work of Levinas and Derrida, among others, to connect the ideas of violence and religion and to explore how repressed violence can be disguised as friendship, and hidden hostilities can distort the face, which should be the face of love. Much of his analysis is highly significant. But the definition of violence with which de Vries begins is, I suggest, so wide as to include everything; and thereby becomes unhelpful as a tool to understand the ways in which religion fosters or colludes in thanatos, the escalating love of death and violence of the world. It also occludes the ways in which religion can make for peace, engendering the passion for transformation. This is not insightful ambiguity; it is rather a matter of tarring everything with the same brush.

VIOLENCE AS BOUNDARY

An alternative definition of violence, which again I find problematic, is given by Regina Schwartz in her recent book *The Curse of Cain*.[4] Schwartz asserts that "violence is the very construction of the Other," so that "imagining identity as an act of distinguishing and separating from others, of boundary making and line drawing, is the most frequent and fundamental act of violence we commit."[5] In her account, even to define a term is already a violent act because it excludes some things from the meaning of the term while including others. Now, if this were correct, then the only path to nonviolence would be by collapsing everything into a Sameness, so that all of reality is a thick soup so fully blended that nothing can be distinguished from anything else.

By contrast, I would suggest that it is not the act of distinguishing and separating into self and others that is violent in and of itself; indeed, such separation is essential if we are ever to experience the richness which respectful mutual interaction with others who are genuinely different from ourselves can bring. Violence enters, I would argue, not when difference is *defined* but when difference is perceived as *dangerous*, so that hierarchies are imposed and force is exerted to keep the hierarchies in place. Schwartz's important insights on perceived scarcity and competition for resources rather than mutuality and generosity which she explores in the rest of her book can be preserved, I suggest, without holding to her view that the construction of the other is itself violent. In fact, elsewhere in her book she redefines the concept of violence in a more nuanced way, which specifically repudiates her earlier definition (though she does not acknowledge this). She says: "Violence is not . . . a consequence of defining identity as either particular or universal. Violence stems from any conception of identity forged negatively against the Other, an invention of identity that parasitically depends upon the invention of some Other to be reviled."[6]

Despite this disclaimer, her earlier definition of violence as differentiation continues to percolate through her book. This definition has a direct bearing on questions of creation. If all forms of differentiation or separation were violent, then to create would be the paradigmatic act of violence. Newness can only arise if it is different from what preceded it; if it were not different it would not be new. So if difference itself indicates violence, then creating or transforming anything, making anything new, is a violent act. When we consider the biblical stories of creation, whether the Genesis myth of origins or Isaiah's vision of "new heavens and a new earth," these are stories of the emergence of newness, where things that are made are separated both from their creator and from anything that had gone before: an ordered cosmos replaces chaos; a world of peace and harmony replaces a world of conflict and destruction. Even if one holds, as I do,[7] to a very strong sense of divine immanence in the world, so that all things in some sense participate in the divine, it is still the case that the stars and flowers and birds and mountains are not an undifferentiated soup, a "night in which all cats are gray"; rather, they are glorious in their vibrant particularity. In their identity is their beauty; and in their interaction they can flourish.

As I will argue more fully later, far from this difference indicating violence, it should be understood as the very opposite. Creativity, and with it the beauty of particularity, is an antidote to destruction, not its enactment. Creativity invites harmony and flourishing, where the flourishing of one is interdependent with the flourishing of all. Although that which has been created can fall all too quickly into death-dealing behavior, the violence is not in the creative act itself, the act from which newness and beauty arises. Rather, violence arises when the mutuality of creation is denied, when difference is perceived as threatening rather than enriching, and force is exerted to dominate or stifle the potential of others.

I have not yet mentioned gender, but it is easy to see how the same analysis applies. In the original creation story, God creates Eve out of Adam, giving her a separate identity. Now, suppose one were to hold that the difference is itself violent. On such a view, it would follow that violence between the sexes would be built into this creation of male and female. I would argue the opposite: namely that it is precisely because Eve is a person in her own right, separate from Adam, that the two can enter into mutually fulfilling interaction. It is not in their distinctness that violence lies; on the contrary, their distinctness is what makes their relationship possible. Violence arises, rather, when their distinctness is taken as threatening, and made a pretext for the domination of one by the other. To generalize: I would argue (contrary to the implications of Regina Schwartz's initial definition of violence) that gender difference, like race or class difference, or difference of all other sorts, is neither itself violent nor the cause of violence. Violence in gender relations, as in all other relations, arises when difference is treated as a danger rather than as a resource, so that hostility rather than mutuality characterizes the interaction. Creativity is not violent in itself. Indeed I would argue that creativity and the beauty that can emerge from it is precisely what can stand against violence and destruction. Violence is ugly.

VIOLENCE AND DESIRE

Implicit in the work of both de Vries and Schwartz is a relationship to psychoanalytic theory, in particular to theories of thanatos, desire, and sacrifice. These issues are made central in the work of René Girard, especially in relation to religion. Highly influential as his work has been, however, in my view, Girard is fundamentally misguided in the account he gives of passion, violence, and the possibility of transformation. I first present his position, then explain why it will not do.

At least since Freud, desire and its repression have been taken by psychoanalytic theory as central to human behavior, both at an individual level and at the level of society and civilization. Girard accepts the centrality of desire; but whereas Freud had focused chiefly on the sexual aspect of desire—indeed sometimes seeming to reduce all desire to sexuality—Girard takes a broader view. In particular, Girard pays attention to the imitative dimension of desire. We want what someone else has; more precisely, we want what someone else *wants*. We learn to value things because other people—parents, teachers, peers—value them; this is the basis of education, culture, the development of taste, and much else. All these are founded on imitation, mimetic desire.

But mimetic desire quickly turns to rivalry. Girard gives a simple example: "Place a certain number of identical toys in a room with the same number of children; there is every chance that the toys will not be distributed without quarrels."[8] Each child can have a toy exactly like the toys the others have; but still they are likely to quarrel, each one wanting not a toy like the others have but the very toy that another child has. Girard considers this as characteristic of desire in general. Desire is not just mimetic, it is conflictual and acquisitive.

Moreover, such conflictual mimesis is mutually reinforcing. If I want what you have, value something that you value, then my desire for it causes you to value it even more, in an escalating reciprocity. This feedback process reinforces itself, until the competition becomes rivalry and the frustrated rivalry turns nasty.

Violence is thus generated. Violence is not originary; it is a by-product of mimetic rivalry. Violence is mimetic rivalry itself becoming violent as the antagonists who desire the same object keep thwarting each other and desiring the object all the more. Violence is supremely mimetic.[9]

In fact, the mimetic rivalry can quickly intensify in such a way that the ostensible object of desire—the toy both children want—no longer matters. All that matters is their quarrel.

As rivalry becomes acute, the rivals are more apt to forget about whatever objects are, in principle, the cause of the contest and instead to become more fascinated with one another. In effect, the contest is purified of any external stake and becomes a matter of pure rivalry and prestige. Only the antagonists remain; we designate them as doubles because from the point of view of the antagonism, nothing distinguishes them.[10]

By this time the rivalry can no longer be called acquisitive; the initial object of desire has dropped out. The mimesis is simply conflictual. It is also contagious: Before long each of the rivals will have allies, and the violence snowballs and polarizes the contestants.

Of course, this mimetic violence can take many forms, from overt force to much subtler strategies. All of it, however, has its roots in desire, in mimetic rivalry. As Hamerton-Kelly puts it in his interpretation of Girard: "Violence is the whole range of this deformation of desire . . . not just the obvious physical coercion. It is the driving energy of the social system. On the level of attitude it is envy and the strategies by which desire attempts to possess itself in the other and the other for itself. . . . Thus violence is more inclusive than aggression. . . . Violence describes the deep strategies of deformed desire in pursuit of its ends in all the modalities of culture."[11]

There are obvious resonances here with Hegel's account of the master and the slave, violence between them arising because both desire the recognition of the other. Girard seldom mentions Hegel; and when he does it is usually to dismiss him; but actually both men see desire and the rivalry it generates as the basis of violence and the driving force of history.

Now, animals also display mimetic rivalry. Two puppies will scrap over the same toy even if each is given an identical one, just as children will. But Girard argues that in the case of humans, the contagious effect of mimetic rivalry does not result in two equal groups in conflict with each other, but rather in the formation of one group to which more and more are attracted, and who focus their attention on the other which eventually dwindles to a single victim. Although this victim is the one against whom all the aggression is directed, the very fact that there is such a focus means that all the others unite into a community. Because aggression is focused outward, it becomes possible to develop prohibitions against violence within the community. The other becomes the scapegoat, the sacrifice who must bear the violence of the group. Girard sees this process as the foundation of religion, which develops increasingly formal rituals around the sacrificial victim and increasingly stringent prohibitions on violence within the group itself. Girard sees this whole process as the one that distinguishes humans from animals (who, unlike humans, seldom carry their mimetic rivalries to an actual fight to the death). He puts it bluntly: "The victimage mechanism is the origin of hominization."[12] As he explains: "We can conceive of hominization as a series of steps that allow for the domestication of progressively increasing and intense mimetic effects, separated from one another by crises that would be catastrophic but also generative in that they would trigger the founding mechanism and at each step provide for more rigorous prohibitions within the group, and for a more effective ritual canalization toward the outside."[13]

The surrogate victim is thus fundamental to civilization, enabling communities to act out their aggression in increasingly ritualized ways, gradually replacing actual victims with symbols; Thus the sacrificial system of ancient Israel gives place to the sacrifice once and for all of the Lamb of God, and eventually to the sacrifice of the mass. "All religious rituals spring from the surrogate victim, and all the great institutions of mankind, both secular and religious, spring from ritual. . . . It could hardly be otherwise, for the working basis of human thought, the process of 'symbolization,' is rooted in the surrogate victim."[14]

It is in the gradual substitution of ritual for actual violence that this whole process leads to peace. Rituals are by definition repetitive; by reenactment of the ritual the community comes to peace with itself as the ritual victim bears its aggression: "A trace of very real violence persists in the rite, and there is no doubt that the rite succeeds at least partially because of its grim associations, its lingering fascination; but its essential orientation is peaceful. Even the most violent rites are specifically designed to abolish violence."[15] In this way ritually enacted violence permits people "to escape their own violence . . . and bestows on them all the institutions and beliefs that define their humanity."[16]

According to Girard, therefore, violence and religion are inextricable, not in the sense that religion generates violence but rather in the sense that religion is the structure of beliefs and rituals within which the symbolic victim is sacrificed. In his earlier writings Girard believed that religion would die away as "the rite gradually leads men away from the sacred" and from their own violence.[17] In more recent writings he asserts, rather, that Christianity offers the perfect resolution of violence, because it requires that all mimetic desire shall be channeled into the imitation of Christ, the one who gave himself for others and took violence upon himself.[18]

Up to this point I have put aside difficulties that I have with Girard in an effort to represent him fairly. I wish now to turn to these, because they help to illuminate aspects of the relations between violence and religion, in particular how creativity enters the context. Girard has virtually nothing to say about creativity. In his view, peace and all the other values of civilization are a result of the victimage mechanism. It is thus ultimately through violence, not through creativity, that newness enters the world. By contrast, I suggest that violence of itself does not bring peace or newness; violence repeats itself in escalating patterns. The newness that allows for human flourishing requires transformation, rooted in what I have elsewhere called "natality."

To begin with the obvious: In the twenty-first century the form of violence that is much to the fore is indeed religious, or at least it is violence that relies on religion for its justification, but in a very different way than we might have expected from reading Girard. Girard has focused on violence *within* a group, and the way in which that violence can be resolved and the group become peaceable by means of the victimage mechanism. But the violence of freedom fighters and terrorists, landmines and helicopter gunships, ethnic cleansing and genocide, is violence *between* groups, often groups who assume that God or Allah is on their side and that their violence has divine blessing. While it is certainly true that violence can unite a group, it does so by deepening their division from the other, the victims against the perpetrators (who can quickly exchange roles). And while it is true that individual nations can develop greater internal unity by making a scapegoat of another nation, and perhaps deflect internal disquiet or aggression by doing so, it has not been the case historically that all the nations of the world have united to focus on a single victim or scapegoat. In the world wars of the twentieth century each side was composed of groups of nations; and in the first decade of this century we find one hyperpowerful nation attacking a sequence of relatively weak nations. A few others join in, but most of the rest (and much of the population within the aggressive states) watch in paralyzed disapproval. Girard's victimage mechanism, in which everyone unites against a single scapegoat, is not in evidence. The ancient history of warfare does not show a scapegoat syndrome any more than does the recent past. Very often we find the same pattern of a very strong nation attacking a weaker one while others look on, unable or unwilling to get involved. The spread of the Roman Empire is an obvious example. Sometimes there is rivalry, as in the wars between the European powers over colonial dominance, but in these instances, again, there is no obvious scapegoating.

It will not do for Girard to reply that he has concentrated on violence *within* groups and has left violence *between* groups for others to discuss. This is because it is clear that at least some aspects of violence within a community are very closely related to the warfare it conducts against its external enemies; one cannot be understood without the other. One of the key points of connection is gender, in particular the construction of masculinities. In *Foundations of Violence* I argue that the construction of virile manliness in the Roman Empire was the glue that connected the spectacles of death in the amphitheatres with the ideology and enactment of war (or violent peace) at its frontiers. In *Godly Killing* I discuss the close relationship between the cult of animal sacrifice and the holy wars of ancient Israel as represented in the Hebrew Bible: Neither are thinkable without the idea of the covenant enacted in circumcision, which inscribed a construction of masculinity on the body of every Israelite male. In later volumes of this project I shall show how gender constructions were again involved in European colonization of the New World, which was routinely feminized against the masculinity of the conquerors, a mastering masculinity all too often expressed in violence at home as well as abroad. The links between the violence inside a group—not least its gender violence—and its conduct of warfare are easy to demonstrate.

It is therefore not without significance that just as Girard is silent on the subject of war, so he has very little to say about gender. In his discussion of Dionysus in *Violence and the Sacred*, he notes the minor importance of the "role played by women in the religious and cultural structure of a society," and asserts that "like the animal and the infant but to a lesser degree, the woman qualifies for sacrificial status by reason of her weakness and relatively marginal social status. That is why she can be viewed as a quasi-sacred figure, both desired and disdained, alternately elevated and abused."[19] However, Girard never questions this marginal status, never investigates the violence that keeps women in their place. Gender violence, actual or threatened, is a major dimension of many societies (including all the societies of Western modernity); it is obviously related to the construction of masculinities and thus to ideologies of mastery and warfare; and it is often given religious justification. But none of this falls discernibly into Girard's category of the victimage mechanism. If Girard is attempting to provide an explanation of violence in relation to religion, and yet has nothing to say about war, gender violence, and their religious justifications, then at the very least the gaps in his theory must be of enormous concern.[20]

This brings me to my most fundamental difficulty with Girard. According to his theory, peace, hominization, and all the goods of civilization ultimately have their foundation in the victimage mechanism and thus are a result of violence. In my view, this is, to say the least, counterintuitive. At an international level the result of violence is a spiraling escalation of war, conflict, and terror; within a group, too, violence reproduces itself either immediately or in festering hatred. Violence does not bring peace. Of course the weaker party can be bombed or bludgeoned into submission, but that is not peace. Girard argues that escalating reciprocal violence, as in a blood feud, can only be resolved by both sides venting their violence on a surrogate victim and thus coming to peace between themselves. But is this true? If, for example, there is a major violation of one party by another—if a powerful nation appropriates the land or resources of a weaker nation, subordinating or killing much of its population—then it is highly likely that the weaker party would fester in anger until it could retaliate; but it is hardly plausible that the two would together join forces against a third nation (or that anything would be resolved if they did). Or again at an individual level, if two people who are feuding were to deal with their grievances by attacking a third—say, arguing parents venting their violence on a child—this would hardly count as a resolution of the problem but as a wholly inappropriate displacement.

Girard is of course aware that violence breeds violence, and he never pretends that the achievement of peace is quick or easy. Nevertheless, he holds that the very escalation of violence pushes the community to a point where the chain reaction has to stop; and at that point the surrogate victim will appear. "The sheer escalation of the crisis, linked to progressively accumulating mimetic effects, will make the designation of such a victim automatic" and thus will lead to the resolution of the conflict.[21] But what evidence could Girard bring to support this claim? It is hard to see what his justification for it could possibly be. Even in situations of conflict in which both sides realize that the violence has gone on far too long and must stop, peace is only finally achieved through negotiations that both sides feel to be fair and that result in justice that, although perhaps imperfect, is nonetheless recognized by both sides as a new start. Think, for example, of the collapse of apartheid in South Africa, or the movement toward peace in Northern Ireland. In both cases there was all too much violence and both sides could see that it had to stop, but in neither case was there a turn to a surrogate victim. Nor can I imagine anyone involved in conflict resolution ever advocating that there should be such a turn or that anything would be improved if there were. More sadly, the spiraling violence between Israel and the Palestinians seems out of control and in urgent need of change; but here again it is absurd to think that the situation would be helped if only the two sides could unite against a common target. Examples could be multiplied: I can think of none in which the victimage mechanism could possibly be the foundation of peace. All the evidence points the other way: Violence begets more violence.[22]

DESIRE AND NEWNESS

And yet sometimes peace does come—slowly and imperfectly, but nevertheless it comes. If it does not come out of violence, if Girard's theory of the victimage mechanism cannot be supported by the evidence, then how *does* transformation come? How does newness enter the world? These questions bring me back to the starting point of this paper, on the relationship between violence and creativity. They also bring me back to Girard's starting point: the centrality of desire. Girard argues, as we have seen, that desire is mimetic, that mimetic desire turns into rivalry, and that rivalry turns into violence. I want to argue, by contrast, that not all desire is mimetic; that even mimetic desire need not turn to rivalry; and that rivalry need not beget violence.

Girard holds that mimetic desire leads to rivalry, which degenerates to violence. Even in his later work, where he talks about "good mimesis" as the "imitation of Christ," this "active, positive desire" for the other cannot be part of human nature but can only occur if "there is some kind of divine grace present" "whether or not it is recognized as such."[23] It is not true of normal human beings, for whom desire is mimetic and rivalrous. But need this be the case? Why need desire lead to rivalry rather than to cooperation or sharing? Girard notes that children with equivalent toys still sometimes quarrel; he does not note that sometimes they play together quite happily. But if desire *need* not lead to rivalry and violence, then we require some other explanation or account of how and why violence arises when it does. How is it that sometimes desire—even mimetic desire—can express itself in cooperation and generosity whereas at other times it leads to resentment and hostility? Unless that question can be answered we will be no further forward in understanding the relationship between desire and violence, let alone how violence can be resolved.

I suggest that within Girard's work on rivalry as the inevitable result of mimesis lurk some unacknowledged (but still very common) gender assumptions: first, that the human is normatively male, and second, that masculinity involves mastery and therefore rivalry. Girard's ideas of mimetic rivalry seem plausible if we think about the way in which businessmen operate, or about football, or about all the many ways in which men strive competitively for mastery. But what sense do they make if we think instead, for example, about the relationship between a parent and their child? The child learns by imitation; but if the imitation turns to rivalry and rivalry turns to aggression, this is a sign that something has gone wrong, not that the relationship is progressing appropriately. Similarly, a teacher delights in the learning of a pupil, and recognizes that her chief work is to make herself dispensable, to teach the pupil so well that the pupil can go forward without further assistance, perhaps beyond the skill or knowledge of the teacher herself. An insecure teacher can of course feel resentment when a student surpasses her; but a teacher secure in her own contribution can rejoice and take pleasure in her student's progress. Girard leaves no room for generosity of spirit rather than rivalry and incessant struggle.

This leads to the deeper question of whether desire itself is mimetic. Girard's description is of course true of many desires, which arise out of a wish to have what someone else has, to value what they value. Moreover, Girard is right to say that much of our education and enculturation would be impossible without imitation. In everything from learning to play a musical instrument to building character, we make progress by trying to copy those whom we admire, as Aristotle said.[24] But I would argue that while much desire is mimetic, there is also an immensely important and undertheorized aspect of desire for which mimesis cannot be an adequate explanation. Mimetic desire as Girard defines it is desire that is premised upon a lack: It is desire for what we do not have, or desire that what we have now shall not be taken from us in the future. But what about creative desire: the desire to make something beautiful, something new? The desire to create cannot, I suggest, be reduced to lack. Rather, creativity bespeaks fullness that overflows, that wants to give of its resources, to express itself.

The paradigm case is once again the creation of the world. As God is portrayed in the Hebrew Bible and Christian theology, God does not lack. The divine is in need of nothing. Yet God desires to create the world and desires to make it beautiful. God desires to make a new heaven and a new earth, where peace and beauty will be restored. This creative desire is traditionally represented theologically as springing from infinite divine resources, not out of lack; if God creates in God's own image, this is the profoundly generative mimesis of divine self-extension, not rivalrous but generous. Similarly, it can be argued that there is more to human creativity than mimesis in the Girardian sense. If humans are made in the image of God, they, too, create out of an abundance of resources, not simply out of lack. Of course, imitation plays a great part in learning the skills without which human creativity cannot be expressed; but ultimately that which is genuinely creative is original, not imitative. It must arise out of the resources of the creator and their desire to create. I cannot produce good music or paint a picture or write a book solely out of mimetic rivalry: I can do so only if I have something new or fresh in me to express, something that is not reducible to imitation.

I suggest that the same considerations apply to conflict resolution. It is not a surrogate victim who can bring peace; rather it is creative thinking, new ways of looking at old problems, that can find a way forward. Of course creativity does not come out of the blue; of course it requires skills built up by long imitation and practice, but unless there are inner resources, not just lack, we could not hope for newness to enter the world. In contrast to Girard, therefore, I suggest that it is not violence and the victimage mechanism but creativity, desire springing from full-ness rather than premised upon a lack, which is the root of hominization and the basis of the passion for transformation.

Girard is of course not alone in focusing exclusively on the mimetic aspect of desire, or in defining desire in terms of lack. Ever since Plato's representation of eros as a child of need, it has been virtually taken for granted in Western philosophy and Christian theology that desire is premised upon a lack and that eros is highly suspect.[25] This, coupled with the emphasis on the word, and on power as the key characteristic of the divine, has meant that even when creation has been pondered it has usually been in terms of the divine word of power. Seldom has there been thought given to the passion for beauty and transformation which would motivate creation—divine passion or ours—or the resources from which such passions could overflow.

Even within the biblical texts, however, ambiguous and riddled with violence as they are, there are resources for thinking otherwise. The glory and beauty of the divine and the consequent creativity of divine passion suggests the possibility of a poetics of beauty that could trans-form the symbolic of a death-dealing world. It is precisely in the margin-alized theme of the divine passion for beauty that we can find resources for the transformation of the ugly violence that takes up such a large part of the Bible itself and that has so profoundly misshaped the world in which we live. Beauty and a passion for creativity stand as alternatives to a symbolic obsessed with destruction and thanatos: they raise a theme of resistance to death-dealing in the name of religion. Through the pas-sion for transformation newness enters the world and makes its creatures sing.

PART V

◈ Rereading the Song of Songs

❧ Lyrical Theology: The Song of Songs and the Advantage of Poetry

TOD LINAFELT

When we are considering poetry we must consider it primarily as poetry and not another thing.—T. S. ELIOT, *The Sacred Wood*

The statement by T. S. Eliot with which I begin is not without its problems, the most obvious of them the difficulty of actually defining "poetry." Yet it seems worth sticking with Eliot's formulation for the time being, inasmuch as too often the fact that the Song of Songs is poetry—and not another thing—seems to be forgotten by interpreters, or at least neglected. What would it mean to consider the Song of Songs as poetry? And further, what *kind* of poetry do we find in the Song of Songs? What are the "other things" that it ought not to be considered as? And finally, how might the poetry of the Song of Songs relate to "theologies of eros"?

We can begin by saying more about the Song of Songs than just that it is poetry. We can say, of course, that it is *love* poetry, or perhaps more properly *erotic* poetry. But we can say also, indeed I submit that we *ought* to say also, that it is *lyric* poetry. It is this latter designation that I am most interested in exploring here, partly because I think that the status of the Song of Songs as lyric poetry has been greatly neglected (even by those who pay close attention to its poetic qualities in general), but also because it seems to me a potentially interesting way to connect with the theological theme of the present volume.[1] I admit that my own theological instincts and interests are distinctly underdeveloped, and that my way into the conversation is primarily through literary categories. But given that the last twenty or thirty years have seen so much attention paid to the literary category of *narrative* in relation to theology, it seems natural to me—someone who has been at work on the Song of Songs for a couple of years now—to wonder about the possibilities of *lyrical* theology. That is, if the literary category (mode, or genre) of narrative holds possibilities for enlivening and enriching the theological task, might not the category of lyric hold such possibilities as well?

The lyric mode traditionally—that is, at least since the Renaissance and possibly as far back as Plato and Aristotle, depending on who it is reading Plato and Aristotle[2]—has been considered one of the "big three" modes of literary discourse, along with the dramatic and the epic (more recently, narrative) modes. If literature is indeed, at least to a large extent, about mimesis, that is, about the imitation of reality, then lyric is mimetic in a different way than either drama or narrative. Drama and narrative might be judged with reference to their imitation of humans interacting with the world and with each other. They are essentially social in nature, and they tend to work on the reader through plot and characterization. But lyric directs its mimesis inward rather than outward. Helen Vendler suggests that the proper questions to ask of the lyric are, "How well does the structure of this poem mimic the structure of thinking?"—or of emotion, we might add—and, "How well does the linguistic play of the poem embody that structural mimesis?"[3] Thus, the lyric's concerns are, primarily, with the inner life rather than the outer world, and its tools are the tools of linguistic play, that is, of structure, syntax, metaphor, productive ambiguity, and the like.[4] Moreover, the lyric is generally distinguished from the narrative and dramatic modes in terms of voice. One expects a single voice in lyric (as for example in the psalms)—not necessarily the voice of the author or poet, of course, but the voice of a persona or a fictive speaker. In drama, one hears the voices of the various characters as they speak directly, and in narrative the voice of the narrator is primary, and through it the voices of the characters are mediated.

The Song of Songs is best understood, I want to argue, as lyric poetry and not as dramatic or narrative poetry. But what makes this distinction tricky is that the Song of Songs does not entirely fit the category of lyric as it is traditionally defined and, moreover, contains both dramatic and

narrative elements. One might be tempted then to throw out the categories altogether, to take the position that each poem is a genre unto itself.
But "baby-and-bathwater" clichés aside, to take this position would mean
to lose the tension, so often exploited by poets, between the expectations
of a mode or genre and the thwarting of those expectations, as well as
the tension that arises in the mixing of genres. Or, in the case of the Song
of Songs, it is not so much a mixing of genres as it is a sort of faux
deployment of dramatic and narrative elements in the service of lyrical
ends. In other words, I would argue that there is no real drama and no
real narrative in the poetry, but the poet has clearly made use of both
modes in order to give the reader (or hearer) a richer and more complex
lyrical experience.

The most obvious dramatic element in the poetry is the alternation
between voices, that of a young woman, a young man, and occasional
group voices, both male and female, with the female group voice functioning something like a chorus (although the ancient Egyptian love
poems give us a precedent of sorts for alternating voices). However,
despite the presence of more or less distinguishable voices, we are not
given genuine literary characters or figures, nor are the poems the tran-
scription of the thoughts of real people with lived lives, as they are often
treated. Rather, we are given fictive speakers—personae, perhaps, but
not persons. Or, as Harold Fisch puts it, "What we have really are impas-
sioned voices rather than characters. There is dialogue to be sure, but it
is dialogue that gives us the maximum of relationality, the minimum of
personality or setting."[5] The dialogue between these voices does not
serve to reveal character but to reveal emotion, and any setting that
one might find, as in the following lines from chapter 2, is generally
metaphorical or emblematic.

> The voice of my beloved!
>   Look, he comes,
> leaping upon the mountains,
>   bounding over the hills.
> [9] My beloved is like a gazelle
>   or a young stag.

Look, there he stands behind our wall,
　　gazing in at the windows,
　　　　looking through the lattice.
¹⁰ My beloved speaks and says to me:
"Arise, my love, my fair one,
　　and come away;
¹¹ for now the winter is past,
　　the rain is over and gone.
¹² The flowers appear on the earth;
　　the time of singing has come,
and the voice of the turtledove
　　is heard in our land.
¹³ The fig tree puts forth its figs,
　　and the vines are in blossom;
　　　　they give forth fragrance.
Arise, my love, my fair one,
　　and come away.
¹⁴ O my dove, in the clefts of the rock,
　　in the covert of the cliff,
let me see your face,
　　let me hear your voice;
for your voice is sweet,
　　and your face is lovely.
¹⁵ Catch us the foxes,
　　the little foxes,
that ruin the vineyards—
　　for our vineyards are in blossom."
　　　　　　(2:8–15, NRSV)

If the poetry of the Song of Songs is lacking in character and setting, it is also by and large without plot, perhaps the primary ingredient of narrative. Indeed, this lack of an overarching plot for the book as a whole has often been cited by commentators as evidence for the composite or anthological character of the book; in truth, it is only evidence for the fact that the Song of Songs is not primarily narrative in nature. But to say that the book as a whole is not to be interpreted as narrative is not to say that there are no narrative elements to be found. There are, especially in the night scenes found in chapters 3 and 5, worth quoting here in full:

Upon my bed at night
    I sought him whom my soul loves;
I sought him, but found him not;
    I called him, but he gave no answer.
² "I will rise now and go about the city,
    in the streets and in the squares;
I will seek him whom my soul loves."
    I sought him, but found him not.
³ The sentinels found me,
    as they went about in the city.
        "Have you seen him whom my soul loves?"
⁴ Scarcely had I passed them,
    when I found him whom my soul loves.
I held him, and would not let him go
    until I brought him into my mother's house,
        and into the chamber of her that conceived me.
⁵ I adjure you, O daughters of Jerusalem,
    by the gazelles or the wild does:
        do not stir up or awaken love until it is ready!
        (3:1–5, NRSV)

I slept, but my heart was awake.
    Listen! my beloved is knocking.
"Open to me, my sister, my love,
    my dove, my perfect one;
for my head is wet with dew,
    my locks with the drops of the night."
³ I had put off my garment;
    how could I put it on again?
I had bathed my feet;
    how could I soil them?
⁴ My beloved thrust his hand into the opening,
    and my inmost being yearned for him.

⁵ I arose to open to my beloved,
    and my hands dripped with myrrh,
my fingers with liquid myrrh,
    upon the handles of the bolt.
⁶ I opened to my beloved,
    but my beloved had turned and was gone.
        My soul failed me when he spoke.
I sought him, but did not find him;
    I called him, but he gave no answer.
⁷ Making their rounds in the city
    the sentinels found me;
they beat me, they wounded me,
    they took away my mantle,
        those sentinels of the walls.
⁸ I adjure you, O daughters of Jerusalem,
    if you find my beloved,
tell him this:
    I am faint with love.
                (5:2–8)

There are, I would argue, concrete stylistic indicators of prose narration within these passages that are more apparent in the Hebrew than in translation, most especially the several occurrences of the particle *ʾet*, which functions grammatically to mark the definite, direct object and is often labeled by scholars a "prose particle," since it appears infrequently in biblical poetry but quite often in prose texts. In all 116 verses of the Song of Songs, *ʾet* occurs only twenty-four times, but in the two night scenes alone it occurs eleven times in the space of twelve verses (six times in 3:1–5 and five times in 5:2–8). Likewise, point of view, or perspective, generally missing in lyric poetry, would seem to be marked here by the use in verse 2 of the Hebrew term *qol*, which functions (much like its visually oriented counterpart *hinneh*) not only as an interjection, "Listen!" but also to mark a shift in figural perspective to the "character" of the young woman. That is, we are to hear the knocking of her beloved through her ears, so to speak, in the same way that we are to see her beloved through her eyes in 2:9 (quoted above) as he gazes through the lattice. In addition to the presence of the prose particle *'et* and an identifiable point of view, one finds in these passages typical narrative elements such as action, plot, setting, genuine dialogue, a certain amount of characterization, and the use of past, present and future tenses. And one might even argue that the two night scenes, brief as they are, exhibit elements that in Aristotle's influential theory of narrative raise a plot from the simple to the complex: *peripateia* (reversal of fortune) and *anagnorisis* (a dramatic moment of recognition, moment of truth).[6] The former is present in both passages, in precisely converse ways, as the scene in chapter 3 begins with the absence of the lover and ends with his presence and in chapter 5 the lover is first present but, owing to a delay in response, ends up being absent. And one might well take the statement "my soul failed me when he spoke" (set off for emphasis as a third colon in a pattern that typically works with two cola per line) as a moment of truth, an emphasis on what was lost when the lover was lost and a spur toward the search of the following lines.

As I indicated above I want to maintain that, despite the dramatic and narrative feel of certain parts of the Song of Songs, it is still primarily lyric poetry that we are dealing with, and that in fact the dramatic and narrative elements serve lyrical ends. But it remains to say what those ends are. Allow me to defer for the moment to Barbara Hardy, whose book *The Advantage of Lyric* has given me my title for this essay. She opens the book with the following observation: "Lyric poetry isolates feeling in small compass and so renders it at its most intense." She continues: "The advantage of lyric in itself is its concentrated and patterned expression of feeling. This advantage is negatively definable: The lyric does not provide an explanation, judgment, or narrative; what it does provide is feeling, alone and without histories or characters."[7] It is important to note the twofold character of Hardy's articulation: that lyric excels both in the expression of *feeling* and in its *concentrated and patterned mode* of expression. Or as Jorge Luis Borges puts it, upon discovering Keats's poem "Ode to a Nightingale," "I knew that language could also be a music and a passion. And thus was poetry revealed to me."[8]

"A music and a passion," writes Borges. Let us first consider the passion. That lyric is concerned with the elucidation and development of feeling, emotion, or passion is something of a commonplace observation among literary critics, one that came especially to the fore among romantic poets and critics (Wordsworth, Coleridge, and the like) who prized passion above all else. The romantics perhaps overdid this aspect of lyric, and of course one can imagine lyric poems in which it is less central than others, but it is also the case that lyric is too often ignored in the actual interpretation of poems (as Helen Vendler shows, for example, in relation to Shakespeare's sonnets), as readers tend to expect and to look for narrative development, for genuine characters, or even for straightforward assertion. Results include about equal measures of disappointment in not finding these elements and of "finding" them in the poetry one way or another. Certainly one finds this quite a bit in criticism of the Song of Songs, where interpreters continue to look for a narrative arc or to treat the book as if it were a sort of literal reportage of the sex lives of two real ancient Judeans.

But what makes this aspect of lyric particularly significant for the Song of Songs, and what might be counted as a real advantage of lyric in biblical literature, is that feeling and emotion is most conspicuous in biblical narrative by its absence. Biblical narrative is exceptional for its refusal to give readers insight into the inner lives of its characters. No one recognized or expressed this better than Erich Auerbach, who famously compared Homeric epic with Hebrew biblical narrative. In general Homeric style aims "to represent phenomena in a fully externalized form, visible and palpable, in all their parts and completely fixed in their spatial and temporal relations," whereas in the Bible, and his representative example here is Genesis 22, "it is unthinkable that an implement, a landscape through which the travelers passed, the serving-men, or the ass, should be described, that their origin or descent or material or appearance or usefulness should be set forth in terms of praise; they do not even admit an adjective: they are serving-men, ass, wood, and knife, and nothing else."[9] Auerbach's observations hold true as well, by and large, for the method of characterization in the respective literatures. He writes: "With the utmost fullness, with an orderliness which even passion does not disturb, Homer's personages vent their inmost hearts in speech; what they do not say to others, they speak in their own minds, so that the reader is informed of it."[10] By contrast, "personages speak in the Bible

too; but their speech does not serve, as does speech in Homer, to manifest, to externalize thoughts—on the contrary, it serves to indicate
thoughts which remain unexpressed."[11] It is not the case that it doesn't
matter what characters are thinking or feeling—for example, it matters
greatly what Abraham, Isaac, even God are thinking in Genesis 22—but
only that biblical authors typically refuse to directly reveal those thoughts
or feelings, preferring to rely on action and dialogue to build an always
ambiguous characterization. One finds exceptions, naturally. I think of
the very brief yet telling insight into Jacob's inner life in Genesis 29: "So
Jacob served seven years for Rachel, and they seemed to him but a few
days because of the love he had for her."

The exceptions notwithstanding, the consistency with which this stylistic convention of ancient Hebrew narrative is maintained is quite remarkable. In biblical poetry, however, this convention falls away. Or it
is more accurate to say that in biblical lyric poetry the convention falls
away, since in the occasional narrative poetry that one finds in the Bible
(and there is not much) the same reticence to expose the inner life of a
character. For example, in the poetic version of the death of Sisera in
Judges 5 the thoughts and feelings of Jael, and thus her motivation for
action, are kept hidden from the reader in the same way that they are in
the prose version in Judges 4. So biblical lyric poetry—and one might
include in this category not only the Song of Songs and many of the
psalms, but also Job's curse of his day in Job 3, David's dirge over Jonathan and Saul in 1 Samuel 1, and much of the book of Lamentations—has
the stylistic advantage over biblical narrative (whether prose or verse) of
not being bound by this convention of blocking access to a character's or
speaker's inner life.

I take this willingness to trade in passion as one of the signs that the
night scenes in chapters 3 and 5 of the Song of Songs ought to be considered pseudonarrative rather than genuine narrative. The plot of a young
woman's search for her lover certainly serves to draw the reader in, but
it is a plot without context and without consequences. Because we do
not have full-blooded characters here—we know nothing about them,
including even their names, because in essence there is no "them" apart
from their existence as fictive speakers—the plot with which we are to
concern ourselves, I would argue, is the "plot" that tracks the feeling of

the speaker from (in chapter 3) desire to deprivation to satisfaction and (in chapter 5) from vigilance to indecision to yearning to the pain of separation to vulnerability at the hands of the guard to, finally, love-sickness. One of the benefits of using pseudonarrative to convey these feelings is that the narrative mode is able to make use of past, present, and future tense ("I sought . . . I adjure you . . . If you find") in a way that lyric generally does not, and thus it provides a figural depth for the speaker (while nevertheless not constituting a fully fleshed-out character).

The absence of full characterization in these narrative-like passages, and even more in the rest of the Song of Songs, means that a reader or hearer of the poetry can more easily adopt the words as his or her own, and thus the feeling, passion, or thought of the fictive speaker can also more easily become part of a reader's well of experience. "A lyric wants us to be its speaker. We are not to listen to the speaker, but to make ourselves into the speaker. We speak the words of the poem as though we were their first utterers."[12] Here again we see a distinct advantage of lyric over drama or narrative where dialogue belongs to characters rather than speakers, and thus are less easily adopted as one's own.

If feeling, passion, or the track of thought are what lyric aims at eluci-dating, its means of doing so is the "music," as Borges and others put it, of language, a concentrated and patterned expression that is compelling in some way even apart from any semantic value or "meaning." Even putting it this way is misleading, since it implies too sharp of a distinction between the form of language and the content of feeling. Rather, the feeling with which lyric is concerned is not only elucidated by language but is evoked by it. It is not passion recollected in more tranquil mo-ments, as Wordsworth has put it, but passion produced by the poem in the reader or hearer who, we have noted, potentially becomes the speaker. The music of language is achieved in any number of ways, of course, depending on the conventions and the linguistic resources of whatever language one is dealing with, but common elements that one would want to explore include structure, repetition, rhythm (if not al-ways meter), wordplay, sound play (assonance and alliteration), and imagery.

A brief look again at verses 8 through 15 of chapter 2 in the Song of Songs (quoted above) will show at least some of the complexity with which even one of these elements, that of structure, can be employed. The passage exhibits a complex structure focused around the following series of repeated keywords, phrases, and images, not all of which are obvious in the various English translations (including the NRSV above): my beloved (5x), voice (4x), look (Hebrew *hinneh*; 3x), the image of the woman's lover as a gazelle or stag upon the mountains (2x), and the verb "to be like" (2x). Framing the entire unit is the metaphor of the gazelle or stag, the masculine forms of the same animals on which the daughters of Jerusalem were asked to swear in 2:7. In a nice example of *inclusio*, the lover is first imagined as a gazelle bounding over the mountains toward the woman (verses 8–9), and he is then admonished to leave, after the night's passing, in the same way (verse 17). In the first instance he is *described* in the third person as being "like a gazelle," while in the second instance he is *commanded* to be "like a gazelle." The two sections of the woman's speech are further structured by the fourfold, matching repetition of "my beloved" in verses 8 and 9 and 16 and 17. A fifth repetition of "my beloved" marks the transition, in verse 10a, to the reported speech of the man. The man's speech is likewise roughly symmetrical, with each half introduced by the phrase, "Arise, my love, my fair one, and come away" (verses 10b and 13b), and each closing with a reference to the blossoming or budding (*sᵉmadar*) of vines or vineyards (verses 13 and 15). Tying together the speech of the woman and the reported speech of the man are the repeated words "voice" (verses 9, 12, and 14 [2x]) and "look" (*hinneh*; verses 8, 9, and 11, translated in the NRSV as "for now").

The overall dynamic of 2:8–17 is to move from distance to proximity and, relatedly, from description to address. Initially heralded only by his voice or the sound of his approach, the male lover progresses from bounding over the mountains (verse 8), to peering through the windows of a house (verse 9), to what would appear to be an intimate embrace (verse 16). If one takes verse 17 as an invitation for the man to spend the night in the arms of his lover, as many commentators do, then the passage ends on this note of embrace. If, however, one understands verse 17 as an exhortation for the man to flee, as I am inclined to, then the verse offers a final counterpoint to the movement from distance to proximity that governs most of the passage. In other words it ends where it began, with the man like a gazelle on the mountains; but instead of approaching he is retreating. As the passage moves from distance to proximity, so too the female and the male voices both move from third-person *description* to second-person *address*, the woman's description of "my beloved" in verses 8–9 giving way to her address to "my beloved" in verse 17, and the man's description of springtime in verses 11–13 giving way to his address to "my dove" in verses 14–15. The effect is both to reflect and to amplify the heightened sense of intimacy that is occasioned by the poem's movement from distance to proximity.

But how might all this relate to questions of theology? What might be the advantage of poetry for theology, and more particularly the advantage of lyrical theology? I will do no more than suggest a few lines of inquiry in what follows.

I begin by noting that the analogy with narrative theology seems helpful. Although I would agree with critics of narrative theology that some claims made in its name are over-reaching and not always clearly theorized,[13] its successes lie in its willingness to ask, What are the particular strengths of this *literary* mode and how might those strengths be brought over into *theological* discourse? In response to these questions narrative theologians have tended to focus on its "coherence" and on its "intelligibility." Coherence would seem primarily to refer to the importance of plot for narrative, what Stanley Hauerwas calls "the connected description of action and suffering which moves to a point,"[14] and what Ronald Thiemann describes as "the interaction of circumstance and character, incident and identity, in an ordered chronological sequence."[15] And intelligibility would seem to refer to the ability of a reader not just to understand but also to absorb stories in such a way as to shape their moral and religious character, to provide an "intelligible pattern"[16] that does more effective theological work than propositional discourse. Of course, some narrative theologians would put it even stronger, arguing not that one absorbs the stories but rather that one is absorbed *into* the world of the story.[17]

Lyric poetry, I would argue, has its own version of coherence and of patterned intelligibility. Certainly the more musical rhythms, structures, and repetitions of verse impress themselves upon one at least as much as—and likely more than—the plot of a story. (I confess, for example, that I still have the riffs and rhythms and catchphrases of the heavy metal of my misspent youth running more or less continuously in the background of my psyche.) Moreover, the forms of poetry do more than just give shape to an existing theological content, but have the potential to give rise to genuinely new theological possibilities. I think, for example, of Robert Alter's argument that apocalyptic is in no small measure a product of the intensifying nature of Hebrew poetic parallelism, which pushes the rhetorical tenor ever higher with every line, so that prophetic visions of the future, cast in verse form, move from "mishap to disaster to cosmic cataclysm."[18] But the intelligibility of lyric plays out in different ways than narrative, I think, and even than other nonlyric forms of poetry, in the sense that there is less to "understand" in lyric and more to be "experienced" aesthetically (to use what I know is an old-fashioned sounding phrase). Narratives—for example, the gospels or the exodus story—might be said to present theological content in story form, though certainly this is not all they do; it might be argued that this makes that content more intelligible to an audience. But lyric rarely has such a content that can be absorbed or a moral that can be learned. Let us take, for example, a few very brief lines from the Song of Songs:

> Stamp me as a seal upon your heart,
>   as a seal upon your arm,
> for love is as strong as death,
>   and its passion hard as the grave.
> its sparks will spark a fire,
>   an all-consuming blaze.

The passage represents a sort of crescendo to the book, offering for the first time a second-order reflection on the nature of love, even the metaphysics of love, rather than the first-person declarations and descriptions that one encounters to this point. And yet here, even with the Song of Songs at its most discursive, we are still in the realm of lyric poetry and not philosophy. The primary tools of the passage are not the tools of philosophy but the tools of Hebrew verse: metaphor, diction, alliteration, and assonance. It is worth reading out loud the statement on love in 8:6 as it sounds in the Hebrew:

ki azzah kamavet ahavah
qashah kish'ol qinah
r'shapheyha rishpey esh
shalhevetyah

Undoubtedly the first answer to the question of why the poet compares love to death and passion to the grave must be: Because it *sounds* good. Yet we want to avoid the temptation of thinking that this answer is the only answer. If the poetry is not reducible to a content that can be paraphrased, neither is it reducible to ornamental flourish. The aesthetics of the poetry are in fact intimately related to its meaning. In this case, the hardness of passion is inseparable from the hardness of that alliterated *k*: "*qashah kish'ol qinah*." And while that hardness gives way to the dancing and popping of sparks into flame in the repeated *r* and *sh* sounds (and the single hard consonant *p*) of the phrase *r'shapheyha rishpey esh*, those initial sparks and flames of desire quickly become, in the final phrase of the verse, "an all-consuming blaze."

Moreover, even when we move to explore the very large claim being made about love here—even, that is, when we ask about the "meaning" of the passage—because this is poetry we find a richly ambiguous text. In what does the hardness of passion consist? How do mere sparks burst into flame? And, most centrally, how are we to understand the relationship between love and death? In the end, the question of what it means to say that "Love is as strong as death" resists a definitive answer. To say that the poetry resists a *definitive* answer is not to say, however, that we are absolved of the work of interpretation. Rather, the function of metaphor is to force the reader to explore the possibilities of meaning-making that it provides.[19]

If lyric brings its own version of coherence and intelligibility to the theological task, it also brings its penchant for passion. Rather than suppressing passion in favor of objectivity, as traditional theological discourse tends to do, lyric places it front and center. And, occurring largely in the first and second person, with an "I" speaking to a "you," lyric has the advantage over narrative of making that passion the reader's own passion. One may identify with certain characters in a narrative but, with the exception of a first-person narrator, the inner life of those characters (to the extent that it is revealed at all) is distanced by the formal constraints of narration. In her reflections on "the narrative imagination," Martha Nussbaum writes: "The habits of wonder promoted by storytelling thus define the other person as spacious and deep, with qualitative differences from oneself and hidden places worthy of respect."[20] Narrative thus promotes an interest in and sympathy for others, while nevertheless honoring their differences from "us" or from the reader. Lyric, on the other hand, tends to collapse the distance, but only for a moment, allowing the sympathy to become deeper and sometimes stranger as one takes on the voice of the fictive speaker of the poem and makes that speaker's passions or thoughts one's own.

An attempt at a "lyrical theology," then, would draw on these strengths of lyric: the music of language (including all the tools of poetry) and the elucidation of feeling. It would be a theology that emphasizes metaphor, wordplay, sound play, and rhythm, a theology that speaks in the first and second person, and a theology built on passion and feeling rather than on philosophical or other discursive categories. It would be a theology that persuades by seduction rather than by argument. This is not to say that a lyrical mode of theology is better than other modes, or that a more traditionally discursive theology is bad; only that lyric has its own strengths and tools and perhaps these might be brought to bear on the theological task. The Song of Songs has of course a long tradition of theological interpretation, mostly taking the form of allegory based on the erotic subject matter of the poetry. The contours of this line of interpretation are familiar and, I think, very fruitful, even if they take us beyond the horizon of the poetry itself. But I have begun to wonder if perhaps the popularity of the Song of Songs as a theological resource is only partially due to the eros that lends itself so powerfully to articulating God's relationship to the world and to humanity, if perhaps it is not the power of its lyricism, which provides something otherwise missing in theology.

❧ The Shulammite's Song: Divine Eros, Ascending and Descending

RICHARD KEARNEY

The Song of Songs offers no single, stable perspective from which to view the amorous scenes unveiled on its pages. Most readers of the Song from antiquity to the present have, however, been inclined to identify with the female figure traditionally known as the Shulammite. But who is the Shulammite, and who, for that matter, is her beloved? The sustained ambiguities of identity and fluid reversals of erotic roles have made this text fertile ground for conceiving and reconceiving the mysteries of desire, in particular, the mysteries of *divine desire*—despite (or perhaps because of) the fact that God is never explicitly named in this biblical book. Does the Song celebrate God's desire for us? Our desire for God? Or both? The text appears to cross modes of the erotic that have traditionally been considered antithetical—human and divine, finite and infinite, ascending and descending, Platonic and Jewish or Christian. In particular, it crosses an ontological understanding of desire as a movement from lack toward fullness and an eschatological understanding of desire as a movement from fullness to lack. In this respect, it harbors the potential for a revolutionary reappraisal of our understanding of eros. In the *Song of Songs*, I will suggest, human and divine desire meet and traverse one another, ascending and descending, filling and emptying.

After a brief outline of my hermeneutic hypothesis, I will test it against some of the most influential premodern readings of the Song—Jewish and Christian—before placing my own argument into the context of contemporary interpretations.

ESCHATOLOGICAL EROS IN THE SONG OF SONGS

One of the passages most revealing of the "crossing" to which I have pointed is Song 3:1–4, where the anxious seeking of the love-struck bride is reversed into a being-found and her desiring suddenly becomes a being desired. The bride speaks of her beloved: "Upon my bed at night I sought him whom my soul loves; I sought him but found him not; I called him, but he gave no answer. So I said to myself, 'I will rise now and go about the city, in the streets and in the squares; I will seek him whom my soul loves.' . . . I sought him, but found him not. The sentinels *found me*, as they went about the city. I asked, 'Have you seen him whom my soul loves?' Scarcely had I passed them, when I found him whom my soul loves." Here one may imagine the desired and desiring God appearing in the guise of a sentinel who hails the reader—"Where are you? Who goes there?"—to which she replies, "Here I am! It is me." The lover of God, this passage seems to suggest, is at once the object and the subject of desire.

Indeed, it would appear that the divine lover seeks out the beloved *before* she seeks him. His desire is both before her desire and beyond her desire. This desire is no mere deficiency but its own excess, gift, and grace. It seems to fulfill the promise of Psalm 34 that "those who seek the Lord *lack* no good thing." Why? Because such desire is not a gaping emptiness or negation but an affirmative "yes" to the summons of a superabundant God—"Here I am. Come. Yes, I say, yes I will. Yes."

The lovers' discourse in the Song of Songs testifies as well to the double traversing of sensuality by transcendence and of transcendence by sensuality. On the one hand, Solomon compares his beloved's breasts to "two fawns, / twins of a gazelle" (7:4) while she compares his eyes to "doves at a pool of water" (5:1). On the other hand, the amorous passion testifies to the unnamable alterity of the divine at the very moment when the Song reaches its highest pitch of exchange between lover and beloved and eros is both matched with death and identified with God.

> Stamp me as a seal upon your heart,
> sear me upon your arm,
> for love is as strong as death,

passion as hard as the grave.
Its sparks will spark a fire,
An all-consuming blaze (8:6)

The identification with Yahweh is alluded to through the final word, *shalhevetyah*, referring to a hyperbolically burning flame. As Tod Linafelt notes, "*-yah*, the last syllable of the last word of the verse, is a shortened form of Israel's personal name for God, Yahweh, and serves grammatically as an intensifying particle. . . . In a book that never directly mentions God, this particle of divinity . . . can only add to the freightedness of the line."[1] Thus the all-consuming flame is also the flame of Yahweh; divinity is the measure of the intensity of eros. The very unicity and uniqueness of the word (which appears nowhere else in the Bible) may suggest, furthermore, that it is a fitting—if indirect, figural, masked and oblique—code for the transcendent one (*Un*): the Lord of Lords, King of Kings, Shepherd of shepherds, Lover of lovers. Here we might also detect an allusion to the burning bush episode on Mount Horeb (Exodus 3:15). The transfiguring fire of the bush becomes the blaze of devouring desire where the ecstasy of the beloved traverses, without consuming, the incarnational love of God. In this crisscrossing of divine lover and human beloved, both are transfigured. Divine desire is embodied. Human desire is hallowed.

If Exodus 3 allowed God to speak through an angel and a burning thorn bush, the Song of Songs amplifies the range of divine speech to include lovers' bodies and, by analogy, entire landscapes. The landscapes in turn are brimming with fruits (nuts, figs, pomegranates), harvests (wine, honey, wheat), plants (lilies, cedars, roses, apple-trees), and animals (gazelles, stags, and turtledoves). The divine desire of Yahweh's flame now appears to embrace all that is alive, as though the seed of the thornbush has spread from the dusty heights of Mount Horeb and disseminated its fecundity throughout the valleys and planes below. But above all, the seed has found its way into the embrace of lover and beloved. The love celebrated in this song echoes the innocence of eros prior to the Fall, when God made the first lovers of one flesh and declared it good (Genesis 2). Perhaps even more radically, the Song looks *ahead* to an eschatological kingdom where such innocence may flourish again once

and for all.[2] The reference (backward and forward) to paradise is reinforced by the startlingly suggestive verse: "Under the apple-tree I awak-
ened you" (8:5), an allusion reiterated in the fact that the lover-shepherd
is himself referred to as an apple-tree. These ostensibly retrospective echoes of a lost Eden are thus transformed here into a celebration—without
the slightest hint of melancholy—of a passionate desire in the here and
now for a fuller consummation still to come. This latter eschatological
horizon is indicated by verse 5:1, among others, which sings of the lover
entering a garden full of milk and honey.

These lovers are not just mouthpieces for a theological message. They
are not mere personifications of spiritual wisdom or representations of
Yahweh's continuing love for Israel in spite of infidelity. They are these
things too perhaps, but much more. The lovers come across as carnal
embodiments of a desire that traverses and exceeds them while they
remain utterly themselves. Hence the candid corporality of recurring references to limbs, mouths, breasts, hands, and navels, not to mention the
sense of deep inner yearning and the sheer naturality of description that
brings this Song to vivid life. The woman is a lily, garden, mare, vineyard,
dove, sun, moon; her lover is a gazelle, king, fawn, bag of myrrh and
cluster of blossoming henna. The powerful erotic charge of many of the
amorous idioms defies any purely allegorical interpretation: "His left arm
is under my head and his right makes love to me" (2:6 and 8:2); he
"pastures his flock among the lilies" (6:3); "his fountain makes the garden
fertile" (4:15); or "my beloved thrust his hand / through the hole in the
door; / I trembled to the core of my being" (5:4).

This kind of language is unmatched elsewhere in the Bible, as we
shall see—and it was to prove so controversial in the later rabbinical and
monastic traditions as to be frequently chastened or censored. Equally
unique in this biblical song is the fact that divine love finds privileged
expression in the voice of a young woman. It is the Shulammite who
takes most of the initiative and does most of the talking in the Song of
Songs. And if the lover-king-Solomon speaks at some length in his own
voice, his discourse often quotes the Shulammite and harks back to her
as its source of reference. It is a "woman's song" from first to last and it
keeps the heroine at center stage.[3]

Moreover, since this freedom and centrality of the woman's point of view suggests the possible influence of Egyptian nuptial hymns, one might even see in the Song's dissemination of God's exodic flame (8:6)—that is, its amplification of the voice of the burning bush—a move away from a perspective that pitted Israel against Egypt to a more inclusive voice that brings them together again in an erotic bond.[4] The fact that the Shulammite's passion represents a free love—she is faithful to her lover outside matrimonial demands and social contracts—corroborates the view that the Song puts the entire societal orthodoxy into question.[5]

This breaking open of divine desire beyond tribal or familial confines is in turn reinforced by three crucial references in the Song. We have, first, the reference to the Shulammite as a chariot (6:12), that is, as one who may be said to carry the Ark of the Covenant, a mark of God's love for his people, to those hitherto considered beyond the familiarly acknowledged bounds. Second, we have the reference to a dance (6:13), which seems to allude to the naked David "swirling with all his might" before the Ark (2 Samuel 6:14), a gesture of human desire for God but one that may equally allude to the eschatological figure of a divine-human love-dance in the last days. And, third, we have the verbal play between the terms Shulammite and Shunammite—the latter being the "extremely beautiful girl" brought to warm King David's bed but ultimately shunned and left a virgin. The fact that the formerly rejected Shunammite is here reprised as the liberated Shulammite who captivates her shepherd-king indicates how this revolutionary biblical Song succeeds in turning the once "passive and reified" woman into an "active subject whose first-person pronoun" dominates the love-talk and celebrates the love.[6]

In short, in the very singularity of the Shulammite's embodied voice we can discern a love cry of universal import.

TALMUDIC AND KABBALISTIC READINGS

The influential nineteenth-century Rabbi Hayyim of Volozhyn reinforces the reading of the Song in the double light of revelation and eschatology. He takes the beloved's famous apostrophe—"Kiss me with the kisses of your mouth" (1:2)—as a plea that the revelations on Mt. Sinai eventually be given *directly*,[7] no longer obscurely through a voice disguised as an angel, a bush or the "back of God's head," but given *mouth to mouth*.[8] This intrepid reading is born out by the Volozhyner's conviction, deeply influenced by the kabbalistic *Books of Creation*, that the cosmological orders of nature and the human body are themselves incarnational metaphors for the eschatological expression of a divine flame. He cites Jewish sources that attribute different powers and names of God to different parts of the body, reserving the nameless name of Exodus 3:15 (*ehyeh* or "I shall be") as the only one that perdures throughout the entire history of creation. The rabbi interprets the invocation of the Song 5:2—"My dove, my perfect one"—as an indication of God's deep association with the universe of creatures and, more precisely, of his eschatological "orientation towards the creation of worlds and His union with them."[9]

We see thus how certain Jewish interpretive traditions—traditions that have exerted considerable influence on contemporary thinkers like Levinas, Rosenzweig, and Scholem—came to read the texts of Genesis, Exodus, and the Song of Songs in the light of the kabbalistic premise that creation is, in part at least, God's body and points toward the transfiguration of a new world.[10] In the context of such traditions, the Song may be said to reveal how eschatology repeats cosmology, taking the form of a gradual filling out of the incarnational voices of Genesis, Exodus, and Isaiah. The nuptial promise reads accordingly as a reprise of the promise of Sinai (Exodus), while the lover longing for his "promised bride" anticipates the promised kingdom.[11]

The correlation of the Song with sacred or covenantal events in biblical history—such as creation, revelation, redemption—is found in many prior rabbinic and medieval commentaries.[12] While several of the allegorical readings offered by Christian Patristic thinkers urged a surpassing of carnal love in favor of a purely spiritual one, Jewish commentators were generally less prone to such an "ascetic renunciation."[13] For rabbinical exegetes, writes Elliot Wolfson, "the internal meaning of the Song is not predicated on undermining the external form of the scriptural metaphor. On the contrary, the allegoresis intended by the midrashic reading is an interpretation of the literal carnality and the consequent application of erotic imagery to the divine."[14] Uncovering a certain esoteric tradition stretching from some early midrashic readings to the kabbalistic exegeses of later Jewish history, Wolfson notes: "A number of aphoristic comments scattered throughout Talmudic and midrashic literature, including the critical exegetical remark that every Solomon mentioned in the Song is holy, for the name refers to God, the 'one to whom peace belongs' (li-mi she-ha-shalom shelo), indicate that the allegorical interpretation of the Song for some rabbis seems to have been predicated on a theosophical conception that attributed gender and sexual images to God."[15] This reading finds support in the famous view of R. Aqiva that if all Scripture is holy, the Song is the holy of holies, for it suggests that the Song captures, in nuce, the entire matrimonial and erotic charge of the divine revelation of Torah to the people (a charge also echoed in the Psalms and Hosea, for example). The Song was considered commensurate with the entire Torah by Aqiva and other rabbinic figures who located the utterance of the Song at Sinai. In other words, the recitation of this poem about the love between God and Israel was thought to coincide with the original giving of Torah in the Sinaitic epiphany—a moment itself erotically charged. But the sensual nature of the language used is also deeply linked to the poetical character of the revelation. For, as Wolfson argues, "the very notion of Torah as revealed word entails the structure of the parable, which is predicated on the paradox of metaphorical representation that is basic to the dynamic of eros, with its disclosure of truth through the appearance of image."[16]

Kabbalistic commentaries of the medieval era developed the allegorical reading of the Song as an erotic relationship between the soul and God, engendered respectively as feminine and masculine. These interpretations may have been influenced by Maimonides' philosophical claim in the *Mishneh Torah* that the entire Song is a parable (*mashal*) for the all-consuming love of the soul for God. Maimonides, like many of the Christian medieval commentators indebted to Neoplatonic and Aristotelian sources, takes the amorous symbolism as code for the contemplative ideal of union between the rational soul (the bride) and the Active Intellect (bridegroom), a union thought to be consequent upon a final overcoming of carnal desire originating in imagination.[17] The kiss mentioned in Song 1:2 is thus interpreted as an intellectual communion with the lights of the divine Intellect, predicated on the emancipation of the human mind from the lures of physical pleasure. The human soul, in a state of mere potentiality, is depicted as female, whereas the fully actualized Intellect of God is depicted as male.[18]

Influence from the philosophical tradition of intellectual allegory intersected with inspiration from the Hispano-Jewish poets who combined the genres of Arabic love poetry with the rabbinic-liturgical use of the love Song. In both instances, the erotic relation of human and divine is seen more in terms of personal salvation than in terms of national redemption. In short, if on an exoteric level the Song was construed as a parable of the relationship between Yahweh and his people, at the more esoteric level favored by the kabbalistic allegoresis it relates to the more intimate rapport between individual human lover and God.

The kabbalists tended to see the gendering of the personas in the Song as either a token of the feminization of the male mystic in relation to the masculine God or a symbol of the theosophical rapport between feminine and masculine potencies within divinity itself—e.g., the lower feminine glory (*Shekhinah*) ascending toward the upper masculine glory (*Tif'eret*). In both cases, as Wolfson has argued, we find a certain transformation of the original heterosexual language of the poem into a spiritualized homoeroticism that is itself predicated upon an ascetic renunciation of physical, carnal desire. By means of these various allegorizations—philosophical, soteriological, messianic, mystical, and theosophical—sex is taken out of the Song. Gender becomes a matter of supra-physical symbolism and sublimation. The bride's appeal to the kiss of the mouth, in several of these accounts, has little to do with love between real lovers and everything to do with a code or cipher that might arouse the return journey of the lower spirit to the higher Spirit from which it originated.[19]

In this context, the equation of eros and thanatos in 8:6—"Love is as strong as death"—was read as indicating that the kiss of union with the mouth of the divine is actually a kiss of death identified with the final liberation of the intellectual soul from the body. An ascetic renunciation of the flesh is understood to prepare one for the day when the death of the body coincides with a uniting with God "like the coal bound to the flame." As Wolfson phrases it, the Zohar sees in Song 8:6 the "eternality of the soul . . . attained in its being annihilated in the flame," "the death of eros experienced through the eros of death and the consequent crowning vision of the glory."[20]

But elaborately gendered and eroticized images are still in play. The desire of the fragmented human being for some kind of eschatological consummation is depicted in the Zohar as a holy marriage (*hieros gamos*). "In that moment when the wife remains face-to-face with her husband," we read, "the Song of Songs is revealed."[21] The amorous coupling is said to occur in both orders of being—lower and upper—corresponding to the elevation and augmentation of the female (*Shekhinah*) in union with the male. As the ontological ascension of the female is met by the descent of the male, the female lover becomes an open space or chora. Receiving the male into herself, she subsequently expands and overflows beyond herself. We thus witness an extraordinary reversal and transformation of gender. Restored to the higher *Binah*, the lower *Shekhinah* (represented by the swarthy Shulammite woman) is finally transfigured from a passive receptacle into an active power that overflows into the terrestrial world of differentiation. Binah here takes on the eschatological character of a messianic world-to-come, identified with King Solomon himself.[22] Only when the lower and higher females are thus realigned in one pattern, through a union with the male principle that is also a transformation into a masculine potency, will all the different gradations of creation ultimately correlate and correspond. The eschatological import of this radical transmutation and conjoining of genders is evident.

These zoharic texts thus retrieve the earlier rabbinic interpretations of the Song in terms of an historical allegory about the overcoming of exile and the coming of a messianic age. Moreover, the poetical allegory of the union of the female with the male in the divine realm is now seen to parallel the corresponding redemption, which may unfold in historical time. History repeats eternity forward, so to speak. And the Song is the map or guide that enables us to correlate our actions here below to the peaceful world-to-come, Solomon (*shelemo*) once again resonating with the etymological echoes of *she-ha-shalom*. Hence this telling reading of Aqiva's famous claim for the Song: "This Song is the Song that contains all of the Torah, the Song in relation to which the upper and lower beings are aroused, the Song that is in the pattern of the world above, which is the supernal Sabbath, the Song on account of which the supernal, holy name is crowned. Therefore it is the holy of holies. Why? Because all of its words are in love and in the joy of everything" (*Zohar Hadash* 2: 143b).[23]

The symbolic overcoming of the gender division between male and female in the eschatological Sabbath thus signals in turn the historical overcoming of the divisions and conflicts of exile, death, and separation. The world-to-come is identified with the "place of the hidden wine"—an attribute of Binah—which overflows all divisions in the promised moment of erotic intoxication. There is, then, a double movement of eros from below to above and above to below. Indeed, the Zoharic reading of the kiss in terms of an interplay between the four emanations (Shekhinah, Yesod, Tif'eret, Binah) and the four names for God (Adonai, Sevar'ot, YHWH, and Ehyeh), expresses the "desire of each to enter the other, so that one may be contained in the other."[24] This Zoharic interplay of desires—lower and upper, female and male, earthly and celestial—is not a matter of intellect or reason. It is a truth of the heart. For just as the bride bids her King to stamp her with a seal upon his heart (*simeni kakhotam al-libbeka*, Song 8:6), so too the ultimate mystical union can only be realized by "contemplation of the heart" (*sukhlatenu de-libba*). The heart knows it, claims the Zohar, even though it is not seen at all.[25] What these Zoharic and midrashic passages are ultimately pointing toward is, we might wager, a desire beyond desire that somehow remains desire. As Wolfson puts it, "For the erotic ascetic, desire not to desire is a potent form of desire, for who, after all, affirms more affirmatively than one who resists affirmation in the affirmation of resistance?"[26]

To be sure, as Gershom Scholem pointed out, kabbalistic readings of desire resist the Christian ascetic ideal of total abstinence. Marriage is not viewed by the kabbalists as a necessary evil to keep alive the human race, but as an appropriate symbol of reconciliation between the male and female powers within the divinity itself. In fact, nuptial union is seen—in keeping with the Song of Songs—as the highest idiom of correlation for a proper understanding of divine and human desire. According to Scholem the mystery of sexuality is not a *via negativa* but a *via eminentia* leading us right to the core of divinity itself. Indeed, historically speaking, the Hispano-Jewish kabbalists who wrote commentaries on the Song were functioning within the norms of *halakhah*, which did not affirm celibacy as an ideal. Marriage was a central part of Jewish ethical and religious life. And observance of the Sabbath involved engaging in carnal intercourse by way of facilitating a holy union above. One of the highest zoharic images for the eschatological return to the womb of repair and pardon is, for example, the reversal of eros from pain to pleasure.[27] This expresses itself, for example, in a double gesture of messianic reparation where the upper foundation of the male father (*yesod de-abba*) descends from on high until it meets the ascending lower foundation of the mother womb (*yesod de-imma*).[28] This eschatological return to the restorative womb of the mother might also be said to echo the summons of the Shulammite to her lover to return with her to the place under the tree where she was originally conceived.

But one should be wary of romanticizing Jewish mysticism's affirmation of human sexuality. As Wolfson has argued, most kabbalistic accounts of the Song ultimately serve to displace carnal sexuality with spiritual eroticism. The spiritualization of eros for the purposes of mystical contemplation or communion is based on a form of ascetic renunciation. "The sacralisation of human sexuality attested in kabbalistic lore cannot," Wolfson insists, "be understood in isolation from the ascetic impulse."[29] Indeed, he concludes his comprehensive survey of the kabbalistic tradition by suggesting that the nexus between asceticism and eschatological redemption was one of the central tenets of the zoharic interpretation of the Song, which "embraces an erotic mysticism that affirms the ideal of ascetic eschatology, an ideal that is proleptically realized by kabbalists in their pietistic fraternities principally through communal study of the secrets of Torah."[30] This called for celibacy and abstinence on the Day of Atonement (Yom Kippur), for example, as one identified with Shekhinah as the "virgin that no man has known" (Gen. 24:16). And if a crucial role is indeed attributed to the female potency of the divine, in the figure of Shekhinah ascending to Binah, the ostensibly sovereign feminine is ultimately restored to the male androgyne in the final Great Sabbath. Binah is masculinized as "king." The divine female is reintegrated into the divine male.

Nonetheless, as Wolfson also argues, the eschatological eros adumbrated by the kabbalistic commentaries is less a denial or postponement of human desire than an opening to a form of desire beyond desire that remains desire.[31] Or, to put it in the words of Jewish poet Paul Célan, are we not here encountering that strange and rare phenomenon of a "desire realized as love but remaining desire" (*l'amour realisée du désir resté désir*)? If so, we no longer need to oppose carnal and spiritual desire in terms of a binary dualism, but might envisage a form of eschatological eros that transforms a first desire into a second desire. Thus theoerotics might be construed as an anaerotics where we return to desire having renounced desire, rediscovering in the retrieved or refigured eros a still deeper incarnational connection between Spirit and Flesh.

PATRISTIC AND MEDIEVAL CHRISTIAN READINGS

The first Christian interpretations of the Song date back to the commentaries of Origen and Gregory of Nyssa. In both cases, we find a strong determination to oppose any historical or physical sense of eros by situating the Song as part of a symbolic relationship between the Church and God or the soul and Christ. This might seem, at first, surprising, given the emphasis placed by Christianity on incarnation. But for many of the Church fathers the Word became Flesh not so much to glorify sexuality as to lead it beyond its physical instantiation toward a more spiritual and transcendent expression. The influence of Neoplatonism here was very marked indeed, at times finding voice in vehement resistances to any sensual or embodied sense of the Shulammite's desire. As Origen put it in his second *Homily on the Song of Songs*: "All the movements of the soul, God . . . created for the good, but in practice it often happens that good objects lead us to sin because we use them badly . . . [O]ne of the movements of the soul is love."[32] The worry here is not so much that Origen recognizes that there are good and bad expressions of desire, but that he should make so much of the deviant and sinful potential of sensual desire in his commentary on a poem that celebrates its inherent goodness. The right use of love for Origen is in the service of a higher truth and wisdom, far removed from the embodied love of flesh and blood. Only those who are spiritually detached from their physical desires can raise themselves up to this intellectual form of love. This anti-carnal reading of desire is one of the main motivations behind Origen's insistence on an allegorical interpretation of the Song. It takes the threat out of the sexual imagery by disembodying and depersonalizing the actual lovers in favor of more abstract movements of love—movements that, in Origen's ascetic reading, ultimately subordinate desire to wisdom. Sex in the Song is really just Logos in drag—a way of inveigling the unsuspecting audience into a sensuous-sounding poem that is really a covert homily about how to transcend the senses in pursuit of supersensible divinity.

As a Christian theologian, Origen insists that since God became flesh in Christ so as to teach us how to renounce the flesh in favor of the Word, we should read the Song as a proleptic allegory of this same movement of ascent or anabasis. The bride's desire for the bridegroom is construed accordingly as a coded parable of the soul's ascetic yearning to become one with Christ as the royal way to absolute transcendence via renunciation and sacrifice. It is in this context that Origen spends much of his time establishing the epistemological and soteriological status of Solomon's Song as a book of *Wisdom*. All references to the body, the senses, flowers, animals, landscapes, nature are no more than ciphers for higher spiritual truths. And the bride herself is but a thinly disguised emblem of the soul or Church in its quest for the one true transcendent God. As a result, "eroticism is subsumed under the body of the text rather than the text of the body, which is to say that this (Patristic) approach diminishes the concrete sensuality implied by the contextual meaning."[33]

Writing in the third century, Origen was one of the first church fathers to combine Neoplatonic and biblical discourses in what was to prove a deeply influential move. In later Patristic writers such as Ambrose, Jerome, and Gregory of Nyssa, we find this particular insistence on allegory being employed on behalf of rigorous ascetic renunciation. Nyssa's commentary on the Song of Songs betrays a deep suspicion of corporeal desire of any kind. Interpreting 3:1–4 as an attempt by the bride, who rises up from her bed at night, to go beyond all worldly sensations, feelings, images, names and concepts, Gregory concludes: "She says 'scarcely had I passed them'—meaning that once she left behind all creation . . . she finds her beloved by faith."[34] Gregory goes on to insist that there is in fact an insurmountable gap (*diastēma*) or "impenetrable wall" fencing off the "created essence" from the "uncreated nature" of God.[35] And if Gregory does refer to something called "divine desire" (*theoseros*) in his commentaries on the Song, he makes it clear that this is to be construed in the form of a Neoplatonic analogy of spirit impervious to the corrupting matter of the flesh. Citing the comparison of air and water to illustrate the descent of divine spirit into flesh, he writes: "Air is not retained in water when it is dragged down by some weighty body and left in the depth of the water, but rises quickly to its kindred element."[36] It would be difficult to find more rigorous practitioners of the *via negativa* than these Patristic apologists of the Logos, even in their commentaries of the Song of Songs. For them, desires of the flesh represent a hazardous detour through the lures of the material universe. Only through purgation, abnegation, and sacrifice can they be ultimately renounced in favor of an intellectual devotion to a supernatural deity.

The most influential medieval commentary on the Song was undoubtedly that of Bernard of Clairvaux, founder of Cistercian monasticism. Writing in the twelfth century, Bernard devoted eighteen years of his life to composing the eighty-six sermons that make up his famous *Talks on the Song of Songs*.[37] The fact that he scarcely gets past the second verse of the Song is an indication of just how fascinated he was with this controversial and oft-contested poem of divine Scripture. Clearly there is something of an existential, and perhaps theological, battle going on between the lines, as Bernard vacillates between allegorical and confessional readings of the Song. At times we find him testifying to an ecstatic visitation by divine Love, at other times pulling back and tempering his enthusiasm with a dose of doctrinal caution.

Most of the first forty-eight sermons are in fact an elaborate series of reflections on the opening lines—"Let him kiss me with the kisses of his mouth." Bernard is evidently concerned with drawing the listeners' attention to the secret meaning "hidden in the words." He calls this the "inner music" of the verse, which imparts "the great joy of privately whispered secrets." Unlike his Neoplatonic patristic predecessors, Bernard does not shy from acknowledging that this poem is more about love than wisdom as such (Sermon 8)—and not some purely metaphysical love, it seems, but that of a "passionate wedding song" (Sermon 1). It seems from the outset then that Bernard is preparing to lead us beyond the safe ecclesiastical terrain of doctrines, dogmas and first metaphysical principles to another kind of mystery—one that has less to do with Christ as logos than with Christ as kiss. The "kissing mouth," as he puts it, "is the Word in human flesh" (Sermon 2). It is that point of chiasmic exchange where "the human and the divine are mingled—two become one" (Sermon 2).

There is an ambiguity in the opening avowal of some secret meaning behind the words in that this mystery could be the occasion of either an allegorical or mystical reading. At times Bernard goes so far as to confide that he is speaking of his own experience of being shot through with God's desire. He speaks of God "entering" and completely "flooding" his being (Sermon 74). And on one occasion he identifies with the bride who has been found by her beloved, while at the same time identifying with Paul being mystically visited by the Lord. In fact, there is a curious temporality at work here to the extent that the moment of rapturous indwelling seems to explode the divisions of linear time and open up an eschatological notion of time where divine eros can only be experienced either as already past or as still to come—what Levinas calls the enigma of "anterior posteriority." "He has come to me on numerous occasions," confesses Bernard. "I never notice the precise moment when he arrives. I feel his presence and then I remember that he was with me. Sometimes I have a premonition that he is coming to me. But I have never been able to put my finger on the exact instant when he arrived or departed. What path he uses to enter or leave my soul is a mystery to me" (Sermon 74). And after such momentous entries and exits, Bernard, not unlike other mystics before him, is left talking "like a fool." He sings rather than argues. He chants rather than expounds. Just like the Shulammite in the Song.

On many other occasions, however, Bernard seems to be censoring himself, drawing back from the extraordinary implications of his own existential-mystical testimony. Then we find him resorting to a standard anticarnational interpretation of the Song, seemingly determined to convince his monastic audience—and himself—that all this talk of personal experience of divine desire is really just that—talk: allegory and homiletic preaching with a good moral message to it all! What matters is the ulterior metaphysical meaning. Thus we find him reassuring his listeners, for example, that when it comes to the divine kiss, "far from a mere touching of lips, it is a spiritual union with God." For when it is a question of kissing God's feet and hands and mouth, it is only in a spiritual sense that we can so speak. "Only God," says Bernard, "does not require some kind of body" (Sermon 9). And this from someone who is a devoted believer in the mystery of the Incarnation! These contortions and revisions continue apace as Bernard struggles to contain the erotic fall-out of his own mystical reading. Eventually he contrives to withdraw the drama from the realm of embodied creation altogether, back into the safe superworldly confines of an intradivine Trinity. The kiss now becomes a love affair of God with himself. "The Father kisses. The Son is kissed. The Holy spirit is the kiss. . . . Only God gives himself fully to Christ with a 'kiss of the mouth'" (Sermon 8).

This conflict between what we might call the amorous and the allegorical readings of the Song is carried on through the entirety of Bernard's homilies. In some passages, Bernard attests to an eschatological desire that descends on him from God, provoking his own passionate longing in turn: "I am in love. I have already received much more than I deserve, but less than I desire. I am motivated not by my head, but by my heart. It may be unreasonable to want more, but I am driven by passionate desire. I blush with shame, but love will not be denied. Love does not listen to arguments. It is not cooled by the intellect. I beg. I plead. I burn. 'Let him kiss me with the kisses of his mouth . . . .' 'Let him kiss me,' I plead, 'with the kisses of his mouth'" (Sermon 9). He represents himself as seduced against his will by the Song: "I did not intend to spend so many days on the mystical dimensions of our text. . . . I had no idea I would be diverted" (Sermon 16).

Elsewhere, however, Bernard seems determined to drain the excitement from the text: "Most important is knowledge of self . . . self-knowledge that leads to knowledge of God. . . . You have heard enough for now and grow weary. I see you yawning and dozing. I'm not surprised" (Sermon 36). His tone is moralizing, even censorious: "We are talking about love. This is not about a man and a woman. It is about the Word and a soul—Christ and his church. The hiding places are not locations for lovers to have a secret rendezvous. Another writer (Gregory the Great) understands the clefts of the rock to mean Christ's wounds in crucifixion. . . . It is the same with a Christian martyr. By looking at Christ's wounds, he will not pay much attention to his own. Pain that would have been overwhelming becomes endurable" (Sermon 61).

With repressive zeal, Bernard subjects the Shulammite to rhetorical humiliation, shaming her beauty as "limited" and "earthbound": "It is too soon for her to gaze upon God in the brightness of midday. She is not ready" (Sermon 38). "She wishes she could be in the warm presence of the Bridegroom, but she is instructed to bear and rear children instead" (Sermon 41). The result of the mystical visitation by divine eros is here deformed into an unwanted pregnancy. At the same time, the bride's amorous apostrophe to her divine lover, "Turn, my lover and be like a gazelle or a young stag" (Song 2.17), is interpreted as a summons to *deny* the flesh: According to Bernard, this turn is from the transient world of embodied beings toward a metaphysical God who is unchanging, since "The spirit gives life, the flesh counts for nothing" (1 Cor 14) (Sermons 73–74). The soul-body dualism that had so hampered the Patristic commentaries of the Song seems still to echo in such dismal passages. Desire climbs a one-way ladder of metaphysical ascent in grim flight from the passions of the flesh.

And yet, in the dips, folds, and invaginations of the text, an amorous eschatology persists, as we have seen. There it is revealed that desire ascending is a response to desire descending—an eros that precedes the upward movement of the soul and comes to meet it halfway down, indeed all the way down, in the kiss of perpetual incarnation. When the Novice Master steps aside to let the secret Shulammite in Bernard speak, the message becomes bold. Here we read that "she who loves is also loved"; that the divine loves us first, before we can love in return, and is waiting to claim us in a personal, secret, intimate mystical way—"as though God's love is exclusive" (Sermon 69). This is the lover descending to the flesh without reservation or reserve: "Our love for him became possible when he came down to browse among our lilies. This revelation of himself generated our loving response" (Sermon 70). We find resurfacing idioms of nourishment and feasting, of fragrance and flourishing, of abundance and superabundance, of grace and gift and gratuity, which so marked the original poetics of the Song itself. "Perhaps it is even possible to be overfilled," as he cites the Gospel passage about the measure "running over" into our laps (Luke 6.38) (Sermon 72). This feeling of asymmetrical passivity before the overflowing eros of God leads in turn to an exchange or reversibility of giving and receiving, of ascending and

RICHARD KEARNEY | 323

descending. Commenting on the Shulammite's famous climactic line, "I held him and would not let him go till I brought him down to my mother's house, to the room of the one who conceived me," Bernard notes tellingly: "This is a reciprocal love. . . . She could not endure if she trusted her own grip. She needed to be held" (Sermon 79). Moreover, this holding is, Bernard adds, of the most intimate kind: "She is not simply taking him to her mother's house. She wants the privacy of its bedroom. The savior brings salvation to the house he enters, but when he enters the bedroom there is intimacy" (Sermon 79).

Deeply immersed in the eros of the Shulammite's Song, we seem as far away from the strictly ascending desire of Platonism as could be imagined. Bernard concludes his Sermons with a reaffirmation of this reciprocal nuptial bond between human and divine desire. "When God loves, his only desire is to be loved in return. . . . A soul that loves like this will be loved. This sharing of love results in a perfect marriage" (Sermon 83). The asymmetry and symmetry of the theoerotic bond are here evenly poised, evidencing once again the miraculous paradox of posterior anteriority: "You should understand that if your soul seeks God, God has (already) sought it. . . . She loves because she is loved" (Sermon 84).

Bernard adds—anticipating Johannes de Silentio in Kierkegaard's *Fear and Trembling*—that he cannot legitimately talk about what he has just been talking about for the last 86 Sermons ("Words do not communicate this"). He thereby acknowledges that he is engaged in a *performative contradiction*. From a logical point of view, his propositions are to be regarded, in retrospect, as meaningless. But from a poetical point of view—and songs, hymns and litanies are of course of such an order—his words say much more than they can explain, if also much less than they have received. The sacred gift of eros is here ultimately attested to, even as it is officially quarantined within the cloisters of Bernard's ecclesiastical apologetics. This is eros betrayed, in both senses of the word.

MYSTICAL READINGS

The readings of the Song by later Christian mystics—above all, John of the Cross and his protégé Teresa of Avila—were to become still more forthright. John of the Cross's famous commentary on the Song, "The Spiritual Canticle," was written in Spain, in 1584, almost five hundred years after Bernard's "Talks." These are not delivered in the manner of formal homilies but rather in the guise of a personal testimony addressed to a single spiritual leader, Mother Ana de Jesus, prioress of the discalced Carmelite nuns of St Joseph's in Granada. The Canticle, as the prologue dedicated to Mother Ana makes plain, is not to be taken as a mere gloss on the biblical text but rather as a canticle in its own right. For who, says John in the prologue, can explain the desires that God gives one? All one can do is to respond with a song overflowing with an abundance of figures, comparisons, similitudes, secrets, and mysteries—a song that poetically repeats the biblical song. Departing from Bernard's residual fidelity to some kind of knowledge about such matters, John invokes a new genre of what he calls "mystical wisdom," which, he claims, "comes through love and is the subject of these stanzas and need not be understood distinctly in order to cause love and affection in the soul."[38] And so John proceeds to compose a canticle of forty verses, entitled "Stanzas between the Soul and the Bridegroom." This rewriting in Christian mystical language of the original biblical Song is followed by almost two hundred pages of notation where each stanza is reprised in copious elaborations, digressions, and perorations: a poetic commentary of commentaries that is virtually endless in scope and intent. Indeed, the impression one receives in reading through these pages is that of stepping carefully through a series of concentric cloisters in a circular centripetal movement that leads, gradually but asymptotically, toward the "holy of holies" itself—the Song of Songs. But the reader, like the soul, like the Bride, like Moses, will never actually reach the promised land of desire.

From the opening verses, John bears witness to a wound caused by the divine stag. He has already been shot through with "the thrust of the lance," which now leaves him "moaning" and disoriented—sick with love. And yet this wounding, which leaves him in such destitute loss, is also, he avows, something blissful and benign. It is "*after* the taste of some sweet and delightful" contact with the divine lover that the bride speaks out. In short, the bride's sense of terrible absence is consequent upon a prior visitation of fullness and presence. The goal of her desiring is somehow already the origin of her desire. Its eschatology is its archeology.

John persistently privileges the choice of the sense of taste over that of sight or even sound. For if the soul is indeed wounded through what

John calls a "trace of the beauty of the beloved," this beauty itself remains unseen and unseeable. Indeed, so sublimely unknowable—"I know not what" says John in stanza 7—is this divine eros that the witness is reduced to a state of "stammering." This is precisely how John seems to regard his own "spiritual canticle." And if the vision of divine beauty signals the impossibility of proper thought and speech, it also marks an interruption of life. "May the vision of your beauty be my death" (stanza 11), the wounded lover cries out. Eros reveals itself here as mysteriously bound to thanatos.

As we proceed through the stanzas, a remarkable shift occurs that, I believe, is typical of John's mystical experience. The wound of the bride is reversed into the wound of the bridegroom. The human and divine lovers are now *both* sufferers of the wound, which unites them in blissful-painful desire. This "spiritual betrothal," as John describes it in stanzas 14–15, is profoundly ambivalent. It speaks of a superabundance of love, comparable to Isaiah's "overflowing river" where the soul may "taste a splendid spiritual sweetness"; but it also speaks of terror and fear before the very force of this mystical ecstasy. The soul is compelled to beg the beloved to "withdraw the eyes I have desired"; it is clearly too much for either the senses or mind to endure. This is the bottomless "abyss of knowledge," the colorless void of sensation, the dark night of the soul which the bride must endure before she can move from "spiritual be-trothal" to "spiritual marriage" proper.

By the time we reach stanza 15, we have joined a divine supper that, we are enthusiastically informed, "affords lovers refreshment, satisfaction and love." We have now passed beyond the various vacillations and withdrawals attendant upon the dark night of loss and embarked upon the eschatological drinking and eating of a divine-human marriage feast. Pre-optical images of fragrance, touching and taste abound, from allu-sions to David "drinking the delicious spiritual wine" (Ps. 63:1) to the bride "feeding among the lilies" (Song 6:2–3), "sucking honey from all things" (stanza 28), swallowing the "juice of pomegranates" and imbibing the "flowings from the balsam" of God to the point of rapturous intoxi-cation (stanzas 26–28, 36). Here, John informs us suggestively, "the soul feels that her beloved is within her as in her own bed" (stanza 16). And she responds by offering herself with unconditional abandon. This language of "sweet inebriation by divine wine" (stanza 25) epitomizes the spiritual espousal where the soul "drinks of her beloved in the inner wine cellar" and feels her "heart tremble at his touch" (Song 5:4 and stanzas 25–26).

John here speaks of a progressive journey through the seven wine cellars of love, anticipating Teresa's mystical itinerary through the seven mansions of her Interior Castle. Indeed when the innermost point of divine indwelling (Prov. 30:1) is reached, we witness a mutual surrender of the soul and Christ, and even a reversal of the prior asymmetry between the finite and infinite. Now it is God who becomes the servant of love and the bride the sovereign ruler! (stanza 25). In this paroxysm of "mystical theology" (as John names it with oddly technical precision), we encounter a *jouissance* of incarnation-crucifixion, of eros-thanatos. For here, we are told, the soul "desires to be dissolved" with Christ in a "beatific pasture . . . where pure water flows . . . deep into the thicket" (stanza 36).

But the invocation of a self-reflexive term like *mystical theology* is like a bell that tolls the singer back to his more epistemological and ecclesiastical self. By the end of "The Spiritual Canticle" John is clearly reigning in his own enthusiasms in deference to some higher tribunal of intellect. In stanza 40 he has firmly reintroduced a traditional dichotomy between soul and body, declaring the necessity of "putting the passion in order according to reason" and "mortifying the appetites."[39] But even in his reversion to the old hierarchy of spirit versus sense, soul versus body, reason versus sex, John uses the telling term "descend" in place of the Platonic term "ascend." The dualism is preserved in some kind of dichotomy but the hierarchy is curiously inverted. In the penultimate statement of the last stanza, John makes this startling observation: "The soul declares that they (the corporeal senses) descended—she does not say "they went," or use some other word—in order to point out that in this share that the sensory part has in the spiritual communication, when the soul takes this drink of spiritual goods, the senses discontinue their natural operations and go down from them to spiritual recollection."[40] Down, not up. *Katabasis*, not *anabasis*. Here John seems to be hinting, even in this ostensible return to the border divides of traditional epistemology into rational and embodied experience, that there is perhaps a form of *second* desire, *other* desire, *supplementary* desire. A desire that the senses can reinvest after they have renounced their first attachments and cravings. And this second desire—this eschatological eros beyond biological eros—is less an expression of lack than of surplus. However purged and spiritualized it may have become, it still pertains to what he calls a passion of "heart and flesh." Or, as he cites David, his predecessor in biblical erotics, with evident approval: "My heart and my flesh have rejoiced in the living God" (Ps. 84:2, stanza 40).

John's protégé Teresa is at once more autobiographical and more circumspect. She is highly personal in her utterances but also very aware that her mystical-erotic witness borders on heresy. Perhaps she learned a lesson from John's own incarceration or from his occasional rebukes to her regarding her sensory enthusiasms (he is said to have ensured she always received a small piece of Eucharistic bread at Mass to curb her natural appetite!). Teresa certainly covers herself with all kinds of disclaimers—I am only an ignorant foolish woman! What do I know about anything!—and constantly defers to higher ecclesiastical authorities for proper guidance and judgment. But for all her caveats and proper piety, her testimonies frequently break through with the shock of an explosion. The fallout has scarcely time to register before she retreats again into formulaic devotions. Her salient comments on the Song of Songs in *The Interior Castle*—arguably her most intrepid text—are of particular interest for our present study.

In the first chapter of the Fifth Mansion, Teresa invokes the Bride's confession that "the King had brought her into the cellar of wine" (Song 1:3; 2:4). This particular scene was to become a staple diet in the mystical imaginary of the Song as it developed from Teresa and John down to the Beguines and beyond. Teresa's opening salvo in this line of visionary poetics decisively casts theoeroticism in the form of passionism. Eros is experienced as a form of radical receptivity to the incoming and descending force of love, surpassing all finite human forms of will, capacity or understanding. Commenting on the bride's experience of being led down into the cellar for the pleasure of the King, Teresa writes: "It (the Song) does not say that she *went*. It also says that she was wandering about in all directions seeking her Beloved (Song 3:2). This, as I understand it, *is* the cellar where the Lord is pleased to put us, when He wills and as He wills. But we cannot enter by any efforts of our own; His Majesty must put us right into the center of our soul, and must enter there Himself; and, in order that He may the better show us His wonders, it is His pleasure that our will, which has entirely surrendered itself to Him, should have no part in this."[41]

Teresa proceeds to make suggestive analogies about the way in which divine eros enters and exits from the center of the feminine being—without using doors or removing stones—intimating that this is some mysterious experience of pre-phallic *jouissance*. The associative implications of erotic pleasuring, fecundation and impregnation are powerfully present, if discreetly deferred to the ultimate erotic feast awaiting the pilgrim in the Seventh or Sabbatical Mansion—unmistakable echoes of the Shulammite's deferral to eschatological postponement in the Song. "Later on," she addresses her readers, "you will see how it is His Majesty's will that the soul should have fruition of Him in its very center, but you will be able to realize that in the last Mansion much better than here."[42] The recurring allusion to center, as correlative image to the inner wine cellar of secrecy, intoxication and delight, carries such an obvious sexual charge that a later clerical redactor of Teresa's text, Gracian, saw fit to cross it out *twice* in this very text! Of course, to the degree that Teresa insists on the involuntary and unexpected character of divine ecstasy, she is also cleverly making it plain that it is not *her* moral or intellectual responsibility, but God's.

Mystical sex is safe sex because it is not consensual. Or rather: It is the effect of a divine seduction in which consent is not easily distinguished from coerced submission. Teresa explores this ambivalence as she returns to Song 2:4. Interpreting this verse now to mean that the divine bridegroom put the bride into the cellar so that he could "ordain love of her," she goes on to relate this to the climactic verse of the Song (8:6) where the bride actually bids her lover to stamp her as a seal upon the heart. Here Teresa exposes the soul's willingness to surrender itself to the influx of divine love at a level beneath that of the conscious or the contractual. In a passage that reprises the Shulammite's pivotal apostrophe and anticipates a whole line of mystico-erotic poetry, Teresa writes: "That soul has now delivered itself into His hands and His great love has so completely subdued it that it neither knows nor desires anything save that God shall do with it what He wills. Never, I think, will God grant this favor save to the soul which He takes for His very own. His will is that, without understanding how, the soul shall go thence sealed with His seal. In reality the soul in that state does no more than the wax when a seal is impressed upon it—the wax does not impress itself; it is only prepared for the impress: that is, it is soft—and it does not even soften itself so as to be prepared; it merely remains quiet and consenting."[43] Here, in short, we are speaking of consent beyond consent, just as we are witnessing a desire beyond desire.

Then, in a flash of afterthought, Teresa suggests that in this mystico-erotic union of the divine and the human, the one *becomes* the other in a strange reversibility. The human and divine, lover and beloved exchange places, as human wax suddenly transmutes into the divine wax. "Oh, goodness of God, that all this should be done at Thy cost! Thou dost require only our wills and dost ask that *Thy* wax may offer no impediment."[44] In the next paragraph, Teresa compares this paradox of active passivity experienced by the lover bride to the surrender of Christ himself at the last supper: "With desire have I desired" (Luke 22, 15). Rarely have the words desire, feast, surrender and suffering—as both allowing and enduring—carried such double meanings. Rarely has the term mystical "subject" carried such strong connotations of both subjection and sovereignty. The seed of grain at the center of our being must be consumed and transmuted into a new, risen, reborn being. Indeed Teresa will go on to compare this secret inner event to the miraculous transmutation of the "seed" of a silk worm into a butterfly.[45]

Is it not easy to imagine that Mary Margaret Alacocque had something like this in mind when she experienced her own blissful vision in Paray-le-Monial of an exchange of blazing hearts between herself and Christ? Or John Donne when he composed "Batter my heart, three-person'd God":

Take me to you, imprison me, for I,
Except you enthrall me, never shall be free,
Nor ever chaste, except you ravish me.

Or George Herbert: "when th' heart says (sighing to be approved), / O, could I love! And stops: God writeth *loved*." ("A True Hymn") You must sit down, says Love, and taste my meat: / So I did sit and eat" ("Love III") Or, finally, the driven Gerard Manley Hopkins when he celebrated the erotico-mystical sacrifice of the Nun in *The Wreck of the Deutschland*:

> [She] was calling "O Christ, Christ, come quickly" . . .
> Is it love in her of the being as her lover had been? . . . .
> What by your measure is the heaven of desire,
> The treasure never eyesight got . . .
> *Ipse*, the only one, Christ, King, Head:
> He was to cure the extremity where he had cast her;
> Do, deal, lord it with living and dead;
> Let him ride, her pride, in his triumph . . .
> What was the feast followed the night
> Thou hadst glory of this nun?—
> Feast of one woman without stain. . . .
> Is the shipwreck then a harvest, does tempest carry the grain for
> thee? . . .
> For the lingerer with a love glides
> Lower than death and the dark;
> A vein for the visiting of the past-prayer, pent in prison,
> Our passion-plunged Giant risen. . .

The images that recur in these examples of what we might call a Christian mystical poetics are remarkably reminiscent of, if not directly indebted to, Teresa's own mystical imaginary as response to the Shulammite's song: cellar, womb, core, heart, seal, feast, sacrifice, seed, passion, ravishment, and rapture.

Before we leave Teresa I would like, however, to follow up on her promise, given the reader in the Fifth Mansion of "spiritual betrothal," to reveal an even fuller form of divine-human union later in her journey. True to her word, Teresa returns to the Shulammite woman later in the text, focusing this time on verse 3:2. The bride rising from her bed at night and wandering the streets and squares is compared to the mystical lover who is prepared to let go of her ego attachments, to surrender her conventional and controlling self, and to welcome the arrival of absolute desire into the core of her being. The release of the lover into an open space of exposure and quest corresponds, curiously, to her being discovered by the beloved in the most inner mansion of the castle where divinity dwells. The images of expenditure and loss are thus counterposed with images of enclosure and concentration, a paradoxical movement of mutual traversal and reversal echoed in similar contrapuntal metaphors of waking/sleeping, pleasure/pain, living/dying, breathing/not-breathing, etc. "He at once commands that all the doors of the Mansion shall be shut, and only the door of the Mansion in which He dwells remains open so that we may enter. . . . For when He means to enrapture this soul, it loses its power."[46] "This lasts only for a short time," Teresa explains, "because, when this profound suspension lifts a little, the body seems to come partly to itself again, and draws breath. . . . Complete ecstasy, therefore, does not last long . . . to this it is fully awake, while asleep. . . . Oh, what confusion the soul feels when it comes to itself again and what ardent desires it has to be used for God in any and every way in which He may be pleased to employ it!"[47] It is in the same Mansion that Teresa chooses to deliver her most notorious and audacious account of divine ecstasy, which has so preoccupied commentators of mystical desire down through the ages from prurient redactors and inquisitors to subversive anthropologists (Georges Bataille) and bemused psychoanalysts (Marie Bonaparte, Jacques Leuba, and Jacques Lacan), who coined the term erotic "transverberation." Given the decisive influence this text has exerted on most attempts to comprehend the mystery of theoretic ecstasy, I cite it here in full:

So powerful is the effect of this upon the soul that it becomes consumed with desire, yet cannot think what to ask, so conscious is it of the presence of its God. Now, if this is so, you will ask me what it desires or what causes it distress . . . I cannot say; I know that this distress seems to penetrate to its very bowels; and that, when He that has wounded it draws out the arrow, the bowels seem to come with it, so deeply does it feel this love. I have just been wondering if my God could be described as the fire in a lighted brazier, from which some spark will fly out and touch the soul, in such a way that it will be able to feel the burning heat of the fire; but as the fire is not hot enough to burn it up, and the experience is very delectable, the soul continues to feel that pain and the mere touch suffices to produce that effect . . . and just as the soul is about to become enkindled, the spark dies, and leaves the soul yearning once again to suffer that loving pain of which it is the cause.[48]

Teresa is adamant on this point: Mystical *jouissance* is not a permanent condition but a passing experience of divine rapture, which stems from desire and returns once again to desire. It is not a fullness that consummates eros—either divine or human—in any final sense. On the contrary, the more ravished the lover bride the more ardent her desire. And as one moves from a primary desire of attachment and craving to a second desire of freedom and bliss, Teresa insists that one not abandon the world of created bodies and things. On the contrary, Teresa's testimony to this second, eschatological desire is accompanied by a summons to return to the ordinary universe. We must not "flee from corporeal things," she warns us, for that would be to deny our "greatest blessing"—namely, "the sacred *Humanity*" of the incarnate God.[49] Love of the embodied everyday is crucial to Teresa's vision. It defies all attempts to construe the mystical-erotic experience in terms of metaphysical or Platonic polarities. And in this she certainly seems faithful to the prophetic erotics of the Shulammite herself whom she discreetly cites and celebrates.[50]

Bernard, John, and Teresa all challenged standard Platonic dualisms between the divine and the human, the spiritual and the corporeal. All three acknowledged that theoerotics, since the Incarnation, involves both ascending and descending eros. (The later notion of a divine desire descending from the Highest Cause or Form to embrace the human would have been anathema to Plato and Aristotle).[51] But these Christian saints lived their mystical witness to divine desire in diverse ways and to different degrees. Where Bernard betrays a contradiction between carnal and spiritual eros, and John a dichotomy, Teresa lives the tension as a fecund paradox that provokes further contemplation and action. Divine eros always calls for *more* of the same, while simultaneously summoning us back to the ordinary universe of everyday love.

Indeed, of all the Christian readings of the Song we have reviewed above, Teresa's is the most incarnational. In this, she might be said to be most faithful not only to Christ's own message of "enfleshment" (*ensar-kosis*) but equally to the message of the Shulammite's song, as voiced by Jewish as well as Christian interpreters. For Christ and the Shulammite sing from the same theoerotic sheet. The divine cries out to be made flesh in both the testimony of the Shulammite bride and of the incarnate Nazarene. Teresa, by doing justice to both, restores the hyphen between Judeo and Christian, where it belongs. Divine desire is, she shows us, but another name for this hyphen.[52]

Our hermeneutic wager may be reformulated thus: The Song of Songs is a chiasm where Judaism and Christianity may interweave and interact. It is a common source and resource for both hermeneutic traditions, a poem of being-between.

READING THE SONG IN THE CONTEXT OF CONTEMPORARY THOUGHT

Jacques Lacan gives a tantalizing nod to the conundrum of mystical eros in his *Encore* essay, "God and Woman's *Jouissance*" (1972–73). Here, referring by name to celebrated mystics like Bernard, Hadewijch, John of the Cross, and most especially Teresa, Lacan speaks of a new form of *jouissance*. This "extra" *jouissance* he terms "supplementary" in that it goes beyond normal phallic *jouissance* where a woman's desire is considered in terms of a lack or a not-all (vis-à-vis the phallus taken as signifier of plenitude, fullness, allness). In the phallic—or to use Derrida's variation, phallogocentric—regime woman's desire is considered as a *pas-tout* that is said to combine with male desire to form a totality or *Tout*. As such it is complementary rather than supplementary. Referring to the famous depiction of the swooning Teresa in Bernini's statue in Rome, Lacan insists that here we are witnessing an "other" bliss that is supplementary rather than complementary (in an ontological, biological or genital sense). At this level, eros functions as surplus (*en-plus*) rather than as lack (*pas-tout / tout*). Or, to rephrase it in our own terms, as an eros that appears to be more eschatological than ontological—moving from more to less rather than less to more.

In a highly dense and arcane passage full of mischievous wordplay and rhetorical brio, Lacan writes of Teresa's *jouissance*: "She's coming [*elle jouit*]. There's no doubt about it. But what is she getting off on? It is clear that the essential testimony of the mystics consists in saying that they experience it, but know nothing about it. These mystical jaculations are neither idle chatter nor empty verbiage; they provide, all in all, some of the best reading one can find on the subject."[53] That is, of course, up to Lacan's own psychoanalytic *Ecrits*, which, he insists, is of the "same order"! Then, entertaining the hypothesis that many of his readers may now think that he, the atheist Jacques Lacan, believes in God, he adds: "I believe in the *jouissance* of woman insofar as it is extra [*en plus*]."[54] And referring to a number of early psychoanalytic attempts—around Charcot and various late-nineteenth-century experiments with hysterical eroticism in women—to reduce mysticism to a matter of sexual repression and deferred genital gratification, he rejoins that this is not it at all. This "other bliss" of the mystics is not reducible to a matter of *foutre*. On the contrary, rejoins Lacan, "doesn't this *jouissance* one experiences and yet knows nothing about put us on the path of ex-sistence? And why not interpret one face of the Other, the God face, as based on feminine desire?"[55]

Does this make God an unconscious projection of feminine desire? Or does it make feminine desire (and Lacan is quite prepared to admit that such mystics as John of the Cross were "feminine" too in this respect) a privileged landing site for incoming divinity? What precisely does Lacan mean by "ex-sistence" anyway? A Heideggerean being-toward-death, as the term first seems to imply? Or a Kierkegaardian openness toward a transcendent "good at one remove" (*bien au second degré*), as he seems to hint in his final paragraph? Lacan does not resolve the issue. The jury is still out. But perhaps the Shulammite woman is prompting from the wings. (To mix poor-taste Lacanian wordplay with a well-known English verse, we might ask: "If Theresa comes, can the Shulammite be far behind?" Though coming—*jouir, venire*—in Lacan's reading is also a matter of coming-out, that is, finding psychoanalytic formulations for this "other bliss" which otherwise remains unsayable in anything but the coded "jaculations" of the mystics themselves.)

What remains but a tantalizing hint in Lacan receives sustained treatment in Georges Bataille, another French thinker fascinated by what he calls "divine love." Drawing on both psychoanalytic and anthropological insights, Bataille focuses sustained attention on the liaison *dangereuse* between mysticism and sensuality. Indeed, Bataille gives us the added advantage of explicitly referencing the Song in his controversial deliberations. In a section of *The Accursed Share* entitled "From the *Song of Songs* to the Formless and Modeless God of the Mystics," a subsection of "Divine Love," Bataille makes this provocative statement: "Only eroticism is capable . . . of admitting the lovers into that void . . . where it is no longer just the other but rather the bottomlessness and boundlessness of the universe that is designated by the embrace . . . [B]y holding resolutely to purity, but at the same time to the desire for the *other*, for that which is missing and which alone might yield us the totality of being, we are in search of God."[56] But for Bataille, God understood as "supreme being" is a denial of the totality of reality understood as contingency and immanence. In settling for such a logical formulation we lose what he terms God's "sensible presence." To try to regain this and rediscover the "burning" divine love that "consumes" us, we need to retrace our search for God back to the "darkness of eroticism" with its concomitant experiences of "horror, anguish, death."[57]

These are kept alive in the violent and transgressive "throes of sacrifice," which, according to Bataille's anthropology, lie at the root of all religious experience. This is not something we will find access to in any kind of positive theology but only in the most extreme forms of negative theology—or what he will call "theopathy"—practiced by the mystics. The mystic who identifies his or her own wounds and lacerations with the "horror and suffering" of the dying God of the Cross no longer speaks logically or theologically but according to a discourse of "human love." And it is precisely here that Bataille locates the language of the Song as prototype of the legacy of biblical mysticism. In this respect, he approvingly cites a believer who claims that the great mystics "saw in the *Song* the most adequate grammar of the effects of divine love and never tired of annotating it, as if those pages had contained a prior description of their experiences."[58] But Bataille makes it clear that he is not reducing mystical states to sexual neuroses. He is simply pointing to the tacit analogy that these two forms of desire share as modes of "*consumption* of all the individual beings' resources."[59] The erotic effusions of the mystics may, Bataille suggests, be construed accordingly as expressions of extreme expenditure and transgression that consume all the energy that sets their life "aflame." They thus bear witness, unbeknownst to themselves, to a deviant sensuality that returns the God of metaphysics, morality and transcendence, to the abyss of formless *jouissance*—a void where the self is subsumed back into the seamless fusion and continuity of brute being. The descent from the elevated sublime of Kant to the abyssal sublime of the Marquis de Sade could not be more direct. Bataille's conclusion is as chilling as it is candid: "Whatever one makes of the erotic language of the mystics, it must be said that their experience, having no limitation, transcends its beginnings and that, pursued with the greatest energy, it finally retains only eroticism's transgression in a pure state, or the complete destruction of the world of common reality, the passage from the perfect Being of positive theology to that formless and modeless God of a 'theopathy' akin to the 'apathy' of Sade."[60]

The jury that remained out with Lacan returns here with a vengeance. The verdict is unambiguous. Divine eros, as evidenced in the long religious tradition ranging from the Song to the mystics, is really about a desire to blissfully and sublimely dissolve into limitless fusion. With what? With what behind the illusory veil of an imaginary God is nothing other than nothingness, death, indifferentiation. In short, the ultimate aim of eros is thanatos. The link between self-annihilation and the *jouissance* of sensual excitement is unequivocal. But this does not, for Bataille any less than for Lacan, mean a reduction of mystical-religious desire to animal or biological drive. On the contrary, what is unique about mystical eros is precisely its ability to use the illusion of ascent as a demonic means to descend far *lower* than the animal order, to a zone of objectless immanence and intimacy never dreamed of by other living beings. What is so special about the divine eros of the mystics is its sense of *waste*, its sheer gratuity. And if the Shulammite, like her eponymous mystics, is indeed "sick with love," it is precisely because she has traded the normal behavior of *"life against death"* (governed by fear, control, taboo, property, convention, survival) for an abnormal *life for death*. She is sublimely disoriented and undone as she errs hysterically through the streets at night, "losing her footing without falling irrevocably."[61] She risks her existence to the point of illness, folly, disequilibrium, violation, and self-destruction. For mystical eros is defined, above all else, by its *assent to life up to the point of death.* It is committed to the quest of an impossible "life through death." This, at bottom, is divine desire—"the desire to live while ceasing to live, or to die without ceasing to live."[62]

It is not surprising, therefore, to find in Bataille's *Eroticism*—a work that explicitly acknowledges its debt to both Jacques Lacan and the aberrant sensuality of de Sade—this unambiguous statement of intent: "The human spirit is prey to the most astounding impulses. Man goes constantly in fear of himself. His erotic urges terrify him. The saint turns from the voluptuary in alarm; she does not know that his unacknowledgable passions and her own are really one . . . [I]n this work flights of Christian religious experience and bursts of erotic impulses are seen to be part and parcel of the same movement."[63] Whether the saintly "she" Bataille invokes here is the Shulammite woman, or Teresa of Avilla, or his own contemporary Simone Weil (another devotee of "divine desire" whom Bataille loved to meet in late-night Parisian cafes, after he had frequented his regular brothels, to discuss questions of depravity and salvation), it is uncertain. Perhaps none? Perhaps a combination of all three? But later in the text, his explicit comment on Saint Teresa's alleged *jouissance* could not be more explicit: "One essential element of excitement is the feeling of being swept off one's feet, of falling headlong. If love exists at all it is, like death, a swift movement of loss within us, slipping into tragedy and stopping only at death."[64] This, he says, is the "desire of an extreme state that Saint Teresa has perhaps been the only one to depict strongly enough in words: 'I die because I cannot die.'"[65] Bataille concludes that the "longed for swoon is thus the salient feature not only of man's sensuality but also of the experience of the mystics . . . Temptation is the desire to fall, to fail, and to squander all one's reserves until there is no firm ground beneath one's feet."[66] If Bataille is to be believed, Teresa yielded to this ultimate temptation of eros lived as thanatos, as did all the great mystical lovers before and after her, starting with the daring bride of the Song of Songs. What else, after all, could be meant by the immortal line "Love is as strong as death"?

These critical readings throw down the gauntlet to allegorical readings. For while the latter saw desire as ascending—often on Platonic wings—from below to above, the former signal a reverse direction of descent to the most abyssal (and at times abject) depths of the unconscious psyche.

Indeed, theopathy and apathy are, in Bataille, just cover names for the perverse pathologies of the erotic psyche he is determined to chronicle. Not that he or Lacan—I repeat—wish to reduce this ontology (or meontology) of eros to a mere biology of animal or genital instincts. They believe they are onto something far more complex and intriguing than anything that could be found in a manual of sex instincts. This is more a matter of jaculation than ejaculation, of psychic *jouissance* than of physiological *foutre*, of eros-thanatos (something alien to the evolutionary animal species drive) than of eros-bios. It is metaphysics, in other words, but metaphysics in reverse. Metaphysical desire turning around in mid orbit and gravitating back to the darkest entrails of the earth, all the way down, to its fathomless, bottomless core (*abgrund/béance/vide*).

There is, of course, something strangely complicit about the two brands of metaphysical eros—the allegorical ascent and psychoanalytic descent—in that both see more in sex than sex. But where the allegorical tends to follow the mystic beyond sexuality the psychoanalytic tends to follow the mystic beneath it. Either way, we eventually follow the respective trajectories, upward and downward, until they disappear off the radar screen. Until we reach what both agree is a zone of pure silent, deathlike stillness. If we live after eros, we live posthumously.

But these are not the only options. There is, as suggested several times in our discussion of the mystical testimonies, a third way that combines the two directions of divine eros. Here we encounter an enigmatic phenomenon of mutual traversal, where ascending and descending desires cross and exchange without fusing into one. This crossing occurs at the site of metaphor. As Wolfson puts it, with reference to rabbinic interpretation but in terms that also resonate with Christian readings: "The implication of the symbolic reading of the Song . . . is well captured in Rosenzweig's recognition of the essentially metaphorical nature of eros and the concurrent affirmation of the essentially erotic nature of metaphor. In his words, 'love is not "but a metaphor"; it is metaphor in its entirety and its essence; it is only apparently transitory: in truth it is eternal. The appearance is as essential as the truth here, for love could not be eternal as love if it did not appear to be transitory. But in the mirror of appearance, truth is directly mirrored.'"[67]

The surplus of metaphoricity in the Song, whereby an eschatological symbolism of nuptial love is enmeshed in erotics of the body without ever being reducible to it, gives rise to what Paul Ricoeur calls "a phenomenon of indetermination."[68] This is evinced in the fact that many readers have difficulty identifying the lover and the beloved of the poem, for the lovers never clearly identify themselves or go by proper names: the term Shulammite itself is not a proper name. So we find ourselves forced to admit that we are never really sure who exactly is speaking, or to whom. We can even imagine that there are up to *three* different characters involved—a shepherdess, a shepherd, and a king (Solomon).[69] This puts us on a constant state of alert, like the amorous fiancée herself, as we keep vigil for the arrival of the divine lover. "Who is coming up from the desert?" (3:6) we too find ourselves asking. Or to frame our question in more eschatological terms: "Is it not from the end of the world and the depth of time that love arises?"[70] Moreover, we might add that it is precisely the primacy of the indeterminately fluid "movements of love" over the specific identities of the lover and the beloved that guards the open door. We are kept guessing. This guarding of the Song as an open text of multiple readings and double entendres—divine and human, eschatological and carnal—provokes a hermeneutic play of constant "demetaphorizing and remetaphorizing," which never allows the Song to end.[71]

In sum, what we have here is a story of transfiguring eros as the making possible of the impossible.[72] This sets the biblical eros celebrated in the Song off from other kinds of erotic expression: e.g., romantic infatuation, courtly *fine amour,* not to mention libertine pornography. But if the Song extends the standard range of Western love literatures, it also amplifies the range of religious expression. The Song marks an opening of religion to what we might call a *poetics of aporetics.* The *persona* of the Song may thus be seen as a figure who promises the coupling without final consummation of God and desire—"sensuous and deferred love . . . passion and ideal."[73]

The Song of Songs confronts us with a desire that desires beneath desire and beyond desire while remaining desire. It is a desire that spills out beyond the limits of the Song itself, sending innumerable ripples throughout many readings—rabbinic, kabbalistic, Patristic, mystical, and more. Indeed, I have been claiming that it reverberates right down into the most contemporary of voices, not only in philosophy and theology but in art and literature too. Let us leave the last words to Molly Bloom, one of the most powerful contemporary reincarnations of the Shulammite woman. Here is Molly's unconditional *yes* to love:

> What else were we given all those desires for I'd like to know I cant help it if Im young still . . . of course a woman wants to be embraced 20 times a day almost to make her look young no matter by who so long as to be in love or loved by somebody if the fellow you want isn't there sometimes by the Lord God I was thinking . . . and I thought well as well him as another and then I asked him with my eyes to ask again yes and then he asked me would I yes to say yes my mountain flower and first I put my arms around him yes and drew him down to me so he could feel my breasts all perfume yes and his heart was going like mad and yes I said yes I will Yes.[74]

❧ Suffering Eros and Textual Incarnation: A Kristevan Reading of Kabbalistic Poetics

ELLIOT R. WOLFSON

WORD / FLESH: METAPHORICAL VEILING AND THE EROS OF EMBODIMENT

I commence with a passage from Julia Kristeva's essay "Stabat Mater" that will serve as the inspiration as we set out on our way:

> FLASH—instant of time or of dream without time; inordinately swollen atoms of a bond, a vision, a shiver, a yet formless, unnamable embryo. Epiphanies. Photos of what is not yet visible and that language necessarily skims over from afar, allusively. Words that are always too distant, too abstract for this underground swarming of seconds, folding in unimaginable spaces. Writing them down is an ordeal of discourse, like love. What is loving, for a woman, the same thing as writing. Laugh. Impossible. Flash on the unnamable, weavings of abstractions to be torn. Let a body venture at last out of its shelter, take a chance with meaning under a veil of words. WORD FLESH. From one to the other, eternally, broken up visions, metaphors of the invisible.[1]

The intertwining of language, eros, being, and time that may be elicited from Kristeva's words complements a cluster of motifs that I recovered in my excavation of the textual landscape of kabbalistic

hermeneutics and poetic imagination.[2] Utilizing a number of philosophical and theoretical perspectives, but most notably Merleau-Ponty's phenomenological ontology, I characterized the erotic play in traditional
kabbalah in incarnational terms that, in a manner surprisingly similar to
Kristeva, revolves about the encircling of flesh and word, the opening
where word is embodied as flesh and flesh embodied as word.[3] The body,
on this score, is configured as textual, the text serving as the link that
loops flesh and word in a bond that nonetheless preserves their difference.[4] For traditional kabbalists this form of semiotic embodiment signifies, more specifically, that the body of the text is inscribed on the text
of the body, which in its most precise sense is constricted to the cir-
cumcised Jewish male,[5] a body that is composed of limbs corresponding
to the twenty-two ciphers of Torah, the Hebrew consonants contained
in the root word, the Tetragram, which may be described as the name of
the nameless, the image of the imageless—a necessary corollary to the
belief in the triune identity of God, Torah, and Israel, widely affirmed by
kabbalists through the generations.[6] From the kabbalistic perspective we
can say as well that language—the ordeal of discourse that is love—
weaves its veil of words, metaphors of the invisible, to reveal the veil of
the veiling.

The metaphoricity of language is captured distinctively in the net of
amorous figures of speech, verbal images that conceal as much as they
reveal in the incandescent shadow of eros, the tension between desire
and denial, binaries that are not resolved in dialectical resolution—the
Hegelian sublation (*Aufheben*)—but which persist in the identity of indifference. The role assigned to metaphor may be better appreciated if we
attend to the philological root *meta-pherein*, "to put one thing in place of
another," "to transport." Thus, as Aristotle long ago noted, the principal
function of metaphor is to transfer meaning from one word to another
(*Poetics* 1457b 9–10), a transference that presupposes a gap that is continuously crossed though never collapsed, an opening that allows disparate
entities to meet without any resolution of their difference. Rendered
metaphorically, then, the metaphor is the bridge that spans the breach
between literal and figurative, the rift between reality and appearance,
the chasm between truth and fiction, the verbal leap that propels one

across the space of an irreducible opposition. As Charles P. Bigger has recently put it, "Metaphors disclose identities over differing ontic realms . . . My use of 'between' . . . signifies the gap [Greek *chaos*] between the margins of supplements beyond the gap between being and becoming within which creatures come to be, a cosmological theme and, phenomenologically, the open or clearing in which they appear. . . . The being and becoming gap and its crossing is the domicile of metaphor. Like *Eros*, also a creature of the between, it is concerned to bring together in a new creation what otherwise might seem estranged. . . . Creative metaphor is a crossing, not a transporting."[7]

Metaphor, on this score, may be thought of as a form of *diastemic discourse*, that is, a mode of language that materializes in the fissure that connects by keeping apart.[8] The understanding of metaphor as the bridging rather than the effacing of difference reflects a distinctively Heideggerian turn beyond the dichotomy that Nietzsche presumed in his understanding of metaphor as dissimulation,[9] a covering of truth by the illusory mask of image.[10] Even more germane to this aspect of kabbalistic hermeneutics is the insight of Derrida that metaphor entails a withdrawal (*re-trait*) of "truth as non-truth," a withdrawal that "is no more proper or literal than figurative," "neither thing, nor being, nor meaning," as it "withdraws itself both from the Being of being as such and from language, without being or being said elsewhere; it *incises* ontological difference itself."[11] What is implied in this *re-trait*, this withdrawal of truth as non-truth? How can we juxtapose truth and non-truth in this manner such that the truth withdrawn as non-truth remains the truth that is withdrawn? For truth to be withdrawn as non-truth it must persist as the truth of non-truth, which can only be as the non-truth of truth, but a truth that is true as non-truth can be neither literally nor figuratively so. Alternatively expressed, it can be literal only as figurative and figurative only as literal, literally figurative, figuratively literal.[12] The metaphor, accordingly, signifies that which is neither being nor without being, the incision of ontological difference, the cut between, writing the supplementary trace, withdrawal of withdrawal.

To elucidate the matter, especially as it relates to the intertwining of the metaphoric and erotic, I invoke the mythical teaching preserved by

Plato in the *Symposium*,[13] attributed to Diotima, the priestess of Manti-neia, though voiced through the persona of Socrates,[14] to depict the "idealized object" of a desexualized "sublime eros," a "transcendental sensuality" or a "sensual metaphysics,"[15] the ideal known in Western culture as "Platonic" love.[16] Eros is cast as the male offspring of the copulation of Poros and Penia, resource and need, rendered more abstractly, as form and matter, the fullness of being and the privation of nonbeing.[17] As the son that issues from the pairing of these opposites, the fate of Eros is "to be always needy . . . barefoot and homeless," discarding whatever he gains, partaking equally of his "mother's poverty" and his "father's resourcefulness . . . at once desirous and full of wisdom . . . neither mortal nor immortal," a lifelong "seeker after truth" positioned "midway between ignorance and wisdom."[18] Through philosophic exegesis of the myth, Plato gave expression to what he considered a basic feature of being human in the world, an ideal embodied in the philosopher, the lover of wisdom: Unlike gods who possess wisdom and hence have no need to desire it (a philosophic truism represented mythopoeically by the fact that Penia had not been invited to the banquet of the gods), humans desire wisdom precisely because they lack it. Yet within this lack is possession, for if there were no lack to possess, there would be no possession of lack, and, consequently, no love of which to speak.[19] Erotic energy, it would seem, issues from the space between satisfaction and want, the space that partakes of both at once, wanting satisfaction in the want of satisfaction, a space we occupy by being uprooted from the space we occupy, a form of possession predicated on possessing naught but the possession of being possessed.[20]

The point was well captured by Luce Irigaray in her exegesis of Diotima's views transmitted by Socrates in the Platonic dialogue:

For, if love possessed all that he desired, he would desire no more. He must lack, therefore, in order to desire still. But, if love had nothing at all to do with beautiful and good things, he could not desire them either. Thus, he is an *intermediary* in a very specific sense. . . . He is neither mortal nor immortal: he is between the one and the other. Which qualifies him as demonic. Love is a *demon*—his function is to transmit to the gods what comes from men and to men what comes from the gods.[21]

Eros, therefore, assumes the veneer of the demonic intermediary, the liaison through which one grasps "the existence or instance of what is held between, what permits the passage between ignorance and knowledge," a passage that has no terminus as it can never attain stasis. "Everything is always in movement, in becoming. . . . Never completed, always evolving."[22]

In slightly different but allied terms, Kristeva offered the following reading of the myth of the begetting of Eros, which she relates, more specifically, to her Heideggerian-inspired characterization of Poros as the "supreme path" that "knows neither device nor mediation":

> Path of want, a want on the way, want blazing a trail for itself. But also a path wanting in devices, a path without essence. Through such an alliance of want and path, could Eros be the place where dialectic takes shape but also opens up to a daimon that overwhelms it? Love as a path that leads nowhere . . . unless it be no immediate sight, scattered totality. We shall thus love what we do not have; the object (of love) is the lacking object.[23]

To suffer eros one must succumb to the restlessness of craving that resists the lure of gratification, to walk the path of want that can want no path if the path it wants wants no path, to love what can be present only in the absence of what is absent in presence.

FLESH / WORD: POETIC INCARNATION AND THE EMBODIMENT OF EROS

It goes without saying that, in my judgment, philosophical assertions of this sort have to be tested and refined by philological investigations apposite to different cultural contexts. In this study, I turn my gaze again on aspects of the erotic imaginary that may be elicited from medieval kabbalistic literature, taking my initial cue, as I often do, from *Sefer ha-Zohar*, the "Book of Splendor,"[24] an anthology of mystical lore that began to assume redactional form in Castile in the late thirteenth and early four-teenth centuries.[25] I shall also cite later sources that make explicit or expand upon themes implicit in passages from the *Zohar*, a strategy of reading indicative of my belief that it is legitimate to speak of a zoharic kabbalah, an edifice of mystical teaching and practice constructed over the course of many centuries by an ever-growing community of readers who study, interpret, and reinscribe the text. Let me note in passing that the current trend to view the *Zohar* as made up of multiple compositional layers and redactional accretions does not preclude the soundness of pos-iting a system of thought unique to this literary entity; on the contrary, as I have argued elsewhere, innovation and repetition are not to be set in diametric opposition. Iteration of structure is what facilitates original-ity and change.[26]

It should be noted that the intricate ideas that may be extracted from the different literary strata of the *Zohar*, and other kabbalistic texts influ-enced thereby, rest heavily on ideas expressed in earlier rabbinic sources. Especially pertinent are ideas about the Song of Songs, the scriptural book that has served more than any other as the textual prism through which images of sacred eros have been projected. Perhaps the most fa-miliar of rabbinic views, and surely the one that was most influential, is that the text should be read as an allegorical depiction of God's (hetero)-erotic relationship to Israel, the stronger partner engendered as male and the weaker as female. In the course of time this way of reading would claim for itself a privileged status as it provided a good rationale to ex-plain the canonical status of the text, though it must be underscored that this is by no means the only perspective attested in rabbinic sources.

In a previous study, I proposed that a feature of rabbinic allegory, which had a significant impact on medieval kabbalists, relates to the as-sumption that the Song is equivalent to Torah in its entirety.[27] I suggested further that this point underlies the oft-cited remark attributed to Aqiva that all of Scripture is holy, but the Song is the holy of holies: Just as the sanctity of the latter outweighs the sanctity of every other place, so the Song is the most hallowed of books, indeed, it embodies the holiness of the canon at large since its metaphorical nature—its literal sense is con-strued as figurative, and the figurative as literal—reveals something basic concerning the very possibility of speaking about divine revelation. It should come as no surprise, therefore, that some rabbis surmised that the initial recitation of the poem occurred at Sinai, precisely at the moment and in the place where the divine glory was manifest—or, in the formulation that I prefer, the glory was incarnate in imaginal form—and the Torah was bequeathed to the people of Israel. The link between narration of the Song and this event intimates that revelation—the be/coming of the word, which is the utterance of the name—is itself erotically charged, the eros of language unveiled in the veil of the language of eros. This can be explained exoterically in terms of the description of the Sinaitic theophany as the conjoining of God and the Jewish nation in holy matrimony, a portrayal quite prevalent in rabbinic literature through the ages,[28] but it also embraces the more esoteric contention that Torah as the divine word displays the parabolic nature of which I spoke above. Within the contours of a religious sensibility that renders the scriptural aniconism in decidedly apophatic terms, how else could one make sense of the notion of God's revelation? The unapparent cannot appear and remain unapparent but through the appearance of its nonappearance; the appearance of its nonappearance, however, necessarily entails the nonappearance of its appearance. Insofar as Scripture is interpreted as the written record of divine speech, it represents the nonrepresentable in verbal icons that showcase what cannot be shown. Theological language exhibits, in Kristeva's locution, the paradox of "metaphorical proliferation," which is "present at the foundations of amorous discourse."[29] The Song embodies this form of discourse in a unique way, the panoply of poetic tropes that disclose truth in the concealment of image through the concealment of truth in the disclosure of image.

From the equation of Torah and the Song we can extrapolate a key assumption that informed the rabbinic conception of the poetic. Just as in the particular case of the Song the contextual meaning is discerned as allegorical, the hermeneutical pattern of Scripture in general is related to the poetic structure of metaphor, the *mashal* in Hebrew, which presumes the dual structure of two layers of signification, the double-sign, outer and inner. Semiotically, it is possible to distinguish these two levels, but semantically they cannot be separated, for the face of the secret (*sod*) is hidden beneath and therefore only accessible through the veil of the literal (*peshaṭ*).[30] In a number of studies, I have discussed this duplicity of secrecy, the convergence of exoteric and esoteric, which yields the inescapable paradox that every revelation is concealment and every concealment revelation,[31] a paradox that renders language in its literalness metaphorical, every saying an unsaying, a saying otherwise.[32]

In this context, I will cite a passage from Abraham Joshua Heschel that complements the hermeneutical standpoint I have assumed in my own thinking.[33] Commenting on the Talmudic dictum that one who is blind in one eye is exempt from the biblically ordained pilgrimage to Jerusalem incumbent on all Israelite males during the three festivals (Exod. 23:17, 34:23) since the fulfillment of the injunction is dependent on the twin possibility of seeing and being seen,[34] Heschel writes:

> Jewish thought is nourished from two sources, and it follows two parallel paths: the path of vision and the path of reason. With respect to those things that are given to objective measurement, reason is primary. With respect to things of the heart, vision is primary. . . . A great principle was enunciated concerning religious faith: "'Observe' and 'Remember' were said in a single utterance."[35] Observe the plain meaning, but remember the esoteric meaning. Just as we are obligated to observe, so are we required to remember. The Torah cannot be fulfilled unless one safeguards the plain meaning of the text and also remembers the revelation at Sinai. Torah can only be acquired in two ways: with reason's lens and the heart's lens. One who is blind in one eye is exempt from the pilgrimage.[36]

In a manner reminiscent of the Hasidic masters to whom he was greatly indebted, Heschel interprets the halakhic ruling as an expression of a hermeneutical truth that was the foundation of the tradition he absorbed, transformed, and transmitted. There are two aspects of Torah, exoteric (*peshaṭ*) and esoteric (*sod*), and both must be affirmed, an idea that is linked exegetically to another rabbinic teaching concerning the simultaneous utterance of the two words associated with the Sabbath command in the Decalogue, *shamor*, "observe" (Exod. 20:7) and *zakhor*, "remember" (Deut. 5:11): The former corresponds to the external and the latter to the internal.[37] What is particularly important about this motif is the implicit kabbalistic interpretation of the rabbinic idea that the two words were uttered in one breath, at one time, something that is not humanly possible. Esoterically rendered, the simultaneous utterance conveys the joining of female and male, shadow and light, the evident and latent layers of meaning.[38] If one sees only with a single eye, one does not possess the bifocal vision that makes it possible to envision the twofold nature of mystery, the seeing of the visibly invisible from and within the invisibly visible, and thus such a person is exempt from making the journey to the Jerusalem Temple. Ever an astute interpreter of kabbalistic and Hasidic teachings, Heschel draws the obvious inference regarding the inseparability of the two levels of meaning; what is hidden can be seen only through the garment, the symbolic through the literal, the invisible through the visible,[39] two hermeneutical propositions connected to the nature of the parable (*mashal*) that many kabbalists in the thirteenth century, and beyond, have appropriated from Maimonides:[40]

> The visionary knows that truth is expressed only in fragments and is revealed only through the lens of metaphors and parables. Is it really possible to see what is concealed without a veil? Or to peek past our bounds without metaphors? What is revealed and what is concealed coexist in admixture, and what is revealed is nothing more than a shroud that the Holy and Blessed One has placed upon that which is concealed.[41]

The Song enunciates this wisdom more than any other biblical book as it is marked by a convergence of the literal and figurative, the iteration of the same that is different in virtue of being the same,[42] and thus it can be branded the paradigm of paradigms, that is, the book that, paradigmatically, demonstrates the paradigmatic nature of paradigm, the duplicity intrinsic to the play of metaphor. If we join the chorus of thinkers who have speculated on the metaphoricity of language as such, then we can speak of the Song as a dialogue that is just as much about language as it is about eros—indeed, the two are indistinguishable inasmuch as the erotic object of the Song is language and the subject of that language is eros. The representation of the Song along these lines is particularly relevant in the realm of theological discourse: To speak of a God that is unspeakable, an apparently endless proposition, is to utilize poetic images, figurative tropes that correlate the ostensibly divergent through the prism of symbolic likeness.[43] The overlapping of *peshaṭ* and *mashal*—surface enfolded in surface, wheel turning within wheel—points to a larger claim regarding the poiesis of Torah, which, in turn, expresses and is expressed by the erotic desire peering through the lattices of the Song.

At this juncture it is prudent to return to the image of the bridge. Common sense dictates that without distance there is no need for a bridge. The bridge, accordingly, brings together what it keeps apart and keeps apart what it brings together. In the semiotic function of comparing things dissimilar, and thereby relating what is not natively related, metaphor is transportive, "a way to reproduce the perpetual connections made within a living and creative reality," a "continuous chain of circles" that "serves to guide the surface of signs toward depth."[44] From the standpoint of what I have termed poetic incarnation, that is, the belief that the body in its most abstract tangibility is the letter,[45] the metaphor is a bridge sited between presence and absence, the interlude where difference is laid bare in the guise of indifference. Eros partakes of the middle ground, presencing absence by way of absencing presence—the former depicted as male and the latter as female[46]—and in this respect it participates in the structural dynamic of metaphoricalness, "the economy that modifies language when subject and object of the utterance act muddle their borders," a process that can be translated psychoanalytically into the "complex process of identification," which involves narcissism and idealization.[47]

The Song, accordingly, may be designated profitably as the *metaphor of metaphors*, the textual embodiment of an embodied textuality, a showing marked by the paradox of the open secret, the concealment disclosed as concealed. Kristeva seems to have an excellent purchase on this dimension of the Song's importance in Judaism and the larger contribution it has made to amorous literature more generally: "It is true that the presence of the loved one is fleeting, it is eventually no more than an expectation. . . . Nevertheless, and through the very flight that is assumed by both protagonists—lovers who do not merge but are in love with the other's absence—no uncertainty affects the *existence* of the one who is loved and loves."[48] In another passage, Kristeva audaciously claims that when compared to erotic literature in the West and in the East the portrayal of love in the Song is distinctive, utterly new.[49] This may be something of an exaggeration, but her observation that this literary exposé of eros is predicated on the pining for (hetero)sexual fulfillment, on the one hand, and the impossibility of its being fully realized, on the other, is unassailable. Her own words are far more eloquent than my paraphrase: "The amorous dialogue is tension and jouissance, repetition and infinity; not as communication but as *incantation*."[50] With remarkably keen insight, Kristeva notes that the allegorical interpretation of the Song promoted by the rabbis only enhanced the tension of love for the other:

> Supreme authority, be it royal or divine, can be loved as flesh while remaining essentially inaccessible; the intensity of love comes precisely from that combination of received jouissance and taboo, from a basic separation that nevertheless unites—that is what love issued from the Bible signifies for us, most particularly in its later form as celebrated in the Song of Songs. Indeed, as soon as the evocation of the amorous experience begins we step into a world of undecidable meaning—the world of *allegories*. . . . The sensitive and the significant, the body and the name, are thus not only placed on the same level but fused in the same logic of undecidable infinitization, semantic polyvalence brewed by the state of love—seat of imagination, source of allegory.[51]

The Song typifies the nature of allegory insofar as the desire of which it speaks separates and unifies—indeed, separates that which it unifies and unifies that which it separates—and it is precisely in this coincidence of opposites that one encounters what Kristeva referred to as the "logic of undecidable infinitization," the "semantic polyvalence" characteristic of the erotic experience of jouissance. Alternatively rendered, the jubilation of eros is equivalent to the semantic process of desemanticization, a curbing of desire in language through the language of desire, an excess of meaning delimited in the "fragmentation of syntax by rhythm."[52] The proximity of Kristeva's thought and insights that may be gleaned from traditional kabbalah is brought into even sharper relief when she expounds the figurative comparison of the Song to a body: "Because of its corporeal and sexual thematics . . . indissolubly linked with the dominant theme of absence, yearning to merge, and idealization of the lovers, sensuality in the Song leads directly to the problematics of incarnation."[53] Given the separation inescapably implied by the topos of erotic flight, it follows that the incarnation of love will be both sensual and ideal—indeed, the more ideal, the more sensual, the more abstract, the more concrete, a state of "pure joy" wherein reality is imagined and the imagined is real, "where life is indistinguishable from an impression of truth."[54] Kristeva draws the obvious inference: "The allegorical rabbinic interpretation that sees God himself in the loved one actually favors the 'incarnational' potentiality of the Song of Songs: how can it indeed be avoided, if I love God, if the loved one is beyond Solomon's body, God himself? As intersection of corporeal passion and idealization, love is indisputably the privileged experience for the blossoming of metaphor (abstract for concrete, concrete for abstract) as well as incarnation (the spirit becoming flesh, the word-flesh)."[55]

It is apposite to cite one more passage from Kristeva that proffers a revision of the Platonic notion of eros,[56] a revision, moreover, that will prove useful in the effort to thematize insights about suffering eros culled from kabbalistic sources:

Metaphoricalness consequently appears to me as the utterance not only of a being as One and acting, but rather, or even on the contrary, as the indication of uncertainty concerning the reference. *Being like* is not only *being* and *nonbeing*, it is also a longing for unbeing in order to assert as only possible "being," not an ontology, that is, something outside of discourse, but the constraint of discourse itself. The "like" of metaphorical conveyance both assumes and upsets that constraint, and to the extent that it probabilizes the identity of signs, it questions the very probability of the reference. Being?—*Unbeing.*[57]

The sensual quality of metaphor and the concomitant metaphorical quality of sensuality are rooted not in an ontology of presence but in what may be called a meontology of absence, the realm of the semiotic, the poetic-maternal linguistic practice that disrupts the hegemonic universality of symbolic-paternal discourse.[58] "Being-like," the watchword of figurative representation, is not reducible to the standard metaphysical binary but it is related to the third term excluded by the principle of the excluded middle, "unbeing," which is neither being nor nonbeing, but the prospect of being that always entails the possibility of nonbeing. This third term, moreover, does not imply, as champions of Neoplatonic apophaticism would have argued, an entity beyond discourse, but rather the inescapable constraint of discourse, the limit of possibility that delimits the impossible, the saying of what cannot be said except in and through the unsaying of what is said.

AS A SEAL UPON THE HEART / EXILE OF DESIRE

I begin the analysis of the kabbalistic material with the following zoharic passage:

> R. Eleazar and R. Abba were held over in a cave in Lod, which they entered on account of the strength of the sun as they were going on the way. R. Abba said: Let this cave be encircled by words of Torah. R. Eleazar began to expound and said: "Let me be as a seal upon your heart, like the seal upon your arm. [For love is as strong as death, passion as mighty as Sheol.] Its darts are darts of fire, a blazing flame" (Song 8:6). We have studied this verse, but one night I was standing before [my] father, and I heard a word from him, that there is no perfection, will, or desire of the Community of Israel for the blessed holy One except through the souls of the righteous, as they arouse the spring of water of the lower beings in relation to the upper beings. In that moment there is the perfection of will and desire in one conjunction to produce offspring. Come and see: After they cleave one to the other, and she receives the will, she says "Let me be as a seal upon your heart." Why "as a seal"? It is the way of the seal that when it cleaves to a place, even after it is removed from there, a trace remains in that place that is not removable, for every trace and every image of it remains there. Thus the Community of Israel said: I have been conjoined to you, and even though I am removed from you and I have gone into exile, "Let me be as a

seal upon your heart," so that my image in its entirety will remain in you like that seal that leaves its whole image in that place to which it was conjoined.[59]

The teaching of R. Simeon ben Yoḥai that is transmitted by R. Eleazar—in several places in zoharic literature these two figures together with R. Abba constitute the three pillars upon which the entire fraternity rests, corresponding to the left, right, and center columns of the sefirotic edifice[60]—is framed as an interpretation of the verse "Let me be as a seal upon your heart" (Song 8:6). In line with a prevailing symbolic explication of the Song adopted by kabbalists beginning in the thirteenth century as a dialogue between the feminine and masculine potencies of the divine,[61] transforming the text thereby into a "nuptial hymn of the Godhead,"[62] the particular verse is applied to *Shekhinah* (designated as *kenesset yisra'el*, the "Community of Israel," one of the rabbinic names for the collectivity of the Jewish people)[63] addressing her male consort *Tif'eret*. R. Simeon's exposition discloses something fundamental about desire as it pertains primarily to the sefirotic realm, but, consistent with kabbalistic doctrine, what is spoken about the divine reflects and is reflected in the sphere of human interaction; the contemporary analytic categories "theosophical" and "psychological"—often utilized by scholars to delineate discrete typological approaches—are two sides of one coin, two ways of viewing the selfsame phenomenon.

The first point that is made in an effort to clarify the nature of desire is that righteous men serve as the conduit between *Tif'eret* and *Shekhinah*, a central idea in zoharic kabbalah that is expressed variously in other passages including the image of the orgasmic fluids, that is, the righteous stimulate the female waters (*mayyin nuqvin*) of *Shekhinah* (occasionally the righteous are even identified as the very stuff that constitutes the substance of the female waters) that ascend and in turn arouse the male waters (*mayyin dukhrin*) to overflow and to produce offspring.[64] But the crucial idea promulgated by this passage is the second point as it relates to the interface of presence and absence at play in the drama of eros. According to the zoharic exegesis, the critical verse from the Song is uttered at the interval/space (temporal and spatial coordinates in the realm of the imaginal are not so easily distinguished) subsequent to the unification of male and female.[65] *Shekhinah* addresses *Tif'eret*, requesting that she should be as a seal upon his heart. Philological attunement is here in order: The verse does not say "Let me be a seal upon your heart" (*simeni ḥotam al libbekha*) but rather "Let me be *as* a seal upon your heart" (*simeni kha-ḥotam al libbekha*)—"as a seal," a turn of phrase that expresses the metaphorical comportment, as it were, the comparison and linking together of entities ostensibly incomparable and disparate. Rather than viewing the qualifying phrase as a caveat that diminishes the force of the symbolic utterance, as Scholem in one place suggested,[66] I would argue that the qualifier enhances the significance of the symbol immeasurably by underscoring that the figure of speech bridges the gap between imaginary and real, and thereby juxtaposes that which is incongruent.

How fitting it seems that to depict the metaphorical nature of eros the biblical author enlists an elocution that denotes the erotic nature of metaphor, to be positioned as a seal upon the heart. But what is the feature of the seal that makes it worthy of this semiotic marking? The answer is given in the zoharic text itself: "It is the way of the seal that when it cleaves to a place, even after it is removed from there, a trace remains in that place that is not removable." The distinctiveness of the seal, therefore, must be thought from the vantage point of the trace it leaves behind, the mark it imprints on the place to which it has been affixed. Hence, the feminine voice implores her male consort to preserve the memory of their conjunction as a seal upon his heart—the seal tattooed on the heart, a sign that signifies the presence of what is absent by demarcating the absence of what is present.[67] Metaphor, analogously, is the mode of language that bespeaks the presence of absence manifestly concealed in the absence of presence.

This commingling, which sheds light on the metaphoric condition, is illumined further by the claim that the verse "Let me be as a seal upon your heart" is uttered by *Shekhinah* in exile,[68] a motif appropriated by kabbalists from rabbinic sources to articulate the ontic state of rupture, the separation of feminine and masculine potencies in the Godhead, respectively the attributes of judgment and mercy, the capacity to receive and the impulse to overflow.[69] Erotically speaking, exile is the intermediate state, the midpoint that makes possible the transmutation of one attribute into the other, the space of desire enrapt by the appetite that arises from and is sustained within the interval (a term that is meant to convey both temporal and spatial meaning along the lines of Bakhtin's chronotope[70]) situated between satisfaction and want. From the kabbalistic standpoint the mending (*tiqqun*) of the blemish (*pegam*) consists of the re/pairing of the heterosexual union that has been torn asunder.[71] For the male to incorporate the female as a seal upon the heart is a crucial metaphorical way of discoursing about this rectification. To plumb these depths, however, we must go deeper into understanding the nature of the seal inscripted on the surface of the heart.

RE/TRACING THE TRACE: DESIRE OF EXILE

The intricate nexus of the erotic and exilic is drawn overtly in the interpretation of Song 8:6 in a passage from *Tiqqunei Zohar*, a later stratum of zoharic literature, presumably composed by an anonymous Spanish kabbalist sometime in the fourteenth century: "It is not written 'Let me be a seal' [*simeni ḥotam*] but 'as a seal' [*kha-ḥotam*]. *Shekhinah* said: Master of the worlds, 'Let me be as a seal,' as that imprint of your seal [*reshimu de-ḥotama dilakh*], for even though the seal remains in your hands, your imprint is in the document, and from that imprint the upper and lower beings tremble."[72] The *ḥotam*, the imprint that is left behind, is compared to an inscription in a document, a figurative turn that highlights the connection of the image of the seal to the gesture of writing. From the juxtaposition we may deduce a larger conceptual point: Writing and erasure are not binary opposites, for what has been written is a remnant of what has been erased and what has been erased a vestige of what has been written. Exile, accordingly, may be depicted as the scripting of the trace, a presence that is absent in the absence of its presence as the absence that is present in the presence of its absence.

The point is made poignantly in the part of the passage that immediately precedes the aforementioned portion:

The "image of man" [*demut adam*] (Ezek. 1:26), surely this refers to *Shekhinah*, which is "his image" [*diyoqneih*], concerning whom it says "behold the likeness of the Lord" [*temunat yhwh yabiṭ*] (Num. 12:8), and it[73] is from the side of the garment [*mi-siṭra di-levusha*]

whereas from the side of the body [*mi-siṭra de-gufa*] it is the unification of the central pillar [*yiḥuda de-ammuda de-emṣa'ita*], which[74] is
the seal from the side of the body [*ḥotama mi-siṭra de-gufa*], and since
he is the seal, *Shekhinah* says to YHWH, which is from within, "Let
me be as a seal on your heart," for even though you departed from
me in exile, your seal will remain with me and it will never depart
from me.[75]

Significantly, the feminine, the visual pole, is cast as the image of the
anthropos, that is, the image through which the invisible is visualized,[76]
and thus it is aligned with the "side of the garment" in contrast to the
masculine, which is aligned with the "side of the body." I have explored
these symbolic complexes at length elsewhere, but what is necessary to
emphasize in this context is that the motif of the garment conveys the
idea that the feminine simultaneously reveals and conceals the male, or
better, the phallic potency within, the seal from the side of the body, the
potency to which is assigned the ineffable name, YHWH, the secret of
the covenant, also identified as the mystical body of Torah. From an
engendered perspective it is worthy to note the somewhat unexpected
shift at the conclusion of the passage: The verse "Let me be as a seal on
your heart" is addressed by *Shekhinah* to the male to indicate that the
breach created by exile, indeed exile is by nature this breach, will not be
absolute since the seal of the male remains imprinted on the female. The
contextual meaning of the text, however, suggests that the request of the
female is to be borne as a seal impressed on the heart of the male and
not to bear the seal of the male impressed on her own body. To lay hold
of the spot where this reversal is itself reversed, so that to speak of the
female desiring to have the seal of the male imprinted on her own heart
is symbolically equivalent to the female desiring to have her seal imprinted on the heart of the male, is to think the metaphoric nature of the
erotic in light of the erotic nature of the metaphoric.

The matter is clarified in the continuation of the homily, where alternative ways of reading the verse are proposed. For our purposes I will
mention only one other interpretation as it provides a way to account
for the aforementioned turnaround. The interpretation I have in mind
purports that the verse is spoken by the soul (*nishmata*) in relation to

its supernal image in the sefirotic pleroma. According to the pneumatic explication, the scriptural petition relates to the dialogue between the soul, the "trace of the seal" (reshimu de-ḥotam) below, and its inscription (gelifu) imprinted above, an idea that is supported by the aggadic theme of the icon (diyoqna) of Jacob engraved upon the throne.[77] The reference to this older motif affords the anonymous kabbalist (and all subsequent readers of his text) an opportunity to embrace the image of the ladder in Jacob's dream-vision, an image that is interpreted (again on the basis of older sources) in a liturgical manner. The casting of the verse from the Song in terms of worship provides the link that connects the theosophic and pneumatic explanations:

> "Let me be as a seal"—this is the Prayer [ṣelota] in which is engraved and inscribed the Life of the Worlds [ḥai almin] in the eighteen blessings of the prayer, and this is the trace of the seal in the text [reshimu de-ḥotama be-fitqa], which is the Torah, the inscription of the letters of the seal [gelifu de-atwwan de-ḥotama], the Righteous, Life of the Worlds [ṣaddiq ḥai almin]. . . . "Let me be as a seal"—this is the soul [nishmata], which is engraved upon the throne. When it is aroused below in prayer, the throne is aroused above.[78]

The two forms of reading are intricately connected, for just as the soul below is a trace of the image that is engraved above, so Shekhinah is a trace of the seal, which is the phallic potency of Yesod, designated by the technical expression "Righteous, Life of the Worlds." Shekhinah is inscripted by the force of Yesod, which consists of the twenty-two letters of the Hebrew alphabet, and she thus assumes the title "prayer" (ṣelota), a clear reference to the amidah, the standing prayer of eighteen benedictions—the Hebrew notation for the number eighteen consists of the letters yod (10) and ḥeit (8), which are the consonants of the word ḥai in the expression ḥai almin. Without engaging all of the details of the zoharic text, we can draw the main point for our purposes: The entreaty to be placed as a seal upon the heart reflects the desire of the feminine to receive the seminal efflux from the divine phallus. To quote from the continuation of the passage from Tiqqunei Zohar:

Another matter: "Let me be as a seal upon your heart." This verse is said with respect to *Shekhinah* who is in exile. It does not say "a seal" [*ḥotam*] but "as a seal" [*kha-ḥotam*], like that seal of the signet [*ḥotam de-gushppanqa*], which is the seal of truth [*ḥotam emet*], and through it [we recite liturgically] "let us be sealed for life" [*ḥotmenu le-ḥayyim*]. And what is that seal in which there is life? This is the Tree of Life whence issue children, livelihood, and sustenance.[79]

The seal corresponds to the Tree of Life, the phallic potency or *Yesod*, which is described as the source whence issue forth children, livelihood, and sustenance, a description based on a Talmudic delineation of the items that are dependent on fortune (*mazzal*) as opposed to merit (*zekhut*).[80] The expression "let us be sealed for life," *ḥotmenu le-ḥayyim*, which is derived from the liturgical formula for the closing service (*ne'ilah*) on Yom Kippur when the fate of each Jew according to rabbinic tradition is thought to be sealed in the book of life, *ḥotmenu be-sefer ha-ḥayyim*,[81] is explained as well in terms of this symbolic association: the Jewish worshiper entreats God to be sealed by the seal of life, which is also the seal of truth.[82] What is crucial for this analysis is the exegetical attribution of the key verse from the Song to *Shekhinah* when she is in exile. In the state of banishment, the female calls out to the male, a yearning for union that is expressed in the wish to be fastened as a seal upon the heart of her lover so that she will not be forgotten even in times of separation. In this craving is the ontic condition that may be rendered poetically as the desire of exile, a desire that arises from the trace left behind, the mark of the seal that is the exile of desire. In another passage from *Tiqqunei Zohar*, the matter is extended to the people of Israel, as their geographical banishment below is a correlate to the separation of *Shekhinah* from *Tif'eret* above:

And the secret of the matter "Each of them had a human face, each of the four had the face of a lion on the right" (Ezek. 1:10), each creature had four faces, and these are the four letters of the holy name, YHWH, which shines within them. The king over all these creatures is the human [*adam*], which is *yw"d h"a wa"w h"a*, for they are numerically equal. The "image of a human" (Ezek 1:5)—this is the holy *Shekhinah*, for she is his image [*diyoqneih*], and she is his seal [*hotam dileih*], and concerning this it says "Let me be as a seal upon your heart." Thus *Shekhinah* said, "Even though you ascend above, your image [*diyoqnakh*] will never be removed from me just like that seal [*hotam*] in the place to which the trace of the master of the seal [*reshimu de-ma'rei hotama*] is conjoined, the image of the seal [*diyoqna de-hotama*], does not depart from it so that it is known through it." Accordingly, *Shekhinah* in exile said, "Let me be as a seal upon your heart. . . ." Israel says, "Master of the world, even though I am in exile far from you, 'Let me be as a seal upon your heart,' your image [*diyoqnakh*], which is your seal [*hotam dilakh*], which is your *Shekhinah*, should not depart from us. On account of this you will remember us in exile, and the seal [*hotama*] of the holy One, blessed be he, is surely the *Shekhinah*."[83]

The critical verse "Let me be as a seal upon your heart," according to the zoharic reading, is uttered by both *Shekhinah* and the Jewish people, a doubling that is to be expected as in the symbolic world of medieval kabbalistic theosophy *Shekhinah* is the divine attribute that corresponds to the community of Israel, and hence what applies to the one applies to the other. Notwithstanding the ontological reciprocity, there is an interesting shift in gender valence connected to the images of the trace and the seal as they apply to each of these referents.

Shekhinah is identified as the figure of the human assumed by the four creatures who bore the throne. Following a careful rendering of the scriptural account of Ezekiel's chariot vision, the anonymous author of the passage from *Tiqqunei Zohar* presumes that each of the four creatures had four faces, but that the composite form of each was that of a human. The point is supported by the numerological equivalence of the word *adam* and the four letters of the Tetragrammaton written out in full as *yw"d h"a wa"w h"a*, that is, both expressions have the sum of forty-five. Read kabbalistically, the human figure is identified as *Shekhinah*, the last of the *sefirot*, which is the anthropomorphic image through and by which the supernal aspect of the divine is revealed. This is the intent of her identification as the image (*diyoqan*) and/or seal (*hotam*) of the male potency. Based on these symbolic identifications the scriptural entreaty ascribed to *Shekhinah*, "Let me be as a seal upon you heart," is interpreted as the request of the female to bear the imprint of the male in the time they are separated just as the seal leaves an impression on the material surface to which it has been affixed after it has been removed. In the exact language of the text: *Shekhinah* says to the male potency of which she is the image/seal, "Even though you ascend above, your image will never be removed from me." Given the prevailing assumptions about heterosexual behavior in the time that this stratum of zoharic literature was composed, this interpretation makes sense empirically, but it is not justified textually as it is the female who says to the male "Let me be as a seal upon your heart." The inversion, however, betokens the gender transformation that can be explained by the fact that the imprinting of the masculine seal on the female is on a par with the feminine image being imprinted as a seal on the heart of the male. Alternatively expressed, as the form of the seal's imprint—the "trace of the seal" (*reshimu de-ḥotama*)[84]—takes shape on the material surface, there is a reversal of image such that right and left, inside and outside, are transposed.[85] The change of position is made clear in the exegetical application of the verse to Israel, that is, the collectivity of Jews, who are symbolically feminized, address the masculine attribute of God in emulation of *Shekhinah*, but in their case the wish to be secured as a seal upon the heart is interpreted as their appeal for the divine presence to accompany them in exile, a kabbalistic reworking of an interpretation attested in other medieval commentators on this verse.[86]

The gender implications of this image are rendered even more complex when we take into account on the basis of numerous passages from *Tiqqunei Zohar* as well as other kabbalistic sources that the word *ḥotam* is a symbolic circumlocution for the phallus or the attribute in the divine that is imaged in phallic terms. To cite one illustration of this symbolic association:

> "Let me be as a seal" (Song 8:6), this is the sign of the covenant of circumcision . . . for it is the mark of the holy name [*reshimu di-shema qaddisha*], in the manner [of the verse] 'Who among us can go up to the heavens' [*mi ya'aleh lanu ha-shamaimah*] (Deut 30:12), the first letters spell *milah* and the final letters *yhwh*.[87] He who guards this mark [*reshimu*] it is as if he guards the holy name, and he who

lies with respect to this mark it is as if he lies with respect to the holy name. . . . The letters of [the word] *mezuzot* are verily *zaz mawet*, and thus concerning the one who protects the covenant of circumcision, which is his seal [*hotama dileih*], death is removed from him [*zaz mawet minneih*] . . . and the one who lies with respect to the covenant of circumcision lies with respect to the seal of the king [*hotama de-malka*], which is inscribed with Shaddai on the outside and YHWH on the inside.[88]

With this understanding of the notion of the seal we can revisit the zoharic delineation of exile in the image of the remnant left behind by the imprint of the signet of truth. Just as the trace is marked by the confluence of presence and absence—the presence of what is absent is discerned in and through the absence of what is present—so exile is demarcated by the erotic longing of the female for the male and reciprocally of the male for the female, a longing that issues from the commingling of want and provision, a commingling in the middle ground where being and nonbeing persevere in the (in)difference of their (non)identity.

The intent of the above citation from *Tiqqunei Zohar* is rendered more transparent in the following remark of the sixteenth-century kabbalist, Moses Cordovero:

Yesod is called the "unblemished ox" [*shor tam*] and with regard to his name *Malkhut* is called "unblemished [*tam*].[89] Indeed, [the word] "unblemished" [*tam*] alludes to their supernal existence . . . and when she is united with *Tif'eret* above, then her existence is named with regard to him in the secret of "Let me be as a seal," and he is called *emet* on account of her name, and since he is like a seal that inverts the reality that remains in it [the letters *mem* and *tau* from the word *emet*] are inverted to *tam* [which is made up of *tau* and *mem*] in the secret of the permutation and the sealing.[90]

It goes without saying that the implications of the zoharic exegesis of Song 8:6 are drawn explicitly by many other kabbalists. In deference to space, however, I will limit myself to one passage from Ḥayyim Vital in which he expounds the notion of the trace (*reshimu*) in terms of the mytho-theosophic speculation that evolved from the teachings of Isaac Luria. To date, most scholars have turned their attention to this notion as it relates to the residue that remains after the primordial withdrawal (ṣimṣum) of the light of Ein Sof to create a space (ḥalal) within itself devoid of itself, a paradox that is explained according to the more exoteric explanation as a clearing of space so that there may be the emanation of being other than the Infinite, or according to the more esoteric explanation as the beginnings of the process of catharsis of the unbalanced forces of judgment from the divine economy.[91] By contrast, I am focusing on another aspect related to the trace, one that contributes more specifically to our thinking of the dynamic between eros and metaphor, though, to be sure, the different issues are textually and conceptually interrelated. Given the importance of this passage as an articulation of the nexus of the trace, eros and exile, I shall cite an extensive portion of the text:

> Now we must explain the matter of this impression [inyan ha-reshimu ha-zeh] that withdraws at night, and through it we will explicate as well the verse "Let me be as a seal upon your heart," which is explained in Sefer ha-Zohar and in the Tiqqunim in relation to the arm phylacteries.[92] Know that there is a distinction between Ze'eir Anpin and Nuqba, for the trace of Ze'eir Anpin withdraws and ascends to the top of his head, but the trace of the consciousness [reshimu de-moḥin] of Nuqba stays within Ze'eir Anpin, verily within his chest wherein the heart of Ze'eir Anpin is found, and from there the illumination goes out to Nuqba. . . . It follows according to this that Nuqba does not dissipate as much as he does, and this is the matter of the verse "Let me be as a seal etc." This is the language of the request of the female in relation to him that he should set her as a seal, that is, the consciousness [moḥin] that enters into the head of Ze'eir Anpin is the essential consciousness [moḥin iqqariyyim] for the aspects of consciousness itself enter into him. . . . But consciousness of the head of Nuqba is called the seal [ḥotam] alone, for they are only the illumination of the seal that is affixed in her from the consciousness of the head of Ze'eir Anpin, which is the essential consciousness, as was mentioned. It is known that in the day there is

drawing near [qeruv] of Ze'eir Anpin and his Nuqba, for they have the aspect of consciousness within them. But during the night when the consciousness entirely disappears, and even the trace disappears, then is the time of separation [perud] of Ze'eir Anpin from his Nuqba, for the aspect that bound them was the [states of] consciousness that came forth from and were bestowed by him upon her, and now with their disappearance there is separation between them. And then she asks him "Let me be as a seal etc.," that is, "even though now your illumination is removed from me . . . act in such a way that you place this seal and my trace on your heart, and it will remain there in the place of the chest . . . and they will not disappear entirely to the place whence they came forth as is the case with your [states of] consciousness that disappeared entirely. By contrast, they remain on your heart, as was mentioned, and the reason for this is on account of the abundance of love [rov ha-ahavah] that I have for you, and this is [the import of] what is written 'love is as strong as death' (Song 8:6). I cannot be separated from you entirely and hence by my trace remaining on your heart the illumination can proceed to me from there, which could not transpire if it disappeared further above.[93]

Beneath the layers of the intricate Lurianic symbolism expounded in the above passage one can discern continuity with the zoharic teaching regarding the gender dynamic that is linked to the notion of the trace or, in its scriptural idiom, the seal upon the heart. I will limit my comments to two points most salient to the theme of this essay. The first thing to note is that, according to Vital's exposition, Song 8:6 is addressed by Nuqba to Ze'eir Anpin, technical terms that denote the last two of the five configurations (parṣufim) within the Godhead, the other three consisting of Arikh Anpin, Abba, and Imma. It is beyond the scope of this essay to enter into a lengthy discussion of the notion of the parṣufim in Lurianic kabbalah, which are based on the Idrot sections of zoharic literature and especially the Idra Zuṭa.[94] Suffice it here to say that the five configurations correspond to five of the ten emanations, which encompass the entire sefirotic edifice: Arikh Anpin corresponds to Keter, Abba to Ḥokhmah, Imma to Binah, Ze'eir Anpin to Tif'eret, and Nuqba di-Ze'eir to Malkhut. For our

purposes what is most important to note is that *Nuqba* and *Ze'eir* person-
ify respectively the daughter and son, which complement *Imma* and *Abba*,
the mother and father.

The second point worthy of note is that Vital makes explicit an underlying assumption that has informed the kabbalistic conception of eros
from its inception: The erotic is commensurate with the noetic.[95] Hence,
consciousness, which is designated by the technical term *mohin*,[96] is portrayed as the medium that draws together *Nuqba* and *Ze'eir*. More specifically, in the day, when consciousness is in them, they are contiguous,
but in the night, when there is no consciousness, they are separated. It is
thus in the nocturnal state, which is emblematic of exile, that the feminine says to the masculine "Let me be as a seal upon your heart," an
utterance that is reflective of the desire to have her trace imprinted on
the chest of the male whence she receives the efflux of consciousness.
The twofold bind attested in the verse—the female desiring to be incorporated in the male so that the male may be incorporated in the female—is indicative of the gender metamorphosis that characterizes both
the metaphoric conception of eros and the erotic conception of metaphor
that may be elicited from kabbalistic sources. The bent circularity is embodied, as it were, in the words "Let me be *as* a seal upon your heart,"
the verse that dissembles the dissemblance and thereby displays the inexorable fold of metaphoric gesticulation, to couple the incomparable in
the bond of comparability. To be enfolded within that fold is to suffer
the eros of textual incarnation, the concomitant desire to inscript and to
be inscripted, indeed to inscript by being inscripted, to be, in the language
of the thirteenth-century Spanish kabbalist Isaac Ibn Sahula in his commentary on the critical verse from the Song, "the seal that is sealed
within the seal" (*hotam be-tokh hotam hatumah*).[97] The mystery of the dual
sealing is imparted as well in the supplication that is assigned in one
zoharic passage to the female persona of the people of Israel addressing
the male deity, "Let it be [your] will that our icon be engraved on your
heart just as your icon is engraved on our hearts."[98] The eros of metaphor ensues from the metaphor of eros occasioned by the bearing of this
double seal.

❧ Afterword: A Theology of Eros, After Transfiguring Passion

CATHERINE KELLER

So many loves. A time of depletion after excess. Afterward—is it the lull of exhaustion or satisfaction, disappointment or fulfillment, detumescence or engorgement? Or some uneasy incompletion? The seduction has been attempted, we may be falling in love or out, getting up or going down, ascending, descending or just turning, oh, God. An afterword comes too late, or too soon; the double entendres are dissipating, the flesh has confessed, the closet is open, the book is closing, and still we may not have figured it out. "It" almost came, is still to come, may have come and gone already. And we, too empty or too full—we still reach "toward." A theology of eros.

Eros in theology may signify the lure of the not-yet. But as this volume demonstrates, there is nothing new about theological realizations of eros. "Theology" and "eros" are more or less co-originate Platonic notions. Yet theology as a work of Jewish and Christian hermeneutics arises from another matrix of love: *agape*, not *eros*, translated the Hebrew *ahabah*, inclusive of human and divine loves, transcendent and carnal, for the New Testament. In other words, the history and future of theology circulate among a multiplicity of loves, a tensive field of mutually contesting, translating loves, competing as much as they cooperate—love of friend and of foe, of neighbor and of stranger, sexual and spiritual, human and divine, intimate and political, self-sacrificial, self-transforming or selfish, passionate and dispassionate, celibate, marital and extra-, mystical and mundane, hetero-, homo-, hetairic, or queer. *Ahabah, eros, philia, agape, caritas, cupiditas.* Carnality and the incarnation—the various theologies of love do not readily love each other, we must admit, even when they lie together. Here Jean-Luc Nancy utters a bit of gospel for postmodernity: "To think love would thus demand a boundless generosity toward all these possibilities, and it is this generosity that would command reticence: the generosity not to choose between loves, not to privilege, not to hierarchize, not to exclude. . . ."[1]

Perhaps then, if love can be practiced in relation to the multiplying loves, if we can love the many loves, if we can indeed rehearse a thinking love, an ethico-intellectual love, the afterword of our symposium takes place not in depletion but in Nancy's imperative reticence. The reticence, like Keats's "negative capability," would leave open the uncertainty within which the erotic risk, the agapic gift, or the *ahabah*-justice become possible. Would this tensive openness not emulate a divine reserve, an apophatic power of attraction? Perhaps even the divine seduction with which Virginia Burrus initiated this volume?

The plurality of loves has not resolved into a tidily Western dyad of Greek and Hebrew traditions, mediated and sublated by a victorious Christian theology. Yet the discourse of Christian theology does live from the interpretation of biblical metaphor in terms of Hellenized *theoria*. How well it honors or even recognizes the eros driving both its philosophy and its scripture is another question. The theological heritage endlessly reevaluates, reviles, or recycles its various Platonic loves—and this volume is no exception. It is no coincidence that its chapters could organize themselves as though around the two magnetic poles represented by the *Symposium* and the *Song of Songs*.

If in this tradition and in this volume we have enjoyed (not without pain) a multiple, ambiguous evaluation of the decorporealizing Platonic eros itself, we have with some consistency attempted to redeem corporeal sex, the sexed bodies and the sexes of bodies, indeed the scents, colors, temperatures, fluids, and fields of bodies. Whether we are saving that sexual flesh *from* or *through* the return to Diotima; whether we consider the Platonic effect from the disciplinary vantage point of theology proper or through the willful transdisciplinarities of our symposium, we do on the whole reinscribe a certain classical gesture: the transformation of the human through a discipline of love, indeed a love that was from its genesis implicated in divinity. Whether or not these love-bodies are *having* sex, and whichever sex they are *being*, their eros marks them as creatures of a good creation, citizens of an unrealized justice, and subjects of a theology to come. But then we have already crossed over to Israel.

Not much later than Plato, the barbarian poetry of the Song was composed, more earthen, sensuous, and conjugal in its intoxication. Its *ahabah* can readily be translated as "eros." Yet the specific form of love that gathered force in the New Testament as an intensification of the Levitico-Deuteronomic teachings of the love of God, neighbor, and stranger had another resonance altogether. Its particular *ahabah* could not have been translated as "eros": The mischievous love god belongs to another mood. So it is perhaps not so surprising that early Christian absorptions of Platonism had recourse to the exegesis of the Song, that piece of erotic scripture odd for the Bible if also alien to Platonism. It became the primary site for an allegorical mysticism of love. In its exegesis the mandated love for God becomes coterminous with the heavenly eros of Plato, and thus with an upwardly mobile desire for God. This syncretistic eros would have as little to do with the Song's highly sexual context as with a merely charitable *imitatio* of the downward-flowing love of God for the creation. Already with Gregory of Nyssa, the infinity of the love object was refracted in the infinity of the love itself: as the infinity of the God who is love, and as the infinite desire of the finite creature for its infinite source. And as Burrus suggested "tentatively" (we begin and end in bold reticence), "If 'God is eros,' as Pseudo-Dionysius (following Plotinus) insists in his erotic transposition of 1 John 4:8 and 4:16, then perhaps eros is God."

And yet how often in the intervening centuries of Judaism and Christianity has the theologoumenon of *God as Eros* been named, the eros that is the *divine desire* for the creation, for the creature? A desire that would not be merely and primly for the sake of the other, but in some no less and no more imaginable sense, also for God's sake. The Christian Father's passionate love of the Son, and by implication the rest of us, found rich symbolization. But the metaphor of divine Eros, as the very God of monotheism rather than a cute iconic residue of polytheism, remained until the twentieth century virtually unspeakable in theology. For the metaphysics cut in the opposite direction: Whether eros signifies too much sex or too little, mere lack seeking fullness or an interplay of want and plenitude, it could not stand for the (differently classicized) God of closed perfection, the *actus purus* incapable of reception, of feeling, and so of change. The Aristotelinized deity could not by definition desire; desire had come to signify lack—and isn't "He" already perfect and self-sufficient? Eros could never encode the dispassionate father, unmoved mover, whose love, as Anselm clarified it, only *appears* to us to be compassionate: "Thou art compassionate in terms of our experience, and not compassionate in terms of thy being."[2] For compassion is a compounded *passion*—a state of being moved, receptive, responsive—inimical with pure act. The God of ontotheology can only "love" us in the sense of "doing what is good for us" for our sake, and never also for God's own.

Anders Nygren would harden this understanding of the New Testament agape as love only for the good of the other, self-sacrificing love, a passion without passion. He did not need to oppose any idea of *God* as eros—this possibility was not in play. Even such an adventurous theologian as Paul Tillich, contesting Nygren, affirmed only the human, not the divine eros. Nygren's polemic directed itself against the human eros, not in its "vulgar" sexuality, but in its always already sublimated Platonic forms: that is, in its delusion that it could attain to God through striving. It is the mystical passion within Christian history that he sought to purge from theology, destroying the delusion that our eros could in any sense pass over or up into agape. In his retro-reformation zeal, he did not notice how it is also pagan philosophy that has already pre-constructed his orthodox presumption of a purely active, and thus unilaterally giving, divine love.

Despite what we call the Passion, the semantic force field of classical theology—in which one form of Platonism beat out the others—could not stretch to encompass the notion of a passionate God. For such a God might *be* the very desire driving the wild, self-organizing, fathomless excess we decorously call cosmos: a God who is "the Eros of the Universe." Or so Alfred North Whitehead, the mathematician turned cosmological pluralist, named it in the 1920s, rereading Plato, Christianity, physics and biology with his own transdisciplinary passion. His Eros urges us at any moment to materialize "a new fact which is the Appearance woven out of the old and the new—a compound of reception and anticipation, which in turn passes into the future."[3] He would mobilize the figure of the "divine Eros" as an alternative to "the divine Dictator," the God of doctrinal omnipotence and imperial politics. "When the Western world accepted Christianity, Caesar conquered."[4] Whitehead's eros embodied not the fiat of force but a power of persuasion akin to rhetoric, with a cosmic appetite for novelty, for complexity, for connection. If the way of eros takes us anew into a space of reticence, in Whitehead's case forged in the teeth of the quantum uncertainty, it simultaneously inspires one of the most radical redistributions of subjects and objects accomplished in twentieth century thought.

Process theology is the strongest effect of this philosophical relationalism. Whitehead's postmodern relevance may itself be undergoing a revival through the discovery of Deleuze, whose concepts of multiplicity, event, fold, and line of flight bear the marks of his own discreet Whiteheadianism. And it is expressly the cosmic unfolding of Whitehead's divine Eros that the normally theophobic Deleuze registers in the prehensive speeds of the "chaosmos."[5] If Deleuze and Guattari have influenced much current exploration of the sexual, the perverse, the queer, and the sadomasochistic, it is by their opening of the body into intensities and interactions belying a hierarchical arrangements of objects or organs into transcendent subjects.[6] Rarely until recently has the relation of this opening to the cosmological (or chaosmological) theism of Whitehead been noted, however.

Let me suggest that the *cosmos* of *eros* matters—if the materiality of eros actually matters to theory. "Bodies that matter"—when they are human, at least—find themselves enmeshed in the irreducible compound of inhuman and cultural materializations. Our necessarily endless attempts to displace the naturalized cultures and the cultured natures of the body can paradoxically capture it in a sophisticated autism of disembodiment. In this way poststructuralism and classical theism are differently tempted to let the Word transcend the flesh and its world, the "flesh of the world" (Merleau-Ponty). For this reason, the emergent conversation of poststructuralism and process thought may prove helpful to the ecological work of incarnation.

Process theology, with its own early notion of the postmodern as radical critique of modern certainties (dualisms, monisms, mechanisms and hierarchies, theism or atheism), translated the Whiteheadian hint of the eros of the universe into a systematic Christian theology. For John Cobb the divine eros is "the lure to enjoyment" (even in this restrained Methodist form, a seminary-shocker within the sacrificial economies of the conventionally agapic).[7] All actual occasions participate, precisely as actualizations—different degrees of incarnation—in this God, arrayed as the palette of possibilities. But differently than the Deleuzian process of infinite speeds, nomadism, and mobility, process theology privileges the constitutive relatedness of process. It would be the emergence of every actuality as an event of interrelation that would provide the evanescent satisfactions of eros, in its lure toward ever more intensity of compound connection. This God desires—not only for our sake but also for God's sake—ever richer forms of materialization, and is at one and the same time relating to each creature and experiencing it as a particle in the universe. Charles Hartshorne described that universe as "the body of God."

Related to this tradition there has emanated a richly woman-inflected body of texts. For example, Sallie McFague developed into a full ecotheology the model of the universe as the body of God, metonymous with her figure of God as lover. Rita Nakashima Brock's "christology of erotic power" draws on Whiteheadian thinkers such as Loomer, Meland, and Wieman to move beyond the apathetic God to eros as "the energy of incarnate love."[8] Beverly Harrison, who always worked closely with the models of theological relationalism for her social ethics, recently reflected on how easily much feminist theology, specifically that influenced by Whitehead, was missed or misperceived as mere modernism; yet it is, she avows, "if properly understood, a postmodern style of metaphysics."[9]

In the interest of this minor archeology of the twentieth-century theology of eros, let me mention those early sources of feminist eros in its spiritual vocation that have nothing to do with theology proper, with Whitehead, or perhaps even with Plato. Preeminent is Audre Lorde's essay "Uses of the Erotic," which understands eros as an intensity that "flows through and colors my life with a kind of energy that heightens and sensitizes and strengthens all my experience." Lorde makes the political potentiality of this joy-rooted energy explicit: "Recognizing the power of the erotic within our lives can give us the energy to pursue genuine change within our world, rather than merely settling for a shift of characters in the same weary drama."[10] Or consider Susan Griffin's *Pornography and Silence*—a compelling attempt to distinguish eros from the pornographic subjugation of the tender mortal flesh, which is a mirror inversion of the Christian denigrations of the flesh.[11] More recent feminist and queer rereadings of Christian asceticism might have put another spin on her critique. However, current (feminist) attempts to avoid feminist puritanisms would do well to recapture her key point: Eros, allied to Psyche, poses a salutary threat to the substantial, self-immortalizing ego. "The psyche is simply world. And if I let myself love, let myself touch, enter my own pleasure and longing, enter the body of another, the darkness, let the dark parts of my body speak, tongue into mouth, in the body's language, as I enter, a part of me I believed was real begins to die, I descend into matter, I know I am at the heart of myself, I cry out in ecstasy. For in love, we surrender our uniqueness and become world."[12] A process-brushed cosmology might reply: Yes, eros takes me into the heart of matter where I become world, there where the world itself is becoming, where the event "passes into its future." But it is in my singularity that I become world. My difference is the self-differentiation of world. And the Eros calls it forth.

Of course this feminist Eros desires a world whose beauty is steeped in justice. Yet the metaphor in Whiteheadian form favors the aesthetic and embeds *ethos* in *cosmos*. Otherwise, perhaps, ethics becomes cloyingly anthropocentric, abstracting justice from its planetary flesh and obligation. Ethics dries out without eros: Lorde's point, wrapped in a wider ecology. As our Introduction suggests, the tension of ethics and eros cannot be escaped—least of all by thinkers who seek justice in the realm of sex. For eros severed from ethics will stimulate the ravishing violations that belong to a social structure of dominance and submission, which will strangle eros itself. Yet an anti-erotic ethos ironically yields the same result: an incapacity to distinguish sexual justice from sexual repression that can shut down the very energies of social transformation. Along these lines, Herbert Marcuse—another twentieth-century prophet of eros, hardly a theologian, but articulating faith of another sort—analyzed the dilemma in Freud, for whom civilization is necessarily built of repressive sublimation. Repression will finally undermine the eros that drives culture itself, that is, the aesthetic impulse. The Freudian prognosis for our discontents was therefore pessimistic: A libidinal entropy would gradually wear down human creativity. Returning with and against Freud to Diotima, Marcuse argued for the possibility of a "non-repressive culture" akin to Schiller's "aesthetic state." A social order in which beauty is cultivated without slaves or scapegoats—hopelessly utopian, or the substance of hope?—would entail "the transformation of sexuality into Eros." In the meantime, Marcuse notes, "the insights contained in the metaphysical notion of Eros were driven underground. They survived, in eschatological distortion, in many heretic movements, in the hedonistic philosophy. Their history has still to be written—as has the history of the transformation of Eros in Agape."[13] Startlingly, he recruits the Christian gospel's unsublimated Agape—as originally identical with Eros—for his hope.

Eros without agape is little more than a greedy grasp; agape without eros issues straightaway in moralism. Both outcomes merge, as we see currently in the wedding of predatory transnational corporate power with that of a theocratically inclined state. If I read the shared tendency of this volume rightly, we are indeed still hoping for a transformation of sexuality into the larger eros; we are soliciting eros as the attractive force, indeed the productive power, of a social cosmos—or chaosmos—that will seek justice without systemic repression, enjoyment without systemic robbery. While avoiding Marcuse's collapse of eros into agape, or vice versa, theology may help to heal the schism between these two loves.

The dualism may better be healed by transmuting it into a figure of *amatory oscillation*. Eros irreducibly encodes desire for something more, for an other in excess of the self. Agape just as stubbornly signifies the gift of that excess. Eros may drive either greed or invitation; agape may express either domination or welcome. If, however, they oscillate as complementary flows or gestures of love, the desire grows in generosity, even as the gift becomes ever more inviting. This oscillation would also, in the process of figuration, obtain of God, itself a dipolar dynamic of primordial lure—an eros, and an eschatological reception emerging at every moment as the "consequent nature of God." That consequent relation suggests the way in which divinity itself is affected, vulnerable, receptive. Quite the contrary of the standard notion of agape as dispassionate, unilateral act, here the gift takes place only in its reception.

We could imagine a theology like this, in miniature, as a wave or spiral of relation: The lure, the prevenient eros, invites—and something comes to be, a subject, human or nonhuman. Then whatever becomes is taken agapically into the becoming divinity, which, like and unlike everything else, emerges within the fluid matrix, that *tehom* or "aquatecture" of relations. And the relation of the human oscillation to the divine analogue would comprise, then, a chaosmic chiasmus. Its double helix or crossover may appear as cruel as crucifixion when passion splits from compassion. In its moments of grace, it moves as rhythmically as dance, evanescent and yet "strong as death."

But all of this theology is excess, an overflow from the essays. Theology also can turn greedy, seeking to possess what it multiplies. So even theologians must accept agape in the midst of our eros—which might mean forgiveness for our projections and displacements, our new binaries arising in the deconstruction of old ones, new con/fusions generated even in love of multiplicity. "The thinking of love should learn to yield to this abandon: to receive the prodigality, the collisions, and the contradictions of love, without submitting them to an order that they essentially deny."[14] The ancient transdisciplinarity of theology has always risked too much, not too little, love. Perhaps the thinking of love, *ahabah*, might yet teach the friends of theology to embrace a revolting multiplicity of passions. Where eros enters into positive feedback with its full amatory spectrum, even Christian love may break through its sentimental rigidities. Agape turns elemental, like the rain and the sun.[15]

NOTES

INTRODUCTION: THEOLOGY AND EROS AFTER NYGREN | VIRGINIA BURRUS

1. Anders Nygren, *Agape and Eros*, trans. Philip S. Watson (Philadelphia: Westminster Press, 1953), 31.
2. Ibid., 52.
3. Ibid., 125–27.
4. Ibid., 49–50.
5. Ibid., 243.

WHAT DO WE TALK ABOUT WHEN WE TALK ABOUT PLATONIC LOVE? | DANIEL BOYARIN

This essay is dedicated to Carlin Barton.

1. Anders Nygren, *Agape and Eros*, trans. Philip S. Watson (New York: Harper & Row, 1969), 303.
2. This point is not uncontroversial; some would read "Platonic love" as a summation of all of the discourses on love in the *Symposium*, while others (notably Mark Jordan, in this volume) take the final speech of Alcibiades as more transformative and decisive than I would.
3. Nygren, *Agape and Eros*, 51.
4. Throughout much of the history of Western (English and German) writing about Greek love, it was understood implicitly and explicitly that no sex was involved. Kenneth Dover eloquently makes this point on the very first page of his book. One of the scholars whom he cites goes so far as to refer to "homosexuality" as a Dorian perversion adopted only by a tiny minority in Athens. K. J. Dover, *Greek Homosexuality*, rev. ed. (Cambridge, Mass.: Harvard University Press, 1989), vii.

5. Michel Foucault, *The Use of Pleasure*, vol. 2 of *The History of Sexuality*, trans. Robert Hurley, rpt., 1984 (New York: Random House, Vintage, 1986), 245.

6. Dover, *Greek Homosexuality*, 163.

7. Peter Brown, *The Body and Society: Men, Women, and Sexual Renunciation in Early Christianity* (New York: Columbia University Press, 1988), 9.

8. See also Gregory Vlastos, "The Individual as Object of Love in Plato," in *Platonic Studies* (Princeton, N.J.: Princeton University Press, 1981), 39–40, whose view of the matter is very like Foucault's.

9. Virginia Burrus, *The Sex Lives of Saints: An Erotics of Ancient Hagiography* (Philadelphia: University of Pennsylvania Press, 2003).

10. I am not, however, ascribing to Christianity some kind of contamination from Hellenism, as, e.g., in Nygren, *Agape and Eros*, 228–29 (for Catholicism). Still less am I trying covertly to argue for a Judaism uncontaminated by Platonism, as perhaps I once did. For some preliminary revision of the claims I made in *Carnal Israel: Reading Sex in Talmudic Culture* (Berkeley and Los Angeles: University of California Press, 1993), see my "Why is Rabbi Yoḥanan a Woman? or, a Queer Marriage Gone Bad: 'Platonic Love' in the Talmud," in *Authorizing Marriage? Canon, Tradition, and Critique in the Blessing of Same-Sex Unions*, ed. Mark Jordan (Princeton, N.J.: Princeton University Press, 2005).

11. After doing so much work in the 1980s to disrupt this hyphenated term, I find myself coming back to it as a convenient moniker for the cultural complex formed by what might be called Jewish Hellenisms, including the various Judaisms of the first centuries B.C. and A.C., rabbinic Judaism and late ancient Christianity. See Daniel Boyarin, *Border Lines: The Partition of Judaeo-Christianity* (Philadelphia: University of Pennsylvania Press, 2004)

12. David M. Halperin, "Why Is Diotima a Woman?" in *One Hundred Years of Homosexuality and Other Essays on Greek Love* (New York: Routledge, 1990), 124.

13. For a discussion of Aspasia's probable status as *pallakē*, or concubine, see Madeleine Mary Henry, *Prisoner of History: Aspasia of Miletus and Her Biographical Tradition* (New York: Oxford University Press, 1995), 14–15. While surely not a fully honorable wife, a concubine like Aspasia was much more legitimate than a courtesan. Henry suggests that the reason that Pericles didn't marry her was owing to her status as *metic*.

14. Halperin, "Why Is Diotima a Woman?" 124. Cf. Martha Nussbaum's version of Halperin's point: "Here, then, Socrates too takes a mistress: a priestess instead of a courtesan, a woman who prefers the intercourse of the pure

mind to the pleasures of the body, who honors (or is honored by) the divine rather than the merely human." Martha Nussbaum, *The Fragility of Goodness: Luck and Ethics in Greek Tragedy and Philosophy* (Cambridge: Cambridge University Press, 1986), 177. While still representing Aspasia as *hetaira*, Nussbaum does hint at the point that I would make: Diotima is the woman—philosopher—who "prefers the intercourse of the pure mind." From Diotima to Hypatia is not, I think, such an enormous epistemic leap. And let us not forget the strong ancient traditions that there were (a few) women in the Academy; Konrad Gaiser, *Philodems Academica: Die Berichte über Platon und die Alte Akademie in zwei herkulanensischen Papyri* [Stuttgart-Bad Canstatt: Frommann-Holzboog, 1988], 154, cited in Pierre Hadot, *What Is Ancient Philosophy?* (Cambridge, Mass.: Harvard University Press, 2002), 61. Diogenes Laertius reports two women among the members of the Academy in Plato's time; see John M. Dillon, *The Heirs of Plato: A Study of the Old Academy, 347–274 B.C.* (Oxford: Oxford University Press, 2003), 13.

15. Halperin, "Why Is Diotima a Woman?" 129.

16. I hasten to make clear that by writing "counterpolitical" I am not indicating that Platonic love escapes the political but that it claims and aspires to do so.

17. My colleague G. R. F. Ferrari has pointed out to me that he has only recently come to realize that this is not a necessary conclusion; neither the text nor Greek custom would demand that a priestess be celibate. However, the very fact that it is only recently that such an assiduous reader of Plato has sensed this suggests to me that it is, indeed, deeply encoded within the text that Diotima is a virginal or celibate woman (if not priestess, then philosopher). Whether or not Lady Diotima had children, the tradition could hardly be faulted, I think, for assuming that it is implied in the text that she had none.

18. Which, in the end, is quite different from Halperin's in *its* end. For Halperin, Diotima turns out to be "not so much a woman as a 'woman,' a necessary female absence" (Halperin, "Why Is Diotima a Woman?" 149). For me, Diotima *is* a woman, but a woman who represents the absence of another woman—Aspasia. At stake is not the politics of gender but the opposition of the academy to the democratic polis.

19. Plato, *Gorgias: A Revised Text*, ed. and trans. E. R. Dodds, rpt. 1959 (Oxford: Oxford University Press, 2002), 129; Dennis Proctor, *The Experience of Thucydides* (Warminster, England: Aris & Phillips, 1980), 6; Nicole Loraux, *The Invention of Athens: The Funeral Oration in the Classical City* (Cambridge, Mass.: Harvard University Press, 1986), 311–27.

20. Reginald E. Allen, "Comment, Menexenus," in *Euthyphro, Apology, Crito, Meno, Gorgias, Menexenus* (New Haven: Yale University Press, 1984), 320. The only thing that puzzles me about this comment is the implication that according to Plato base rhetoric is badly organized while philosophical rhetoric is artistic. I would have thought almost the opposite to be true: "Base" rhetoric is overly artistic, while philosophical speech is marked by its artlessness. See *Menexenus* 234c5–6: "Wise men lavish praise on him, and not at random but in speeches prepared long in advance" (Ibid., 129), which is hardly meant as a complement to the *epitaphios*. Cf. Loraux, *The Invention of Athens*, 314.

21. Halperin, "Why Is Diotima a Woman?" 138–39.

22. Plato, *The Republic*, ed. G. R. F. Ferrari, trans. Tom Griffith (Cambridge: Cambridge University Press, 2000), 200–201.

23. Andrea Wilson Nightingale, *Genres in Dialogue: Plato and the Construct of Philosophy* (Cambridge: Cambridge University Press, 1995), 43.

24. Unlike David Cohen, *Law, Sexuality, and Society: The Enforcement of Morals in Classical Athens* (Cambridge: Cambridge University Press, 1991), 175, who thinks that Uranian love is unconsummated, I see no evidence to that effect in Pausanias's speech. On my interpretation, then, demotic love is always consummatable, however high-minded it may get, while Platonic love is never consummated.

25. See, too, Halperin, "Why Is Diotima a Woman?" 148, and Allan David Bloom, "The Ladder of Love," in *Plato's Symposium*, trans. Seth Benardete (Chicago: University of Chicago Press, 2001), 77.

26. "Perhaps also Plato thought the intellectual free-for-all at Athens a special obstacle to such a gradual doling out of wisdom as Diotima proposed; cf. *Rep.* VI 498a–c"; G. R. F. Ferrari, "Platonic Love," in *The Cambridge Companion to Plato*, ed. Richard Kraut (Cambridge: Cambridge University Press, 1992), 262. To which I can only respond: Indeed!

27. See, too, Nightingale's positioning of Aristophanes as "insider" critic of the democratic city as opposed to Plato as "outsider / socially disembedded" (*Genres*, 190–92). See also the discussion in Josiah Ober, *Political Dissent in Democratic Athens: Intellectual Critics of Popular Rule* (Princeton, N.J.: Princeton University Press, 1998), 48–51.

28. In another part of my present research I shall be arguing that the doubled hermeneutic space of the literal and the figural is homologous with these as well. This, in turn, is part of a larger project to study the place of rhetoric versus philosophy in ancient Athens and its political consequents in late ancient Judeo-Christianity.

29. Dover, *Greek Homosexuality*, 155. In this matter, I am entirely in agreement as well with Foucault, *The Use of Pleasure*, 236. Kathy L. Gaca, in her attempt to contrast Plato with later Judeo-Christian Platonism, focuses almost exclusively on the regulation of sexual practice in the *Republic* and the *Laws*, which is, I submit, by no means the most relevant aspect of Plato's work for the formation of late antiquity. Gaca, *The Making of Fornication: Eros, Ethics, and Political Reform in Greek Philosophy and Early Christianity* (Berkeley: University of California Press, 2003), 41–58. Her account of Platonic love (35–41), while showing compelling and convincing interpretations in some matters, seems almost totally to ignore the distinction that Plato makes between the ordinary lot of human beings whose sexual practice must be regulated and the philosophers in whom sexual desire can be eradicated entirely, leaving only Platonic love. It is this distinction, I think, that made the difference in late antiquity. Another problem that I have with Gaca's account of Plato is that she seemingly ignores chronological development within his thought and writing, treating the *Laws* as if it represented his views always and forever. As Vlastos has pointed out, there is a big gap, precisely on this issue, between the *Laws* and the Middle Dialogues, which are—on Vlastos's theory, accepted by Gaca—also Plato speaking in propria persona (Vlastos, "The Individual," 22).

30. Plato, *Symposium*, ed. Paul Woodruff, trans. Alexander Nehamas (Indianapolis: Hackett, 1989), 7.

31. Ibid., 31.

32. Halperin, "Why Is Diotima a Woman?" 132.

33. Ibid., 133.

34. Ibid., 136–37.

35. Here we see how Nygren's refusal to read Plato's views as anything other than Pausanias's blinds him to much more nuanced possibilities than the stark opposition of eros to agape. See Robert Markus: "We know by now that desire for [the beautiful itself] is 'desire' in a very queer sense: it is desire to give rather than to receive, a kind of generosity rather than a kind of need"; R. A. Markus, "The Dialectic of Eros in Plato's *Symposium*," in *Plato: A Collection of Critical Essays*, ed. Gregory Vlastos (Garden City, N.Y.: Anchor Books, 1970), 140. For Markus, Platonic eros is nothing else than agape itself.

36. Benjamin Jowett, *The Dialogues of Plato* (Oxford: Clarendon Press, 1875), ii, 15.

37. Plato, *Symposium*, 37–39.

38. Leo Strauss, *Leo Strauss on Plato's Symposium*, ed. Seth Benardete (Chicago: University of Chicago Press, 2001), 155.

39. Jowett, *The Dialogues of Plato*, ii, 15.

40. Dover, *Greek Homosexuality*, 164.

41. Plato, *Symposium*, 44.

42. Steven Lowenstam, "Paradoxes in Plato's Symposium," *Ramus* 14 (1985): 90.

43. Bloom, "Ladder," 121–22. Bloom himself seems to admire this behavior of Socrates, but perhaps I am projecting something here.

44. *Symposium*, ed. C. J. Rowe (Warminster, England: Aris & Phillips, 1998), 166–67.

45. See similar formulation in Bloom, "Ladder," 123.

46. I thus could not disagree more with Halperin's remark that "The Platonic dialogue is true to this model of philosophical inquiry," namely, "the atmosphere of good will and ungrudging exchange of questions and answers." David M. Halperin, "Plato and Erotic Reciprocity," *Classical Antiquity* 5 (1986): 78. Plato no more imagines dialectic as reciprocal than he conceives eros as mutual, although he does mystifyingly present it as such. The *anterōs* of all the young men for Socrates serves to convey Plato's revisionist aesthetics. Perhaps it is not going too far to say that this love of all is for Socrates a parable of the way that the truly beautiful (or God) participates in love by stimulating it, but not by feeling it.

47. Plato's moves here have to be correlated with other, even earlier, movements within Athenian thought. Plato's own vision of philosophia, of course, owes much to Parmenides, but also, as Froma Zeitlin has argued, much as well to Aeschylus. The very foundations of philosophy, as a specifically European practice according to her, are grounded in "bring[ing] together phallos and head . . . for the ending of the [*Oresteia*] is also concerned with a shift in modes and behavior, as it charts a progression from darkness to light, from obscurity to clarity. Representation of symbolic signs [symbolic here is not in the Lacanian sense] perceived as a form of female activity gives way to the triumph of the male *Logos*. Representation and lyric incantation yield to dialectic and speech, and magic to science. Even more, this 'turning away from the mother to the father,' as Freud observed, 'signifies victory of intellectuality over the senses.'" Froma Zeitlin, "The Dynamics of Misogyny: Myth and Mythmaking in Aeschylus's *Oresteia*," in *Playing the Other: Gender and Society in Classical Greek Literature* (Chicago: University of Chicago Press, 1996), 211. Zeitlin proceeds to provide an extensive list of the ontological oppositions grounded in the primary opposition of male as Apollo and female as Erinyes that grow from

this "turning" or "victory" (ibid., 112) and that are characteristic of Greek philosophy from some Pre-Socratics to Plato and Aristotle. These relations will be further worked out, Deo volente, in the longer version of this study.

48. Pierre Hadot writes: "Socrates's task—entrusted to him, says the *Apology*, by the Delphic oracle (in other words, the god Apollo)—was therefore to make other people recognize their lack of knowledge and of wisdom. In order to accomplish this mission, Socrates himself adopted the attitude of someone who knew nothing—an attitude of naiveté. This is the well-known Socratic irony: the feigned ignorance and candid air with which, for instance, he asked questions in order to find out whether someone was wiser than he. . . . According to Cicero, 'Socrates used to denigrate himself, and conceded more than was necessary to the interlocutors he wanted to refute. Thus, *thinking one thing and saying another,* he took pleasure in that dissimulation which the Greeks call "irony."'" And yet again, "Socratic irony consists in pretending that one wants to learn something from one's interlocutor, in order to bring him to the point of discovering that he knows nothing of the area in which he claims to be wise." The question, of course, is, how this sits with the vaunted "say what you mean" principle that Nehamas makes the hallmark of Socratean sincerity, as contrasted with his sophistic opponents. Alexander Nehamas, "Eristic, Antilogic, Sophistic, Dialectic," *History of Philosophy Quarterly* 7 (1986): 3–16. It would seem that the principle of sincerity applies only to the opponents while Socrates is permitted to utilize rhetoric, *mirabile dictu,* to convince of his point, once again completely disrupting any notion of mutuality in the "conversation." I wonder if Hadot himself is aware of the irony in his own phrasing: "the mutual accord which Socrates *demands* from his interlocutor at each stage of the discussion" (Hadot, *What Is,* 26–27, emphases added). Or yet again: "A true dialogue is possible only if the interlocutors *want* to dialogue. Thanks to this agreement between the interlocutors, which is renewed at each stage of the discussion, neither one of the interlocutors imposes his truth upon the other" (Hadot, *What Is,* 63).

49. Eugene F. Rogers, *Sexuality and the Christian Body: Their Way Into the Triune God* (Oxford: Blackwell, 1999).

50. Foucault, *The Use of Pleasure,* 240.

51. Dover, *Greek Homosexuality,* 164–65.

52. David M. Halperin, "Platonic *Erōs* and What Men Call Love," *Ancient Philosophy* 5 (1985): 161–204, is, in itself, a profound interpretation of the *Symposium,* to my mind the most compelling I have seen yet. It underplays, on my reading, the sharpness of the value-distinction that Plato makes here

and elsewhere between two kinds of lovers, who are different *ab ovo*, as it were. See especially Halperin, "Platonic," 183–87, for both the profundity of his account and this one elision. The elision shows up particularly on page 187, when Halperin asks (but does not answer; his promised answers never, to the best of my knowledge, appeared) a remarkable set of questions about "what a properly Platonic love-affair [would] look like in practice. . . . How would it differ from what Plato's contemporaries considered normal in the way of erotic relations?" My reading, following in part Ferrari, hazards an answer to these questions. This point is crucial, on my view, for perceiving the Platonic affinities of late ancient thinking about sexuality. Halperin's account opens up, at the same time, other interesting points of contact (whether genetic or typological, I cannot yet say) between Platonic and rabbinic ways of thinking. In particular, I think we need a study in depth of the ways that Platonic *erōs* as creative force (Halperin, "Platonic," esp. 182) approaches rabbinic accounts of the *yeṣer*, on which, see Ishay Rosen-zvi, "The Evil Instinct, Sexuality, and Forbidden Cohabitations: A Chapter in Talmudic Anthropology," *Theory and Criticism: An Israeli Journal* 14 (summer 1999): 55–84. I am thinking particularly of accounts that describe the demise of the *yeṣer* (imagined as a daimon!) as the end of all human and animal creativity.

53. Foucault, *The Use of Pleasure*, 225.

54. Ibid., 238.

55. For this argument to different ends, see J. M. E. Moravcsik, "Reason and Eros in the 'Ascent'—Passage of the *Symposium*," in *Essays in Ancient Greek Philosophy*, ed. John P. Anton (Albany: State University of New York Press, 1971), 291.

56. Interestingly, Ludwig (*Eros and Polis*, 313) seems not to consider this a reductio ad absurdum and actually suggests that it is through a recommended promiscuity that the young Socrates is supposed to become contemptuous of all bodies: "Promiscuity is initially attractive but quickly becomes boring." I find this interpretation unconvincing, to say the least. Elsewhere Ludwig adopts the same, to my mind, somewhat odd interpretation of Diotima's words: "Child production required bodily contact, and even the philotimic couple were allowed to touch; but 'correct' pederasty (211b 5–6) means leaving bodies behind, at first leaving other people's bodies but eventually also leaving one's own body. Diotima counsels promiscuity for Socrates as a young man as a way of making his taste go off bodies" (*Eros and Polis*, 368). Taking the "promiscuity," however, as a promiscuity of

visual pleasure alone, as I think we are almost bound to, makes Diotima's recommendation considerably less grotesque.

57. For another endorsement of Ferrari's position that there are two ladders (without, however, referring to him), see Corrigan and Glazov-Corrigan, *Plato's Dialectic*, 50.

58. Nightingale, *Genres*, 55–59, citing *Symposium* 203a as compared with *Republic* 495d–e, suggested by Kenneth James Dover in his edition of *Symposium* (Cambridge: Cambridge University Press, 1980), 141.

59. See the profound discussion of this passage in Seth Benardete, *Plato's "Laws": The Discovery of Being* (Chicago: University of Chicago Press, 2000), 240–44. Each of the types of love of which Plato speaks has a body kind and a soul kind, and it is clear which of these is favored by Plato (without denying that he makes place for the first as well). Benardete here (*Plato's "Laws,"* 242) partly misleads, as he glosses this passage as referring to two different impulses within the lover and not two different kinds of lovers. The passage is, however, clear. There are two conflicting impulses within each lover, but crucially there are two different kinds of lovers, those who follow the first and those who follow the second of these impulses. Gaca, *Making*, 37, partly gets this right but then muddles it with a fuzzy reading of the Platonic text. The "third kind of love" there is not the one of those for whom the desire of the body is incidental; this is a subdivision *within* the third kind of love.

60. Thus I can agree with Halperin that "a coherent account can be given of Platonic eroticism without collapsing either its sexual or its metaphysical dimension into the other," that sexual desire is not a metaphor for philosophy in Plato nor philosophy a "sublimation" of sexual desire, and still disagree with Halperin in the implication that there is only one way of relating the two faces of eros.

61. Hadot, *What Is*, 56, writes that for Diotima/Socrates/Plato "the highest form of intelligence consists in self-mastery and justice, and these are exercised in the organization of cities or other institutions. Many historians have seen in this mention of 'institutions' an allusion to the founding of Plato's school, for in the following lines Plato clearly gives us to understand that the fruitfulness he is talking about is that of an educator." Unfortunately, I have been able to divine neither the exact Platonic passage to which Hadot refers nor the identity of these "many historians." The closest I can come is 209a, where the Greek has *"peri ta tōn poleōn te kai oikēseōn diakosmēsis"* (*Symposium*, ed. Dover, 59–60). All of the translations that I have consulted render the second term in its seemingly obvious sense of "households" or

"dwellings," so I am unsure upon what Hadot is leaning here, much as I would love to be able to lean, in turn, on his interpretation.

62. Foucault, *The Use of Pleasure*, 230, emphasis added; see also 244–45, drawing a fairly sharp distinction between Plato and the later (Christian) tradition that was to follow in his wake.

63. On the next page, Foucault somewhat confusingly seems to allow as much when he writes of "the raw material that Plato elaborates and transforms when he replaces the problematics of 'courtship' and honor with that of truth and ascesis" (Foucault, *The Use of Pleasure*, 230–31).

64. Jowett, *The Dialogues of Plato*, II 18.

65. Although, of course, the Stranger in the *Laws* would dearly like it to have been so (835c1–8). See the discussion in Benardete, *Plato's "Laws,"* 239.

66. Ferrari, "Platonic Love," 256: "The transition from the Lesser to Greater bears comparison with the crucial shift of focus in the *Republic* from institutions grounded in the honor code (Books II–IV) to those derived from rule by philosopher-kings (Books V–VII)."

67. Upon presentation of this paper at the conference which this volume documents, I was confronted by some of the less happy implications of my writing here, namely, a tendency toward a normativization of an *oikos*-based vanilla sexuality (although not heterosexist necessarily). This is not really where I want to be going, and the dilemma posed by Virginia Burrus's question to me about whether good politics and good sex are possible in the same theory (pointing toward the oppressiveness of political correctness) is one that will haunt (and animate) this entire project as it develops.

68. Burrus, *Sex Lives*. But where can we go with that version of the "queer"? This is not a rhetorical but a genuine question.

FLESH IN CONFESSION: ALCIBIADES BESIDE AUGUSTINE | MARK D. JORDAN

1. Benjamin Jowett, "Introduction" to the *Symposium*, in *The Works of Plato*, ed. B. Jowett (New York: Tudor, 1937), 286.

2. Ibid., 290.

3. See Boyarin's essay in this volume.

4. Because this is a response and not a full counterproposal, I keep secondary references to a minimum. Boyarin has already provided a rich and well-judged list of other interpretations.

5. Not all, of course. One notable exception is Martha C. Nussbaum, *The Fragility of Goodness: Luck and Ethics in Greek Tragedy and Philosophy*, rev. ed. (Cambridge: Cambridge University Press, 2001), 165–99.

6. Boyarin and I would not be having this conversation except for that ravishing essay by David Halperin, "Why Is Diotima a Woman?" in *One Hundred Years of Homosexuality and Other Essays on Greek Love* (New York: Routledge, 1990), 113–51. Reading that essay for the first time, while standing in Toronto's Glad Day bookstore, I decided to change how and what I studied. I, too, am a sort of Apollodorus.

7. I translate from the Greek in Plato, *Symposium*, ed. Kenneth J. Dover (Cambridge: Cambridge University Press, 1980).

8. Susan Guettel Cole, "Procession and Celebration at the Dionysia," in *Theater and Society in the Classical World*, ed. Ruth Scodel (Ann Arbor: University of Michigan Press, 1993), 25–38, at 26, 28.

9. The use of *pais* for the socially approved object of male-male love does say something about age-graded relations, but does not specify any particular age—any more than "boy" does in contemporary gay slang. A "boy" is supposed to be younger, though not always young, and submissive, though not by any means supine. Of course, *pais* also has the connection with slavery that "boy" had in the segregated American South. In his speech, Alcibiades uses *pais* both for an erotic role and for slaves—who are relatively unregulated sexual targets.

10. Alcibiades's speech and the narrative around him are filled with allusions both to the mysteries and to his earlier prosecution. For some samples, see Kevin Corrigan and Elena Glazov Corrigan, *Plato's Dialectic at Play: Argument, Structure, and Myth in the Symposium* (University Park: Pennsylvania State University Press, 2004), 164; Elizabeth Belfiore, "*Elenchus, Epode*, and Magic: Socrates as Silenus," *Phoenix* 34 (1980): 128–137, at 134, 136–37.

11. For a few other examples, see Halperin, "Why Is Diotima a Woman?" 147–48; Daniel E. Anderson, *The Masks of Dionysos: A Commentary on Plato's Symposium* (Albany: State University of New York Press, 1993), 51–53; Corrigan and Glazov Corrigan, *Plato's Dialectic*, 111–18.

12. Jacob Klein describes the "dianoetic extension" of image reading as the power relied on in Socratic teaching. See his *A Commentary on Plato's Meno* (Chapel Hill: University of North Carolina Press, 1965), 112–25.

13. See Mackendrick's essay in this volume.

14. I translate from the Latin in Augustine, *Confessions*, ed. James J. O'Donnell, vol. 1, *Introduction and Text* (Oxford: Clarendon Press, 1992). The text is cited according to the traditional books, chapters, and sections.

15. For her probable age, and the social context of the match, see Peter Brown, *The Body and Society: Men, Women, and Sexual Renunciation in Early Christianity* (New York: Columbia University Press, 1988), 392–93. Compendia of Roman civil law set the minimum age for both partners as puberty.

16. I am not claiming, of course, that Augustine denied the incarnation. On the contrary, he taxes the Platonic books for not knowing of it (7.9.14). I am reflecting on the absence of the incarnation from the narrative of Augustine's decisive turn to God—and away from the bonds of erotic flesh.

FOR THE LOVE OF GOD: THE DEATH OF DESIRE AND THE GIFT OF LIFE | MARIO COSTA

1. Plato, *The Symposium*, trans. R. E. Allen (New Haven: Yale University Press, 1991), 200a–b.

2. Much has been written about the complex relationships among Socrates, Diotima, and Plato. Whose voice and ideas are represented here? Is Diotima merely one more device of Socratic irony by which he can critique the preceding speeches about Eros, but in someone else's voice? And to whom should Plato's ideas be attributed, Socrates or Diotima? Or some combination of the two? By making a distinction here between Socrates and Diotima it is not my intention to resolve, or even address, these questions. I merely want to exploit a tension that appears to be inherent in the text in order to suggest that Diotima offers a correction to Socrates's view.

3. Luce Irigaray, "Sorcerer Love: A Reading of Plato, *Symposium*, 'Diotima's Speech,'" *An Ethics of Sexual Difference*, trans. Carolyn Burke and Gillian C. Gill (Ithaca, N.Y.: Cornell University Press, 1993), 20–21.

4. Ibid., 21.

5. Irigaray, too, as this brief discussion indicates, argues that Diotima's conception of Eros differs from Socrates's. However, despite this difference, Irigaray concludes that Diotima finally succumbs to Platonic metaphysics, and thus whatever difference between them that might initially obtain is undone. See ibid., 26–33. For a compelling, if at some times overstated, counter-argument to Irigaray's, one that argues more carefully (than I do in this essay) the difference between Socrates/Plato and Diotima, see Andrea Nye, "Irigaray and Diotima at Plato's Symposium," *Feminist Interpretations of Plato*, ed. Nancy Tuana (University Park: Pennsylvania State University Press, 1994), 197–215.

6. For instance, Michael Joyce translates this phrase as "to make the beautiful his own"(204d) and "[t]o make the good his own"(204e); *Symposium*, in *The Collected Dialogues of Plato*, ed. Edith Hamilton and Huntington Cairns (Princeton, N.J.: Princeton University Press, 1989), and in Alexander Nehemas and Paul Woodruff's translation, the phrase is rendered "[t]hat they become his own"(204d, 204e); *Symposium* (Indianapolis: Hackett, 1989).

7. Andrea Nye, "Irigaray and Diotima at Plato's Symposium," 200. My argument in this paragraph has been greatly influenced by parts of Nye's essay.

8. Andrea Nye argues a similar point, ibid., 198–201.

9. For a different and far more critical reading of this part of the *Symposium*, see Daniel Boyarin's carefully argued essay "What Do We Talk About When We Talk About Platonic Love?" in this volume.

10. Friedrich Nietzsche, *The Gay Science*, ed. Bernard Williams, trans. Josefine Nauchoff and Adrian Del Caro (Cambridge: Cambridge University Press, 2001), 199.

11. Ibid., 120.

12. Ibid., 119.

13. Ibid., 120.

14. Ibid., 235.

15. Ibid., 234.

16. See Friedrich Nietzsche, *The Birth of Tragedy*, in *Basic Writings of Nietzsche*, ed. and trans. Walter Kaufmann (New York: Modern Library, 1992), 33.

17. In fact, one need only look to Nietzsche's "Attempt at a Self-Criticism," added to *The Birth of Tragedy* some fourteen years after its first publication, to see that the Apollonian had almost completely vanished from Nietzsche's thinking. Here Nietzsche explains and clarifies his notion of the Dionysian without referring at all to the Apollonian.

18. Although James Strachey translates *Trieb* as "instinct," a better choice would be "drive." In the Freudian literature, a distinction is drawn between *Instinkt* and *Trieb*, the former referring to an inherited behavioral response common to all members of a particular species, the latter referring to predetermined factors in mental life. For a more detailed account of this distinction, see the entry on "Instinct (or Drive)" in J. Laplanche and J.-B. Pontalis, *The Language of Psychoanalysis*, trans. Donald Nicholson Smith (New York: Norton, 1973). Throughout my discussion of Freud, I will substitute "drive" for "instinct" for the sake of clarity.

19. Sigmund Freud, "Instincts and Their Vicissitudes," trans. James Strachey, *On Metapsychology* (London: Penguin Books, 1991), 119.

20. Ibid.

21. See Laplanche and Pontalis, *The Language of Psychoanalysis*, 214.

22. Jacques Lacan, *The Four Fundamental Concepts of Psycho-Analysis*, ed. Jacques-Alain Miller, trans. Alan Sheridan (New York: Norton, 1978), 168.

23. Ibid., ix.

24. According to Lacan, there are four drives, each with its own source or erogenous zone and *objet a*. There is the oral drive, with the mouth or lips as its source and the breast as its *objet a*. There is the anal drive, with the nose as its source and feces as its *objet a*. There is the scopic drive, with the

eye as its source and the gaze as its *objet a*. And there is the invocative drive, with the ear as its sources and the voice as its *objet a*.

25. Sigmund Freud, *Civilization and Its Discontents*, trans. James Strachey (New York: Norton, 1961), 13.

26. Ibid., 15.

27. Ibid., 12.

28. Jacques Derrida, *On the Name*, trans. John P. Leavey Jr., ed. Thomas Dutoit (Stanford: Stanford University Press, 1995).

29. Jacques Derrida, "How to Avoid Speaking: Denials," *Derrida and Negative Theology*, ed. Harold Coward and Toby Foshay (Albany: State University of New York Press, 1992), 77. This text marks Derrida's first explicit engagement with negative theology. One of his strategies in this text is to displace and thus free God, or God's name, from the singular proprietary claims of theology, particularly Christian theology. *Sauf le nom* is, in many respects, a continuation of the train of thought first developed in "How to Avoid Speaking: Denials."

30. Derrida, *On the Name*, 37.

31. Ibid.

32. Ibid.

33. Ibid.

34. Like both Freud and Lacan, for Derrida the desire of God is essentially unsatisfiable: Desire is not completed in the full presence of God, nor is God ever made present to desire. The desire of God might very well aim at satisfaction—here Derrida is closer to Freud—but such satisfaction is rendered impossible by the very structure of desire (and *différance*), where the object of desire is necessarily lacking or absent—here he is closer to Lacan.

35. Derrida, *On the Name*, 55–56.

36. Ibid., 58.

37. Ibid., 67.

38. Ibid., 74.

39. Ibid., 37.

40. Ibid., 76.

41. Richard Kearney, "Desire of God," *God the Gift and Postmodernism*, ed. John D. Caputo and Michael J. Scanlon (Bloomington: Indiana University Press, 1999), 125.

42. Jacques Derrida, *The Gift of Death*, trans. David Wills (Chicago: University of Chicago Press, 1995), 83.

43. Jacques Derrida, *Aporias*, trans. Thomas Dutoit (Stanford: Stanford University Press, 1993), 22.

44. Derrida, *The Gift of Death*, 55–56.

45. Hent de Vries, *Philosophy and the Turn to Religion* (Baltimore: Johns Hopkins University Press, 1999), 257. With equal succinctness, John Caputo makes a similar point when he writes, "[T]he name of God is also the name of death." *The Prayers and Tears of Jacques Derrida: Religion Without Religion* (Bloomington: Indiana University Press, 1997), 300.

46. Such definitions of eros and agape are, of course, given their classic articulation in Anders Nygren's *Agape and Eros*, trans. Philip S. Watson (Philadelphia: Westminster Press, 1953).

47. Jean-Luc Marion, *Being Given*, trans. Jeffrey L. Kosky (Stanford: Stanford University Press, 2002), 53.

48. Ibid., 54.

49. Ibid., 312.

50. Jean-Luc Marion, *God Without Being*, trans. Thomas A. Carlson (Chicago: University of Chicago Press, 1991), 102.

51. For Marion's discussion of revelation or Jesus Christ as the saturated phenomenon par excellence, see *Being Given*, 24.

52. Jean-Luc Marion, *The Idol and Distance: Five Studies*, trans. Thomas A. Carlson (New York: Fordham University Press, 2001), 200.

53. Ibid., 198. In drawing from Marion's insights into the constitutive elements of God's relationship with the creation, the traditional and sexist language of "Father" and "Son" can be rejected without losing his point. What is at stake here, for my purposes, are not the fixed identities of the persons of the Trinity, but the dynamic and fluid coincidence of withdrawal and intimacy in divine relationality. Thus, in place of the language of "Father" and "Son" I will use withdrawal and intimacy.

54. It should be noted that the remainder of this paper, while indebted to Marion, is not an elaboration of his thought. To the best of my knowledge, he does not address the relationship between eros and agape in his work, nor is it clear to me that the argument I put forward here would meet with his approval.

55. For a more detailed discussion of beauty's prompting an unceasing reproduction of beauty, see the opening pages of Elaine Scarry, *On Beauty and Being Just* (Princeton, N.J.: Princeton University Press, 1999).

56. St. Gregory of Nyssa, *On the Soul and the Resurrection*, trans. Catharine P. Roth (Crestwood, N.Y.: St. Vladimir's Seminary Press, 1993), 77.

57. Marion, *God Without Being*, 107.

SEXING THE PAULINE BODY OF CHRIST: SCRIPTURAL SEX IN THE CONTEXT OF THE AMERICAN CHRISTIAN CULTURE WAR | DIANA M. SWANCUTT

This essay is dedicated to David Bartlett, for his friendship and support of the LGBT community, on the occasion of his retirement from Yale Divinity School.

1. Groups that support gay civil rights include the American Friends Service Committee, California Council of Churches, the Ecumenical Catholic Church, Hawai'i Council of Churches, Interfaith Working Group, Pacific Congress of Quakers, Presbyterian Church (USA), United Churches of Christ, and Universal Fellowship of Metropolitan Community Churches. The MCC and ECC bless same-sex unions; PCUSA does so with terminological restrictions. In the UCC and among the Quakers, local representatives decide.

2. William Countryman, "The Acceptance of Gay/Lesbian People in the Episcopal Church in the United States—and What it Signifies for the Anglican Communion," a communication to the Lambeth–Eames Commission.

3. For analyses of church positions, see Kathy Rudy, *Sex and the Church: Gender, Sexuality, and the Transformation of Christian Ethics* (Boston: Beacon, 1997); Mary McClintock Fulkerson, "Church Documents on Human Sexuality and the Authority of Scripture," *Interpretation* 49 (1995): 46–58; J. G. Melton, *The Churches Speak on Homosexuality: Official Statements from Religious Bodies and Ecumenical Organizations* (Detroit: Gale Research, 1991).

4. "Keeping Body and Soul Together," in Melton, *Churches Speak*, 94.

5. Andrew Sullivan, "Alone Again, Naturally: The Catholic Church and the Homosexual," in *Que(e)rying Religion: A Critical Anthology*, ed. Gary David Comstock and Susan E. Henking (New York: Continuum, 1997), 238–50, esp. 243.

6. Statement of Rev. Jimmy Creech at his UMC church trial (1999) for performing a same-sex blessing. He was defrocked.

7. As so well put by Dennis Williams, a retired Methodist minister, district superintendent, and defense counsel for defrocked UMC pastor Elizabeth Stroud. He now teaches at Evangelical School of Theology in Myerstown, Pennsylvania.

8. Robin Scroggs, *The New Testament and Homosexuality: Contextual Background for Contemporary Debate* (Philadelphia: Fortress, 1983), 111; quoted by David McCarthy Matzko, "Homosexuality and the Practices of Marriage," *Modern Theology* 13 no. 3 (1997): 371–97, esp. 390.

9. This is true regardless of whether they believe homosexuality is a choice or an orientation. Focus on the Family and ex-gay evangelical groups think homosexuality is a modern, alterable set of practices enacted by "heterosexuals out of depravity, curiosity, impulse, predisposition, or bad moral guidance." (Sullivan, "Alone Again," 242; Rudy, *Sex*; Exodus International, http://exodus.to/exodus_faqs_political.shtml; Comiskey, "Understanding Homosexuality." www.desertstream.org/homosexuality.htm). Proponents of this view assume sexuality: they use the term "homosexuality" and the conceptual apparatus of orientation (two sexes, a sexual drive, and an object-orientation) to describe same-sex intercourse. In the December 1994 issue of *Focus on the Family*, James Dobson referred to a "non-gay homosexual," a celibate person of homosexual orientation. (If homosexuality is a lifestyle choice, there should be no homosexuality beyond homosexual acts; a "non-practicing homosexual" would not homosexual, but chaste androgynes or celibate.) Likewise, Exodus members describe homosexuals as those "motivated, in adult life, by a definite preferential *erotic attraction* to members of the *same sex* and who usually, *but not necessarily*, engage in overt sexual relations with them"; F. Worthen, "What Is Homosexuality?" http://home.messiah.edu/~chase/h/articles/worthen2.htm. My emphasis.

10. *The Church and Human Sexuality: A Lutheran Perspective*, first draft of a social statement. Division of Church in Society, Department for Studies of the ELCA (October 1993). Cf. Fulkerson, "Church Documents," 58 note 7.

11. Worthen, "What Is Homosexuality?"

12. Matzko, "Homosexuality," 383.

13. Richard B. Hays, *The Moral Vision of the New Testament: A Contemporary Introduction to New Testament Ethics* (San Francisco: HarperCollins, 1996), 386 (my emphasis); cf. "Relations Natural and Unnatural: A Response to John Boswell's Exegesis of Romans 1," *Journal of Christian Ethics* 14 (1986): 184–215.

14. Hays, *Moral Vision*, 390.

15. Robert Gagnon, *The Bible and Homosexual Practice: Texts and Hermeneutics* (Nashville, Tenn.: Abingdon, 2001); Dan O. Via and Robert Gagnon, *Homosexuality and the Bible: Two Views* (Minneapolis, Augsburg, 2003). I focus on the work of Hays, on which Gagnon builds.

16. Comiskey, "Understanding Homosexuality," www.desertstream.org/homosexuality.htm.

17. The contradiction typifies the church's dilemma over homosexuality: "What in 1975 had been a pathological constitution judged to be incurable was, [by 1986], a homosexual person made in the image and likeness of

God." See Sullivan, "Alone Again," 242, 245. On Hays's treatment of homosexuality, see "Relations," 200. Hays describes Paul as censuring homosexuality despite knowing that Paul had no concept of it, a problem that
continues in *Moral Vision* (387–88). In *Moral Vision* he even says that Paul's
theological anthropology ("the fallen human condition") implicates "homosexual inclination" as sin (390). On this subject, see Dale Martin, "Heterosexism and the Interpretation of Rom. 1:18–32," *Biblical Interpretation* 3,
no. 3 (1995): 332–55.

18. Hays, "Relations," 200, emphasis mine.

19. Sullivan, "Alone Again," 244.

20. Ibid.

21. Ibid.; Matzko, "Homosexuality," 381.

22. For Ratzinger's treatment of complementarity, see Matzko, "Homosexuality," 380–81.

23. Ibid., 376–77.

24. David Halperin, *One Hundred Years of Homosexuality and Other Essays on
Greek Love* (New York: Routledge, 1990), 25–26; Dale Martin, "Heterosexism
and the Interpretation of Rom. 1:18–32," 340 note 21.

25. Halperin, *One Hundred Years*, 15.

26. Ibid., 15–16.

27. George Chauncey Jr., "From Sexual Inversion to Homosexuality: Medicine
and the Changing Conceptualization of Female Deviance," *Salmagundi*
58–59 (Fall–Winter 1982–83): 114–46, esp. 116.

28. Thomas Laqueur, *Making Sex: Body and Gender from the Greeks to Freud*
(Cambridge, Mass.: Harvard University Press, 1990).

29. Laqueur, *Making Sex*, 62; cited by Dale Martin, *The Corinthian Body* (New
Haven: Yale University Press, 1995), 230.

30. Martin, *Corinthian Body*, 230–31, 294 note 6. See Aristotle, *Generation of Animals* 1.20, 728a217, 4.6 775a15. All quotations of classical texts are from the
Loeb Classical Library unless otherwise noted.

31. Judith Butler, *Gender Trouble* (New York: Routledge, 1990), 17, 151 note 6.

32. Anne Fausto-Sterling, *Sexing the Body: Gender Politics and the Construction of
Sexuality* (New York: Basic Books, 2000), 78–114.

33. Ibid., 51–53, 109.

34. Ibid., 109.

35. Marjorie Mandelstam Balzer, "Sacred Genders in Siberia: Shamans, Bear
Festivals, and Androgyny," in *Gender Reversals and Gender Cultures*, ed. Sa-
brina Petra Ramet (London: Routledge, 1996), 164–82, esp. 164–65.

36. Serena Nanda, "Hijras as Neither Man nor Woman," in *The Lesbian and Gay Studies Reader,* ed. Henry Abelove, Michele Barale, and David Halperin (New York: Routledge, 1993), 542–52.

37. Sabine Lang, "There is More than Just Women and Men: Gender Variance in North American Indian Cultures," in *Gender Reversals and Gender Cultures,* 183–96, esp. 190; Will Roscoe, "We'wha and Klah: The American Indian Berdache as Artist and Priest," in *Que(e)rying Religion,* 89–106, esp. 91; Harriet Whitehead, "The Bow and the Burden Strap: A New Look at Institutionalized Homosexuality in Native North America," in *The Lesbian and Gay Studies Reader,* 498–527, esp. 505.

38. Anthropological studies suggest that social attributes constituting Native American gender construction and Western gender ideology are compatible (occupation, dress/demeanor, and identity of sexual partner) but the order of importance is reversed (Whitehead, "Bow," 513).

39. Lang, "More than Just Women," 193.

40. Fausto-Sterling, *Sexing,* 268.

41. Lang, "More than Just Women," 185, 188.

42. Alice Domurat Dreger, *Hermaphrodites and the Medical Invention of Sex* (Cambridge, Mass.: Harvard University Press, 1998).

43. Ibid., 25–26.

44. Ibid., 45–77, 78–114.

45. Ibid., 35.

46. Mary McClintock Fulkerson, "Gender—Being It or Doing It? The Church, Homosexuality, and the Politics of Identity?" *Union Seminary Quarterly Review* 4 no. 1–2 (1993): 29–46, esp. 34.

47. Butler, *Gender Trouble,* 7; Fausto-Sterling, *Sexing,* 3, 5, 20.

48. Matzko, "Homosexuality," 382–83. On complementarity as a product of late-nineteenth-century urban work environments that forced American men to leave home-based labors for the industrial city, see Roselyn Rosenberg, *Beyond Separate Spheres* (New Haven: Yale University Press, 1982); Alice Kessler-Harris, *Out to Work* (New York: Oxford University Press, 1982). On its insertion into Genesis 1, see Rodney Clapp, *Families at the Crossroads* (Downer's Grove, Ill.: InterVarsity, 1993). On the differences between complementarity in ancient Israelite extended families and the modern nuclear family, see Carol Meyers, *Discovering Eve: Ancient Israelite Women in Context* (Oxford: Oxford University Press, 1988), 92, 132–38.

49. Cf. David Balch, ed., *Homosexuality, Science, and the "Plain Sense" of Scripture* (Grand Rapids, Mich.: Eerdmans, 2000); and Alice Ogden Bellis and Terry

L. Hufford, *Science, Scripture, and Homosexuality* (Cleveland, Ohio: Pilgrim, 2002).

50. Diana Swancutt, " 'The Disease of Effemination': The Charge of Effeminacy and the Verdict of God (Romans 1:18–2:16)," in *New Testament Masculinities*, ed. Stephen Moore and Janice Capel Anderson (Atlanta: Society of Biblical Literature, 2003), 193–234, esp. 207–8.

51. Augustine, *Corpus Scriptorum Ecclesiasticorum Latinorum* 81:47, 49, 51, 53 (Vienna: Tempsky, 1966).

52. Halperin, *One Hundred Years*, 21, 32–33; David Halperin et al., eds., *Before Sexuality: The Construction of Erotic Experience in the Ancient Greek World* (Princeton, N.J.: Princeton University Press, 1990); Judith Hallett and Marilyn Skinner, eds. *Roman Sexualities* (Princeton, N.J.: Princeton University Press, 1997); Saul Olyan, "And with a Male You Shall Not Lie the Lying Down of a Woman," *Journal of the History of Sexuality* 5 (1994): 179–206; Daniel Boyarin, "Are There Any Jews in *The History of Sexuality?" Journal of the History of Sexuality* 5 (1995): 333–55; Michael Satlow, "They Abused Him like a Woman": Homoeroticism, Gender Blurring, and the Rabbis in Late Antiquity," *Journal of the History of Sexuality* 5 no. 1 (1994): 1–25; Dale Martin, "Contradictions of Masculinity: Ascetic Inseminators and Menstruating Men in Greco-Roman Culture," in *Generation and Degeneration*, ed. V. Finucci and K. Brownlee (Durham, N.C.: Duke University Press, 2001), 81–108.

53. As Brent Nongbri ably describes in his unpublished essay, "Self-Mastery When There is No Male and Female': Paul and the Masculinization of the Gentiles in Galatians," critiques of Laqueur are largely misplaced (8–9 note 23). Even the strand of Hippocratic medicine that treats women as wholly other exhibits the fluidity to which Laqueur points. For critiques, see Helen King, *Hippocrates Woman: Reading the Female Body in Ancient Greece* (London: Routledge, 1998), 11; Rebecca Fleming, *Medicine and the Making of Roman Women: Gender, Nature, and Authority from Celsus to Galen* (Oxford: Oxford University Press, 2000), 120–21.

54. Peter Brown, *The Body and Society: Men, Women, and Sexual Renunciation in Early Christianity* (New York: Columbia University Press, 1988), 11.

55. Aileen Ajootian, "The Only Happy Couple: Hermaphrodites and Gender," in *Naked Truths*, ed. A. O. Koloski-Ostrow and C. L. Lyons (New York: Routledge, 1997), 200–242; Luc Brisson, *Sexual Ambivalence: Androgyny and Hermaphroditism in Graeco-Roman Antiquity*, trans. J. Lloyd (Berkeley: University of California Press, 2002).

56. Ajootian, "The Only Happy Couple," 221.

57. Brisson, *Sexual Ambivalence*, 7–40.

58. Ibid., 49–53. Translations of Diodorus Siculus by Brisson.

59. Pseudo-Lucian *Amores* 21; Philostratus on Favorinus, *Vita Sophistarum* 489. See Tim Whitmarsh, *Greek Literature and the Roman Empire: The Politics of Imitation* (Oxford: Oxford University Press, 2004), 114–15: "Eunuchs were often viewed as lusty" and sometimes convicted of adultery (Philostratus *VS* 489). See also Matthew Kuefler, *The Manly Eunuch: Masculinity, Gender Ambiguity, and Christian Theology in Late Antiquity* (Chicago: University of Chicago Press, 2001). "Pseudoetymologically, a *eunoukhos* is sometimes interpreted as the 'possessor' (*-okhos*) of a 'bed' (*eunē*)" (Whitmarsh, *Greek Literature*, 115). Their androgyny may explain why eunuchs are exempt from the Genesis-based ruling on divorce in Matthew 19:10–12: Whether born or made eunuchs, the rule against divorce did not apply because they were neither male nor female.

60. John Winkler, *The Constraints of Desire: The Anthropology of Sex and Gender in Ancient Greece* (New York: Routledge, 1989), 50.

61. For this argument, see Swancutt, "Still Before Sexuality."

62. Ibid. For *tribades'* masculine characteristics, cf. Bernadette Brooten, *Love Between Women: Early Christian Responses to Female Homoeroticism* (Chicago: University of Chicago Press, 1996), 25, 46; K. J. Dover, *Greek Homosexuality* (Cambridge, Mass.: Harvard University Press, 1978, rpt. 1989), 60–68; Laqueur, *Making Sex*, 53; Halperin, *One Hundred Years*, 166 note 83.

63. Winkler, *Constraints of Desire*, 61. Cf. *De Vita Beata* 13.4.

64. Swancutt, "Disease," 225.

65. Origen, *Against Celsus* 4.14 (*Scriptorum Vetus Fragmenta* 2.1052); Diogenes Laertius 7.134, 137 (*SVF* 2.300, 2.299, 2.526); Aristocles (Eusebius, *Evangelical Preparation* 15.14; *SVF* 1.98). See Alexander *On Mixture* 225.1–2 (*SVF* 2.310); Aetius 1.7.33 (*SVF* 2.1027); Diogenes Laertius 7.135–36 (*SVF* 1.102). See also A. A. Long and D. K. Sedley, *Hellenistic Philosophers* (Cambridge: Cambridge University Press, 1987), 273–74.

66. Epicurus, *Letter to Menoeceus* 123–24; Cicero, *On the Nature of the Gods* 1.43–49.

67. Seneca, *On Kindness* 4.19.1–4; 4.4.1–3; *The Beautiful Life* 7.4; Cicero, *On the Nature of the Gods* 2.75–76.

68. See Brooten, *Love*, 245–46.

69. Swancutt, "Disease," 207 n 31.

70. Swancutt, "Still Before Sexuality."

71. James Miller, "The Practices of Romans 1:26: Homosexual or Heterosexual?" *Novum Testamentum* 35 (1995): 1–11. The category of "sexuality" skews

Miller's helpful analysis. Pregnancy in women was a form of female self-mastery; channeling energy to the growth of the fetus controlled *voluptas*. This may explain why the author of 1 Timothy 2:19–15 asserted that women "could be saved" by it (it was masculinizing in a positive sense). Some thought female virginity functioned similarly (see Nongbri, "Self-Mastery," 12; Brown, *Body*, 11; Philo, *Questions and Answers on Exodus* 2.3).

72. Augustine also argued that polygamous women acted unnaturally—although polygamous men did not—because female polygamy did not increase procreativity. As Augustine said, only a lust-driven whore would do such a thing (*Nuptials* 10.11). On the stereotype that too much sex physically masculinized prostitutes, rendering them androgynous, see Swancutt, "Still Before Sexuality."

73. John Boswell, *Christianity, Social Tolerance, and Homosexuality* (Chicago: University of Chicago Press, 1980), 358; contra Brooten, *Love*, 331. Cf. Wisdom of Solomon 14:24–26, where *enallage geneseōs* refers to the "exchange of genitals" (shape-shifting), not "sexual perversion." Likewise, *gamon ataxia* is probably "disorder in marriage," that is, sex-role reversal (active / penetrative women; passive/penetrated men).

74. Swancutt, "Disease," 212. Patristic interpreters focused on the men.

75. Brooten, *Love*, 245, 250; Martin, "Heterosexism," 339–49.

76. Swancutt, "Disease," 211–12. *Aschēmosynē* and its synonym, *aischros*, referred to a "want of form," "deformity," or "disfigurement" of body or mind, often as a result of indulgence of passion. Aristotle, *Physica* 190b15, cf. 188b20; *Politics* 1341b5; Plato, *Symposium* 201a; Xenophon, *Cyropaedia* 2.2.29; Philo, *Embassy to Gaius* 3.156–57; Plutarch, *Moralia* 997 2b–c.

77. Swancutt, "Disease," 211.

78. *Corpus Scriptorum Ecclesiasticorum Latinorum* 81:47, 49, 51, 53.

79. Boswell, *Christianity*, 137–38.

80. Boswell, *Christianity*, 141. Novatian, *De cibis Judaicos* (PL 3:957–58).

81. Boswell, *Christianity*, 140, 356–57.

82. Brooten, *Love*, 338–43; Swancutt, "Disease," 214 note 42.

83. Jonathan Walters, "Invading the Roman Body: Manliness and Impenetrability in Roman Thought" in *Roman Sexualities*, 29–43.

84. See Stephen Moore, *God's Gym* (New York: Routledge, 1996), 4–8.

85. Halvor Moxnes, *Putting Jesus in His Place: A Radical Vision of Household and Kingdom* (Louisville, Ky.: Westminster John Knox, 2003), 72–90.

86. John Collins, *The Scepter and the Star: The Messiahs of the Dead Sea Scrolls and Other Ancient Literature* (New York: Doubleday, 1995).

87. Adela Collins, "Mark and His Readers: The Son of God Among Greeks and Romans," *Harvard Theological Review* 93 (2000): 85–100; Stephen Moore, *God's Gym*, 108.

88. Eric Thurman, "Looking for a Few Good Men," in *New Testament Masculinities*, 137–62; Chris Frilingos, "Sexing the Lamb," in ibid., 297–318.

89. See Thurman, "Looking," 153–56; Dale Martin, *Slavery as Salvation: The Metaphor of Slavery in Pauline Christianity* (New Haven: Yale University Press, 1990), 85–116, 124–26, 134–35; Epictetus, *Discourses* 3–4.

90. Thurman, "Looking," 152.

91. Homi Bhabha, *The Location of Culture* (New York: Routledge, 1994), 85–92, 102–22, esp. 94. See Thurman's helpful summary, "Looking," 139–140, which I paraphrase.

92. Frilingos, "Sexing," 299, 309; Thurman, "Looking," 140, 157.

93. Wayne Meeks, "The Image of the Androgyne: Some Uses of a Symbol in Earliest Christianity," *History of Religions* 13 (1973): 165–208; Dennis MacDonald, *There Is No Male and Female: The Fate of a Dominical Saying in Paul and Gnosticism* (Philadelphia: Fortress, 1987), 98–101; Martin, *Corinthian Body*, 230–33. Cf. Daniel Boyarin, *Carnal Israel: Reading Sex in Talmudic Literature* (Berkeley: University of California Press, 1993), 36–44.

94. *On the Contemplative Life* 63; *Allegorical Interpretation* 2.13; Nongbri, "Self-Mastery," 5.

95. Cited by Nongbri, "Self-Mastery," 4. As Nongbri indicates (note 12), the Hebrew terms for "androgynes" and "two-faced" transliterate Greek equivalents that appear in *Symposium* 189e as *androgynon* and *prosōpa du*.

96. Paraphrase, Stephen Moore, *God's Gym*, 86–91, esp. 90; Boyarin, *Carnal Israel*, 43; *Leviticus Rabbah* 14.1; b. *Berakhot* 61a; b. *Erubin* 18a.

97. Martin, *Corinthian Body*, 230–33; MacDonald, *No Male*, 98–101.

98. Nongbri, "Self-Mastery," 5–7, esp. 5 note 16 for his critical engagement with readings of Philo by Daniel Boyarin, *Carnal Israel*; Richard Baer, *Philo's Use of the Categories Male and Female* (Leiden: E. J. Brill, 1970).

99. Tertullian, *On the Apparel of Women* 1.2; quoted by Martin, *Corinthian Body*, 231.

100. The subjunctive reading is far better attested.

101. Meeks, "Image," 185.

102. Dennis MacDonald, "Corinthian Veils and Gnostic Androgynes," in *Images of the Feminine in Gnosticism*, ed. Karen L. King (Philadelphia: Fortress, 1988), 276–92, esp. 285; Martin, *Corinthian Body*, 231, 295 note 13; Nongbri, "Self-Mastery," 15, note 40.

398 | NOTES TO PAGES 89-94

103. Martin, *Corinthian Body*, 1–37.
104. *On Hippocrates and Plato's Doctrines* 5.2.49 (*SVF* 2.841).
105. The relationship between Platonic and Stoic ideas of physiology within the work of first- to second-century Stoics like Epictetus, Seneca, and Marcus Aurelius was dynamic. In the period, platonized Stoic or stoicized Platonic philosophy permeated elite Roman gender and political ideologies. I am interested in this permeation, the equation of commonplace ideas about Stoic thought with "elite" notions of gender.
106. J. Albert Harrill, "Coming of Age and Putting on Christ: The *Toga Virilis* Ceremony, Its Paraenesis, and Paul's Interpretation of Baptism in Galatians," *Novum Testamentum* 44 (2002): 252–77.
107. Chrysostom, *Homily on Galatians* 3.27 (*Interpretatio Omnium Epistularum Paulinarum* 4:65–66 [ed. F. Field; Oxford: Clarendon, 1849–1862]).
108. Augustine, *Epistle to the Galatians* 1B.3.28–29 (Migne *Patrilogia Latina* 35:2125).
109. Jerome, *Epistle to the Galatians* 2.3.27–28 (Migne *Patrilogia Latina* 26:369B [445]).
110. 1 Cor. 7:22–23; Wayne Meeks, *The First Urban Christians: The Social World of the Apostle Paul* (New Haven: Yale University Press, 1983).
111. Martin, *Corinthian Body*, 175–76.
112. Nongbri, "Self-Mastery," ties the discourse explicitly to Gal. 3:28. See also Stanley Stowers, *A Rereading of Romans: Justice, Jews, and Gentiles* (New Haven: Yale University Press, 1994), 42–65; Troels Engberg-Pedersen, *Paul and the Stoics* (Louisville, Ky.: Westminster John Knox, 2000).
113. Nongbri, "Self-Mastery," 14, citing Philo *QE* 1.8.
114. E.g., Plato, *Timacus* 69d 81e; Aristotle, *Generation of Animals* 775h.
115. Cf. Halvor Moxnes, "Honor, Shame, and the Outside World in Paul's Letter to the Romans," in *The Social World of Formative Christianity and Judaism* (Philadelphia: Fortress Press, 1988).
116. Herman Waetjen, "Same-Sex Sexual Relations in Antiquity and Sexuality and Sexual Identity in Contemporary American Society," in *Biblical Ethics and Homosexuality: Listening to Scripture*, ed. Robert L. Brawley (Louisville, Ky.: Westminster John Knox, 1996), 103–16. As Waetjen puts it, "The moral order of the new creation and its ministry of justice . . . is the emerging reality of . . . the Body of Christ" (1 Cor. 12:12).
117. Jo-Ann Brant, "The Place of Mimesis in Paul's Thought," *Studies in Religion* 22 (1993), 285–300. Cf. Whitmarsh, *Greek Literature*.
118. Although scholars typically treat this passage as a censure of individual *porneia*, Paul could use the plural, bodies (*sōmata*), when he wished (6:15).

His point, missed by individualistic readings of 1 Cor. 6, is that an individual's *sōma cannot* be separated from the whole *sōma* of Christ.

119. Aetius 4.21.1–4 (*SVF* 2.836); Martin, *Corinthian Body*, 201.

120. Martin, *Corinthian Body*, 200.

121. Ibid., 176. Martin focuses on the "inward" danger this sex act poses to the body of Christ, since the believer and Christ are one (177). I focus on the "outward" danger, the danger of expelling Christ's seed.

122. Ibid., 209–17.

123. Ibid., 218.

124. Eugene Rogers, *Sexuality and the Christian Body: Their Way into the Triune God* (London: Blackwell, 1999).

125. Standard translations of Rom. 1 (v. 23: *allasō* as "exchange" rather than "change"; *doxa* as "glory" rather than "appearance"; *en* as "for" rather than "into"; verse 24 *atimadzesthai* as "dishonoring" rather than "degrading"; verse 26: the addition of "women" as direct objects; verse 27: *homoiōs* as linkage of objects rather than as adverb; *tēn aschemosynēn katergazomenoi* as "committing shameless acts" rather than "working degradation") are so structured by modern ideas about biology and homosexuality that we have eliminated the ancient focus on gender morphing and guaranteed a homosexual reading. We must correct this translational practice.

126. Hays, *Moral Vision*, 389.

127. *Third Wave Agenda: Being Feminist, Doing Feminism*, ed. L. Heywood and Jennifer Drake (Minnesota: University of Minnesota, 1997), as quoted by Dale Martin, "Galatians 3:28: "No Male and Female," National SBL Presentation, November 23, 1998.

128. Martin, "Galatians 3:28," 8.

129. Cited by Martin, "*Arsenokoitês* and *Malakos*: Meanings and Consequences," in *Biblical Ethics and Homosexuality*, 117–36, esp. 130.

HOMOEROTIC SPECTACLE AND THE MONASTIC BODY IN SYMEON THE NEW THEOLOGIAN | DEREK KRUEGER

1. Throughout this essay, I have where possible used published English translations, modified to articulate the sense of the Greek. However, I have retranslated much of Hymn Fifteen. I have transliterated the Greek according to conventions for ancient Greek, although this does not reflect middle Byzantine pronunciation. This essay began as a presentation to the Thirty-ninth Spring Symposium of Byzantine Studies at Queen's University, Belfast, in April 2005. A slightly different version with more complete citations of the Greek texts will appear in *Performing Byzantium*, ed. Margaret Mullett

(Aldershot: Ashgate, forthcoming). I thank Margaret Mullett, Elizabeth Jeffreys, Averil Cameron, Gene Rogers, and Jeff Mortimore for their comments on earlier drafts.

2. See, for example, *On the Mystical Life: The Ethical Discourses*, trans. Alexander Golitzin, 3 vols. (Crestwood, N.Y.: Saint Vladimir's Seminary Press, 1995–97), 3:69–79, 90–94, 107–11; Basil Krivocheine, *In the Light of Christ: St. Symeon the New Theologian: Life, Spirituality, Doctrine*, trans. Anthony P. Gythiel (Crestwood, N.Y.: St. Vladimir's Seminary Press, 1986), 361–70. For other important studies of Symeon, see H. J. M. Turner, *St. Symeon the New Theologian and Spiritual Fatherhood* (Leiden: Brill, 1990); Ilarion Alfeyev, *St. Symeon the New Theologian and the Orthodox Tradition* (New York: Oxford University Press, 2000); Anestes Keselopoulos, *Man and the Environment: A Study of St. Symeon the New Theologian*, trans. Elizabeth Theokritoff (Crestwood, N.Y.: St. Vladimir's Seminary Press, 2001).

3. Symeon introduces the passage in question: "But I will illustrate this for you with an example" (*Ethical Discourses* 10.234); *On the Mystical Life*, 1:149 (translation modified).

4. See *On the Mystical Life*, 3:37. Symeon's exile resulted from conflict with Stephen of Nikomedeia, a member of the patriarchal staff, over a number of issues, including Symeon's devotion to icons of his deceased mentor, Symeon the Stoudite. See Alfeyev, *St. Symeon*, 39–41; *On the Mystical Life*, 3:30–32.

5. Darrouzès (*Traités théologiques et éthiques*, 1:8–10) believed it was intended primarily for a reading audience. See *On the Mystical Life*, 1:8–9; Turner, *St. Symeon*, 11–12.

6. See *Ethical Discourses* 10.1, 154, 159, 197, 304, 318, 350, 471, 480, 612, 802, 861, 911.

7. "Malgré certains détails plausible, en particulier la collation des insignes au co-empereur, le récit tombe dans une sensiblerie un peu équivoque. . . . Il donne l'impression d'oublier cette 'sensation parfaite' qu'il défende." Darrouzès, *Traités théologiques et éthiques*, 2:278–79 note 1.

8. *On the Mystical Life*, 1:151n2.

9. See for instance, ibid., 3:73–79, 90–94; Krivocheine, *In the Light of Christ*, 361–70.

10. In the subsequent section, Symeon interprets this bride to be Mary (*Ethical Discourses* 1.9.43).

11. Virginia Burrus, *The Sex Lives of Saints: An Erotics of Ancient Hagiography* (Philadelphia: University of Pennsylvania Press, 2004).

12. Symeon the New Theologian, *Catechetical Discourses* 30.84, also refers to the parable of the prodigal son. For a translation, see *Symeon the New Theologian: The Discourses*, trans. C. J. deCantanzaro (New York: Paulist, 1980). See also Turner, *St. Symeon*, 44.

13. That Symeon's rapid shift risks the impression of incest only heightens the shock of Christ's perverse desire for the sinner. God's slippage from parent to lover is not without biblical precedent. In the Synoptic Gospels, God the Father declares of Jesus, "You are my son, my [or: the] beloved [*Su ei ho huios mou ho agapētos*]" (Lk. 3:22; compare Mk. 1:11; Mt. 3:17). For a discussion of this mix of Son and Beloved, see Eugene F. Rogers, *Sexuality and the Christian Body: Their Way into the Triune God* (Oxford: Blackwell, 1999), 219–22.

14. Mt. 22:2, compare Lk. 14:16–24. And see Mk. 2:18–19; Mt. 25:1; Lk. 12:35; Mk. 13:34.

15. *Ethical Discourses* 4.81–83; trans. Golitzin, 2:14. For the robe of glory, see, for example, *Ethical Discourses* 4.254–79. On Symeon's discussions of being clothed in light, see *On the Mystical Life*, 3:75. For Symeon's discussion of divine light more generally, see Alfeyev, *St. Symeon*, 226–41.

16. *Ethical Discourses* 10:354; *On the Mystical Life*, 1:153.

17. In the *Alexiad*, Anna Komnene describes how Isaac the Sebastokrator arrived at Philippopolis to find his brother Alexius I "sleeping in his imperial tent, but Isaac went in noiselessly and lay down on the second of his brother's beds." While Anna does not place her father and uncle in the same bed, this does attest that men might sleep near their intimates nonsexually. *Alexiad* 8.8.1. I thank Michael Grünbart for this reference.

18. For Symeon's citations of the Bible, see Turner, *St. Symeon*, 40.

19. A negative example sustains the connection between sleep coverings and sexuality. In the story of Noah (Gen. 9), Shem and Japheth cover their father with a *himation* by walking backward so as not to see their father's nakedness, as their brother Ham had.

20. Niketas Stethatos, *Vie de Syméon le nouveau théologien*, ed. Irénée Hausherr (Rome: Pontifical Institute of Oriental Studies, 1928), 2.25. See Turner, *St. Symeon*, 37–39.

21. Plato, *Symposium* 219b.

22. See Jordan's essay in this volume.

23. *Catechetical Discourses* 26.80–113.

24. *Evergetis Typikon* 24; *Byzantine Monastic Foundation Documents: A Complete Translation of the Surviving Founders'* Typika *and Testaments*, ed. John Thomas and Angela C. Hero (Washington, D.C.: Dumbarton Oaks, 2000), 2:490.

25. See *On the Mystical Life*, 3:26–28; Turner, *St. Symeon*, 63–64. On the master/ disciple relationship in Symeon's works, see ibid., esp. 52–58.

26. Compare 1 Cor. 12:23 and Symeon the New Theologian, *Hymns* 15.165; *Syméon le nouveau théologien: Hymnes*, ed. Johannes Koder, 3 vols. (Paris: Cerf, 1969–73); *Hymns of Divine Love*, trans. George A. Maloney (Denville, N.J.: Dimension, n.d.). On the deification of the body, see Alfeyev, *St. Symeon*, 255–69.

27. In preparing his edition of the *Hymns*, Niketas wrote scholia defending Hymn Fifteen (see Koder, *Hymnes*, 1:70–73). In his 1790 edition of Symeon's *Hymns*, Dionysios Zagoraios omitted Hymn Fifteen, presumably because he regarded it as shocking (Koder, *Hymnes*, 1:276–77 note 1).

28. On this passage, see Dale B. Martin, *The Corinthian Body* (New Haven: Yale University Press, 1995), 92–96.

29. *Hymns* 15.141–145; Maloney, *Hymns of Divine Love*, 54.

30. See Koder, *Hymnes*, 1:71–73.

31. Thus Koder and Maloney; Alfeyev (*St. Symeon*, 267) supplies "pudendum."

32. There is here striking resonance with the ascetic homoeroticism that pervades kabbalistic texts, which likewise exploit the play between the concealment and the exposure of the crown of the phallus, read as a privileged sign of divine potency, as Elliot Wolfson has argued: "The dimension of God that is, paradoxically, present in its absence is the corona of the phallus." *Language, Eros, Being: Kabbalistic Hermeneutics and Poetic Imagination* (New York: Fordham University Press, 2005), 133.

33. *Hymns* 15.187: *emou lalountos ta phrikta peri melōn hagiōn*, "When I utter these formidable [things] about holy members."

34. *On the Mystical Life*, 3:75.

35. *Ethical Discourses* 4.372–375; *On the Mystical Life*, 2:23–24.

36. *Ethical Discourses* 4.375–378; *On the Mystical Life*, 2:24.

37. *Ethical Discourses* 4.486; *On the Mystical Life*, 2:27.

38. The strongest case is argued in Turner, *St. Symeon*, 18–22. But see Kathryn M. Ringrose, *The Perfect Servant: Eunuchs and the Social Construction of Gender in Byzantium* (Chicago: University of Chicago Press, 2003), 86, 234 note 86, and Alfeyev, *St. Symeon*, 30 note 90. Rosemary Morris suggests that Symeon was a eunuch in "The Political Saint of the Eleventh Century," in *The Byzantine Saint*, ed. Sergei Hackel (London: Fellowship of St. Alban and St. Sergius, 1981), 44; but did not repeat the claim in *Monks and Laymen in Byzantium, 843–1118* (Cambridge: Cambridge University Press, 1995), 77–78.

39. See Ringrose, *The Perfect Servant*, 18–24, 57–61; and Matthew Kuefler, *The Manly Eunuch: Masculinity, Gender Ambiguity, and Christian Ideology in Late Antiquity* (Chicago: University of Chicago Press, 2001), 96–102, 260–282.

40. See also *Hymns* 15.134: "You make your home in each one and you dwell in everyone."

41. Resonances with the fluid erotic imagery found in the texts of the medieval mystics discussed by Amy Hollywood in this volume are notable.

42. For an example of monastic anxieties about same-sex attraction, see the twelfth-century *Phoberos Typikon* 58 (*Byzantine Monastic Foundation Documents*, ed. Thomas and Hero, 3:942). See also Catia Galatariotou, "*Eros* and *Thanatos*: A Byzantine Hermit's Conception of Sexuality," *Byzantine and Modern Greek Studies* 13 (1990): 116–17.

43. *Life* 150.20. I thank Eustratios Papaioannou for bringing this passage to my attention.

44. For ancient constructions of sexuality, see David Halperin, *One Hundred Years of Homosexuality* (New York: Routledge, 1990), 15–40; and John J. Winkler, *The Constraints of Desire: The Anthropology of Sex and Gender in Ancient Greece* (New York: Routledge, 1990), 17–44. For the state of the question regarding the need to historicize sexualities, see David Halperin, *How to Do the History of Homosexuality* (Chicago: University of Chicago Press, 2002).

45. In support of such a reading, I note that Symeon terms the rebel's bowing down and embrace of the emperor's feet as "humility" (*Ethical Discourses* 10.256).

46. What exactly a "sodomite" is, is also open to question, and may include nonprocreative cross-sex sexual activity in addition to same-sex sexual activity. On the confessions in Hymn Twenty-Four, see Turner, *St. Symeon*, 28–29; *On the Mystical Life*, 3:26–27. On confession and the formation of identity, see Michel Foucault, *The History of Sexuality*, vol. 1, *An Introduction*, trans. Robert Hurley (New York: Vintage, 1978), 59–62.

47. For Symeon's views of *apatheia*, see Turner, *St. Symeon*, 170–178.

48. Alfeyev (*St. Symeon*, 24–25) reminds us that the Stoudion Monastery contained a bath.

49. *Thēlymanēs* literally means something like "girl-crazy" and thus may suggest cross-sex sexual desire. But perhaps it merely means "horny."

50. Rowan D. Williams, "The Body's Grace," in *Theology and Sexuality: Classic and Contemporary Readings*, ed. Eugene F. Rogers (Oxford: Blackwell, 2002), 317.

SEXUAL DESIRE, DIVINE DESIRE; OR, QUEERING THE
BEGUINES | AMY HOLLYWOOD

This essay was first published in *Queer Theology: New Perspectives on Sex and Gender*, ed. Gerard Loughlin (Oxford: Blackwell Publishing, 2006), and is reprinted here with permission.

1. Judith Bennett, "'Lesbian-Like' and the Social History of Lesbianisms," *Journal of the History of Sexuality* 9 (2000): 7. See also the essays collected in Francesca Canadé Sautman and Pamela Sheingorn, ed., *Same Sex Love and Desire Among Women in the Middle Ages* (New York: Palgrave, 2001) and for groundbreaking theoretical and historical work on the early modern period, Valerie Traub, *The Renaissance of Lesbianism in Early Modern England* (Cambridge: Cambridge University Press, 2002). For materials directed toward specifically religious texts, see Jeffrey Jerome Cohen, *Medieval Identity Machines* (Minneapolis: University of Minnesota Press, 2003), esp. 154–87; Ulrike Wiethaus, "Female Homoerotic Discourse and Religion in Medieval Germanic Culture," in *Gender and Difference in the Middle Ages*, ed. Sharon Farmer and Carol Braun Pasternack (Minneapolis: University of Minnesota Press, 2003), 288–321; Carolyn Dinshaw, *Getting Medieval: Sexualities and Communities, Pre- and Postmodern* (Durham, N.C.: Duke University Press, 1999), esp. 143–82; Karma Lochrie, "Mystical Acts, Queer Tendencies," in *Constructing Medieval Sexuality*, ed. Karma Lochrie, Peggy McCracken, and James A. Schultz (Minneapolis: University of Minnesota Press, 1997), 180–200; Bruce Holsinger, "The Flesh of the Voice: Embodiment and the Homoerotics of Devotion in the Music of Hildegard of Bingen (1098–1179)," *Signs* 19 (1993): 92–125; Mary Anne Campbell, "Redefining Holy Maidenhead: Virginity and Lesbianism in Late Medieval England," *Medieval Feminist Newsletter* 13 (1992): 14–15; and Kathy Lavezzo, "Sobs and Sighs between Women: The Homoerotics of Compassion in *The Book of Margery Kempe*," in *Premodern Sexualities*, eds. Louise O. Fradenburg and Carla Freccero (New York: Routledge, 1996), 175–98.

2. Lochrie does not provide a full history of the image. An early, intensely erotic and eucharistic example can be found in Aelred of Rievaulx, "Rule of Life for a Recluse," a general guide to the religious life written, perhaps not surprisingly, for women. In meditating on Christ's body, Aelred encourages the reader: "Hasten, linger not, eat the honeycomb with your honey, drink your wine with your milk. The blood is changed into wine to gladden you, the water into milk to nourish you. From the rock streams have flowed for you, wounds have been made in his limbs, holes in the wall of his body, in which, like a dove, you may hide while you kiss them

one by one. Your lips, stained with his blood, will become like a scarlet ribbon and your word sweet." Aelred of Rievaulx, *Treatises and the Pastoral Prayer*, trans. Theodore Berkeley, Mary Paul Macpherson, R. Penelope Lawson (Kalamazoo, Mich.: Cistercian Publications, 1971), 90–91. Cited by Thomas Bestul, *Texts of the Passion: Latin Devotional Literature and Medieval Society* (Philadelphia: University of Pennsylvania Press, 1996), 39. As Bestul points out, the passage brings together language from the Psalms and the Song of Songs. Although this kind of highly erotic devotion to Christ's wounds becomes characteristic of late medieval meditational practice, the example from Aelred shows that it has roots in mid-twelfth-century texts and practices. For further examples from fourteenth-century and fifteenth-century devotional texts, see Bestul, *Texts of the Passion*, 56–57, 59, and 62; Douglas Gray, "The Five Wounds of Our Lord," *Notes and Queries* 10 (1963): 50–51, 82–89, 127–34, 163–68; Lewis Flora, "The Wound in Christ's Side and the Instruments of the Passion: Gendered Experience and Response," in *Women and the Book: Assessing the Physical Evidence*, ed. Lesley Smith and Jane H. M. Taylor (Toronto: University of Toronto Press, 1996), 204–29; David S. Areford, "The Passion Measured: A Late Medieval Diagram of the Body of Christ," in *The Body Broken: Passion Devotion in Late-Medieval Culture*, ed. A. A. MacDonald, H. N. B. Ridderbos, and R. M. Schlusemann (Groningen: Egbert Forsten, 1998), 211–38; and Amy Hollywood, "'That Glorious Slit': Irigaray and the Medieval Devotion to Christ's Side Wound," in *Luce Irigaray and Premodern Culture: Thresholds of History*, ed. Elizabeth D. Harvey and Theresa Krier (New York: Routledge, 2005), 105–25. See also Michael Camille, "The Image and the Self: Unwriting Late Medieval Bodies," in *Framing Medieval Bodies*, ed. Sarah Kay and Miri Rubin (Manchester: Manchester University Press, 1994), 77.

3. Both Bynum and Lochrie cite Raymond of Capua's *Life* of Catherine of Siena (1327–80): "With that, he tenderly placed his right hand on her neck and drew her towards the wound on his side. 'Drink, daughter, from my side,' he said, 'and by that draught your soul shall become enraptured with such delight that your very body, which for my sake you have denied, shall be inundated with its overflowing goodness.' Drawn close in this way to the outlet of the Fountain of Life, she fastened her lips upon that sacred wound, and still more eagerly the mouth of her soul, and there she slaked her thirst." Caroline Walker Bynum, *Holy Feast and Holy Fast: The Religious Significance of Food to Medieval Women* (Berkeley: University of California Press, 1987), 172; and Lochrie, "Mystical Acts," 188.

Bynum, in reading the side wound as a breast and Christ's blood as milk, explicitly rejects a sexualized reading, whereas Lochrie insists that the maternal does not exclude the sexual. In the Middle Ages, it was believed that breast milk was created from surplus menses not released in childbirth. The association of the blood with Christ's side wound, then, ties it both to the vagina *and* breast milk, thereby enabling the threefold association of wound, vulva, and breast. On these associations, see Charles Wood, "The Doctor's Dilemma: Sin, Salvation, and the Menstrual Cycle in Medieval Thought," *Speculum* 56 (1981): 710–27. For the highly suggestive and erotic visual images, see Lochrie, "Mystical Acts"; Lewis, "Wound"; and Hollywood, "Glorious Slit." On the linguistic association of the Latin for wound and for vulva, see Lochrie, "Mystical Acts," 189, 198 note 26; and Wolfgang Riehle, *The Middle English Mystics*, trans. Bernard Sandring (London: Routledge and Kegan Paul, 1981), esp. 46. One wonders about the relationship between these vulvic wound images and the blood-drenched Christ discussed by Jeffrey Hamburger, *Nuns as Artists: The Visual Culture of a Medieval Convent* (Berkeley: University of California Press, 1997), plate 1. For a warning against the dangers of assuming all penetrable sites are feminine, see Richard Rambuss, *Closet Devotions* (Durham, N.C.: Duke University Press, 1998), 19–32.

4. This queering can also be seen in a text that Lochrie mentions but does not cite, Angela of Foligno's (c. 1248–1309) *Book*, particularly the *Memorial*, dictated by Angela to a Friar. In two places she discusses the wound in Christ's side: "In the fourteenth step, while I was standing in prayer, Christ on the cross appeared . . . to me. . . . He then called me to place my mouth to the wound on his side. It seemed to me that I saw and drank the blood, which was freshly flowing from his side. His intention was to make me understand that by this blood he would cleanse me." And later, she writes that "At times it seems to my soul that it enters into Christ's side, and this is a source of great joy and delight." Angela of Foligno, *The Complete Works*, trans. Paul Lachance (New York: Paulist Press, 1993), 128 and 176 (and also see 246).

These two passages are compressed in a highly erotic and homosexuated or queered reading by Luce Irigaray: "Could it be true that not every wound need remain secret, that not every laceration was shameful? Could a sore be *holy*? Ecstasy is there in that glorious slit where she curls up as if in her nest, where she rests as if she had found her home—and He is also in her. She bathes in a blood that flows over her, hot and purifying." Luce Irigaray, *Speculum of the Other Woman*, trans. Gillian C. Gill (Ithaca, N.Y.:

Cornell University Press, 1985), 200. For other examples of "possibly queer female desire for Christ's wounds," see Lochrie, "Mystical Acts," 199 note 34. For more on Irigaray and mysticism, see Amy Hollywood, *Sensible Ecstasy: Mysticism, Sexual Difference, and the Demands of History* (Chicago: University of Chicago Press, 2002), esp. 187–210; and Hollywood, "Glorious Slit."

5. Lochrie, "Mystical Acts," 195.

6. Bennett, "'Lesbian-Like,'" 8.

7. Ibid., 8–9.

8. Ibid., 14–15. For related work, see Judith Bennett and Amy Froide, eds., *Single Women in the European Past, 1250–1800* (Philadelphia: University of Pennsylvania Press, 1999).

9. I realize that this is not quite where Bennett places the implausibility—for her it is the purported jump between religious representations and actual sexual practices between women that is implausible. But I think that behind her sense that religious representation tells us little about "actual people" lies the irreality of medieval religious beliefs for many modern readers.

10. Judith C. Brown's descriptions of the trial records concerning Sister Benedetta Carlini (1590–1661) suggest that one *might* in fact lead to the other. In this case, Benedetta Carlini's visions, in which she speaks as Christ and as a male angel, serve as the pretext for her sexual relationship with another nun assigned to care for her. As Brown explains, Benedetta's "male identity consequently allowed her to have sexual and emotional relations that she could not conceive between women." In addition, the requests she made as the angel Splenditello did not differ substantially from erotic mystical language. See Judith C. Brown, *Immodest Acts: The Life of a Lesbian Nun in Renaissance Italy* (New York: Oxford University Press, 1986), 127.

11. On the potential problems with using modern notions of normativity to understand medieval materials, see Amy Hollywood, "The Normal, the Queer, and the Middle Ages: Remarks on Carolyn Dinshaw's *Getting Medieval: Sexualities and Communities, Pre- and Postmodern," Journal for the Study of Sexuality* 10 (2001): 173–79.

12. Rambuss, *Closet Devotions*, 48. Rambuss points to similar problems with Leo Steinberg's theological readings of Christ's penis as it appears in Renaissance art. See Leo Steinberg, *The Sexuality of Christ in Renaissance Art and in Modern Oblivion*, 2nd ed. (Chicago: University of Chicago Press, 1996). For a related argument about the body of Christ in the York cycle, see Garrett J. Epp, "Ecce Homo," in *Queering the Middle Ages*, ed. Glenn Burger and Steven F. Kruger (Minneapolis: University of Minnesota Press, 2001), 236–51.

13. Bynum, *Holy Feast and Holy Fast*, 178. For many, this would be an apt description of intense sexual desire.

14. The beguines did not marry, but lived singly or in groups. They often supported themselves through manual labor and sometimes refused or attempted to escape from the strict jurisdiction of male ecclesial or monastic hierarchies. They were thus "lesbian-like" in the terms discussed by Bennett. Their modes of religious imagery, however, as I will argue in what follows, were queer in varying degrees.

15. Rambuss, *Closet Devotions*, 58.

16. At least from the standpoint of the contemporary reader. Whether these idealized conceptions of divine-human relations would have been similarly queer for medieval readers is not yet clear to me. See again Hollywood, "The Normal, the Queer, and the Middle Ages."

17. Michael Warner, "Tongues Untied: Memoirs of a Pentacostal Boyhood," in *The Material Queer: A LesBiGay Cultural Studies Reader*, ed. Donald Morton (Boulder, Colo.: Westview Press, 1996), 43.

18. See Rambuss, *Closet Devotions*, esp. 11–71; Georges Bataille, *Eroticism: Death and Sensuality*, trans. Mary Dalwood (San Francisco: City Lights, 1986); Hollywood, *Sensible Ecstasy*, 36–119.

19. For a useful introduction to Origen and his interpretation of the Song of Songs, see Bernard McGinn, *The Foundations of Mysticism: Origins to the Fifth Century* (New York: Crossroads, 1992), 108–30. On the queering of the Song of Songs in the Christian tradition, see Stephen D. Moore, "The Song of Songs in the History of Sexuality," *Church History* 69 (2000): 328–49. The "individual believer" is a potentially gender-neutral category, yet in many male-authored texts on the Song of Songs the presumption of *reversal* in calling oneself a bride depends on the marking of that believer as male.

20. See Bernard McGinn, *The Growth of Mysticism: Gregory the Great Through the 12th Century* (New York: Crossroads, 1994), 158–224, 225–74, and 328–33; and Shawn M. Krahmer, "The Virile Bride of Bernard of Clairvaux," *Church History* 69 (2000): 304–27.

21. For the intensity of such gender crossings (and re-crossings) in seventeenth-century English devotional poetry, and the ways in which they destabilize sex, gender, and sexual categories, see Rambuss, *Closet Devotions*. The texts of a number of medieval male authors might usefully be subjected to a similar analysis, most particularly, Rupert of Deutz, Bernard of Clairvaux, Richard of St. Victor, and Heinrich Suso.

22. For an overview of Mechthild's life and work, see Amy Hollywood, "A Vision of Flowing Light," in *The New History of German Literature*, ed. David

E. Wellbery (Cambridge, Mass.: Harvard University Press, 2005), 161–31; Amy Hollywood, *The Soul as Virgin Wife: Mechthild of Magdeburg, Marguerite Porete, and Meister Eckhart* (Notre Dame, Ind.: Notre Dame University Press, 1995), 1–86; Bernard McGinn, *The Flowering of Mysticism: Men and Women in the New Mysticism—1200–1350* (New York: Crossroads, 1998), 222–44.

23. Mechthild of Magdeburg, *The Flowing Light of the Godhead*, trans. Frank Tobin (New York: Paulist Press, 1998), 1.44, 59.

24. Ibid., 61.

25. Ibid., 62.

26. This leads in the latter books of the *Flowing Light* to Mechthild's claim that the "well-ordered" soul becomes the "housewife" of God. See *Flowing Light*, 7.3, 277; and Hollywood, *Virgin Wife*, 78–86.

27. For a general overview, see McGinn, *Flowering*, 199–222. On the homoeroticism of her poems and letters, see E. Ann Matter, "My Sister, My Spouse: Woman Identified Women in Medieval Christianity," in *Weaving the Visions: New Patterns in Feminist Spirituality*, ed. Judith Plaskow and Carol P. Christ (San Francisco: Harper, 1989), 54–55. On the "queering" effect of the intensity of her desire, see Lochrie, "Mystical Acts," 184. For a more "normalizing" reading of Hadewijch's language, in relationship to late medieval theology, see Saskia Murk-Jansen, "The Use of Gender and Gender-Related Imagery in Hadewijch," in *Gender and Text in the Later Middle Ages*, ed. Jane Chance (Gainesville: University Press of Florida, 1996), 52–68.

28. Hadewijch, *Complete Works*, trans. Mother Columba Hart (New York: Paulist Press, 1980), 356.

29. Lochrie, "Mystical Acts," 184.

30. Hadewijch, *Complete Works*, 61.

31. Ibid., 280.

32. Ibid.

33. Ibid., 281–82.

34. For Hadewijch's debts to secular courtly love lyric, see Saskia Murk-Jansen, "The Mystic Theology of the Thirteenth-Century Mystic, Hadewijch, and Its Literary Expression," *The Medieval Mystical Tradition in England* 5 (1992): 117–28; Murk-Jansen, "The Use of Gender," 54–55; and the literature cited there. According to Bynum, medieval religious men used gender reversal (the soul as the Bride of Christ) to stress their humility in the face of the divinity. Murk-Jansen carries this argument to Hadewijch's poems, arguing that, since "within the conventions of the courtly love lyric it is the lady who has all the power" and "the man who is represented as of lower status," Hadewijch too uses gender reversal as a form of renunciation. This

is certainly right, at least in part. However, as I will argue here, Hadewijch's knight is not simply passive in face of the unattainable Love but actively seeks her, through pain, passion, and desire. In this he combines activity and passivity (as does the bride in the Song of Songs, who goes into the streets looking for her beloved).

35. Cited and trans. Murk-Jansen, "Use of Gender," 58.

36. On the one hand, Hadewijch stresses that this is the case as long as the soul is in the body or on earth, holding forth the promise of the continual union and coming to fruition of the soul and the divine after death. Yet at other times the doubleness and cruelty of desire and its passionate, painful ecstasy seem literally endless.

37. Murk-Jansen, "Use of Gender," 58. This is reminiscent of *The Rothschild Canticles'* representation of Song of Song's 4:9 ("You have wounded my heart, my sister, my spouse.") in which the bride holds the lance with which Christ's side is wounded on the verso side, and Christ on a stylized cross displays his side wound on the recto. *Rothschild Canticles*, New Haven, Beinecke Rare Book and Manuscript Library, MS 404, fols. 18v–19r.

38. Hadewijch, *Complete Works*, 162.

39. According to Murk-Jansen, "the fluid movement between masculine and feminine imagery emphasizes the basic similarity of male and female before God," leaving any account of Hadewijch's own understanding of "woman-hood" "necessarily speculative." Yet doesn't the fluidity of human gender before God tell us *something* about how Hadewijch experienced gender, at least on the level of her relationship to the divine (itself central to her life)? Murk-Jansen, "Use of Gender," 66.

40. See Michael Sells, *Mystical Languages of Unsaying* (Chicago: University of Chicago Press, 1994), 180–217; and Hollywood, *Virgin Wife*, 87–119, 180–93.

41. Marguerite Porete, *The Mirror of Simple Souls*, trans. Ellen Babinsky (New York: Paulist Press, 1993), chap. 131, 213–14.

42. Nicholas Watson, "'If wommen be double naturelly': Remaking 'Woman' in Julian of Norwich's Revelation of Love," *Exemplaria* 8 (1996): 3.

43. For the "fall into nothingness" and the dialectic of All and Nothing in Porete, see Porete, *Mirror*, chap. 118, 192–93.

44. The term grace rarely appears in the *Mirror*, and then to refer to the very lowest stages of the soul, which are clearly subordinated to the life of the spirit and that of the annihilated soul. See, for example, Porete, *Mirror*, chap. 60, 137–38.

45. Watson, "Remaking 'Woman,'" 6.

46. Porete deploys gendered language in a number of different ways through-out the *Mirror*. Her dialectical subversions of the gap between the soul and

love (or the Trinity), for example, often depend for their linguistic operation on the fact that these terms are feminine and so take feminine pronouns. The resultant pronominal ambiguity elides the gap between the soul and the divine. There may also be echoes in Porete of the uniting of male and female characteristics in Christ's body through the bloody side wound. In general, Porete focuses attention on Christ in the third and fourth realms. Yet she calls the divine in the higher realms the "Farnear," thereby evoking both courtly and biblical allusions to the beloved. This male beloved, moreover, in the sixth stage (the highest the soul can achieve in this life), opens an "aperture" to the soul in which she sees her own eternal glory. Porete, *Mirror*, chap. 61, 138. For more on this and other uses of gendered language in the *Mirror*, see Hollywood, *Virgin Wife*, 100–101, 108–9; and Sells, *Languages of Unsaying*, 180–217.

47. Although Porete retains the orthodox position that full union between the soul and the divine can only occur after death, she clearly holds that the soul, while on earth, can annihilate its will and desire. In doing so, the soul overcomes the need for corporeal aids to salvation and is able to "give to nature what it wills." But it is able to do so only because the body is fully subservient to the virtues and so asks nothing contrary to God's will. See Hollywood, *Virgin Wife*, 109–12.

48. Mechthild of Magdeburg, *Flowing Light*, 335–36.

49. Ibid., 336.

50. For a related argument about the self-subverting nature of sexual desire, see Leo Bersani, "Is the Rectum a Grave?" in *AIDS: Cultural Analysis, Cultural Activism*, ed. Douglas Crimp (Cambridge, Mass.: MIT Press, 1988), 197–222.

FEETISHISM: THE SCENT OF A LATIN AMERICAN BODY THEOLOGY | MARCELLA MARÍA ALTHAUS-REID

For the full text of the sonnet cited in the epigraph at the beginning of this chapter, together with the translation by Carlos Akiro Nishimura, see http://formattoso.sites.uol.com.br/performative.htm.

1. Glauco Mattoso is the pseudonym of Pedro José Ferreira da Silva. Born in 1951, Mattoso belonged to a generation of political and sexually transgressive poets in Brazil known as the "mimeographic generation" because they printed and distributed their poems using that medium. Glauco Mattoso is a pun for *glaucomattoso*, that is, someone suffering from glaucoma, reflecting the fact that Glauco suffered that illness for many years till he became blind. His poetry also reflects the aesthetic quest of someone losing his sight and seeking the meaning of blindness. He is the author of several books and poems as well as comic strips in Brazilian cartoon journals.

2. See Steven Butterman's original study of Mattoso, *Perversions on Parade: Brazilian Literature of Transgression and Postmodern Anti-Aesthetics in Glauco Mattoso* (San Diego: Hyperbole Books, 2005).

3. Some years ago I helped with the translation of a final document from an international Quaker women's conference gathered in Birmingham, England. A phrase containing the words "women's empowerment" created an agitated debate among Mexican delegates who explained that they didn't want more power in the church; on the contrary, they wanted less, in order to be faithful to their desire to be with the disempowered of their country.

4. Glauco Mattoso, poem 9.5.3 (1977), from his "Poemas en Castellano," collected in *Galleria Allegria* (Sao Paulo: Memorial da America Latina, 2002), my translation. See http://www.poesia.com/n14/n14itg.html.

5. W. Hamacher, "The End of Art with the Mask," in *Hegel After Derrida,* ed. S. Barnett (London: Routledge, 1998), 105.

6. Roland Barthes, *Mythologies* (New York: Hill and Wang, 1972), 9. A different analysis of this passage in Barthes can be found in William Pietz, "Fetishism and Materialism," in *Fetishism as Cultural Discourse*, ed. E. Apter and W. Pietz (Ithaca, N.Y.: Cornell University Press, 1993), 121.

7. For the methodology of queer theology and its starting point of the body, see Robert Goss, *Queering Christ: Beyond Jesus Acted Up* (Cleveland: Pilgrim Press, 2002).

8. Michael Taussig, "Maleficium: State Fetishism," in *Fetishism as Cultural Discourse*, ed. E. Apter and W. Pietz (Ithaca, N.Y.: Cornell University Press, 1993), 217.

9. Christopher Kocela, "A Myth Beyond the Phallus," *Genders* 34 (2001): 13.

10. M. Yegenoglu, "Sartorial Fabric-actions: Enlightenment and Western Feminism," in *Postcolonialism, Feminism and Religious Discourse*, ed. L. Donaldson and K. Pui-Lan (London: Routledge, 2000), 96.

11. A. Ploeger, *Dare We Observe? The Importance of Art Works for Consciousness of Diakonia in (Post-) Modern Church* (Leuven: Peeters, 2002), chapter 1.

12. Ibid., 16.

13. Jacques Derrida, *Glas* (Lincoln: University of Nebraska Press, 1974).

14. Ibid., 227.

15. C. Classen, D. Howes, and A. Synnott, *Aroma: The Cultural History of Smell* (London: Routledge, 1994), 132.

16. Ploeger, *Dare We Observe*, 7.

17. Jacques Derrida, *Acts of Religion*, ed. Gil Anidjar (London: Routledge, 2002), 251.

18. Jacques Derrida and Hèlene Cixous, *Velos*, trans. Mara Negrón (Buenos Aires: Siglo, 2001).

19. Ibid., 17.

20. In *Specters of Marx: The State of the Debt, The Work of Mourning, and the New International* (New York: Routledge 1994), Derrida seems to confuse commodity fetishism with his own play on spectrality or ghostliness. That is, Derrida removes the historical concreteness of fetishism by ignoring the processes of ideological formation behind them. See Michael Sprinker, ed., *Ghostly Demarcations: A Symposium on Jacques Derrida's Specters of Marx* (New York: Verso, 1999).

21. Derrida and Cixous, *Velos*, 51.

22. Ibid., 81.

23. Ibid.

24. Ibid.

25. Ploeger, *Dare We Observe*, 17.

26. Jacques Derrida, *Memoirs of the Blind: The Self-Portrait and Other Ruins* (Chicago: University of Chicago Press, 1993).

27. From an interview with Francisco Ernesto Molina by Ernesto Castrillón and Luis Casabal in *La Nación*, July 23, 2002, www.lanacion.com.ar/02/07/23/dg_416182.asp.

28. For this point, see Marcella Althaus-Reid, *Indecent Theology: Theological Perversions in Sex, Gender and Politics* (London: Routledge, 2000), chapter 2.

29. Juan Manuel de Rosas was a nationalist Argentinean president in the nineteenth century who died in exile in France. During many decades people fought for his body to be repatriated to Argentina. That finally happened a few years ago. The slogan "Rosas returns" referred both to the idea of repatriating his body and to the return of nationalist ideas in some political sectors of the country.

30. E. Apter, introduction, *Fetishism as Cultural Discourse,* ed. E. Apter and W. Pietz (Ithaca, N.Y.: Cornell University Press, 1993), 3.

31. Martin Piro, "Un tiempo de horror eficaz," www.clarin.com/suplementos/cultura/2002/06/29/u-00601.html.

32. Gilles Fraser, *Redeeming Nietzsche: On the Piety of Unbelief* (London: Routledge, 2002), 125.

33. The words *tradition* and *betrayal* share a common etymology: the Latin *tradere,* "to give up" or "to hand over."

34. Alistair Kee, "Nietzsche and Christians with Beautiful Feet," in *Philosophy of Religion for a New Century: Essays in Honour of Eugene T. Long,* ed. J. Hackett and J. Wallulis (Dordrecht: Kluwer Academic).

35. For this point of betrayal and disloyalty in theology, see Marcella Althaus-Reid, *The Queer God* (London: Routledge, 2003).
36. John Caputo, *On Religion* (London: Routledge, 2001), 5.
37. Ibid.
38. Rowan Williams, "Forms of Literature in 1848," in *Literature, Politics and Theory*, ed. Francis Barker et al. (London: Methuen, 1986). Williams distinguishes between indicative and subjunctive texts. Indicative texts are those that relate to what happens in the world, while subjunctive texts introduce radical or transgressive perspectives. Subjunctive texts push the limits and go beyond the ideological reproduction of the world present in the indicative ones.
39. Hélène Cixous, "The Laugh of Medusa," in *New French Feminisms: An Anthology*, ed. E. Marks and I. de Courtivron (Brighton: Harvester, 1981).
40. On Mattoso's visual and blind poetic phase, see "The Visual Poet," http://formattoso.sites.uol.com.br/visual poet.htm.
41. Kee, "Nietzsche and Christians with Beautiful Feet," 19.
42. Ibid.

DIGITAL BODIES AND THE TRANSFORMATION OF THE FLESH | SHEILA BRIGGS

1. See Leo Steinberg, *The Sexuality of Christ in Renaissance Art and in Modern Oblivion* (Chicago: University of Chicago Press, 1996).
2. Elaine Graham, "Post/Human Conditions," *Theology and Sexuality* 10, no. 2 (2004): 24.
3. Frank Tipler, *The Physics of Immortality: Modern Cosmology, God, and the Resurrection of the Dead* (New York: Anchor Books, 1995).
4. Marcella Althaus-Reid, *Indecent Theology: Theological Perversions in Sex, Gender and Politics* (London: Routledge, 2000).

PASSION—BINDING—PASSION | YVONNE SHERWOOD

1. Erich Auerbach, "Passio as Passion [*Passio als Leidenschaft*]," trans. Martin Elsky, *Criticism*, summer 2001. The essay was written during the Second World War and was first published in the United States while Auerbach was in exile in Istanbul.
2. Gilles Deleuze, *The Logic of Sense*, trans. Mark Lester (New York: Columbia University Press, 1992), 75.
3. For Derrida's comments on the rhetorical ruse of the "at the same time," see "The Deconstruction of Actuality," in *Negotiations: Interventions and Interviews 1971–2001*, ed. Elizabeth Rottenberg (Stanford, Calif.: Stanford University Press, 2002), 85–116, esp. 93.

4. Julia Kristeva, "Reading the Bible," in *New Maladies of the Soul* (New York: Columbia University Press, 1995), 115–26.

5. This is a brutal summary of five pages on "subject" in the OED—pages that seem to me to be a poignant summary of the ambiguity of human living positions writ large. The fractured sense of what it means to be a subject is nowhere better illustrated than in contributions to postmodern theory that lurch, uncomfortably, between extremes of the passive (subjected) subject, helplessly inscribed in the world of language, and the pure voluntarist subject who suffers absolutely no impediment in her/his desire to change words and worlds. For discussion of the, to say the least, divided, postmodern subject, see Herman Rapaport, *The Theory Mess: Deconstruction in Eclipse* (New York: Columbia University Press, 2001), 124.

6. At the same time that English speakers were speaking of a "passion" of the belly, Grünewald's Isenheim altarpiece (c. 1515) performed an alliance between hostile forces inside and outside the skin in its interpretation of the Passion. In the green-gray body of Christ (a body that one certainly would not relish taking into one's body through the Eucharist) the marks on Jesus' body caused by the nails and the lashes are transformed into the lesions and eruptions of St. Anthony's fire.

7. Georges Bataille, "The Notion of Expenditure," in *Visions of Excess: Selected Writings 1927–1939*, trans. Allen Stoekel (Minneapolis: University of Minnesota Press, 1985), 116–29.

8. Michael Roemer, *Telling Stories: Postmodernism and the Invalidation of Traditional Narrative* (Lanham, Md.: Rowman and Littlefield, 1995). Seeking alternatives to literary theory and narratology's triumphant stories of creation that revolve around huge authors and/or readers—as "HyperSubjects"—Roemer attempts to write about story in a way that replicates the belittling of human agency. He takes story itself as the central force. The irony (which makes the second half of his book so much weaker than the first), is that one of the main tasks of the book seems to be to rant against postmodernism as a pure Citadel of Positivism (?). This styles Roemer as the lone hero-crusader, cut off from all the other contemporary writers who are trying to perform the vulnerability of the thinking/writing/written subject.

9. Roemer argues that modern formulations of positivism amplify what has always been a fundamental human response to fiction and the conditions of human impotence it imposes (by definition). He uses the term positivism in this broader sense. The particularly forceful modern denigration of story does not mean that human beings have not always been anxious around

the acute performances of subjection in story. The modern antithesis between fact and fiction is the latest and strongest symptom of the need to
reassert control.

10. Roemer, *Telling Stories*, 47.

11. I am sticking to the traditional "he" because "s/he" would be misleading
in ways that I can only begin to sketch out here. The role of hero, even
qualified hero, has not traditionally been available to women in the same
way that it has been available to men. One of the traditional devices for
making the figure of the subjected hero more palatable has been to juxtapose him against a more subjected female, in relation to whom he is always
relatively heroic/salvific (hence in a sense redeemed). Gender complicates
the conditions of story because the sense of relative objecthood and subjecthood shift radically across that line dividing s/he.

12. Honoré de Balzac, cited without reference by Frank O'Connor, *The Mirror
in the Roadway: A Study of the Modern Novel* (New York: Knopf, 1956), 87;
Roemer, *Telling Stories*, 47.

13. The conditions of narrative, which mean that it is impossible to create a
sense of pure (sole) agency, are demonstrated even, and in fact especially,
in the versions of the Passion story (Johannine, Pauline) that stress the
absolute agency of God. They still rely on, and indeed emphasize, the idea
of God entering a world gone astray from his desiring—and the Bible is
constantly stressing how *extremely* it has gone astray from his desiring. And
they enforce a *must* around his dying that is variously attributed to, and
distributed among, different counteragents (of which God can be only one,
and, arguably, the most problematic one). All kinds of problems for philosophical theology and its conditions of omnipotence follow from the narrative condition that God *must* experience the pain of an intractable plot.

14. Though the cracks show in all the gospels, the impossibility of the narrator/
author and the character/victim being one is most overtly demonstrated
in Mark, where Jesus experiences distress and agitation in the garden and
foregrounds "in a loud voice" the gulf between himself and God (Mark
14:32–42; 15:34).

15. A lot could be said about this little particle *for*, which seems to me to play
a helpfully obfuscating role in its relationship to the Passion and the torrent
of questions concerning divine agency that it implies. Mainstream Christian
theology seems to tell us both that Jesus dies "for" us (i.e., because of us,
because of a compulsion necessitated by us, along the lines of He was
wounded for our transgressions / He was crushed for our iniquities [Isa.
53.5]), and also that he dies "for" us (i.e., in place of us, on our behalf). As

soon as we stop to think about them, significant cracks seem to open up between these two different senses of *for* as causation and substitution. The idea of humanity as the rightful victim / object of death and the killer are hardly one and the same. Holding both senses together means that we can watch humanity hammer the nails in (in Mel Gibson's far from maverick interpretation of the Passion) without asking what kind of hyper-subject the Human has become if it has the power to so sway—indeed replace—the father's hand. The far less palatable (but more theological) idea that the hand of the Father must (ultimately) hold the nails is pursued by Mark, up to the point where the narrative suddenly breaks off, as if aware of the impossibilities that it is opening up. The gospel tails off, interestingly enough, with the last word "for" (of *gar*).

16. Roemer, *Telling Stories*, 35.

17. Marie-Louise von Franz, *On Dreams and Death* (Boston: Shambhala, 1986), 72; Roemer, *Telling Stories*, 85

18. Roemer, *Telling Stories*, 47.

19. Frederick Sands, "Interview with Carl Jung: Why I Believe in God," *Good Housekeeping* (December 1961), 138–41.

20. For important discussions of the element of torture in the passion see Jennifer Glancy, "Torture: Flesh, Truth and the Fourth Gospel," *Biblical Interpretation* 13, no. 2 (2005): 107–36, and Stephen D. Moore, *God's Gym: Divine Male Bodies of the Bible* (London: Routledge, 1996).

21. Compare Geoffrey Bennington's discussion of the aporia whereby "the necessary possibility of the worst is a positive condition of the (unconditionally demanded) better" in "Deconstruction and Ethics," in Nicholas Royle, ed., *Deconstructions: A User's Guide* (New York: Palgrave, 2000), 64–82.

22. In Leviticus 1 there is no mention of binding, and slaughtering precedes the placing of the pieces of animal on the altar.

23. See, for example, the curiously sanguine gloss of Gordon Wenham: "The OT nowhere speaks of sacrificial animals having their legs bound before the slaughter, and if Isaac had been reluctant to be sacrificed, it would have been easier for Abraham to have cut his throat or stabbed him rather than tie him up first and place him on the altar." Gordon Wenham, *Genesis 16–50* (Waco, Tex.: Word Biblical Commentary, 1994), 115. The implication is that Isaac is an active subject, not an object. For more tangled interpretations of the binding, see for example the Isaacs of *Pesikta Rabbati* or Midrash Tanhuma who, somewhere between subject and object, implore the father to bind tightly because they might kick against their bonds (Ps. R. 40; *Tanh.* on Gen. 22.9; cf. *Midrash Bereshit Rabbati* 55, 90).

24. See note 19.

25. In Rembrandt's *The Angel Preventing Abraham from Sacrificing Isaac* (1653; Hermitage State Museum, St. Petersburg), Isaac lies face up, his face entirely obliterated by his father's hand and his arms tied behind his back. In Caravaggio's *Sacrifice of Isaac* (1603; Uffizi Gallery, Florence), Isaac is held face-down firmly by the neck while his hands are tied behind him.

26. See Lacan's "Introduction to the Names-of-the-Father Seminar" (November 20, 1963), from *Television*, ed. Joan Copjec (New York: Norton, 1990). The edition I am using can be found in *The Postmodern Bible Reader*, ed. David Jobling et al. (Oxford: Blackwell, 2001), 102–16.

27. Wenham, *Genesis 16–50*, 105.

28. Cf. Malcolm Bowie, *Lacan* (London: Fontana Press, 1991), 136. It is an interesting twist that the Abraham who can thus unreservedly answer God's demand is more godlike than the god who demands this of him. Certain Midrashim thrive on our unbelief in this Abraham, not to mention this Isaac, by imagining residual anger or accusation after the event. Even the traditional Jewish reading (proclaimed on Rosh Hashanah and running through the liturgy) can be seen as interpreting Abraham's yes as an extreme, but not unconditional, one. On the basis of what they have (impossibly) given, Abraham and Isaac make ongoing demands for mercy. Paradoxically, God willingly binds himself to Israel's demands through the excessiveness of his original request.

29. The traditional argument is that the *real* (that is, quite well-hidden) purpose of the story is to open the eyes of human beings and teach them that the widely practiced act of human sacrifice is no longer required. The now well-worn (though still not always heard) responses are that the historical evidence for widespread child sacrifice is very thin and that, given that Abraham is *rewarded* for being prepared to kill his son, this is a very poor piece of anti–child sacrifice polemic. It now strikes me that the emphasis on the *covert* lesson of what humanity sees and learns may also, perhaps more importantly, be a way of detracting from the overt emphasis on what God sees (and learns or confirms). The emphasis on human eyes/learning and the distraction of a deeper hidden reading leads us to turn a blind eye (as they say) to the surface sense of the deficiency of divine seeing and knowledge implied in Genesis 22:12.

30. Puns on "to see," "to fear," and "to provide" run throughout the text. The verb translated by the English *to provide* (Gen. 22:8; 14) is the niphal of the verb *to see* (*ra-ah*).

31. This cross-reference to the voracious eye in Ecclesiastes was inspired by a comment by Alicia Ostriker, for which grateful thanks.

32. This is a very crude attempt to gesture in a clause to all that Lacan says about the eye of the other as the zone in which the self recognizes his/her own impotence, as a subject "shorn of his recourse" ("Introduction to the Names-of the Father-Seminar," 106–7).

33. Caravaggio's Isaac is clearly groaning in pain and looks for all the world as if he does not want to be there. Though I stand to be corrected, I cannot recall a similar look on the face of any Jesus on the cross.

34. Bowie, *Lacan*, 29.

35. Brian S. Hook and R. R. Reno, "Abraham and the Problems of Modern Heroism," in *Sacred Text, Secular Times: The Hebrew Bible in the Modern World*, ed. Leonard Jay Greenspoon and Bryan F. LeBeau (Omaha: Creighton University Press, 2000), 135–61. The analogy between this article and Roemer's conception of story is striking, again confirming the sense of Akedah as hyperstory.

36. Auerbach, "Odysseus' Scar," in *Mimesis: The Representation of Reality in Western Literature* (Princeton, N.J.: Princeton University Press, 1991), 3–23; "Die Narbe des Odysseus," *Mimesis: Dargestellte Wirklichkeit in der abendländischen Literatur* (Bern: A. Francke, 1946), 7–30. The popular misreading (in which lacunae become spaces for the readerly imagination) ignores the aspect of extreme "sacrificial poetics." For Auerbach, narrative holes are testimonies to all that has been—and that under these extreme, uncompromising narrative conditions must be—stripped away.

37. The word-set that Auerbach uses to talk about the Akedah links *kneten* (kneading), *knechten* (to subjugate or to oppress), and the related noun *Knechte* (servants). In an image pertinent to our argument here, he reads the Akedah as testimony to the "stern hand of God" (*harten Zugriff Gottes*) "that is ever upon the Old Testament figures" as he "continues to work upon them, bends them and kneads them [*sie biegt und knetet*] . . . without destroying them in essence [*ohne doch sie im Wesen zu zerstören*]" ("Odysseus' Scar," 18; "Die Narbe," 23).

38. Cf. Nietzsche: "This shattering of oneself, this scorn for one's own nature . . . which religions have made so much out of, is actually a very high degree of vanity. . . . Man takes a truly voluptuous pleasure in violating himself by exaggerated demands and then deifying this something in him that is so tyrannically taxing" (*Human, All Too Human* [1878], trans. Marion Faber with Stephen Lehman [Lincoln: University of Nebraska Press, 1984], section 140). Apart from that minor detail about Abraham getting up early

(Gen. 22:3), the text refuses any hook on which to hang fantasies of ecstatic submission. Only in later words and images do we get joyful self-immolation, as when Isaac cries "Father bind me!" or Abraham, disappointed by the arrival of the angel, says, "Please let me give you a little drop of blood, at least."

39. The text goes as far as possible in insisting that we read this as an act of God by leaving us with only one other—extremely perverse—alternative, in which *eros* hangs out with *thanatos* and the intensity / proliferation of life bound to, and achieved through, the intensity of death. If the outcome of the text at least can be read as an (in some sense straightforward) fantasy of the *Ich* ("You Abraham are going to be the Father of a great nation, living on, through your progeny, eternally, across the heavens"), the route by which we get there is counterintuitive in the extreme. Forcing us to choose between an act of God or a perverse love act of Abraham, the text forbids an exegesis in tandem with the dream of the integrated, controlling human subject, according to the models of the logical human (social) sciences. It forces us into the sub- or sur-terrains of psychoanalysis or religion.

40. A notable exception would be Ilana Pardes's *The Biography of Ancient Israel: National Narratives in the Bible* (Berkeley: University of California Press, 2000).

41. As Derrida points out, the promise is necessarily logically unstable, for in order to promise, and ask us to believe the promise, it is necessary that the one who promises might be lying, or joking, or might die before they have a chance to keep it. The figure of Israel can be read as the fragility of the promise (barely) incarnate, never more so when it is in potentia, in the body of Isaac, perched on the altar between the angel / ram and knife.

42. To summarize briefly, at the very moment of the giving of the promise of land, God already tells Abraham that it is full of Canaanites (Gen. 12:1–9), so bringing in an excessive and overwhelming plot complication that counterattacks the land promise from the first. Abraham then journeys into the land only to be driven out of it repeatedly by famine, and by the end of the Abraham saga has managed to gain only a grave-size piece of Canaan, which he has purchased from the Hittites in order to bury his dead wife (Gen. 23). The land-possession saga, never consummated within the bounds of Torah, culminates in the death of Moses who collapses without having ever entered or possessed the land (Deut. 34).

43. In her important book *God, Gender and the Bible* (London: Routledge, 2002), Deborah Sawyer argues that the subject of the Hebrew Bible is characteristically the emasculated male as foil to God as supermale. As one of the first

attempts to explore the implications of divine omnipotence (domination), it is highly relevant to some of the issues we are discussing here.

44. According to the student's bibliography, she is quoting from Jonathan Sacks, *Radical Then, Radical Now: The Legacy of the World's Oldest Religion* (New York: HarperCollins, 2002), 20.

45. See Sherwood, "Prophetic Scatology: Prophecy and the Art of Sensation," in *In Search of the Present: The Bible Through Cultural Studies,* ed. Stephen D. Moore (Atlanta: Scholars Press, 2000), 183–224, and "'Darke Texts Needs Notes': On Prophetic Poetry, John Donne and the Baroque," *Journal for the Study of the Old Testament* 27, no. 1 (2002): 47–74.

46. Judith Butler, *Bodies That Matter: On the Discursive Limits of "Sex"* (New York: Routledge, 1993), 90–91.

47. Cited without reference in Roemer, *Telling Stories,* 85.

48. Of course there are theological models that can countenance such a lower-case god. But in Judaism and Christianity, God is author and creator with a world to remake otherwise and (which is to say the same thing) a story to tell.

49. Emphatically not a spokes*person.* Culturally, the Bible speaks in the solid, bass notes of a (true) male voice; it is emphatically not female, and emphatically not queer.

50. Even the rabbis, on whom I usually rely for this kind of thing, did not notice this one.

51. For sacrifice as "birth done better," see Nancy Jay, *Throughout Your Genera-tions Forever: Sacrifice, Religion, and Paternity* (Chicago: University of Chicago Press, 1992), xiii and throughout. Jay argues that, just as still-sacrificing cul-tures seem, without exception, to exclude all potentially childbearing women (in some cases admitting only old women and prepubescent girls), so the biblical (or biblically inspired) sacrifice scenes are a remedy for, and symbolic inflation of, natural reproduction. In a way that helps us under-stand those curious male genealogies in Genesis, strung out like male um-bilical cords between the generations, she argues that the purpose of sacrifice is to socially legitimate the patrilineage and to confirm lines of descent through fathers and sons. On the symbolic compulsion that forces biblical mothers to be barren see Esther Fuchs's important essay "The Lit-erary Characterisation of Mothers and Sexual Politics in the Hebrew Bible," in *Women in the Hebrew Bible,* ed. Alice Bach (London: Routledge, 1999), 127–39.

52. Demurely registering the problem, translators often render this vaguely, as God *dealt with* Sarah (so NRSV).

53. For a wonderful description of the "phantasmagorical" and "alien" body of Mary, see Marcella Althaus-Reid, *Indecent Theology: Theological Perversions in Sex, Gender and Politics* (New York: Routledge, 2001), esp. 39, 71. For a now-classic discussion of the shift of symbolic freight from birth to death, see Grace Jantzen, *Becoming Divine: Towards a Feminist Philosophy of Religion* (Manchester: Manchester University Press, 1998).

54. At the time of writing this paper, I was also cowriting an SBL presentation with Stephen Moore. The observation about the gush of eucharistic blood and baptismal water comes from that discussion.

55. Those quarters, of course are not biblical commentary nor (at least self-consciously) mainstream Christian theology. Instead, see Karmen MacKendrick, *Counterpleasures* (Albany: State University of New York Press, 1999), esp. 65–85; Anita Phillips, *A Defence of Masochism* (London: Faber and Faber, 1998), 59, 135–64.

56. Abraham J. Heschel, *The Prophets* (New York: Harper & Row, 1969), 50. As should become clear, I mean to respectfully point to the erotics of submission, rather than to mock submission or make a cheap joke at religion's expense.

57. I am grateful to Mark Brummitt for pointing me in the direction of this Christian chorus. Should you want to check it (or sing it) you can find it in *Songs of Fellowship*, no. 510. For a more self-conscious meditation on this passage see Ken Stone, "'You seduced me, You overpowered me, and you prevailed': Religious Experience and Homoerotic Sadomasochism in Jeremiah," in *Patriarchs, Prophets, and Other Villains*, ed. Lisa Isherwood (London: Equinox, 2006). Compare also Richard Kearney's allusion in this volume to Donne's "Batter My Heart," which, though English critics in general seem to have missed it, has obvious resonances with Jer. 20.7.

58. For a particularly lucid discussion of how Freud is begging to be read beyond Freud see MacKendrick, *Counterpleasures*, 6–11.

59. Ibid., 151.

60. These observations grew from the discussion at Drew. I am grateful—not least for the opportunity to disseminate responsibility around the table.

61. See Elaine Scarry, *The Body in Pain: The Making and Unmaking of the World* (New York: Oxford University Press, 1985).

62. For a recent interpretative history of the Song of Songs, far more nuanced than the brutal reduction I'm giving here, see Virginia Burrus and Stephen

D. Moore, "Unsafe Sex: Feminism, Pornography and the Song of Songs," *Biblical Interpretation* 11, no. 1 (2003): 24–52.

63. See, for example, Tod Linafelt, "Biblical Love Poetry (. . . and God)," *Journal of the American Academy of Religion* 70, no. 2 (1998): 323–45; Roland Boer, "Night Sprinkle(s): Pornography and the Song of Songs," in *Knockin' on Heaven's Door: The Bible and Popular Culture* (New York: Routledge, 1999), 53–70. Gregory of Nyssa is added into the mix in Burrus and Moore, "Unsafe Sex," 45–47.

64. MacKendrick, *Counterpleasures*, 126.

65. For a classic and still-important analysis of the Song and the Prophets as antithetical spaces, see Fokkelien van Dijk-Hemmes, "The Imagination of Power and the Power of Imagination: An Intertextual Analysis of Two Biblical Love Songs: The Song of Songs and Hosea 2," *Journal for the Study of the Old Testament* 44 (1989): 75–88.

66. See Linafelt, "Biblical Love Poetry," 325. See also Linafelt, "The Arithmetic of Eros," *Interpretation* 59 (2005): 244–59. Lest I conscript Linafelt into my argument too easily, I quote him in full: "Let me be clear that I am not saying that sexual desire is somehow magnified by violence, or that this passage is somehow to be understood as an ancient Israelite version of sadomasochistic practices. Rather, the watchmen are one of the tropes put in the mouth of the speaker by the poet in order to represent what it feels like to discover that one's nephesh has 'gone out,' that one has been ravished by desire—and that feeling, at this moment in the poetry at least, is the feeling of vulnerability, violation, assault."

67. Burrus and Moore, "Unsafe Sex," 41.

68. First introduced to the arena of biblical studies by feminist scholars back in the 1970s, the question of divine violence is now integrated to the point where it can feasibly be the topic of an SBL presidential address. See John J. Collins, *Does the Bible Justify Violence?* (Minneapolis: Fortress, 2004).

69. I do not mean to claim that there are no meeting points between biblical religion and the modern discourse of rights—just that they are overemphasized, while the obvious collision points between theocracy and democracy tend to remain in the shadows.

70. For discussion of how commentators identify, *to a man*, with God, rather than taking up the bowed addressee position of Gomer-Israel, see Sherwood, *The Prostitute and the Prophet* (London: Continuum, 2004), 262. Without wanting to make a cheap, snide point about a generous review, I find it interesting that Paul J. Kissling sees my book as particularly valuable for

424 | NOTES TO PAGES 187-190

those who "value autonomy as among our most cherished ideals" (citing my own comments on 302), as if to imply that there is a whole group who do not see autonomy as so important (see Kissling's review in *Review of Biblical Literature*, 15 January 1998). The implication—that there are those who are more open to embracing radical biblical heteronomy—may be true in theory, but it is not (yet?) demonstrated in readings of the text.

71. For an unequivocal rejection see, for example, Carol Delaney, *Abraham on Trial* (Princeton, N.J.: Princeton University Press, 1998). If this paper allows itself to be seen, simplistically, as a postfeminist alternative to that position, it will have failed. A less overt rejection—that is a rejection nonetheless—is implied by the now traditional reading that places all the focus on the ram and the angel, and reads the story as *opposed* to sacrifice and Isaac's suffering. In this reading the text becomes a modern manifesto advocating *care* of the self.

72. In biblical studies thus far I hear only Moore and Burrus, "Unsafe Sex," and, in a very different style, various chapters in Boer's *Knockin' on Heaven's Door*. Unlike Boer, Burrus and Moore are anxious to work through the relationship between feminism and sadomasochism in ways that ensure that they cannot come out looking like simple alternatives, even in this relatively untheorized space.

73. Frank Browning, *The Culture of Desire: Paradox and Perversity in Gay Lives Today* (New York: Crown, 1993), 104, cit. MacKendrick, *Counterpleasures*, 122.

74. See Phillips, *A Defence of Masochism*, 49–55. I prefer this definition to Mac-Kendrick's bad girl feminism, which seems to momentarily trespass against her own warnings about being "too impressed with our own transgressivity," and being "radical, subversive, and unspeakably cool" (*Counterpleasures*, 16; cf. 10–12).

75. Phillips, *A Defence of Masochism*, 4.

76. See, for example, *Counterpleasures* 4, 19, 57. Note particularly how MacKendrick distinguishes what she is doing from the hypersovereign subject of a certain kind of "postmodernism" (12).

77. Certain boundary-breaking hypersubjects strike me as very similar to the wall-vaulting David of 2 Sam 22.30. For the popular preference for deconstruction as an active verb to Derrida's definitions of deconstruction as a contestation of *pouvoir* as power / being able, see the discussion in Sherwood and Hart, "Other Testaments," in *Derrida and Religion: Other Testaments* (New York: Routledge, 2004).

78. Phillips, *A Defence of Masochism*, 136.

79. My point here is by no means to offer an *alternative* to such theologies or in any way to qualify their importance. Rather, acts of human-sexual mimicry (by which I emphatically do not mean straight performance and consolidation) of that which we try to approach (philosophically and theologically) through ideas of transcendence, may also imply some stubborn content of "God" that yet remains resistant to translation to the horizontal and the humane.

80. For Judaism, of course, the Old Testament is not old in the sense that it has a new one, but Oral Torah / Mishnah is an adaptation, masked as repetition, of that which is already old. Torah without repetition/expansion/clarification is assumed to be a dangerous concept (hence the outsider status of the Karaites, who adhered only to Written Torah).

81. Compare Burrus and Moore: "At issue here is the potential, indeed the propensity, of erotic fantasy not merely to resemble, but also dissemble, and thereby reassemble, reality, engaging in a transgressive mimicry, rather than a compliant mimesis" ("Unsafe Sex," 48).

82. Even as I use the term I cannot help noting in passing how even the curiously euphemistic term *practitioner*—implying a skill set or sexual CV item—turns this into something at which one is accomplished or which one does.

83. When reading OT/Tanakh for the first time, first-year religion and Bible students often conclude that to be an Israelite/Judean (which they dangerously equate with being a contemporary Jew) is to be a victim or an object. It is striking how often—though the curriculum hardly leads them there—first attempts to translate biblical theology into modern terms come out as accusations of masochism in the sense of a willing (unhealthy) embrace of suffering for God.

84. For example, several Midrashim describe how God knocked on the door of other nations and sought consent to the gift of Torah, but was refused (e.g., *Pesikta Rabbati* 21, *Sifre Deut*, 343). Only Israel was risk-inclined enough to take the Torah on, and to do so in a way that involved obeying/doing before hearing/understanding *(B. Shab* 88a). From an early stage, the Song of Songs was bound up with the Sinai event partly to create mutuality from nonreciprocity. But these traditions coexist with traditions that, for example, expand the "And they stood under [*tahat*; txt] the mount" (Exod. 19.17) as "This verse implies that the Holy One overturned the mountain upon them, like an inverted cask, and said to them: If you accept the Torah, it is well; if not, your grave will be right here" (*B. Shab* 88a; *Avod. Zar.* 2b).

85. For the binding/restraining the hand of God, see for example the midrashic angels who protest against God's anomalous, outsider, out-Torah act, who melt the knife with their tears, or take Isaac off to Eden-hospital for three years for recuperation (*Pes R.* 40, *Gen. R. Vayera* 56.7; *Midrash haGadol* on Gen. 22.19). The death of Sarah and the struggles of Isaac against his binding are also frequently used to criticize an act of demanded not-withholding that has gone too far. For further discussion see Sherwood, "Textual Carcasses and Isaac's Scar: What Jewish Interpretation Makes of the Violence that Almost Takes Place on Mount Moriah," in *Sanctified Aggression: Legacies of Biblical and Post-Biblical Vocabularies of Violence*, ed. Jonneke Bekkenkamp and Sherwood (London: Continuum, 2004), 22–43.

86. For famous examples of God submitting to the greater authority of Torah, see the image of God putting on tefillin and studying in the Heavenly Academy (*B. Berakhot* 6a and 7a), and, most famously, the case of the oven of Achnai, in which God, bested by the majority and by Torah, concedes (laughing?) "My children have defeated me" (*B. Bava Metzia* 59b).

87. For now classic descriptions of the masochistic textual pleasures of Midrash (which are never labeled as such) see, for example, Jankelevitch, "You must entangle [note not disentangle] the inextricable and only ever stop when it becomes impossible to go any further . . . you leave [the safety of] your starting point behind and the starting point ends up by refuting the finishing point"; *Quelque part dans l'inacheve* (Paris: Gallimard, 1978), 18–19.

88. Cf. MacKendrick, *Counterpleasures*, 33.

89. David Stern, "Imitatio Hominis: Anthropomorphism and the Character(s) of God in Rabbinic Literature," *Prooftexts* 12 (1992): 151–74. For classic rabbinic articulations of the bound and trapped (lowercase?) god, see *Eikah Rabbah*. For biblical accusations that God is not fulfilling his side of the contract, see Lamentations and the so-called psalms of complaint. See particularly the accusation that God is sleeping too much and not making his power actively felt. For early hints of divine abjection (role-switch) see Micah 1.8–9 and the discussion in Timothy K. Beal, "The System and the Speaking Subject in the Hebrew Bible: Reading for Divine Abjection," *Biblical Interpretation* 2, no. 2 (1994): 171–89.

90. Guy Baldwin, "Radical Rite," in *Ritual Sex*, ed. David Aaron Clark and Tristan Taormino (New York: Rhinoceros Books, 1996), 126; cited in MacKendrick, *Counterpleasures*, 66.

91. MacKendrick, *Counterpleasures*, 129; italics mine.

PRAYING IS JOYING: MUSINGS ON LOVE IN EVAGRIUS PONTICUS | VIRGINIA BURRUS

1. Translations generally follow John Eudes Bamberger, trans., *Evagrius Ponticus: The Praktikos, Chapters on Prayer* (Kalamazoo, Mich.: Cistercian Publications, 1981). The Greek text is found in MPG 79 under the works of Nilus of Sinai.

2. Cf. Luke 5:5.

3. Cf. John 21:11.

4. On the doubled address of prayer—or rather of the supplement of prayer qua writing—cf. Derrida's reading of Dionysius's *Mystical Theology*: "The one who asks to be led by God turns for an instant toward another addressee, in order to lead him in turn"; Jacques Derrida, "How to Avoid Speaking: Denials," in *Derrida and Negative Theology*, ed. Harold Coward and Toby Foshay (Albany: State University of New York Press, 1992), 117.

5. The controversial nature of Evagrius's embrace of apatheia within ancient Christian ascetic circles can be measured by, e.g., Jerome's Epistle 133.1: "To maintain such a doctrine is to take man's nature from him, to forget that he is constituted of body as well as soul, to substitute mere wishes for sound teaching." In this letter, Jerome brings together his critique of the "Origenist" Rufinus (possibly the recipient of Evagrius's *Chapters on Prayer*) with his denunciation of the teachings of Pelagius. Regarding the convergence of Origenist and Pelagian teachings in Jerome's heresiological construction, see the excellent account of Elizabeth A. Clark, *The Origenist Controversy: The Cultural Construction of an Early Christian Debate* (Princeton, N.J.: Princeton University Press, 1992), 221–27. Robert Somos, "Origen, Evagrius Ponticus and the Ideal of Impassibility," in *Origeniana Semptima*, ed. W. A. Bienert and U. Kuuauhneweg (Leuven: Leuven University Press, 1999), 365–73, makes a case (against prior scholarly consensus) for Evagrius's debts to Origen's understanding of apatheia. Jeremy Driscoll, "*Apatheia* and Purity of Heart in Evagrius Ponticus," in *Purity of Heart in Early Ascetic and Monastic Literature: Essays in Honor of Juana Raasch, O.S.B.*, ed. Harriet A. Luckman and Linda Kulzer (Collegeville, Minn.: Liturgical Press, 1999), 141–59, suggests that language of "apatheia" and "purity of heart" is used by Evagrius interchangeably, an overlooked fact that partly explains John Cassian's prominent use of the latter terminology.

6. Peter Brown, *The Body and Society: Men, Women, and Sexual Renunciation in Early Christianity* (New York: Columbia University Press, 1988), 406, notes that for the ancient ascetic, "sexuality . . . lacked a distinctive flavor,"

whereas Augustine "could no longer regard sexual desire as no more than one irritant among so many others. It edged itself forward, in his thought, with ever-increasing circumstantiality." The contrast that Brown here insightfully draws should not, however, obscure the importance of sexual temptation in the writings of many "ascetics."

7. As Karmen MacKendrick, *Counterpleasures* (Albany: SUNY Press, 1999), 108, puts it, pain and restraint "provide both active and mnemonic techniques of subversion. . . . They teach us that our flesh may surpass our subjectivity, that we are stronger and more powerful than our selves."

8. Jean-Luc Nancy, *The Inoperative Community*, ed. Peter Connor (Minneapolis: University of Minnesota Press, 1991), 106.

9. A recent treatment of the topic, negotiating the apparent tension in Evagrius's thought between the concept of "imageless prayer" and his incarnational and scriptural piety, is offered by Columba Stewart, "Imageless Prayer and the Theological Vision of Evagrius Ponticus," *Journal of Early Christian Studies* 9, no. 2 (2001): 173–204.

10. See Clark, *The Origenist Controversy*, 58–60.

11. I hasten to add that such a "pure" language is always threatened by impure thoughts. The problems attending the particular masculinist nomenclature of trinitarian address are of central concern in my *"Begotten, not Made": Conceiving Manhood in Late Antiquity* (Palo Alto: Stanford University Press, 2000).

12. Derrida nuances the point: Theology emerges as the supplement of prayer. "If there were a purely pure experience of prayer, would one need religion and affirmative or negative theologies? Would one need a supplement of prayer? But if there were no supplement, if quotation did not bend prayer, if prayer did not bend, if it did not submit to writing, would a theology be possible? Would a theology be possible?" (Derrida, "How to Avoid Speaking," 131).

13. Nancy, *Inoperative Community*, 119.

14. Ibid., 150.

15. Ibid., 97.

16. Cf. Derrida's reading of Dionysus, in which "the place" is located "where the two modes [of apophatic and symbolic inscription] cross—such that, properly speaking, the crossing itself . . . belongs to neither of the two modes and doubtless even precedes their distribution." He adds, "God is not simply His place; He is not even in His most holy places. He is not and He does not take place, or rather He is and takes place, but without Being

and without place, without being His place" (Derrida, "How to Avoid Speaking," 94, 96).

17. Nancy, *Inoperative Community*, 97.

18. Ibid., 150.

19. In a complex passage in "Of Divine Places," Nancy suggests that "in order to speak of God, we have to speak of something other than the Other, the Abstruse, and their infinite remoteness (if indeed it is still a matter of 'speaking of something'). . . . In baptizing our abysses with the name of God, we are guilty of at least two errors or two incoherencies: we fill in the abysses by attributing a bottom to them, and we blaspheme (in the true sense of the word) the name of God by making it the name of some*thing*" (Nancy, *Inoperative Community*, 113).

20. Karmen MacKendrick, *Immemorial Silence* (Albany: SUNY Press, 2001), 109.

21. Far juicier, for example, are the hagiographical writings that are the focus of my *The Sex Lives of Saints: An Erotics of Ancient Hagiography* (Philadelphia: University of Pennsylvania Press, 2004).

22. Richard Rambuss, *Closet Devotions* (Durham, N.C.: Duke University Press, 1998).

23. Nancy, *Inoperative Community*, 90.

24. Burrus, *Sex Lives of Saints*, 1–18.

25. Michel Foucault, "About the Beginning of the Hermeneutics of the Self," in *Religion and Culture: Michel Foucault*, ed. Jeremy R. Carrette (New York: Routledge, 1999), 175–81.

26. "Postmodern" is, of course, not Foucault's language, nor is it language with which I am always comfortable. Nonetheless, it does helpfully reference broad schema of historical periodization that give shape to the "genealogical" project.

27. Foucault's fascination with "sacrifice" owes much to Georges Bataille's study of eroticism; see his "A Preface to Transgression," in Carrette, *Religion and Culture*, 57–71. Nancy's "Of Divine Places" likewise enters into dialogue with Bataille at crucial points. On the engagements of both Foucault and Nancy with Bataille's "atheological" project, see the nuanced study of Laurens ten Kate, "The Gift of Loss: A Study of the Fugitive God in Bataille's Atheology, with References to Jean-Luc Nancy," in *Flight of the Gods: Philosophical Perspectives on Negative Theology*, ed. Ilse N. Bullhof and Laurens ten Kate (New York: Fordham University Press, 2000), 250–92.

28. Mark D. Jordan, *The Ethics of Sex* (Oxford: Blackwell, 2002), 165, 168. Note that Graham Ward in particular has stridently rejected the analogy with contemporary theories and practices of sadomasochism, as part of his

broader rejection of poststructuralist discourses of eroticism, and "postmodern secularity" more generally, as "pathological"; see his "Suffering and Incarnation," in *Postmodern Theology*, ed. Graham Ward (Oxford: Blackwell, 2001), 192–208. Where I differ from Ward is less in his own constructive theology of eros—which I find in many respects compatible with Nancy's philosophy of eros—than in his generalizations regarding poststructuralist thought.

29. Nancy, *Inoperative Community*, 148.

30. Ibid, 101–102.

CARTHAGE DIDN'T BURN HOT ENOUGH: SAINT AUGUSTINE'S DIVINE SEDUCTION | KARMEN MACKENDRICK

1. Augustine, *Confessions*, trans. Henry Chadwick (Oxford: Oxford University Press, 1991), II.ii.2.

2. Ibid., II.iii.8. In contrast, note the use of "convert" in VI.iv.5: "Even if it was not yet evident that the Church taught the truth, yet she did not teach the things of which I harshly accused her. So I was confused with shame. I was being turned around (*itaque confundebar et convertebar*). And I was glad, my God, that your one Church, the body of your only Son in which on me as an infant Christ's name was put, did not hold infantile follies."

3. Alicia Ostriker, "Anne Sexton and the Seduction of the Audience," in *Seduction and Theory: Readings of Gender, Representation and Rhetoric*, ed. Dianne Hunter (Chicago: University of Illinois Press, 1989), 154–55.

4. Pamela Haag, *Consent: Sexual Rights and the Transformation of American Liberalism* (Ithaca, N.Y.: Cornell University Press, 1999), 181. Haag goes on to note, "At the same time, however, sexual 'rights'—and rights discourse generally—are tremendously powerful and patently important and foundational concepts in liberal culture"; Ibid.

5. Most extensively in Karmen MacKendrick, *Counterpleasures* (Albany: SUNY Press, 1999).

6. Augustine, *Confessions*, X.vi.

7. Ibid., X.xxix.40. See also: "For my part, I carry out your command by actions and words; but I discharge it under the protection of your wings (Ps. 16:8, 35:8). It would be a far too perilous responsibility unless under your wings my soul were submissive to you." X.iv.6.

8. Ibid., X.xxxv.56.

9. Ibid., X.xxxi.47.

10. Ibid., X.xxxiii.49–50.

11. Ibid., X.xxiv.51–52.

12. Ibid., VII.xvii.23.

13. Ibid., X.vi.9.

14. One possible exception is book VIII, in the famous "Take and read" episode that marks the moment of his conversion. Even here, however, we must bear in mind Augustine's own warnings, from books XII and XIII, against overly literal readings; something tells him to take and read, but this does not make it a "fact" that he hears voices.

15. Ibid., VII.xvii.23.

16. Gloria Steinem, "Erotica vs. Pornography," in *Transforming a Rape Culture*, ed. E. Buchwald et al. (Minneapolis: Milkweed Editions, 1993), 41.

17. "Pornography is the graphic sexually explicit subordination of women through pictures and/or words that also includes one or more of the following: (i) women are presented dehumanized as sexual objects, things or commodities; or (ii) women are presented as sexual objects who enjoy pain or humiliation; or (iii) women are presented as sexual objects who experience sexual pleasure in being raped; or (iv) women are presented as sexual objects tied up or cut up or mutilated or bruised or physically hurt; or (v) women are presented in postures or positions of sexual submission, servility, or display; or (vi) women's body parts—including but not limited to vaginas, breasts, or buttocks—are exhibited such that women are reduced to those parts; or (vii) women are presented as whores by nature; or (viii) women are presented being penetrated by objects or animals; or (ix) woman are presented in scenarios of degradation, injury, torture, shown as filthy or inferior, bleeding, bruised, or hurt in a context that makes these conditions sexual.

    The use of men, children, or transsexuals in the place of women in [the paragraph] above is also pornography." http://www.nostatusquo.com/ACLU/dworkin/other/ordinance/newday/T2c.htm.

18. Thus, perhaps, the frequent and often comic censoring of naughty bits, notable at least since the 1870s compilation of the "secret" exhibits of the British Museum. See Walter Kendrick, *The Secret Museum: Pornography in Modern Culture* (New York: Penguin Books, 1987).

19. Jean Baudrillard, *Seduction*, trans. Brian Singer (New York: St. Martin's Press, 1991), 2–4.

20. Peg Miller and Nancy Biele, "Twenty Years Later: The Unfinished Revolution," in *Transforming a Rape Culture*, 59.

21. Haag, *Consent*, 31. "The postbellum inflection of seduction is a violence against an 'ordinary' individual's contract, rather than a violation of extraordinary female character. Most states, to be sure, stipulated in criminalization that seduction could only occur under a 'promise of marriage,' such that criminal seduction from the start encompassed aspects of contractual violation or fraud—but those aspects were often grace notes in earlier trials that focused on chastity and female character more energetically than on the specific relation between the 'beautiful victim' and the seducer."

22. Augustine, *Confessions*, X.vi.8.

23. Ibid., X.xxvii.38.

24. Ibid., I.i.1.

25. Ibid., III.iv.8.

26. Ibid., XIII.ix.10. See also: "What is the light which shines right through me and strikes my heart without hurting? It fills me with terror and burning Love: with terror inasmuch as I am utterly other than it, with burning love in that I am akin to it." XI.viii.10.

27. Ibid., I.v.5; also XIII.viii.9.

28. Ibid.

29. Jane Gallop, *The Daughter's Seduction: Feminism and Psychoanalysis* (Ithaca, N.Y.: Cornell University Press, 1982), 28. Citation from Jacques Lacan, *Écrits* (Éditions du Seuil, 1966).

30. Ibid., 30.

31. Susan David Bernstein, "Confessing Lacan," in *Seduction and Theory: Readings of Gender, Representation and Rhetoric*, ed. Dianne Hunter (Champaign: University of Illinois Press, 1989), 203.

32. Jacques Lacan, "The Subversion of the Subject and the Dialectic of Desire in the Freudian Unconscious," in *Écrits*, 804, cited in Gallop, 11. Lacan here is specifically concerned with desire's inarticulability in the ethical, but I suspect that there is to this metonymic urge something more fundamentally inarticulable.

33. Bernstein, "Confessing Lacan," 204.

34. Baudrillard, *Seduction*, 142.

35. Augustine, *Confessions*, X.ixxix.39.

AMERICAN TRANSCENDENTALISM'S EROTIC AQUATECTURE | ROBERT S. CORRINGTON

1. Ralph Waldo Emerson, *Emerson: Essays and Lectures*, ed. Joel Porte (New York: Library of America, 1983), 119.

2. Ibid., 546.

"SHE TALKS TOO MUCH": MAGDALENE MEDITATIONS | CATHERINE KELLER

This essay was first delivered as a public lecture in a conference on Mary Magdalene organized by the Rice University Rockwell Series, with publication also intended. I am grateful to Rice, Rockwell, and Continuum Press for permission to publish this paper here. Let me also thank my research assistant Nick Stepp for his editorial help on this chapter and the afterword.

1. *Pistis Sophia* I.17. English translation, *Pistis Sophia*, ed. Carl Schmidt, trans. Violet MacDermot (Leiden: E. J. Brill, 1978), 53. I have replaced "thou" with "you" in the translation.

2. Ibid., I.34; Schmidt and MacDermot, 113.

3. Ibid.

4. Karen L. King, *The Gospel of Mary of Magdala: Jesus and the First Woman Apostle* (Santa Rosa, Calif.: Polebridge Press, 2003), 7.

5. Jane Schaberg, *The Resurrection of Mary Magdalen: Legends, Apocrypha, and the Christian Testament* (New York: Continuum, 2002), 14–17. Schaberg offers superb recapitulations of the relevant scholarship, including the feminist revisionist contributions, as well as her own reconstruction. As this volume goes to press, even *Ms. Magazine* has joined the magdalogical moment, with an article by Schaberg and Melanie Johnson-DeBaufre entitled "There's Something about Mary Magdalene" (Spring 2006).

6. King, *The Gospel of Mary of Magdala*, 3.

7. Susan Haskins, *Mary Magdalene: Myth and Metaphor* (New York: Riverhead Books, 1993), 5. Haskins's book is the most complete source of Magdalene traditions from antiquity to the present.

8. Schaberg, *The Resurrection of Mary Magdalene,* 350.

9. Ibid., 203.

10. Esther de Boer, *Mary Magdalene: Beyond the Myth*, trans. John Bowden (Harrisburg, Pa.: Trinity Press International, 1997), 56.

11. *Pistis Sophia* II.72; Schmidt and MacDermot, 325.

12. King, *The Gospel of Mary of Magdala*, 15.

13. Ibid., 17.

14. Ibid., 3.

15. P.-M. Guillaume, "Ste. Marie-Madeleine," *Dictionnaire de spiritualité ascétique et mystique: Doctrine et histoire*, ed. Marcel Viller et al., vol. 10 (Paris: Beauchesne, 1977), col. 565.

16. Pamela Thimmes, "Memory and Re-Vision: Mary Magdalene Research Since 1975," *Currents in Research: Biblical Studies* 6 (1998): 214.

17. The Gospel of Philip (II.3), in *The Nag Hammadi Library*, ed. James M. Robinson (San Francisco: Harper & Row, 1977), 139.

18. Robert M. Price, "Mary Magdalene: Gnostic Apostle?" *Grail* 6, no. 2 (1997): 59.

19. Gregory the Great, Homily 33, *Patrologia Latina* 76, col. 1239.

20. Jane Schaberg, "How Mary Magdalene Became a Whore," *Bible Review* 8 (1992): 37.

21. Rosemary Radford Ruether, *Women-Church: Theology and Practice of Feminist Liturgical Communities* (San Francisco: Harper & Row, 1985), 43 note 1. See also Rosemary Radford Ruether, *Womanguides: Readings Toward a Feminist Theology* (Boston: Beacon Press, 1985), 177–78.

22. Elizabeth Schussler Fiorenza, *In Memory of Her: A Feminist Theological Reconstruction of Christian Origins* (London: Herder & Herder, 1983), 60.

23. Elaine Pagels, *The Gnostic Gospels* (New York: Random House, 1979), 60–68.

24. Virginia Burrus, "The Heretical Woman as Symbol in Alexander, Athanasius, Epiphanius, and Jerome," *Harvard Theological Review* 84 (1991): 232.

25. The description of Mary Magdalene at Jesus' tomb is perhaps the most erotic passage in all of Gregory's oeuvre. From Gregory's "Gospel Homily," 25. B. McGinn, *The Presence of God: A History of Western Christian Mysticism* (New York: Crossroad, 1992), 2:61.

26. The tradition of the Song of Songs is exhibiting ever more queer potential. See Virginia Burrus and Stephen Moore, "Performing Sadomasochism in the Song of Songs," *Women & Performance: A Journal of Feminist Theory* 13, no. 1 (2002): 25.

27. Marcella Althaus-Reid, *Indecent Theology* (New York: Routledge, 2001), 25.

28. Virginia Burrus, *The Sex Lives of Saints: An Erotics of Ancient Hagiography* (Philadelphia: University of Pennsylvania Press, 2004), 162.

29. Amy Hollywood, *Sensible Ecstasy: Mysticism, Sexual Difference, and the Demands of History* (Chicago: University of Chicago Press, 2002), 278.

30. Mayra Rivera, *The Touch of Transcendence* (Louisville, Ky.: Westminster John Knox Press, 2006).

31. Luce Irigaray, *Sexes and Genealogies*, trans. Gillian C. Gill (New York: Columbia University Press, 1993), 68.

32. Emmanuel Levinas, *Totality and Infinity: An Essay on Exteriority*, trans. A. Lingis (Pittsburgh: Duquesne University Press, 1969), 50.

33. Edith Wyschograd, in John Milbank, Graham Ward, and Edith Wyschograd, eds., *Theological Perspectives on God and Beauty* (Philadelphia: Trinity Press International, 2003).

34. King, *The Gospel of Mary Magdala*, 13.

35. Jean-Luc Nancy, *Being Singular-Plural* (Stanford, Calif.: Stanford University Press, 2000), 3.
36. King, *The Gospel of Mary Magdala*, 45.
37. Or it may be, as King suggests, a belief that the self is its "spirit-infused soul," and not its matter, which will dissolve in the end along with our material actions. "Like adultery, sin joins together what should not be mixed: in this case, material and spiritual natures" (King, *The Gospel of Mary Magdala*, 50). This would be the predictable Gnostic dualism of matter and spirit.
38. Alfred North Whitehead, *Science and the Modern World* (New York: Macmillan, 1925), 91.
39. Indeed, it does not divinize the All as such (as the Magdalene texts do not seem to do, either), but rather articulates a panentheism of All in God. God is, then, an infinite medium by and in which all are redistributed—flung in utter fragmentarity—into each other. I have elsewhere discussed this process panentheism in relation to apophatic mystical traditions in which the interrelationship of all creatures is drawn into the mutual immanence and transcendence of God and the world. See Catherine Keller, *Face of the Deep: A Theology of Becoming* (New York: Routledge, 2003), esp. Part IV.
40. "The Thunder, Perfect Mind," intro. and trans. George W. McRae, in Robinson, *The Nag Hammadi Library*, 271–76.

ETHICAL DESIRES: TOWARD A THEOLOGY OF RELATIONAL TRANSCENDENCE | MAYRA RIVERA

1. Luce Irigaray, "Each Transcendent to the Other," in *To Be Two* (New York: Routledge, 2001).
2. Ibid., 86.
3. Ibid.
4. Ibid., 88.
5. Luce Irigaray, *An Ethics of Sexual Difference* (New York: Cornell University Press, 1993), 12, 17.
6. Luce Irigaray, *I Love to You: Sketch of a Possible Felicity in History*, trans. Alison Martin (New York and London: Routledge, 1996), 104.
7. Irigaray, *An Ethics of Sexual Difference*, 17.
8. *An Ethics of Sexual Difference* closes with an essay on Levinas, but his thought is throughout the volume, not least in its title. Irigaray refuses to be described as a disciple of Levinas, however. In fact she explains that when she "sought dialogue with Levinas" through her reading of his texts and the publication of "The Fecundity of Caress," "each time, it was a failure";

Luce Irigaray, "What Other Are We Talking About?" in *Encounters with Levinas*, ed. Thomas Trezise (New Haven: Yale University Press, 2004), 68.

9. Emmanuel Levinas, *Totality and Infinity: An Essay on Exteriority* (Pittsburgh: Duquesne University Press, 1969), 43.

10. Ibid., 41.

11. Derrida, "Violence and Metaphysics," 92.

12. Levinas, *Totality and Infinity*, 34.

13. The structure of this outward moving ethics is replayed in the unreturnability of the gift as described by Derrida.

14. Levinas, *Totality and Infinity*, 254.

15. Ibid., 39.

16. Levinas's depiction of the feminine has been the subject of much feminist scholarship. See, for instance, Tina Chanter, ed., *Feminist Interpretations of Emmanuel Levinas: Re-Reading the Canon* (University Park: Pennsylvania State University, 2001); Stella Sandford, *The Metaphysics of Love: Gender and Transcendence in Levinas* (New Brunswick, N.J.: Athlone, 2000); Claire Elise Katz, *Levinas, Judaism, and the Feminine: The Silent Footsteps of Rebecca*, ed. Merold Westphal (Bloomington: Indiana University Press, 2003).

17. An appreciative note on the distinction between erotic love and ethical love frames, for instance, Claire Elise Katz's insightful reading of Levinas's portrayal of the feminine against the backdrop of Jewish thought (Katz, *Levinas, Judaism, and the Feminine*).

18. Emmanuel Levinas, *Nine Talmudic Readings*, trans. Annette Aronowicz (Bloomington: Indiana University Press, 1990), 76. Significantly, the images of creation over a reviled chaos are evoked here. For an assessment of the influence and ethical repercussions of this theological trope, see Catherine Keller, *Face of the Deep: A Theology of Becoming* (London and New York: Routledge, 2003).

19. Levinas, *Nine Talmudic Readings*, 76. Significantly, the images of creation over a reviled chaos are evoked here. For an assessment of the influence and ethical repercussions of this theological trope see Keller, *Face of the Deep*.

20. Levinas, *Totality and Infinity*, 264.

21. Levinas, *Nine Talmudic Readings*, 76.

22. Diane Perpich, "From the Caress to the Word: Transcendence and the Feminine in the Philosophy of Emmanuel Levinas," in *Feminist Interpretations of Emmanuel Levinas*, ed. Tina Chanter (University Park: Pennsylvania State University Press, 2001), 44.

23. Luce Irigaray, *The Way of Love*, trans. Heidi Bostic and Stephen Pluhácek (New York: Continuum, 2002), 131; italics added.

24. Irigaray, *An Ethics of Sexual Difference*, 193.

25. Irigaray remarks that the world of the womb "is not to be confused with her. It is destroyed forever at birth and it is impossible ever to return to it. All kinds of veils may claim to take its place, seek to repeat it, but there can be no return to that first dwelling place"; Luce Irigaray, *Sexes and Genealogies* (New York: Columbia University Press, 1993), 33.

26. Irigaray, *An Ethics of Sexual Difference*, 186.

27. Ibid., 187.

28. Luce Irigaray, "Questions to Emmanuel Levinas: On the Divinity of Love," in *Re-Reading Levinas*, ed. Robert Bernasconi and Simon Critchley (Bloomington: Indiana University Press, 1991), 110.

29. Ibid., 110.

30. Gayatri Chakravorty Spivak, "French Feminism Revisited," in *Outside in the Teaching Machine*, ed. Gayatri Chakravorty Spivak (New York and London: Routledge, 1993), 171.

31. Luce Irigaray, "Sexual Difference," in *French Feminist Thought: A Reader*, ed. Toril Moi (New York: Basil Blackwell, 1987), 124.

32. Irigaray, "Questions to Emmanuel Levinas," 111.

33. Ibid., 36.

34. Latin American liberation thinkers have challenged this aspect of Levinas's thought. For instance, Enrique Dussel contends that for Levinas: "The poor provokes, but in the end is always poor, miserable" (Enrique Dussel and Daniel E. Guillot, *Liberación latinoamericana y Emmanuel Levinas* [Buenos Aires, Argentina: Editorial Bonum, 1975], 9).

35. Irigaray, "What Other Are We Talking About?" 69.

36. Irigaray, *An Ethics of Sexual Difference*, 13. Similarly, she states, "One of the dangers of love between women is the confusion of their identities, the lack of respect for or of perception of their differences" (63).

37. Amy Hollywood, *Sensible Ecstasy: Mysticism, Sexual Difference, and the Demands of History* (Chicago: University of Chicago Press, 2002), 232.

38. Irigaray, *An Ethics of Sexual Difference*, 12.

39. Ibid.

40. Ibid.

41. Challenging the common confusion of ground with "fixity, the self-present, the changeless . . . the Same," Keller proposes thinking of the metaphor of ground not as something that discourses provide, but which they "variously inhabit and honor." Concepts "will either attend to their own

'ground,' the earthly habitat that endlessly and differently gives rise to thought, or they will drift in the conventional groundlessness that has provided the very foundation for *classical* metaphysics"; Catherine Keller and Anne Daniell, ed., *Process and Difference: Between Cosmological and Poststructuralist Postmodernisms* (Albany: State University of New York Press, 2002), 13.

42. Irigaray, *An Ethics of Sexual Difference*, 100.

43. Tina Chanter, *Ethics of Eros: Irigaray's Rewriting of the Philosophers* (New York and London: Routledge, 1995), 219.

44. Irigaray, *An Ethics of Sexual Difference*, 195.

45. Ibid., 48; italics added.

46. In a more recent essay on Levinas's work, Irigaray restates her opinion of the necessary priority of the gender difference in discourses about the other. Cf. Irigaray, "What Other Are We Talking About?"

47. Luce Irigaray, *This Sex Which Is Not One*, trans. Catherine Porter and Carolyn Burke (Ithaca, N.Y.: Cornell University Press, 1977), 279.

48. Irigaray's single focus has been strategically crucial for challenging the ubiquitous erasure of the female subject in Western thought. However, the urgent needs for resisting the global force of imperialism demands attention to other Others also forcefully excluded from Western thought.

49. These scholars do not work from within the Western philosophical tradition, as Irigaray, Levinas, and Dussel do, but at the intersection of ethnic, literary and cultural studies. Therefore, the term *transcendence* is absent from their discourse. It is in their allusions to transformation and rebirth that I find the potential points of connection with Irigaray's project.

50. The African ancestry, so central to the Caribbean imaginary, is notably absent from the work of most Chicana scholars. U.S. Hispanic theologians have adopted the term *mulatez* in conjunction to mestizaje to highlight its significance.

51. Irigaray, *This Sex Which Is Not One*, 272. "The work of mestiza consciousness is to break down the subject-object duality which keeps her prisoner and to show in the flesh and through images in her work how duality is transcended"; Gloria Anzaldúa, *Borderlands / La Frontera: The New Mestiza* (San Francisco: Aunt Lute Books, 1999), 151.

52. Anzaldúa, *Borderlands*, 104.

53. Irigaray, *An Ethics of Sexual Difference*, 193.

54. Yvonne Yarbro-Bejarano, *The Wounded Heart: Writing on Cherríe Moraga*, ed. Deena J. González and Antonia Castañeda (Austin: University of Texas, 2001), 19.

55. Ibid., 92.

56. Do "we need to think this body as quite so pure, so new-born as Irigaray's woundless utopia of the flesh," Catherine Keller wonders. "I suspect," Keller proposes, "that the deep flesh, even in its resurrection, will carry the redemptive scars" (Keller, *Face of the Deep*, 221).

NEW CREATIONS: EROS, BEAUTY, AND THE PASSION FOR TRANSFORMATION | GRACE JANTZEN

1. Grace M. Jantzen, *Death and the Displacement of Beauty*, vol. 1, *Foundations of Violence* (New York: Routledge, 2004).

2. Hent de Vries, *Religion and Violence: Philosophical Perspectives from Kant to Derrida* (Baltimore: Johns Hopkins University Press, 2002).

3. Ibid., 1.

4. Regina Schwartz, *The Curse of Cain: The Violent Legacy of Monotheism* (Chicago: University of Chicago Press, 1997).

5. Ibid., 3.

6. Ibid., 88.

7. Grace M. Jantzen, *Becoming Divine: Towards a Feminist Philosophy of Religion* (Manchester: Manchester University Press, 1998), 270.

8. René Girard, *Things Hidden Since the Foundation of the World*, trans. Stephen Bann and Michael Metteer (Palo Alto, Calif.: Stanford University Press, 1987), 9.

9. René Girard, *The Girard Reader*, ed. James G. Williams (New York: Crossroad, 1996), 12–13.

10. Girard, *Things Hidden*, 26.

11. Robert G. Hamerton-Kelly, *Sacred Violence: Paul's Hermeneutic of the Cross* (Minneapolis: Fortress Row, 1992), 21.

12. Girard, *Things Hidden*, 97.

13. Ibid., 96.

14. René Girard, *Violence and the Sacred*, trans. Patrick Gregory (Baltimore: Johns Hopkins University Press, 1977), 306.

15. Ibid., 103.

16. Ibid., 306.

17. Ibid.

18. Girard, *The Girard Reader*, 63; Girard, *Things Hidden*, 430.

19. Girard, *Violence and the Sacred*, 140–42.

20. Girard rejects out of hand feminist critics of his theory, suggesting that they simply "want now to join the power games of the males" and thereby lose "their real moral superiority" (Girard, *The Girard Reader*, 226–27). But this

misses the point that violence is always already involved in gender construction, and that Girard's analysis of violence cannot account for it, thereby omitting a huge dimension of what it purports to explain.

21. Girard, *Things Hidden*, 25.

22. Sometimes Girard writes as though this victimage mechanism should be read back into prehistory as the origin of religion, not as an account of violence today. If that is how he means to be read, then my objections drawn from contemporary events would not stand. But then Girard faces two questions. First, given the difference between his view of violence in prehistory and what we see today, what evidence could he possibly adduce for his theory that it was the victimage mechanism that brought peace? Secondly, if his theory is not an account of how violence functions today, then is it of any but historical interest? Surely the whole point of his theory is that it claims to gives insight into *present* violence?

23. Girard, *The Girard Reader*, 65.

24. See my discussion of this in *Foundations of Violence*.

25. There have been some notable exceptions: Spinoza among the philosophers; and medieval women mystics like Julian of Norwich.

LYRICAL THEOLOGY: THE SONG OF SONGS AND THE ADVANTAGE OF POETRY | TOD LINAFELT

1. On the specifically lyrical qualities of the Song of Songs, see especially F. W. Dobbs-Allsopp, "The Delight of Beauty and Song of Songs 4:1–7," and Tod Linafelt, "The Arithmetic of Eros," both in *Interpretation* 59 no. 3 (2005), 260–77 and 245–58, respectively.

2. For a brief account of the place of lyric in the traditional threefold division of literature, see René Wellek, "Genre Theory, the Lyric, and *Erlebnis*," in *Discriminations: Further Concepts of Criticism* (New Haven: Yale University Press, 1970), 223–52. A more in-depth account of the history of the threefold division since the Renaissance, with a warning about tracing it back to classical sources, can be found in Gerard Genette, *The Architext*, trans. J. Lewin (Berkeley: University of California Press, 1992). The most influential modern attempt to reword the three categories is perhaps Northrop Frye's *Anatomy of Criticism* (Princeton, N.J.: Princeton University Press, 1957). On the category of lyric alone, see W. R. Johnson, *The Idea of Lyric: Lyric Modes in Ancient and Modern Poetry* (Berkeley: University of California Press, 1982).

3. Helen Vendler, *The Art of Shakespeare's Sonnets* (Cambridge, Mass.: Harvard University Press, 1997), 3.

4. I am aware that there are problems attendant on the use of the term "inner life" here, most especially that it might presume, as Virginia Burrus puts it, "a distinctly modern construction of subjectivity as an enfolded interiority." I agree that one needs to be careful not to project such modern notions onto the ancient texts I am considering here, and it is important to note that ancient notions of subjectivity, interiority, the self, and the like, would have been very different from modern notions (of which there are of course more than one). Nevertheless, the notion of an inner life, *mutatis mutandis*, would seem to obtain for Hebrew biblical texts at least, which have no qualms about distinguishing between inner and outer when it comes to human experience: thus, for example, the common idiom, "to say in one's heart" (as in "the fool says in his heart, 'There is no God'" in Ps. 14:1), and God's claim to Samuel that while humans look only on the "outer appearance, the Lord sees into the heart" (1 Sam. 16:7).

5. Harold Fisch, *Poetry with a Purpose: Biblical Poetics and Interpretation* (Bloomington: Indiana University Press, 1988), 104.

6. Aristotle, *Poetics*, trans. M. E. Hubbard, in *Ancient Literary Criticism: The Principal Texts in New Translations*, ed. D. A. Russell and M. Winterbottom (Oxford: Oxford University Press, 1972), 1452a.

7. Barbara Hardy, *The Advantage of Lyric: Essays on Feeling in Poetry* (Bloomington: Indiana University Press, 1977), 1.

8. Jorge Luis Borges, *This Craft of Verse* (Cambridge, Mass.: Harvard University Press, 2000), 99.

9. Erich Auerbach, *Mimesis: The Representation of Reality in Western Literature*, trans. W. R. Trask (Princeton, N.J.: Princeton University Press, 1953), 7, 9.

10. Ibid., 6.

11. Ibid., 11.

12. Helen Vendler, *Poems, Poets, Poetry*, 2nd ed. (New York: St. Martin's Press, 2002), 183.

13. See, for example, the critiques of Frederick J. Ruf, *Entangled Voices: Genre and the Religious Construction of the Self* (New York: Oxford University Press, 1997), chapters 1 and 4, and of Daniel Beaumont, "The Modality of Narrative: A Critique of Some Recent Views of Narrative in Theology," *Journal of the American Academy of Religion* 65, no. 1 (1997): 125–39.

14. Stanley Hauerwas, *Truthfulness and Tragedy* (South Bend, Ind.: Notre Dame University Press, 1977), 28.

15. Ronald Thiemann, *Revelation and Theology: The Gospel as Narrated Promise* (South Bend, Ind.: Notre Dame University Press, 1985), 86.

16. Hauerwas, *Truthfulness and Tragedy*, 76.

17. Amos Niven Wilder, "Story and Story-World," in *The Bible and the Literary Critic* (Minneapolis: Fortress Press, 1991), 132–48.
18. Robert Alter, *The Art of Biblical Poetry* (New York: Basic Books, 1985), 153–55.
19. For more on this passage in particular, see Tod Linafelt, "Biblical Love Poetry (. . . and God)," *Journal of the American Academy of Religion* 70, no. 2 (2002): 323–45. See also Virginia Burrus and Stephen D. Moore, "Unsafe Sex: Feminism, Pornography, and the Song of Songs," *Biblical Interpretation* 11, no. 1 (2003): 24–52, who make good use of Jeanette Winterson's allusion to these verses in her novel *Oranges Are Not the Only Fruit*, and who offer an alternative to the unmitigated celebration of the Song of Songs that one tends to find among interpreters these days.
20. Martha Nussbaum, *Cultivating Humanity* (Cambridge, Mass.: Harvard University Press, 1997), 90.

THE SHULAMMITE'S SONG: DIVINE EROS, ASCENDING AND DESCENDING | RICHARD KEARNEY

1. Tod Linafelt, "Biblical Love Poetry (. . . and God)," *Journal of The American Academy of Religion* 70 (2002): 332. The cited translation is also Linafelt's.
2. See also Karl Barth's eschatological reading of the Song in the light of Genesis 2 in *Church Dogmatics*, vol. 3, part 2, trans. H. Knight (Edinburgh: T&T Clark, 1960), as interpreted by Paul Ricoeur, "The Nuptial Metaphor," in *Thinking Biblically: Exegetical and Hermeneutical Studies*, trans. David Pellauer (Chicago: University of Chicago Press, 1998), 298–99. The eschatological reading of the Song is by no means confined to Christian interpretations of the Kingdom, as evidenced, e.g., in the commentaries by Rabbi Hayyim of Volozhyn.
3. André LaCocque, "The Shulammite," in *Thinking Biblically: Exegetical and Hermeneutical Studies*, trans. David Pellauer (Chicago: University of Chicago Press, 1998), 243. See also Michael Fox, *The Song of Songs and the Ancient Egyptian Songs* (Madison: University of Wisconsin Press, 1985), 309: "All events are narrated from her point of view, though not always in her voice, whereas from the boy's angle of vision we know little besides how he sees her."
4. See Fox, *The Song of Songs*, and LaCocque, "The Shulammite," 243f. Neither Fox nor LaCocque reads this passage, as I do, in the eschatological light of an ultimate nuptial reconciliation between traditional enemies, Israel and Egypt, Jew and Gentile, and other adversarial brothers. For us this is, of course, only one of many readings possible within the semantic surplus of this text as hermeneutically reread and reused throughout the history of

its constant reinterpretation and re-enactment. See Ricoeur, "The Nuptial Metaphor," 291f.

5. LaCocque, "The Shulamite," 245. He adds: "The family and familiar guardians of women's chastity, namely the 'brothers' and the night watchmen in the Song, are largely outdone by events over which they have lost control. Those who consider the future marriage of their son or daughter as a commercial transaction are derided. The institution in general is swept aside and the event of love is glorified" (253).

6. Ibid., 259 and 260–62.

7. Rabbi Hayyim de Volozhyn, *Nefesh Hahayyim / L'Ame de la vie*, ed. B. Gross (Paris: Verdier, 1986), 51–52.

8. Ibid., 77. This anticipates in some respects the three parts of Rosenzweig's *Star of Redemption*—Creation, Revelation, Redemption—and Levinas's related schema of immemorial beginning, ethical relation, and eschatological-messianic peace. In his preface to the French translation of Hayyhim of Volozhyn's book, Levinas hails it as an "exceptional" work from one of "the most eminent Talmudists of our epoch and founder of a school which formed the greatest Talmudic masters up to the present time." He goes on to praise it as expressing "the intimate thinking of a rabbinical authority . . . who devoted his days to what he deemed to be the kernel of all Jewish existence: study" (vii–x).

9. Ibid., 110.

10. Ibid., 294, 322–25, 363. See also ibid., 292, citing Levinas's interpretation of the relationship between cosmology, anthropology, and eschatology as a mark of the primacy of the ethical in Emmanuel Levinas, *L'au-dela du Verset* (Paris: Editions Seuil, 1982), 194.

11. For an analysis of this eschatological reading of biblical and messianic desire in contemporary Jewish authors like Levinas and Derrida, see the chapter "Desiring God" in my *The God Who May Be* (Bloomington: Indiana University Press, 2002), 62–79. Parts of that chapter contain earlier versions of the present analysis.

12. Elliot R. Wolfson, *Language, Eros, Being: Kabbalistic Hermeneutics and Poetic Imagination* (New York: Fordham University Press, 2005), 334.

13. Ibid., 335. See also Ricoeur's critical account of certain allegorical readings of the Song, "The Nuptial Metaphor," 287–90.

14. Ibid., 335.

15. Ibid.

16. Ibid., 336.

17. Ibid., 346. See also my analysis of *yester hara* and good and evil desire in chapter 1 of *The Wake of Imagination* (London: Hutcheson, 1988), and my more recent essay "Desire: Between Good and Evil," in *Evil and Religion*, ed. David Eckel and David Nichols (Boston: Boston Institute of Religion and Philosophy, 2006).

18. Ibid., 347.

19. Ibid., 351.

20. Ibid., 353.

21. Ibid., 355.

22. Ibid., 358.

23. Cited by ibid., 359.

24. Wolfson views *Zohar* accordingly as "an extended and multivalent commentary on the erotic mysticism celebrated in the Song" (ibid., 361). He goes on to comment on the gender implications of this eschatological paradigm of mutual interplay and reversibility: "Each gender contains the other in itself, the principle that is basic to the kabbalistic notion of androgyny. The conjunction of male and female yields the intertwining, cohabiting, of male in female and female in male. Mathematically framed, the twofold that is one becomes four. . . . The eros of the kiss is thus associated with the emanative process by means of which the androgynous being emerges from the union of the spirits of the mouth, male and female. This being is the perfect spirit, the son that contains the daughter as his sister, or as the breath of prophecy, the inarticulate masculine voice articulated through the articulation of feminine speech" (362).

25. Cited by ibid., 362.

26. Ibid., 297.

27. See G. Scholem, *Major Trends in Jewish Mysticism* (New York: Schocken Books, 1954, 235); see also Wolfson's comments, *Language, Eros, Being*, 363–67.

28. Ibid., 370.

29. Ibid., 363.

30. Ibid., 371.

31. See ibid., 296–97.

32. Cited by Ricoeur, "The Nuptial Metaphor," 271.

33. Wolfson, *Language, Eros, Being*, 335.

34. Gregory of Nyssa, *In Canticum Canticorum, Gregorii Nysseni Opera*, ed. W. Jaeger (Leiden: Brill, 1960), 6:181–83.

35. Gregory of Nyssa, *Contra Eunomium II, Gregorii Nysseni Opera*, 1:1, 246.

36. Gregory of Nyssa, *Contra Eunomium III, Gregorii Nysseni Opera*, 2:131–32.

37. Bernard of Clairvaux, *Talks on the Song of Songs*, ed. Bernard Bangley (Brewster, Mass: Paraclete Press, 2002). The sermons are modernized and annotated for the contemporary reader.

38. John of the Cross, "The Spiritual Canticle," in *The Selected Works of St. John of the Cross*, trans. Kieran Kavanaugh and Otilio Rodriguez (Washington, D.C.: ICS Publications, 1991), 470.

39. This dichotomy, it has to be said, is already anticipated in a number of passages and asides prior to this—e.g., stanzas 16 and 24—where John seems to reach out, uncharacteristically, for a more allegorical or intellectualist reading of the bride-bridegroom relationship.

40. John of the Cross, "The Spiritual Canticle," 630.

41. *Teresa of Avila*, trans. and ed. E. Allison Peers (New York: Doubleday, 1961), 103.

42. Ibid.

43. Ibid., 109.

44. Ibid.

45. Ibid., 111.

46. Ibid., 153.

47. Ibid.

48. Ibid., 136.

49. Ibid., 172.

50. Teresa does not actually quote the biblical verses in her own text but refers to them by allusion and familiarity, as if the Bride being led to the wine cellar by God was almost a personal acquaintance of hers, if not a pseudonym for the author herself!

51. See my reading of Platonic and metaphysical eros, as contrasted with biblical eros, in "Desire: Between Good and Evil."

52. I do not however wish to deny that there are other religious traditions with analogous or contrasting hermeneutics of divine desire, e.g., Rumi and Al-Arabi in the Sufi Islamic tradition; the *Gita Govinda*, *Saundarya Lahari*, and *Gitanjali* (by Tagore) in the Hindu tradition; Tantric interpretations of divine bliss in Buddhist traditions. See Lama Thubten Yeshe, *The Bliss of Inner Fire* (Boston: Wisdom Publications, 1998).

53. This is my own modified translation from the conclusion of Jacques Lacan's "Dieu et la jouissance de la femme," in *Encore* (Paris: Le Seuil, 1975), 70–71.

54. Ibid., 71.

55. Ibid. See also William Richardson, "Philosophy and Psychoanalysis: The Spelling of Marilyn Monroe," Thomas Blakely Memorial Lecture, Boston College, March 1990: "The *jouissance* can be of two kinds, Lacan claims:

phallic (sexual) and non-phallic (non-sexual) (or simply an 'other *jouis-sance*'). Phallic *jouissance* is associated with the phallus, to be sure, but where phallus is understood as the signifier par excellence of desire, and where desire is filtered through the demands of the symbolic order structured like a language. Phallic *jouissance*, then, is inevitably associated with the functioning of language. Lacan argues that all males are subjected to, and normally limited to, this kind of *jouissance*, but woman, though also subjected to phallic *jouissance*, is yet not completely so. Woman has access to an 'other' *jouissance*, the *jouissance* of 'being,' a specifically feminine *jouis-sance*. Lacan finds an example of this represented in a statue of Bernini in Rome to understand immediately that she is experiencing *jouissance* (*qu'elle jouit*). It would be this 'other *jouissance*,' then, which is the prerogative of Woman that makes her unique. Such questions as these still remain unanswered."

56. Georges Bataille, *The Accursed Share*, trans. Robert Hurley (Cambridge, Mass.: Zone Books, 1991), 2:169.
57. Ibid.
58. Ibid., 2:170.
59. Ibid.
60. Ibid., 2:170–71.
61. Georges Bataille, *Erotism: Death and Sensuality*, trans. Mary Dalwood (San Francisco: City Lights Books, 1986), 244.
62. Ibid., 239. Tod Linafelt gives an intriguing critical reading of The Song of Songs in the light of Bataille's theory of transgression, sacrifice and expenditure in "Biblical Love Poetry," 340–42.
63. Bataille, *Eroticism*, 7–9.
64. Ibid., 239.
65. Ibid.
66. Ibid., 240.
67. Elliot Wolfson, *Language, Eros, Being*, 336.
68. See Ricoeur's detailed analysis of the indetermination and proliferation of metaphorical meaning in the Song, "The Nuptial Metaphor," 268–70.
69. Ricoeur, "The Nuptial Metaphor," 269: "Is it a question, for example, in 1:6–8 of shepherd and a shepherdess, or in 1:4 and 3:2 and 11 of a king and a woman who might be a townswoman, or of a peasant in 1:12–14 and 7:6 and 13? What is more, the dialogue is rendered even more complex by internal explicit and implicit quotations. Nor is it sure that certain scenes are not dreamed or that they might consist of dreams. . . . These features

of indetermination are incontestably favorable to the freeing of the nuptial held in reserve within the erotic."

70. Ibid., 270.

71. Ibid., 271 and 274–75.

72. Ibid., 274. Julia Kristeva, *Tales of Love*, trans. Leon Roudiez (New York: Columbia University Press, 1987), 97, also speaks of "an impossibility set up as amatory law." She understands religion here as "the celebration of the secret of reproduction, the secret of pleasure, of life and death" within, over and against the limits of law and language.

73. Kristeva, *Tales of Love*, 96.

74. James Joyce, *Ulysses* (New York: Penguin Classics, 1992), 932–33.

SUFFERING EROS AND TEXTUAL INCARNATION: A KRISTEVAN READING OF KABBALISTIC POETICS | ELLIOT R. WOLFSON

To Virginia, for suffering eros in the eros of suffering.

1. Julia Kristeva, *Tales of Love*, trans. Leon S. Roudiez (New York: Columbia University Press, 1987), 234–35.

2. Elliot R. Wolfson, *Language, Eros, Being: Kabbalistic Hermeneutics and Poetic Imagination* (New York: Fordham University Press, 2004).

3. Ibid., 191–97. On the meeting of word and flesh in Kristeva, see Diane Jonte-Pace, "Situating Kristeva Differently: Psychoanalytic Readings of Woman and Religion," in *Body/Text in Julia Kristeva: Religion, Women, and Psychoanalysis*, ed. David R. Crownfield (Albany: State University of New York Press, 1992), 7–12.

4. My analysis accords in significant ways with the feminist reading of Merleau-Ponty's notion of the lived body and the phenomenology of the flesh offered by Elizabeth Grosz, *Volatile Bodies: Toward a Corporeal Feminism* (Bloomington: Indiana University Press, 1994), 86–111. For a nuanced description of the body as an inscriptive surface, a conception that may be usefully applied to kabbalistic sources, see ibid., 138–59. See also Henri Maldiney, "Flesh and Verb in the Philosophy of Merleau-Ponty," in *Chasms: Merleau-Ponty's Notion of Flesh*, ed. Fred Evans and Leonard Lawlor (Albany: State University of New York Press, 2000), 51–76. On the textual nature of the semiotic process of signifying the feminine body in the thought of Kristeva, see Shari Benstock, *Textualizing the Feminine: On the Limits of Genre* (Norman: University of Oklahoma Press, 1991), 23–46.

5. Elliot R. Wolfson, "Ontology, Alterity, and Ethics in Kabbalistic Anthropology," *Exemplaria* 12 (2000): 129–55, reprinted in *"Turn It Again": Jewish*

Medieval Studies and Literary Theory, ed. Shelia Delany (Asheville, N.C.: Pegasus Press, 2004), 119–44.

6. Wolfson, *Language, Eros, Being*, 245, and 539 note 370, for citation of other scholarly discussions of this motif to which one may now add Moshe Idel, *Enchanted Chains: Techniques and Rituals in Jewish Mysticism* (Los Angeles: Cherub Press, 2005), 133–44. A moving theological reflection on this kabbalistic motif, which I neglected to mention in previous publications, is offered by Abraham Joshua Heschel, "God, Torah, and Israel," trans. Byron Sherwin, in Abraham Joshua Heschel, *Moral Grandeur and Spiritual Audacity: Essays*, ed. Susannah Heschel (New York: Farrar, Straus, Giroux, 1996), 191–205. I was reminded of Heschel's essay by Idel's reference to it in *Enchanted Chains*, 141 note 92.

7. Charles P. Bigger, *Between Chora and the Good: Metaphor's Metaphysical Neighborhood* (New York: Fordham University Press, 2005), 64–65; for further elaboration on metaphor and the space of the between, see 77–82. For an innovative characterization of the openness of metaphorical discourse as a temporal mode of inquiry that gives one access to truth, see Carl G. Vaught, *Metaphor, Analogy, and the Place of Places: Where Religion and Philosophy Meet* (Waco, Tex.: Baylor University Press, 2004), 137–9, 167–70.

8. My formulation is indebted to Scot Douglass, "A Critical Analysis of Gregory's Philosophy of Language: The Linguistic Reconstitution of Metadiastemic Intrusions," in *Gregory of Nyssa: Homilies on the Beatitudes: An English Version with Commentary and Supporting Studies*, ed. Hubertus R. Drobner and Albert Viciano (Leiden: Brill, 2000), 447–65, esp. 449–51.

9. The point is expressed most poignantly in the short composition "On Truth and Lying in a Non-Moral Sense" included in Friedrich Nietzsche, *The Birth of Tragedy and Other Writings*, ed. Raymond Geuss and Ronald Speirs (Cambridge: Cambridge University Press, 1999), 144–46: "We believe we speak of trees, colours, snow, and flowers, we have knowledge of the things themselves, and yet we possess only metaphors of things which in no way correspond to the original entities. . . . What, then, is truth? A mobile army of metaphors, metonymies, anthropomorphisms, in short a sum of human relations which have been subjected to poetic and rhetorical intensification, translation, and decoration, and which, after they have been in use for a long time, strike a people as firmly established, canonical, and binding; truths are illusions of which we have forgotten that they are illusions, metaphors which have become worn by frequent use and have lost all sensuous vigour, coins which, having lost their stamp, are now regarded as metal and no longer as coins." See also ibid., 43: "For the genuine poet metaphor

is no rhetorical figure, but an image which takes the place of something else, something he can really see before him as a substitute for a concept. To the poet, a character is not a whole composed of selected single features, but an insistently alive person whom he sees before his very eyes, and distinguished from a painter's vision of the same thing only by the fact that the poet sees the figure continuing to live and act over a period of time."

10. See Jane Love, "Appetite and Violability: Questioning a Platonic Metaphor," in *Crises in Continental Philosophy*, ed. Arleen B. Dallery, Charles E. Scott, with P. Holley Roberts (Albany: State University of New York Press, 1990), 184–85: "In a different context, Heidegger speaks of the between as that which, reaching from the earth to the sky, is measured out for the dwelling of man. Perhaps the function of metaphor can be thought of in the same way, as a spanning of the 'between' that rests within the poles of, or the movement from, literal to metaphorical. For Heidegger, the possibility of measuring lies with the disclosure of the unknown, insofar as it remains unknown and against which man's familiarity shines forth. Something similar happens within a metaphor, although reversed: as meaning is carried across the span, the meaning itself, like man in his measuring, shines forth. But what shines forth is what is known; the familiarity of meaning is what allows the metaphor, and the discretion of metaphor protects this familiarity. And yet behind this shining forth stands, obscured, the between itself, which is unknown as long as the metaphor goes unquestioned. Once questioned, however, metaphor reveals an innocent literalism at its core. Difference is always assumed in the metaphorical leap, difference that the leap proposes to bridge."

11. Jacques Derrida, "The Retrait of Metaphor," in *The Derrida Reader: Writing Performances*, ed. Julian Wolfreys (Lincoln: University of Nebraska Press, 1998), 128.

12. On the collapse of the distinction between the literal and figurative in Derrida's thinking about the inherent metaphoricity of language, see John Llewelyn, *Derrida on the Threshold of Sense* (New York: St. Martin's Press, 1986), 74–80; Marian Hobson, *Jacques Derrida: Opening Lines* (London: Routledge, 1998), 207–11; Christian Howells, *Derrida: Deconstruction from Phenomenology to Ethics* (Cambridge: Polity Press, 1999), 60–64; Giuseppe Stellardi, *Heidegger and Derrida on Philosophy and Metaphor* (Amherst, N.Y.: Humanity Books, 2000), 67–126. For discussion of other contemporary views on metaphor that resonate with this perspective, see C. A. Van Peursen, "Metaphor and Reality," *Man and World* 25 (1992): 165–80, esp. 169–71.

13. On Plato's attitude toward myth, see Luc Brisson, *Plato the Myth Maker*, ed. Gerard Naddaf (Chicago: University of Chicago Press, 1998), and *How Philosophers Saved Myths: Allegorical Interpretation and Classical Mythology* (Chicago: University of Chicago Press, 2004), 15–28.

14. For a brief summary of this aspect of Plato's dialogue, and references to other critical assessments, see Rhoda H. Kotzin, "Ancient Greek Philosophy," in *A Companion to Feminist Philosophy*, ed. Alison M. Jaggar and Iris Marion Young (Malden: Blackwell, 1998), 17–18. See also the important observation of James M. Rhodes, *Eros, Wisdom, and Silence: Plato's Erotic Dialogues* (Columbia: University of Missouri Press, 2003), 317, that Diotima describes herself as a *daimonios anēr*, a "daimonic male," which indicates, consequently, that she is a "spiritual androgyne," the masculine aspect of her soul related to her activism and the feminine aspect to her receptivity. Rhodes concludes, moreover, that her androgyny "mirrors that of her alter ego, Socrates, who is both himself and Diotima."

15. I appropriate this expression to describe the Platonic perspective from Love, "Appetite and Violability," 185.

16. Kristeva, *Tales of Love*, 71–72.

17. *Symposium*, 203b–c. I am indebted to the analysis of the Platonic text in Julius Evola, *Eros and the Mysteries of Love: The Metaphysics of Sex* (Rochester, N.Y.: Inner Traditions, 1983), 57–58. For a more recent analysis along similar lines, see Rhodes, *Eros, Wisdom, and Silence*, 313–63.

18. *Symposium*, 203c–e. I have availed myself of the English translation of Michael Joyce in *The Collected Dialogues of Plato*, ed. Edith Hamilton and Huntington Cairns (Princeton, N.J.: Princeton University Press, 1961), 555–56.

19. Compare the depiction of the phenomenon of the caress in Emmanuel Levinas, *Time and the Other*, trans. Richard A. Cohen (Pittsburgh: Duquesne University Press, 1987), 89: "The seeking of the caress constitutes its essence by the fact that the caress does not know what it seeks. This 'not knowing,' this fundamental disorder, is the essential. It is like a game with something slipping away, a game absolutely without project or plan, not with what can become ours or us, but with something other, always other, always inaccessible, and always still to come [*à venir*]. The caress is the anticipation of this pure future [*avenir*], without content. It is made up of this increase of hunger, of ever richer promises, opening new perspectives onto the ungraspable. It feeds on countless hungers." See Levinas, *Totality and Infinity: An Essay on Exteriority*, trans. Alphonso Lingis (Pittsburgh: Duquesne University Press, 1969), 257–58.

20. I am here influenced by the characterization of the mystic in William Everson, *Earth Poetry: Selected Essays and Interviews, 1950–1977*, ed. Lee Bartlett (Berkeley: Oyez, 1980), 18, as "insatiable, because the food that feeds him incites him in his hunger. Hunger is his need and his need is unstanchable. Reason may balk, but imagination knows no end. Never exhausting the modes of its obsession, because love is inexhaustible, like the lover who never possessed his beloved in all the possessable ways, he relinquishes possession in order to be trapped, in order to be possessed."

21. Luce Irigaray, "Sorcerer Love: A Reading of Plato's Symposium, Diotima's Speech," in *Revaluing French Feminism: Critical Essays on Difference, Agency, and Culture*, ed. Nancy Fraser and Sandra Lee Bartky (Bloomington: Indiana University Press, 1992), 66. The essay is reprinted in *Feminist Interpretations of Plato*, ed. Nancy Tuana (University Park: Pennsylvania State University Press, 1994), 181–95, followed by the analysis of Andrea Nye, "Irigaray and Diotima at Plato's Symposium," 197–215.

22. Irigaray, "Sorcerer Love," 65.

23. Kristeva, *Tales of Love*, 73.

24. There are a number of important studies dealing with the historical, literary, and thematic issues pertaining to the *Zohar*. Here I will mention only a handful: Gershom Scholem, *Major Trends in Jewish Mysticism* (New York: Schocken Books, 1956), 156–204; Isaiah Tishby, *The Wisdom of the Zohar: An Anthology of Texts*, trans. David Goldstein (Oxford: Oxford University Press, 1989), 1–126; Yehuda Liebes, *Studies in the Zohar*, trans. Arnold Schwartz, Stephanie Nakache, and Penina Peli (Albany: State University of New York Press, 1993), 85–138; Boaz Huss, "*Sefer ha-Zohar* as a Canonical, Sacred and Holy Text: Changing Perspectives of the Book of Splendor between the Thirteenth and Eighteenth Centuries," *Journal of Jewish Thought and Philosophy* 7 (1998): 257–307; Boaz Huss, "The Appearance of *Sefer ha-Zohar*," *Tarbiz* 70 (2001): 507–42 (Hebrew); Charles Mopsik, "Le corpus Zoharique ses titres et ses amplifications," in *La Formation des Canons Scripturaires*, ed. Michel Tardieu (Paris: Cerf, 1993), 75–105; Charles Mopsik, "Moïse de León, le Sheqel ha-Qodesh et la rédaction du Zohar: Une réponse à Yehuda Liebes," *Kabbalah: Journal for the Study of Jewish Mystical Texts* 3 (1998): 117–218; Daniel Abrams, "Critical and Post-Critical Textual Scholarship of Jewish Mystical Literature: Notes on the History and Development of Modern Editing Techniques," *Kabbalah: Journal for the Study of Jewish Mystical Texts* 1 (1996): 17–71, esp. 61–64; Daniel Abrams, "The *Zohar* as a Book: On the Assumptions and Expectations of the Kabbalists and Modern Scholarship," *Kabbalah: Journal for the Study of Jewish Mystical Texts* 12 (2004): 201–32; Ronit

Meroz, "Zoharic Narratives and their Adaptations," *Hispania Judaica Bulletin* 3 (2000): 3–63; Pinchas Giller, *Reading the Zohar: The Sacred Text of Kabbalah* (Oxford: Oxford University Press, 2001), 3–33. For a lucid, albeit prosaic, introduction, see Arthur Green, *A Guide to the Zohar* (Stanford: Stanford University Press, 2004). For a more elaborate account of my own view, though surely not sufficient, see Wolfson, *Language, Eros, Being*, 47–48.

25. My most sustained analysis of the contours of the erotic experience in zoharic kabbalah can be found in *Language, Eros, Being*. Also noteworthy are the studies by Yehuda Liebes, "Zohar and Eros," *Alpayyim* 9 (1994): 67–115; Liebes, "Eros and Anti-Eros on the Jordan," in *Life as a Midrash: Perspectives in Jewish Psychology*, ed. Shahar Arzy et al. (Tel-Aviv: Yediot Ahranot, 2004), 152–67, esp. 160–65 (Hebrew); Moshe Idel, "Eros in der Kabbala: Zwischen gegenwärtiger physischer Realität und idealen metaphysischen Konstrukten," in *Kulturen der Eros*, ed. Detlev Clemens and Tilo Schabert (Munich: Fink, 2001), 59–102; Idel, *Kabbalah and Eros* (New Haven: Yale University Press, 2005); Charles Mopsik, *Sex of the Soul: The Vicissitudes of Sexual Difference in Kabbalah*, ed. Daniel Abrams (Los Angeles: Cherub Press, 2005).

26. Wolfson, *Language, Eros, Being*, 47–48, 92–94. My discussion there already anticipates the criticism leveled against me by Idel, *Kabbalah and Eros*, 129.

27. Wolfson, *Language, Eros, Being*, 335–36.

28. See Elliot R. Wolfson, *Circle in the Square: Studies in the Use of Gender in Medieval Kabbalistic Symbolism* (Albany: State University of New York Press, 1995), 3–9.

29. Kristeva, *Tales of Love*, 99.

30. Wolfson, *Language, Eros, Being*, 222–33.

31. Elliot R. Wolfson, *Abraham Abulafia—Kabbalist and Prophet: Hermeneutics, Theosophy and Theurgy* (Los Angeles: Cherub Press, 2000), 14–38; Wolfson, "Divine Suffering and the Hermeneutics of Reading: Philosophical Reflections on Lurianic Mythology," in *Suffering Religion*, ed. Robert Gibbs and Elliot R. Wolfson (London: Routledge, 2002), 107–17; Wolfson, *Language, Eros, Being*, 7–10, 17–21, 25–27, 134–35, 160, 195–96, 220–24.

32. See note 12.

33. The resonance should come as no surprise, since Heschel was indebted to similar intellectual currents that have informed my work, to wit, kabbalistic esotericism and hermeneutical phenomenology.

34. Babylonian Talmud, Ḥagigah 2a, 4b.

35. *Mekhilta de-Rabbi Ishmael*, ed. Hayyim S. Horovitz and Israel A. Rabin (Jerusalem: Wahrmann Books, 1970), Baḥodesh, sec. 7, 229; *Sifre on Deuteronomy*,

ed. Louis Finkelstein (New York: Jewish Theological Seminary of America, 1969), sec. 233, 265–66; Palestinian Talmud, Nedarim 3:2, 37d; Babylonian Talmud, Rosh ha-Shanah 27a, Shavu'ot 20b.

36. Abraham Joshua Heschel, *Heavenly Torah as Refracted through the Generations*, ed. and trans. with commentary by Gordon Tucker and Leonard Levin (New York: Continuum, 2005), 708.

37. Heschel is here following older kabbalistic and Hasidic sources according to which *zakhor* and *shamor* refer respectively to the male and female potencies of the divine. See Tishby, *Wisdom*, 1221–23; Elliot K. Ginsburg, *The Sabbath in the Classical Kabbalah* (Albany: State University of New York Press, 1989), 107–8. The two levels of meaning, moreover, are engendered, the internal or mystical corresponding to the male and the external or literal to the female. On the correlation of the revealed with the feminine and the concealed with the masculine, see, for instance, *Zohar* 1:64b. For different articulations of the point, see Elliot R. Wolfson, "Occultation of the Feminine and the Body of Secrecy in Medieval Kabbalah," in *Rending the Veil: Concealment and Secrecy in the History of Religions*, ed. Elliot R. Wolfson (New York: Seven Bridges Press, 1999), 143–45; Wolfson, *Abraham Abulafia*, 32–33; Wolfson, *Language, Eros, Being*, 132–33.

38. *Zohar Ḥadash*, ed. Reuven Margaliot (Jerusalem: Mosad ha-Rav Kook, 1978), 120a (*Tiqqunim*).

39. Elliot R. Wolfson, "Beautiful Maiden Without Eyes: Peshat and Sod in Zoharic Hermeneutics," in *The Midrashic Imagination: Jewish Exegesis, Thought and History*, ed. Michael Fishbane (Albany: State University of New York Press, 1993), 155–203; Wolfson, *Language, Eros, Being*, 224–25.

40. See Elliot R. Wolfson, "Beneath the Wings of the Great Eagle: Maimonides and Thirteenth-Century Kabbalah," in *Moses Maimonides (1138–1204): His Religious, Scientific, and Philosophical Wirkungsgeschichte in Different Cultural Contexts*, ed. Görge K. Hasselhoff and Otfried Fraisse (Würzburg: Ergon Verlag, 2004), 212–21.

41. Heschel, *Heavenly Torah*, 710. It is not the right context to delve more deeply into Heschel's thought, but suffice it to state that the appropriation of the kabbalistic hermeneutic mentioned briefly here has relevance to the critical question regarding Heschel's own understanding of the symbolic nature of religious language, a point that, in my judgment, has not been adequately assessed by scholars who have written on the subject, partially misled by the critique of symbolism offered by Heschel himself. Perhaps one day I shall return to investigate this matter more thoroughly.

42. My thinking here betrays the intricate interplay of consciousness, body, and language in the thought of Merleau-Ponty. The bibliography on Merleau-Ponty is enormous so I will mention here only one readable but sophisticated account that is greatly indebted to—indeed, can even be read as a summary account of—Merleau-Ponty's reflections on these matters: Remy C. Kwant, *Phenomenology of Language* (Pittsburgh: Duquesne University Press, 1965).

43. For a contemporary theological exposition along these lines, see Sallie Mc-Fague, *Speaking in Parables: A Study in Metaphor and Theology* (Philadelphia: Fortress Press, 1975), and *Metaphorical Theology: Models of God in Religious Language* (Philadelphia: Fortress Press, 1982).

44. Julia Kristeva, *Time and Sense: Proust and the Experience of Literature*, trans. Ross Guberman (New York: Columbia University Press, 1996), 213.

45. Wolfson, *Language, Eros, Being*, 190–260. Consider the following remarks in Brian Cosgrove, "Murray Krieger: Ekphrasis as Spatial Form, Ekphrasis as Mimesis," in *Text Into Image: Image Into Text*, ed. Jeff Morrison and Florian Krobb (Amsterdam: Rodopi, 1997), 30–31: "Modernism, indeed, is at its most ambitiously mimetic when it adopts, far too readily, an incarnationism which is *au fond* derivative from a theological source. The paradoxical reconciliation of the temporal sequence of language with the stasis or permanence of literary form . . . is both persistently and uncritically dependent 'upon the two-in-one paradox of the primal Christian metaphor' . . . the hypostatic union of the two natures, human and divine, in Christ. Such a dependence becomes fully explicit in T. S. Eliot's *Four Quartets*, where time 'incarnates' the timeless, and the poetic word aspires to emulate the Word or Logos. In this poetics of presence, we find what is arguably the most ambitiously mimetic of all poetic undertakings: the attempt to create a language which, even as it moves in time, reveals the timeless, or an 'ultimate' reality—just as, analogously, the historical Jesus reveals the eternal Godhead." In the kabbalistic worldview, the focal point of the incarnation is different from the Christological doctrine, but the portrayal of the poetic nature of language as the temporal disclosure of the timeless bears an interesting comparison to the Jewish mystical teaching. Compare also the title of the introduction in *Dark God of Eros: A William Everson Reader*, ed. Albert Gelpi (Berkeley: Heyday Books, 2003), xv–xxxvii: "Under the Sign of Woman: The Poetics of Incarnation." Everson's own words in *Earth Poetry*, 17, resonate in a remarkable way with kabbalistic poetics according to my understanding: "In the essential speechlessness that mysticism is, poetry

finds its voice. Like prayer, it moves forever beyond itself to its own extinction. . . . This is a feature it shares with physical love. The phallus knocking at the womb, like the tongue stuttering in the throat, achieves at climax that expenditure which is its failure, the quintessence of success. I think more than any other form of art, poetry is mysticism's flesh."

46. Jonte-Pace, "Situating Kristeva," 12–22.
47. Kristeva, *Tales of Love*, 268.
48. Ibid., 89 (emphasis in original).
49. Ibid., 60: "Never would Eastern eroticism, even when celebrated in the most erotic Hindu or Bangali poems, equal the joyful, quivering passion of the Song of Songs. For in the East, a body joys, lays out the pleasure of its organs, swells to infinite proportions in the bursting of its pleasure, quietly dependent upon the nourishing mother. But those are pleasures whose expanse is in itself differentiated, joys devolving upon a cosmos-speech, which set themselves aflame in their elements. While love for the other, and even more so for the other sex, came to us for the first time through king Solomon and the Shulammite—a precocious yet fragile triumph of heterosexuality, tinged with impossibility."
50. Ibid., 93. Compare Jacques Derrida, *Of Grammatology*, trans. Gayatri Chakravorty Spivak, corrected edition (Baltimore: John Hopkins University Press, 1997), 280: "Articulation is the dangerous supplement of fictive instantaneity and of the good speech: of full pleasure [*jouissance*]. . . . The present is always the present of a pleasure; and pleasure is always a receiving of presence. What dislocates presence introduces difference and delay, spacing between desire and pleasure."
51. Kristeva, *Tales of Love*, 90.
52. Julia Kristeva, *Desire in Language: A Semiotic Approach to Literature and Art*, ed. Leon S. Roudiez (New York: Columbia University Press, 1980), 142.
53. Kristeva, *Tales of Love*, 94.
54. Kristeva, *Time and Sense*, 202.
55. Kristeva, *Tales of Love*, 95.
56. Ibid., 269–70, where the views of Plato are dealt with more explicitly.
57. Ibid., 273 (emphasis in original). See 332–33.
58. On the distinction between the symbolic and semiotic, see Julia Kristeva, *Revolution in Poetic Language*, trans. Margaret Waller (New York: Columbia University Press, 1984), 21–106; and the critical appraisals in Diana T. Meyers, "The Subversion of Women's Agency in Psychoanalytic Feminism: Chodorow, Flax, Kristeva," in *Revaluing French Feminism*, 144; Ann Brooks, *Postfeminisms: Feminism, Cultural Theory and Cultural Forms* (London:

Routledge, 1997), 81–82; and the critique of Judith Butler, "The Body Politics of Julia Kristeva," in *Revaluing French Feminism*, 162–76. The link between metaphor and the image of the mother is explored in Marilyn Edelstein, "Metaphor, Meta-Narrative, and Mater-Narrative in Kristeva's 'Stabat Mater,'" in *Body / Text*, 27–52. See also Eva Feder Kittay, "Women as Metaphor," *Hypatia* 3 (1988): 63–86, esp. 69–72. Finally, we should recall the nexus between the originary nature of language as metaphor and the maternal characteristics affirmed in the reading of Rousseau offered by Derrida, *Of Grammatology*, 271.

59. *Zohar* 1:244b–245a.

60. On this point, see Liebes, *Studies in the Zohar*, 9–10.

61. For references, see Wolfson, *Language, Eros, Being*, 584 note 128.

62. Gershom Scholem, *On the Mystical Shape of the Godhead: Basic Concepts in the Kabbalah*, ed. Jonathan Chipman (New York: Schocken Books, 1991), 184.

63. Scholem, *Major Trends*, 233; Scholem, *On the Mystical Shape*, 145–46, 163, 168; Tishby, *Wisdom*, 381; Yehuda Liebes, *Studies in Jewish Myth and Jewish Messianism*, trans. Batya Stein (Albany: State University of New York Press, 1993), 42–54.

64. Wolfson, *Circle in the Square*, 110–12, and further references cited on 227 notes 158–60 and 228 note 168; Wolfson, "Eunuchs Who Keep the Sabbath: Becoming Male and the Ascetic Ideal in Thirteenth-Century Jewish Mysticism," in *Becoming Male in the Middle Ages*, ed. Jeffrey J. Cohen and Bonnie Wheeler (New York: Garland, 1997), 166–67; Wolfson, *Language, Eros, Being*, 76, 182, 185–86.

65. See the interpretive gloss on this zoharic passage in the pietistic work *Taharat ha-Qodesh* (Jerusalem, 1929), 179. "After the union has been achieved she certainly says 'Place me as a seal upon your heart,' for she is called by his name, that is, after the union she is called by the name of her husband." It is worth noting that in a parallel passage in *Zohar* 2:114a, the verse "Let me be as a seal upon your heart" (Song 8:6) is said to have been uttered by *Shekhinah*, the "Community of Israel," when she is conjoined to her spouse and not in the moment of separation consequent to the unification. See Tishby, *Wisdom*, 301.

66. Gershom Scholem, *Sabbatai Ṣevi: The Mystical Messiah 1626–1676* (Princeton, N.J.: Princeton University Press, 1973), 27: "The kabbalists, whose mystical thinking strained after expression in symbolic forms, endeavored to evade responsibility for their symbols by the frequent use of qualifying phrases such as 'so to speak,' 'as if,' 'as it were,' and the like. These reservations were supposed to minimize the real significance of the symbols employed."

While I do not deny that Scholem's assessment may apply in some instances, I would maintain that the qualifying phrases to which he refers generally maximize rather than minimize the significance of the symbol to serve as a mirror wherein the real appears as the image that is imagined as real.

67. The intent of the zoharic image is made explicit by Moses Cordovero, *Zohar im Perush Or Yaqar*, (Jerusalem, 1974), 6:260: "The reason for this request ['Place me as a seal upon your heart'] is that with regard to every reality in which her form is formed, that reality is the source whence she is illumined through it even if she is separated, and even though she is rooted in it, for every effect is rooted in its cause, she wants to be rooted in the aspect of her arrayments after she has been adorned for the unification and after he descends to the lower entities." The point is well captured in the depiction of the relationship between *Ḥokhmah* and *Binah*, the attributes of the divine that correspond respectively to the father and mother, in Moses Cordovero, *Pardes Rimmonim* (Jerusalem, 1962), 9:5, 58b: "In *Binah* there is an aspect of *Ḥokhmah*, and in *Ḥokhmah* an aspect of *Binah*, in the secret of 'Let me be as a seal' (Song 8:6), for after the two are united, they are sealed within one another and they are formed within one another."

68. The zoharic interpretation is anticipated in the kabbalistic commentary on the Song by Ezra of Gerona, printed in *Kitvei Ramban*, ed. Ḥayyim D. Chavel (Jerusalem: Mosad ha-Rav Kook, 1964), 2:514: "'Let me be as a seal upon your heart' (Song 8:6), when we separate in the time of exile [place me] as the seal that is known."

69. On the motif of the exile of *Shekhinah*, see Scholem, *Major Trends*, 232–33, 275; Scholem, *On the Kabbalah*, 58–59, 70–71, 107–9, 113–15, 141–53; Scholem, *Kabbalah*, 164, 167, 194, 335; Tishby, *Wisdom*, 382–85; Moshe Idel, *Messianic Mystics* (New Haven: Yale University Press, 1998), 317–18. The strong distinction between the rabbinic and kabbalistic approaches to this motif promulgated by Scholem and Tishby does not seem fully warranted; on the contrary, a close reading of the relevant texts suggests that the "gnostic paradox" (the language used by Scholem, *On the Kabbalah*, 113) that presumes that exile and redemption are processes that occur within God's own nature is already operative in the older sources. See Liebes, *Studies in Jewish Myth*, 52–54; Wolfson, "Divine Suffering," 105–07, 116–17, 145–46 note 34; Wolfson, *Language, Eros, Being*, 374–75; Michael Fishbane, *Biblical Myth and Rabbinic Mythmaking* (Oxford: Oxford University Press, 2003), 134–46, 156–59, 195–99, 215–16, 223, 265–66, 285, 296, 357–70.

70. Mikhail Bakhtin, *The Dialogic Imagination*, trans. Caryl Emerson and Michael Holquist (Austin: University of Texas Press, 1981), 1:258.

71. Liebes, *Studies in the Zohar*, 67–71, offers a typical account of this element in kabbalistic doctrine with special reference to zoharic symbolism. The emphasis on heterosexual coupling as the distinctive mark of the kabbalistic understanding of divine unity is the standard perspective affirmed by most scholars who have weighed in on the nature of eros in medieval Jewish mysticism. See, for example, Charles Mopsik, *Lettre sur la sainteté: Le secret de la relation entre l'homme et la femme dans la cabale* (Paris: Verdier, 1986), 45–163; Mopsik, *Sex of the Soul*, 128–49; Idel, *Kabbalah and Eros*, 53–103. On divine pathos and the longing for reunion, see also Fishbane, *Biblical Myth*, 296–300.

72. *Tiqqunei Zohar*, ed. Reuven Margaliot (Jerusalem: Mosad ha-Rav Kook, 1978), sec. 22, 65b.

73. In the interests of full disclosure, the word I have rendered as "it" is *ihi*, the third-person feminine pronoun.

74. In some versions of the text, the third-person pronoun is in the masculine (*ihu*) while according to other versions it is in the feminine (*ihi*).

75. *Tiqqunei Zohar*, sec. 22, 65b.

76. For more extensive discussion of the kabbalistic depiction of *Shekhinah* as the archetypal image, see Wolfson, *Through a Speculum*, 306–17, and esp. 313–15.

77. I explored this aggadic theme and some of its later reverberations in depth in "The Image of Jacob Engraved Upon the Throne: Further Speculation on the Esoteric Doctrine of the German Pietism," in *Massu'ot Studies in Kabbalistic Literature and Jewish Philosophy in Memory of Prof. Ephraim Gottlieb*, ed. Michal Oron and Amos Goldreich (Jerusalem: Mosad Bialik, 1994), 131–85 (Hebrew), and in an expanded and revised English version in Elliot R. Wolfson, *Along the Path: Studies in Kabbalistic Myth, Symbolism, and Hermeneutics* (Albany: State University of New York Press, 1995), 1–62.

78. *Tiqqunei Zohar*, sec. 22, 65b-66a.

79. Ibid., 67b.

80. Babylonian Talmud, Mo'ed Qatan 28a.

81. In *Tiqqunei Zohar*, sec. 18, 32b, the expression *ḥotmenu le-ḥayyim* is applied to the supernal Mother, that is, the third emanation *Binah*, on account of which the ninth emanation *Yesod* (or *Ṣaddiq*) is called the "book of life" (*sefer ḥayyim*). On the expression *ḥotmenu le-ḥayyim* and its theosophic significance, see Ḥayyim Vital, *Sha'ar ha-Kawwanot* (Jerusalem, 1963), Inyan Yom ha-Kippur, sec. 5, 102c–d.

82. Implicit in this expression is the rabbinic tradition that the seal (*ḥotam*) of God is truth, a motif that is applied by many kabbalists to the phallic potency of the divine. See Babylonian Talmud, Shabbat 55a.

83. *Tiqqunei Zohar*, Introduction, 18a, and compare parallel in *Tiqqunei Zohar*, sec. 22, 65b.

84. *Tiqqunei Zohar*, sec. 22, 65b.

85. A similar dynamic is attested in a number of medieval Jewish thinkers who utilize the image of the seal and its imprint to convey the overflow from the form of the Active Intellect upon the matter of the human soul, engendered respectively as male and female. See Moshe Idel, *The Mystical Experience in Abraham Abulafia* (Albany: State University of New York Press, 1988), 194, 216–17 note 96; and for the later reverberation of this motif, see Bezalel Naor, "'A Raised Seal and Sunken Seal' in the Teachings of Abraham Abulafia and Lubavitch," *Sinai* 107, (1991): 54–7 (Hebrew). See below, note 97. Finally, it is worth noting that the reversal implied by the image of the seal is emphasized by Moses Alshikh in his commentary on Song 8:6 in *Shoshannat ha-Omaqim* (Venice, 1591), 55a.

86. Especially close to the language in the passage from *Tiqqunei Zohar* is the description of the "third explanation" of the words "Let me be as a seal" (Song 8:6) offered by Abraham Ibn Ezra: "These are the words of the community of Israel to the *Shekhinah* that I should be conjoined to you forever." See also *Numbers Rabbah* 5:6.

87. On this philological usage, see further evidence adduced in Elliot R. Wolfson, "Circumcision and the Divine Name: A Study on the Transmission of Esoteric Doctrine," *Jewish Quarterly Review* 78 (1987): 77–112, esp. 102–9. Needless to say, many passages from *Tiqqunei Zohar* and other kabbalistic treatises could have been cited to substantiate the point. On the symbolic significance of circumcision in *Tiqqunei Zohar*, see also Pinchas Giller, *The Enlightened Will Shine: Symbolization and Theurgy in the Later Strata of the Zohar* (Albany: State University of New York Press, 1993), 90–3, 115.

88. *Tiqqunei Zohar*, sec. 22, 65b–68a.

89. Compare *Tiqqunei Zohar*, sec. 22, 68a: "Another interpretation: 'Let me be as a seal' [*simeni kha-ḥotam*], the power of the unblemished one [*koaḥ tam*], the power of the supernal *Shekhinah* . . . the unblemished one [*tam*] refers to Israel above, and on the basis of its name Jacob is called 'unblemished' [*tam*], as it says 'and Jacob the unblemished man' [*we-yaʿaqov ish tam*] (Gen. 25:27). And since he is the image of the seal of truth [*diyoqna de-ḥotam emet*] that is above, it says concerning him, 'Bestow truth upon Jacob' (Micah 7:20)."

90. Cordovero, *Pardes Rimmonim*, 23:1, s.v. "emet": Cf. ibid., 27:5, 61a: "There are those who explain that the [letter] *beit* refers to *Malkhut*, and since she united with her consort, there were formed in her the two arms that she embraces and he is in the middle . . . and this is the secret of 'Let me be as a seal,' for his form is engraved in her." And ibid., 28:5, 66b: "She discloses the seal of the king [*ḥotam ha-melekh*] that is engraved in her as in the matter of 'Let me be as a seal.'"

91. On the notion of the *reshimu* in Lurianic theosophy, see Scholem, *Major Trends*, 264, 267; Scholem, *Sabbatai Ṣevi*, 29–31; Isaiah Tishby, *The Doctrine of Evil and the 'Kelippah' in Lurianic Kabbalism*, rev. ed. (Jerusalem: Magnes Press, 1984), 58–59 (Hebrew); Lawrence Fine, *Physician of the Soul, Healer of the Cosmos: Isaac Luria and His Kabbalistic Fellowship* (Stanford: Stanford University Press, 2003), 130–31, 147–48.

92. *Tiqqunei Zohar*, sec. 22, 65b.

93. Vital, *Shaʿar ha-Kawwanot*, Inyan Tefillin, sec. 5, 9c, and parallel in Vital, *Peri Eṣ Ḥayyim* (Dubrowno, 1804), Shaʿar Tefillin, ch. 7, 21b–d. The latter version is cited and explicated by Zevi Aryeh ben Eleazar, *Imrei Binah al Megillat Shir ha-Shirim* (M.-Sziget: Mendel Wider, 1897), 92c–93b.

94. Scholem, *Major Trends*, 269–73; Scholem, *Kabbalah*, 140–44; Giller, *Reading the Zohar*, 105–24; Fine, *Physician of the Soul*, 138–41.

95. Wolfson, *Language, Eros, Being*, 269–71. My discussion there includes a brief analysis of Vital on the matter of the convergence of the noetic and erotic in kabbalistic symbolism.

96. See Giller, *Reading the Zohar*, 151–52; Fine, *Physician of the Soul*, 236–39. For the attentive reader I note that the Hebrew *moḥin* is plural, but I have rendered it in the singular "consciousness." As a consequence, I have translated verbal expressions associated with it in the singular as well, even though the precise Hebrew equivalent is in the plural.

97. Arthur Green, "Rabbi Isaac Ibn Sahola's Commentary on the Song of Songs," *Jerusalem Studies in Jewish Thought* 6, nos. 3–4 (1987): 483. The expression *ḥotam be-tokh ḥotam* is used in Babylonian Talmud, Avodah Zarah 29b and 31a, with reference to the practice of double-sealing a container of wine placed in the hand of a Gentile, and it is found as well in any number of later medieval rabbinic sources. An application of the idiom beyond its halakhic intent is attested in the writings of Abraham Abulafia. See, for instance, *Ḥayyei ha-Olam ha-Ba*, 3rd ed. (Jerusalem, 2001), 77 and 79; *Oṣar Eden Ganuz* (Jerusalem, 2000), 3, 111, 168, 278, 368, 371, 372, 373; *Maṣref la-Kesef we-Khur la-Zahav* (Jerusalem, 2001), 21; *Ḥotam ha-Hafṭarah* in *Maṣref ha-Sekhel*

(Jerusalem, 2001), 113. On the use of the term *ḥotam* in Abulafia, see note 85. The expression also appears frequently in kabbalistic sources of a theosophic orientation and in some contexts it clearly denotes the ontic enfolding of the feminine in the masculine. A typical example of this application is Ḥayyim Vital, *Eṣ Ḥayyim* (Jerusalem, 1963), 35:3, 52a: "This is the secret of what the rabbis, blessed be their memory, said that in order to protect the container of wine there must be a seal within a seal . . . for *Yesod* is the first seal and *Malkhut* is the second seal." See Vital, *Sha'ar ha-Kawwanot*, Inyan Sefirat ha-Omer, sec. 11, 85b, and further elaboration in ibid., Inyan Yom ha-Kippur, sec. 102d–103a, and Inyan Sukkot, sec. 6, 106b; Vital, *Sefer ha-Liqquṭim* (Jerusalem, 1963), 117c. For other contexts wherein the expression *ḥotam be-tokh ḥotam* appears, see Cordovero, *Pardes Rimmonim*, 23:19, 39b, 27:15, 62d; Vital, *Eṣ Ḥayyim*, 5:5, 23d, 34:6, 50b, 35:2, 52a; Vital, *Sha'ar ha-Kawwanot*, Inyan Yom ha-Kippur, sec. 3, 102b, sec. 5, 102c.

98. *Zohar* 2:114a. The intent of the zoharic passage is made explicit in Elijah de Vidas, *Re'shit Ḥokhmah ha-Shalem* (Jerusalem: Or ha-Musar, 1984), Sha'ar ha-Ahavah, ch. 1, 365: "From this the one who investigates will discern the matter of the love of the Lord, for when a man engraves the form of the name YHWH in his heart constantly . . . he causes the form of his soul to be engraved above, and the holy One, blessed be he, will love him. . . . When a man rouses his heart to love the Lord, the man is called in the secret of *yw"d h"a wa"w h"a*, which numerically equals *adam*, for the Lord will love him and be bound to him." An interpretation of the image of the seal in Song 8:6 that emphasizes the conjunction (*devequt*) of the soul and God is attested in Elisha Gallico, *Perush Shir ha-Shirim* (Venice, 1587), 59b–60a.

Finally, it is worth noting the following comment from *Ṭaharat ha-Qodesh*, 173, which immediately precedes the citation of the zoharic passage cited above (n. 59): "I have also already notified you that you should not wonder that the names of all the emanations are equivalent, and particularly that the husband is called by the name of the wife and all the more so that the wife is called by the name of the husband. And this is the secret of 'Place me as a seal upon your heart.'" The verse from the Song is utilized to anchor the conceptual point that the gender transformation is twofold, that is, as a consequence of the intercourse the male assumes the name of the female and the female assumes the name of the male, and thus both man and woman can utter the request to be placed as a seal upon the heart of the other with whom he or she has been united.

AFTERWORD: A THEOLOGY OF EROS, AFTER
TRANSFIGURING PASSION | CATHERINE KELLER

1. Jean-Luc Nancy, *Inoperative Community,* ed. Peter Connor (Minneapolis: University of Minnesota Press, 1991), 83.

2. "When thou beholdest us in our wretchedness, we experience the effect of compassion, but thou dost not experience the feeling." Anselm, *Proslogium* VI and VII, in *Proslogium; Monologium; An Appendix, et al.,* trans. S. N. Deane (New York: Open Court, 1945), 11, 13.

3. Alfred North Whitehead, *Adventures of Ideas* (New York: Free Press, 1967), 275.

4. "The brief Galilean vision of humility flickered uncertainly through the ages": Alfred North Whitehead, *Process and Reality* (New York: Free Press, 1978 [1928]), 342.

5. Gilles Deleuze, *The Fold: Leibniz and the Baroque* (Minneapolis: University of Minnesota Press, 1992). Deleuze rereads Leibniz via Whitehead to account for the high-speed expansion of a postmodern universe. See also Catherine Keller and Anne Daniell, ed., *Process and Difference: Between Cosmological and Poststructuralist Postmodernisms* (Albany: State University of New York Press, 2002).

6. For the problematic and promising effects of Deleuzian theory upon sexual and specifically feminist theory, see Elizabeth Grosz, *Volatile Bodies: Toward a Corporeal Feminism* (Bloomington: Indiana University Press, 1994); Rosi Bradotti, *Metamorphoses: Towards a Materialist Theory of Becoming* (Cambridge: Polity Press, 2002); and Lynda Hart, *Between the Body and the Flesh: Performing Sadomasochism* (New York: Columbia University Press, 1998).

7 The classic process *aperitif* is John Cobb Jr. and David Ray Griffin, *Process Theology: An Introductory Exposition* (Louisville, Ky.: Westminster, 1977). See Catherine Keller, *From a Broken Web: Sexism, Separation and Self* (Boston: Beacon, 1986), for a more feminist and psychoanalytic introduction.

8. Rita Nakashima Brock, *Journeys by Heart: A Christology of Erotic Power* (New York: Crossroads, 1994), 49. Other feminist theologies of eros also germinated in this relational medium, such as Carter Heyward's theology of mutuality, with its consecration of same-sex love: *Touching Our Strength: The Erotic as Power and the Love of God* (San Francisco: Harper & Row, 1989). See also Wendy Farley, *Eros for the Other: Retaining Truth in a Pluralistic World* (University Park: Pennsylvania State University Press, 1996). For an incisive critique of the first wave of feminist theological affirmations of eros, see Kathleen Sands, *Escape from Paradise: Evil and Tragedy in Feminist Theology* (Minneapolis: Augsburg Fortress, 1994).

9. Beverly Wildung Harrison, *Justice in the Making: Feminist Social Ethics*, ed. Elizabeth Bounds, Tracy West, et al. (Louisville, Ky.: Westminster John Knox Press, 2004), 115.

10. Audre Lorde, *Sister / Outsider: Essays and Speeches* (Freedom, Calif.: Crossing Press, 1984), 59.

11. Audre Lorde, *Uses of the Erotic: The Erotic as Power* (New York: Crossing, 1981); Susan Griffin, *Pornography and Silence: Culture's Revenge Against Nature* (New York: Harper, 1981).

12. Griffin, *Pornography and Silence*, 260.

13. Herbert Marcuse, *Eros and Civilization: A Philosophical Inquiry Into Freud* (Boston: Beacon, 1955). He footnotes without comment Nygren's then recently published *Agape and Eros* (70, 126).

14. Nancy, *Inoperative Community*, 83.

15. For an exegesis of the politics of love in Mt. 5.45, see Mario Costa, Catherine Keller, and Anna Mercedes, with a response by Michael Hardt and Antonio Negri, "Love in Times of Empire: Theopolitics Today," forthcoming in *Evangelicals and Empire*, ed. Bruce Ellis Benson and Peter Heltzel (Oxford: Oxford University Press).

Marcella M. Althaus-Reid, an Argentinean theologian, holds the chair of contextual theology in the School of Divinity of the University of Edinburgh in Scotland. Her area of research is liberation theology and queer theory. Her publications include *Indecent Theology* (2000), *The Queer God* (2003), *From Feminist Theology to Indecent Theology* (2005), *The Sexual Theologian* (2004; co-editor), and *Liberation Theology and Sexuality* (2006).

Daniel Boyarin is Taubmann Professor of Talmudic Culture in the Departments of Near Eastern Studies and Rhetoric at the University of California at Berkeley. He has published numerous books and articles on subjects relating to gender and sexuality in ancient Judaism and Christianity, as well as other issues of identity politics in late antiquity. His books include *Carnal Israel: Reading Sex in Talmudic Culture* (1993), *A Radical Jew: Paul and the Politics of Identity* (1994), *Unheroic Conduct: The Rise of Heterosexuality and the Invention of the Jewish Man* (1997), *Dying for God: Martyrdom and the Making of Christianity and Judaism* (1999), and *Border Lines: The Partition of Judaeo-Christianity* (2004). His current project is a study of dialogue and power in Platonism and early Judaism.

Sheila Briggs is associate professor of religion and gender studies at the University of Southern California. Her areas of research interest encompass feminist theology, nineteenth- and twentieth-century German theology, early Christianity, theories of history, and modern liberation movements. She is currently studying the relation of attitudes toward gender and attitudes toward the Jewish Torah in the writings of Paul. Other projects focus on an ancient past that never happened except in the imagination of contemporary popular culture.

Virginia Burrus is professor of early church history at Drew University. Her research interests in the field of late ancient Christianity center on issues of gender, sexuality, and the body; orthodoxy and heresy; and the literatures of martyrdom and hagiography. Her publications include *The Making of a Heretic: Gender, Authority, and the Priscillianist Controversy* (1995), *"Begotten, Not Made": Conceiving Manhood in Late Antiquity* (2000), *The Sex Lives of Saints: An Erotics of Ancient Hagiography* (2004), and *Late Ancient Christianity* (2005; editor). She is currently working on a book about ancient Christian views of shame.

Robert S. Corrington is professor of philosophical theology in the Graduate and Theological Schools of Drew University. He is the author of nine books, over seventy articles, and co-editor of five other works. Among his books are: *Nature and Spirit* (1992), *Ecstatic Naturalism* (1994), *A Semiotic Theory of Theology and Philosophy* (2000), and his autobiography *Riding the Windhorse* (2003). His work is in the areas of metaphysics, semiotics, depth-psychology, liberal theology, and pragmatism.

Mario Costa is completing his PhD in theological and religious studies at Drew University. His research interests currently center on the political possibilities of philosophical and theological views of love. He has several forthcoming publications that address the topic of Christian love, power, and justice.

Amy Hollywood is the Elizabeth H. Monrad Professor of Christian Studies at Harvard Divinity School. She is the author of *The Soul as Virgin Wife: Mechthild of Magdeburg, Marguerite Porete, and Meister Eckhart* (1995) and *Sensible Ecstasy: Mysticism, Sexual Difference, and the Demands of History* (2002). She is currently working on a manuscript entitled *Acute Melancholia*.

Grace Jantzen was Research Professor of Religion, Culture and Gender at the University of Manchester in England from 1996 until her tragic death from cancer in May 2006. Her wide-ranging scholarly interests have intersected especially with continental philosophy and western Christian mysticism. She is the author of many books and articles, including *Power, Gender and Christian Mysticism* (1995), *Becoming Divine: Towards a Feminist Philosophy of Religion* (1998), and *Foundations of Violence: Death and the Displacement of Beauty* (2004).

Mark D. Jordan is Asa Griggs Candler Professor of Religion at Emory University. His teaching and research range from the rhetorical critique of contemporary Catholicism to innovations in the performance of LGBT religious identities. His books include *The Invention of Sodomy in Christian Theology* (1997), winner of the 1999 John Boswell Prize for lesbian and gay history, *The Silence of Sodom: Homosexuality in Modern Catholicism* (2000), a Lambda Literary Award finalist, *Telling Truths in Church: Scandal, Flesh, and Christian Speech* (2003), *Blessing Same-Sex Unions: The Perils of Queer Romance and the Confusions of Christian Marriage* (2005), and *Rewritten Theology: Aquinas after His Readers* (2005).

Richard Kearney holds the Charles B. Seelig Chair of Philosophy at Boston College and has served as a visiting professor at University College Dublin, the University of Paris (Sorbonne), and the University of Nice. He is the author of more than twenty books on European philosophy and literature, as well as two novels and a volume of poetry, and has edited or coedited fourteen other volumes. His most recent work in philosophy comprises a trilogy entitled "Philosophy at the Limit." The three volumes are *The God Who May Be: A Hermeneutics of Religion* (2001), *On Stories* (2001), and *Strangers, Gods and Monsters: Ideas of Otherness* (2002).

Catherine Keller is professor of constructive theology in the Graduate and Theological Schools of Drew University. Her interests span a wide theopoetic/theopolitical spectrum, embracing feminist, ecological, process and poststructuralist investigations. Her publications include *From a Broken Web: Separatism, Sexism, and Self* (1986), *Apocalypse Now and Then: A Feminist Guide to the End of the World* (1996), *Face of the Deep: A Theology of Becoming* (2003), and *God & Power: Counter-Apocalyptic Journeys* (2005). She is currently working on a book for seminarians called *On the Mystery*, as well as a scholarly text entitled *The Absolute and the Dissolute: Exercises in Truth*.

Derek Krueger is professor of religious studies at the University of North Carolina at Greensboro. A student of late ancient and Byzantine Christian hagiography, hymnography, and ritual practice, his publications include *Symeon the Holy Fool: Leontius's Life and the Late Ancient City* (1996), *Writing and Holiness: The Practice of Authorship in the Early Christian East* (2004), and *Byzantine Christianity* (2006; editor). He is currently writing on the liturgical formation of identity in Byzantine Christianity and on the place of eros in the Byzantine monastic tradition.

Tod Linafelt is associate professor of biblical literature at Georgetown University. He is the author of *Surviving Lamentations* (2000) and of a commentary on the book of Ruth for the Berit 'Olam series (1999), and has edited or coedited four books, the most recent being *Mel Gibson's Bible* (2005). He is coeditor, with Timothy K. Beal, of the University of Chicago Press book series *Afterlives of the Bible*. His recent work centers on the poetry of the Hebrew Bible, and he is currently writing a commentary on the Song of Songs.

Karmen MacKendrick is associate professor of philosophy at Le Moyne College in Syracuse, New York. Her diverse research interests in philosophy and theology tend to center on the corporeal and the sensual. Her publications include *counterpleasures* (1999), *Immemorial Silence* (2001), and *Word Made Skin: Figuring Language at the Surface of Flesh* (2004), along with essays on pleasure, dance, body art, and other eclectic subjects. She is currently at work on a project involving the intersections of memory and fragmentation.

Mayra Rivera is assistant professor of theology at the Pacific School of Religion in Berkeley, California. Her research is in the field of constructive theology with special interest in feminist, liberation and postcolonial thought. She is coeditor of *Postcolonial Theologies: Divinity and Empire* (2004) and is currently working on a book about divine transcendence.

Yvonne Sherwood is senior lecturer in Old Testament / Tanakh and Judaism at the University of Glasgow. Her previous publications include *The Prostitute and the Prophet* (1996), *A Biblical Text and Its Afterlives: The Survival of Jonah in Western Culture* (2000), *Derrida and Religion: Other Testaments* (2004; coeditor), and *Derrida's Bible* (2004; editor). She is currently working on a project on the history of interpretation of the sacrifice of Isaac/Ishmael.

Diana M. Swancutt is assistant professor of New Testament at Yale Divinity School. Combining interests in gender, ethnicity, rhetoric, ideological criticism, and empire studies, her research focuses on identity formation in Pauline communities, particularly the resocialization of Greeks into Pauline Christian Judaism. Her first book, *Pax Christi: Empire, Identity, and Protreptic Rhetoric in Paul's Letter to the Romans*, will be published this year. Current projects include monographs on the effects of Roman imperialism on education in Pauline communities and on gender ideology and the Pauline "body of Christ."

Elliot R. Wolfson is the Abraham Lieberman Professor of Hebrew and Judaic Studies at New York University. His main area of scholarly research is the history of Jewish mysticism but he has brought to bear on that field training in philosophy, literary criticism, feminist theory, postmodern hermeneutics, and the phenomenology of religion. His publications include ten books and four edited volumes, among them *Through a Speculum That Shines: Vision and Imagination in Medieval Jewish Mysticism* (1994), which won the 1995 American Academy of Religion's Award for Excellence in the Study of Religion in the Category of Historical Studies and the 1995 National Jewish Book Award for Excellence in Scholarship; *Language, Eros, Being: Kabbalistic Hermeneutics and the Poetic Imagination* (2005), which won the 2006 National Jewish Book Award for Excellence in Scholarship; *Alef, Mem, Tau: Kabbalistic Musings on Time, Truth, and Death* (2006); and *Venturing Beyond Law and Morality in Kabbalistic Mysticism* (2006).